Group Policy: Management, Troubleshooting, and Security

Mark Minasi
Windows® Administrator
Library

Group Policy: Management, Troubleshooting, and Security

For Windows Vista™, Windows® 2003, Windows® XP, and Windows® 2000

Jeremy Moskowitz

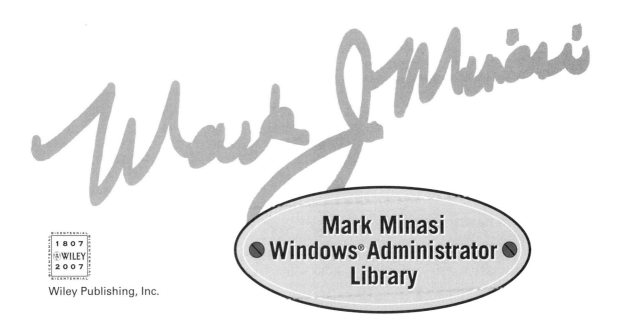

BICENTENNIAL
1807
WILEY
2007
BICENTENNIAL

Wiley Publishing, Inc.

Mark Minasi
Windows® Administrator
Library

Acquisitions and Development Editor: Tom Cirtin

Technical Editor: Darren Mar-Elia

Production Editor: Elizabeth Campbell

Copy Editor: Sally Engelfried

Production Manager: Tim Tate

Vice President and Executive Group Publisher: Richard Swadley

Vice President and Executive Publisher: Joseph B. Wikert

Vice President and Publisher: Neil Edde

Compositor: Craig Woods, Happenstance Type-O-Rama

Proofreader: Rachel Gunn

Indexer: Jack Lewis

Anniversary Logo Design: Richard Pacifico

Cover Designer: Ryan Sneed

Copyright © 2007 by Wiley Publishing, Inc., Indianapolis, Indiana

Published by Wiley Publishing, Inc., Indianapolis, Indiana

Published simultaneously in Canada

ISBN-13: 978-0-7821-10642-6

For general information on our other products and services or to obtain technical support, please contact our Customer Care Department within the U.S. at (800) 762-2974, outside the U.S. at (317) 572-3993 or fax (317) 572-4002.

Wiley also publishes its books in a variety of electronic formats. Some content that appears in print may not be available in electronic books.

Library of Congress Cataloging-in-Publication Data

Moskowitz, Jeremy.

 Group policy : management, troubleshooting, and security / Jeremy Moskowitz.

   p. cm.

 ISBN 978-0-470-10642-6 (paper/website)

 1. Microsoft Windows (Computer file) 2. Operating systems (Computers) I. Title.

 QA76.76.O63M69675 2007

 005.4'46--dc22

                          2007002732

10 9 8 7 6 5 4 3 2 1

To Our Valued Readers:

Thank you for looking to Sybex for your technical information needs. The Sybex team at Wiley is proud of its reputation for providing IT professionals with the practical knowledge and serious skills needed to succeed in the highly competitive workplace. The author and editors have worked hard to ensure that the new edition of this highly acclaimed book you hold in your hands is comprehensive and in-depth, as well as readable and engaging.

As always, your feedback is important to us. If you believe you've identified an error in the book, please visit Wiley's Technical Support web site at `wiley.custhelp.com`. If you have general comments or suggestions, feel free to drop me a line directly at nedde@wiley.com. At Sybex we're continually striving to meet the needs of dedicated technology professionals.

All the best.

Neil Edde
Vice President & Publisher
Sybex, an Imprint of Wiley

To everyone I've ever had the chance to meet in "real life." Your energy and excitement make it all worthwhile.

Acknowledgments

We've renamed the title, but this is the 4th edition of "the Big Green Group Policy Book" (as we've come to call it). Lots of things have changed since I wrote the first edition. We have a new head of Group Policy at Microsoft, Mr. Kevin Sullivan, who, interestingly, was the technical editor of this book for the 3rd edition. A hearty congratulations, Kevin! And an equally hearty thank you to the outgoing lead Michael Dennis for his continuous support of all my efforts.

Why do I always wait until the end of the book to write the acknowledgements? This is a mystery to me. If I were really smart, I would have kept better notes about everyone who hand in helping out, since the list of people who helped contribute grows and grows.

First, I want to thank my pal Darren Mar-Elia who runs SDM Software, for joining on as the book's Technical Editor, and big-time contributor to Chapter 4. If there are still any technical problems with the book, blame me, not him. He was great.

I also want to thank Ron Montgomery and Eric Johnson, two regular guys from GPanswers.com who stepped up to help me shoulder some of the grunt work of the book, namely taking screenshots while I was busy writing. For "regular guys" you're the tops in my book (literally)!

When I tell you that an army of people have contributed in some fashion to this book, it would be a huge understatement. I want to thank the Sybex and Wiley magicians, especially Tom Cirtin and Elizabeth Campbell (whom I called out of "retirement" just for this project). To Jay Lessandrini, Dave Mayhew, and Joe Wikert: Once again, your dedication to my book's success means so much to me. You take everything I create and deal with it so personally, and I really know that. Thank you, very sincerely.

Mark Williams from the Group Policy team at Microsoft has always been a huge supporter of my efforts for this book. And in this fourth go-around, his tenacity did not wane. Not only did he provide the Foreword, but he also helped review chapters, answered the hard questions I had, and located reviewers for each and every chapter—sometimes as many as four reviewers for a single chapter! Thank you to the other folks on the Group Policy team who always support me: Mark Lawrence, Erik Vosukil, Mike Stephens, David Power, Craig Marl, John Kaiser, Judith Herman, Dilip Radhakrishnan, and Jason Leznek (who isn't on the Group Policy team, but is awesome nonetheless). Thank you also to the other members of the Group Policy team who support me directly and indirectly and help me out whenever you can.

Additional thanks to the battalion of technical reviewers at Microsoft: Michael Niehaus, Josh Edwards, Paul Barr, Puneet Arora, Gene Ferioli, Jason Popp, Sarah Wahlert, David Abzarian, Mark Vayman, Chris Mitchell, Chris Black, Brian Aust, Navjot Virk, Dan Boldo, Anshul Rawat, Ming Zhu, Ken Maybee, Gurjot Barr, Ian Hameroff, Chris Corio, Saad Sycd, Jim Hong, and Steve Hiskey. Special thanks to Scott Dickens and Darren Canavor who made incredible "above and beyond" contributions.

All of these amazing people didn't review my chapters because they had to; they did it because they wanted to. Each one has a clear dedication to their craft, and I'm thrilled that they took the time out of their work lives to help this book be its best.

To my friends Jill, Alisa, Tom, Jennifer, Chris, and Laura, and to my parents, thank you for your support during the long working hours. To my assistant Mark who was able to magically make big problems disappear, especially when I suddenly decided to move from Delaware to Philadelphia while I was writing the book. (Note to self: Don't do that again.) And, thanks to my ever diligent `GPanswers.com` assistant, Adam Vero who does so much behind the scenes, I don't even know what he does (in a good way).

Thank you, Mark Minasi, for asking me to be a part of your series and giving me all the time and allowance to write about the subject that I love most. Thanks to Scott Fenstermacher for updating Bill Boswell's Chapter 7.

This list would not be complete without mentioning Ron Hrehirchuk. Ron was such an integral part of the previous edition, and he's served as my behind-the-scenes right-hand man for the `GPAnswers.com` forums, giving his time and expertise to the cause, and always with a smile. My most sincere, heartfelt prayers and warm wishes to Ron and his family for a speedy recovery. We miss you, Ron—hurry back! Finally, I want to thank all the readers of the previous editions who believed in Group Policy and have used it daily to make their administration experiences even better. And a heartier thanks to those folks on `GPAnswers.com` who ask questions, help others, and help me make this book the best it can be.

Foreword

I first met Jeremy when he approached the Microsoft Group Policy team with a handful of questions for the second edition of this book. All of us were very busy getting Windows Server 2003 and GPMC to ship; we couldn't answer Jeremy's questions right away. But with his deadlines looming, Jeremy was persistent. He wanted answers to the toughest Group Policy questions, so he could deliver them to you.

His persistence and dedication to Group Policy paid off. Because of his Group Policy training classes and his community engagement at GPanswers.com, he was recognized as a Group Policy "thought leader" and was given the title of *Microsoft MVP (Most Valuable Professional) for Group Policy*—an honor to which only six other people worldwide—at the time of writing—can also lay claim. With this title comes some responsibility, and we regularly ask him to provide our team with feedback on documents in progress before we release them.

At Microsoft, we have a lot of downloadable documentation on Group Policy and the other topics in this book. What Jeremy's book provides is a one-stop shop for practical, how-it-works information, including real-world examples of implementing and troubleshooting Group Policy and creating a managed desktop. Indeed, his digging and prodding into the Group Policy internals, plus his relationship with the various product teams at Microsoft, means that there is information in his book that you simply cannot find anywhere else. Jeremy has always provided an independent perspective on how Group Policy works. Best of all, his unique, friendly and informative writing style will keep you engaged throughout the book.

The goal of the Group Policy team is to give you the power you need to control your desktops and servers in the most efficient way possible. This vision began in Windows 2000, it continued on with the development of the Group Policy Management Console (GPMC), and continues still with the release of Windows Vista.

Windows Vista brings more of what you already love about Group Policy—more Group Policy settings, more security functions, and a greater ability to configure your network the way you want. And, our expectation is that the power of Group Policy will only increase. The time to learn Group Policy is now, and this book delivers that information to you efficiently.

Jeremy's book covers the basics of Group Policy and GPMC and then reveals the hidden features that truly unleash the power of Group Policy. Each version of Windows is a little different in the way it handles Group Policy and what Group Policy functions are supported. And this book takes special care to ensure that the nuances of each version are revealed. The practical, often prescriptive, technical information just keeps coming, chapter after chapter.

Many teams within Microsoft have provided input to Jeremy's book: from our folks on the Group Policy team (Chapters 1, 2, 3, 4, 5 and 8), multiple teams within Security (Chapters 6 and 7), as well as other teams like the Folder Redirection, Offline Folders, and Microsoft Office teams (Chapters 9, 10, and 11), as well as the Windows Deployment Services and Shadow Copies teams (Chapter 12). Jeremy kept sending all of us at Microsoft the tough questions so that he could make Group Policy more accessible to you with this book.

At Microsoft, we've enjoyed working with Jeremy, and reviewing his chapters to make this the best book possible. It's our hope that you enjoy the power and control Group Policy provides. It's also our hope that you enjoy the additional power and control you'll have after reading Jeremy's very practical book on Group Policy.

—Mark Williams
Program Manager, Group Policy, Microsoft

Contents at a Glance

Table of Contents

What's New (in Vista Group Policy and in This Book)

If you're like me, you just want to get right to the good stuff and find out what's new: both with Group Policy for Vista, and in the book.

And, that's exactly what we're going to do here—ensure that you can find the new stuff in this book if you're *just* looking for updates.

For newcomers to Group Policy, I suggest that you start with the Introduction and read all the way through. What's new in Vista Group Policy won't matter much to you at this point.

Again, *this* section is for people already accustomed to Group Policy, and who are just looking for pointers to the updates. So, if you're not accustomed to Group Policy, you might find some areas of this section a little obtuse. I promise in the rest of the book, I'll ensure that everything is well spelled out to give you a clear understanding of all of the topics.

And, for everyone who chooses to read this section, I also want to give you a sneak peek about where Vista (and Longhorn Server) Group Policy is going, and how we plan to make sure that you stay current, even though we know the technology is going to be updated.

What's New in Vista Group Policy

If all goes well with the upcoming Vista deployments around the world, most administrators really shouldn't notice any *big* changes. With that said, you might think I should just stop the book here and call it quits, as seemingly there's nothing left to say.

But, I assure you, for administrators with modest goals, as well as the "Power Administrator," there's lots of great stuff to discover.

Nuts and Bolts Changes in Vista Group Policy

The under-the-hood changes are numerous and should be discussed so we can get a handle where things are going. Let's take a tour of what's new in the Group Policy nuts and bolts.

Group Policy Becomes a Client Service   Prior to Vista, the "moving parts" of Group Policy were contained within a process called winlogon. Winlogon had a lot of responsibility, including getting people logged on and doing the Group Policy chores. Now Group Policy has been designated as its own Windows Service. And what's more, it's hardened. That is, it cannot be stopped, nor can an administrator take ownership of the permissions on it and turn it off. These changes enhance the overall reliability of the Group Policy engine. Read more about this in Chapter 4.

GPMC Built-in   The Group Policy Management Console, or GPMC, which was previously only available as a download, is now just built into Vista. This means that whenever you're ready to create or edit GPOs, you'll already have the best tools for the job. Read more about this in Chapter 1.

Updated Network Awareness The Vista Group Policy engine has a new way to determine if the link is truly fast or not. It also determines if there's a Domain Controller available to deliver Group Policy. Read more about Network Location Awareness ("NLA 2.0") in Chapter 4.

Multiple Local GPOs This is a big, new feature in Vista. In addition to a GPO which affects everyone on the machine, you can also layer additional GPOs at the local level. That is, you can now have additional multiple local GPOs—one that affects mere-mortal accounts and one that affects administrator accounts. Read more about this in Chapter 1.

Error Messages and Troubleshooting Windows Vista has a whole new Event Log system (which could be a whole article in and of itself). However, in short, the Group Policy engine now leverages this new event system, and splits up events into two particular logs. Read more about this in Chapter 4.

ADM versus ADMX files ADM files are the underlying definitions for what's possible in Group Policy. But Vista bring a new format—ADMX. The ADMX files are replacements for ADM, and with them come new management techniques and things to watch out for. We'll spend a great deal of time on ADMX files in Chapter 5.

New Stuff to Control

Windows Vista brings about 700 new policy settings to the table. To cover *all* of these settings would make this book too huge. Our goal is to cover the settings which most help you manage your world.

There are already categories of settings which you know and love. And Vista brings some new categories to the table which lacked any Group Policy controls, or simply hadn't existed. Enhanced areas in Group Policy are:

- Wired and Wireless policy (covered in Chapter 7)
- Windows Firewall and IPsec (covered in Chapter 7)
- Print Management (covered in Chapter 12)
- Desktop Shell (covered in various places)
- Remote Assistance (not specifically covered)
- Tablet PC (not specifically covered)

New areas in Vista Group Policy are:

- Removable Storage Device management (covered in Chapter 7)
- Power Management (not specifically covered)
- User Account Control (covered in Chapter 7)
- Network Access Protection (covered briefly in Chapter 8)
- Windows Defender (not specifically covered)

Microsoft has a nice concise document about what's new and expanded here: http://tinyurl.com/ffelo

On the Table for Vista/SP1 and Longhorn Server Timeframe

Additional Group Policy features are scheduled to come out in Vista's first service pack, which should be around the same time that Longhorn Server comes out. Microsoft is calling this the "Longhorn Server Timeframe." And the idea is that these new features will likely come out with Vista's Service Pack 1, which should be around the same time Longhorn server ships. And, because they're not out at the time of this writing—I can't really write about them. So, while these upcoming features are subject to change, there are three major areas of improvements slated for the Longhorn timeframe future:

Comments   One often requested feature is the ability to put in comments about what the GPO does, or what any specific Group Policy setting is meant to do. Right now, the only way to make comments is to keep track of your GPOs and settings in, say, a spreadsheet and then make comments there. This feature will be a welcome addition.

Templates   Oftentimes, administrators want to give other administrators a starting point when creating their own GPOs. Group Policy Templates allow administrators to create GPOs from these templates. Microsoft will likely also include their "common scenarios" to the initial set of templates which will have some specific guidance for how to control different types of machines. (Check out the Common Scenarios documentation and files at http://tinyurl.com/jpn5p.)

Searching and Filters   With what feels like a million policy settings, sometimes it's just too hard finding the one policy setting you need. This upcoming feature will make it easier to search inside the policy setting's title, Explaintext, and comments. You'll also be able to see at a glance which policy settings are Enabled or Disabled within a GPO so you can make quick changes to a misbehaving GPO.

All Settings Node   The Group Policy editor will contain a new node which will show, in a flat list, every Group Policy setting, and show if it's set or not. On the surface, this feature sounds almost as if it has no purpose. However, the goal is to show you a sortable list of all policy settings and determine which ones are set by having those bubble to the top.

Again, Comments, Templates, Searching and Filters, and the All Settings Node are *not* going to be part of Vista when it initially ships. Heck, their names might change or these features might not show up at all. Again, however, the plan as stated is that these features will be added on, most likely via a Service Pack, or some other add-on mechanism, around the time Longhorn Server ships. And to be clear, no feature here requires Longhorn server to actually work.

What Happens when Vista/SP1 Comes Out?

As I've already stated, in the Vista/SP1 timeframe there are going to be some whiz-bang new features which we won't be able to cover in the book you're holding in your hands. However, here's the promise: Soon after Vista/SP1 comes out, I'll make a free downloadable update available for anyone who owns this edition of the book.

That way, you'll be ready for today, and for tomorrow.

Just check in every so often at www.GPanswers.com in the Book Resources page, or sign up for the GPanswers.com newsletter, where I'll announce it.

What's Kept and What's History

Even though the title has changed, you could think of this book as the "Fourth Edition" of the original Group Policy book I published back in 2000. This edition will revise all examples with Vista instead of Windows XP or Windows 2000.

Some things are history because, well, they're history. The Remote Installation Service (RIS) has been replaced with a free upgrade called Windows Deployment Services (WDS). So, that's what we're going to cover in Chapter 11 instead of RIS.

It's my goal that this book becomes a useful resource to people getting started with Group Policy (of which there are thousands every day) or to seasoned Group Policy professionals. However, I will essentially retain the same flow, stories, and advice. Some of the examples may have changed, but the way I introduce concepts won't change from the way you've already come to know and love. It's my goal to simply "Vista-ize" this edition of the book, and make sure that a good thing continues to be useful for you.

Introduction

If you've got an Active Directory, you need Group Policy. Group Policy has one goal: to make your administrative life easier. Instead of running around from machine to machine tweaking a setting here or installing some software there, you'll have ultimate control from on high.

Turns out that you're not alone in wanting more power for your desktops and servers. Managing user desktops (via Group Policy) was the top-ranked benefit of migrating to Active Directory, according to 1000 members who responded to a poll from TechTarget.com. You can find the study at `http://tinyurl.com/47wrg`.

Like Zeus himself, controlling the many aspects of the mortal world below, you will have the ability, via Group Policy, to dictate specific settings pertaining to how you want your users and computers to operate. You'll be able to shape your network's destiny. You'll have the power. But you need to know exactly how to tap into this power and exactly what can be powered, and what can only *appear* to be powered.

In this Introduction and throughout the first several chapters, I'll describe just what Group Policy is all about and give you an idea of its tremendous power.

> To get the most out of this book, you'll likely want to utilize our suggested setup lab environment in Chapter 1. What's needed is a Windows 2003 Server machine (which will be the Domain Controller) and with at least one Windows XP client (preferably running SP2) a Windows Vista machine, and possibly a Windows 2000 Professional machine (running at least SP4). If you don't have a copy of Windows 2003 Server, you can download a free evaluation copy from Microsoft (`http://tinyurl.com/pgqz`), or have them send you a CD. (You pay only for shipping.) Again, check out Chapter 1 for complete details.

Group Policy Defined

If we take a step back and try to analyze the term *Group Policy*, it's easy to become confused. When I first heard the term, I thought it was an NT 4 System Policy that applied to Active Directory groups. But, thankfully, it's much more exciting. Microsoft's perspective is that the name "Group Policy" is derived from the fact that you are "grouping together policy settings." Group Policy is, in essence, rules that are applied and enforced at multiple levels of Active Directory. All policy settings you dictate must be adhered to. This provides great power and efficiency when manipulating client systems.

When going though the examples in this book, you will play the parts of the end user, the OU administrator, the domain administrator, and the enterprise administrator. Your mission is to create and define Group Policy using Active Directory and witness it being automatically enforced. What you say goes! With Group Policy, you can set policies that dictate that users quit messing with their machines. You can dictate what software will be deployed. You can determine how much disk space users can use. You can do pretty much whatever you want—it is really up to you. With Group Policy, you hold all the power. That's the good news. The bad news is that this magical power only works on Windows 2000 or later machines. That includes Windows 2000, Windows XP, and Windows 2003 Server. That's right; there is no way—no matter what anyone tells you—to use the magic that is known as Group Policy in a way that affects Windows 95, Windows 98, or Windows NT workstations or servers. But, since this is 2007, you likely don't have many of these kicking around anymore.

The application of Group Policy does not concern itself with the mode of the domain. Windows 2000 or Windows 2003 domains need not be in any special functional mode. Windows 2000 domains can be in Mixed or Native mode. Windows 2003 domains can be in domain mode: Mixed, Interim, or Functional.

If the range of control scares you—don't be afraid! It just means more power to hold over your environment. You'll quickly learn how to wisely use this newfound power to reign over your subjects, er, users.

Group Policy versus Group Policy Objects

Before we go headlong into Group Policy theory, let's get some terminology and vocabulary out of the way:

- The term *Group Policy* is the concept that, from upon high, you can do all this "stuff" to your client machines.

- A *policy setting* is just one individual setting that you can use to perform some specific action.

- *Group Policy Objects (GPOs)* are the "nuts-and-bolts" contained within Active Directory Domain Controllers, each of which contain anywhere from one to a zillion individual policy settings.

It's my goal that after you work through this book, you'll be able to jump up on your desk one day and declare: "Hey! Group Policy isn't applying to our client machines! Perhaps a policy setting is misconfigured. Or, maybe one of our Group Policy Objects has gone belly up! I'd better read what's going on in Chapter 3, 'Group Policy Processing Behavior.'"

This terminology can be a little confusing—considering that each term includes the word *policy*. In this text, however, I've tried especially hard to use the correct nomenclature for what I'm trying to describe.

 Note that there is never a time to use the phrase "Group Policies." Those two words together shouldn't exist. If you're talking about "multiple GPOs" or "multiple policy settings" these are the preferred phrases to use.

Where Group Policy Applies

Group Policy can be applied to many machines at once, or it can be applied only to a specific machine. For the most part in this book, I'll focus on using Group Policy within an Active Directory environment where it affects the most machines.

A percentage of the settings explored and discussed in this book are available to member or stand-alone Windows machines—which can either participate or not participate in an Active

Directory environment. However, the Folder Redirection settings (discussed in Chapter 10) and the Software Distribution settings (discussed in Chapter 11) are not available to stand-alone machines (that is, computers that are not participating in an Active Directory domain). In some cases, I will pay particular attention to non–Active Directory environments. However, most of the book deals with the more common case; that is, we'll explore the implications of deploying Group Policy in an Active Directory environment.

Most of the book shows screens of Windows Vista and Windows XP; but most of the book is still applicable for domains with Windows 2000 clients. Indeed, you should not be scared off even if you're stuck with 100% Windows 2000 Domain Controllers. Where appropriate, I've noted the differences between the operating environments.

This Book and Beyond

Group Policy is a big concept with some big power. This book is intended to help you get a handle on this new power to gain control over your environment and to make your day-to-day administration easier. This book is filled with practical, hands-on examples of Group Policy usage and troubleshooting. It is my hope that you enjoy this book and learn from my experiences so you can successfully deploy Group Policy and manage your desktops to better control your network. I'm honored to have you aboard for the ride, and I hope you get as much out of Group Policy as I do from writing and speaking about it in my hands-on workshops.

As you read this book, it's natural to have questions about Group Policy or managing your desktops. To form a community around Group Policy, I have started a free service that can be found at www.GPanswers.com. My Technical Editor, Darren Mar-Elia (fellow Group Policy MVP) also runs GPOguy.com, which has different resources.

I encourage you to visit our websites and post your questions to the community forum or peruse the other resources that will be constantly renewed and available for download. For instance, in addition to the forum at GPanswers.com, you'll find the full scripts for Chapter 7 and ADM and ADMX templates to download, tips and tricks, a third-party Group Policy Solutions Guide and more!

If you want to meet me in person, my website at GPanswers.com has a calendar of all my upcoming appearances at various conferences, events, and intensive workshop classes. I'd love to hear how this book met your needs or helped you out.

Group Policy Essentials

In this chapter, you'll get your feet wet with the concept that is Group Policy. You'll start to understand conceptually what Group Policy is and how it's created, applied, and modified, and you'll go through some practical examples to get at the basics.

The best news is that the essentials of Group Policy are the same in all versions of Windows 2000 onward. This includes server products (Windows 2000 server, Windows Server 2003, and the upcoming Longhorn server) and all client versions of Windows including Windows 2000, Windows XP, and Windows Vista. And, when Longhorn server is released, the good news is that there won't be a lot of new stuff to learn. You already have the right book you need until the next "big iteration" of Windows comes out.

Indeed, Group Policy isn't really a "server driven" technology. As you'll learn in depth a little later, the magic of Group Policy happens (mostly) on the target (client) machine, say, Windows XP or Windows Vista. So, if your Active Directory Domain Controllers are a mixture of Windows 2000 and/or Windows 2003 and/or Longhorn server, nothing much changes. And, it doesn't matter if your domain is in Mixed, Native, or another mode—Group Policy works exactly the same in all of them.

So, regardless of what your server architecture is, I still encourage you to read and work through the examples in this chapter.

Getting Ready to Use This Book

This book is full of examples. And, in order to work through these examples, I'm going to suggest a sample test lab for you to create. It's pretty simple really, but in its simplicity we'll be able to work though dozens of real-world examples to see how things work. Here are the computers you need to set up and what I suggest you name them (if you want to work through the examples with me in the book):

DC01.corp.com   This is your Windows Server 2003 Active Directory Domain Controller. I'll assume you've loaded Windows Server 2003/SP1 on this computer. For this book, I'll also assume you'll create a domain called Corp.com.

In real life you would have multiple Domain Controllers in the domain. But here in the test lab, it'll be okay if you just have one. I'll be using Windows Server 2003, but if by the time you read this Longhorn server comes out, you can choose to make this machine a Longhorn Domain Controller and the examples will just work fine. I'll refer to this machine as DC01 in the book. We'll also use DC01 as a file server, software distribution server, and a lot of other roles we really shouldn't. That's so you can work though lots of examples without bringing up lots of servers.

XPPRO1.corp.com   This is some user's Windows XP machine and it's joined to the domain Corp.com. I'll assume you've loaded Windows XP's SP2. Sometimes it'll be a Sales computer, other times a Marketing computer, other times a Nursing computer. To use this machine as such, just move the computer account around in Active Directory when the time comes. You'll see what I mean. I'll refer to this machine as XPPRO1 in the book.

Vista1.corp.com   This is some user's Windows Vista machine and it's joined to the domain Corp.com. I'll refer to this machine as VISTA1 in the book. Like XPPRO1, this machine will move around a lot to help us "play pretend" when the times arise.

Vistamanagement.corp.com   This is your machine—the IT pro who runs the show. You could manage Active Directory from anywhere on your network, but you're going to do it from here. This is the machine that you'll run the tools you need to manage both Active Directory and Group Policy. I'll refer to this machine as VISTAMANAGEMENT. As the name implies, you'll run Windows Vista from this machine.

Figure 1.1 shows a diagram of what our test network should look like if you want to follow along.

FIGURE 1.1   Here's the configuration you'll need for the test lab in this book. Note the Domain Controller can be 2000 or above, but 2003 and above will allow you to work through all the examples in this book.

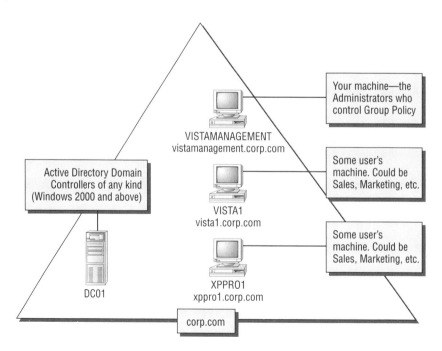

WARNING   Because Group Policy can be so all-encompassing, it is highly recommended that you try these examples in a test lab environment first, before making these changes for real in your production environment.

Note that in the book, from time to time I might describe other machines for example. However, this is the minimum configuration you'll need to get the most out the book.

Some Group Policy History

If you've done any work at all with Group Policy and Active Directory before Windows Vista came out, you're likely familiar with the "usual" Group Policy interface, which was "in the box." Microsoft then went on to provide the free downloadable tool called the GPMC, or Group Policy Management Console. The GPMC is an add-on for Windows XP (or Windows Server 2003) machines to make the task of managing Group Policy easier. Windows Vista comes with the GPMC preloaded—so there's nothing to download. And, you already know this, but it's good to repeat anyway: you can manage your entire Active Directory from any computer on your network. Therefore, for the majority of tasks in this book, we're going to be using our Windows Vista machine (named Vistamanagement1) to perform the majority of Active Directory and Group Policy tasks.

So the goal of the GPMC is to give us an updated, refreshing way to view and manage Group Policy, indeed, this tool enables us to view and manage Group Policy the way it was meant to be viewed and managed. The new GPMC interface provides a one-stop shop for managing nearly all aspects of Group Policy in your Active Directory.

To use the new GPMC tool, it doesn't matter if your entire Active Directory (or individual domains) have Windows 2000, Windows 2003 or Longhorn server Domain Controllers. And it doesn't matter what kind of Windows clients you have (from Windows 2000 onward). It just matters that you have Active Directory.

And did I mention it's free? And in Windows Vista, it's in the box?

Stay tuned, dear reader. We'll get to that exciting new and free stuff right away in this first chapter. I don't want to keep you in suspense for too long.

Getting Started with Group Policy

Group Policy is a big, big place. And you need a roadmap. Let's try to get a firm understanding of what we're about to be looking at for the next several hundred pages.

Group Policy Entities and Policy Settings

Every Group Policy contains two halves: a User half and a Computer half. These two halves are properly called *nodes*, though sometimes they're just referred to as either the *User half* and the *Computer half* or the *User branch* and the *Computer branch*. A sample Group Policy Object Editor screen with both the Computer Configuration and User Configuration nodes can be seen back in Figure 1.1. (Don't worry, we'll show you how to get there in just a second.)

The first level under both the User and the Computer nodes contains Software Settings, Windows Settings, and Administrative Templates. If we dive down into the Administrative Templates of the Computer node, underneath we discover additional levels of Windows Components, System, Network, and Printers. Likewise, if we dive down into the Administrative Templates of the User node, we see some of the same folders plus some additional ones, such as Shared Folders, Desktop, and Start Menu And Taskbar.

In both the User and Computer halves, you'll see that policy settings are hierarchical, like a directory structure. Similar policy settings are grouped together for easy location. That's the idea anyway; though, admittedly, sometimes locating the specific policy you want can prove to be a challenge.

When manipulating policy settings, you can choose to set either Computer policy settings or User policy settings (or both!). You'll see examples of this shortly. (See the section "Minimizing the View with Policy Setting Filtering" in Chapter 2 for tricks on how to minimize the effort of finding the policy setting you want.)

Most policy settings are not found in both nodes. However, there are a few that overlap. In that case, if the computer policy setting is different from the user policy setting, the computer policy setting generally overrides the user policy setting. But to be sure, check the Explain text associated with the policy.

The 18 Categories of Group Policy

In this first section, you'll learn how to gain access to the interface, which will let you start configuring these categories.

TABLE 1.1   In this book, you'll learn about the 18 major categories of Group Policy. Here's a table that should be helpful if you're looking to get started working right with a category.

Group Policy Category	Where in Group Policy Interface	Which Operating Systems support it	Where to find information in the book	Notes
Administrative Templates (also known as Registry Settings)	User or Computer ➢ Administrative Templates	Windows 2000+	Many examples throughout the book	

TABLE 1.1   In this book, you'll learn about the 18 major categories of Group Policy. Here's a table that should be helpful if you're looking to get started working right with a category. *(continued)*

Group Policy Category	Where in Group Policy Interface	Which Operating Systems support it	Where to find information in the book	Notes
Security Settings	Computer or User Configuration ➢ Windows Settings ➢ Security Settings	Windows 2000+	Chapter 6 and 7	
Wired Network (802.3) settings	Computer Configuration ➢ Windows Settings ➢ Security Settings ➢ Wired Network (IEEE 802.3) Policies	Windows Vista only	Chapter 7	Be sure to read Chapter 7 before attempting to use these settings.
Wireless Network (802.11) settings	Computer Configuration ➢ Windows Settings ➢ Security Settings ➢ Wired Network (IEEE 802.3) Policies	Windows XP and Windows Vista (set independently)	Chapter 7	Be sure to read Chapter 7 before attempting to use these settings for Windows Vista.
Scripts	Computer Configuration ➢ Windows Settings ➢ Scripts (Startup/Shutdown) And User Configuration ➢ Windows Settings ➢ Script (Logon/Logoff)	Windows 2000+	Chapter 6	

TABLE 1.1   In this book, you'll learn about the 18 major categories of Group Policy. Here's a table that should be helpful if you're looking to get started working right with a category. *(continued)*

Group Policy Category	Where in Group Policy Interface	Which Operating Systems support it	Where to find information in the book	Notes
RIS (Remote Installation Services)			Chapter 12	RIS has been deprecated in lieu of Windows Deployment Services (WDS). However, WDS can run in Mixed mode where it can emulate a RIS setup. These settings are not available in Windows Vista and only accessible when editing GPOs on previous versions of Windows. If you want to specifically control RIS, it is suggested you manage the machine directly, without GPOs. We won't cover the RIS aspects in this book. For RIS information, see previous editions of the book.
Group Policy Software Installation (also known as Application Management)	Computer or User Configuration ➢ Software Settings	Windows 2000+	Chapter 11	
Folder Redirection	User Configuration ➢ Windows Settings ➢ Folder Redirection	Windows 2000+; some additional options for Windows XP; many additional options for Windows Vista	Chapter 10	
Disk Quotas	Computer Configuration ➢ Administrative Templates ➢ System ➢ Disk Quotas	Windows 2000+	Chapter 10	

TABLE 1.1 In this book, you'll learn about the 18 major categories of Group Policy. Here's a table that should be helpful if you're looking to get started working right with a category. *(continued)*

Group Policy Category	Where in Group Policy Interface	Which Operating Systems support it	Where to find information in the book	Notes
Encrypted Data Recovery Agents (EFS Recovery Policy)	Computer Configuration ➢ Windows ➢ Security settings ➢ Public Key Policies ➢ Encrypting File System	Windows 2000+	Chapter 6	
Internet Explorer Maintenance	User Configuration ➢ Windows Settings ➢ Internet Explorer Maintenance	Windows 2000+	Chapter 7	
Software Restriction Policies	Computer or User ➢ Windows ➢ Security Settings ➢ Software Restriction Policies	Windows XP+	Chapter 6	
Quality of Service (QoS) Packet Scheduler and Policy-Based QoS	Computer or User Configuration ➢ Windows Settings ➢ Policy-based QoS	Windows XP+; Policy-based QoS is Vista-only	Not covered	You can start your Windows Vista QoS journey here: http://tinyurl.com/yxglpp
IPSec (IP Security) Policies	In XP: Computer Configuration ➢ Windows Settings ➢ Security Settings ➢ IP Security Policies	Windows 2000+	Chapter 7	In Vista, this is now part of the Advanced Firewall and Security Section located Computer Configuration ➢ Windows Settings ➢ Security Settings.

TABLE 1.1   In this book, you'll learn about the 18 major categories of Group Policy. Here's a table that should be helpful if you're looking to get started working right with a category. *(continued)*

Group Policy Category	Where in Group Policy Interface	Which Operating Systems support it	Where to find information in the book	Notes
Windows Search	Computer Configuration ➢ Administrative Templates ➢ Windows Components ➢ Search	Windows Vista	Not covered	http://www.microsoft.com/windows/desktopsearch
Deployed Printer Connections	Computer or User Configuration ➢ Windows Settings ➢ Deployed Printers	Technically, Vista-only; workaround available for Windows 2000+	Chapter 12	
Offline Files	Computer Configuration ➢ Administrative Templates ➢ Network ➢ Offline Files	Vista has different Group Policy "moving parts" than other operating systems; feature available in Windows 2000+	Chapter 10	

Group Policy is a twofold idea. First, without an Active Directory, there's one and only one Group Policy available, and that lives on the local Windows XP or Windows 2000 workstation (note that this changes in Windows Vista—but we'll discuss that later). Officially, this is called a *local policy*, but it still resides under the umbrella of the concept of Group Policy. Later, once Active Directory is available, the nonlocal (or, as they're sometimes called, *Domain-based* or *Active Directory–based*) Group Policy Objects come into play, as you'll see later. Let's get started and explore both options.

While you're plunking around inside the Group Policy Object Editor, you'll see lots of policy settings that are geared toward Windows 2000, Windows XP, Windows Vista, and/or Windows 2003. Some are geared only for Windows Vista, and others are geared only for Windows 2003. If you happen to apply a policy to a system that isn't listed, the policy is simply ignored. For instance, policy settings described as working for Windows XP will not typically work on Windows 2000 machines. Each policy setting has a "Supported on" field which should be consulted to know which operating systems can embrace what policy setting.

Understanding Local Group Policy

Before we officially dive in to what is specifically contained inside this magic of Group Policy or how Group Policy is applied when Active Directory is involved, you might be curious to see exactly what your interaction with the Local Group Policy might look like.

Local Group Policy is best used when Active Directory isn't available, say, either in a Netware environment or when you have a gaggle of machines that simply aren't connected to a domain.

Local Group Policy is different for Windows Vista versus the other Windows operating systems. Let's explore Local Group Policy on non-Vista machines first, then move on to the Vista-specific features.

Local Group Policy on Non-Vista Computers

The most expeditious way to edit the local Group Policy on a machine is to click Start ➢ Run and type in **GPEDIT.MSC**. This pops up the Local Computer Policy Editor.

You are now exploring the Local Group Policy of this Windows XP workstation. Local Group Policy is unique to each specific machine. To see how a Local Group Policy applies, drill down through the User Configuration ➢ Administrative Templates ➢ System ➢ Ctrl+Alt+Del Options and select **Remove Lock Computer** as seen in Figure 1.2. Once selected, click "Enabled" and select OK.

FIGURE 1.2   You can edit the local Group Policy once you use the local Group Policy editor (GPEDIT.MSC)

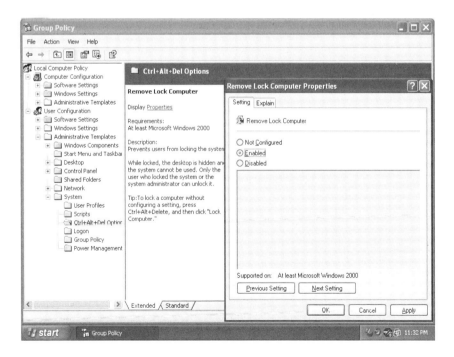

When you do, within a few seconds, you should see that if you press Ctrl+Alt+Del, the "Lock Computer" option is unavailable.

To revert the change, simply re-select **Remove Lock Computer** and select "Not Configured." This reverts the change back to the way the operating system works by default.

> You can think of Local Group Policy as a way to perform decentralized administration. A bit later, when we explore Group Policy with Active Directory, we'll saunter into centralized administration.

This Local Group Policy affects everyone who logs on to this machine—including normal users and administrators. Be careful when making settings here; you can temporarily lock yourself out of some useful functions. For instance, frequently administrators want to remove Run from the Start Menu for Windows XP machines. Then, the first time they themselves want to go to a command prompt, they can't choose Start ➢ Run. It's just gone!

> If this happens, to get that Run command back, you'll have to click the MMC.exe icon in Explorer (or via command line) and manually load the Group Policy Snap-in.

As I stated in the Introduction, most of the settings we'll explore in this book are available to workstations or servers that aren't joined to an Active Directory domain. However, many functions, like Folder Redirection settings (discussed in Chapter 10), the Software Distribution settings (discussed in Chapter 11), and others are not available to stand-alone machines without Active Directory present.

> You can point toward other computers by using the syntax gpedit.msc / gpcomputer:"*targetmachine*" or gpedit.msc /gpcomputer:"*targetmachine* .domain.com"; the machine name must be in quotes.

Local Group Policy on Vista computers

It's true that you can also type **GPEDIT.MSC** at the Vista command prompt and get the same Local Computer Policy Editor you just saw in Windows XP. However, Windows Vista takes Local Group Policy to the next level.

Remember how, not more than four paragraphs ago, I stated:

> "This Local Group Policy affects everyone who logs on to this machine—including normal users and administrators. Be careful when making settings here; you can temporarily lock yourself out of some useful functions."

True: for pre-Vista machines. On Vista, the super-power is that you can decide who gets what settings at a local level. This feature is called Multiple Local GPOs, or MLGPOs for short.

This is most often handy when you want your users to get one gaggle of settings (that is, desktop restrictions) but you want to ensure your access is unfettered for day-to-day administration.

Understanding Multiple Local GPOs

The best way to understand MLGPOs is by thinking of the end product. That is, when we're done, we want our users to embrace some settings, and we'll want us (administrators) to potentially embrace some settings. Or, perhaps you want just one specific user to embrace a particular combination of settings.

When you type **GPEDIT.MSC** at a command prompt, it's just like you did it on Windows XP: you're affecting all users—mere mortals *and* administrators.

However, with just a little bit of extra knowledge you can tap into one of Vista's "secret features." That is, Windows Vista actually has three "layers" that can be leveraged to ensure that some settings affect regular users and other settings affect you (the administrator).

Let's be sure to understand all three layers before we get too gung-ho and try it out. When MLGPOs are processed, it checks to see if the layer is being used, and if that layer is supposed to apply to that user.

Layer 1 (lowest priority)   The Local Computer Policy. You create this by running GPEDIT.MSC.

- The settings you make on the Computer Configuration side are guaranteed to affect all users on this computer (including administrators).

- The settings you make on the User Configuration side may be trumped by Layer 2 or Layer 3 (see below).

Layer 2 (next highest priority)   Is the user a mere-mortal user, OR a local administrator? (One account cannot be both.) This layer cannot contain computer configuration settings.

Layer 3 (most specific)   Am I a specific user who is being dictated a specific policy? This layer cannot contain computer configuration settings.

You can see this graphically laid out in Figure 1.3.

If there are no conflicts amongst the levels, the effect is additive. For instance, let's imagine the following:

- Layer 1 (the Local Computer Policy level): The wish is to **Remove Lock Computer** from the Ctrl+Alt+Del area.

- Then, at Layer 2: We say "All local users" will have "Search" gone from the Start Menu.

- Then, at Layer 3: We say Fred, a local user will be denied access to the Control Panel.

The result for Fred will be the sum total of all edicts at all layers.

But what if there's a conflict between the levels? In that case the layer that's "closest to the user" wins (also known as "Last Writer Wins"). So, if at the Local Computer Policy the wish is to **Remove Lock Computer** from the Ctrl+Alt+Del area, but that area is expressly granted to Sally, a local user on that machine, Sally will still be able to use the "Lock" command. That's because we're saying that she is expressly granted the right at Layer 3, which "wins" over Layers 1 and 2.

Trying out Multiple Local GPOs on Windows Vista

Just typing GPEDIT.MSC at the Vista "Start Search" prompt doesn't give you the magical "Laying" superpower. Indeed, just typing GPEDIT.MSC performs the exact same function as it did in Windows XP. That is, every edit you make while you run the Local Computer Policy affects all users logged on to the machine.

FIGURE 1.3 A block diagram of how Multiple Local GPOs (MLGPOs) are applied to a system

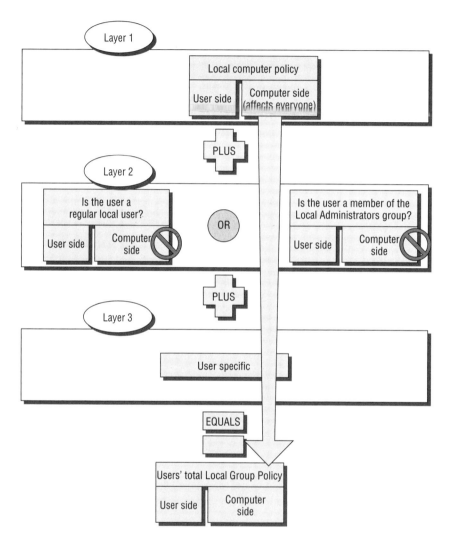

To tell Vista you want to edit one of the layers (as just described), you need to load the Group Policy Object Editor by hand. We'll do this on VISTA1.

On VISTA1, to load the Group Policy Object Editor by hand, follow these steps:

1. Click Start, then in the "Start Search" box, (which will run things) type **MMC**. A "naked" MMC appears. Note, you will have to approve the User Access Control message (UAC is discussed in detail in Chapter 7).

2. From the File menu, choose Add/Remove Snap-in to open the Add/Remove Snap-in dialog box.

3. Locate and select the Group Policy Object Editor Snap-in and click Add (don't choose the Group Policy Management Snap-in—that's the GPMC which we'll use a bit later).

4. At the "Select Group Policy Object" screen, note that the default "Local Computer Policy" is selected, then click "Browse" as seen in Figure 1.4.

5. The "Browse for a Group Policy Object" dialog appears and contains two tabs. Select the "Users" tab and select the layer you want. That is, you can pick "Non-Administrators," "Administrators," or click a specific user as seen in Figure 1.4.

> You can also see in the "Users" tab if a local GPO layer is being used or not in the "Group Policy Object Exists" column.

6. At the "Select a Group Policy Object" dialog select Finish

7. At the "Add or Remove Snap-ins" dialog select OK.

You should now be able to edit that layer of the local GPO. For instance, in Figure 1.5, I've chosen to edit the Non-Administrators portion of the GPO (which is on level 2.)

FIGURE 1.4 Edit specific layers of Windows Vista's MLGPOs by first adding the Group Policy Object Editor into a "naked" MMC. Then, Browse for the Windows Vista Local Group Policy by firing up GPEDIT.MSC.

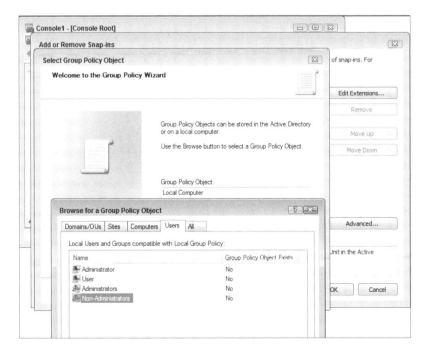

FIGURE 1.5   Below the words "Console Root" you can see which layer of the local GPO you're specifically editing.

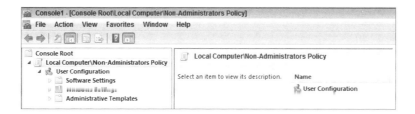

To edit additional or other layers of the local GPO, repeat the previously laid-out steps.

Here's an important point which bears repeating: Layers 2 and 3 of the MLGPO cannot contain computer settings. That's why in Figure 1.5, you simply don't see them—they're not there. If you want to introduce a computer-side setting which affects everyone on the machine, just fire up GPEDIT.MSC and you'll be off and running. That's Layer 1, and it affects everyone.

Local GPOs Final Thoughts

You can think of Local Group Policy as a way to perform desktop management in a decentralized way. That is, you're still running around, more or less, from machine to machine where you want to set the Local Group Policy.

The other strategy is a centralized approach. Centralized Group Policy administration works only in conjunction with Active Directory and is the main focus of this book.

For more information, check out the "Step-by-Step Guide to Managing Multiple Local Group Policy" from Microsoft. At last check the URL was http://tinyurl.com/e4e9k, but it could change by the time you read this.

Local Group Policy is stored in the c:\windows\system32\grouppolicy directory. The structure found here mirrors what you'll see later in Chapter 4 when we inspect the ins and outs of how Group Policy applies from Active Directory.

Active Directory–based Group Policy

To use Group Policy in a meaningful way, you need an Active Directory environment. An Active Directory environment needn't be anything particularly fancy; indeed, it could consist of a single Windows 2000, Windows 2003, or Longhorn Server Domain Controller and perhaps just one Windows XP or Windows Vista workstation joined to the domain.

But Active Directory can also grow extensively from that original solitary server. You can think of an Active Directory network as having four constituent and distinct levels that relate to Group Policy:

- The local computer
- The site
- The domain
- The organizational unit (OU)

The rules of Active Directory state that every server and workstation must be a member of one (and only one) domain and be located in one (and only one) site.

In Windows NT, additional domains were often created to partition administrative responsibility or to rein in needless chatter between Domain Controllers. With Active Directory, administrative responsibility can be delegated using OUs.

Additionally, the problem with needless domain bandwidth chatter has been brought under control with the addition of Active Directory sites, which are concentrations of IP (Internet Protocol) subnets with fast connectivity. There is no longer any need to correlate domains with network bandwidth—that's what sites are for!

Group Policy and Active Directory

When Group Policy is created at the local level, everyone who uses that machine is affected by those wishes. But once you step up and use Active Directory, you can have nearly limitless Group Policy Objects (GPOs)—with the ability to selectively decide which users and which computers will get which wishes (try saying that five times quickly). The GPO is the vessel that stores these wishes for delivery.

     Actually, you can have only 999 GPOs applied to a user or a computer.

When we create a GPO that can be used in Active Directory, we actually create some brand-new entries within Active Directory, and we automatically create some brand-new files on our Domain Controllers, both of which are known as GPOs.

You can think of Active Directory as having three major levels:

- Site
- Domain
- OU

Additionally, since OUs can be nested within each other, Active Directory has a nearly limitless capacity for where we can tuck stuff away.

In fact, it's best to think of this design as a three-tier hierarchy: site, domain, and each nested OU. When wishes, er, policy settings, are set at a higher level in Active Directory, they automatically flow down throughout the remaining levels.

So, to be precise:

- If a GPO is set at the site level, the policy settings contained within affect those accounts within the geography of the site. Sure, their user and computer accounts will be in one or more domains (and/or possibly in an OU), but the account is affected only by the policy settings here because the account is in a specific site.

- If a GPO is set at the domain level, it affects those users and computers within the domain and all OUs and all other OUs beneath it.

- If a GPO is set at the OU level, it affects those users or computers within the OU **and all** other OUs beneath it (usually just called child OUs).

By default, when a policy is set at one level, the levels below *inherit* the settings from the levels above it. You can have "cumulative" wishes that keep piling on.

You might wonder what happens if two policy settings conflict. Perhaps one policy is set at the domain level, and another policy is set at the OU level, which reverses the edict in the domain. The result is simple: Policy settings further down the food chain take precedence. For instance, if a policy setting conflicts at the domain and OU levels, the OU level "wins." Likewise, domain-level settings override any policy settings that conflict with previously set site-specific policy settings. Take a look at the following graphic to get a graphical view of the order of precedence.

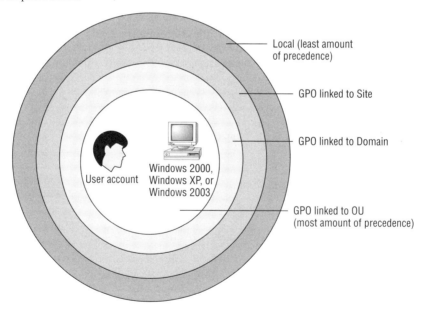

However, don't forget about any Local Group Policy that might have been set on a specific workstation. Recall that for pre-Vista machines, everyone logging on to that workstation is affected by that policy setting. For Vista machines, you just learned how Vista's MLGPOs add up to three layers (where Windows XP's local GPOs has just one).

Regardless, once that local policy is determined, only *then* do policy settings within Active Directory (the site, domain, and OU) apply. So, sometimes people refer to the *four* levels of

Group Policy: local workstation, site, domain, and OU. Nonetheless, GPOs set within Active Directory always "trump" the Local Group Policy should there be any conflict.

If this behavior is undesired for lower levels, all the settings from higher levels can be blocked with a "Block Inheritance" attribute. Additionally, if a higher-level administrator wants to guarantee that a setting is inherited down the food chain, they can apply the "Enforced" attribute via the GPMC interface (or "No Override" attribute in the old-school parlance) (Chapter 2 explores both "Block Inheritance" and "Enforced" attributes in detail).

Don't sweat it if your head is spinning a little bit now from the Group Policy application theory. I'll go through specific hands-on examples to illustrate each of these behaviors so that you understand exactly how this works.

Linking Group Policy Objects

Another technical concept that needs a bit of description here is the "linking" of GPOs. When a GPO is created at the site, domain, or OU level, via the GUI (which we'll do in a moment), the system automatically associates that GPO with the level in which it was created. That association is called *linking*.

Linking is an important concept for several reasons. First, it's generally a good idea to understand what's going on under the hood. However, more practically, the Group Policy Management Console, or GPMC, as we'll explore in just a bit, displays GPOs from their linked perspective.

You can think of all the GPOs you create in Active Directory as children within a big swimming pool. Each child has a tether attached around their waist, and an adult guardian is holding the other end of the rope. Indeed, there could be multiple tethers around a child's waist, with multiple adults tethered to one child. A sad state indeed would be a child who has no tether but is just swimming around in the pool unsecured. The "swimming pool" in this analogy is a specific Active Directory container named Policies (which we'll examine closely in Chapter 4). All GPOs are born and "live" in that specific domain. Indeed, they're replicated to all Domain Controllers. The adult guardian in this analogy represents a *level* in Active Directory—any site, domain, or OU.

In our swimming pool example, multiple adults can be tethered to a specific child. With Active Directory, multiple levels can be linked to a specific GPO. Thus, any level in Active Directory can leverage multiple GPOs, which are standing by in the domain ready to be used.

Remember, though, unless a GPO is specifically linked to a site, a domain, or an OU, it does not take effect. It's just floating around in the swimming pool of the domain waiting for someone to make use of it.

I'll keep reiterating and refining the concept of linking throughout these first four chapters. And, in Chapter 3, I'll discuss why you might want to "unlink" a policy.

This concept of linking to GPOs created in Active Directory can be a bit confusing. It will become clearer a bit later as we explore the processes of creating new GPOs and linking to existing ones. Stay tuned. It's right around the corner.

An Example of Group Policy Application

At this point, it's best not to jump directly into adding, deleting, or modifying our own GPOs. Right now, it's better to understand how Group Policy works "on paper." This is especially true if you're new to the concept of Group Policy, but perhaps also if Group Policy has been deployed by other administrators in your Active Directory.

By walking through a fictitious organization that has deployed GPOs at multiple levels, you'll be able to better understand how and why policy settings are applied by the deployment of GPOs. Let's start by taking a look at Figure 1.6, the organization for our fictitious example company, Corp.com.

This picture could easily tell 1000 words. For the sake of brevity, I've kept it down to around 200. In this example, the domain Corp.com has two Domain Controllers. One DC, named CORPDC1, is physically located in the California site. Corp.com's other Domain Controller, CORPDC2, is physically located in the Phoenix site.

As for PCs, Sally's PC is in the California Site, Brett's PC and Adam's PC are in the Delaware Site. And Adam's PC is specifically placed within the High Security OU.

Using Active Directory Sites and Services, a schedule can be put in place to regulate communication between CORPDC1 located in California and CORPDC2 located in Phoenix. That way the administrator controls the chatter between the two Corp.com Domain Controllers, and it is not at the whim of the operating system.

Inside the Corp.com domain are two OUs: **Human Resources** and (inside **Human Resources**) another OU called **High Security**. FredsPC is located inside the **Human Resources** OU and also in the California site, as are Dave's user account and Jane's user account. There is also JoesPC, which is a member of the Corp.com domain. It physically resides at the Phoenix site and isn't a member of any OU.

Another domain, called Widgets.corp.com, has an automatic transitive two-way trust to Corp.com. There is only one Domain Controller in the Widgets.corp.com domain, named WIDDC1, and it physically resides at the Phoenix site. Last, there is MarksPC, a member of the Widgets.corp.com domain, which physically resides in the New York site and isn't in any OU.

Understanding where your users and machines are is half the battle. The other half is understanding which policy settings are expected to appear when they start logging on to Active Directory.

Examining the Resultant Set of Policy

As stated earlier, the effect of Group Policy is cumulative as GPOs are successively applied—starting at the local computer, the site, the domain, and each nested OU. The end result of what affects a specific user or computer—after all Group Policy at all levels has been applied—is called the *Resultant Set of Policy*, or *RSoP*. This is sometimes referred to as the *RSoP Calculation*.

Throughout your lifetime working with Group Policy, you will be asked to troubleshoot the RSoP of client machines.

FIGURE 1.6 This fictitious Corp.com is relatively simple. Your environment may be more complex.

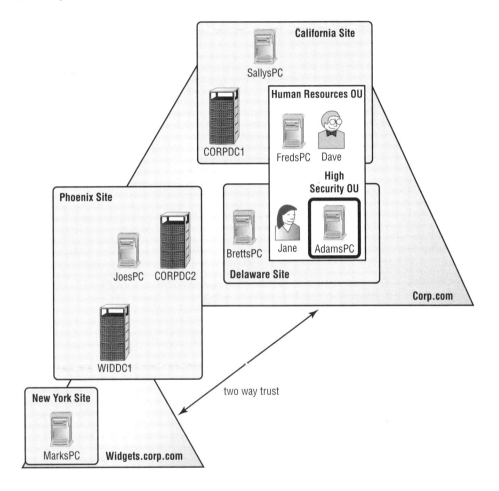

 Much of our dealings with Group Policy will be trying to understand and trouble-shoot the RSoP of a particular configuration. Getting a good understanding early of how to perform manual RSoP calculations on paper will be a useful trouble-shooting skill. In Chapter 3 and Chapter 4, we'll also explore additional RSoP skills—with tools and additional manual troubleshooting.

Before we jump in to try to discover what the RSoP might be for any specific machine, it's often helpful to break out each of the strata—local computer, site, domain, and OU—and examine, at each level, what happens to the entities contained in them. I'll then bring it all together to see how a specific computer or user reacts to the accumulation of GPOs. For these examples, assume that no local policy is set on any of the computers; the goal is to get a better feeling of how Group Policy flows, not necessarily what the specific end-state will be.

At the Site Level

Based on what we know from Figure 1.6, the GPOs in effect at the site level are as follows:

Site	Computers Affected
California	SallysPC, CORPDC1, and FredsPC
Phoenix	CORPDC2, JoesPC, and WIDDC1
New York	MarksPC
Delaware	AdamsPC and BrettsPC

If we look at the graphic again, it looks like Dave, for instance, "resides" in California and Jane, for instance, resides in Delaware. But I don't like to think about it like that. Their accounts "reside" in OUs.

But, users are affected by site GPOs *only* when they log on to computers that are at a specific site.

In Figure 1.6, we have Dave in California (because he's using a PC in California) and Jane is in Delaware (because she's using a PC in Delaware). So, don't think that they "reside" at the site level. Rather, they reside in the OU level, but are using computers in the site, and hence, get the properties assigned to all users at that site.

At the Domain Level

Here's what we have working at the domain level:

Domain	Computers/Users Affected
Corp.com Computers	SallysPC, FredsPC, AdamsPC, BrettsPC, JoesPC, CORPDC1, and CORPDC2
Corp.com Users	Dave and Jane
Widgets.corp.com Computers	WIDDC1 and MarksPC

At the OU Level

At the organizational unit level, we have the following:

Organizational Unit	Computers/Users Affected
Human Resources OU Computers	FredsPC is in the Human Resources OU; therefore it is affected when the Human Resources OU gets GPOs applied. Additionally, the High Security OU is contained inside the Human Resources OU. Therefore, AdamsPC, which is in the High Security OU, is also affected whenever the Human Resources OU is affected.
Human Resources OU Users	The accounts of Dave and Jane are affected when the Human Resources OU has GPOs applied.

Bringing It All Together

Now that you've broken out all the levels and seen what is being applied to them, you can start to calculate what the devil is happening on any specific user and computer combination. Looking at Figure 1.6 and analyzing what's happening at each level makes adding things together between the local, site, domain, and organizational unit GPOs a lot easier.

Here are some examples of RSoP for specific users and computers in our fictitious environment:

FredsPC   FredsPC inherits the settings of the GPOs from the California site, then the Corp.com domain, and last, the Human Resources OU.

MarksPC   MarksPC first accepts the GPOs from the New York site and then the Widgets.corp.com domain. MarksPC is not in any OU; therefore, no organizational unit GPOs apply to his computer.

AdamsPC   AdamsPC is subject to the GPOs at the Delaware site, the Corp.Com domain, the Human Resources OU, and the High Security OU.

Dave using AdamsPC   AdamsPC is subject to the computer policies in the GPOs for the Delaware site, the Corp.com domain, the Human Resources OU, and finally the High Security OU.

When Dave travels from California to Delaware to use Adam's workstation, his user GPOs are dictated from the Delaware site, the Corp.com domain, and the Human Resources OU.

 At no time are any domain GPOs from the Corp.com parent domain automatically inherited by the Widget.corp.com child domain. Inheritance for GPOs only flows downward to OUs within a single domain—not between any two domains—parent to child or otherwise, unless you explicitly link one of those parent GPOs to a child domain container.

If you want one GPO to affect the users in more than one domain, you have four choices:

- Precisely re-create the GPOs in each domain with their own GPO.

- Copy the GPO from one domain to another domain (using the GPMC, as explained in the Appendix).

- Use a third-party tool that can perform some magic and automatically perform the copying between domains for you. (Check out www.GPanswers.com for a list of tools.)

- Do a generally recognized no-no called *cross-domain policy linking*. (I'll describe this no-no in detail in Chapter 4 in the "Group Policy Objects from a Domain Perspective" section.)

Also, don't assume that linking a GPO at a site level necessarily guarantees the results to just one domain. In this example, as in real life, there is not necessarily a 1:1 correlation between sites and domains.

Group Policy, Active Directory, and the GPMC

Active Directory administrators already somewhat familiar with Group Policy will tell you that finding what you need and understanding what's going on under the hood can sometimes be confusing. The interface used to create, modify, and manipulate Group Policy in the original iteration of Active Directory on Windows 2000 has led to numerous missteps and head scratching when people try to figure out why something isn't going the way it should.

Occasionally, Microsoft has recognized that the first iteration of a product release has missed the mark a little in the way the product works, acts, or interfaces. They often request additional customer feedback, embrace it, regroup, and return a "2.0 version" of the product.

To make optimal use of Group Policy in an Active Directory environment, the Group Policy team at Microsoft introduced a free, downloadable "2.0 version" for managing Group Policy in Active Directory. It's called the Group Policy Management Console, or GPMC, as mentioned earlier. The GPMC isn't part of the Windows 2000, Windows 2003, or Windows XP operating systems; you need to fetch it and install it. It is, however, part of the shipping Windows Vista, so no extra effort is required.

Kickin' It Old School

Out of the box, the tools built-in to Windows 2000 and Windows 2003 domains use the old-style interface. This interface is built in to the Active Directory Users and Computer and Active Directory Sites and Services.

If you've never seen the old-style interface, you can do so right now before we leave it in the dust for the new GPMC in the next section.

To see the old-style interface and create your first GPO at the domain level, follow these steps:

1. Log on to the Domain Controller DC01 as the Administrator account (which is a Domain Administrator).

2. Choose Start ➢ All Programs ➢ Administrative Tools and select Active Directory Users And Computers. Alternatively, select Start ➢ Run and select dsa.msc to open up Active Directory Users and Computer.

3. Right-click the domain name and choose Properties from the shortcut menu, as shown in Figure 1.7, to open the Properties dialog box for the domain.

4. Click the Group Policy tab.

There is a "Default Domain Policy" GPO, but you won't modify it at this time. (I'll talk about it in Chapter 6.)

FIGURE 1.7   Right-click the domain name and choose Properties.

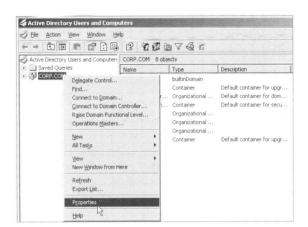

5. Click the New button to spawn the creation of your first GPO.

6. For this first example, type **My First GPO**, as shown in Figure 1.8.

7. Highlight the policy and click Edit to open the Group Policy Object Editor.

At this point, things should look familiar, just like the Local Group Policy Object Editor, with the user and computer nodes. For example, if you drill down into the Administrative Templates folder in the User Configuration folder, you can make a wish at the domain level, and all your computers will obey.

For now, don't actually make any changes; just close the Group Policy Object Editor and read on.

FIGURE 1.8   You've just created your first GPO in Active Directory.

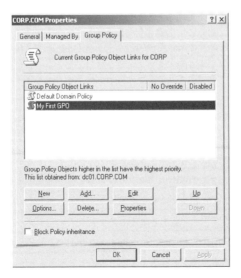

GPMC Overview

The Group Policy Management Console (GPMC) was created to help administrators work in a "one-stop-shop" place for all Group Policy management functions. Since 2003, it was freely downloadable as an add-on to either Windows XP or Windows Server 2003 systems. In Windows Vista, it's included in-the-box! And, best part, it doesn't matter if your Active Directory or domains are Windows 2000 or Windows 2003; it just matters that you have Active Directory.

Why Abandon Old School?

In Figure 1.8, we were able to create our first GPO (even though we didn't actually place any policy settings in there). The interface seems reasonable enough to take care of such simple tasks. And, heck, this interface is already part of the operating system, so, why move away from it?

The old-school way of viewing and managing Group Policy just isn't scalable over the long haul. This interface doesn't show us any relationship between the GPO we just created and the domain it's in. As you'll see in this chapter, the new interface demonstrates a much clearer relationship between the GPOs you create, the links it takes to use them, and the domains where the GPOs actually "live."

The old-style interface also provides no easy way to figure out what's going on inside the GPOs you create. To determine what changes are made inside a GPO, you need to reopen each GPO and poke around. I've seen countless administrators open each and every GPO in their domain and manually document their settings on paper for backup and recovery purposes.

Indeed, backup and recovery is a really, really big deal, and the old-school mechanism (via NTBACKUP) provided no realistic way to back up and recover GPOs without copious amounts of surgery. The GPMC makes it a snap.

With that in mind, I encourage all of you—those currently using the original Windows 2000 old-school way (and those who haven't even yet been to school)—to step up and try the new way of doing things, the GPMC.

Even though you cannot load the GPMC on a Windows 2000 Domain Controller or a Windows 2000 Professional machine, it's still capable of controlling Windows 2000 domains.

About the GPMC

The GPMC's name says it all. It's the Group Policy Management Console. Indeed, this will be the MMC snap-in that you use to manage the underlying Group Policy mechanism. The GPMC just helps us tap into those features already built into Active Directory. I'll highlight the mechanism of how Group Policy works throughout the next three chapters.

One major design goal of the GPMC is to get a Group Policy–centric view of the lay of the land. Compared with the old interface, the GPMC does a much better job of aligning the user interface of Group Policy with what's going on under the hood.

The GPMC also provides a programmatic way to manage your GPOs. In fact, the GPMC scripting interface allows just about any GPO operation (other than to dive in and create or modify actual policy settings). We'll explore scripting with the GPMC in Chapter 7. So, if you're interested in scripting, you'll need to have the GPMC bits loaded on the XP or Vista systems you want to script. The GPMC is (yay!) included in Windows Vista—Microsoft has already loaded it for you!

> The GPMC scripts, which were previously part of the downloadable GPMC package are not included in Windows Vista. You have to specifically download them from the GPMC scripting center at www.microsoft.com/technet/ scriptcenter/hubs/gp.mspx.

There are lots of ways you *could* manage your Group Policy universe. Some people walk up to their Domain Controllers, log on to the console, and manage their Group Policy infrastructure there. Others use a *management workstation* and manage their Group Policy infrastructure from their own Windows XP or Windows Vista workstations.

I'll talk more about the use and best practices of a Windows Vista management workstation in Chapter 5.

Implementing the GPMC on Your Management Station

As I mentioned, the GPMC isn't part of the standard Windows 2003 or Windows XP package out of the box. But, if you're holding this book in your hands, it doesn't matter. That's because the GPMC is built right in to Windows Vista. That's right—there's nothing to download, nothing to install, and nothing to worry about.

Remember earlier we stated that you could manage your Active Directory from anywhere. And this is true. You *could* walk up to a Domain Controller, you *could* install the GPMC on a Windows XP or Windows Server 2003 server, or you *could* use Terminal Services to remotely connect to a Domain Controller.

But in this book, you won't be.

Upgrading from NT 4 to Windows 2000, Windows 2003, or Windows 2003/ SP1: Cleaning Up Old GPOs

If you have any remaining Windows 2000 Domain Controllers, you should have at least SP2 and preferably SP3 applied to them. This is because most Windows 2003 tools, including the GPMC, use LDAP (Lightweight Directory Access Protocol) signing for all communication. For more information, see the Microsoft Knowledge Base article 325465.

After you run the GPMC, you may be prompted to "clean up" older GPOs the first time you touch one. You should do so. Under the hood, the GPMC is adjusting some key security descriptors in Active Directory.

The precise error message you'll get is, "The permissions for this GPO in the SYSVOL folder are inconsistent with those in Active Directory. It is recommended that these permissions be consistent. To change the SYSVOL permissions to those in Active Directory, click OK."

By allowing this, you can do some fancy footwork later, as you'll see in the section "Advanced Security and Delegation with the GPMC" in Chapter 2. You will see this message if your Windows 2000 PDC-Emulator domain was upgraded from anything prior to SP4.

Using a Windows Vista Management Station

You'll be using what's known as a Windows Vista "Management Station."

I delve into this in serious detail in Chapter 5, but here's the CliffsNotes, er, Jeremy's Notes version:

- Always use Windows Vista as your management station, and you'll always be able to control all operating systems' settings: Windows Vista and earlier.

- If you have even one Windows Vista client machine (say, in Sales, Marketing, etc.) you're going to need to manage it using a Windows Vista management station.

- If you create a GPO using Windows Vista but then edit it using an older operating system, you might not be able to "see" all the settings. And, what's worse, some might actually be set (but you wouldn't see them!).

- The GPMC is already preloaded on Vista, and it's updated with the latest bug fixes and the like, so it makes sense to use Windows Vista.

- You can always (if you need to) remote control a Windows Vista machine via Terminal Services (also known as Remote Desktop) in order to access the GPMC and Group Policy goodies on Vista.

So—good news! If you've got even one Windows Vista box up and running—you're done! That is, you don't need to install anything on your machine. Again, for our examples we'll call our machine VISTAMANAGEMENT. So, on VISTAMANAGEMENT click Start and in the "Start Search" prompt type the **gpmc.msc** command.

If You Must Use a Windows XP or Windows Server 2003 Management Station

Again, I recommend against using the GPMC on Windows XP or Windows 2003 if you've even got just one Windows Vista machine to use. Read Chapter 5 for the full rundown about why.

However, if you feel you must continue to use Windows XP or Windows Server 2003 as your management station, you can download the GPMC for free from www.microsoft .com/grouppolicy. Click the link for the Group Policy Management Console to locate the download.

Once it's downloaded, the GPMC is called GPMC.MSI. You can install this on either Windows 2003 or Windows XP with at least SP1, but nothing else. That is, you cannot load the GPMC on Windows 2000 servers or workstations; but, as I noted before, the

GPMC can manage Windows 2000 domains with Windows 2000 and Windows XP clients as well as Windows 2003 domains with Windows 2000 or Windows XP clients.

Installing the GPMC does require certain prerequisites, which must be loaded in the order listed here.

Loading the GPMC on Windows XP

If you intend to load the GPMC on a Windows XP machine to manage Group Policy in your domain, follow these steps:

1. At least Windows XP Service Pack 1 is required. If you are unsure whether SP1 (or later) is installed, run the WINVER command, which will tell you whether a service pack is installed. So, if your Windows XP system doesn't have at least SP1 installed, you should install it.

2. The GPMC requires the .NET Framework 1.1 to run properly. Note that if you only have the newer .NET Framework (2 or higher), it won't work. It simply must be .NET Framework 1.1. If it's not installed, you'll need to download and install it. At last check, the .NET Framework download was at a URL I've shortened to http://tinyurl.com/ 7vshz. If it's not there, Google for ".NET Framework 1.1."

   After downloading .NET Framework, double-click the install to get it going on your target Windows XP/SP1 (or greater) machine. It isn't a very exciting or noteworthy installation.

3. To install the GPMC, double-click the GPMC.MSI file you downloaded. If you're running Windows XP with SP1, the GPMC installation routine will report that a hotfix (also known as a QFE) is required and then proceed to automatically install the hotfix on the fly. This hotfix (Q326469) is incorporated into Windows XP's SP2. So, if installing on a Windows XP/SP2 machine, you won't be asked to bother to install it.

Technically the GPMC runs fine on .NET 2 only, but the MSI installer chokes when checking .NET versions. If you have the skills to get around that, you're theoretically good to go with just .NET 2.

Loading the GPMC on a Windows 2003 Domain Controller

If you intend to load the GPMC on a Windows 2003 Domain Controller or a member server, there are just a couple of things to do:

1. Although there aren't any Windows 2003 prerequisites, it's a good idea to install the .NET Framework 1.1. If the operating system tells you that it's already installed; you're a-ok. If not, load it up.

2. To install the GPMC, double-click the GPMC.MSI file you downloaded.

The Results of Loading the GPMC on Windows XP

After the GPMC is loaded on the machine from which you will manage Group Policy (the management workstation), you'll see that the way you view things has changed. If you take a look in Active Directory Users And Computers (or Active Directory Sites And Services) and try to manage a GPO, you'll see a curious link on the existing Group Policy tab (as seen in Figure 1.9).

FIGURE 1.9   The Group Policy tab now refers you to the GPMC and provides a link.

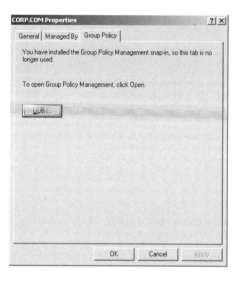

Additionally, you'll see a Group Policy Management icon in the Administrative Tools folder in the Start Menu folder.

Creating a One-Stop Shop MMC

As you'll see, the GPMC is a fairly comprehensive Group Policy management tool. But the problem is that right now, the GPMC and the Active Directory Users And Computers snap-ins are not integrated beyond what you see in Figure 1.9.

Often, you'll want to change a Group Policy on an OU and then move computers to that OU. Unfortunately, you can't do so from the GPMC; you must to return to Active Directory Users And Computers to finish the task. This can get frustrating quickly. The GPMC does allow you to right-click at the domain level to choose to launch the Active Directory Users And Computers console when you want, but I prefer a one-stop shop view of my Active Directory management. It's a matter of taste.

To that end, my preference is to create a custom MMC by running MMC from the Run dialog box and then add in both Active Directory Users And Computer and Group Policy Management snap-ins as shown in Figure 1.10.

You might be wondering at this point "So, Jeremy, what are the steps I need in order to create this unified MMC console you've so neatly described and shown in Figure 1.10?" Well, that's the bit of bad news. As of this writing, Windows Vista doesn't yet have the Administration Pack which would have the tools you need to make this magic happen on your Windows Vista management station. But, the previous version of the Adminpak (for Windows Server 2003) can run on Windows Vista—with a bit of elbow grease (until the Windows Vista Adminpak is finally released).

FIGURE 1.10   Use the MMC to create a unified console.

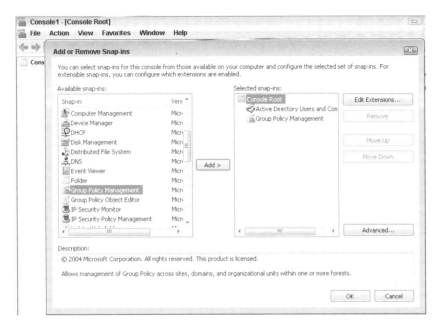

If you want to run the Windows Server 2003 Adminpak on your Windows Vista management station (VistaManagement), check out `http://support.microsoft.com/default.aspx/kb/930056` for the gory step-by-steps and gotchas. Get the latest version of the Windows Server 2003/SP1 Adminpak here `http://tinyurl.com/9f2wm`. Ultimately, going through the pain will be worth it, because you'll then have both the Active Directory Users and Computer (from the Adminpak) and the GPMC (pre-loaded with Windows Vista) in one place. Then, you can just fire up `mmc.exe` and add in the two snap-ins you need, and it'll look just like Figure 1.10 (except it'll be on your Windows Vista management station).

Once you have added both snap-ins into your console, you'll really have a near-unified view of most of what you need at your fingertips. Both Active Directory Users And Computers and the GPMC can create and delete OUs. Both tools also allow administrators to delegate permissions to others to manage Group Policy, but that's where the two tools' functionality overlap ends.

The GPMC won't show you the actual users and computer objects inside the OU; so deleting an OU from within the GPMC is dicey at best, because you can't be sure of what's inside!

You can choose to add other snaps-ins too, of course, including Active Directory Sites And Services or anything else you think is useful. The illustrations in the rest of this book will show both snap-ins loaded in this configuration.

You can launch the GPMC from either the new link in Active Directory Users And Computers (or Active Directory Sites And Services) or directly from the new icon in the Start Menu. However, clicking Open in the existing tools has a slight advantage of telling the GPMC to "snap to" the location in Active Directory on which you are currently focused.

I came across this tip a liiiiiittle too late while writing this book. This means that many, many screenshots show Active Directory Users and Computers being used on Windows Server 2003 and not on Windows Vista (like Figure 1.11). Don't let that throw you. My advice still stands: use Windows Vista whenever you can as your management station. We discuss this is gory detail in Chapter 5, and believe me—it pays off.

Using the GPMC in Active Directory

For the examples in this book, I'll refer to our sample Domain Controller, DC01, which is part of my example Corp.com domain. For these examples, you can choose to rename the Default-First-Site-Name site or not—your choice.

Let's start with some basics to ensure that things are running smoothly. For most of the examples in this book, you'll be able to get by with just the one Domain Controller and one or two workstations that participate in the domain, for verifying that your changes took place.

Again, I encourage you to not try these examples on your production network, in order to avoid a CLM (Career-Limiting Move).

For our examples, we'll assume you're using VISTAMANAGEMENT as your management station.

Active Directory Users And Computers versus GPMC

The main job of Active Directory Users And Computers is to give you an "Active Directory object-centric" view of your domain. Active Directory Users And Computers lets you deal with users, computers, groups, contacts, the operations masters (FSMOs), and delegation of control over user accounts as well as change the domain mode and define advanced security and auditing inside Active Directory. You can also create OUs and move users and computers around inside those OUs. Other administrators can then drill down inside Active Directory Users And Computers into an OU and see the computers, groups, contacts, and so on you've moved to those OUs.

But the GPMC has one main job: to provide you with a "Group Policy-centric" view of all you control. All the OUs that you see in Active Directory Users And Computers are visible in the GPMC. Think about it—it's the same Active Directory behind the scenes "storing" that OU.

However, the GPMC does *not* show you users, computers, contacts, and such. When you drill down into an OU inside the GPMC, you'll see but one thing: the GPOs that affect the objects inside the OU.

In Figure 1.11, you can see the Active Directory Users And Computers view as well as the GPMC view—rolled up into one MMC that we created earlier. The Active Directory Users And Computers view of **Temporary Office Help** and the GPMC view of the same OU is radically different.

FIGURE 1.11   GPMC shows the same OUs as Active Directory Users And Computers. However, the GPMC shows GPO relationships, not users, computers, or other objects.

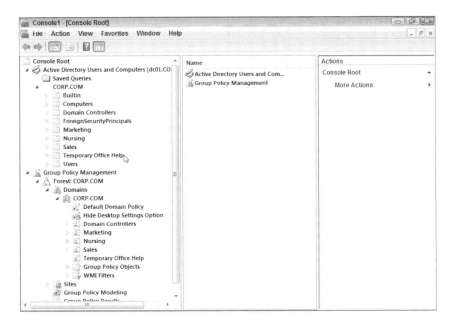

When focused at a site, a domain, or an OU within the GPMC, you see only the GPOs that affect that level in Active Directory. You don't see the same "stuff" that Active Directory Users And Computers sees, such as users, computers, groups, or contacts.

The basic overlap in the two tools is the ability to create and delete OUs. If you add or delete an OU in either tool, you need to refresh the other tool by pressing F5 to see the update. For instance, in Figure 1.11, you can see that my Active Directory has several OUs, including one named **Temporary Office Help**.

Deleting an OU from inside the GPMC is generally a bad idea. Because you cannot see the Active Directory objects inside the OU (such as users and computers), you don't really know how many objects you're about to delete. So be careful!

If I delete the **Temporary Office Help** OU in Active Directory Users And Computers, the change is not reflected in the GPMC window until it's refreshed. And vice versa.

Adjusting the View within the GPMC

The GPMC lets you view as much or as little of your Active Directory as you like. By default, you view only your own forest and domain. You can optionally add in the ability to see the sites in your forest, as well as the ability to see other domains in your forest or domains in other forests, although these views might not be the best for seeing what you have control over.

Viewing Sites in the GPMC   When you create GPOs, you won't often create GPOs that affect sites. The designers of the GPMC seem to agree; it's a bit of a chore to apply GPOs to sites. To do so, you need to link an *existing* GPO to a site. You'll see how to do this a bit later in this chapter.

However, you first need to expose the site objects in Active Directory. To do so, right-click the Sites object in GPMC, choose "Show Sites" from the shortcut menu (see Figure 1.12), and then click the check box next to each site you want to expose.

In our first example, we'll use the site level of Active Directory to deploy our first Group Policy Object. At this point, go ahead and enable the Default-First-Site so that you can have it ready for use in our own experiments.

Viewing Other Domains in the GPMC   To see other domains in your forest, drill down to the Forest folder in Group Policy Management, right-click Domains, choose Show Domains, and select the other available domains in your forest. Each domain will now appear at the same hierarchical level in the GPMC.

Viewing Other Forests in the GPMC   To see other forests, right-click the root (Group Policy Management), and choose "Add Forest" from the shortcut menu. You'll need to type the name of the Active Directory forest you want to add. If you want to add or subtract domains within that new forest, follow the instructions in the preceding paragraph.

FIGURE 1.12   You need to expose the Active Directory sites before you can link GPOs to them.

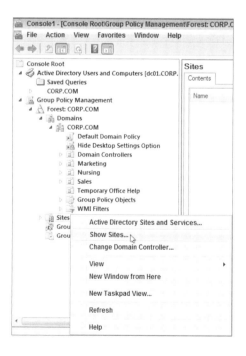

You can add forests with which you do not have a trust. However, GPMC defaults will not display these domains as a safety mechanism. To turn off the safety, choose View ➢ Options to open the Options dialog box. In the General tab, clear "Enable Trust Detection" and click OK.

Now that we've adjusted our view to see the domains and forests we want, let's examine how to manipulate our GPOs and GPO links.

The GPMC-centric View

As I stated earlier, one of the fundamental concepts of Group Policy is that the GPOs themselves live in the "swimming pool" that is the domain. Then, when a level in Active Directory needs to use that GPO, there is simply a link to the GPO.

Figure 1.13 shows what our swimming pool will eventually look like when we're done with the examples in this chapter.

FIGURE 1.13   Imagine your about-to-be-leveraged GPOs as just hanging out in the swimming pool of the domain.

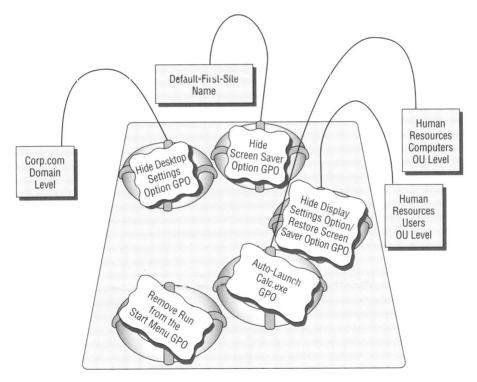

The Corp.com GPO Swimming Pool

Our swimming pool will be full of GPOs, with various levels in Active Directory "linked" to those GPOs. To that end, you can drill down, right now, to see the representation of the swimming pool. It's there, waiting for you. Click Group Policy Management ➢ Forest ➢ Domains ➢ Corp.com ➢ Group Policy Objects to see all the GPOs that exist in the domain (see Figure 1.14).

FIGURE 1.14   The Group Policy Objects folder highlighted here is the representation of the swimming pool of the domain that contains your actual GPOs.

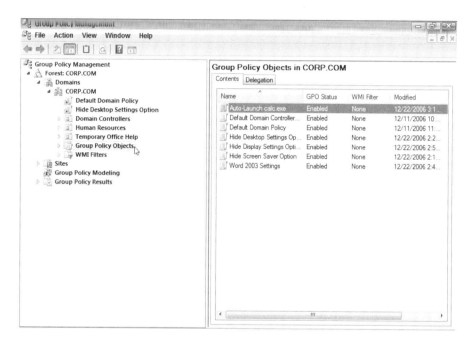

 If you're just getting started, it's not likely you'll have more than the "Default Domain Controllers Policy" GPO and "Default Domain Policy" GPO. That's OK. You'll start getting more GPOs soon enough. Oh, and for now, please don't modify the default GPOs. They're a bit special and are covered in great detail in Chapter 6.

All GPOs in the domain are represented in the Group Policy Objects folder. As you can see, when the **Temporary Office Help** OU is shown within the GPMC, a relationship exists between the OU and the "Enforce 50MB Disk Quotas" GPO. That relationship is the tether to the GPO in the swimming pool—the GPO link back to "Enforce 50MB Disk Quotas." You can see this linked relationship because the "Enforce 50MB Disk Quotas" icon inside **Temporary Office Help** has a little arrow icon, signifying the link back to the actual GPO in the domain.

Our Own Group Policy Examples

Now that you've got a grip on honing your view within the GPMC, let's take it for a quick spin around the block with some examples!

For this series of examples, we're going after the users who keep fiddling with their display gadgets in Windows Vista, Windows XP, and Windows 2000.

If you want to see these examples in action using Windows XP, first start out on XPPRO1 by checking out the default Display Properties dialog box. Just right-click the Desktop and choose Properties from the shortcut menu. You'll see several tabs, including Screensaver, Appearance, and Settings, as shown in Figure 1.15 (left screen).

If you want to see these examples in action using Windows Vista, first start out on VISTA1 by looking at the "Personalize appearance and sounds" page, which is located by right-clicking the Desktop and choosing Personalize. You'll see several entries including Screen Saver, Windows Color and Appearance, and Display Settings as shown in Figure 1.15 (right screen).

FIGURE 1.15 In Windows XP, all the tabs in the Display Properties dialog box are available by default (left screen). In Windows Vista, we can see lots of available areas in the "Personalization" screen, shown on right.

Since they're called "tabs" in Windows XP and "entries" or "options" in Windows Vista, I'll just generally call them "options" from here on out.

For our first use of Group Policy, we're going to produce four "edicts" (for dramatic effect, you should stand on your desk and loudly proclaim these edicts with a thick British accent):

- At the site level, there will be no more ability to change Screen Savers.
- At the domain level, there will be no Desktop Settings option in the Windows Vista Personalization page (or Desktop tab in the Display Properties dialog box for Windows XP).

- At the **Human Resources Users** OU level, there will be no Display Settings option in the Windows Vista Personalization page (or Settings tab in the Display Properties for Windows XP). And, while we're at it, let's bring back the ability to change Screen Savers!

- At the **Human Resources Computers** OU, we'll make it so whenever anyone uses a Human Resources computer, `calc.exe` automatically launches after login.

Following along with these concrete examples will reinforce the concepts presented earlier. Additionally, they are used throughout the remainder of this chapter and the book.

Understanding GPMC's Link Warning

As you work through the examples, you'll do a lot of clicking around. When you click a GPO link the first time, you'll get this message:

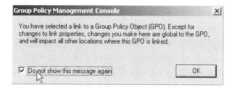

This message is trying to convey an important sentiment. That is, multiple levels in Active Directory may be linked back and use the exact same GPO. The idea is that multiple levels of Active Directory could use the exact same Group Policy Object contained inside the Group Policy Objects container—but just be linked back to it.

What if you modify the policy settings by right-clicking a policy link and choosing Edit from the shortcut menu? All instances in Active Directory that link to that GPO embrace the new settings. If this is a fear, you might want to create another GPO and then link it to the level in Active Directory you want. More properties are affected by this warning, and we'll explore them in Chapter 3.

If you've squelched this message by selecting "Do not show this message again," you can get it back. In the GPMC in the menus, choose View ➢ Options and select the General tab and select "Show Confirmation Dialog To Distinguish Between GPOs And GPO Links" and click OK.

More about Linking and the Group Policy Objects Container

The GPMC is a fairly flexible tool. Indeed, it permits the administrator to perform many tasks in different ways. One thing you'll do quite a lot in your travels with the GPMC is to actually create your own Group Policy Objects. Again, GPOs live in a container within Active Directory and are represented within the Group Policy Objects container (the swimming pool) inside the domain (seen in Figure 1.14, earlier in this chapter). Any levels of Active Directory—site, domain, or OU—simply link back to the GPOs hanging out in the Group Policy Objects container.

To apply Group Policy to a level in Active Directory (site, domain, or OU) using the GPMC, you have two options:

- Create the GPOs in the Group Policy Objects container first. Then, while focused at the level you want to command in Active Directory (site, domain, or OU), manually add a link to the GPO that is in the Group Policy Objects container.

- While focused at the level you want to command in Active Directory (domain or OU), create the GPOs in the Group Policy Objects container and automatically create the link. This link is created at the level you're currently focused at *back* to the GPO in the Group Policy Objects container.

Which is the correct way to go? Both are perfectly acceptable, because both are really doing the same thing.

In both cases the GPO itself does not "live" at the level in Active Directory at which you're focused. Rather, the GPO itself "lives" in the Group Policy Objects container. The link back to the GPO inside the Group Policy Objects container is what makes the relationship between the GPO inside the Group Policy Objects container swimming pool and the level in Active Directory you want to command.

To get the hang of this, let's work through some examples. First, let's create our first GPO in the Group Policy Objects folder. Follow these steps:

1. Launch the GPMC.

2. Traverse down by clicking Group Policy Management ➤ Forest ➤ Domains ➤ Corp.com ➤ Group Policy Objects.

3. Right-click the Group Policy Objects folder and choose New from the shortcut menu to open the New GPO dialog box as seen in Figure 1.16.

4. Let's name our first edict, er, GPO, something descriptive, such as "Hide Screen Saver Option."

5. Once the name is entered, you'll see the new GPO listed in the swimming pool. Right-click the GPO, and choose Edit to open the Group Policy Object Editor as seen in Figure 1.17.

6. To hide the Screen Saver option, drill down by clicking User Configuration ➤ Administrative Templates ➤ Control Panel ➤ Display. Double-click the **Hide Screen Saver tab** policy setting to open the "Hide Screen Saver tab Properties" screen, as shown in Figure 1.18. Select the "Enabled" setting, and click OK.

7. Close the Group Policy Object Editor.

FIGURE 1.16   You create your first GPO in the Group Policy Object container by right-clicking and choosing New.

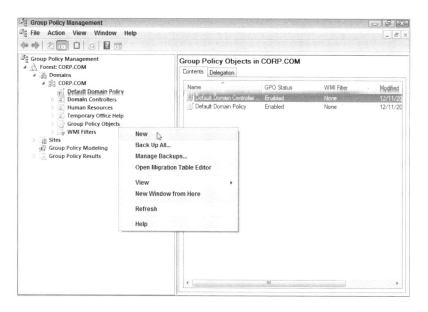

FIGURE 1.17   You can right-click the GPO in the Group Policy Objects container and choose Edit from the shortcut menu to open the Group Policy Object Editor.

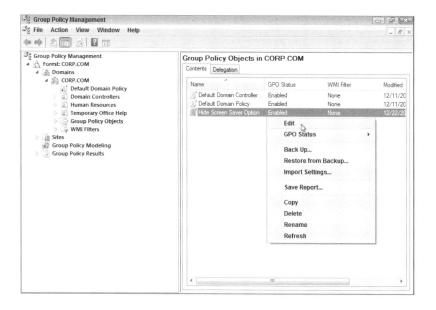

FIGURE 1.18   Double-click the policy setting and "Enable" it.

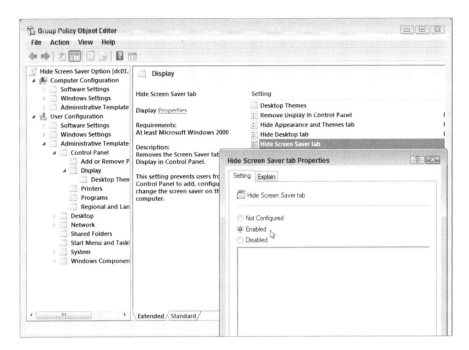

 Note how the policy setting name is called **Hide Screen Saver Tab**. However, in Windows Vista, there isn't a "tab" like there is in either Windows 2000 or Windows XP. It's more like an option on the "Personalization" page. You'll see this later. Just note that not all policy settings have a 100 percent direct meaning sometimes, in rare occurrences like this.

Understanding Our Actions

Now that we have this "Hide Screen Saver Option" edict, er, GPO floating around in the Group Policy Objects container—in the representation of the swimming pool of the domain—what have we done? Not a whole lot, actually, other than create some bits inside Active Directory and upon the Domain Controllers. By creating new GPOs in the Group Policy Objects folder, we haven't inherently forced our desires on *any* level in Active Directory—site, domain, or OU.

To actually make a level in Active Directory accept our will, we need to link this new Group Policy Object to an existing level. Only then will our will be accepted and embraced. Let's do that now.

Applying Group Policy Object to the Site Level

The least-often-used level of Group Policy application is at the site. This is because it's got the broadest stroke but the bluntest application. Additionally, since Active Directory states that only members of the Enterprise Administrators (EAs) can modify sites and site links, it's equally true that only EAs (by default) can add and manipulate GPOs at the site level.

When a tree or a forest contains more than one domain, only the EAs and the Domain Administrators (DAs) of the root domain can create and modify sites and site links. When multiple domains exist, DAs in domains other than the root domain cannot create sites or site links (or site-level GPOs).

However, site GPOs might come in handy on an occasion or two. For instance, you might want to set up site-level GPO definitions for network-specific settings, such as Internet Explorer proxy settings or an IP security policy for sensitive locations. Setting up site-based settings is useful if you have one building (set up explicitly as an Active Directory site) that has a particular or unique network configuration. You might choose to modify the Internet Explorer proxy settings if this building has a unique proxy server. Or in the case of IP security, perhaps this facility has particularly sensitive information, such as confidential records or payroll information.

Therefore, if you're not an EA (or a DA of the root domain), it's likely you'll never get to practice this exercise outside the test lab. And, note in the upcoming chapters, we'll show you how to delegate these rights to other administrators, like OU administrators around the bend.

In this example, we'll work with a basic example to get the feel of the Group Policy Object Editor.

Implementing GPOs linked to sites can have a substantial impact on your logon times and WAN (Wide Area Network) traffic if not performed correctly. For more information, see Chapter 4 in the "Group Policy Objects from a Site Perspective" section.

We already stood on our desks and loudly declared that there will be no Screen Saver options at our one default site. The good news is that we've already done two-thirds of what we need to do to make that site accept our will: we exposed the sites we want to manage, and we created the "Hide Screen Saver Option" GPO in the Group Policy Objects container.

Now, all we need do is to tether the GPO we created to the site with a GPO link.

To remove the Screen Saver option using the Group Policy Object Editor at the site level, follow these steps:

1. Inside the GPMC snap-in, drill down by clicking the Group Policy Management folder, the Forest folder, and the Sites folder.

2. Find the site to which you want to deliver the policy. If you have only one site, it is likely called Default-First-Site-Name.

3. Right-click the site, and choose "Link an Existing GPO," as shown in Figure 1.19.

4. Now you can select the "Hide Screen Saver Option" GPO from a list of GPOs in the Group Policy Objects container in the domain.

FIGURE 1.19   Once you have your first GPO designed, you can link it to your site.

Once you have chosen the GPO, it will be linked to the site. You can also view it in the "Linked Group Policy Objects" tab in the right pane.

  Did you notice that there was no "Are You Sure You Really Want To Do This?" warning or anything similar? The GPMC trusts that you set up the GPO correctly. If you create GPOs with incorrect settings and/or link them to the wrong level in Active Directory, you can make boo-boos on a grand scale. Again—this is why you want to try any setting you want to deploy in a test lab environment first.

Verifying Your Changes at the Site Level

Now, log onto any workstation or server that falls within the boundaries of the site to which you applied the site-wide GPO. If you didn't change any of the defaults, you should be able to log on to any computer in the domain (say, XPPRO1 or VISTA1) as any user you have defined—even the administrator of the domain.

By right-clicking the Desktop and selecting Personalize (for Vista) or Properties (for Windows XP) you'll see that the Screen Saver option is gone as seen in Figure 1.20.

  Don't panic if you do not see the changes reflected the first time you log on. See Chapter 3, particularly the section "Windows XP/Windows Vista and Background Processing" and "Initiating a Manual Background Refresh for Windows XP, Windows Vista and Windows 2003" to find out how to encourage changes to occur. To see the Screen Saver tab disappear on Windows XP or Windows Vista machines right now, log off and log back on. The policy should take effect.

This demonstration should prove how powerful Group Policy is, not only because everyone at the site is affected, but more specifically because administrators are not immune to Group Policy effects. Administrators are not immune because they are automatically members in the Authenticated Users security group. (You can modify this behavior with the techniques explored in Chapter 3.)

FIGURE 1.20   The Screen Saver tab in Windows XP (shown on the left) is missing because the site policy is affecting the user. In Vista, (shown on the right) the "Screen Saver" entry in the Personalization page is missing.

Applying Group Policy Objects to the Domain Level

At the domain level, we want an edict that says that the Desktop Settings option in the Windows Vista Personalization page (or Desktop tab in the Display Properties dialog box for Windows XP) should be removed.

Active Directory domains allow only members of the Domain Administrators group the ability to create Group Policy over the domain. Therefore, if you're not a DA (or a member of the EA group), or get delegated the right, it's likely that you'll never get to practice this exercise outside the test lab.

To apply the edict, follow these steps:

1. In the GPMC, drill down by clicking Group Policy Management ≻ Forest ≻ Corp.com.

2. Right-click the domain name to see the available options, as shown in Figure 1.21.

FIGURE 1.21   At the domain level, you can create the GPO in the Group Policy Objects container and then immediately link to the GPO from here.

"Create a GPO in this domain, and Link it here..." versus "Link an Existing GPO"

In the previous example we forced the site level to embrace our "Hide Screen Saver Option" edict. First, we created the GPO in the Group Policy Objects folder, and then in another step we linked the GPO to the site level. However, at the domain level (and, as you're about to see, the OU level), we can take care of both steps at once via the "Create a GPO in this domain, and Link it here" command. (Note, in previous versions of the GPMC, this was confusingly called "Create And Link A GPO Here." Being a grammar snob, this was a personal wish of mine to have clarified, and I'm happy to see Microsoft agreed and corrected it.)

This command tells the GPMC to create a new GPO in the Group Policy Objects folder and then automatically link the new GPO back to this focused level of Active Directory. This is a time-saving step so we don't have to dive down into the Group Policy Objects folder first and then create the link back to the Active Directory level.

So why is the "Create a GPO in this domain, and Link it here" option possible only at the domain and OU level and not the site level? Because Group Policy Objects linked to sites can often cause excessive bandwidth troubles using the old-school way of doing things. With that in mind, the GPMC interface makes sure that when you work with GPOs that affect sites, you're consciously choosing from *which* domain the GPO is being linked.

I'll talk more about this concept and how it's rectified with the GPMC way of doing things at the top in Chapter 3.

Don't panic when you see all the possible options. We'll hit them all in due time; right now we're interested in the first two: "Create a GPO in this domain, and Link it here" and "Link an Existing GPO."

Since you're focused at the domain level, you are prompted for the name of a new Group Policy Object when you right-click and choose to "Create a GPO in this domain, and Link it here." For this one, type a descriptive name, such as "Hide Desktop Settings Option." Your new "Hide Desktop Settings Option" GPO is created in the Group Policy Objects container and, automatically, a link is created at the domain level from the GPO to the domain.

 Take a moment to look in the Group Policy "swimming pool" for your new GPO. Simply drill down through Group Policy Management ➤ Forest ➤ Domains ➤ Corp.com and locate the Group Policy Objects note. Look for the new "Hide Desktop Settings Option" GPO.

Right-click either the link to "Hide Desktop Settings Option" (or the GPO itself) and choose Edit to open the Group Policy Object Editor. To hide the Desktop Settings option in the Windows Vista Personalization page (or Desktop tab in the Display Properties dialog box for Windows XP), drill down through User Configuration ➤ Administrative Templates ➤

Control Panel ➢ Display, and double-click **Hide Desktop Tab**. Change the setting from "Not Configured" to "Enabled," and click OK. Close the Group Policy Object Editor to return to the GPMC.

Verifying Your Changes at the Domain Level

Now, log on as any user in the domain. You can log on to any computer in the domain (say, XPPRO1 or VISTA1) as any user you have defined—even the administrator of the domain.

In Vista, right-click the Desktop and click Personalize. In Windows XP right-click the Desktop and click Properties.

You'll see the Desktop Settings option in the Windows Vista Personalization page (or Desktop tab in the Display Properties dialog box for Windows XP) is missing, as in Figure 1.22.

FIGURE 1.22   The Desktop tab is now also missing because the user is affected by the domain-level policy (left). In Vista, the "Desktop Background" entry is gone from the Personalization page (right).

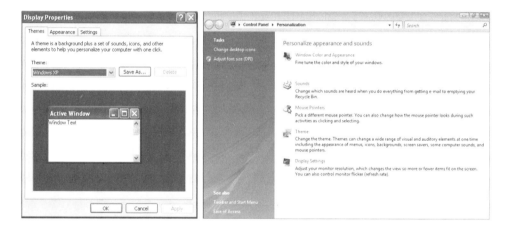

Once again, administrators are not immune to Group Policy effects. You can change this behavior, as you'll see in Chapter 3.

Applying Group Policy Objects to the OU Level

OUs are wonderful tools for delegating away unpleasant administrative duties, such as password resets or modifying group memberships. But that's only half their purpose. The other half is to be able to apply Group Policy.

You'll likely find yourself making most of Group Policy additions and changes at the OU level, because that's where you have the most flexibility, and the OU is the most refined instrument to affect users. Once OU administrators become comfortable in their surroundings, they want to harness the power of Group Policy.

Preparing to Delegate Control

To create a GPO at the OU level, you must first create the OU and a plan to delegate. For the examples in this book, we'll create three OUs that look like this:

- Human Resources
  - Human Resources Users
  - Human Resources Computers

Having separate OUs for your users and computers is a good idea—for both delegation of rights and also GPO design. Microsoft considers this a "best practice."

In the **Human Resources Users** OU in our Corp.com domain, we'll create and leverage an Active Directory security group to do our dirty work. We'll name this group HR-OU-Admins and put our first users inside the HR-OU-Admins security group. We'll then delegate the appropriate rights necessary for them to use the power of GPOs.

To create the **Human Resources Users** OU using your VISTAMANAGEMENT machine, follow these steps:

1. Earlier, you created a "unified console" where you housed both Active Directory Users and Computer and the GPMC. Simply use Active Directory Users And Computers, right-click the domain name, and choose New ➢ Organizational Unit, which will allow you to enter in a new OU name. Enter **Human Resources** as the name.

2. Inside the **Human Resources** OU, create two more OUs—**Human Resources Computers** and **Human Resources Users**, as shown in Figure 1.23.

> Alternatively, you can create the OU in the GPMC. Just right-click the domain and choose "New Organizational Unit" from the shortcut menu.

FIGURE 1.23   When you complete all these steps, your Human Resources OU should have a Human Resources Users OU and Human Resources Computers OU. In the users side, put Frank Rizzo and the HR-OU-Admins.

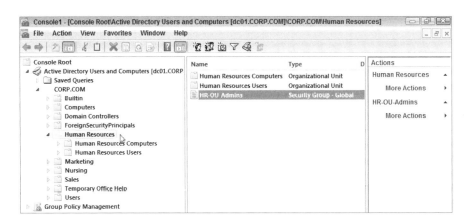

To create the HR-OU-Admins group, follow these steps:

1. In Active Directory Users And Computers, right-click the new **Human Resources Users** OU and choose New ➢ Group.

2. Create the new group HR-OU-Admins as a new Global Security group.

To create the first user to go inside HR-OU-Admins, follow these steps:

1. In Active Directory Users And Computers, right-click the **Human Resources Users** OU and choose New ➢ User.

2. Name the user Frank Rizzo, with an account name of **frizzo,** and click Next.

3. If you've established a Windows 2003 domain, you must now enter a complex password for a user. My suggested password in all my books is: "p@ssw0rd." That's a lowercase p, "at sign," an s, an s, a double-U, a zero, then, r, d.

4. Finish and close the wizard.

If you're following along, Frank Rizzo's login will be `frizzo@corp.com`.

Easily Manage New Users and Computers

The Computers folder and Users folder in Active Directory Users And Computers are not OUs. They are generic containers. You'll notice that they are not present in the GPMC view of Active Directory. Because they are generic containers (and not OUs), you cannot link Group Policy Objects to them.

These folders have two purposes:

- If an NT 4 domain is upgraded, the User and Computer accounts will wind up in these folders. (Administrators are then supposed to move the accounts into OUs.)

- It's the default location where older tools create new users and computers. These older tools are in the Windows NT 4 User Manager (which still works in a Windows 2000 or Windows 2003 domain). Additionally, command-line tools, such as the `net user`, `net group`, will add accounts to this location. Similarly, the Computers folder is the default location for any new client workstation or server that joins the domain. Or, similarly, should you pre-create computer accounts using the `net computer` command.

If you execute one of these commands, the objects you create will wind up in either the Users folder or the Computers folder. But really, you don't want your users or computers to be in these folders—you want them in OUs. That's where the action is because you can apply Group Policy to OUs, not to these folders! Yeah, sure, these users and computers are affected by site- and domain-level GPOs. But really the action is at the OU level, and you want your computer and user objects to be placed in OUs as fast as possible—not sitting around in these generic Computers and Users folders.

To that end, Windows 2003 domains (in full functional level) have two tools to redirect the default location of new users and computers to the OUs of your choice. For example, suppose you want all new computers to go to a **NewComputers** OU and all new users to go to a **NewUsers** OU. And you want to link several GPOs to the **NewUsers** and **NewComputers** OUs to ensure that new accounts immediately have some baseline level of security, restriction, or protection. Without a little magic, new user accounts created using older tools won't automatically be placed there.

In Windows 2003 Active Directory, Microsoft has provided REDIRUSR and REDIRCMP commands that take a distinguished name, like:

```
REDIRCMP ou=newcomputers,dc=corp,dc=com and/or
REDIRUSR ou=newusers,dc=corp,dc=com
```

Now if you link GPOs to these OUs, your new accounts will get the Group Policy Objects dictating settings to them at an OU level. This will come in handy when users and computers aren't specifically created in their final destination OUs.

To learn more about these tools, see the Microsoft Knowledge Base article 324949.

To add Frank Rizzo to the HR-OU-Admins group, follow these steps:

1. Double-click the HR-OU-Admins group.

2. Click the Members tab.

3. Add Frank Rizzo.

When it's all complete, your OU structure with your first user and group should look like Figure 1.23, shown previously.

Delegating Control for Group Policy Management

Now that you've created the **Human Resources** OU, which contains the **Human Resources Users** OU and the **Human Resources Computers** OU and the HR-OU-Admins security group, and put Frank inside the **HR-OU-Admins group**, you're ready to delegate control.

Performing Your First Delegation

You can delegate control to use Group Policy in two ways: using Active Directory Users And Computers and using the GPMC.

For this first example, we'll kick it old school and use the Active Directory Users And Computers way. Then, in Chapter 2, I'll demonstrate how to delegate control using the GPMC.

To delegate control for Group Policy management, follow these steps:

1. In Active Directory Users And Computers, right-click the top-level **Human Resources** OU you created and choose Delegate Control from the shortcut menu to start the "Delegation of Control Wizard."

2. Click Next to get past the wizard introduction screen.

3. You'll be asked to select users and/or groups. Click Add, add the HR-OU-Admins group, and click Next to open the "Tasks to Delegate" screen, as shown in Figure 1.24.

4. Click "Manage Group Policy Links," and then click Next.

5. At the wizard review screen, click Finish.

FIGURE 1.24   Select the "Manage Group Policy Links" task.

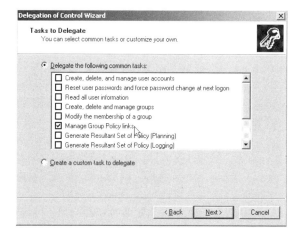

 You might want to click some or all the other check boxes as well, but for this example, only "Manage Group Policy Links" is required. Try to avoid selecting "Generate Resultant Set of Policy (Planning)" and "Generate Resultant Set of Policy (Logging)" at this time. You'll see where they come in handy in Chapter 3.

 The Manage Group Policy Links task assigns the user or group "Read" and "Write" access over the gPLink and gPOptions properties for that level. To see or modify these permissions by hand, open Active Directory Users And Computers and choose View ➢ Advanced Features. If later you want to remove a delegated permission, it's a little challenging. You can locate the permission that you set by right-clicking the delegated object (such as OU), then click the Properties tab, click the Security tab, choose Advanced, and dig around until you come across the permission you want to remove. Finally, delete the corresponding access control entry (ACE).

Adding a User to the Server Operators Group (Just for This Book)

Under normal conditions, nobody but Domain Administrators, Enterprise Administrators, or Server Operators can walk up to Domain Controllers and log on. For testing purposes only, though, we're going to add our user, Frank, to the Server Operators group so he can easily work on our DC01 Domain Controller.

To add a user to the Server Operators group, follow these steps:

1. In Active Directory Users And Computers, double-click Frank Rizzo's account under the **Human Resources Users** OU.

2. Click the Member Of tab and click Add.

3. Select the Server Operators group and click OK.

4. Click OK to close the Properties dialog box for Frank Rizzo.

Normally, you wouldn't give your delegated OU administrators Server Operators access. You're doing it solely for the sake of this example to allow Frank to log on locally to your Domain Controllers.

Testing Your Delegation of Group Policy Management

At this point, log off as Administrator and log in as the Frank Rizzo (frizzo@corp.com).

Now follow these steps to test your delegation:

1. Choose Start and type in GPMC.MSC at the "Start Search" prompt to open the GPMC.

2. Drill down through Group Policy Management, Domains, Corp.com, and Group Policy Objects. If you right-click Group Policy Objects in an attempt to create a new GPO, you'll see the shortcut menu shown in Figure 1.25.

As you can see, Frank is unable to create new GPOs in the swimming pool of the domain. Since Frank has been delegated some control over the **Human Resources** OU (which also contains the other OUs), let's see what he *can* do. If you right-click the **Human Resources** OU in the GPMC, you'll see the shortcut menu shown in Figure 1.26.

FIGURE 1.25   Frank cannot create new GPOs in the Group Policy Objects container.

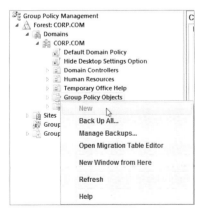

FIGURE 1.26   Frank's delegated rights allow him to link to existing GPOs but not to create new GPOs.

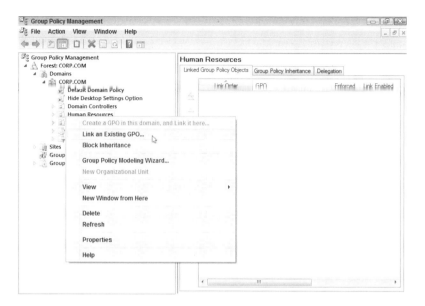

Because Frank is unable to create GPOs in the swimming pool of the domain (the Group Policy Objects container), he is also unable by definition to "Create a GPO in this domain, and Link it here." Although Frank (and more specifically, the HR-OU-Admins) has been delegated the ability to "Manage Group Policy links," he cannot *create* new GPOs. Frank (and the other potential **HR-OU-Admins**) has only the ability to *link* an existing GPO.

Understanding Group Policy Object Linking Delegation

When we were logged on as the Domain Administrator, we could create GPOs in the Group Policy Objects container, and we could "Create a GPO in this domain, and Link it here" at the domain or OU levels. But Frank cannot.

Here's the idea about delegating the ability to link to GPOs: someone with a lot of brains in the organization does all the work in creating a well-thought-out and well-tested GPO. Maybe this GPO distributes software, maybe it sets up a secure workstation policy, or perhaps it runs a startup script. You get the idea.

Then, others in the organization, like Frank, are delegated just the ability to *link* to that GPO and use it at their level. This solves the problem of delegating perhaps too much control. Certainly some administrators are ready to create their own users and groups, but other administrators may not be quite ready to jump into the cold waters of Group Policy Object creation. Thus, you can design the GPOs for other administrators; they can just link to the ones you (or others) create.

When you (or someone with the right to link GPOs) selects "Link an Existing GPO," as seen in Figure 1.26, you can choose a GPO that's already been created—and hanging out in the domain swimming pool—the Group Policy Objects container.

In this example, the HR-OU-Admins members, such as Frank, can leverage any currently created GPO to affect the users and computers in their OU—even if they didn't create it themselves. In this example, Frank has linked to an existing GPO called "Word 2003 Settings." Turns out that some other administrator in the domain created this GPO, but Frank wants to use it. So, because Frank has "Manage Group Policy Links" rights on the **Human Resources** OU (and OUs underneath it), he is allowed to link to it.

But, as you can see in Figure 1.27, he cannot edit the GPOs. Under the hood, Active Directory doesn't permit Frank to edit GPOs he didn't create (and therefore doesn't own).

FIGURE 1.27   The GPMC will not allow you to edit an existing GPO if you do not own it (or do not have explicit permission to edit it).

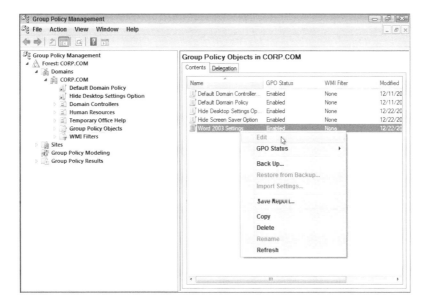

 In Chapter 2, I'll show you how to grant specific rights to allow more than just the original creator (and now owner) of the object to edit specific GPOs.

Giving the ability to just link to existing GPOs is a good idea in theory, but often OU administrators are simply given full authority to create their own GPOs (as you'll see later). For this example, don't worry about linking to any GPOs. Simply cancel out of the Select GPO screen, close the GPMC, and log off from the server as Frank Rizzo.

Granting OU Admins Access to Create New Group Policy Objects

By using the Delegation of Control Wizard to delegate the Manage Group Policy Links attribute, you performed half of what is needed to grant the appropriate authority to Frank (and any additional future HR-OU-Admins) to create GPOs in the Group Policy Objects container and link them to the **Human Resources** OU, the **Human Resources Users** OU, or the **Human Resources Computers** OU. (Though we really don't want to link many GPOs directly to the **Human Resources** OU.)

You can grant the HR-OU-Admins the ability to create GPOs in the Group Policy Objects container in two ways. For now, I'll show you the old-school way; in Chapter 3, I'll show you the GPMC way.

One of Active Directory's built-in security groups, "Group Policy Creator Owners," holds the key to the other half of our puzzle. You'll need to add those users or groups whom you want to have the ability to create GPOs to a built-in group, cleverly named Group Policy Creator Owners. To do so, follow these steps:

1. Switch-User back to Domain Administrator.

2. Fire up Active Directory Users And Computers.

3. By default, the Group Policy Creator Owners group is located in the Users folder in the domain. Double-click the "Group Policy Creator Owners" group and add the HR-OU-Admins group and/or Frank Rizzo.

 If you just created a new Windows 2003 domain or upgraded your domain from NT 4, you will not be able to add the HR-OU-Admins group until the domain mode has been switched to Windows 2000 Native or Windows 2003 Functional level. Switch the domain by using Active Directory Domains and Trusts. Switching the domain mode is a one-way operation, which shuts out older Domain Controllers. If you are not prepared to make the switch to Native mode, you'll only be able to add individual members, such as Frank Rizzo—and not a group.

 In Chapter 2, you'll see an alternate way to allow users to create GPOs.

Creating and Linking Group Policy Objects at the OU Level

At the site level, we hid the Screen Saver option. At the domain level, we chose to get rid of the Desktop Settings option in the Windows Vista Personalization page (or Desktop tab in the Display Properties dialog box for Windows XP). At the OU level, we have two jobs to do:

- Hide the Display Settings option for Windows Vista (or Settings tab in Windows XP)

- Restore the Screen Saver option that was taken away at the site level.

To create a GPO at the OU level, follow these steps:

1. Since you're on VISTAMANAGEMENT, log off as Administrator and log back on as Frank Rizzo (frizzo@corp.com)

2. Choose Start and type GPMC.MSC in the "Start Search" prompt.

3. Drill down until you reach the **Human Resources Users** OU, right-click it, and choose "Create a GPO in this domain, and Link it here" from the shortcut menu to open the "New GPO" dialog box.

4. In the "New GPO" dialog box, type in the name of your new GPO, say "Hide Display Settings Option/Restore Screen Saver Option." This will create a GPO in the Group Policy Objects container and link it to the **Human Resources Users** OU.

5. Right-click the Group Policy link and choose Edit from the shortcut menu to open the Group Policy Object Editor.

6. To hide the Display Settings option in the Windows Vista Personalization page (or Settings tab in the Display Properties for Windows XP), drill down through User Configuration ➢ Administrative Templates ➢ Control Panel ➢ Display and double-click the **Hide Settings Tab** policy setting. Change the setting from "Not Configured" to "Enabled," and click OK.

7. To restore the Screen Saver setting for Windows Vista (or Screen Saver tab in Windows XP), double-click the **Hide Screen Saver Tab** policy setting. Change the setting from "Not Configured" to "Disabled," and click OK.

8. Close the Group Policy Object Editor to return to the GPMC.

 By disabling the **Hide Screen Saver Tab** policy setting, you're reversing the Enable setting set at a higher level. See the sidebar "The Three Possible Settings: 'Not Configured,' 'Enabled,' and 'Disabled'" later in this chapter.

Verifying Your Changes at the OU Level

On your test Windows XP or Windows Vista machine in the domain (XPPRO1 or VISTA1), log back on as Frank.

On XP, right-click the Desktop and choose Display from the shortcut menu to open the Display Properties dialog box. Note that the Display Settings Option (on Windows Vista) or Settings tab (on Windows XP) is missing, but that the Screen Saver option is back, as shown on the left in Figure 1.28.

On Windows Vista, right-click the Desktop and choose Personalize. Note that the Windows Vista behavior is somewhat different this time: the "Display Settings" field is still available, but clicking on it yields an access error due to Group Policy enforcement. And, because of our edict, note the Screen Saver entry has returned and is clickable (as seen in the right screen of Figure 1.28).

This test proves, once again, that even OU administrators are not automatically immune from policy settings. Chapter 3 explains how to change this behavior.

FIGURE 1.28   On Windows XP, the Settings tab is missing along with the Desktop tab, but the Screen Saver tab has returned (left). The Windows Vista Personalization page is a bit different. It continues to show the Display Settings entry, but denies access. And, the Screen Saver entry has return as expected (right).

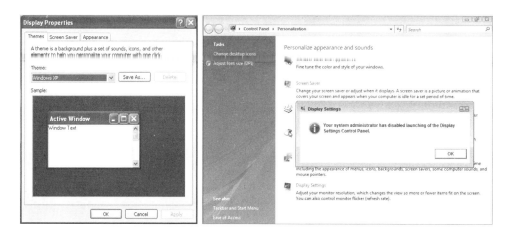

Group Policy Strategy: Should I Create More or Fewer GPOs?

At times, you'll want to lock down additional functions for a collection of users or computers. For example, you might want to specify that no users in the **Human Resources Users** OU can use Control Panel.

At the **Human Resources Users** OU level, you've already set up a GPO that contained a policy setting to hide the Display Settings option in the Windows Vista Personalization page (or Settings tab for Windows XP). You now have a decision to make. You can create a new GPO that affects the **Human Resources Users** OU, give it a descriptive name, say "No One Can Use Control Panel," and then drill down through User Configuration ➢ Administrative Templates ➢ Windows Components ➢ Control Panel and enable the policy setting named **Prohibit Access to Control Panel**.

Or you could simply modify your existing GPO, named "Hide Display Settings Option/Restore Screen Saver Option" so that it contains additional policy settings. You can then rename your GPO to something that makes sense and encompasses the qualities of all the policy changes, say, "Our Human Resources Users' Desktop Settings."

Here's the quandary: The former method (one policy setting per GPO) is certainly more descriptive and definitely easier to debug should things go awry. If you have only one policy set inside the GPO, you have a better handle on what each one is affecting. If something goes wrong, you can dive right into the GPO, track down the policy setting, and make the necessary changes, or disable the ornery GPO (as discussed later).

The second method (multiple policy settings per GPO) is teeny weeny bit faster for your computers and users at boot or logon time, because each additional GPO takes some miniscule fraction of additional processing time. But if you stuff too many settings in an individual GPO, the time to debug should things go wrong goes up exponentially. Group Policy has so many nooks and crannies that can be difficult to debug.

So, in a nutshell, if you have multiple GPOs at a particular level, you can do the following:

- Name each of them more descriptively.

- Debug them easily if things go wrong.

- Disable individually misbehaving GPOs.

- Associate that GPO more easily to a WMI filter (explored in Chapter 10).

- More easily delegate permissions to any specific GPO (explored in Chapter 3).

If you have fewer GPOs at a particular level, the following is the case:

- Logging on is slightly faster for the user (but really only slightly).

- Debugging is somewhat more difficult if things go wrong.

- You can disable individually misbehaving GPOs or links to misbehaving GPOs. (But if they contain many settings, you might be disabling more than you desire.)

So, how do you form a GPO strategy? There is no right or wrong answer; you need to decide what's best for you. Several options, however, can help you decide.

One middle-of-the-road strategy is to start with multiple GPOs and one lone policy setting in each. Once you are comfortable that they are individually working as expected, you can create another new GPO that contains the sum of the settings from, in this example, **Hide Settings Tab** and **Prohibit Access to Control Panel** and then delete (or disable) the old individual GPO.

Another middle-of-the-road strategy is to have a single GPO that contains only the policy settings required to perform a complete "wish." This way, if the wish goes sour, you can easily address it or disable it (or whack it) as needed.

Here's yet another strategy. Some Microsoft documentation recommends that you create GPOs such that they affect only the User half or the Computer half. You can then disable the unused portion of the GPO (either the Computer half or the User half). This allows for policy settings affecting one node to be grouped together for ease of naming and debugging and allows for flexible troubleshooting. However, be careful here because after you disable half the GPO, there's no iconic notification, and, in my opinion, troubleshooting can become harder if not performed perfectly and consistently. In all, I'm not a huge fan of disabling "half" the GPO.

Creating a New Group Policy Object for Computers in an OU

For the sake of learning and working through the rest of the examples in this section, you'll create another GPO and link it to the **Human Resources Computers** OU. This GPO will auto-launch a very important application for anyone who uses these machines: `calc.exe`.

> The setting we're about to play with also exists under the User node, but we'll experiment with the Computer node policy.

First, you'll need to create the new GPO and modify the settings. You'll then need to move some client machines into the **Human Resources Computers** OU in order to see your changes take effect.

To auto-launch `calc.exe` for anyone logging in to a computer in the **Human Resources Computers** OU, follow these steps:

1. If you're not already logged in as Frank Rizzo, the **Human Resources** OU administrator, do so now on VISTAMANAGEMENT.

2. Choose Start and type **GPMC.MSC** in the "Start Search" prompt.

3. Drill down until you reach the **Human Resources Computers** OU, right-click it, and choose "Create a GPO in this domain, and Link it here" from the shortcut menu.

4. Name the GPO something descriptive, such as "Auto-Launch calc.exe."

5. Right-click the GPO, and choose Edit to open the Group Policy Object Editor.

6. We want to affect our client computers (not users), so we need to use the Computers node. To auto-launch `calc.exe`, drill down through Computer Configuration ➢ Administrative Templates ➢ System ➢ Logon, and double-click **Run these programs at user logon**. Change the setting from "Not Configured" to "Enabled."

7. Click the "Show" button, and the "Show Contents" dialog appears. Click "Add" and in the "Add item" dialog, enter the full path to calc.exe as **c:\windows\system32\calc.exe** then click OK as shown in Figure 1.29. Click OK to close the "Show Contents" dialog, and click OK again to close the "Run these programs at user logon" policy setting.

8. Close the Group Policy Object Editor to return the GPMC.

> Be aware of occasional strange Microsoft verbiage when you need to enable a policy to *disable* a setting. In Windows 2003, most policy settings have been renamed to "Prohibit *<whatever>*" to reflect the change from confusion to clarity.

FIGURE 1.29   By enabling this policy setting and specifying calc.exe, all computers in this OU will launch calc.exe when a user logs in.

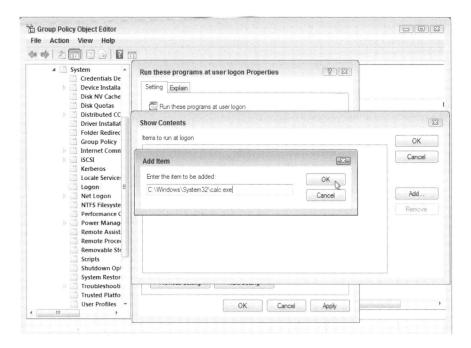

Moving Computers into the Human Resources Computers OU

Since you just created a policy that will affect computers, you'll need to place a workstation or two inside the **Human Resources Computers** OU to see the results of your labor. You'll need to be logged on as Administrator to DC01 to do this.

Quite often computers and users are relegated to separate OUs. That way, certain GPOs can be applied to certain computers but not others. For instance, isolating laptops, desktops, and servers is a common practice.

In this example, we're going to use the Find command in Active Directory Users And Computers to find a workstation named XPPRO1 and the Windows Vista workstation named VISTA1 and move it into the **Human Resources Computers** OU.

To find and move computers into a specific OU, follow these steps:

1. In Active Directory Users And Computers, right-click the domain, and choose Find from the shortcut menu, as shown in Figure 1.30, to open the Find Users, Contacts, and Groups dialog box.

2. From the Find drop-down menu, select Computers. In the Name field, type **VISTA1** to find the computer account of the same name. Once you've found it, right-click the account and choose Move from the shortcut menu. Move the account to the **Human Resources Computers** OU.

   Repeat these steps for XPPRO1 and all other computers that you want to move to the **Human Resources Computers** OU.

3. Now that you've moved VISTA1 (and maybe also XPPRO1) into the new OU, be sure to reboot those client computers.

WARNING   After you move the computer accounts into the **Human Resources Computers** OU, it's very important to reboot your client machines. As you'll see in Chapter 3, the computer does not recognize the change right away when computer accounts are moved between OUs.

As you can see in this example (and in the real world), a best practice is to separate users and computers into their own OUs and then link GPOs to those OUs. Indeed, underneath a parent OU structure, such as the **Human Resources** OU, you might have more OUs, (that is, **Human Resources Laptops** OU, **Human Resources Servers** OU, and so on). This will give you the most flexibility in design between delegating control where it's needed and the balance of GPO design within OUs. Just remember that in order for GPOs to affect either a user or computer, that user or computer must be within the scope of the GPO—site, domain, or OU.

FIGURE 1.30   Use the Find command to find computers in the domain so you can move them.

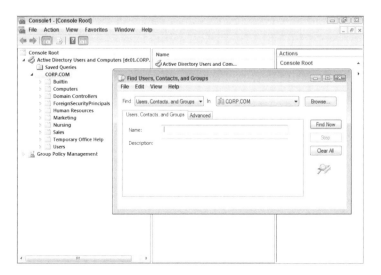

Verifying Your Cumulative Changes

At this point, you've set up three levels of Group Policy that accomplish multiple actions:

- At the site level, the "Hide Screen Saver Option" GPO is in force for users.

- At the domain level, the "Hide Desktop Settings Option" GPO is in force for users.

- In the **Human Resources Users** OU, the "Hide Display Settings Option/Restore Screen Saver Option" GPO is in force for users.

- In the **Human Resources Computers** OU, the "Auto-Launch Calc.exe" GPO is in force for computers.

At this point, take a minute to flip back to Figure 1.13 (the swimming pool graphic) to see where we're going here. To see the accumulation of your policy settings inside your GPOs, you'll need to log on as a user who is affected by the **Human Resources Users** OU and at a computer that is affected by the **Human Resources Computers** OU. Therefore, log on as Frank Rizzo on XPPRO1.

If you're using Windows XP, right-click the Desktop and choose Display from the shortcut menu to open the Display Properties dialog box. Note that the Settings tab is still missing from the previous exercise (and the Screen Saver tab is restored). You should also see Windows Calculator jumping at you as soon as you log on (because your computer GPO told it to).

If you're using Windows Vista, right-click the Desktop and choose Personalize. Note that the Desktop Settings option is still missing from the previous exercise (and the Screen Saver entry is restored.) And, when you logged in, did the computer GPO auto-launch Windows Calculator?

 These tests prove that even OU administrators are not automatically immune from GPOs and the policy settings within. Under the hood, they are in the Authenticated Users security group. See Chapter 3 for information on how to modify this behavior.

The Three Possible Settings: "Not Configured," "Enabled," and "Disabled"

As you saw in Figure 1.29 earlier in this chapter, nearly all administrative template policy settings can be set as "Not Configured," "Enabled," or "Disabled." These three settings have very different consequences, so it's important to understand how each works.

"Not Configured"   The best way to think about "Not Configured" is to imagine that it really says, "Don't do anything" or even "Pass through." Why is this? Because if a policy setting is set to "Not Configured," then it honors any previously set setting (or, the operating system default).

"Enabled" When a specific policy setting is enabled, the policy will take effect. In the case of the **Hide Screen Saver Tab** policy setting, the effect is obvious. However, lots of policy settings, once enabled, have myriad possibilities *inside* the specific policy setting! (For a gander at one such policy setting, use the Group Policy Object Editor and drill down to User Configuration ➢ Administrative Templates ➢ Windows Components ➢ Internet Explorer ➢ Toolbars and select the policy setting named **Configure Toolbar Buttons**.) So, as we can see, "Enabled" really means "Turn this policy setting on." It will then either do what it says, or there will be more options inside the policy setting that can be configured.

"Disabled" This setting leads a threefold life.

- "Disabled" usually means that if the same policy setting is enabled at a higher level, reverse its operation. For example, we chose to enable the **Hide Screen Saver Tab** policy setting at the site level. If at a lower level (say, the domain or OU level), we chose to disable this policy setting, the Screen Saver tab will pop back at the level at which we disabled this policy.

- Additionally, "Disabled" often forces the user to accept the administrator's will. That is, if a policy setting is Disabled, some default behavior of the policy setting is enforced, and the user cannot change it. To see an example policy setting like this, use the Group Policy Object Editor and drill down through User Configuration ➢ Administrative Templates ➢ Control Panel and select the policy setting named **Force Classic Control Panel Style**. Once this policy setting is Disabled, the policy forces Windows XP users to use the Control Panel in the new task-based style. The point here is that the "Disabled" setting is a bit tricky to work with. You'll want to be sure that when you disable a policy setting, you're doing precisely what you intend.

- "Disabled" sometimes has a special and, typically, rare use. That is, something might already be hard-coded into the Registry to be "turned on" or work one way, and the only way to turn it off is to select "Disabled." One such policy setting is the **Shutdown Event Tracker**. You Disable the policy setting, which turns it off, because on Windows 2003 it's already hard-coded on. In Windows XP and Windows Vista, it's already hard-coded off. Likewise, if you want to kill Windows XP/SP2's or Windows Vista's firewall, you need to set **Windows Firewall: Protect All Network Connections** to "Disabled." (You can find that policy setting at Administrative Templates ➢ Network ➢ Network Connections ➢ Windows Firewall ➢ Domain Profile while editing GPOs on Windows XP/Service Pack 2 computers.)

So, think of "Not Configured" as having neither Allow nor Deny being set. "Enabled" will turn it on and possibly have more functions. "Disabled" has multiple uses, and be sure to test, test, test to make sure that once you've manipulated a policy setting, it's doing precisely what you had in mind.

Things That Aren't Group Policy but *Look* Like Group Policy

Windows is a big place. There are a lot of nooks and crannies, and occasionally things start to look similar, even though they're unrelated. Indeed two sections inside Windows 2000 and Windows 2003 sometimes look like they might have some tie-ins to Group Policy. Actually, they're totally separate.

Terminal Services

Both Windows 2000 Server and Windows Server 2003 come with a built-in Terminal Services service. To configure the service in Windows 2000, you have only one option: use the Terminal Services Configuration utility.

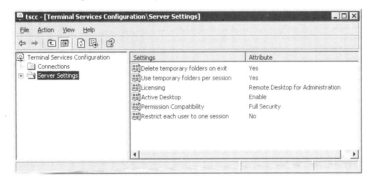

Don't let the little binary 1/0 icons fool you into thinking this window is Group Policy related. It is not. However, Windows 2003 Terminal Services does have multiple policy settings, and once they are set, the outcome is reflected in this window. (See Chapter 3 for information about how to locate the applicable policy settings.)

Routing and Remote Access

Routing and Remote Access (RRAS) allows users to connect to Windows 2003 servers over dial-in or VPN (virtual private network) connections, among other functions. To specify who can and cannot get through the gates, Windows Server 2003 has a facility to create rules to allow or deny access. Those rules happen to be called "Policies," as shown in Figure 1.31.

Don't let the little "scroll" icons fool you into thinking these are somehow related to Group Policy. They're not.

FIGURE 1.31   RRAS policies are not associated with Windows 2003 Group Policy.

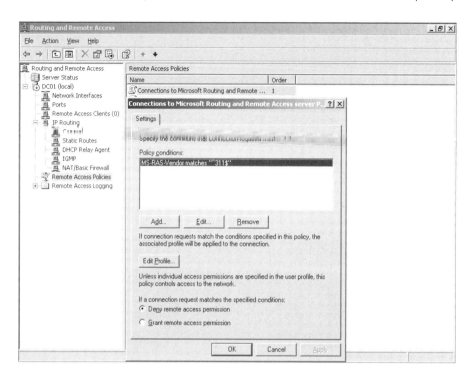

Final Thoughts

The concepts here are valid regardless of what your domain is running. It doesn't matter if you have a pure or mixed Active Directory domains with Windows 2000, Windows 2003, or Longhorn Domain Controllers. The point is that to make the most use of Group Policy, you'll need an Active Directory.

You'll also need a Vista management station to do the work. Again, we talk more about why you need a Windows Vista management station in Chapter 5. Regardless, the GPMC is built-in to Windows Vista and that's a Good Thing™. And, the best news is that the GPMC can control any type of Active Directory you have.

The more you use and implement GPOs in your environment, the better you'll become at the basic use while at the same time avoiding pitfalls when it comes to using them. The following tips are scattered throughout the chapter but are repeated and emphasized here for quick reference, to help you along your Group Policy journey:

GPOs don't "live" at the site, domain, or OU level.   GPOs "live" in Active Directory and are represented in the swimming pool of the domain called the Group Policy Objects container. To use a GPO, you need to link a GPO to a level in Active Directory that you want to affect: a site, a domain, or an OU.

GPOs apply to Active Directory sites, domains, and OUs.   Active Directory is a hierarchy, and Group Policy takes advantage of that hierarchy. There is one local GPO that can be set, which affects everyone who uses that machine. Then, Active Directory Group Policy Objects apply: site, domain, and then OU. Active Directory GPOs "trump" any local policy settings if set within the Local Group Policy.

Avoid using the site level to implement GPOs.   Users can roam from site to site. When they do, they can be confused by the settings changing around them. Use GPOs linked to the site only to set up special site-wide security settings, such as IPsec or the Internet Explorer Proxy. Use the domain or OU levels when creating GPOs whenever possible.

Implement common settings high in the hierarchy when possible.   The higher up in the hierarchy GPOs are implemented, the more users they affect. You want common settings to be set once, affecting everyone, instead of having to create additional GPOs performing the same functions at other lower levels, which will just clutter your view of Active Directory with the multiple copies of the same policy setting.

Implement unique settings low in the hierarchy.   If a specific collection of users is unique, try to round them up into an OU and then apply Group Policy to them. This is much better than applying the settings high in the hierarchy and using Group Policy filtering later.

Use more GPOs at any level to make things easier.   When creating a new wish, isolate it by creating a new GPO. This will enable easy revocation by unlinking it should something go awry.

Strike a balance between having too many and too few GPOs.   There is a middle ground between having one policy setting within a single GPO and having a bajillion policy settings contained within a single GPO. At the end of your design, the goal is to have meaningfully named GPOs that reflect the "wish" you want to accomplish. If you should choose to end that wish, you can easily disable or delete it.

As you go on your Group Policy journey…   Don't go at it alone. There are some nice third-party independent resources to help you on your way. I run www.GPanswers.com, which has oodles of resources, downloads, a community forum, links to third party software and my hands-on training. My pal (and Technical Editor of this edition) Darren Mar-Elia runs www.GPOguy.com. There's also Microsoft's independent Group Policy Wiki at http://grouppolicy.editme.com/. All of these locations are here to help you get more advanced with Group Policy as you progress.

2

Managing Group Policy with the GPMC

In the last chapter, you got to know how and when Group Policy works. We used Active Directory Users And Computers to create and manage users and computers, but we used the GPMC to manage Group Policy. We got a little workout with the GPMC when creating new GPOs and linking them to various levels in Active Directory.

And, for just a moment, we went back to the old-school way to delegate control to Frank and the HR-OU-Admins group to link existing GPOs to their **Human Resources** OU structure.

In this chapter, I'll cover the remainder of daily tasks you can perform using the GPMC. As a reminder, the GPMC is for all implementations of Active Directory. That is, you can use the GPMC to manage your Active Directory—whatever the Domain Controllers are that constitute it. You just need the GPMC loaded up on some machine. Now, in the previous chapter, I put a pretty fine point on it: you want this machine to be a Windows Vista machine. In short, if you don't use a Windows Vista machine, you won't have access to all the settings. So, in this chapter, you're going to be working, again, with your VISTAMANAGEMENT machine which is already preloaded with the GPMC.

In Chapter 5, I delve into deep detail about expressly why you want to ensure your management station is a Windows Vista machine.

I'll tackle most of the remaining features the GPMC has to offer in this chapter, but we'll handle the remaining GPMC features in other chapters as the occasion arises.

One of those goodies is the ability to migrate GPOs between domains. For additional information, see the Appendix.

So, with that in mind, let's get to know the GPMC a bit better.

If you're not already logged in to your VISTAMANAGMENT machine, go ahead and do so now. Since the GPMC is already built in to Windows Vista, just click Start and in the Start Search box, type **GPMC.MSC** to get started.

Common Procedures with the GPMC

In the last chapter, we created and linked some GPOs, which we can see in the Group Policy Objects container, to see how, at each level, we were affecting our users. In this section, we'll continue by working with some of the more advanced options for applying, manipulating, and using Group Policy.

Clicking either a GPO itself (or a link) lets you get more information about what they do. For now, feel free to click around, but I suggest that you don't change anything until we get to the specific examples.

Various tabs are available to you once you click the GPO itself or a link. For instance, let's locate the GPO that's linked to the **Human Resources Users** OU. We'll do this by drilling down to Group Policy Management ➢ Forest ➢ Domains ➢ corp.com ➢ Human Resources ➢ Human Resources Users and clicking the one GPO that's linked there: "Hide Display Settings Option/ Restore Screen Saver Option." Let's take a look at the results of that action now.

The Scope Tab   Clicking a GPO or a GPO link opens the Scope tab. The Scope tab gives you an at-a-glance view of where and when the GPO will apply. We'll examine the Scope tab in the sections "Deleting and Unlinking Group Policy Objects" and "Filtering the Scope of Group Policy Objects" in this chapter, and "WMI Filters" in Chapter 11. For now, you can see that the "Hide Display Settings Option/Restore Screen Saver Option" GPO is linked to the **Human Resources Users** OU. But you already knew that.

The Details Tab   The Details tab contains information describing who created the GPO (the owner) and the status (Enabled, Disabled, or Partially Disabled), as well as some nuts-and-bolts information about its underlying representation in Active Directory (the GUID.) We'll examine the Details tab in the sections "Disabling 'Half' (or Both Halves) of the Group Policy Object" and "Understanding GPMC's Link Warning" in this chapter and again in Chapter 4.

Should you change the GPO status here, say, by disabling the User Configuration of the policy, you'll be affecting all other levels in Active Directory that might be using this GPO by linking to it. See the section "Understanding GPMC's Link Warning" section as well as the sidebar "On GPO Links and GPOs Themselves" a bit later in the chapter.

The Settings Tab   The Settings tab gives you an at-a-glance view of what's been set inside the GPO. In our example, you can see the Enabled and Disabled status of the two policy settings we manipulated. You can click Hide (or Show) to contract and expand all the configured policy settings:

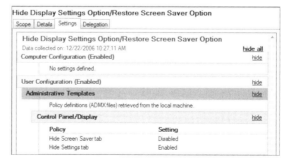

- Clicking Hide at any level tightens that level. You can expose more information by clicking the inverse of Hide when available, which is Show.

- Clicking the actual policy setting name, for example, **Hide Settings Tab** displays the help text for the policy setting (but note that this is only applicable to Administrative Template settings). This can be useful if someone set up a GPO with a kooky name, and you want to know what's going on inside that GPO.

- If you want to change a setting, you can right-click the settings area and select Edit. The familiar Group Policy Object Editor will appear. Note, however, that the Group Policy Object Editor will not "snap to" the policy setting you want to edit. The editor always starts off at the root.

- Additionally, at any time, you can right-click over this report and select Save Report, which does just that. It creates an HTML or XML report that you can then e-mail to fellow administrators or the boss, and so on. This is a super way of documenting your Group Policy environment instead of writing down everything by hand.

I've said it before, but it bears repeating: you can also edit the settings by clicking the GPO or any GPO link for that object and choosing Edit. However, you *always* affect all containers (sites, domains, or OUs) to which the GPO is linked. It's one and the same object, regardless of the way you edit it. See the sidebar "On GPO Links and GPOs Themselves" a bit later in the chapter to get the full gist of this.

 If you chose to load the GPMC on a Windows 2003 machine, you may run into an initial problem when clicking the Settings tab. That is, certain aspects of the GPMC, such as the Settings tab, tap into Internet Explorer. Since Internet Explorer is hardened on a Windows 2003 machine, you will have limited access to the whole picture. If you're presented with a warning box, simply add the security_mmc.exe as a trusted website. This should make your problems go away. You can also turn off "Internet Explorer Enhanced Security Configuration" in Windows 2003 in Add/Remove Programs. This is recommended in test labs but not really recommended on production servers.

The Delegation Tab   The Delegation tab lets you set the security for who can do what with GPOs, their links, and their properties. You'll find the Delegation tab in a lot of places, such as when you:

- Click a GPO link or clicking a GPO in the Group Policy Objects container
- Click a site
- Click a domain
- Click an OU
- Click the WMI Filters node
- Click a WMI filter itself

At each of these locations, the tab allows you to do something different. I'll discuss what each instance of this tab does a bit later in the "Advanced Security and Delegation with the GPMC" section.

WMI, which stands for Windows Management Instrumentation, is discussed in Chapter 11.

Minimizing the View with Policy Setting Filtering

Imagine you were just given the task to prevent all your users from accessing the Control Panel. Where do you start to look for that policy setting?

Sometimes, you just don't know where to start clicking inside the Group Policy Object Editor. You could be in the editor for a variety of reasons. Perhaps you want to locate a new policy setting to enable. With more than 1800 possible settings in Windows 2003, 1200 in Windows XP/Service Pack 2, and 2400 in Windows Vista, finding the specific policy setting you want can sometimes be a challenge.

To that end, the updated Group Policy Object Editor has a way to filter the view. The good news is that this feature is very powerful. The bad news is that this feature works only while browsing the Administrative Templates branch.

While in the Group Policy Object Editor, to examine the filtering option, choose either User Configuration ➤ Administrative Templates or Computer Configuration ➤ Administrative Templates. Then, choose View ➤ Filtering to display what's in Figure 2.1, which is described in the following sections.

The Filter settings are independent on each of the User and Computer nodes. Additionally, should you close the Group Policy Object Editor and come back into it, those filters are not preserved.

Filtering doesn't specifically help you "find" a GPO, per se. For instance, you can't "find" policy settings based on names and Explaintext.

When editing a GPO from a Windows Vista management station, it would appear that the final policy settings appear not to be scrubbed so that there was simply one "At least" requirement for Vista.

There are two main sets of Vista-specific policy settings, each with their own "Requirements." One set is: "At least Windows Vista" The other set is: "At least Microsoft Windows Vista." Most are in the latter set. However, the *first* set appears first when you click "Filter by Requirements information", so most people will likely click the one that comes up first, "At least Windows Vista." And when you do, you simply won't see most Vista-specific policy settings. Again, you'll need to click *both* filters to see all Vista-specific policy settings. This will likely be fixed in a Vista service pack or updated ADMX template download. (See Chapter 5 for more on ADMX files.)

FIGURE 2.1   The Group Policy Object Editor allows for filtering of the Administrative Template branch.

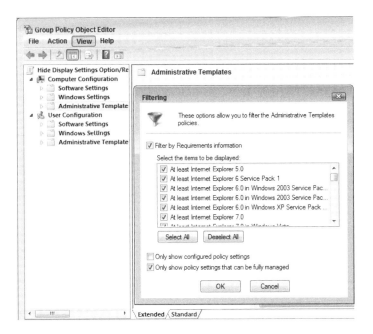

The "Only show configured policy settings" Setting

If you want to modify an existing policy setting, you needn't click every branch in one of the Administrative Templates folder in order to hunt-and-peck. Once the "Only show configured policy settings" option, as seen in Figure 2.1, is selected, you will see only policy settings that have been enabled or disabled within either the User Configuration ➢ Administrative Templates or Computer Configuration ➢ Administrative Templates.

By default, the "Only show configured policy settings" check box is not checked, and therefore you can see policy settings that are enabled, disabled, and not configured. The "Only show configured policy settings" check box is independent for both the Computer and User node settings. Additionally, when you close the editor, the check box is always reset.

Policy Setting Filtering Based on Operating System and Service Pack

As you learned in the Introduction, policy settings are specific to the operating system. For instance, a Windows XP policy setting such as **Turn off creation of System Restore Checkpoints** makes no sense to a Windows 2000 machine. This is because Windows 2000 doesn't have the System Restore feature.

There are times when you want to search for policy settings specific to the computers you want to target. Simply click the "Filter by Requirements information" check box as seen in Figure 2.1, and then proceed to check the items on which you want to filter.

You have a huge variety of criteria to choose from, including operating system, service pack, and even unique items such as Internet Explorer level and Windows Media Player.

 If the description of the filter is too long to read, simply hover the mouse over the description (don't click) to display the entire description in a floating ToolTip style window.

Using the "Only show policy settings that can be fully managed" Option

As we'll explore in Chapter 5, there's a difference between "true policies" and "preferences." Here's the deal: some settings are "bad" because they don't modify the "correct" portion of the Registry. In general, this is highly undesirable because in this way they won't act like Group Policy. That is, these settings usually permanently "tattoo" the target machine until the settings are explicitly removed.

For more on the distinction between policies and preferences with respect to Group Policy settings, see the "Policies vs. Preferences" section in Chapter 5.

This check box is checked by default, as seen in Figure 2.1. This gives a gentle persuasion to avoid the importation of implementing old-school preferences instead of true policies.

 You can choose to ensure this check box is permanently checked by using the "Enforce Show Policies Only" policy setting as described Chapter 3, in the "Using Group Policy to Affect Group Policy" section.

Locating Specific Policy Settings

I get tons of e-mails that ask the following question: "Jeremy, do you know if there's a policy setting that does <insert crazy thing here>?" My typical answer is, "I don't know. I'll have to look it up." Then I do. That's because there are more than 2400 policy settings, each contained within some nook or cranny.

To that end, you can (hopefully) hunt down your own policy setting that does what you want in several ways.

GP.CHM   GP.CHM is part of the Windows 2000 Resource Kit. It's a .CHM file, which means it's a compiled HTML file, and that basically means it's a help file like other help files. The good news is that it mirrors the hierarchy of the Windows 2000 Group Policy Object Editor. That is, it has both user and computer nodes and then all the levels of Group Policy nooks and crannies underneath in a beautiful hierarchical manner. Best of all, you can search within the text file for the policy setting's help text and get what you want. The bad news is that it's getting kind of old. Many policy settings have been renamed since Windows 2000, but GP.CHM is still useful.

hh <admtemplate>.chm (not for Windows Vista)   This one is most easily explained if you just go ahead and try it. Open a command prompt on your Windows 2003 machine and type **hh system.chm** or **hh inetres.chm** or **hh <name_of_any_other_adm_template>.chm**, and out pops a searchable help file with the stuff contained within the corresponding ADM file. Keen!

hh SPOLSCONCEPTS.CHM (not for Windows Vista)   This .CHM file is built into Windows XP and Windows 2003 Server. To open it, choose Start ➤ Run to open the Run dialog box and enter **hh spolsconcepts.chm** in the Open box. You'll then see another help file that discusses only the security-related settings, such as the meaning of each of the User Rights Assignments, what each of the Audit Policies is, and all the Security Options. This is truly a nice built-in resource.

PolicySettings.XLS and VistaGPSettings.XLS   If you want a definitive list of all Administrative Template policy settings that can affect Windows 2000 and Windows 2003 Server, XP, and Vista machines, you can download a spreadsheet from Microsoft from my website at www.GPanswers.com. Note, however, that Microsoft's spreadsheet doesn't go into much detail beyond the "Explain Text" setting for each policy setting. But they're all there and searchable, and you can sort by which operating systems will embrace which policy settings. It's quite good. Also, if you've got an older version, you should note that these are always updated whenever a service pack comes out. And, starting with Windows XP/SP2, they've started to document some of the "Security" settings as well. And the Windows Vista version tries to express when a specific policy setting requires a logoff or a reboot. Nice touch!

Raising or Lowering the Precedence of Multiple Group Policy Objects

You already know the "flow" of Group Policy is inherited from the site level, the domain level, and then from each nested OU level. But, additionally, *within* each level, say at the **Temporary Office Help** OU, multiple GPOs are processed in a ranking precedence order. Lower-ranking GPOs are processed first, and then the higher GPOs are processed.

In Figure 2.2, you can see that some administrator has linked two GPOs to the **Temporary Office Help** OU. One GPO is named "Enforce 50MB Disk Quotas," and another is named "Enforce 40MB Disk Quotas."

If the policy settings inside these GPOs both adjust the disk quota settings, which one will "win"? Client computers will process these two GPOs from lowest-link order to highest-link order. Therefore, the "Enforce 40MB Disk Quotas" GPO (with link order 2) is processed before "Enforce 50MB Disk Quotas" (link order 1). Hence, the GPO with the policy settings to dictate 50MB disk quotas will "win."

So, if two (or more) GPOs within the same level contain values for the same policy setting (or policy settings), the GPOs will be processed from lowest-link order to highest-link order. Each consecutively processed GPO overlays (and perhaps overwrites) overlapping policy settings. This could happen where one GPO has a specific policy setting enabled and another GPO at the same level has the same policy setting disabled.

Changing the order of the processing of multiple GPOs at a specific level is an easy task. For instance, suppose you want to change the order of the processing such that the "Enforce 40MB Disk Quotas" GPO is processed after the "Enforce 50MB Disk Quotas" GPO. Simply click the policy setting you want to process last and click the down arrow icon. Similarly, if you have additional GPOs that you want to process first, click the GPO and click the up arrow icon. The multiple arrow icons will put the highlighted GPO either first or last in the link order—depending on the icon you click.

FIGURE 2.2 You can link multiple GPOs at the same level.

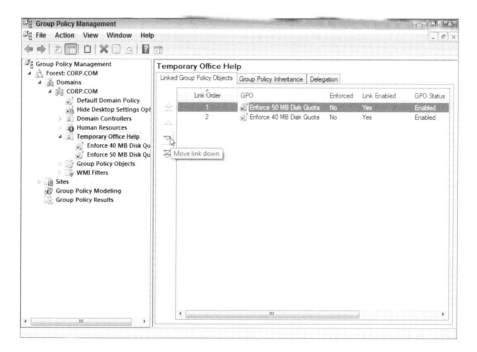

Again—the last applied GPO "wins." So the GPO with a link order of 1 is always applied last and, hence, has the "final" say at that level. This is always true unless the "Enforced" flag is used (as discussed later).

Understanding GPMC's Link Warning

In the previous chapter, I pointed out that any time you click a GPO link, you get the informational (or perhaps it's more of a warning) message shown in Figure 2.3.

This message is trying to convey an important sentiment: no man is an island, and neither is a Group Policy Object. Just because you created a GPO and it is seen swimming in the Group Policy Objects container doesn't mean you're the only one who is possibly using it.

FIGURE 2.3   You get this message any time you click the icon for a link.

As we work through examples in this chapter, we'll manipulate various characteristics of GPOs and links to GPOs. If we manipulate any characteristics of a GPO we're about to play with, such as the following:

- The underlying policy settings themselves
- The security filtering (on the Scope tab)
- The WMI filtering (on the Scope tab)
- The GPO status (on the Details tab)
- The delegation (on the Delegation tab)

then all other levels in Active Directory that also link to this GPO will be affected by our changes.

This is sometimes a tough concept to remember, so it's good to see it here again. You can choose to squelch the tip if you like. Just don't forget its advice.

The difference between the GPO itself and the links you can create can be confusing. Be sure to check out the sidebar "On GPO Links and GPOs Themselves," a bit later in the chapter.

You can see this principle in action if you like by locating the "Auto-Launch Calc.exe" GPO. In either the link upon the **Human Resources Computers** OU or the object itself with "GPOs," go to the Details tab and change the GPO status to some other setting. Then, go to the link or the actual GPO and see that your changes are reflected. You can even create a new OU, link the GPO, and see that the change is still there. This is because you're manipulating the actual GPO, not the link. If you choose to squelch the message, you can get it back by choosing View ➢ Options ➢ General and selecting "Show confirmation dialog to distinguish between GPOs and GPO links."

Stopping Group Policy Objects from Applying

After you create your hierarchy of Group Policy that applies to your users and computers, you might occasionally want to temporarily halt the processing of a GPO—usually because some user is complaining that something is wrong. You can prevent a specific GPO from processing at a level in Active Directory via several methods, as explained in the following sections.

Preventing Local GPOs from Applying

Before we get too far down the path with Active Directory–based GPOs, let's not forget that you might also want to stop a local GPO from applying. For instance, you might have walked up to 50 sales computers and created a local GPO that prevents access to the Control Panel. However, now you want to release that edict. Instead of walking around to those 50 computers, you can just zap a Group Policy to those computers to inhibit the processing of local GPOs. Here's the trick though: this technique only works for Windows Vista—not for earlier versions of the operating system. To do this trick, you'll use the policy setting found at Computer Configuration ➢ Administrative Templates ➢ System ➢ Group Policy, and it's called **Turn off Local Group Policy objects processing**. Just remember to ensure that your computers are in the OU where this GPO is targeted to take affect.

Disabling the "Link Enabled" Status

Remember that all GPOs are contained in the Group Policy Objects container. To use them at a level in Active Directory (site, domain, or OU), you link back to the GPO. So, the quickest way to prevent a GPO's contents from applying is to remove its "Link Enabled" status. If you right-click a GPO link at a level, you can immediately see its "Link Enabled" status, as shown in Figure 2.4.

To prevent this GPO from applying to the **Human Resources Users** OU, simply click "Link Enabled" to remove the check mark. This will leave the link within the OU back to the GPO but disable the link, rendering it innocuous. The icon to the left of the name of the GPO will change to a scroll with the link arrow dimmed. You'll see a zoomed-in picture of this later in the "GPMC At-a-Glance Icon View" section.

FIGURE 2.4   You can choose to enable or disable a GPO link.

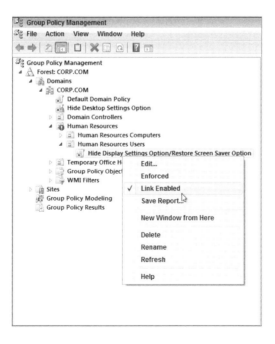

Disabling "Half" (or Both Halves) of the Group Policy Object

The second way to disable a specific GPO is by disabling just *one-half* of a Group Policy Object. You can disable either the user half or the computer half. Or, you can optionally disable the entire GPO.

You might be wondering why you might want to disable only half of a GPO. On the one hand, disabling a GPO (or half of a GPO) actually makes startup and logon times a teeny-weeny bit faster for the computer or user, because each GPO you add to the system adds a smidgen of extra processing—either for the user or the computer. Once you disable the unused portion of the GPO, you've shaved that processing time off the startup or logon time. Microsoft calls this "modifying Group Policy for performance."

Don't go bananas disabling your unused half of GPO just to save a few cycles of processing time. Trust me, it's just not worth the headaches figuring out later where you did and did not disable a half of a policy.

So, disabling half of the GPO makes troubleshooting and usage quite a bit harder, as you might just plumb forget you've disabled half the GPO. Then, down the road, when you modify the disabled half of the policy for some future setting, it won't take effect on your clients! You'll end up pulling your hair out wondering why, once things *should* change, they just don't!

Why Totally Disable a Group Policy Object?

One good reason to disable a specific GPO is if you want to manually "join" several GPOs together into one larger GPO. Then, once we're comfortable with the reaction, we can re-create the policy settings from multiple GPOs into another new GPO and disable the old individual GPOs. If there are signs of trouble with the new policy, you can always just disable (or delete) the large GPO and reenable the individual GPOs to get right back to where you started.

You might also want to immediately disable a new GPO even before you start to edit it. Imagine that you've chosen "Create and link a new GPO here" for, say, an OU. Then, imagine you have lots of policy settings you want to make in this new GPO. Remember that each setting is immediately written inside the Group Policy Object Editor, and computers are continually requesting changes when their Background Refresh interval triggers. The affected users or computers might hit their Background Refresh cycle and start accepting the changes before you've finished writing all your changes to the GPO! Therefore, if you disable the GPO before you edit and re-enable the GPO after you edit, you can ensure that your users are getting all the newly changed settings at once.

This tip works best only when creating new GPOs; if you disable the GPO *after* creation, there's an equally likely chance that critical settings will be removed while the GPO is disabled when clients request a Background Refresh. We'll discuss the ins and outs of Background Refresh in Chapter 3.

To disable an unused half of a GPO, follow these steps:

1. Select the GPO you want to modify. In this case, select "Auto-Launch Calc.exe" and select the Details tab in the right pane of the GPMC.

2. Since the policy settings within the "Auto-Launch Calc.exe" GPO modify only the Computer node, it is safe to disable the User node. Select the "User configuration settings disabled" drop-down box, as shown in Figure 2.5.

3. You will be prompted to confirm the status change. Choose to do so.

FIGURE 2.5   You can disable half the GPO to make Group Policy process a weeee bit faster.

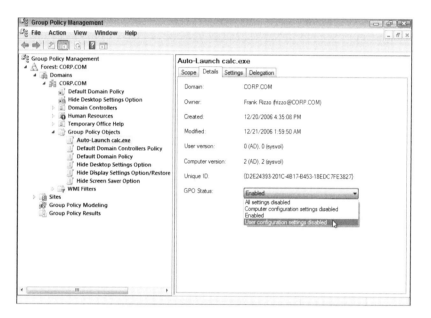

Here are some additional items to remember regarding disabling portions of a GPO:

- It is possible to disable the entire GPO (both halves) by selecting the GPO, clicking the Options button, and selecting the "All Settings Disabled" option. If you select "All Settings Disabled," the scroll icon next to the name of the GPO "dims" a bit to show that there is no way it can affect any targets. You'll see a zoomed-in picture of this later in the "GPMC At-a-Glance Icon View" section.

- As I stated in the "Understanding GPMCs Link Warning" section, changing the "GPO Status" entry (found on the Details tab) will affect the GPO—everywhere it is linked—at any level, anywhere in Active Directory!! You cannot just change the GPO status for the instance of this link—this affects all links to this GPO! The only good news here is that only the person who created the GPO itself (or anyone who has rights to it) can manipulate this setting. To get the full thrust of this, be sure to read the "On GPO Links and GPOs Themselves" sidebar a bit later in this chapter.

- The GPMC does not have any indication, other than this "GPO status," that the link has been fully or half-disabled. However, the old-school "Active Directory Users and Computers" interface in Windows 2003 will alert you to a GPO that is "half disabled." You'll see a yellow triangle warning icon next to the name of the GPO.

Deleting and Unlinking Group Policy Objects

As you just saw, you can prevent a GPO from processing at a level by merely removing its "Link Enabled" status. However, you can also choose to remove the link entirely. For instance, you might want to return the normal behavior of the computers such that calc.exe isn't launched whenever someone uses that machine. You have two options:

- Delete the link to the GPO
- Delete the GPO itself

Deleting the Link to the Group Policy Object

When you right-click the GPO link of "Auto-Launch Calc.exe" in the **Human Resources Computers** OU, you can choose Delete. When you do, the GPMC will confirm your request and remind you of an important fact, as shown in Figure 2.6.

FIGURE 2.6   You can delete a link (as opposed to deleting the GPO itself).

Recall that the GPO itself doesn't "live" at a level in Active Directory; it really lives in a special container in Active Directory (and can be seen via the Group Policy Objects Container in the GPMC). We're just working with a link to the real GPO. And, in Chapter 4, you'll see where this folder relates directly within Active Directory itself.

When you choose to delete a GPO link, you are simply choosing to stop using it at the level it was created, but keep the GPO itself alive in the representation of the swimming pool—the Group Policy Objects container. This leaves other administrators at other levels to continue to link to that GPO if they want.

Truly Deleting the Group Policy Object Itself

You can choose to delete the GPO altogether—lock, stock, and barrel. The only way to delete the GPO itself is to drill down through Group Policy Management ➤ Domains ➤ Corp.com, locate the Group Policy Objects container, and delete the GPO. It's like plucking a child directly from the swimming pool. Before you do, you'll get a warning message as shown in Figure 2.7.

FIGURE 2.7 Here, you're actually deleting the GPO itself.

This will actually remove the bits on the Domain Controller and obliterate it from the system. No other administrators can then link to this GPO.

Once it's gone, it's gone (unless you have a backup).

If you delete the GPO altogether, there's only one problem. There is no indication sent to the folks who are linking to this GPO that you've just deleted it. The idea is simple: you might be done with the "Auto-Launch Calc.exe" GPO and don't need it anymore to link to *your* locations in Active Directory. But what about other administrators? In this case, while I was out to lunch, Freddie, the administrator for the **Temporary Office Help** OU, has already chosen to link the "Auto-Launch Calc.exe" GPO to his OU, as shown in Figure 2.8.

What if I had deleted the "Auto-Launch Calc.exe" GPO? I'm pretty sure I would have received an angry phone call from Freddie. Or, maybe not—if Freddie didn't know who created (and owned) the GPO.

FIGURE 2.8 The "Auto-Launch Calc.exe" GPO (lowest circle) is linked at both the Temporary Office Help OU (middle circle) and this Human Resources Computers OU (topmost circle).

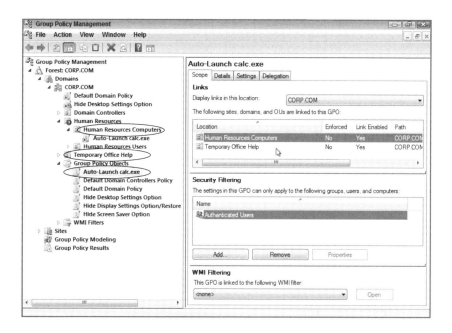

Since we only have a handful of OUs, this link back to the GPO was easy to find. However, once you start getting lots of OUs, locating additional links back to a GPO will become much harder. Thankfully, the GPMC shows you if anyone else is linked to a GPO you're about to delete. I call this ability "look before you leap." You can just look in the Scope tab under the Links heading as indicated in Figure 2.8 by the mouse pointer. There you can see that both the **Temporary Office Help** OU and the **Human Resources Computers** OU are utilizing the GPO named "Auto-Launch Calc.exe."

If you're confident that you can still continue, you can delete the GPO contained within the Group Policy Objects container. However, for now, let's leave this GPO in place for use in future examples in the book.

The Scope tab shows you the links to the GPOs from your own domain. It is possible for other domains to leverage your GPOs and link to them. When you delete a GPO forever, you're deleting the ability for other domains to use that GPO as well. Note that there is a drop-down in the scope tab labeled "Display links in this location." If you want, you can show "Entire Forest." That way, if a GPO is being leveraged by doing a no-no like "Cross Domain Linking" you can see if this GPO is linked to other areas you might not have intended it to be.

For now, don't delete the GPO. We'll use it again in later chapters. If you want to play with deleting a GPO, create a new one and delete it.

Block Inheritance

As you've already seen, the normal course of Group Policy inheritance applies all policies settings within GPOs in a cumulative fashion from the site to the domain and then to each nested OU. A setting at any level automatically affects all levels beneath it. But perhaps this is not always the behavior you want. For instance, we know that an edict from the Domain Administrator states there will be no Desktop Settings option in the Windows Vista Personalization page (or Desktop tab in the Display Properties dialog box for Windows XP).

This edict is fine for most of the OU administrators and their subjects who are affected. But Frank Rizzo, the administrator for the **Human Resources** OU structure, believes that the folks contained within his little fiefdom can handle the responsibility of the Desktop Settings option for Windows Vista (or Desktop tab for Windows XP) and the Screen Saver option, and he wants to bring them back to his users. (But he's not ready to give back the Display Settings option in the Windows Vista Personalization page or Settings tab for Windows XP.)

In this case, Frank Rizzo can prevent GPOs (and the policy settings within them) defined at higher levels (domain and site) from affecting his users, as shown in Figure 2.9. If Frank chooses to select "Block Inheritance," Frank is choosing to block the flow of *all* GPOs (with all their policy settings) from *all* higher levels.

When Frank does this, the **Human Resources** OU icon changes to include a blue exclamation point (!) as seen in Figure 2.9. Once the check is present and the GPOs are reprocessed on the client, only those settings that Frank dictates within his **Human Resources** OU structure will be applied.

If you want to see the effect of "Block Inheritance," ensure the check is seen as shown in Figure 2.9. Then, log on as any user affected by the **Human Resources** OU—say, Frank Rizzo. You'll notice that the Desktop Settings option in the Windows Vista Personalization page (or

Desktop tab in Windows XP) has reappeared. But you'll also notice that the Display Settings option in the Windows Vista Personalization page (or Settings tab in Windows XP) is still absent because that edict is contained within a GPO that's explicitly defined at the **Human Resources Users** OU level, which contains Frank's user account.

FIGURE 2.9   Use the "Block Inheritance" feature to prevent all GPOs (and the policy settings within them) from all higher levels from affecting your users and computers.

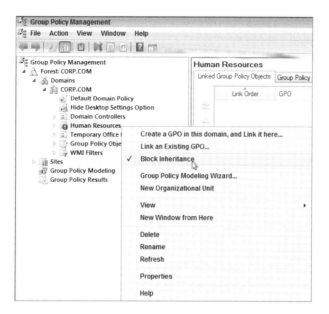

The "Enforced" Function

Frank Rizzo and his Human Resources folks are happy that the Screen Saver and Desktop Settings options in Vista (or Screen Saver and Desktop tabs for Windows XP) have made a triumphant return. There's only one problem: the Domain Administrator has found out about this transgression and wants to ensure that the Desktop Settings option in Vista (or Desktop tab in Windows XP) is permanently revoked.

The normal flow of inheritance is site, domain, and then OU. Super. If you've set a "Block Inheritance" on an OU (say, the **Human Resources** OU) then all settings to that OU are null and void.

But, shouldn't there be some power to allow "bigger" administrators to get their wills enforced? Enforced! Heck, what a great term. I should patent that. To trump a lower level's "Block Inheritance," a higher-level administrator will use the "Enforced" function.

"Enforced" was previously known as "No Override" in old-school parlance.

The idea behind the "Enforced" function is simple: it guarantees that policies and settings within a specific GPO at a higher level are always inherited by lower levels. It doesn't matter if the lower administrator has blocked inheritance or has a GPO that tries to disable or modify the same policy setting or settings.

In this example, you'll log on as the Domain Administrator and set an edict to force the removal of the Desktop Settings option in the Windows Vista Personalization page (or Desktop tab in the Display Properties dialog box for Windows XP).

To use "Enforced" to force the settings within a specific Group Policy Object setting, right-click the "Hide Desktop Settings Option" GPO link and select "Enforced," as shown in Figure 2.10.

FIGURE 2.10 Use the "Enforced" option to guarantee settings contained within a specific GPO affect all users downward via inheritance.

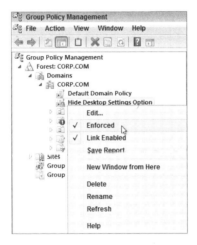

Notice that the GPO link now has a little "lock" icon, demonstrating it cannot be trumped. You can see this in the "Hide Desktop Settings Option" GPO link icon in Figure 2.10. You'll see a zoomed-in picture of this later in the "GPMC At-a-Glance Icon View" section.

To test your "Enforced" edict, log on as a user affected by the **Human Resources** OU— Frank Rizzo. In the Display Properties dialog box, the Desktop Settings option in the Windows Vista Personalization page (or Desktop tab in Windows XP) should be absent because it is being forced from the "Enforced" edict at the domain level even though "Block Inheritance" is used at the OU level.

On GPO Links and GPOs Themselves

The GPMC is a cool tool, but, in my opinion, it actually shows you a bit *too* much. Sometimes, it can be confusing what can be performed on the GPO's link and what can be performed on the GPO itself. Remember that GPOs themselves are displayed in the GPMC via the Group Policy Objects container. The links back to them are shown at the site, domain, and OU levels. So here's a list of what you can "do" to a GPO link and what you can "do" to a GPO *itself*.

You can only do three things on a GPO link that applies to a site, a domain, or an OU:

- Link Enable (that is, enable or disable the settings to apply at this level).

- Enforce the link (and force the policy settings).

- Delete the link.

Everything else is always done on the *actual* GPO itself:

- Change the policy settings inside the GPO (found on the Settings tab).

- Apply security filters, rights (such as the "Apply Group Policy" privilege), and delegation (such as the "Edit this GPO" privilege) discussed in the "Advanced Security and Delegation with the GPMC" section.

- Enable/disable the computer and/or user half of the GPO via the GPO status (found on the Details tab).

- Place a WMI filter upon the GPO (discussed in Chapter 11).

If this seems clear as mud, consider this scenario:

- Fred and Ginger are the two Domain Administrators. By definition, they can create GPOs.

- Imagine that Fred designs the "Desktop Settings" GPO, which contains policy settings that affect both users and computers. Perhaps one user policy setting is **Remove Run off Start Menu**. Perhaps one computer policy setting is **Enforce disk quota limit**. And Fred sets the quota limit to 50MB.

- Fred links the "Desktop Settings" GPO to the **Dancers** OU as well as the **Audition Halls** OU.

- Ginger gets a phone call from the folks in the **Audition Halls** OU. The users in the **Audition Halls** OU report that the 50MB disk quotas are too restrictive. "Can they just turn off the computer-side settings for us Audition Halls folks?" one of them cries.

- Ginger goes to the "Desktop Settings" GPO link (which is linked to the **Audition Halls** OU), clicks the Details tab, and disables the computer settings using the "GPO Status" setting drop-down box.

- Fred then gets a phone call that the **Dancers** OU no longer has disk quotas being applied.

Why did this happen?

Because the Group Policy engine has certain controls on the GPO *itself* and has other controls on the Group Policy *link*. Because Fred and Ginger are both Domain Administrators, they jointly have ownership of the ability to change the GPO and the GPO link.

Whenever Ginger modifies any characteristic in the previous bulleted list, she's changing it "globally" for any place in Active Directory that might be using it. That's what the warning in Figure 2.3, earlier in this chapter, is all about.

If you'll allow me to get on my soap box for the next 10 seconds, the level of finite control over what Ginger can and cannot do to the GPO itself is fairly limited. In the future, I'd love to see the Group Policy engine extended so that we can delegate more aspects of control about the GPO link, not just about the GPO itself.

In any event, delegating what we can control over the GPO itself is precisely what the next section is about, specifically the "Granting User Permissions on a GPO" section.

Advanced Security and Delegation with the GPMC

Mere mortals' access to Group Policy can be and, indeed, should be controlled. Users' access to all things Group Policy related is judged in many forms. However, the first question you'll want to answer and understand well is basic: To whom should Group Policy be applied, and to whom should it not be applied?

Once we can answer that, we can move on to some more advanced topics:

- What kind of access can I grant to mere mortals to manipulate the GPO itself? That is, can a user read or modify the GPO's settings or security?

- How can I grant a mere mortal access to create GPOs in the domain?

- Can a user perform special Group Policy–related stuff, such as the creation and management of WMI filters or access to RSoP tools?

You can answer all these questions by determining what security is placed on Active Directory and specific GPOs. Let's tackle these questions one at a time to locate all the places users' access touches our Group Policy infrastructure and where that access can be managed.

Filtering the Scope of Group Policy Objects

The normal day-to-day Human Resources workers inside the **Human Resources** OU structure are fine with the facts of life:

- The Enterprise Administrator says that no one at the site will have the Screen Saver option.

- The Domain Administrator says that no one will have the Desktop Settings option in the Windows Vista Personalization page (or Desktop tab in the Display Properties dialog box for Windows XP). He is forcing this edict with the "Enforced" option.

- Frank Rizzo, the **Human Resources** OU Manager, says that for the **Human Resources Users** OU he will remove the Settings tab but restore the Screen Saver option. For the **Human Resources Computers** OU, he'll want to make sure that calc.exe launches whenever someone uses a Human Resources computer.

- Additionally, at the top-level **Human Resources** OU, he will enable the "Block Inheritance" setting to give back the Screen Saver option removed by the Enterprise Administrator at the site level. But Frank is forced to live with the fact that he won't be able to return to his people the Desktop Settings option in the Windows Vista Personalization page (or Desktop tab in the Display Properties dialog box for Windows XP). The Domain Administrator has taken this away and that's that.

But Frank and other members of the HR-OU-Admins Security group are getting frustrated that they cannot access the Settings tab. And they're also getting a little annoyed that every time they use an Human Resources machine, calc.exe pops up to greet them.

Sure, it was Frank's own idea to make these two policy settings—one that affects the users he's in charge of and one that affects the computers he's in charge of. The problem is, however, it also affects Frank (and the other members of the HR-OU-Admins team) when they're working, and you can see where that can be annoying.

Frank needs a way to filter the "Scope of Management" (*SOM*) of the "Hide Display Settings Option/Restore Screen Saver Option," as well as the "Auto-Launch Calc.exe" GPOs. By scope or SOM, I mean "how far and wide" the GPOs we set up will be embraced.

Occasionally you will see references to SOM in your travels with Group Policy. An SOM is simply a quick-and-dirty way to express where and when a GPO might apply. An SOM can be nearly any combination of things: linking a GPO to the domain, linking a GPO to an OU, and linking a GPO to a site. However, if you start to filter GPOs within the domain, that's also an SOM. In essence, an SOM indicates when and where a GPO applies to a level in Active Directory.

In our case, the idea is twofold:

- Frank and his team are excluded from the "Hide Display Settings Option/Restore Screen Saver Option" GPO edict.

- The specific computers that Frank and his team use are excluded from the "Auto-Launch Calc.exe" GPO edict.

Recall from Chapter 1 that, despite the wording of the term *Group Policy*, Group Policy does not directly affect Security groups. You cannot just wrap up a bunch of similar users or computers in a Security group and thrust a GPO upon them. There's nowhere to "link" to. You need to round up the individual user or computer accounts into an OU first and then link the desired GPO on that OU.

Here's the truly strange part: even though you can't round up users in Security groups and apply GPOs to them, it's the Security group that we'll leverage (in most cases) in order to enable us to filter Group Policy application!

In order for users to get GPOs to apply to them, they need two under-the-hood access rights to the GPO itself:

- Read

- Apply Group Policy

These permissions must be set on the GPO in question. By default, all Authenticated Users are granted the "Read" and "Apply Group Policy" rights to all new GPOs. Therefore, anyone who has a GPO geared for them will process it.

How Is a Computer an Authenticated User?

I was shocked to learn that a computer falls under the category of an Authenticated User. It's true: the computer account has the Authenticated User's SID in its access token. I was skeptical, but über-guru Bill Boswell (and author of Chapter 7) proved it to me. And you can prove it to yourself by following these steps on a Windows XP machine (they won't work on Windows Vista):

1. Use the at command and specify a time at least one minute ahead of the current time to open a system-level console:

   at <one minute in the future> /interactive cmd

2. Use WHOAMI to verify that the cmd has run as System. Now use WHOAMI /ALL to verify that you have the Authenticated Users group in the access token.

Note that the System does not have domain credentials. When it touches another machine, it uses the Kerberos ticket issued to the local computer. You can take advantage of this for this experiment.

1. Set the NTFS permissions on a folder in a shared volume on another machine to deny access to Authenticated Users but allow access by Everyone.

2. Map a drive from the system console to the share point and try to access the contents of the protected folder. You'll be denied access.

Because Deny for Authenticated Users comes before Allow for Everyone, you've proved that the computer account has the Authenticated Users group in its access token.

The following two things might not be immediately obvious:

- Administrators are not magically exempt from embracing Group Policy; they, too, are members of "Authenticated Users." You can change this behavior with the techniques described in the very next section.

- Computers need love, too. And for computers to apply their side of the GPO, they need the same rights: "Read" and "Apply Group Policy." Since computers are technically Authenticated Users, the computer has all it needs to process GPOs meant for it.

With this fundamental concept in mind, let's look at several ways to filter who gets specific GPOs.

If you want to filter GPOs for either specific users or specific computers, you have three distinct approaches. For our three examples (which will all do the exact same thing), we want the "Hide Display Settings Option/Restore Screen Saver Option" GPO to "pass over" our heroes in the HR-OU-Admins Security group but to apply to everyone else who should get them. We also want the "Auto-Launch Calc.exe" GPO to pass over the specific computers our heroes use at their desks.

Group Policy Object Filtering Approach #1: Leverage the Security Filtering Section of the Scope Tab in GPMC

In the first approach, you'll round up only the users, computers, or Security groups who should get the GPO applied to them. To make things easier, let's first create two Active Directory Security groups—one for our users who will get the GPO, and one for computers who will get the GPO. Good names might be:

- People-Who-Get-the-Hide-DisplaySettingsOption-GPO

  and

- Computers-That-Get-the-Auto-Launch Calc.exe-GPO.

  Go ahead and do this in Active Directory Users And Computers as seen in Figure 2.11. Next, add all user accounts you want to embrace the GPO into the first Security group.

  You would then add all computer accounts you want to get the GPO into the Security group named Computers-That-Get-the-Auto-Launch-Calc.exe-GPO.

FIGURE 2.11   Create a new Active Directory Security group for whom you want the GPO to apply. Create security groups for both users and computers based on the GPO you want to filter.

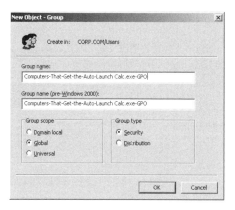

Because we don't want these GPO to apply to Frank or Frank's computer (XPPRO1 or VISTA1), don't add Frank to the first group (which contains users) and don't add XPPRO1or VISTA1 to the second group (which contains computers).

Next, click the link to the "Hide Display Settings Option/Restore Screen Saver Option" GPO found in Group Policy Management ➤ Forest ➤ Domains ➤ Corp.com ➤ **Human Resources** OU ➤ **Human Resources Users** OU. In the Security Filtering section, you can see that Authenticated Users is listed. This means that any users inside the **Human Resources Users** OU will certainly get this GPO applied.

However, now we're about to turn the tables. We're going to click the "Remove" button to remove the Authenticated Users in the Security Filtering section; then we're going to add the People-Who-Get-the-Hide-DisplaySettingsOption-and-Restore-GPO Security group, as shown in Figure 2.12.

Next, click the "Auto-Launch Calc.exe" GPO link (which is under the **Human Resources Computers** OU). In the Security Filtering section of the Scope tab, you'll remove Authenticated Users and add the Computers-That-Get-The-Auto-Launch-Calc.exe-GPO Security group.

 In both cases, what we're really doing under the hood is giving these new Security groups the ability to "Read" and "Apply Group Policy." You'll see this under-the-hood stuff in a minute.

FIGURE 2.12   When you remove "Authenticated Users," no one will get the effects of the GPO. Add only the users or groups you want the GPO to affect.

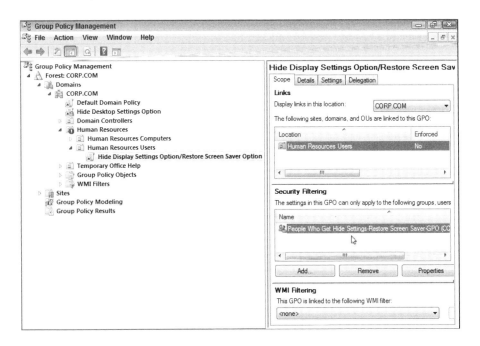

Testing Your First Filters

To see if this is working, log on XPPRO1 or VISTA1 as Frank (Frizzo). Even though the GPO applies to the **Human Resources Users** OU, the GPO will pass over him and anyone else not explicitly put into that Security group since Frank is not a member of the People-Who-Get-the-Hide-DisplaySettingsOptionGPO Security group.

For another test, add a new user account or two to the **Human Resources Users** OU (via Active Directory Users And Computers.) Then, log on as one of these new users (in the OU) and verify that they, indeed, do not get the GPO. This is because the GPO is only set to apply to members of the Security group. Then, add the user to the Security group and log on again. The GPO will then apply to your test users (inside the Security group) as well. In fact, you can add users to the Security group by simply clicking the Properties button in the Security Filtering section. Doing so opens the Security Group Membership dialog in which you can add or delete users or computers.

Repeat your tests by adding XPPRO1or VISTA1 into the Security group named Computers That Get The Auto-Launch Calc.exe GPO. When the computer is in the group, it will apply the GPO. Now, try removing XPPRO1 or VISTA1 and see what happens. When the computer is out of the group, the GPO will pass over the computer.

You will have to reboot the machine to immediately see computer-side results.

What's Going on Under the Hood for Filtering

As I implied, when you add Security groups to get the GPOs in the Security Filtering section, you're really doing a bit of magic under the hood. Again, that magic is simply granting two security permissions: "Read" and "Apply Group Policy" to the users or Security groups that you want to apply the GPOs in the OU.

To see which security permissions are really set under the hood for a particular GPO (or GPO link, because it's the same information), click the Delegation tab and select the Advanced button as shown in Figure 2.13.

When you do, you can see the actual permission on the GPO itself. You can easily locate the Security group named People-Who-Get-the-Hide-DisplaySettingsOption-GPO and see that they have both the "Read" and "Apply Group Policy" access rights set to "Allow." This is why they will process this GPO.

Filtering Approach #2: Identify Who You Do Not Want to Get the Policy

The other approach is to leave the default definition in for the GPO such that the "Authenticated Users" group is granted the "Read" and "Apply Group Policy." Then, figure out who you *do not* want to get the policy applied to them, and use the "Deny" attribute over the "Apply Group Policy" right.

When Windows security is evaluated, the designated users or computers will not be able to process the GPO due to the "Deny" attribute; hence, the GPO passes over them.

FIGURE 2.13   Selecting "Advanced" in the Delegation tab for the GPO (or GPO link) shows the under-the-hood security settings for the GPO.

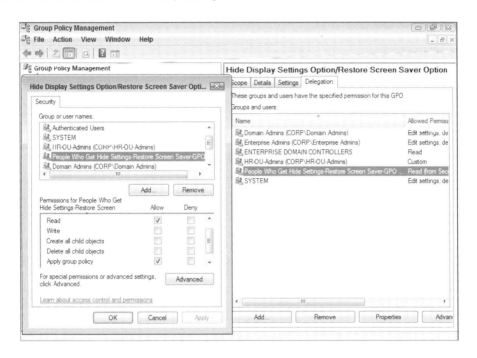

 See tho "Positive ur Negative?" sidebar later in this chapter before doing this in your real environment.

For our examples, we want the "Hide Display Settings Option/Restore Screen Saver Option" GPO to pass over our heroes in the HR-OU-Admins Security group, but apply to everyone else by default. We also want the "Auto-Launch Calc.exe" GPO to pass over the specific computers our heroes use at their desks.

To use this second technique, we'll use the "Deny" permission to ensure that the HR-OU-Admins Security group cannot apply (and hence process) the "Hide Display Settings Option/Restore Screen Saver Option" GPO. We'll also additionally prevent Frank's computer, XPPRO1 or VISTA1, from processing the "Auto-Launch Calc.exe" GPO.

Again, you'll do this on the GPO (or the GPO link, because it's the same information), click the Delegation tab, and then click the Advanced button. Follow these steps:

1. Locate the "Pcople-Who-Get-the-Hide-DisplaySettingsOption-GPO" Security group and remove it.

2. Locate the "Authenticated Users" group, select the "Read" permission, select Allow, select "Apply Group Policy" permission, and select Allow.

3. If you used Frank's account to originally create this GPO, he is specifically listed in the security list. You want to remove Frank and add the HR-OU-Admins group. Click Frank, and then click Remove. Click Add, and add the HR-OU-Admins group.

4. Make sure the "Apply Group Policy" check box is set to "Deny" for the HR-OU-Admins group, as shown in Figure 2.14.

Do not set the Deny check box for the "Read" or "Write" attributes from the HR-OU-Admins (the group you're currently a member of when logged in as Frank). If you do, you'll essentially lock yourself out, and you'll have to ask the Domain Administrator to grant you access again.

1 Click OK to close the Group Policy Settings dialog box. In the warning box that tells you to be careful about Deny permissions, click Yes.

2. Click OK to close the OU Properties dialog box.

To test your first filter again, log on to XPPRO1 or VISTA1 as Frank Rizzo. Note that the Settings tab has returned to him because he is part of the HR-OU-Admins group. The "Hide Display Settings Option/Restore Screen Saver Option" GPO has passed over him because he is unable to process the GPO.

To bypass "Auto-Launch Calc.exe" GPO on XPPRO1 or VISTA1, you'll perform a similar operation. That is, you'll modify the security on the GPO to pass over the computers our heroes use by denying those specific computer accounts the ability to "Apply Group Policy." You can then test your second filter by logging on as anyone to XPPRO1 or VISTA1. You should then see that calc will not launch when a user uses that machine.

FIGURE 2.14 Use the "Deny" bit on the "Apply Group Policy" right to prevent Group Policy from applying.

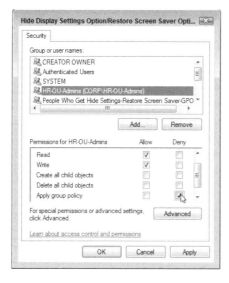

Turns out, however, there's a major problem in using the aforementioned method. That is, if you performed the previous exercise and used the "Deny" attribute to pass over the HR-OU-Admins group using the Security on the GPO, you've got a small problem. Sure, it worked! That's the good news. The bad news is that GPMC isn't smart enough to interpret quite what you did back on the Scope tab in the Security Filtering section as shown in Figure 2.15.

Yes, it's technically true what the Security Filtering section says: Authenticated Users will apply this GPO. However, it doesn't tell us the other important fact: that the HR-OU-Admins group *will not* process this GPO, because they were denied the ability to "Apply Group Policy."

The only way to get the full, true story of who will actually get the GPO applied to them is to look back within the GPO (or GPO link, because it's the same information), select the Delegation tab, and click the Advanced button to see who has "Read" and "Apply" Group Policy; then also see who is denied access to process the GPO via the "Deny" attributes.

The moral of the story? Always consult the Advanced tab to get the whole truth as to the security on the GPO.

FIGURE 2.15   The Security Filtering section on the Scope tab will not show you any use of "Deny" bits under the hood.

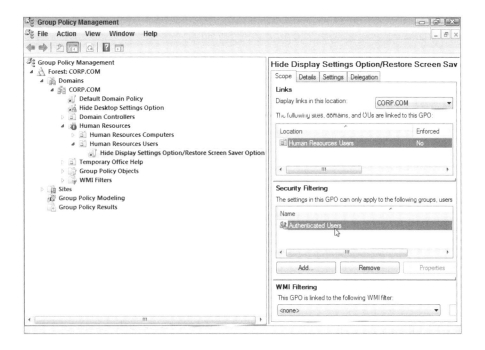

Positive or Negative?

Now that you can see the two ways to filter users from processing GPOs, which should you use? Approach 1 (adding only those you want to get the GPO) or Approach 2 (denying only those you don't want to get the GPO)? The data reflected within the GPMC's Scope tab clearly wants you to take the first approach. However, many Active Directory implementations I know take the second approach (and, in fact, it was my advice to do so in the first edition of this book).

Now, you and your team need to make a choice for your approach. As you saw, when you create new GPUs, you can choose to filter via the Scope tab or the Advanced Delegation. So which do you choose? If you're going to be religious about using the first approach, you can then be reasonably confident that only the users, groups, and computers listed in the Security Filtering section of the Scope tab will, in fact, be the only users, groups, and computers who will get the GPO. You can then reduce your need to dive into the Security Editor as seen in Figures 2.13 and 2.14, earlier in this chapter.

However, if you (or other administrators) occasionally choose to use the "Deny" attribute upon users, computers, and groups from getting the GPO, you'll need to additionally inspect the Advanced Security Editor dialog in the Delegation tab as in Figures 2.13 and 2.14.

The GPMC clearly encourages you to use Approach 1 for filtering. If you have older GPOs in your Active Directory that already use Approach 2 for filtering, consider changing it so that GPMC's Scope tab will actually reflect who will get the GPO.

Granting User Permissions upon an Existing Group Policy Object

You already know the three criteria for someone to be able to edit or modify an existing GPO:

- They are a member of the Domain Admins group.
- They are a member of the Enterprise Admins group.
- They created the GPO themselves and hence are the owner. (We saw this in Figure 1.22 in Chapter 1 when Frank couldn't edit the GPOs he didn't create.)

But sometimes, you also want to add rights to a user on a GPO so that they can modify it. As we foreshadowed, the Delegation tab for a GPO (or GPO link, which reflects the same information) has a second purpose: to help you grant permissions to groups or users over the security properties of that GPO. If you click Add on the Delegation tab, you can grant any mere mortal user or group (even in other domains) the ability to manipulate this GPO, as seen in Figure 2.16.

FIGURE 2.16   The Delegation tab helps you set permissions on a GPO.

Once the permissions settings have been applied, the user has that level of rights over the GPO, as seen in Table 2.1.

TABLE 2.1   GPMC vs. Genuine Active Directory Permissions

Permissions Option	Actual Under-the-Hood Permissions
"Read"	Sets the Allow permission for "Read" on the GPO.
"Edit settings"	Sets the Allow permission for "Read," "Write," "Create Child Objects," and "Delete Child Objects." See the note regarding "Under the hood" attributes.
"Edit settings, delete, modify security"	Sets the Allow permission for "Read," "Write," "Create Child Objects," "Delete Child Objects," "Delete," "Modify Permissions," and "Modify Owner." This is near-equivalent to full control on the GPO, but note that "Apply Group Policy" access permission is not set. (This can be useful to set for administrators so they can manipulate the GPO but not have it apply to themselves.)
"Read (from Security Filtering)"	This isn't a permission located in the ACL Editor (see Figure 2.14); rather this is only visible if the user has "Read" and "Apply Group Policy" permissions on the GPO. This is a reflection of what is on the Scope tab.
Custom	Any other combinations of rights, including the use of the Deny permission. Custom rights are only added via the ACL editor but can be removed here. They can be removed using the Remove button as in the Delegation tab.

If you look really, really closely at the "Under the hood" attributes specifically granted to the user when they are given "Edit settings" or "Edit setting, delete, modify security" rights, you'll note that "Write" isn't expressly listed. However, the ability to perform writes is granted because other subattributes which do permit writing are granted on the entry. To see those attributes for yourself, click the Advanced button while looking at the properties of the security on a GPO (like what we see in Figure 2.14).

Granting Group Policy Object Creation Rights in the Domain

As you learned in Chapter 1, a user cannot create new GPOs unless that user is a member of the Group Policy Creator Owners group. Dropping a user into this group is one of two ways you can grant this right.

However, the GPMC introduces another way to grant users the ability to have Group Policy Creator Owner–style access. Traverse to the Group Policy Objects container as seen in Figure 2.17, and click the Delegation tab. You can now click Add and select any user, including any user in your domain, say a user named Joe User, or users across forests, such as Sol Rosenberg, who is in a domain called bigu.edu. As you can see in Figure 2.17, both users have been added.

This can be handy if you have trusted administrators in other domains that you want to have create GPOs in your domain. You might want to round them up into a group (instead of just listing them individually as Sol is listed here), but that's your option.

Special Group Policy Operation Delegations

You can delegate three special permissions at the domain and OU levels, and you can set one of those three special permissions at the site level. Clicking the level, such as an OU, and then click-ing the Delegation tab for that level shows the available permissions as seen in Figure 2.18.

FIGURE 2.17   You can choose to delegate to users in your domain, in other domains, or in domains in other forests.

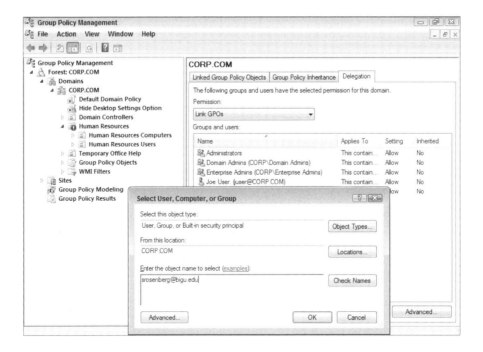

FIGURE 2.18 These operations are equivalent to the Active Directory Users And Computers "Delegation Wizard."

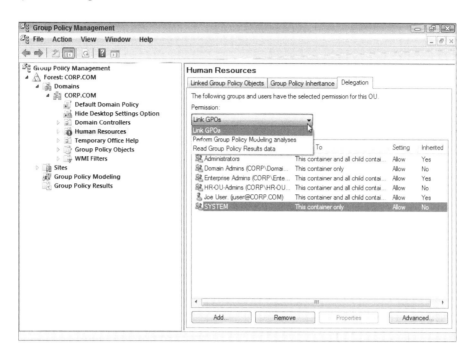

The interface is a bit confusing here. Specifically, you must first select the permission from the drop-down box. This lists the current users who can have permissions to use the right. You can then click the "Add," "Remove," or "Advanced" button to make your changes.

There are three Permissions that may be selected from the drop-down box, as seen in Figure 2.18. They are:

Link GPOs Of the three permissions here, this is the only permission that can be configured at all levels: site, domain, and OU. Recall in Chapter 1 that you ran the Active Directory Users And Computers "Delegation of Control Wizard" (see Figure 1.19). Instead of using Active Directory Users And Computers to perform that task, the GPMC can do the same job—right here.

Perform Group Policy Modeling analyses This right performs the same function as if we had used the Active Directory Users And Computers "Delegation of Control Wizard" to grant the "Generate Resultant Set of Policy (Planning)" permissions, as seen previously in Figure 1.19. The next section describes how to get more data about what's happening at the client. You'll see how to use this power in the "What-If Calculations with Group Policy Modeling" section later in this chapter. Group Policy Modeling lets you simulate what-if scenarios regarding users and computers.

By default, only Domain Admins have the right to perform this task. Domain Admins can grant other users or groups the ability to perform this function, such as the Help Desk,

HR-OU-Admins, or your own desktop-administrator teams. You can choose to grant people the ability to perform Group Policy Modeling analyses on this specific container or this specific container and child containers. When you assign this right, the user performing the Group Policy Modeling analysis must have the delegated right upon the container containing the what-if user and also the container containing the what-if computer. If you don't grant rights in both containers, only half the analysis is displayed.

This right is available only if the domain AD schema has been updated for Windows 2003. Additionally, Group Policy Modeling analyses function only when at least one Windows 2003 Domain Controller is available in the domain.

Read Group Policy Results Data   This right performs the same function as if we used the Active Directory Users And Computers "Delegation of Control Wizard" to grant the "Generate Resultant Set of Policy (Logging)" permission, as seen previously in Figure 1.19. You'll see how to use this power in the "What's-Going-On Calculations with Group Policy Results" section later in this chapter. However, if you want to grant this power to others, you can. Again, a typical use is to grant this right to the Help Desk or other administrative authority.

When you assign this right, the user performing the Group Policy Results analysis must have the delegated right upon the container containing the target computer. Or this right can be applied at a parent container, and the rights will flow down via inheritance. The user or group must also have this right delegated upon any container containing any users who have logged on to the machine you want to analyze. If you don't grant rights in both containers, no analysis is displayed.

This right is available only if the domain AD schema has been updated for Windows 2003 and later.

Who Can Create and Use WMI Filters?

Okay, okay, okay. I know the subject of WMI filters has come up about 3000 times already, and every time I refer you, the poor reader, to Chapter 11. Once you've read what they are and how to create them in Chapter 11, please come back here and read how to manage them.

Two types of people are involved in the management of WMI filters:

- Those who can create them
- Those who can use them

Delegating Who Can Create WMI Filters

By default, only the Domain Administrator can create WMI filters. However, you might have some WMI whiz-kid in your company (and it's a good chance this isn't the same person as the Domain Administrator). With that in mind, the Domain Administrator can grant that special someone the ability to create WMI filters. To do this, drill down to the domain ➢ WMI Filters node, and then select Delegation in the pane on the right. You can now grant one of two rights, as shown in Figure 2.19.

In Figure 2.19, we can see the two rights that appear in the drop-down box:

- Once a user has "Creator owner" rights here, they can create and modify their own WMI filters, but they cannot modify others' WMI filters.

- A user with "Full control" rights here can create and modify their own WMI filters or anyone else's.

FIGURE 2.19 These are controls over the creation of WMI filters.

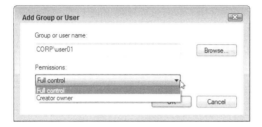

 These rights are available only if the domain AD schema has been updated for at least Windows 2003.

Delegating Who Can Use WMI Filters

Once WMI filters are created (again, see Chapter 11), you'll likely want to assign who can apply them to specific GPOs. To do this, drill down to the specific WMI filter, as shown in Figure 2.20. Then click Add, and you'll see that two rights are available for the user you want.

In Figure 2.20, we can see the two rights that appear in the drop-down box:

- Once a user has "Edit" rights here, they can edit and tailor the filter, as we do in Chapter 11.

- A user with "Full control" rights here can edit the filter as well as delete it and modify the security (that is, specify who else can get "Edit" or "Full Control" rights here).

 These rights are available only if the domain AD schema has been updated for at least Windows 2003.

FIGURE 2.20   These are controls over the WMI filters themselves.

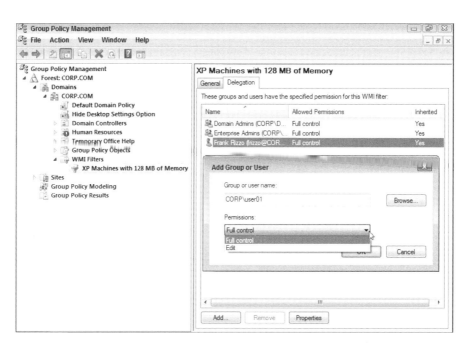

Performing RSoP Calculations with the GPMC

In Chapter 1, we charted out a fictitious organization's GPO structure on paper. We looked and saw when various GPOs were going to apply to various user and computers. Charting out the RSoP (Resultant Set of Policies) for users and computers on paper is a handy skill for basic understanding of GPO organization and flow; but in the real world, you'll need a tool that can help you actually figure out what's going on at your client desktops.

The GPMC has a handy feature to show us all the GPOs that are going to apply for the users and computers at a specific level in Active Directory. In Figure 2.21, when you click the **Human Resources Users** OU and then click the Group Policy Inheritance tab, you can see a list of all the GPOs that should apply to the **Human Resources Users** OU.

The site level is not shown in this Group Policy Inheritance tab. Because computers, particularly laptops, can travel from site to site, it is impossible to know for sure what site to represent here.

FIGURE 2.21   The Group Policy Inheritance tab shows you which GPOs should apply.

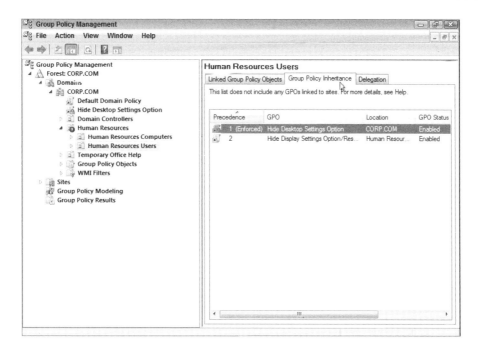

As I said, this tab in Figure 2.21 should really tell you what's going to happen. The operative word here is *should*. That's because a lot can go wrong between your wishes and what actually happens on the client systems. For instance, you already saw how to filter GPOs using Security groups, which would certainly change the experience of one user versus another on the very same machine. And in Chapter 11, you'll learn about WMI filters, which limit when GPOs are applied even more.

The point of all this RSoP stuff is to help us know the score about what's going on at machines that could be many hundreds of millimeters, meters, or kilometers away. When users freak out about getting settings they don't expect or when they freak out about lacking settings they do expect, the point is to know which setting is causing the stir and which GPO is to blame for the errant setting.

We know one thing's for sure: users do freak out a lot if anything changes, and it's our job to douse water on the problem (but not the user or computer). So the point of performing an RSoP calculation is to help you know what is going on and why it's going on that way. The GPMC can help with that.

What's-Going-On Calculations with Group Policy Results

If someone calls you to report that an unexpected GPO is applying, you can find out what's going on via the GPMC. You can find out what's going on if the machine in question is a Windows Vista,

Windows XP, Windows 2003, and presumably later clients. Sorry, Windows 2000 computers are left in the dust.

Windows 2000 computers are not left in the dust for the what-if calculations with Group Policy Modeling in the next section.

Once the user with the problem has logged on to the machine in question, you can tap into the WMI provider built in to Windows Vista, Windows XP, and Windows 2003. Without going too propeller-head here, the upshot of this magic is that the GPMC (and the GPRESULT command, as you'll see in Chapter 4) can query any particular user that has ever logged on locally. It's then a simple matter to display the sexy results within the GPMC.

Once the results are displayed, you can right-click over them and save them as an HTML or XML report.

The magic happens when the computer asking "What's going on?" (in this case, the computer running the GPMC) asks the target client computer. The target client computer responds with a result of what has happened—which GPOs were applied to the computer side and to the user side (provided the user has ever, at least once, logged on).

Let me expand on this important point: this Group Policy Results magic only works if the target user has ever logged on to the target machine. They only need to have ever logged on once, and here's the amazing part: They don't even need to be logged on while you run the test. But if the target user has *never* logged on to the target machine, the Group Policy Results will not allow you to select that user.

You can run your what's-going-on calculations inside the GPMC by right-clicking the Group Policy Results node at the bottom of the GPMC's hierarchy as shown in Figure 2.22. When you do, you can select the user and the computer and see their interaction.

FIGURE 2.22 The Group Policy Results Wizard performs what's-going-on calculations.

You need to remember the following before trying to run the Group Policy Results Wizard to figure out what's going on:

- The target computer must be Windows Vista, Windows XP, Windows Server 2003, or later. Again, Windows 2000 machines are left out of the fun here.

- The target computer must be actually turned on and on the network. If this is not the case, you'll get an error regarding this fact. It will state that it cannot contact the WMI service via RPC.

- If the target machine is Windows Vista, Windows XP/Service Pack 2, or Windows 2003/Service Pack 1, the Windows Firewall must be disabled. Alternatively (in advance), you can open up ports 135 and 445 on the target machine. See the sidebar entitled "Understanding Windows XP/SP2 and Windows Vista's Firewall Settings (and Dealing with Group Policy Results)" for some ideas on how to mitigate this. If the machine is unreachable because the firewall is blocking access to port 135 or port 445, you'll get the same "RPC Error" as if the computer was off.

- The Windows Management Instrumentation service must be started.

Remember: the user you want to find out about must have logged on to the target computer *at least once* to be eligible to perform a Group Policy Results calculation.

Understanding Windows XP/SP2 and Windows Vista's Firewall Settings (and Dealing with Group Policy Results)

Once SP2 is loaded upon Windows XP (or you load Windows Vista), the Windows Firewall is automatically engaged. As you just learned, getting Group Policy Results is effectively disabled when the Windows Firewall is engaged. It's like the target computer is turned off.

There was always a firewall built in to Windows XP, but with Windows XP/Service Pack 2 and Windows Vista, the firewall is turned on by default. To boot, it's now much more controllable via Group Policy. The policy settings used to control the Windows Firewall can be found in two locations: Administrative Templates ➤ Network ➤ Network Connections ➤ Windows Firewall ➤ Domain Profile, and Administrative Templates ➤ Network ➤ Network Connections ➤ Windows Firewall ➤ Standard Profile.

You can see that the exact same policy settings are listed for both the Standard Profile and Domain Profile nodes. The Domain Profile settings are what will take effect when users are inside your corporate network; that is, when they're actively logged in by a Domain Controller. The Standard Profile, on the other hand, is used for when users are out of the office (perhaps in a hotel or other public network where they cannot reach your company's Domain Controllers for authentication).

Once a Windows Vista or Windows XP/Service Pack 2 computer receives the policy settings for both the Domain Profile and Standard Profile, that computer is ready to travel both in and out of the office. You can be sure that machine is embracing your company's firewall security policy both in the office and on the road.

If you're interested in learning more about how a computer makes a determination if it is supposed to use "Domain Profile" or "Standard Profile" policy settings, be sure to read Microsoft's document entitled "Determination Behavior for Network-Related Group Policy Settings" at www.microsoft.com/technet/community/columns/cableguy/cg0504.mspx (shortened to http://tinyurl.com/cao73).

You have three options if you want to restore the Group Policy Results functionality when you have Windows XP/SP2 or Windows Vista clients. Note that if you cannot locate the following policy settings to control the Windows XP/SP2 and Windows Vista firewalls, be sure to read Chapter 5, which explains ADM and ADMX Template management.

Approach 1: Kill the Windows XP/SP2 and Windows Vista Firewall   Now that you understand how to control Windows XP's and Windows Vista's Firewall Settings, one approach is to kill the firewall completely. If you do this, you understand that you're giving up any of the protection that Windows Firewall affords. However, by doing so, you will restore communication to the target Windows XP/SP2 or Windows Vista computer. To kill the Vista or XP/SP2 firewall, drill down to Administrative Templates ➤ Network ➤ Network Connections ➤ Windows Firewall ➤ Domain Profile and select **Windows Firewall: Protect all network Connections.** But here's the thing. You don't Enable this policy to kill the firewall. You Disable it. Yes, you read that right, you Disable it. Read the Explaintext help inside the policy for more information on specific usage examples.

Approach 2: Poke Just the Required Holes in Firewall   Instead of killing the firewall dead, you can simply open up the one port you need. Again, the idea is that if the target computer responds on port 135, you're golden. Windows Vista has a policy setting you can enable named **Windows Firewall: Allow Inbound Remote Administration Exception** (**Windows Firewall:Allow Remote Administration Exception** on Windows XP/Service Pack 2), which is located in Computer Configuration ➤ Administrative Templates ➤ Network ➤ Network Connections ➤ Windows Firewall ➤ Domain Profile. Again, when you do this, you're opening up the necessary port 135 (RPC). Note, however, that enabling this policy setting also opens up port 445 (SMB), which might be more than you need.

Approach 3: Keep the Firewall Engaged, and Don't Use Group Policy Results   You might opt for this third approach. That is, you really, really want to keep the firewall enabled and all ports closed on that target Windows XP or Windows Vista machine. If so, how will you find out "what's going on" on a target machine? There are two ways, both explored a bit later. One way is to trot out to the machine (or take remote control of it somehow) and run the GPRESULT command, which will tell you what's going on. Or, you can use a tool called GPMonitor (which we explore in the Appendix). The idea is to have the target machines periodically push their Group Policy Results data to a location of your choosing. So, even if they're behind a firewall, you're still periodically able to see what's going on.

The output generated from the GPMC version when performing Group Policy Results RSoP calculations is quite powerful, as shown in Figure 2.23.

Similar to the Settings tab, you can expand and contract the report by clicking Show and Hide. Inside, you can clearly see which GPOs have been applied and any major errors along the way. At a glance, you can see which GPOs have Applied and which were Denied (passed over) for whatever reason, such as filtering or that one-half of the GPO was empty.

FIGURE 2.23 The Group Policy Results report shows lots of useful information.

The WMI filters category (shown in Figure 2.23) will not display data unless the target machine is running Windows 2003, Windows XP with SP2, or Windows Vista.

If you click the Settings tab here, you get an extra bonus. That is, if there are conflicts along the scope of the GPO, you can see which other GPOs "won" in the contest for the ultimate Group Policy smackdown! Indeed, you can see this in Figure 2.24. Note, however, that the GPMC doesn't show you which GPOs "lost" when there was a conflict. This can sometimes mean more troubleshooting to determine other GPOs with conflicting settings. In Chapter 4, you'll learn how to locate "losing" GPOs.

FIGURE 2.24 If specific settings conflict, you can quickly determine which GPO "wins."

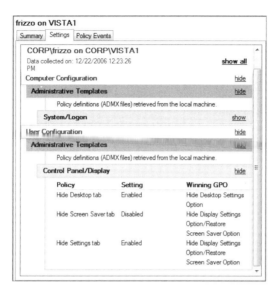

FIGURE 2.25 The Policy Events tab shows you events specific to this target computer.

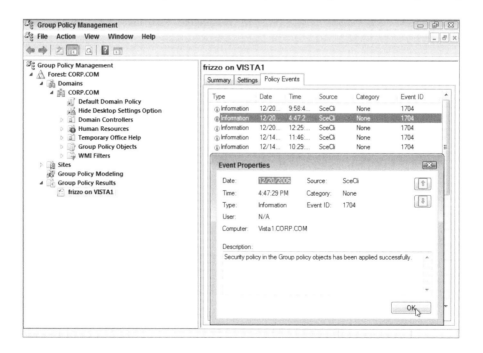

There are one or two caveats about Group Policy Results data. Specifically, when you produce a Group Policy Results report, some data simply isn't reported! Specifically, here's what you won't see in a report:

- IPsec
- Wireless
- Disk quotas
- Third-party policy add-ins

Note, however, that after the report runs, you can right-click the entry for the report (located right under the Group Policy Results node, as seen in Figure 2.25) and select "Advanced View." When you do this, you'll see an alternate view of the report, which isn't HTML, but does show all the attributes—even the stuff listed above which isn't normally reported. Since the report isn't HTML, however, it's not really "portable" and you can't print it or send it in an e-mail.

Additionally useful here is the Policy Events tab, which will dive into the target machine's Event Viewer and pull out the events related to GPOs, as shown in Figure 2.25. Just double-click the event to open it. Talk about handy!

The GPMC will also save the query so you can reuse it later if you want to retest your assumptions. For example, you might want to retry this after you've corrected your software installation failure, added a new GPO to the mix, or moved a machine from one OU to another.

If you move a computer from one OU to another, you might not get the correct results right away, because the computer may not immediately recognize that it has been moved. If you move a computer from one OU to another, you might want to synchronize your Domain Controllers and then reboot the target machine to get accurate results right away. This is discussed in more detail in Chapter 3.

What-If Calculations with Group Policy Modeling

Finding out what's going on is useful if someone calls you in a panic. However, you might also want to plan for the future. For instance, would you be able to easily determine what would happen to the users inside the **Human Resources Users** OU if a somewhat indiscriminately named GPO called "Desktop Settings" was linked to it? Maybe or maybe not. (With a horribly named GPO like that, likely not.)

Or, what might happen if Frank Rizzo took a trip to another site? Which GPOs would apply to him then? Or which GPOs would apply if the HR-OU-Admins were granted (or revoked) different security rights? The Oracle, er, the Group Policy Modeling Wizard found in the GPMC can answer a million of these questions. Its job is to answer "What happens if?"

This function is available only if the domain schema has been updated for Windows 2003 and you have at least one Windows 2003 Domain Controller available. This is because a Windows 2003 Domain Controller runs a service that must be running for the calculation to occur.

The best news about what-if calculations is that Windows 2000 computers aren't left out of the picture. But the bad news is that the calculations shown for Windows 2000 machines are likely inaccurate. Modeling will happily tell you that your Windows 2000 machines will apply things only available for Windows XP and Windows Vista, such as Wireless policy (when it's not possible for Windows 2000 machine to get these at all).

The only catch to this magic is that when you want to run what-if modeling calculations, the processing of the calculations must actually occur on a Windows 2003 Domain Controller. Even if you have the GPMC loaded on a Windows Vista or Windows XP management station, you'll still have to make contact with a Windows 2003 Domain Controller to assist in the calculations.

> This is the biggest warning icon the publisher gives me, but it isn't big enough for this message. If your Windows 2003 domain has been upgraded from Windows 2000, and you want to perform Group Policy Modeling between domains, it is likely it will not work without some manual attention. There are ACL permission problems on GPOs upon performing a domain upgrade. To fix the problem in a flash you run the GrantPermissionOnAllGPOs.wsf script that is included with the GPMC. Specifically, you run cscript GrantPermissionOnAllGPOs.wsf /FullEdit "Enterprise Domain Controllers". This will "touch" all GPOs in SYSVOL, which will force replication to all Domain Controllers and, hence, may cause a lot of network traffic. This could be an issue with environments with many GPOs.

You can kick off a modeling session by right-clicking the domain or any OU (as well as the Group Policy Modeling node) and selecting "Group Policy Modeling Wizard." When you do, you'll be presented with the Group Policy Modeling Wizard Welcome screen.

You then choose which Windows 2003 Domain Controller will have the honor of performing the calculation for you. It doesn't matter which Windows 2003 Domain Controller you choose—even those in other domains. Just pick one. Just note that it does need to be a Windows 2003 Domain Controller and not anything less.

You'll then get to play Zeus and determine what would happen if you plucked a user and/or computer out of a current situation and modified the circumstances. In the wizard screens, you get to choose the following:

- Which user and/or computer (or container) you want to start to play with

- Whether to pretend to apply slow-link processing (if not already present on the target)

- Whether to pretend to apply loopback processing (if not already present on the target)

- The site in which you want to pretend the object is starting

- Where to move the user (if the user account moves at all)

- Where to move the computer (if it moves at all)

- Whether to pretend to change the user's Security group membership

- Whether to pretend to change the computer's Security group membership

- Whether to pretend to apply WMI filters for users or computers (if not already present on the target)

You will likely get inaccurate results if you try to do something that isn't really possible. For instance, you can force the wizard into seeing what happens if Frank Rizzo's account is moved to another domain. But, since there isn't a way to actually move Frank's account, the displayed results will be cockeyed. You'll learn more about some of the new concepts, such as slow-link processing and loopback processing in Chapter 3. You'll learn more about WMI filters in Chapter 11.

The output in Figure 2.26 shows what would happen if Frank Rizzo were removed from the **Human Resources Users** OU (and plopped into the root of the domain).

FIGURE 2.26 Here, the Group Policy Modeling summary screen shows you what you're about to simulate. For instance, you can simulate moving a computer and/or a user to other locations, among other scenarios.

What to Expect from the Group Policy Modeling Wizard

When you first use the Group Policy Modeling Wizard, you may be surprised to see that it has "Loopback," "WMI Filters," and "Slow Links" options. At first, I was curious about why these were options in the wizard—if the wizard's whole job is to figure out what will be at the end of the simulation.

In a nutshell, the Group Policy Modeling Wizard allows you to simulate these additional items as if they all were *actually* going to be true. This way, you don't have to create an OU and/or a GPO with the specific policy settings (Loopback, and so on) *just* to turn it on. This makes sense: if you enable these options on the real OU, you change the live environment.

The point of the Group Policy Modeling Wizard is to let you just simulate *what if* you did this on the target. When using the wizard and selecting "Loopback," "Slow Links," or "WMI Filters," don't expect it to tell you that any of these things *are* true in the target. The simulation demonstrates what would happen *if* these properties came into the mix.

Note that the Group Policy Modeling Wizard is unable to take into account any Local Group Policy Object settings on the potential target workstation. That's because this wizard never actually queries a target computer. The calculations all happen on a Windows 2003 Domain Controller and are then outputted in the GPMC.

When the calculations are complete, you'll get a results dialog that looks quite similar to Figures 2.23 and 2.24. There, you can see how results will be displayed in both the Summary and Settings tabs. As a reminder, the Summary tab shows you which GPOs applied; the Settings tab shows you which policies inside the GPOs will "win" if there's a conflict. Present only in Group Policy Modeling output (not shown) is another item, called the Query tab, which can remind you of the choices you made when generating the query.

Backing Up and Restoring Group Policy Objects

Inadvertently deleting a single GPO can wreak havoc on your domain. Imagine what happens when a bunch of GPOs are inadvertently deleted. Let's just say that the users are suddenly happy because they can do stuff they couldn't, and you're not happy because now they're happy. Ironic, isn't it?

An administrator inadvertently deleting a portion of a SYSVOL container of one Domain Controller will quickly damage your GPOs, and you'll need a way to restore.

> The Backup and Restore functions for GPOs are only meant to work within the same domain. However, you'll see in the Appendix how the GPMC can be used to back up and import a GPO to get the same effect *between* domains.

In our cases, if the policy settings inside the "Auto-Launch Calc.exe" GPO were wiped out, the name of the GPO can surely help us put it back together. But the name alone might not be an accurate representation of what's really going on inside the GPO.

Then, there are still other questions: Where was this GPO linked? What was the security on the GPO? Who owned it?

All said and done, you don't want to get stuck with a deleted or damaged GPO without a backup. Thankfully, the GPMC makes easy work of the once-laborious task of backing up and restoring GPOs.

> These techniques are valid for both Windows 2000 and Windows 2003 domains, as I stated in the Introduction. So, back up those GPOs today with the GPMC regardless of your domain structure!

Backing Up Group Policy Objects

When you back up a GPO within the GPMC, you also back up a lot of important data:

- The settings inside the GPO.
- The permissions upon that GPO (that is, the stuff inside the Delegation tab).

- The link to the WMI filter—however, the actual filter itself is not preserved. (Again, I'll talk about WMI filters in Chapter 11.)

However, it's also important to know what won't be backed up:

- Any WMI filters are contained within Active Directory. You must back them up separately. You can see one way to do this in the "Backing Up and Restoring WMI Filters" section later in this chapter.

- IPsec settings aren't backed up via the GPMC Backup and Restore function. They are backed up during a Domain Controller's System State backup. But discussing backing up and restoring them is a bit beyond the scope of this book. My best suggestion: Manually document any GPOs with IPsec settings.

- GPO links aren't specifically backed up. Yes, you read that right. But before you panic, let me first explain how this is for your own protection. We'll examine this phenomenon in a little bit and try to make you a believer in why this is a good thing.

As you'll learn in Chapter 4, there are two parts of GPOs: the GPT (Group Policy Template) from Active Directory and the GPC (Group Policy Container) from within the SYSVOL. When a backup is performed, the GPT and GPC are wrapped up and placed as a set of files that can be stored or transported.

What's additionally neat is that contained within the backup is a report of the settings inside that GPO you just backed up. So, if someone backs up a GPO named "Desktop Settings" (again, a horrible name), you can at least see the report of just what is inside the GPO before you restore it to your domain.

To back up a GPO, you need "Read" access to that GPO, as shown earlier in an example back at Figure 2.16. You can start by locating the GPO node in the GPMC and right-clicking it. Select either "Back up All" or "Manage Backups." For this first time, select "Back up All."

You then select the location for the backup (hopefully some place secure) and click Backup. You'll then see each GPO being backed up to the target location as shown in Figure 2.27. When you're finished, you can rest easy (or at least easier) that your GPOs are safe.

You can inspect the directories the backup produced if you like. You'll see a directory for each GPO, the XML file representing the GPT, and an XML report showing the settings. In the next section, you'll learn how to view the report (easily) by utilizing the "View settings" button (as shown a bit later in Figure 2.28).

In Chapter 4, we'll learn more about the underlying "nuts and bolts" of GPOs. Specifically, you'll learn that the underlying name of a GPO relies on a unique GUID name being assigned to the GPO. What isn't immediately obvious here is that the directory names produced by the backup (which take the form of GUIDs) are *not* the same GUIDs that are actually used for the underlying identification of the GPO. These are additional, unique, random GUID directory names generated just for backup. This seemingly bizarre contradiction becomes useful, when you read the next paragraph.

The backup is quick, painless, and rather reasonably sized. The best part about the backup facility is that it's flexible. When you choose to run your next backup, you can keep your backups in the same directory you just chose, and you'll keep a history of the GPOs, should anything change. It's the underlying random and unique GUID names for the directories that allow you to keep plowing more GPO backups right into the same backup directory—there's no fear of overlap. Or you can keep the backups in their own directory; it's your choice.

FIGURE 2.27   You can back up all your GPOs at once, if desired.

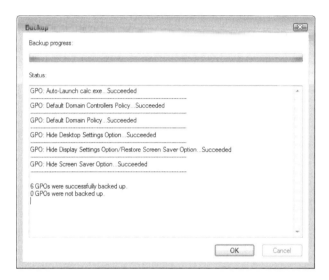

If you dare, go ahead and delete the "Hide Display Settings Option/Restore Screen Saver Option." GPO. You'll restore it in the next section (I hope).

Now that you've backed up the whole caboodle, it should also be noted that you can back up just a solitary GPO. Right-click the *actual* GPO (which is located only in the Group Policy Objects container) and choose Backup. In Chapter 7, you'll find a script that enables you to script and automate your backups.

Be sure the place in which you back up your GPOs is secure. You don't want the knowledge stored within the GPOs to possibly be used as an attack against you.

Restoring Group Policy Objects

The restore process is just as easy. It works for GPOs that were backed up in the same domain. Note that it's also possible to back up and restore between domains, but this is called a GPO Migration (see the Appendix).

When you restore a GPO, the file object you created in the backup process is "unrolled" and placed upon Active Directory. As you would expect, the following key elements are preserved:

- The settings inside the GPO
- The friendly name (which comes back from the dead)

- The GUID (which comes back from the dead)
- The security and permissions on that object (which come back from the dead)
- The link to WMI filters (which comes back from the dead)

 Whomping a GPO doesn't delete any WMI filters associated with a GPO itself. Any WMI filters are stored in a separate place in Active Directory. It's sort of like the Jacuzzi next to the swimming pool.

The GPO does not have to be deleted to do a restore. For instance, if someone changed the settings and you want to simply restore the GPO to get an older version of the policy settings, you can certainly restore over an existing GPO to put a previously known "good" version back in play.

Restoring GPOs requires the following security rights:

- If you want to restore on top of a GPO that already exists, you need Edit, Delete, and Modify rights, as seen back in Figure 2.16.
- If you want to restore a deleted GPO, you need to be a member of the Group Policy Creator Owners (or Domain Admins or Enterprise Admins) Security group.

Warning: A Deleted GPO's Links Are Not Restored!

Assuming you went ahead in the last example and deleted the "Hide Display Settings Option/ Restore Screen Saver Option" GPO and are now ready to restore it, there is something you need to know before proceeding. That is, one critical item is missing: the Group Policy links to the GPO are *not* restored in this operation. The location of links is backed up, but upon a restore, the links are *not* restored. You might be scratching your head wondering why this is.

Let's examine a theoretical timeline.

- On Day 0, a GPO named "Desktop Settings" is linked to two OUs named **Doctors** and **Nurses**.

- On Day 1, the GPO is backed up.

- On Day 2, a fellow administrator unlinks the GPO from **Doctors**. Now, the GPO is linked only to **Nurses**.

- On Day 3, someone deletes the whole GPO (and hence its links).

- On Day 4, someone recognizes this deleting and restores the GPO.

Here's the $50,000 question: Upon restore, where should the links be restored to?

Should the links be restored back to the last way it was *just before* the catastrophe on Day 3? Sure, that would be ideal, but how would the system know what happened between Day 2 and Day 4? As it is, on Day 4, the GPO is now linked *only* to **Nurses**, but how could the system know that now?

Should it link the GPO back to the *original* locations, as it was on Day 1? On Day 1, it was linked to **Doctors** and **Nurses**? But restoring those links back to the same location could be a catastrophic mistake. Clearly, on Day 2 an administrator unlinked it from **Doctors** for some good reason! Restoring the link back upon the **Doctors** could be detrimental to their health!

Instead, of restoring the links, the GPMC does the smartest thing it can do during a restore: it doesn't restore the links. That's right — by not restoring the links, it is ensured that you're not inadvertently relinking the GPO back upon some location in Active Directory that shouldn't have it anymore.

However, as stated, the backup process does record where the links were at the time of backup. To that end, you can easily see where the links were at the time of backup and, if desired, you can manually relink the GPO back to the locations you want. To see where a GPO had links upon backup time, here's what to do:

- Right-click over the Group Policy Objects node and select "Manage Backups."

- In the "Manage Backups" dialog, ensure you're looking at the directory with the contents of the backup.

- Locate then select the GPO which was deleted.

- Then click on the "View Settings" button (as seen in Figure 2.28).

A report will be generated that, among other things, shows you where the GPO was linked. Then, once the GPO is restored, you can manually relink the GPO where you need it to be linked.

You can start a restore by right-clicking the Group Policy Objects container and choosing "Manage Backups." You'll be able to select a location from which to locate your GPO backups; you might have multiple locations.

If you've chosen to keep backing up the GPOs into the same backup directory, you can select the "Show only the latest version of each GPO" option, which shows you only the last backed-up version. If you've forgotten what is contained in a backup, simply click the backup name and choose "View Settings." You can see these options in Figure 2.28.

When you're ready, click the GPO to restore, and then click Restore. It's really that easy.

You can also right-click the GPO itself (found only in the Group Policy Objects container) and choose "Restore from Backup," which in fact performs the same function. (See Chapter 7 for a script that will enable you to script and automate your restores.)

FIGURE 2.28   You can see all backups or just the latest versions.

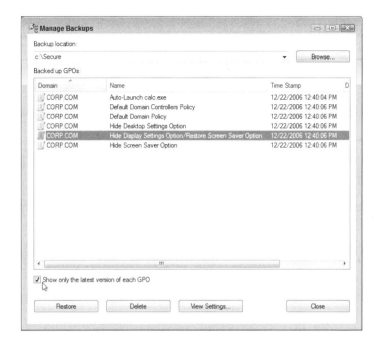

Backing Up and Restoring WMI Filters

As you read about WMI filters in Chapter 11 and learn what a pain in the tush they are to create, you'll be thankful that there's a mechanism that can back up and restore them. They are not backed up or restored in the process we just used. Rather, you must individually back up each WMI filter. Simply right-click the filter, and choose Export. To restore, right-click WMI Filters node and choose Import. Sometimes restoring a WMI filter adds excess and invalid characters to the query. Simply re-edit the query and clean up the characters, and you're back in business.

In the previous section, you saw that GPO links are not restored when the GPO is restored. The same is true for WMI filters: the WMI filter links are not restored when the WMI filter is restored. Again, for information on how to automatically document this information, see Chapter 7.

Searching for Group Policy Objects with the GPMC

As your Active Directory grows, so will your use of GPOs. However, sometimes remembering the one GPO that you used to do some magic a while ago can be difficult. To that end, the GPMC has some basic searching functionality.

With the search feature, you can search for GPOs with any (and all) of the following characteristics:

- Display name (that is, friendly name)

- GUID

- Permissions on the GPO itself

- A link, if it exists (used in conjunction with the name, and so on)

- WMI filters used

- Specific client-side-extensions if they were used for either the user or computer side

To search for a GPO that matches the characteristics you're after, right-click the domain and choose Search. In the Search Item dialog box, enter your criteria in the condition fields. The Value field will change based on the Search Item field. In Figure 2.29, I'm searching corp.com for all GPOs with the word *Hide* in the name.

 The one thing this search engine cannot do is to poke through each and every GPO to see where you enabled some policy setting.

FIGURE 2.29   You can locate GPOs with lots of characteristics.

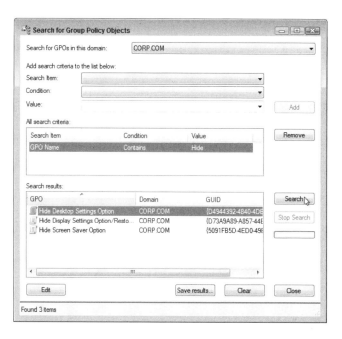

GPMC At-a-Glance Icon View

Because the GPMC contains so many icon types, it can be confusing to know specifically what an icon represents. That's what Table 2.2 is all about.

TABLE 2.2   GPMC Icon List

Icon	Description	What the Icon Means
	Scroll.	A GPO itself. You'll only see this in the Group Policy Objects container.
	Scroll with arrow.	A link to an actual GPO.
	Scroll with arrow. Just the arrow is dimmed.	GPO link that has Link Status disabled.
	Scroll with arrow. The whole icon is dimmed.	A link to a GPO whose status (on the Details tab) has been set to "All settings disabled."
	Scroll. Whole icon is dimmed.	The GPO whose status (on the Details tab) has been set to "All settings disabled."
	Scroll with arrow; additional lock icon.	"Enforced" link to this level.
	Blue exclamation point.	Block inheritance at this level.
	Folder with scroll.	Group Policy Objects container that actually holds the GPOs themselves.
	Folder with filter.	WMI Filters node.
	Filter.	A WMI filter.

The GPMC At-a-Glance Compatibility Table

You learned a lot in this chapter. Sometimes it can be confusing to know just when a feature is compatible with your setup in the office or the test lab. Hopefully, Table 2.3 will clear things up.

TABLE 2.3   Group Policy Functionality Compatibility Table

Function	Requirement	Where Discussed
Create and link GPOs and apply them to client systems	Any Active Directory domain with Group Policy-capable clients (Windows 2000, Windows XP, Windows Server 2003 or Windows Vista)	Chapter 1
Load the GPMC console	Pre-Loaded on Windows Vista. You need any Active Directory domain.	Chapters 1 and 2
Back up and restore GPOs	Any Active Directory domain plus GPMC console.	Chapter 2
Transfer (migrate) GPOs between same forest	Any Active Directory domain plus GPMC console.	Appendix
Run Group Policy Results reports	Any Active Directory domain plus GPMC console. Targets must be Windows Vista, Windows XP, or Windows 2003. Target user must have logged on to target machine at least once.	Chapter 2
Run Group Policy Modeling reports	Any Active Directory domain plus GPMC console. Must have one Windows Server 2003 Domain Controller (or Longhorn Domain Controller) available to run the calculations. Targets may be Windows 2000, but you might get inaccurate results with Windows 2000 clients.	Chapter 2
WMI filters	Windows 2003 domain or Windows 2000 with an updated Windows 2003 schema via the ADPREP /Domainprep command. Additionally, Windows Vista, Windows XP, or Windows 2003 clients required. Windows 2000 clients ignore WMI filters.	Chapter 11

TABLE 2.3   Group Policy Functionality Compatibility Table *(continued)*

Function	Requirement	Where Discussed
Delegate Group Policy Results ability	Windows 2003 forest, or Windows 2000 updated schema via ADPREP /forestprep. Use Active Directory Users And Computers or GPMC to delegate rights.	Chapter 2
Delegate Group Policy Modeling ability	Windows 2003 forest or Windows 2000 updated schema via ADPREP /forestprep. Use Active Directory Users And Computers or GPMC to delegate rights.	Chapter 2

Final Thoughts

While using the GPMC throughout this chapter, you ran queries and created several reports. What you possibly didn't know is that all that time you were creating HTML reports you can use to document your environment.

Back when you were first exploring a GPO's settings (see the graphic in the "Common Procedures with the GPMC" section earlier in the chapter) and when you were creating RSoP reports (that is, Figures 2.23 and 2.24 and what would result after Figure 2.26), you were really generating HTML reports. Any time you create those reports, you can right-click anywhere in the report and choose "Save Report." Since these are standard HTML, you have an incredibly easy way to document just about every aspect of your Group Policy universe.

Backing up and restoring with the GPMC is simply awesome. But as you'll recall, when you restore a deleted GPO, you don't restore the links. You'll have to bring them back manually. Having good backups and good documentation about where each GPO is linked will always be your ace in the hole.

I stopped short in this chapter of demonstrating two of the GPMC's major additional functions. That is, the GPMC provides a scriptable interface for many of our day to day GPO functions—including backups, creation, and management. You'll see that in Chapter 7. Additionally, you can use the GPMC to migrate GPOs from one domain to another. I'll tackle that in the Appendix.

The GPMC is now built in to Windows Vista. So, if in the past you were avoiding it, it's time to stop avoiding it and embrace it.

Here are some parting tips for daily Group Policy Object management with the GPMC:

Check out these Microsoft documentation links.   Microsoft GPMC documentation is available at `http://go.microsoft.com/fwlink/?LinkId=14320`. Additionally, Microsoft has some other RSoP documentation available at `www.microsoft.com/technet/prodtechnol/windowsserver2003/proddocs/entserver/rspintro.asp` (or shortened to `http://tinyurl.com/4ngbw`).

Use "Block Inheritance" and "Enforced" sparingly.   The less you use these features, the easier it will be to debug the application of settings. Figuring out at which level in the hierarchy one administrator has "Blocked Inheritance" and another has declared "Enforced" can eat up days of fun at the office. The GPMC makes it easier to see what's going on, but still, minimize your use of these two attributes.

Remember what can only be applied at the link.   Three and only three attributes are set on a GPO link: Link Enable (Enable or Disable the settings to apply at this level), Enforce the link (and force the policy settings), and Delete the link.

Remember what can be applied only on the actual GPO itself.   The following attributes must be set on the GPO itself: the policies and settings inside the GPO (found on the Settings tab), Security filters, rights (as in the "Apply Group Policy" permission), delegation (as in the "Edit this GPO" permission), Enabling/Disabling half (or both halves) of the GPO via the GPO Status (found on the Details tab), and WMI filtering (discussed in Chapter 11).

Remember Group Policy is notoriously tough to debug.   Once you start linking GPOs at multiple levels, throwing in a "Block Inheritance," an "Enforced," and a filter or two, you're up to your eyeballs in troubleshooting. The best thing you can do is document the heck out of your GPOs. The GPMC helps you determine what a GPO does in the Settings tab, but your documentation will be your sanity check when trying to figure things out.

Use Microsoft's spreadsheet.   Microsoft has an Excel spreadsheet of all the administrative templates for Windows 2000, Windows XP, and Windows 2003 and another for Windows Vista. (You'll learn more about why this is when you read Chapter 5.) My suggestion is to leverage this file every single time you create a new GPO and keep it in a common place for all administrators to reference to see what anyone else did inside a GPO. Be religious about it, and keep these files updated within your company. To locate the spreadsheet, go to www.GPanswers.com, in the "Microsoft Resources section" where I always have a link to it that's easy to find.

3

Group Policy Processing Behavior

After you create or modify a GPO in the domain, the policy "wishes" are not immediately dropped on the target machines. In fact, they're not dropped on the target machines at all; they're requested by the client computer at various times throughout the day. GPOs are processed at specific times, based on various conditions. You could basically say that GPOs are "pulled" by the client but originate at the server.

Indeed, it's likely that you have Windows 2000, Windows XP, Windows 2003, and now Windows Vista machines in your environment. Each operating system that receives Group Policy instructions processes Group Policy at different times in different ways. With different operating systems requesting different things at different times, the expected behaviors can really get confusing quickly.

Additionally, other factors determine when and how a GPO applies. When users dial in over slow links, things can be—and usually are—different. And you can instruct the Group Policy engine (on specific or all computers) to forgo its out-of-the-box processing behaviors for a customized (and often more secure) way to process.

Also, if you are using Active Directory's Cross-Forest Trusts (available only in native Windows Server 2003 mode and presumably Windows Server Longhorn Active Directory mode), Group Policy will process differently, depending on each operating system (and service pack) you use; understanding what is going on is paramount.

Often, people throw up their hands when the Group Policy engine doesn't seem to process the GPOs they dictate in an expected manner. Group Policy doesn't just process when it wants to; rather, it adheres to a strict set of processing rules. This chapter's goal is to answer the question, *when* does Group Policy apply? Understanding the processing rules will help you better understand when Group Policy processes GPOs the way it does. Then, in the next chapter, you'll get a grip on *why* Group Policy applies. Between these two chapters, your goal is to become a better Group Policy troubleshooter.

Group Policy Processing Principles

To best understand how Windows XP or Windows Vista processes its policy, I'll first describe how Windows 2000 does its thing. Then, we'll better understand how and why Windows XP and Vista's processing is different.

To better understand how GPO processing works, we're going to walk through what happens to three users:

- Wally, who only uses a Windows 2000 Professional machine
- Xavier, who only uses a Windows XP machine
- Victoria, who only uses a Windows Vista machine

By using Wally, Xavier, and Victoria as our three sample users (on our three sample computers), we can see precisely when Group Policy applies to them—when they're using Windows 2000, Windows XP machines, and Windows Vista machines.

Before we go even one step further, let me debunk a popular myth about Group Policy processing. That is, Group Policy is never *pushed* from the server and forced upon the clients. Rather, the process is quite the opposite. Group Policy occurs when the Group Policy engine on a Windows client requests Group Policy. This happens at various times, but at no time can you magically declare from on high: "All clients?! Go forth and accept my latest GPOs!" It doesn't work like that. Clients request GPOs according to the rules listed in this chapter.

 In Chapter 7, I'll show you a technique that emulates the same effect as if you were performing a push to all your clients. Additionally, on GPanswers.com, in the "Third-Party Tools section," I have a pointer to two free downloads that perform similar functions: one is a command-line tool (rGPrefresh), the other is a graphical snap-in to Active Directory Users and Computers (Specops GPUpdate).

In a nutshell, Group Policy is potentially triggered to apply at four times. Here's a rundown of those times; I'll discuss them in grueling detail in the next sections.

Initial Policy Processing   For Windows 2000 and Windows 2003 machines, processing occurs when the computer starts up or when the user logs on. By default, in "daily life" there is no initial policy processing for Windows XP machines or Windows Vista machines.

There is, however an exception, which we'll note later when a user has never logged in before a computer first joins the domain.

Background Refresh Policy Processing (Member Computers)   For Windows 2000, Windows 2003, Windows XP, and Windows Vista member machines, processing occurs some time after the user logs on (usually at 90-minute intervals or so). A bit later, you'll see how Windows XP and Windows Vista leverage the background policy processing mechanism to a distinct advantage.

Background Refresh Policy Processing (Domain Controllers)   Windows 2000 and Windows 2003 Domain Controllers need love too, and to that end, they perform a background refresh every five minutes (after replication has occurred).

Security Policy Processing   For all operating systems, only the security settings within all GPOs are reprocessed and applied every 16 hours regardless of whether they have changed. This safety mechanism prevents unscrupulous local workstation administrators from doing too much harm.

You can change the default behavior of certain nonsecurity policy settings so that they are enforced in a manner similar to the way that security settings are automatically enforced. But you have to explicitly turn this feature on, and you have to do so correctly. In the "Security Policy Processing" section later in this chapter, I describe how to do this and give you several examples of why you would want to do so.

Special Case: Moving a User or Computer Object   Although all the previous items demonstrate a trigger of when Group Policy applies, one case isn't trigger-specific; however, it's important to understand a special case of Group Policy processing behavior. You might think that if you move a user or computer around in Active Directory (specifically, from one OU to another), then Group Policy is set to reapply—the system would "know" it's been moved around in Active Directory. But that doesn't happen. When you move a user or a computer from one OU to another, background processing may not immediately understand that something was moved. Some time later, the system should detect the change, and background processing should start normally again.

Don't Get Lost   There are definitely nuances in the processing mechanism among the various operating systems. The good news, if your head starts to swim a bit, is that you can dog-ear this page and highlight this little area for quick reference. If you remember one "takeaway" coming out of this chapter, there is one big message: there are three behavior types for target computers:

- Behavior type 1: Windows 2000 Workstations, Windows 2000 member servers, Windows Server 2003 member servers (and presumably Windows Server Longhorn)

- Behavior type 2: Domain Controllers of all sorts: Windows 2000 and Windows Server 2003 (and presumably Windows Server Longhorn)

- Behavior type 3: Windows XP and Windows Vista

So, the point is that there are three behavior types. And it's important to understand the difference between them. And, once you understand the difference between them you can decide if you want to take the machines which are in Behavior type 3 (Windows XP and Windows Vista) and make them act like machines which are in Behavior type 1 (Windows 2000 and Windows Server 2003.)

By now, you might have expunged Windows 2000 systems from your domain. However, I would strongly encourage you to read how all systems are processed.

This is for three reasons:

1. The behaviors described below are all "based" upon the original Windows 2000 behavior.

2. It's easier to understand the Windows XP and Windows Vista behavior if you understand the original Windows 2000 behavior, and

3. Later in the chapter I'm going to encourage you to "Make your Windows XP and Windows Vista machines act like Windows 2000." So, if you don't understand the Windows 2000 behavior, you won't know what I'm talking about.

Initial Policy Processing

Recall that each GPO has two halves: a computer half and a user half. This is important to remember when trying to understand when GPOs are processed. Windows 2000 and Windows 2003 perform what is called *initial policy processing*. Windows XP and Windows Vista are also capable of initial policy processing, but it doesn't work quite the same as its Windows 2000 counterpart.

Windows 2000 (and Windows Server 2003) Initial Policy Processing

Wally walks into his office and turns on his Windows 2000 Professional machine. The computer half of the policy is always processed at the target machine upon startup as his machine reboots. When a Windows 2000 or Windows 2003 machine starts up, it states that it is "Processing security policy." What this really should say is "Processing Group Policy" (but it doesn't).

At that time, the workstation logs on to the network by contacting a Domain Controller. The Domain Controller (based upon DNS information) then tells the workstation which site it belongs to, which domain it belongs to, and which OU it is in. The system then downloads and processes the computer half of Group Policy in that order. When the processing is finished, the "Press Ctrl+Alt+Delete to begin" prompt is revealed, and Wally can log on by pressing Ctrl+Alt+Delete and giving his username and password.

After Wally is validated to Active Directory, the user half of the GPO is downloaded and then processed in the same precise order: site, domain, and then each nested OU.

Wally's Windows 2000 Desktop is manipulated by the policy settings inside any GPOs targeting Wally's user or computer account. Wally's Desktop is displayed only when all the user-side GPOs are processed.

If you look at how all this goes, you'll see it's a lock-step mechanism: the computer starts up and then processes GPOs in the natural order: site, domain, and each nested OU. The user then logs on, and Group Policy is processed, again in the natural order: site, domain, and each nested OU. This style of GPO processing is called *synchronous processing*. That is, in order to proceed to the next step in either the startup or logon processes, the previous step must be completed. For example, the GPOs at the OU level of the user are never downloaded before the GPOs at the site level. Likewise, the GPOs at the domain level for the Windows 2000 (and Windows Server 2003) are never downloaded before the site GPOs that affect a computer.

Therefore, the default for Windows 2000 (and Windows Server 2003) for both the computer startup and user logon is that each GPO is processed synchronously. This same process occurs every time a user booting a Windows 2000 (or Windows Server 2003) machine turns on the machine and then logs on.

Windows XP and Windows Vista Initial Policy Processing

Xavier walks into his office and turns on his Windows XP machine. For a moment, let's assume this is the *first time* that this Windows XP machine has started up since joining the domain. Perhaps it just landed on Xavier's desk after a new desktop rollout of Windows XP. If this is the case, the

Windows XP machine will act just like Windows 2000 (and Windows 2003). It will look to see which site, domain, and OUs the computer account is in and then applies GPOs synchronously.

Likewise, let's assume this is the first time Xavier is logging in to this Windows XP machine with his user account which lives in Active Directory. Again, imagine that this machine just arrived after a desktop rollout. In this case, again, Windows XP will act like Windows 2000 (and Windows 2003) and synchronously process GPOs based on the site, domain, and OU Xavier is logging on from.

So far, so good. However, Windows XP performs this initial synchronous processing only in this special case described here. That is, either the computer has never started in the domain before, or the user has never logged on to this particular Windows XP machine before. To understand Windows XP's normal default processing mode, take a deep breath and read on.

Victoria's experience on Windows Vista will be the same as Xavier's. That is, if Victoria walks into her office and turns on her Windows Vista machine for the first time and logs into the machine for the first time, it will act like Windows 2000 and process GPOs synchronously for both the computer (during startup) and for the user (during login).

Background Refresh Policy Processing

Once Wally is logged on to Windows 2000 (or Windows 2003) and Xavier is logged on to Windows XP, and Victoria is plugging along on Windows Vista, things are great—for everyone. As the administrator, we're happy because Wally, Xavier, and Victoria are all receiving our wishes. They're happy because, well, they're just happy, that's all.

But, now, we decide to add a new GPO or to modify a policy setting inside an existing GPO. What if something is modified in the Group Policy Object Editor that should affect a user or a computer? Aren't Wally, Xavier, and Victoria already logged on—happy as clams? Well, a new setting is destined for an already-logged-in user or computer, and the new changes (and only the new changes) are indeed reflected on the user or computer that should receive them. But this delivery doesn't happen immediately; rather the changes are delivered according to the *background refresh interval* (sometimes known as the *background processing interval*).

The background refresh interval dictates how often changed GPOs in Active Directory are pulled by the client computer. As I implied earlier, there are different background intervals for the different operating systems' roles (that is, member vs. Domain Controller).

When the background refresh interval comes to pass, GPOs are processed *asynchronously*. That is, if a GPO that affects a user's OU (or other Active Directory level) is changed, the changes are pulled to the local computer when the clock strikes the processing time. It doesn't matter if the change happens at any level in Active Directory: OU, domain, or site. When changes are available to users or computers after the user or computer is already logged on, the changes are processed asynchronously. Whichever GPOs at any level have changed, those changes are reflected on the client.

Standard *application rules* still apply, and the precedence order is still reflected: site, domain, OU. In other words, even though a new GPO linked to a site is ready, it isn't necessarily going to trump a GPO linked to the OU.

When does this happen? According to the background refresh interval for the operating system (discussed next).

Background Refresh Intervals for Windows 2000/2003 Members

It stands to reason that when we change an existing GPO (or create a new GPO) we want our users and computers to get the latest and greatest set of instructions and wishes. With that in mind, let's continue with our example. Remember that Wally is on his Windows 2000 machine and Xavier is on his Windows XP machine.

By default, the background refresh interval for Windows 2000 workstations and Windows 2000 and Windows 2003 member servers is 90 minutes, with a 0–30 minute positive random differential added to the mix to ensure that no gaggle of PCs will refresh at any one time and clog your network asking for mass GPO downloads from Domain Controllers. Therefore, once a change has been made to a GPO, it could take as little as 90 minutes or as long as 120 minutes for each user or workstation that is already logged on to the network to see that change.

Microsoft documentation isn't consistent in this description. Often, Microsoft documentation will say the offset is 30 minutes (which could be interpreted as positive or negative 30 minutes). Indeed, in the first edition of this book, I incorrectly reported that "fact." However, since then, I have verified with Microsoft that the refresh interval is (and has always been) 90 minutes plus (not minus) 0–30 minutes.

Again, this is known as the background refresh interval. Additionally, the background refresh interval for the computer half of Group Policy and the user half of Group Policy are on their own independent schedules. That is, the computer or user half might be refreshed before the other half; they're not necessarily refreshed at the exact moment because they're on their own individual timetables. This makes sense: the computer and user didn't each get Group Policy at the precise moment in time in the first place, did they?

You can change the background refresh interval for the computer half and/or the user half using Group Policy, as described later in this chapter in the section cleverly entitled "Using Group Policy to Affect Group Policy."

You can set individual policy settings to prevent specific areas of Group Policy from being refreshed in the background, such as Internet Explorer Maintenance and Administrative Templates. See the "Using Group Policy to Affect Group Policy" section later in the chapter.

How Does the Group Policy Engine Know What's New or Changed?

The Group Policy engine on Windows 2000 and Windows XP can keep track of what's new or changed via a control mechanism called *version numbers*. Each GPO has a version number for each half of the GPO, and this is stored in Active Directory. If the version number in Active Directory doesn't change, nothing is downloaded. Since nothing has changed, the Group Policy engine thinks it has all the latest-greatest stuff—so why bother to redownload it (which takes time) and reprocess it (which takes more time)?

By default, when a background refresh interval arrives, a time-saving mechanism, "checking the GPO version numbers," is employed to minimize the time needed to get the latest-greatest GPOs. You'll learn more about GPO version numbers in Chapter 4.

To reiterate, when the background refresh interval arrives, only the new or changed GPOs are downloaded and processed.

Background Refresh Intervals for Windows 2000/2003 Domain Controllers

Even though neither Wally nor Xavier are logging on to Domain Controllers, other people might. And because Domain Controllers are a bit special, the processing for Domain Controllers is handled in a special way.

Because Group Policy contains sensitive security settings (for example, Password and Account Policy, Kerberos Policy, Audit Policy), any policy geared for a Domain Controller is refreshed within five minutes. This adds a tighter level of security to Domain Controllers. For more information on precisely how the default GPOs work, see Chapter 6.

You can change the background interval for Domain Controllers using Group Policy (as described later in the "Using Group Policy to Affect Group Policy" section). However, you really shouldn't mess with the default values here. They work pretty well.

You'll learn more about affecting Domain Controllers' security in Chapter 6.

Background Refresh Exemptions

Wally has been logged onto his Windows 2000 machine for four hours. Xavier has been logged on to his Windows XP machine and Victoria has been logged on to her Windows Vista machine for the same amount of time. Clearly, the background refresh interval has come and gone—somewhere between two and three times.

If any GPOs had been created or any existing GPOs had changed while Wally, Xavier, and Victoria were logged on, both their user accounts and their computer accounts would have embraced the newest policy settings. However, four policy categories are exceptions and are never processed in the background while users are logged on:

Folder Redirection (Explored in Detail in Chapter 10)   Folder Redirection's goal is to anchor specific directories, such as the My Documents folder, to certain network shared folders. This policy is never refreshed during a background refresh. The logic behind this is that if an administrator changes this location while the user is using it (and the system responds), the user's data could be at risk for corruption. If the administrator changes Folder Redirection via Group Policy, this change affects only the user at next logon.

Software Installation (Explored in Detail in Chapter 11)   Software Installation is also exempt from background refresh. You can use Group Policy to deploy software packages, large and small, to your users or to your computers. You can also use Group Policy to revoke already-distributed software packages. Software is neither installed nor revoked to users or computers when the background interval comes to pass. You wouldn't want users to lose applications right in the middle of use and, hence, lose or corrupt data. These functions occur only at startup for the computer or at logon for the user.

There are third-party tools that hook into Group Policy that will permit the deployment of software while the user is logged on. Check out GPanswers .com in the "Third Party Solutions Guide" section.

Logon, Logoff, Startup, and Shutdown Scripts (Explored in Detail in Chapter 6)   These scripts are run only at the appointed time (at logon, logoff, startup, or shutdown). These are not run again and again when the background processing interval comes around. Note that script updates (for example, location and path changes) are updated while the user is already logged on. It's just that, of course, they won't run again until the appointed time.

Disk Quotas (Explored in Detail in Chapter 10)   These are not run when the background processing interval comes around. They are only run (changed, really) at computer startup.

Windows XP/Windows Vista and Background Processing

As I stated in the introduction to this section, Windows XP and Windows Vista do not process new Group Policy updates in the same way that Windows 2000 and Windows Server 2003 do. Let's get a grip on how Windows XP and Windows Vista work.

Now that Xavier has logged on to his Windows XP machine for the first time and Victoria has logged on to her Windows Vista machine for the first time, their sessions will continue to process GPOs in the background as I just described: every 90 minutes or so if any new GPOs appear or any existing GPOs have changed. Xavier now goes home for the night. He logs off the domain and shuts down his machine. When he comes in the next morning, he will not process GPOs the same way that Wally will on his Windows 2000 machine.

When Xavier (or Victoria) logs on the second time (and all consecutive times) to a Windows XP or Windows Vista machine, initial policy processing will no longer be performed as described in the "Initial Policy Processing" section earlier in this chapter. From this point forward, at startup or logon, Windows XP and Windows Vista will not process GPOs synchronously like Windows 2000; rather, GPOs will be processed only in the background.

If you're scratching your head at this point as to why Windows 2000 is different than Windows XP and Windows Vista, here's the short answer. When Windows XP was in development, all the stops were pulled to make the "XPerience" as fast as possible. Both boot times and logon times were indeed faster than ever, but the tradeoff came at a price.

By default, Windows XP and Windows Vista process GPOs asynchronously—both at computer startup and at user logon. Upon startup, the computer doesn't wait for the network interface to initialize before starting to process computer GPOs. Windows XP and Windows Vista use the last-known downloaded GPOs as its baseline, even if GPOs have changed in Active Directory while the Windows XP or Windows Vista machine was turned off.

While the network card is still warming up and finding the network and the first Domain Controller, the last-used computer GPOs are already being used. Then, the "Press Ctrl+Alt+Delete to begin" prompt is presented to the user. While this prompt is presented, Windows XP downloads any new computer GPOs. These new computer GPOs are not applied until a bit later.

Assuming the user is now logged on, the Desktop and Start Menu appear. Again, the system will not synchronously download the latest site, domain, and OU Group Policy Objects and apply them before displaying the Desktop. Instead, other activity is happening while the latest-greatest Group Policy is being downloaded. So, the user might not see the latest-greatest Group Policy effects right away.

Once the computer has started, the user is logged on, and any previously known computer and user GPOs are applied, newly downloaded GPOs (and the policy settings inside) are then processed asynchronously in the background. This net result is a bit of a compromise. The user feels that there is a faster boot time (when processing GPOs with computer policy settings) as well as faster logon time (when processing GPOs with user policy settings). The most important policy settings, such as updated Security settings and Administrative Templates (Registry updates), are applied soon after logon—and no one is the wiser. Microsoft calls this Group Policy processing behavior *Fast Boot* (sometimes called "Logon Optimization"). Yes, it does speed things up a bit, but at a cost.

To keep things simple, we just walked through what would happen for Xavier on his Windows XP machine. However, the exact same behavior would occur for Victoria on her Windows Vista machine. There is no difference between Windows Vista and Windows XP in this respect.

Windows XP/Windows Vista Fast-Boot Results

Fast Boot affects two major components: Group Policy processing and user-account attribute processing. The (sometimes strange) results occur for both Xavier on his Windows XP machine and Victoria on her Windows Vista machine when they have previously logged on to it. On his Windows 2000 machine, Wally is spared the "Fast Boot" behavior.

WINDOWS XP/WINDOWS VISTA FAST BOOT GROUP POLICY PROCESSING DETAILS

The immediate downside to the Windows XP and Windows Vista Fast Boot approach is that, potentially, a user could be totally logged on but not quite have all the GPOs processed. Then, once they are working for a little while—pop! A setting takes effect out of the blue. This is because not all GPOs were processed before the user was presented with the Desktop and Start Menu. Your network would have to be pretty slow for this scenario to occur, but it's certainly possible.

The next major downside takes a bit more to wrap your head around. Some Group Policy (and Profile) features can potentially take Windows XP and Windows Vista several additional logons or reboots to actually get the changes you want on them. This strange behavior becomes understandable when we take a step back and think about how certain policy categories are processed on Windows 2000. Specifically, we need to direct our attention to Software Distribution and Folder Redirection policy. I mentioned that on Windows 2000 these two types of policy categories *must* be processed in the foreground (or synchronously) to prevent data corruption. That is, if there are Software Distribution or Folder Redirection edicts to embrace, then they can *only* happen during startup or login.

But we have a paradox: If Windows XP and Windows Vista only process GPOs asynchronously, how are the Software Distribution and Folder Redirection polices handled if they must be handled *synchronously*?

Windows XP and Windows Vista fake it and tag the machine when a Software Package is targeted for a Windows XP client. The next time the user logs on (or the computer is rebooted for computer-side policy), the Group Policy engine sees that the machine is tagged for Software Distribution and switches, just for this one time, back into synchronous mode. The net result: Windows XP and Windows Vista machines typically require two logons (or reboots) for a user or computer to get a software distribution package.

Again, note that Windows 2000 Professional machines only require one logon (for user settings) or one reboot (for computer settings).

Folder Redirection, as you'll see in Chapter 9, is a wonderful tool. It has two modes: Basic Folder Redirection (which applies to everyone in the OU) and Advanced Folder Redirection (which checks which security groups the user is in). Windows XP and Windows Vista machines won't get the effects of Basic Folder Redirection for two logons! And Windows XP and Windows Vista machines won't get the effects of Advanced Folder Redirection for a whopping three logons. The first logon tags the system for a Folder Redirection change; the second logon figures out the user's security group membership; and the third logon actually performs the new Folder Redirection—synchronously for just that one logon.

Again, remember that Fast Boot is automatically disabled the first time any Windows XP or Windows Vista machine is started as a member of the domain. It is also disabled the first time any new user logs on to a Windows XP or Windows Vista client. In these situations, Windows XP and Windows Vista assume (correctly) that no GPO information is known and therefore must go out to Active Directory to get the latest GPOs. The net effect is that if settings for either (or both) Folder Redirection policy and Software Distribution policy already exist, the user will not require additional logons or reboots *the first time* they log on to a Windows XP or Windows Vista machine or when the computer is started for the first time after joining the domain.

FAST BOOT USER-ACCOUNT ATTRIBUTE PROCESSING DETAILS

Group Policy is only one of two areas affected by the Windows XP and Windows Vista Fast Boot mechanism. Some Microsoft documentation claims that other parts of the user's information could require several logons or reboots in order to take effect.

The idea is that certain attributes are cached and assumed to be accurate at logon. If, after a background download the information is actually changed, it would only be on the next logon that the change will take effect.

Microsoft says Windows XP takes two logons or reboots to process the following attributes:

- Roaming profile path (discussed in Chapter 8)

- The home directory

- Old-style logon scripts

I have observed this behavior, but I cannot figure out a strict set of rules for when it sometimes takes two logons or reboots and other times it only takes one. However, in my testing, the aforementioned attributes almost never do take two logons or reboots to apply. But it is possible.

So, under certain circumstances (with Fast Boot enabled), the preceding will hold true. So, if the user is using Windows XP or Windows Vista, and any of these properties are changed in Active Directory, it *could* take two logons for these changes to actually take effect.

Turning off Windows XP/Windows Vista Fast Boot

If you want your Windows XP and Windows Vista computers to start up a teeny-weeny bit faster (and have your user's desktops pop up a teeny-weeny bit faster), by all means, leave the default of Fast Boot on.

> If you're doing some no-no's in Group Policy (namely setting up cross-domain Group Policy links or processing a lot of site-based GPOs), leaving Fast Boot on will, in fact, serve its purpose and likely make each and every startup and logon a wee bit faster.

My recommendation, however, is to get all your machines—Windows XP, Windows Vista, and Windows 2000 Professional—to act the same. That is, I suggest that you force your Windows XP and Windows Vista machines to act like Windows 2000 machines and perform synchronous policy processing during their startup and logon. To do this, you need to set a Group Policy that contains a setting to revert Windows XP and Windows Vista machines to the old behavior. It might be a smidgen slower to log on, but no slower than your Windows 2000 machines already experience.

This will make your Windows XP and Windows Vista machines perform initial policy processing at startup and logon—just like your Windows 2000 machines. That is, the computer will start up, locate all GPOs, and then process them—before displaying the "Press Ctrl+Alt+Delete to begin" prompt. Once the user is logged on, all GPOs are processed before the desktop is displayed.

Troubleshooting Group Policy is now a heck of a lot more predictable because you're not trying to guess when Software Distribution, Folder Redirection, or even the errant Administrative Template setting is going to be processed. Since your Windows 2000 machines already act this way (and you can't make Windows 2000 Fast Boot like Windows XP), it probably would be a good enterprise supportability practice to have all machines in your environment act as similarly as possible—even if they are different operating systems.

To set Windows XP and Windows Vista to the Windows 2000 synchronous behavior, for Initial Policy Processing, create and link a GPO (preferably at the domain level) to simply enable the policy setting named **Always wait for the network at computer startup and logon**. This policy can be found in the Computer Configuration ➢ Administrative Templates ➢ System ➢ Logon branch of Group Policy. The name of this policy setting is a bit confusing. It would have been better, in my opinion, to name it **Make All Client Machines Process GPOs Like Windows 2000**. But they didn't.

Don't give the name of the policy setting, **Always wait for the network at computer startup and logon,** too much contemplation, even though it's confusing. It does not mean that the machine will just "hang" there until it sees the network during startup and logon. Its job is really only to make Windows XP and Windows Vista machines act like Windows 2000.

Remember, to force Windows XP and Windows Vista machines to receive this computer policy (or any computer policy), the computer account must be within the site, domain, or OU at which you set the policy. If you set this policy at the domain level (and enforce it to ensure it cannot be blocked), you're guaranteed that all Windows XP and Windows Vista machines in your domain will get the policy.

By performing this at the domain level, all your machines—Windows XP, Windows Vista, Windows 2000, and Windows 2003—will receive the message. But remember that policy settings meant for Windows XP or Windows Vista or Windows Server 2003 won't affect Windows 2000 machines. And it's a moot point for Windows 2003 machines anyway, as you'll see in the next section.

Forcing Background Policy Processing

You get a phone call from the person who handles the firewalls and proxy servers at your company. He tells you that he's added an additional proxy server for your users to use when going out to the Internet. Excitedly, you add a new GPO that affects Wally and Xavier's user objects so they can use the new proxy server via Internet Explorer Maintenance Settings. But you're impatient.

You know that when you make this setting, it's going to take between 90 and 120 minutes to kick in. And you don't want to tell Wally or Xavier to log off and log back on to get the policy—they wouldn't like that much.

In cases like these, you might want to bypass the normal wait time before background policy processing kicks in. The good news is that you can run a simple command that tells the client to skip the normal background processing interval and request an update of new or changed GPOs from the server right now. Again, only new GPOs or GPOs that have changed in some way on the server will actually come down and be reflected on your client machines.

Initiating a Manual Background Refresh for Windows 2000

The command-line tool used to encourage your Windows 2000 machines to kick off a manual background refresh is SECEDIT. SECEDIT can request the refresh of GPOs (and the settings therein) from the User Configuration node, the Computer Configuration node, or both, but you'll need to run the command once for each half.

As I've mentioned, there is no way from up on high to say, "Go forth and refresh, all ye users or computers affected by this recent change in policy!" To utilize SECEDIT, you must physically be present at the Windows 2000 machine and execute the command. Otherwise, you must simply wait for the background refresh interval to kick in.

> You can independently change the background refresh interval of both the user and computer. See the "Using Group Policy to Affect Group Policy" section later in this chapter.

But, because you're impatient, you want to see Wally on his Windows 2000 machine start using that new proxy server setting that you plunked into that GPO right away. So you physically trot out to his machine, log on with administrator-level authority, and enter the following commands to manually refresh the GPOs.

For Windows 2000, follow these steps to request a refresh of GPOs from the User Configuration node:

1. Choose Start ➢ Run to open the Run dialog box, and in the Open box, enter **cmd** to open the command-line window.

2. At the prompt, type **secedit /refreshpolicy user_policy**.

For Windows 2000, follow these steps to request a refresh of GPOs from the Computer Configuration node:

1. Choose Start ➢ Run to open the Run dialog box, and in the Open box, enter **cmd** to open the command-line window.

2. At the prompt, type **secedit /refreshpolicy machine_policy**.

See Chapter 6 for additional uses of the SECEDIT command.

> You might want to create a batch file called ꙅ.bat or even gpupdate.bat, which runs secedit to initiate machine and user policy settings to apply. Then, if you place this batch file on all your workstations, you can perform both in one stroke!

Initiating a Manual Background Refresh for Windows XP, Windows Vista, and Windows 2003

You now want to initiate a manual refresh for Xavier on his Windows XP machine and Victoria on her Windows Vista machine. Windows XP, Windows Vista, and Windows 2003 refresh GPOs using a different command called gpupdate. gpupdate is similar to SECEDIT in that it can refresh either the user or computer half of a GPO, or both. The syntax is gpupdate /Target:Computer, /Target:User, or just gpupdate by itself to trigger both.

Running gpupdate while Xavier is logged on to his Windows XP machine immediately gives him the new settings in the GPO you just set. This is, of course, provided the Domain Controller that Xavier and his Windows XP machine are using has the replicated GPO information. Ditto for Victoria on her Windows Vista machine.

Additionally, gpupdate can figure out if newly changed items require a logoff or reboot to be active. Since Windows XP and Windows Vista's default behavior is to enable Fast Boot, Software Distribution and Folder Redirection settings are processed only at future logon times. Therefore, specifying gpupdate with a /Logoff switch will figure out if a policy has changed in Active Directory such that a logoff is required and automatically log you off. If the updated GPO does not require a logoff, the GPO settings are applied, and the currently logged-on user remains logged on.

Similarly, with Windows XP and Windows Vista's Fast Boot enabled, GPOs that have Software Distribution settings will require a reboot before the software will be available. Therefore, specifying gpupdate with a /boot switch will figure out if a policy has something that requires a reboot and automatically reboot the computer. If the updated GPO does not require a reboot, the GPO settings are applied, and the user remains logged on.

The /Logoff and /boot switches are optional.

> For information about how to turn off Windows XP and Windows Vista's Fast Boot and make it act like Windows 2000, refer to the "Turning Off Windows XP/Windows Vista Fast Boot" section earlier in this chapter.

Security Background Refresh Processing

Even before Microsoft had the big, internal security hurrah, some modicum of security was built into the Group Policy engine. As I've stated, Windows 2000, Windows 2003, Windows XP, and Windows Vista clients process GPOs when the background refresh interval comes to pass—but only those GPOs that were new or changed since the last time the client requested them.

Wally is on a Windows 2000 machine, and he's been logged on for four hours. Likewise, Xavier has been logged on to his Windows XP machine for four hours and Victoria has been logged on to her Windows Vista machine for four hours.

Imagine for a second that there was a GPO in Active Directory named "Remove Run menu from Start Menu" and its function was to do just that. The client would certainly do so according to the initial policy processing rules and/or the background refresh processing rules.

GPUpdate /force **Command for Windows XP and Windows Vista**

There is one peculiarity about the gpupdate /force command when run in Windows XP. If there's a GPO which deploys software to your user or computer and you run the gpudpate /force command, you'll encounter a weird behavior. Sometimes it gets confused and thinks that the underlying GPOs have changed– even though they haven't. So, when it gets confused, gpupdate will express that a reboot (or logoff) is needed in order get the full set of GPOs. However, this isn't strictly correct.

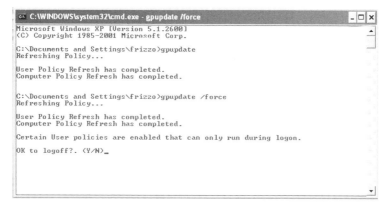

Windows Vista has apparently cured this inconsistency. Windows Vista's gpupdate does something different. It informs you that during the next foreground refresh, it will occur synchronously to ensure all policy is applied.

Assuming that the underlying GPO doesn't get any policy settings modified or any new policy settings or that the GPO itself doesn't get removed, the client already knows to accept this edict. The client just accepts that things haven't changed and, hence, keeps on truckin'. Only a change inside the GPO will trigger the client to realize that new instructions are available, and the client will execute that new edict during its background policy processing.

Now, let's assume that we anoint Wally, Xavier, and Victoria as local administrators of their Windows 2000, Windows XP, and Windows Vista machines, respectively. Since Wally, Xavier, and Victoria are now local administrators, they have total control to go around the Group Policy engine processes and make their own changes. These changes could nullify a policy you've previously set with a GPO and allow them to access and change features on the system that shouldn't be changed. In this case, there are certainly going to be situations in which the GPOs on the domain controllers don't change, but certain parts of the workstation should remain locked down anyway.

Of course, the right answer is to only give people you absolutely trust access to local Administrator accounts. You should never give "regular users" Administrator accounts if you can possibly help it.

But, with that being said, let's examine two potential exploits of the Group Policy engine if a local administrator does choose to do so.

Group Policy Exploit Example #1: Going Around an Administrative Template Consider the `calc.exe` program we forced to run every time someone uses a computer in Human Resources. We created a GPO named "Auto-Launch Calc.exe" and enabled the policy setting named **Run these programs at user logon** within it. We linked the GPO to the **Human Resources Computers** OU. Our edict affected all users on our computers (including our administrators) such that `calc.exe` ran for everyone (because the GPO was linked to an OU containing the computer). Imagine, then, that someone with local administrative privileges (such as Wally) on the workstation changes the portion of the Registry that is affected, as shown in Figure 3.1.

FIGURE 3.1 A simple deletion of the Registry entry will nullify our policy setting.

After the local administrator changes the setting, `calc.exe` simply won't run. (Again, only local administrators can make this change. Mere mortals do not have access to this portion of the Registry.) We're now at risk; a local administrator did the dirty work, and now all users on this workstation are officially going around our policy. Ninety minutes or so later, the background refresh interval strikes, and the client computer requests the background refresh from the GPOs in Active Directory. You might think that this should once again lock down the "Auto-Launch Calc.exe" ability. But it doesn't. This ability won't get relocked down upon a reboot, either. Why? Because the Windows client thinks everything is status quo. Because nothing has changed in the underlying GPO in Active Directory that is telling the client its instruction set changed.

In this example, the Group Policy processing engine on the client thinks it has already asked for (and received) the latest version of the policy; the Group Policy processing engine doesn't know about the nefarious Registry change the local workstation administrator performed behind its back. Windows clients are not protected from this sort of attack by default. However, the protection can be made stronger. (See the "Mandatory Reapplication for Nonsecurity Policy" section later in this chapter.) Okay, this example exploit is fairly harmless, but it could be more or less damaging depending on precisely which policy settings we are forcing on our clients (as seen in this next example).

Group Policy Exploit Example #2: Going Around a Security Policy Setting   Via Group Policy, we use the material in Chapter 6 to create a security template (and corresponding security policy) that locks down the \windows\repair directory with specific file ACLs (for Windows XP machines). For this example, imagine we set the \windows\repair directory so that only the Domain Administrators have access. Then, behind our backs, Xavier, now a local administrator, changes these file ACLs to allow everyone full control to these sensitive files. Uh-oh, now we could have a real problem on our hands.

Windows offers protection to handle clean-up for exploits of these two types. Let's see how that works.

In the first example, we went around the **Run these programs at user logon** policy setting by forcefully modifying the Registry. Running calc.exe for every user on a particular computer isn't considered a security setting. So, *by default* there is no protection for Exploit #1 (note the emphasis on "by default"). But, before you start panicking, let's examine Exploit #2, which attempts to go around a security policy we set.

Background Security Refresh Processing for Windows 2000, Windows 2003, Windows XP, and Windows Vista

The Group Policy engine tries to clean up after examples such as Exploit #2 by asking for a special background refresh—just for the security policy settings. This is called the *background security refresh*. Every 16 hours, a client asks Active Directory for all the security-related GPOs that apply for it (not just the ones that have changed). This ensures that if a security setting has changed on the client (behind the Group Policy engine's back), it's automatically patched up within 16 hours.

 You can manually change this security refresh interval in two ways. First, you can edit the local workstation's Registry at HKEY_LOCAL_MACHINE\SOFTWARE\ Microsoft\Windows NT\CurrentVersion\Winlogon\GPExtensions\ {827D319E-6EAC-11D2-A4EA-00C04F79F83A}\MaxNoGPOListChangesInterval and leverage a REG_DWORD signifying the number of minutes to pull down the entire security policy (by default, every 16 hours, so 960 minutes). You can also use the Security Policy Processing policy, which is described in the "Using Group Policy to Affect Group Policy" section, later in this chapter. For more information, see the Microsoft Knowledge Base article 277543.

To reiterate, background security refresh helps secure stuff on the client only every 16 hours and only if the setting is security related. So, within a maximum of 16 hours, the \windows\repair directory would have the intended permissions rethrust upon it. Okay, great. But in Exploit #1, our evil administrator went around the **Run these programs at user logon** policy setting. And the background security refresh would *not* have re-enforced our intended will upon the system. Running calc.exe is not considered a security policy setting. How do we secure *those* exploits, I hear you cry? Read on, I reply. (Hey, that rhymed.)

Mandatory Reapplication for Nonsecurity Policy

Your network is humming along. You've established the GPOs in your organization, and you've let them sit unchanged for several months. Wally logs on. Wally logs off. So does Xavier. And Victoria. They each reboot their machines a bunch. But imagine for a moment that the GPOs in Active Directory haven't changed in months.

When your users or computers perform initial Group Policy processing or background policy processing, a whole lot of nothing happens. If GPOs haven't changed in months, there's nothing for the clients to do. Since the engine has already processed the latest version of what's in Active Directory, what more could it possibly need?

True, every 16 hours the security-related policy settings are guaranteed to be refreshed by the background security refresh. But what about Exploit #1 in which Wally (who was anointed as a local workstation administrator) went around the **Run these programs at user logon** policy setting by hacking his local Registry?

Well, running calc.exe isn't a security policy. But it still could be thought of as a security hole you need to fill (if you were running something really important every time a user logged in). With a little magic, you can enforce the nonsecurity sections of Group Policy to automatically close their own security holes. You can make the nonsecurity sections of Group Policy enforce their settings, even if the GPOs on the servers haven't changed. This will fix exploits that aren't specifically security related. You'll learn how to do this a bit later in the "Affecting the Computer Settings of Group Policy" section.

The general idea is that once the nonsecurity sections of Group Policy are told to mandatorily reapply, they will do so whenever an initial policy processing or background refresh processing happens.

You can choose to (optionally) mandatorily reapply the following areas of Group Policy, along with the initial processing and background refresh:

- Registry (Administrative Templates)
- Internet Explorer Maintenance
- IP Security
- EFS Recovery Policy
- Wireless Policy
- Disk Quota
- Scripts (by Scripts we mean the notification of changes to scripts, not the actual re-running of scripts after the appointed time)
- Security

- Folder Redirection
- Software Installation
- Wired Policy

Note that most of the new CSEs for Windows Vista (like Printers and Windows Search) aren't in that list. But Wired (new for Windows Vista) and Wireless Policy (updated for Windows Vista) made it. Why some and not others? Beats me. I think someone just forgot to add them in during the rush-rush to get Windows Vista out the door. Maybe the rest will return in Windows Vista service pack or something, but for now, they're not available.

As you'll see in the "Affecting the Computer Settings of Group Policy" section, you can use the GUI to select other areas of Group Policy to enforce along with the background refresh.

To recap, if the GPO in Active Directory has *actually* changed, you don't have to worry about whether it will be automatically applied or not. Rather, mandatory reapplication is an extra safety measure that you can choose to place upon your client systems so your will is always download and re-embraced, not only if an existing GPO has changed or a new GPO has appeared. And, you can specify specific Group Policy sections that you wish to do this for.

 As you'll see in Chapter 4, a bit more is going on between the client and the server. Underneath the hood, the client keeps track of the GPO *version number*. If the version number changes in Active Directory, the GPO is flagged as being required for download; it is then redownloaded and applied. If the version number stays the same in Active Directory, the Group Policy isn't redownloaded or applied. Stay tuned for more on GPO version numbers in Chapter 4.

Manually Forcing Clients to Process GPOs (Revisited)

In the "Forcing Background Refresh Processing" section, I talked a bit about what happens if you set up a new GPO (or change an existing one) and get impatient. That is, you want to force your client systems to embrace your new settings.

As I've said, there's no way (with the tools in the box) from on high to shout to your client computers and proclaim: "Accept my latest GPOs, ye mere mortals and puny systems!"

If you want to kick off policy processing at a client, you need to trot on over to it to kick it in the shins. You use SECEDIT on Windows 2000 machines and gpupdate on Windows XP, Windows Vista, and Windows 2003 machines. But the command-line tools have slightly different switches and behaviors.

Windows 2000 *SECEDIT* with the */enforce* Switch

Recall that you must run the Windows 2000 SECEDIT command-line tool on the client that you want to refresh. SECEDIT has an additional switch, /enforce, that ensures that all policy-related settings are processed by the Windows 2000 workstation—regardless of whether the underlying GPO has changed in Active Directory. Instead of waiting 16 hours, you can rush the hands of time and force the background policy refresh processing to strike.

The commands are either:

```
secedit /refreshpolicy machine_policy /enforce
```

or

```
secedit /refreshpolicy user_policy /enforce
```

Windows XP, Windows Vista, and Windows 2003 *gpupdate* with the */force* Switch

Recall that you must run the Windows command-line tool gpupdate on the clients other than Windows 2000. And that you must be on the machine that you specifically want the refresh to occur. The /force switch looks similar to the /enforce switch for the Windows 2000 command-line tool SECEDIT, but it's not the same—it's better.

gpupdate /force ensures that all settings in all GPOs are processed by the Windows XP, Windows Vista , or Windows 2003—regardless of whether the underlying GPO has changed in Active Directory.

The command is typically specified as:

```
gpupdate /force
```

Other options are available in conjunction with /force, such as the ability to log off the user or reboot the machine should a foreground policy be required (in the case of, say, Software Distribution).

> The Windows Vista /force switch is littttle bit smarter than previous operating system versions. This is because in previous versions of the operating systems (like Windows XP) it might suggest a reboot or a logoff when one wasn't specifically needed. Here in Windows Vista, it seems to "know" better than to make these suggestions when not needed.

Special Case: Moving a User or a Computer Object

When you move a user or a computer within Active Directory, Group Policy may not immediately apply as you think it should. For instance, if you move a computer from the **Human Resources Computers** OU to another OU, that computer may still pull GPOs from the **Human Resources Computers** OU for a while longer. This is because the computer may get confused about where the accounts it's supposed to work with are currently residing.

The userenv process syncs with Active Directory every so often to determine if a user or a computer has been moved.

This happens, at most, about every 30 minutes or so.

Once resynced, background processing continues as it normally would. Only this time the user and computer GPOs are pulled from the new destination. If you move a user or a computer, remember that Group Policy processing continues to pull from the old location until it realizes the switch.

And, don't forget that replication takes a while within your site, and also, potentially *between* Active Directory sites.

Altogether, the maximum wait time after a move to get GPOs pulled from a new location is as follows:

- 30 minutes (the maximum Active Directory synchronization time) *and*
- 90 minutes (the maximum Group Policy default background refresh rate) *and*
- 30 minutes (the maximum Group Policy default background refresh rate offset)

So that's the time it takes to replicate the change, plus a maximum of 150 minutes.

It could and usually does happen faster than that, but it can't take any longer. This behavior is important to understand if you move an entire OU (perhaps with many computers) underneath another OU!

Windows Vista has a special trick, however. If you know the computer or user account has been moved (and, hence, would get different Group Policy settings) you can just run `gpupdate /force`, which double-checks where both the user and computer account "live" in Active Directory. Once the location is found, it applies GPOs specifically for that new location.

> Windows XP/SP2's gpupdate /force is supposed to have the same behavior as Windows Vista. That is, it should be able to figure out if the user or computer account has moved. But in my testing it did not work as well as Windows Vista's.

Policy Application via Remote Access, Slow Links, and after Hibernation

You will certainly have situations in which users take their Windows machines on the road then remote-access your Active Directory and servers via dial-up or VPN.

All versions of Windows, by default, will detect the speed of the connection and make a snap judgment about whether to process Group Policy. However, different operating systems determine the speed differently.

Windows 2000 and Windows XP Group Policy via RAS Speed Determination and Policy Reapplication

If the Windows 2000 or Windows XP machine uses TCP/IP to connect to RAS (Remote Access Service), it is considered "fast enough" to process Group Policy if the connection is 500 kilobits or greater.

However, Windows 2000 and Windows XP sometimes have trouble figuring out what the speed actually is. Windows 2000 and Windows XP use ICMP (the same protocol as ping) to figure out the speed. However, many router administrators have turned off ICMP at the routers. When this happens, and Windows 2000 and Windows XP can't ping their domain controllers, they just give up and don't process Group Policy.

And this is bad—because the whole point in figuring out the speed of the link is to help "hone in" exactly which portions of Group Policy will apply over a slow link or not.

And what happens if your user's laptop is off the network for three days? When they connect back, Windows 2000 and Windows XP laptops will have tried and tried and tried to refresh policy. However, since a Domain Controller wasn't available, it just keeps on trying.

However, when you finally do reconnect back up, Windows 2000 and Windows XP will finally find a Domain Controller. But, this could take (you guessed it) up to 120 minutes (90 minutes, plus the 30 minute offset) to finally occur. Vista improves on this (see next section).

Windows Vista Group Policy via RAS Speed Determination and Policy Reapplication

Windows Vista uses a different mechanism than Windows XP or Windows 2000 to determine if the link is slow. Windows Vista's Group Policy speed detection mechanism depends on an updated Windows component called "Network Location Awareness 2" or NLA 2 for short.

NLA 2 is pretty simple (and there's nothing you need to configure). NLA 2 for Windows Vista has two jobs:

1. NLA checks to see if the link is slow or not. This test doesn't use ICMP, so if router administrators have turned off ICMP, the calculation will still work. (See the section "What Is Processed Over a Slow Network Connection?" for why you care about what is processed over a slow network connection, coming up next.)

2. NLA calls out to the universe every so often and asks "Is there a Domain Controller available NOW?" If the answer is "No!" then Group Policy cannot be updated. Pretty simple. However, if the answer is "Yes!" updated Group Policy could, theoretically, be processed, right?

This might be useful when a user has been working at the beach, disconnected for several days, then finally dials up or comes into the office. However, before actually doing anything, the Group Policy engine kicks in and asks one more question. The Group Policy engine then asks, "Did I miss the last background refresh interval?" (for instance, if the computer was hibernated, and therefore turned off, for three days).

If the answer is "Yes," then the Group Policy engine immediately performs (what amounts to) a gpupdate (no force) to refresh Group Policy since the last time the user and computer made contact.

Why is the Group Policy engine so specific about ensuring that it missed the last background refresh interval? The Group Policy engine asks this question because NLA could have determined that the computer was ever-so-briefly off the network—and then back on again. And, if that's the case, there was nothing to miss, so nothing is updated. You wouldn't really want it to trigger every time it went off and back on the network. That would be a veritable flurry of Group Policy updating! In other words, the Group Policy ensures that the Windows Vista machine was off the network for a goodly amount of time before asking for a refresh.

What Is Processed Over a Slow Network Connection?

So, if the connection is deemed fast enough, *portions* of Group Policy are applied.

Surprisingly, even if the connection is deemed "not fast enough," several sections of Group Policy are *still* applied. Security settings, Software Restriction Policy settings (Windows XP and higher), and Administrative Templates are *guaranteed* to be downloaded during logon over an RAS connection—regardless of the speed. And there's nothing you can do to change that (not that you should really want to). Additionally, included in security settings are EFS (Encrypting File System) Recovery Policy and IPsec (IP Security) policy. They are also always downloaded over slow links.

 WARNING The Group Policy interface suggests that downloading of EFS Recovery Policy and IPsec policy can be switched on or off over slow links. This is not true. (See the note in the "Using Group Policy to Affect Group Policy" section later in this chapter.)

If the user connects using RAS before logging on to the workstation (using the "Logon Using Dial-Up Connection" check box as seen in Figure 3.2), the security and Administrative Templates policy settings of the Computer node of the GPO are downloaded and applied to the computer once the user is authenticated. Then, the security and Administrative Templates policy settings of the User node of the GPO are applied to the user.

If the user connects using RAS after logging on to the workstation (using the "Network and Dial-up Connections" icons), the security policy settings and the Administrative Templates policy settings for the user and computer are not applied right away; rather they are applied during the next normal background refresh cycle (every 90 minutes by default).

Other sections of Group Policy are handled as follows during a slow connection:

Internet Explorer Maintenance Settings These are not downloaded by default over slow links. (You can change this condition using the information in the "Using Group Policy to Affect Group Policy" section later in this chapter.)

Folder Redirection Settings These are not downloaded by default over slow links. (You can change this condition using the information in the "Using Group Policy to Affect Group Policy" section later in this chapter.)

Scripts (Logon, Logoff, Startup, and Shutdown) Script update are not downloaded by default over slow links. (You can change this condition using the information in the "Using Group Policy to Affect Group Policy" section later in this chapter.) Also see the sidebar "Processing and Running Scripts Over Slow Links" later in this chapter.

Disk Quota Settings These are not downloaded by default over slow links. (You can change this condition using the information in the "Using Group Policy to Affect Group Policy" section later in this chapter.) The currently cached disk quota settings are still enforced.

FIGURE 3.2   If you select "Log on using dial-up connection," you first process GPOs in the foreground (when Fast Boot is disabled).

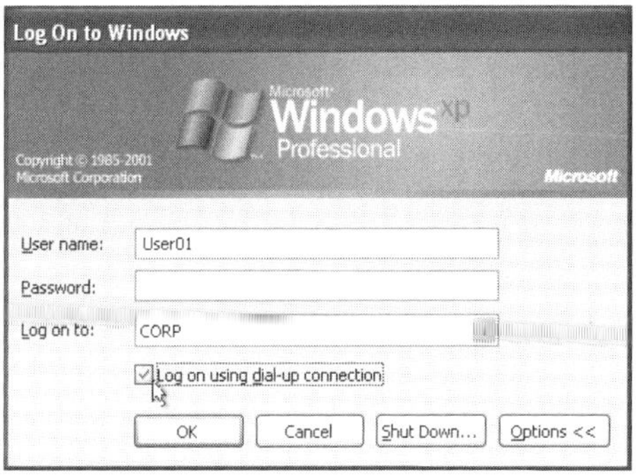

Software Installation and Maintenance   These are not downloaded by default over slow links. More specifically, the offers of newly available software are not shown to users. Users do have the ability to choose whether to pull down the latest versions of applications at their whim, as detailed in Chapter 10. You can torture your dial-in users by changing the behavior of how offers are handled and permit the icons of new software to be displayed. They will hate you after you do this, but that is for you and them to work out. See the corresponding setting described later in this chapter in the "Using Group Policy to Affect Group Policy" section.

Software Restriction Policy (Windows Vista, Windows XP, and Windows 2003 Only)
These are guaranteed to download over slow links. You cannot turn off this ability.

802.11 Wireless Policy (Windows Vista, Windows XP, and Windows 2003 Only)   These are not downloaded by default over slow links. (You can change this condition using the information in the "Using Group Policy to Affect Group Policy" section later in this chapter.) The currently cached 802.11 policy settings are still enforced.

802.3 Wired Policy (Windows Vista Only)   These are not downloaded by default over slow links. (You can change this condition using the information in the "Using Group Policy to Affect Group Policy" section later in this chapter.)

Administrative Templates   These are guaranteed to download over slow links. You cannot turn off this ability.

EFS Recovery Policy   These are guaranteed to download over slow links. You cannot turn off this ability. The interface has an option that makes it appear as if you can turn off this ability, but you can't.

IPsec Policy   These are guaranteed to download over slow links. You cannot turn off this ability. The interface has an option that makes it appear as if you can turn off this ability, but you can't.

What is considered "fast enough" for all these policy categories can be changed from 500Kb to whatever speed you desire (independently for the computer half and the user half), is detailed in the "Using Group Policy to Affect Group Policy" section later in this chapter.

Processing and Running Scripts Over Slow Links

If your users try to run scripts while using slow links, they (and you) might notice some interesting behavior. First, computer startup scripts will not run over slow links. This just isn't supported by the Group Policy engine.

However, one enterprising customer of mine had a service written to explicitly do this after the user was logged on. That said, logon scripts are currently still fair game. However, many factors play into whether the scripts will run.

When a user is dialed in over a slow link, the scripts policy itself will not process. That is, it will not receive information about new or updated scripts. The actual *running* of the scripts is a different matter altogether and is irrespective of whether the user has a slow connection. Therefore, if you applied the script policy while on a high-speed connection (for example, a home office LAN) and then a user should log on over a dial-up connection, scripts will run; the script policy has already been downloaded and set for takeoff. Indeed, your script policy might tell the client to execute the script from the server, which may or may not be available.

But until your users come back to the headquarters, they won't get updates to that script policy if any has occurred. For instance, if the script policy states to run the script from an alternate server location, this information won't be downloaded until they come back into headquarters.

Windows 2000 and Windows XP have slightly different behavior for the actual running of the scripts. Windows 2000 requires that the SYSVOL (NETLOGON share) be accessible for the scripts to even attempt to run. If the machine cannot see SYSVOL, no scripts will run.

Windows XP, Windows Vista, and Windows 2003 have addressed this problem, but it's thorny. If the machine is 100 percent offline (and, hence, SYSVOL isn't available), the scripts will indeed run. But if the system determines it's on a fast connection and SYSVOL is unavailable, scripts won't run.

Using Group Policy to Affect Group Policy

At times, you might want to change the behavior of Group Policy. Amazingly, you actually use Group Policy settings to change the behavior of Group Policy! Several Group Policy settings appear under both the User and Computer nodes; however, you must set the policy settings in each section independently.

Affecting the User Settings of Group Policy

The Group Policy settings that affect the User node appear under User Configuration ➢ Administrative Templates ➢ System ➢ Group Policy. Remember that user accounts must be subject to the site, domain, or OU where these GPOs are linked in order to be affected. Most of these policy settings are valid for Windows 2000, Windows XP, Windows Vista machines and Windows 2003 servers, although some are explicitly designed and will operate only on Windows XP, Windows Vista, and/or Windows 2003 servers.

The following sections list the policy settings that affect the user side of Group Policy.

Group Policy Refresh Interval for Users

This setting changes the default User node background refresh rate of 90 minutes with a 0–30 minute positive randomizer to almost any number of refresh and randomizer minutes you choose. Choose a smaller number for the background refresh to speed up Group Policy on your machines, or choose a larger number to quell the traffic that a Group Policy refresh takes across your network. There is a similar refresh interval for computers, which is on an alternate clock with its own settings. A setting of 0 is equal to 7 seconds. Set to 0 only in the test lab.

Group Policy Slow Link Detection

You can change the default definition of *fast connectivity for users* from 500Kbps to any speed you like. Recall that certain aspects of Group Policy are not applied to machines that are determined to be coming in over slow links. This setting specifies what constitutes a slow link for the User node. There is an identically named policy setting located under the Computer node (explored later in this chapter) that also needs to be set to define what is slow for the Computer node. Preferably set these to the same number.

Group Policy Domain Controller Selection

GPOs are written to the PDC emulator by default. When users (generally Domain Administrators or OU administrators) are affected by this setting, they are allowed to create new GPOs on Domain Controllers other than the PDC emulator. (See Chapter 4 for more information on this setting and how and why to use it.)

Create New Group Policy Object Links Disabled by Default

When users (generally Domain Administrators or OU administrators) are affected by this setting, the GPOs they create will be disabled by default. This ensures that users and computers are not hitting their refresh intervals and downloading half-finished GPOs that you are in the process of creating. Enable the GPOs when finished, and they will download during their next background refresh cycle.

Default Name for Group Policy Objects

If a user has been assigned the rights to create GPOs via membership in the Group Policy Creator Owners group and has also been assigned the rights to link GPOs to OUs within Active Directory, the default name created for GPOs is "New Group Policy Object." You might want all GPOs created at the domain level to have one name, perhaps "AppliesToDomain-GPO," and all GPOs created at the **Human Resources** OU level (and all child levels) to have another name, maybe "AppliestoHR-GPO." Again, in order for this policy to work, the user's account with the rights to create GPOs must be affected by the policy.

Enforce Show Policies Only

When users (generally Domain Administrators or OU administrators) are affected by this setting, the "Only show policy settings that can be fully managed" setting (explored in Chapter 5) is forced to be enabled. This prevents the importation of "bad" ADM templates, which have the unfortunate side effect of "tattooing" the Registry until they are explicitly removed. (See Chapter 5 for more information on using all types of ADM templates with Windows 2003.)

Turn Off Automatic Update of ADM Files

You'll learn all about ADM files (and this particular policy setting) in Chapter 5. But, in essence, ADM template files are the underlying "definitions" of what's possible in Group Policy land (when you use pre-Vista machines). (On Vista machines, a new mechanism called ADMX files is used.)

These ADM files are updated by service packs. The default behavior is to check the launching point, that is, the \windows\inf folder, to see if the ADM template has yet been updated. This check for an update occurs, by default, every time you double-click the Administrative Templates section of any GPO as if you were going to modify it. However, if you enable this setting, you're saying to ignore the normal update process and simply keep on using the ADM template you initially used. In other words, you're telling the system you'd prefer to keep the initial ADM template regardless of whether a newer one is available. (See Chapter 5 for critical information on updating ADM templates when service packs are available for Windows XP or Windows 2003.)

Disallow Interactive Users from Generating Resultant Set of Policy Data

Users affected by this setting cannot use the "Group Policy Modeling" or "Group Policy Results" tasks in the GPMC. Enabling this setting locks down a possible entry point into the system. That is, it prevents unauthorized users from determining the current security settings on the box and developing attack strategies.

This policy setting is only valid when applied to Windows Vista, Windows XP, and Windows 2003 servers.

Affecting the Computer Settings of Group Policy

The Group Policy settings that affect the Computer node appear under Computer Configuration ➢ Administrative Templates ➢ System ➢ Group Policy. Once computers are affected by these policy settings, they change the processing behavior of Group Policy. Remember that the computer accounts must be subject to the site, domain, or OU where these GPOs are linked in order to be affected.

Turn Off Background Refresh of Group Policy

When this setting is enabled, the affected computer downloads the latest GPOs for both the user and the computer, according to the background refresh interval—but it doesn't apply them. The GPOs are applied when the user logs off but before the next user logs on. This is helpful in situations in which you want to guarantee that a user's experience stays the same throughout the session.

Group Policy Refresh Interval for Computers

This setting changes the default Computer node background refresh rate of 90 minutes with a 30-minute randomizer to almost any number of refresh and randomizer minutes you choose. Choose a smaller number for the background refresh to speed up Group Policy on your machines, or choose a larger number to quell the traffic a Group Policy refresh takes across your network. A similar refresh interval for the User node is on a completely separate and unrelated timing rate and randomizer. A setting of 0 equals 7 seconds. Set to 0 only in the test lab.

Group Policy Refresh Interval for Domain Controllers

Recall that Domain Controllers are updated regarding Group Policy changes within five minutes. You can close or widen that gap as you see fit. The closer the gap, the more network chatter. Widen the gap, and the security settings will be inconsistent until the interval is hit. A setting of 0 equals 7 seconds. Set to 0 only in the test lab.

User Group Policy Loopback Processing Mode

We'll explore this setting with an example in the next section.

Allow Cross-Forest User Policy and Roaming User Profiles

This policy is valid only in cross-forest trust scenarios. I'll describe how these work and how this policy works later in this chapter in the "Group Policy with Cross-Forest Trusts" section.

This policy setting is valid only when applied to Windows Vista and Windows XP workstations and Windows 2003 servers (and presumably, Windows Server Longhorn).

Group Policy Slow Link Detection

You can change the default definition of *fast connectivity* from 500Kbps to any speed you like. Recall that certain aspects of Group Policy are not applied to those machines that are deemed to be coming in over slow links. Independently, an identically named policy setting exists under the User node (explored earlier) also needs to be set to define what is slow for the User node. Preferably, set these to the same number.

Turn Off Resultant Set of Policy Logging

As you'll see in Chapter 4, users on Windows XP and Windows Vista machines can launch the Resultant Set of Policy (RSoP) snap-in by typing **RSOP.MSC** at the command prompt. Enabling this policy doesn't prevent its launch but, for all intents and purposes, disables its use. This policy disables the use for the currently logged-on user (known as the interactive user) as well as anyone trying to get the results using the remote features of the RSoP snap-in.

This policy setting is valid only when applied to Windows Vista and Windows XP workstations and Windows 2003 servers (and presumably, Windows Server Longhorn).

 On Windows Vista, regular users can only see the user half of the RSoP by default. They must be delegated the "Read Group Policy Results data" right over the Windows Vista computer they want to gather the information for. We talked about this in Chapter 2's "Special Group Policy Operating Delegations" section.

Remove Users Ability to Invoke Machine Policy Refresh

By default, mere mortal users can perform their own background refreshes using gpupdate, as described in the "Initiating a Manual Background Refresh for Windows XP, Windows Vista, and Windows 2003" section. However, you might not want users to perform their own gpupdate. I can think of only one reason to disable this setting: to prevent users from sucking up bandwidth on Domain Controllers by continually running gpupdate. Other than that, I can't imagine why you would want to prevent them from being able to get the latest GPO settings if they were so inclined. Perhaps one user is performing a denial of service (DoS) attack on your Domain Controllers by continually requesting Group Policy—but even that's a stretch.

Even if this policy is enabled, local administrators can still force a GPUpdate. But, again, gpupdate only works when run locally on the machine needing the update.

This policy setting is valid only when applied to Windows Vista and Windows XP workstations and Windows 2003 servers (and presumably, Windows Server Longhorn).

Disallow Interactive Users from Generating Resultant Set of Policy Data

This policy is similar to the "Turn off Resultant Set of Policy logging" setting but affects only the user on the console. Enabling this setting might be useful if you don't want the interactive user to have the ability to generate RSoP data but still want to allow administrators to get the RSoP remotely. Again, RSoP and its related functions are explored in Chapter 4.

This policy setting is valid only when applied to Windows Vista, Windows XP workstations, and Windows 2003 servers (and presumably Windows Server Longhorn).

Registry Policy Processing

This setting affects how your policy settings in the Administrative Templates subtrees react (and, generally, any other policy that affects the Registry). Once this policy setting is enabled, you have two other options:

Do Not Apply During Periodic Background Processing   Typically, Administrative Templates settings are refreshed every 90 minutes or so. However, if you enable this setting, you're telling the client not ever to refresh the Administrative Templates in the GPOs that are meant for it after the logon. You might choose to prevent background refresh for Administrative Templates for two reasons:

- When the background refresh occurs, the screen may flicker for a second as the system reapplies the changed GPOs (with their policy settings) and instructs `Explorer.exe` to refresh the Desktop. This could be a slight distraction for the user every 90 minutes or so.

- You might choose to disable background processing so that users' experiences with the Desktop and applications stay consistent for the entire length of their logon. Having settings suddenly change while the user is logged on could be confusing, but my advice is to leave this setting alone unless you're seriously impacted by the background processing affecting your users' experience.

Process Even If the Group Policy Objects Have Not Changed   If this setting is selected, the system will update and reapply the policy settings in this category even if the underlying GPO has not changed when the background refresh interval occurs. Recall that this type of processing is meant to clean up should an administrator have nefariously gone around our backs and modified a local setting.

 You cannot turn off Registry policy processing over slow links. They are always downloaded and applied.

Internet Explorer Maintenance Policy Processing

Once enabled, this policy setting has three potential options:

Allow Processing Across a Slow Network Connection   Check this check box to allow Internet Explorer Maintenance settings to download when logging on over slow links. Enabling this could cause your users to experience a longer logon time but adhere to your latest Internet Explorer wishes.

Do Not Apply During Periodic Background Processing   If this option is selected, the latest Internet Explorer settings in Active Directory GPOs will not be downloaded or applied during the background refresh.

Process Even If the Group Policy Objects Have Not Changed   If this option is selected, it updates and reapplies the policy settings in this category even if the underlying GPO has not changed. Recall that this type of processing is meant to clean up should a user or an administrator have nefariously gone around our backs and modified a local setting.

Software Installation Policy Processing

Once enabled, this policy setting has two potential options:

Allow Processing Across a Slow Network Connection   As I stated, by default, software deployment offers are not displayed to users connecting over slow links. This is a good thing; allowing users to click the newly available icons to begin the download and installation of new software over a 56K dial-up line can be tortuous. Use this setting to change this behavior.

If you have already distributed software via Group Policy, and an offer has been accepted by a client computer (but perhaps not all pieces of the application have been loaded), setting this selection will likely not help, and your users may experience a long delay in running their application over a slow link. For more information on how to best distribute software to clients who use slow links, see Chapter 11.

Process Even If the Group Policy Objects Have Not Changed   For Software Installation, I cannot find any difference if this option is selected or not, though Microsoft has implied it might correct some actions should the software become damaged. Since software deployment offers are only displayed upon logon or reboot (otherwise known as foreground policy processing), in my testing, this setting seems not to have any outward effect.

Users can still opt to download software over slow links, even if the "Allow Processing Across a Slow Network Connection" is selected. See the Software Installation settings described in detail in Chapter 11.

Folder Redirection Policy Processing

Once enabled, this policy setting has two potential options:

Allow Processing Across a Slow Network Connection   Recall that the Folder Redirection policy is changed only at logon time. Chances are you won't want dialed-in users to experience that new change. Rather, you'll want to wait until they are on your LAN. If you want to torture your users and allow them to accept the changed policy anyway, use this setting to change this behavior.

Process Even If the Group Policy Objects Have Not Changed   I cannot find any difference if this setting is selected or not, though Microsoft has implied it might correct some folder-redirections woes should the user name get renamed.

Folder Redirection settings are discussed in detail in Chapter 9.

Scripts Policy Processing

Once enabled, this policy setting has three potential options:

Allow Processing Across a Slow Network Connection   Recall that, by default, new or changed startup, shutdown, logon, and logoff scripts are not downloaded over slow networks. Change this to allow the download over slow links. The actual running of the scripts is a different process, as discussed earlier in the "Processing and Running Scripts Over Slow Links" sidebar.

Do Not Apply During Periodic Background Processing   This option will not allow the newest script instructions to be downloaded. See the sidebar "Processing and Running Scripts Over Slow Links" earlier in the chapter.

Process Even If the GPOs Have Not Changed   This option will allow the newest script instructions to be downloaded even if the GPOs have not changed. See the sidebar "Processing and Running Scripts Over Slow Links."

Security Policy Processing

Once enabled, this policy setting has two potential options:

Do Not Apply During Periodic Background Processing   Recall that the security settings are refreshed on the machines every 16 hours, whether they need it or not. Checking this option will turn off the check every 16 hours. It is recommended to leave this as is. However, you might want to consider enabling this setting for servers with high numbers of transactions that require all the processing power they can muster.

Process Even If the GPOs Have Not Changed   Recall that after 16 hours, this policy category is always refreshed. With this option enabled, the security policy will be reprocessed during *every* refresh cycle.

IP Security Policy Processing

Once enabled, this policy setting has three potential options:

Allow Processing Across a Slow Network Connection   When selected, this setting does nothing. IP Security settings are always downloaded, regardless of whether the computer is connected over a slow network. So, you might be asking yourself, what happens when you select this check box, which is shown in Figure 3.3? Answer: nothing—it's a bug in the interface. To repeat: IP Security is always processed, regardless of the link speed.

> IPsec policies act slightly different from other policy setting categories. IPsec policy settings are not additive. For IP Security, the last applied policy wins.

Do Not Apply During Periodic Background Processing   If this option is selected, the latest IP Security settings in Active Directory GPOs will not be downloaded or applied during the background refresh.

Process Even If the Group Policy Objects Have Not Changed   If this option is selected, it updates and reapplies the policy settings in this category even if the underlying GPO has not changed. Recall that this type of processing is meant to clean up should a user or an administrator have nefariously gone around our backs and modified a local setting.

FIGURE 3.3   The "Allow processing across a slow network connection" setting is not used for IP Security or EFS settings (all versions of Windows).

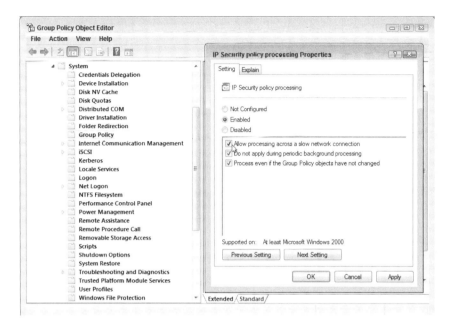

EFS Recovery Policy Processing

Once enabled, this policy setting has three potential options:

Allow Processing Across a Slow Network Connection   When this option is selected, it does nothing. EFS recovery settings are always downloaded, regardless of whether the computer is connected over a slow network.

Like IP Security, the EFS recovery settings are always downloaded—even over slow networks. Once again, this is the same bug as shown in Figure 3.3 earlier in this chapter. To repeat, EFS recovery policy is always processed, regardless of link speed.

   EFS recovery policies act slightly different from other policy setting categories. EFS recovery policies are not additive; the last applied policy wins.

Do Not Apply During Periodic Background Processing   If this option is selected, the latest EFS recovery settings in Active Directory GPOs are not downloaded or applied during the background refresh.

Process Even If the Group Policy Objects Have Not Changed   If this option is selected, it updates and reapplies the policy settings in this category even if the underlying GPO has not changed. Recall that this type of processing is meant to clean up should a user or an administrator have nefariously gone around our backs and modified a local setting.

Wireless Policy Processing

If this policy setting is enabled, it has three potential options:

Allow Processing Across a Slow Network Connection   Check this option to allow the latest wireless policy settings to download when the user is logging on over slow links. Enabling this could cause your users to experience a longer logon time

Do Not Apply During Periodic Background Processing   If this option is selected, the latest wireless policy settings will not be downloaded or applied during the background refresh.

Process Even If the Group Policy Objects Have Not Changed   If this option is selected, it updates and reapplies the policy settings in this category even if the underlying GPO has not changed. Recall that this type of processing is meant to clean up should a user or an administrator have nefariously gone around our backs and modified a local setting.

This policy setting is valid only when applied to Windows Vista and Windows XP workstations and Windows 2003 servers (and presumably, Windows Server Longhorn).

Wired Policy Processing

If this policy setting is enabled, it has three potential options:

Allow Processing Across a Slow Network Connection   Check this option to allow the latest wired policy settings to download when the user is logging on over slow links. Enabling this could cause your users to experience a longer logon time.

Do Not Apply During Periodic Background Processing   If this option is selected, the latest wired policy settings will not be downloaded or applied during the background refresh.

Process Even If the Group Policy Objects Have Not Changed   If this option is selected, it updates and reapplies the policy settings in this category even if the underlying GPO has not changed. Recall that this type of processing is meant to clean up should a user or an administrator have nefariously gone around our backs and modified a local setting.

This policy setting is valid only when applied to Windows Vista (and presumably, Windows Server Longhorn).

Disk Quota Policy Processing

If this policy setting is enabled, it has three potential options:

Allow Processing Across a Slow Network Connection   Check this option to allow the latest disk quota policy settings to download and apply when the user logs on over slow links. Enabling this could cause your users to experience a longer logon time.

Do Not Apply During Periodic Background Processing   If this option is selected, the latest disk quota policy settings will not be downloaded or applied during the background refresh.

Process Even If the Group Policy Objects Have Not Changed   If selected, this option updates and reapplies the policy settings in this category even if the underlying GPO has not changed. Recall that this type of processing is meant to clean up should a user or an administrator have nefariously gone around our backs and modified a local setting.

Disk quotas and their corresponding Group Policy settings are discussed in detail in Chapter 9.

Always Use Local ADM Files for Group Policy Object Editor

 This policy is valid only when applied to Windows 2003 servers and Windows Vista management stations. This is strange, as you might expect it to affect Windows XP management stations as well. But it doesn't. It only affects Windows Server 2003 and Vista management stations.

ADM files are the underlying language that creates policy settings in pre-Windows Vista versions. I'll talk more about ADM files and how to best use them in Chapter 5. However, for reference, if a computer is affected by this policy setting, the Group Policy Object Editor attempts to show the text within the ADM files from your local `%windir%\inf` directory (usually `c:\windows\inf`). If the ADM file is different on the Domain Controller than on your local `c:\windows\inf` directory, you could end up seeing different settings and Explaintext than are really inside the Domain Controller.

Indeed, if this policy is enabled, you might now see totally different policy settings than were originally placed in the GPO. However, you might want to enable this policy setting if you know that you will always be using one specific management station as described in Chapter 5. Stay tuned for Chapter 5 to see how to use this function.

Turn off Local Group Policy Objects Processing

If a Windows Vista computer is affected by this policy setting, then whatever is set within the local GPOs is ignored.

This can be useful if a machine is originally used in a workgroup (nondomain joined environment) and then it's joined to the domain. In that case, you might want to ensure that no user has any lingering policy settings that will specifically affect them. Hence, your desire would be to control everything from Active Directory and not anything from the local level.

Of course, this policy only works when being delivered from Active Directory (not when it's set locally).

This policy only affects Windows Vista machines (and presumably, Windows Server Longhorn machines).

Startup Policy Processing Wait Time

 This policy only affects Windows Vista machines (and presumably, Windows Server Longhorn machines).

This policy setting helps with timeouts when processing Group Policy. The policy setting only exists for Windows Vista (and presumably, Windows Server Longhorn machines), however, the facility to control these timeouts exists in other operating systems (like Windows XP/SP2 with a Registry hack).

Check out KB article 840669 (found here: `http://tinyurl.com/88tbo`) if you want to implement this setting for Windows XP/SP2 and earlier machines.

Group Policy Loopback Processing

As you know, the normal course of Group Policy scope is local computer, site, domain, and then each nested OU. But sometimes it's necessary to deviate from the normal routine. For instance, you might want all users, whoever they are, to be able to walk up and log on to a specific machine and get the same User node settings. For example, this can be handy in public computing environments such as libraries, nurses' stations, kiosks, and manufacturing and production assembly environments. This is also critically necessary for terminal server environments, as discussed in the "Group Policy Loopback—Replace Mode for Terminal Services" section later in this chapter.

Wouldn't it be keen if you could round up all the special computers on which users need the same settings for an OU and force them to use these settings? Whoever logs on to those computers would get the same Internet Explorer settings (such as a special proxy), logon scripts, or certain Control Panel restrictions—just for those workstations.

Reviewing Normal Group Policy Processing

Recall that sometimes computers and users can each be relegated into different OUs. Indeed, a user from any other portion of the domain, say the Domain Administrator (or anyone else), could log on to VISTA1 located under the **Human Resources Computers** OU. When this happens (for example, the computer and user accounts affected by GPOs are located in different processing locations), the normal behavior is to process the computer GPOs based on the normal hierarchy and then process the user GPOs based on the normal hierarchy. This is true just by the rules of time: computers start up, their GPOs are processed, users log on, and their GPOs are processed.

 Even when Windows Vista or Windows XP's default of "Fast Boot" is turned off, that's generally the way things happen.

So, if the Domain Administrator were to sit down at the VISTA1 machine in the **Human Resources Computers** OU, the normal course of events would apply the policy settings in the Computers node from the Default-First-Site, then the Corp.com domain, and then, finally, the **Human Resources Computers** OU. Next, the policy settings in GPOs linked to the user account would apply; first from the Default-First-Site and then only from the Corp.com domain (as the administrator account is not sitting under any OU in our examples).

With Group Policy Loopback processing, the rules change. There are two Group Policy Loopback modes: Merge and Replace. In both, the computer is tricked into forgetting that it's really a computer. It temporarily puts on a hat that says, "I'm a user," and processes the site, domain, and organizational unit GPOs as if it were a user. Kooky, huh? Let's take a look at the Merge and Replace modes.

Group Policy Loopback—Merge Mode

When computers are subject to Group Policy Loopback—Merge mode, GPOs process in the normal way at startup (and at background refresh time): Computer node for site, for domain, and then for each nested OU. The user then logs on, and policy settings meant for that user are applied in the normal way: all GPOs are processed from the site, the domain, and then each nested OU.

But when computers are affected by Group Policy Loopback—Merge mode, the system determines where the computer account is and applies another round of User node settings—those contained in all GPOs that lead to that computer (yes, User node settings). This means that the logged-on user gets whacked with two different sets of User node policy settings. Here's the timeline:

- The computer starts up and gets the appropriate Computer node policy settings.
- The user logs on and gets the appropriate User node policy settings.
- The computer then puts on a hat that says, "I'm a user." Then all *User* node policy settings apply to the *computer*. Again, this happens because the computer is wearing the "I'm a user" hat.

The net result is that the user settings from the user's account and the user settings from the computer (which temporarily thinks it's a user) are on par and equal to each other; neither is more important than the other, except when they overlap. In that case, the computer settings win, as usual.

The Group Policy Loopback—Merge mode is rarely used unless you need to modify a property in the user profile, but do it per computer.

Group Policy Loopback—Replace Mode

When computers are subject to Group Policy Loopback—Replace mode, Group Policy processes in the normal way at startup (and at background refresh time): Computer node for site, domain, and then each nested OU. The user then logs on, and GPOs meant for the user are totally ignored down the food chain for the logged-on user. Instead, the computer puts on an "I'm a user" hat, and the system determines where the computer account is but applies the User node settings contained in all GPOs that lead to that computer. Therefore, you change the balance of power so all users are forced to heed the User settings based on what is geared for the computer. Confused? Let's generate an example to "unconfuse" you.

By and large, Group Policy Loopback—Replace mode is more useful than Merge mode and works well in public computing environments such as labs, kiosk, classrooms, training machines, libraries, and so on. So let's work though an example to solidify our understanding of Replace mode. In this example, we'll perform a variety of steps.

- Create a new OU called **Public Kiosk**.
- Move a Windows Vista machine into the **Public Kiosk** OU.
- Create a new GPO for the **Public Kiosk** OU that performs two functions:
  - Disables the Display Properties dialog box.
  - Performs Group Policy Loopback—Replace mode processing so that all users logging on to the computers in the **Public Kiosk** OU will be unable to use the Display Properties dialog box.

For our examples, we'll pretend to have another machine called Vista2. This is a new machine, just for this set of examples. It is not listed in the "Getting Ready to Use this Book" section in Chapter 1.

Setting All Who Log on to a Specific Computer to Use a Specific Printer

You might want to use the Group Policy Loopback—Merge mode to create a printer and apply it to anyone who uses a particular machine. For instance, you might want anyone who logs on to a machine on the fourth floor to automatically connect to the printer on the fourth floor. One way to do this is to run around to every machine on the fourth floor, log on as the user, and manually connect to the printer on the fourth floor.

If you've ever attempted this feat, you might have also tried to create a Group Policy startup script for a computer to try to connect everyone to a printer on the network; but it won't work. There is no user environment in which to house this newly created printer. So you have a paradox: how do you run a computer startup script for every user who sits down at a machine but run this startup script after the user is logged on? Group Policy Loopback—Merge mode comes to the rescue.

In both loopback processing modes, the computer doesn't think it's a computer. It temporarily puts on a user hat and processes the site, domain, and organizational unit GPOs as if it were a user.

With that in mind, you'll need to do several things:

1. Create a VB script that connects you to the printer you want. (Later in this sidebar, you'll see an example, ASSIGNHP4.VBS.)

2. Create an OU, say "4th Floor Computers," and move the computers on the fourth floor into it.

3. Create a new GPO on that OU and name it, say, "All computers get HPLJ4 Printer."

4. Drill down into the new GPO to Computer Configuration ➤ Administrative Templates ➤ System ➤ Group Policy ➤ User Group Policy Loopback Processing mode, and specify that it be in Merge mode.

5. Drill down into User Configuration ➤ Windows ➤ Scripts ➤ Logon. Click "Add" to add a new file, click "Browse" to open the File Requester, copy the ASSIGNHP4.VBS script, and add it to the list to run.

Remember, in Loopback Processing mode, the computer thinks it's a user, so use User/Logon scripts, not Computer/Startup script.

Now, whenever you log on as any user to a computer in the 4th Floor Computers OU, the GPOs meant for the user will be evaluated and run. The computer will then put on a user hat and run its own logon script, and you will get the printer assigned for every user on a computer.

Here is the ASSIGNHP4.VBS vbscript you can use for the preceding example:

```
Set wshNetwork = CreateObject("WScript.Network")


    PrinterPath = "\\server1\HPLJ4"
    PrinterDriver = "HP LaserJet 4"
    WshNetwork.AddwindowsPrinterConnection PrinterPath, PrinterDriver
    WshNetwork.SetDefaultPrinter "\\server1\HPLJ4"
    Wscript.Echo "Default Printer Created"
```

Thanks to Richard Zimmerman of ABC Computers for the inspiration for this tip. Before you go implementing this tip, be sure to read in Chapter 12 where we'll show you how to use ordinary Group Policy to get the same job accomplished. That is, we'll show you how to zap printers down to specific machines in a more efficient way. However, I'm leaving this example here because it's a firm demonstration, in general, of what Merge mode does.

Creating a New OU

To create a new OU called **Public Kiosk,** follow these steps:

1. Log on to the Domain Controller WINDC01 as Domain Administrator.

2. Choose Start ➤ Programs ➤ Administrative Tools and select Active Directory Users And Computers.

3. Right-click the domain name, and choose New ➤ Organizational Unit. Enter **Public Kiosk** as the name in the "New Object – New Organizational Unit" dialog box.

You are creating this new OU on the same level as **Human Resources**. Do not create this new OU underneath Human Resources.

Moving a Client into the Public Kiosk OU

In this case, we'll move a different computer, say VISTA2, into the **Public Kiosk** OU. Follow these steps:

1. In Active Directory Users And Computers, right-click the domain and choose Find to open the "Find Users, Contacts and Groups" dialog box.

2. In the Find drop-down, select Computers. In the Name field, type **VISTA2** (or the name of some other computer) to find the computer account of the same name. Once you've found it, right-click the account, and choose Move. Move the account to the **Public Kiosk** OU.

    Repeat these steps for all other computers you want to move to the **Public Kiosk** OU.

Creating a Group Policy Object with Group Policy Loopback—Replace Mode

We want the Display Properties dialog box disabled for all users who log on to VISTA2. To do this, we need to set two policy settings within a single GPO: **Remove Display in Control Panel** and **User Group Policy Loopback Processing Mode**. Follow these steps using the GPMC:

1. Right-click the **Public Kiosk** OU, and choose "Create a GPO in this domain, and Link it here."

2. In the "New GPO" dialog box, name the GPO something descriptive, such as "No Display Setting – Loopback Replace."

3. Highlight the GPO and click Edit to open the Group Policy Object Editor.

4. To hide the Settings tab, drill down to User Configuration ➢ Administrative Templates ➢ Control Panel ➢ Display and double-click the **Remove Display in Control Panel** policy setting. Change the policy setting from "Not Configured" to "Enabled," and click OK.

5. To enable loopback processing, drill down to Computer Configuration ➢ Administrative Templates ➢ System ➢ Group Policy and double-click the **User Group Policy Loopback Processing Mode** policy setting. Change the setting from "Not Configured" to "Enabled," select "Replace" from the drop-down box, as shown in Figure 3.4, and click OK.

6. Close the Group Policy Object Editor.

Verifying That Group Policy Loopback—Replace Mode Is Working

You'll want to log on to VISTA2, but you'll need to restart it because loopback processing doesn't seem to ever take effect until a reboot occurs. Since we're using Loopback Policy processing in Replace mode, you can choose any user you have defined—a mere mortal or even the administrator of the domain.

Right-click over the Desktop and select Personalize and note that no one can access the Display settings, as shown in Figure 3.5.

Group Policy Loopback—Replace Mode policy processing is powerful but really is only useful for specialty machines. Additionally, you'll need to use it sparingly, because loopback processing is a bit more CPU intensive for the client and servers and quite difficult to troubleshoot should things go wrong.

FIGURE 3.4 Choose the Loopback Processing mode desired, in this case, "Replace."

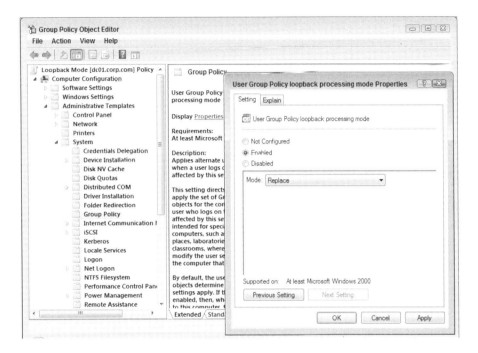

FIGURE 3.5 With Group Policy Loopback—Replace Mode processing enabled, all users are affected by a computer's setting.

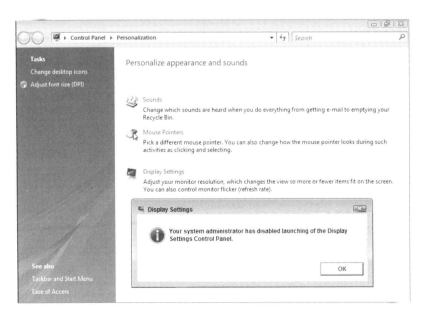

Group Policy Loopback—Replace Mode for Terminal Services

Group Policy Loopback—Replace mode has one other major use: Terminal Services. If you have lots of servers and lots of users logging on to them, chances are you want everyone who logs on to your Terminal Services machines to have precisely the same settings, regardless of who they are.

The process of establishing these settings is straightforward:

- Create an OU for your Terminal Services computers and give it an appropriate name, such as **Terminal Services Computers** OU.

- Set Loopback Replace mode to apply to that OU.

- Stuff your Terminal Services computer objects into the OU and reboot them.

Now any user policy settings within GPOs set upon the Terminal Services computers OU and everyone logging on to the Terminal Services computers will get the exact same settings.

Windows 2000 servers and Windows 2003 Terminal Services respond just fine to Loopback Replace mode. So be sure to stuff your Windows 2000 Terminal Services computer objects into your designated OU too and then manually configure the policy settings on those computers as desired.

> As an administrator, you might want to log on to Terminal Services machines, but you don't want the same settings as everyone else. To configure this, simply use the techniques found in Chapter 2, and filter the GPO containing the Loopback policy for, say, Domain Administrators.

Yet Another Practical Use for Group Policy Loopback—Replace Mode

I don't know about you, but I just hate it when I walk up to a server and log on. Usually, I have no idea what the server's name, function, IP address, and so on could possibly be. In the NT 4 days, I used the following trick:

1. Fire up Windows Paint.

2. Create a .bmp file that detailed the name, function, and IP address and save it as, say, c:\winnt\background.bmp.

3. Modify the .default user profile so that when no one was logged on at the console, the .bmp file was displayed. To do this, open the Registry of the local server and change HKEY_USERS\.DEFAULT\Control Panel\Desktop\Wallpaper to path of c:\winnt\background.bmp.

But there was one major problem—as soon as I logged on to the server, the background went away (because my local profile took over), and 20 seconds later, I forgot what the machine's name, function, and IP address were. With Windows 2003 and the Group Policy Loopback—Replace Mode policy, I've discovered a cool trick; you can now force the same background .bmp for every user who physically logs on to any given machine.

The idea is simple:

- Create the `.bmp` file as explained earlier, and store it once again, locally, as `c:\windows\background.bmp`.

- Create a new GPO on the Domain Controllers OU or on your own OU for your servers. Call the policy "Forced Background Wallpaper—Loopback Replace."

- Modify the User node of the policy as follows:

1. Drill down through User Configuration ➤ Administrative Templates ➤ Desktop ➤ Active Desktop ➤ **Enable Active Desktop**, and set "Enabled."

2. Drill down through User Configuration ➤ Administrative Templates ➤ Desktop ➤ Active Desktop ➤ **Desktop Wallpaper**, and set "Enabled." Set the wallpaper name to `c:\windows\background.bmp`.

3. Drill down through User Node ➤ Administrative Templates ➤ Desktop ➤ Active Desktop ➤ **Allow Only Bitmapped Wallpaper**, and set "Enabled."

4. To modify the Computer node of the policy, drill down through Computer Configuration ➤ Administrative Templates ➤ System ➤ Group Policy ➤ and enable **User Group Policy Loopback Processing Mode**. Set to Loopback—Replace.

   Now, whenever anyone logs on to that server, they will get the exact same background `.bmp`! This is still true even if they usually get a background dictated via some other Group Policy for their own personal account!

   There is one more accompanying tip to seal the deal. If you've enabled Terminal Services Administration mode, by default you cannot see the wallpaper when coming in over Terminal Services. Change the default behavior of Terminal Services by using the Terminal Services Configuration application, right-clicking the RDP protocol, and selecting the Environment tab. Choose to view the wallpaper by deselecting the "Disable the Wallpaper" check box.

   A similar ability is available from the BGINFO tool, which you can download from Microsoft's Sysinternals site at `http://tinyurl.com/u6yy2`. And it's dynamic, so if something changes on the server, the background changes with it. However, this tip in here is a useful example of how to use the Group Policy Loopback—Replace mode.

Additional Terminal Services Tips

As a little side note, additionally, if your Terminal Services are Windows Server 2003, at your disposal is an arsenal of policy settings designed to manage Windows 2003 Terminal Services. You'll find two sets of Terminal Services policy settings for Windows 2003: one for users and one for computers:

- To manipulate Terminal Services computers, drill down through Computer Configuration ➤ Administrative Templates ➤ Windows Components ➤ Terminal Services.

- To manipulate Terminal Services clients, drill down through User Configuration ➢ Administrative Templates ➢ Windows Components ➢ Terminal Services.

Including information on how best to use the policy settings that configure Windows 2003 Terminal Services is beyond the scope of this book. To that end, I recommend Christa Anderson's *Windows IT Pro Magazine* article "Using GPOs to Configure Terminal Services." You can find it at www.winnetmag.com. InstantDoc ID: 38284.

One final parting tip regarding Terminal Services: Microsoft has a nice doc, which has a lot of tips and tricks for Terminal Services admins vis a vis Group Policy. As I write this, the document isn't publicly available. But by the time you read this, you should be able to Google for, and get the document named, "Step-by-Step Guide for Configuring Group Policy for Terminal Services."

Group Policy with Cross-Forest Trusts

Windows 2003 domains bring a new trust type to the table, a forest trust (also known as a cross-forest trust). The idea is that if you have multiple, unrelated forests, you can join their root domains with one single trust; then, any time new domains pop up in either forest, there is an automatically implied trust relationship.

To do this requires a large commitment from all parties involved. All domains must be in Windows 2003 Functional mode, and all forests must be in Windows 2003 Functional mode. Only then is it possible to create cross-forest trusts via the Active Directory Domains and Trusts utility. For an example of an organization that might use this, see Figure 3.6.

In this example, all domains trust all other domains via the cross-forest trust. Indeed, a user with an account housed in bigu.edu, say, Sol Rosenberg, could sit down at a computer in either Corp.com or Widgets.corp.com, and log on to his user account, which is maintained in bigu.edu.

When Sol (srosenberg) from bigu.edu logs on to any computer in domains below Corp.com (that is, Widgets.corp.com), the logon screen will not present BIGU as an option. To log on, Sol will need to type **srosenberg@bigu.edu** as his logon id along with his password. This is one of the limitations of cross-forest trusts.

What Happens When Logging on to Different Clients Across a Cross-Forest Trust?

So what happens when Sol from bigu.edu has access to various computer types in the Corp.com forest? Let's find out.

FIGURE 3.6   Here's one example of how a cross-forest trust can be used.

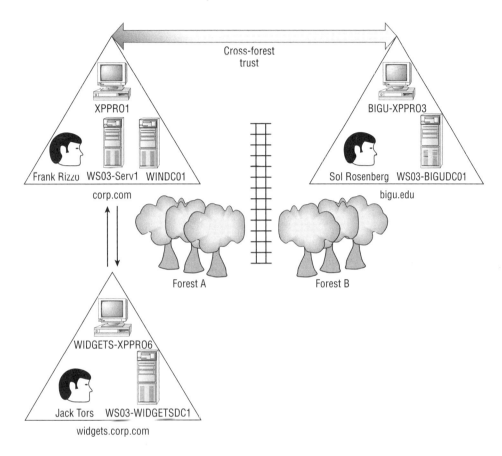

Logging on to Windows XP (with no Service Pack or with SP1) Across a Cross-Forest Trust

For users logging on to Windows XP machines in Windows 2003 domains, Group Policy across forests acts as if it were one big forest. For instance, if Sol Rosenberg logs into WIDGETS-XPPRO6 at Widgets.corp.com or VISTA1 at Corp.com, Sol would get the GPOs that affect his user account and the user policy settings that affect him. The Windows XP computer Sol uses will get the GPOs meant for it. (The computer would embrace the policy settings based on the site, the domain, and the OU it's in.)

Makes sense. Take a deep breath, and then read the next section.

What about Windows XP's SP2 or Windows Vista? They're different, so keep reading.

Logging on to a Windows 2003 Server Across a Cross-Forest Trust

Here's where things get weird, so try to stay with me. Imagine that Sol Rosenberg in bigu.edu is also the SQL database administrator for a server named WS03-Serv1 over in Corp.com in the **Human Resources SQL-Servers** OU. From time to time, Sol gets in his car and travels from the BigU campus over to the WS03-Serv1 computer sitting at the Corp.com headquarters. He sits down, logs on locally to the console (where he's been granted access), and he doesn't get the GPOs meant for him (and therefore doesn't get his own policy settings).

Instead the server processes GPOs as if it was using Group Policy Loopback Processing mode—Replace mode. What does this mean?

- The GPOs that would normally apply to Sol's user account in bigu.edu are ignored by the Windows 2003 server.

- The computer puts on an "I'm a user" hat and says, "Give me the GPOs that would apply to me if I were a user."

So, in our example, we can see that when Sol from bigu.edu logs on to WS03-Serv1, his policy settings are ignored. The computer then looks at the GPOs that would apply to users in the **Human Resources SQL-Servers** OU (where the WS03-Serv1 account resides).

Since no GPOs linked to the **Human Resources SQL-Servers** OU contain policy settings geared for users, Sol gets no policy settings applied.

After logging on, you can check out the Application Event Log and see Event ID 1109, which states that Sol is "from a different forest logged onto this machine. Cross Forest Group Policy processing is disabled and loopback processing has been enforced in this forest for this user account."

 For your own testing and to solidify this concept, you might wish, just for now, to link an existing GPO (which has user policy settings) to the **Human Resources Computers** OU. For instance, link the "Hide Desktop Tab" GPO to the **Human Resources Computers** OU, then log back on as Sol. Sol's user account will be affected by the GPO with the policy setting.

Logging on to Windows 2000 Across a Cross-Forest Trust

Logging on to a Windows 2000 system with SP4 across the trust—either Server or Professional—is just like logging on to Windows 2003 Server. That is, the GPOs that affect the user are ignored, and the computer processes Group Policy Loopback—Replace mode.

Logging on to a Windows 2000 system that doesn't have SP4 (say, SP3 and earlier) across the trust—either Server or Professional—will not perform loopback. The user will get the expected user settings, and the computer will get the expected computer settings.

Logging on to Windows Vista or Windows XP/SP2 Across a Cross-Forest Trust

Logging on to Windows Vista or Windows XP with SP2 installed across the trust is just like logging on to Windows 2003 Server (or Windows 2000 Professional with SP4). That is, GPOs that would normally affect users are ignored, and the computer processes Group Policy Loopback—Replace mode. This might drive system administrators and CIO managers alike nuts.

Imagine that you are halfway through your Windows XP rollout, and then you add Windows XP plus SP2 to the mix. Users will definitely get different settings when logging on to these different machines. So, if things start going haywire, know what the score is by using the chart in the "Cross-Forest Trust Client Matrix" section later in this chapter.

The Big Question: Why Loopback Across Cross-Forest Trusts?

At this point, you're likely scratching your head in disbelief. Why would Sol not get the GPOs that should affect him? The answer is simple: if Sol were assigned software (see Chapter 10), logon scripts, or other potentially dangerous settings, our machine's stability could be affected.

This mechanism protects our systems from stuff that we might not want to happen to it. Since we're not administrating Sol, we don't know what potential harm Sol's settings might do. Then, we need to examine what might happen if the folks at Microsoft decided to do things differently, say, have no GPOs affect Sol when he uses our Corp.com machines. That might be really bad too, because then Sol would have free reign to do whatever he wanted.

So what does Loopback buy us? Loopback makes us think about what happens when users from afar use our systems. Even though, as you know, user policy settings don't affect computers, you can start to design your OUs and GPOs for this occasion. That is, if you set up user policy settings in OUs that just contain servers, and someone in a foreign domain logs on, they'll at least get the user policy settings you intend—not what their administrator wanted.

Strange? Yes, but it works, and this becomes strangely more logical the more you think about it.

What about workstation machines? This is a less-critical problem on workstation machines, because, well, it's just a workstation. If someone is assigned an application (see Chapter 10) that maybe does evil stuff, at least it's only affecting a workstation, not a server that a whole team might have access to.

I have more advice on how to manage this in the "Disabling Loopback Processing When Using Cross-Forest Trusts" section later in this chapter.

Event ID 1109 will be generated in the Application Event log stating that a user is "...from a different forest."

Microsoft has additional documentation about times when you might not get GPOs applied on Windows 2000 systems. See KB article 823862 for more information.

Disabling Loopback Processing When Using Cross-Forest Trusts

If you do not want the default behavior, which is that Loopback Replace processing is enabled for the computer, you can set a specific Group Policy to apply to the computers you want to be normal again. Here are my recommendations:

- Keep the default behavior for all servers: Windows 2000 Server + SP4 and Windows 2003 Server. You want them to process in Group Policy Loopback—Replace mode.

- Return the "normal" behavior for all workstations: Windows Vista, Windows 2000 + SP4, and Windows XP + SP2. Windows 2000 + SP3 (and earlier) and Windows XP + SP1 (and no service pack) are already at the "normal" behavior. You want them to process GPOs using regular processing rules.

To do this, you need to locate the **Allow Cross-Forest User Policy and Roaming User Profiles** policy setting. Drill down through Computer Configuration ➤ Administrative Templates ➤ System ➤ Group Policy. Note that the policy setting says "At least Windows Server 2003" but it will affect Windows XP/SP2 machines as well.

To set it up, follow these steps:

1. Create a new GPO at the domain level, say, "No Loopback for Cross-Forest." Enable the policy setting named **Allow Cross-Forest User Policy and Roaming User Profiles**. This will initially affect all computers, including servers.

   However, I suggest that you filter out your server machines so that they keep the default loopback behavior. I suggest you do this as follows:

2. Create a security group called "AllMyServers."

3. Add all the Windows 2000 and Windows 2003 servers (regardless of service pack) in the domain to the AllMyServers group.

4. Deny the AllMyServers group the ability to process this new GPO.

> In a pure Windows 2003, Windows XP, and Windows Vista environment (that is, no Windows 2000 clients), you can optionally set up a WMI filter to apply the policy just to the servers. See Chapter 10 for information about WMI filters.

This will maintain the loopback behavior for servers but go back to normal processing for absolutely all workstations in the domain. This way your servers are protected from other users in trusted forests from potentially doing bad stuff to your servers. But those same users are free to have normal processing on all your workstations.

> Be careful when using the "Deny" attribute to deny a group the ability to apply Group Policy. The GPMC will not show you that you are passing over specific users or computers from applying the GPO in the Settings tab. I discussed this earlier in Chapter 2.

Cross-Forest Trust Client Matrix

If your head is spinning about what happens to users when they use a specific client across a cross-forest trust, Table 3.1 is for you. Additionally, this table shows which client systems can be set back to normal processing by enabling the **Allow Cross-Forest User Policy and Roaming User Profiles** policy setting.

TABLE 3.1   Cross-Forest Trust Client Matrix

Client	What Happens When a User Logs on Across the Cross-Forest Trust	Can be Changed by the "Allow Cross-Forest User Policy and Roaming User Profiles" Policy Setting
Windows 2000 Server or Professional, with no service pack, SP1, SP2, or SP3	User gets user settings. Computer gets computer settings.	No
Windows 2000 Server or Professional, with SP4	User settings are ignored. Computer gets settings as if it were a user (that is Group Policy Loopback—Replace mode)	Yes
Windows XP with no service pack or SP1	User gets user settings. Computer gets computer settings.	No
Windows XP with SP2	User settings are ignored. Computer gets settings as if it were a user (that is, Group Policy Loopback—Replace mode)	Yes
Windows 2003 Server with or without any service pack	User settings are ignored. Computer gets settings as if it were a user (that is, Group Policy Loopback—Replace mode)	Yes
Windows Vista	User settings are ignored. Computer gets settings as if it were a user (that is, Group Policy Loopback—Replace mode)	Yes

Understanding Cross-Forest Trust Permissions

Windows 2003 cross-forest trusts have two modes: Forest-wide Authentication and Selective Authentication, as shown in Figure 3.7. To view the screen shown in Figure 3.7, open Active Directory Domains and Trusts, locate the properties of the trust, click the Authentication tab.

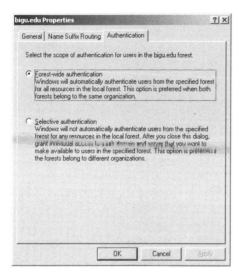

In a Windows 2003 Active Directory domain, Full Authentication mode permits Group Policy across forests to act as if it were one big forest. That is, GPOs are processed according to Table 3.1.

We already know that Sol is the SQL database administrator over at Corp.com, and we saw what happened when he logged on to the Windows 2003 member server WS03-Serv1. Twice a week, however, Sol works at Widgets.corp.com on the WIDGETS-XPPRO3 for some CAD work. Then, the unthinkable happens.

An attack originating at bigu.edu upon Corp.com's computers gets the two Domain Administrators in a heated battle. The Corp.com Domain Administrator decides he wants to prevent attacks from bigu.edu, so he enables "Selective Authentication." Now no one from bigu.edu can log on to any of the machines in Corp.com or Widgets.corp.com. Ergo, Sol will not be able to log on to either his WS03-Serv1 Windows 2003 member server in Corp.com or to his WIDGETS-XPPRO3 machine in Widgets.corp.com. Sol needs the "Allowed to Authenticate" right on the computer objects he will use. In this example, you can see what is done for WIDGETS-XPPRO3, as shown in Figure 3.8.

Additional computers in Corp.com and Widgets.corp.com need these explicit rights if anyone else from bigu.edu is going to use them. Then, Group Policy will process as described earlier and summarized in Table 3.1.

See Chapter 7 for how profiles react in conjunction with cross-forest trusts.

FIGURE 3.8   You need to specifically grant the "Allowed to Authenticate" right in order for Sol to use this machine.

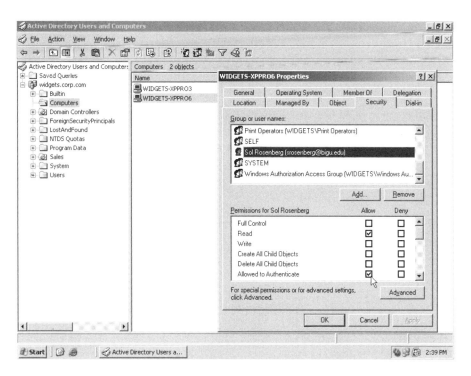

Intermixing Group Policy and NT 4 System Policy

I've already discussed how Group Policy cannot apply to Windows 9X or Windows NT clients. Group Policy applies only to Windows 2000 clients and newer. However, the opposite is not true. That is, NT 4 System Policy (whose filename is NTCONFIG.POL) is perfectly valid and accepted on Windows 2000 and newer. You might have an occasion to use both at the same time—typically if you're in the middle of an NT 4 to Active Directory migration. If this happens, it's likely you'll have both Active Directory Group Policy and legacy NT 4 System Policy on the same network.

If you're trying to migrate from NT to Active Directory, you basically have four major cases:

1. Both computer and user accounts in a Windows NT domain

2. A computer account in Windows NT and a user account in an Active Directory domain

3. A computer account in an Active Directory domain and a user account in Windows NT

4. Both computer and user accounts in Active Directory

You could, if you wanted, have an NT 4 System Policy (named `NTCONFIG.POL`) file in each and every domain—NT 4 or an Active Directory domain. Hopefully, you won't be taking your `NTCONFIG.POL` files with you when you go to Active Directory, but, if you do, you'll need to know how that calculates into the final RSoP. Additionally, it's important to remember that NT 4 System Policy "tattoos" the machines it touches, meaning that even if you're eventually going to phase out NT 4 System Policy, you'll need a battle plan to specifically reverse the settings in `NTCONFIG.POL` so that your clients can phase out the settings.

Let's briefly examine what will happen in each of these cases, which are illustrated in Figure 3.9.

Case 1: Both computer and user accounts are contained in the Windows NT domain.
When the computer starts up, it first applies any settings in the computer-side of the local GPO. Next, the user logs on to the NT 4 domain and obtains the user side settings from the `NTCONFIG.POL` file. If present, the user side of the local GPO applies after the `NTCONFIG.POL` settings. These settings are added cumulatively, except if there is a conflict. If there is a conflict, most often the `NTCONFIG.POL` settings win.

FIGURE 3.9   There are four main cases when dealing with NT 4 System Policy and "modern" clients (Windows 2000, Windows Server 2003, Windows XP, or Windows Vista) clients.

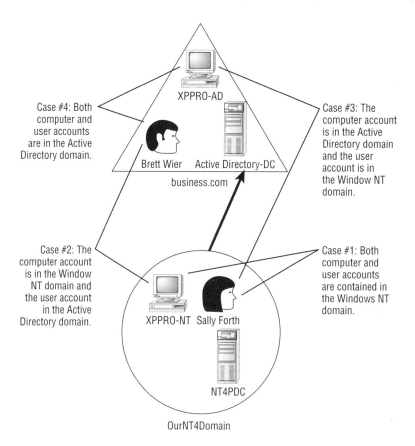

Case 2: The computer account is in the Windows NT domain, and the user account is in the Active Directory domain. When the computer starts up, it logs on to the NT 4 domain. If present, the computer side of the local GPO applies. When the user logs on to Active Directory, two things happen:

- The computer downloads and applies NTCONFIG.POL (from the NT 4 domain).
- The user processes GPOs normally. First, user-side local GPO settings apply, followed by the user-side Active Directory GPOs. As expected, these Active Directory GPO settings are added cumulatively to the local GPO settings, except if there is a conflict. If there is a conflict, the last written Group Policy setting wins. If there is any NTCONFIG.POL file in the domain where the user's account is located, that old System Policy is ignored for the user.

 In some circumstances, it appears that the local Windows 2000 Group Policy wins, such as when you set a background Desktop image. As usual, you'll want to test to make sure that what you want is what you get when you intermix NT 4 System Policy and local GPOs.

Case 3: The computer account is in an Active Directory domain, and the user account is in the Windows NT domain. When the computer starts up, it first applies any settings in the computer side of the local GPO. Then, after the computer logs on to Active Directory, it receives the computer-side GPOs from the site, domain, and OUs.

As expected, these Active Directory GPO settings are added cumulatively to the local GPO settings, except if there is a conflict. If there is a conflict, the last-written Group Policy setting wins. If there is an NTCONFIG.POL file in the domain where the computer's account is located, that old System Policy is ignored for the computer.

Upon logon, if present, the user side of the local GPO applies to the user. Then, the user downloads and applies user-side settings from the NTCONFIG.POL file on the NT domain. These settings are added cumulatively, except if there is a conflict. If there is a conflict, NTCONFIG.POL wins.

Case 4: Both computer and user accounts are in Active Directory. Most of this book is about this case. Both the computer and user apply local GPO settings first, followed by the GPOs from Active Directory: site, domain, and OUs. These Active Directory GPO settings append the local GPO settings, except if there is a conflict. If there is a conflict, the Active Directory GPO settings win over the local GPO settings. No System Policy (NTCONFIG.POL) is downloaded. However, clients that have been tattooed by NTCONFIG.POL will stay tattooed, and it's likely that at least some Registry entries will have to be manually scrubbed. Therefore, it's best to reverse the NTCONFIG.POL settings while you still can—before both the computer and the user accounts have been migrated. After the migration, neither the user nor the computer will read from the NTCONFIG.POL file.

Final Thoughts

Group Policy doesn't just pick and choose when it wants to apply. Rather, a specific set of rules is followed when it comes time to process. Understanding these rules is paramount in helping you pretroubleshoot Group Policy problems. Many other things can affect the Group Policy engine, including loopback policy processing and how users connect over slow links.

Group Policy processing with a cross-forest trust can be tricky because each operating system and service pack has its own way of doing things; but hopefully the text, examples, and Table 3.1 can help you with any problems.

Last, try to get away from any NT 4 System Policy. Remember that they tattoo and are difficult to fully scrub out of your environment.

Here are a few things to keep in mind:

Remember initial policy processing.   Windows 2000 and Windows 2003 machines process all GPOs when the computer starts up or when the user logs on. That is, by default, XP and Vista only performs initial policy processing when a user has never logged in on the machine before (or if the computer has just joined the domain).

Remember background refresh policy processing (member servers).   For Windows 2000, Windows 2003, Windows XP, and Windows Vista member machines, this happens some time after the user is logged on (usually 90 minutes or so).

Remember background refresh policy for Windows Vista and Windows XP.   By default, Windows Vista and Windows XP are unique and process GPOs *only* in the background (asynchronously). Some features, such as Software Distribution, Folder Redirection, and other functions take two reboots or logons to take effect. Advanced Folder Redirection takes three logons to take effect. This is because these special functions can be processed only in the foreground. You can turn off this feature as described earlier in this chapter.

Remember background refresh policy processing (Domain Controllers).   Windows 2000 and Windows 2003 Domain Controllers receive a background refresh every five minutes (after replication has occurred).

Security policy processing occurs every 16 hours.   For all operating systems, every 16 hours, only the security settings within all GPOs are reprocessed and applied, regardless of whether security settings have changed. This ensures that all security functions in all GPOs are reprocessed if someone has manually gone around the security on the system.

Leverage "Process Even If the Group Policy Objects Have Not Changed."   You can tell many other Group Policy categories (such as Administrative Templates) to also refresh at the background refresh interval. This will make those categories more secure and less susceptible to attack.

How Group Policy reacts in cross-domain scenarios depends on the operating system.
Refer to the "Cross-Forest Trust Client Matrix" section earlier in this chapter for information on how specific operating systems react during cross-forest trust scenarios.

Be careful and test when using NT 4 and Active Directory with Group Policy.   If you're still migrating from NT 4 to Windows 2000 or Windows 2003, you'll need to understand the reaction when user and/or computer accounts still have a foot in NT 4. With that in mind, test, test, test before you deploy.

Upgrading a Windows XP Machine to Windows Vista

It's not likely that you'll often do this, but, should you choose to do a mass-upgrade of machines (or even a one-off upgrade of a particular Windows XP machine to Windows Vista), you should know what happens. Don't worry, it's not much:

- Any local Group Policy settings are upgraded to the Windows Vista Layer 1 local GPO (see Chapter 1).

- Any special ADM template settings are retained (see Chapter 5).

- RSoP "calculation data" is expunged. However, it is recreated the first time the computer logs on to the domain and when each user logs on.

- If your Windows XP machine happened to have the downloadable version of the GPMC installed, it's removed. Remember, the GPMC is now part of Windows Vista, so that version is used instead. The GPMC preferences are retained, however.

- Even though a huge number of Windows XP settings are valid on Windows Vista, some settings could have a slightly different outcome when run on Windows Vista. To that end, all policy settings are regrabbed from Active Directory and applied as if the computer had just joined the domain and the user logged on for the first time

4

Troubleshooting Group Policy

Working with Group Policy isn't always a bed of roses. Sure, it's delightful when you can set up GPOs with their policy settings from upon high and have them reflected on your users' Desktops. However, when you make a Group Policy wish, a specific process occurs before that wish comes true. Indeed, the previous chapter discussed *when* Group Policy applies. Now you understand the general rules of the game and when they occur.

But what if the unexpected happens? Most specifically, it's difficult to determine *where* a policy setting comes from and *how* it's applied. Or, if Group Policy isn't working, *why* not, and *what* the heck is going on? Additionally, you're usually after *whom* to blame, but that's actually something that auditing (discussed in Chapter 6) can help with. Additionally, check out our information on third-party tools in the Appendix.

A user might call the Help Desk and loudly declare, "Things have just changed on my Desktop! I want them back the way they were!" Okay, sure, you want things better too. But a lot of variables are involved. First, there are the four levels: Local Group Policy (and potentially multiple local GPOs in Windows Vista), site, domain, and each nested OU (so perhaps even more levels). Then, to make matters worse, what if multiple administrators are making multiple and simultaneous Group Policy changes across your environment? Who knows who has enabled what Group Policy settings and how some user is getting Group Policy applied?

Additional factors are involved as well. For instance, if you have old-style NT 4 System Policy, things can be particularly complex. Or perhaps you have a Windows 2003 forest, with cross-forest trusts to another Windows 2003 forest, and users are logging in all over the place. Not to mention a whole litany of things that could possibly go wrong between the time you make your wish and the time the client is expected to honor that wish.

Here's a foretaste of what to expect while troubleshooting GPOs:

Disabled GPOs   If the GPO is disabled or half the GPO is disabled, you need to hunt it down.

Inheritance Troubles   Between local, site, domain, and multiple nested OUs, it can be a challenge to locate the GPO you need to fix.

GPO Precedence at a Given Level   With multiple GPOs linked to a specific level in Active Directory, you might have some extra hunting to do.

Special thanks to Darren Mar-Elia for his additional contributions to this chapter.

Permissions Problems   Ensuring that users and computers are in the correct site, domain, and OU is one battle; however, ensuring that they have the correct permissions to access GPOs is quite another.

Windows XP and Windows Vista Processing   Windows XP and Windows Vista change the way GPOs are processed. And cross-forest trusts can be somewhat confusing as well.

Replication Problems   The health of the GPO itself on Domain Controllers is important when hunting down policy settings that aren't applying.

Infrastructure Problems   Group Policy processing requires that all pieces of your infrastructure are healthy, including such seemingly unrelated pieces as DNS, the services running on the client and the ability to pass network protocols between clients and domain controllers. Additionally, healthy Active Directory design is where your Domain Controllers are all part of specific Active Directory sites (that is, don't create sites without Domain Controllers). Good Active Directory design equals good (consistent) Group Policy processing.

Loopback Policy Processing   Sometimes, by mistake, an administrator has enabled loopback policy processing for a computer (or multiple computers). When this happens, the user sees unexpected behavior, because the GPOs that would normally apply to him are suddenly out of the ordinary.

Slow Links   You've rolled out your RAS (Remote Access Service). Now how and when are your clients going to process GPOs?

These are just a few places where you might encounter trouble. Between various client types with different processing behavior, these problems and the occasional solar flare make things crazy. Troubleshooting can get complicated. Fast.

In this chapter, we'll first dive into *where* Group Policy "lives" to give you a better sense of what's going on. We'll then explore some techniques and tools that will enable you to get an even better view of *why* specific policies are being applied.

Under the Hood of Group Policy

As stated in Chapter 1, Group Policy scope really has four levels: Local Group Policy and then the three levels of Active Directory–based Group Policy—site, domain, and OU. When troubleshooting Group Policy, one approach is to first get a firm understanding of what's going on under the hood. As a kid, I took things apart all the time. My parents went mental when they came home and the dishwasher was in pieces all over the kitchen floor. It wasn't broken; I just wanted to know how it worked. If you're like me, this section is for you.

Inside Local Group Policy

Remember that a GPO is manipulated when someone walks up to the machine, runs the Local Group Policy Object Editor (GPEDIT.MSC), and makes a wish or three. Remember that in all versions of Windows prior to Vista, there was only one local GPO on a machine and that local GPOs affected everyone who logged on to that machine.

 Enterprise Admins, by default, do not have local administrator rights on individual client machines. Domain Admins, but not Enterprise Admins, have rights to LGPOs.

Where Local Group Policy Lives

Once wishes are made with GPEDIT.MSC and a Local Group Policy is modified, the Local Group Policy lives in two places. The first part is file based, and the second part is Registry based:

The File-Based Part of Local Group Policy (all versions of Windows)   The file-based part of the default local GPO can be found in C:\windows\system32\grouppolicy.

The File-Based Part of Local Group Policy for MLGPOs (Vista Only)   Remember that in Windows Vista, there are now multiple local GPOs (MLGPOs). Because of this, the storage of those user-specific and group-specific GPOs are stored in a different location than the default local GPO. Namely, they are stored in a new subfolder of \Windows\SYSEM32 called GroupPolicyUsers, as shown in Figure 4.1.

FIGURE 4.1   Viewing the directories of Vista local GPOs

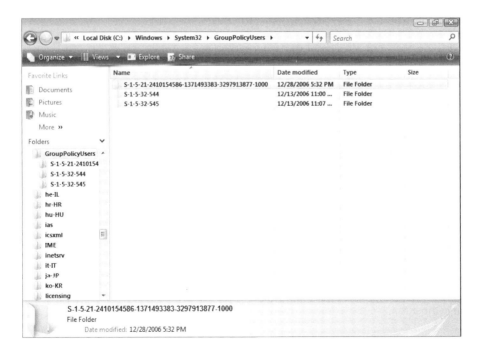

As you can see in the figure, there are three SID-named folders that contain the user-specific portion of the local GPO. (Remember the computer portion applies to everyone, and, hence, there is no computer portion represented here.) You might actually have more than three folders here. In my example, the first SID you see in the list (with a SID of S-1-5-21-2410154586-1371493383-3297913877-1000) is the SID of a user account for whom I created a user-specific local GPO.

And, again, as you know from Chapter 1, I could have any number of user-specific local GPOs defined. And, for each of those user-specific GPOs, one would have its own SID-based folder.

In addition, the two other folders that you see in Figure 4.1 are ones you will find on your Vista systems if you decide to define GPOs specific for the Administrators group and another which applies to nonadministrators local GPOs. The folder called S-1-5-32-544 defines the Administrators GPO (and not coincidentally, that is the SID of the built-in Administrators group). Likewise, the folder named S-1-5-32-545 is the SID of the built-in Users group, which represents the nonadministrators local GPO.

> Again, you should notice one major difference between the default local GPO and these user-specific local GPOs. That is, the default local GPO includes a computer-specific Machine folder in addition to the default User folder. However, any user-specific local GPO only contains a User folder (since it only contains user-specific policy settings).

The files and folders found in the local GPO mirrors, for the most part, are the way the file-based portion of an Active Directory–based GPO stores its stuff. This is good news, as it makes understanding the two types of GPOs (local versus domain-based GPOs) nearly equal.

> Feel free to inspect the C:\windows\system32\grouppolicy folder, and then jump to the "Group Policy Templates" section later in this chapter to get the gist of the file structure. Note, however, that not all the structure may be present until the local GPO is edited. For Windows XP and newer operating systems, one major difference between local and Active Directory–based GPOs is that, when you make a policy change to the security attributes on the local GPO, that change is made directly to the workstation you're editing, instead of being stored in the file system. So, if you change, for example, the password policy on the local GPO, you won't find evidence of it stored anywhere but in the local computer's Security Accounts Manager (SAM) database.

Three Use-at-Your-Own-Risk Local Group Policy Tips

Here are three tips that you are welcome to try—but use at your own risk. I cannot vouch for their validity or soundness, so you're on your own.

Tip #1: Ensure that admins (and other users) avoid Local Group Policy.   Perhaps you've set it up so that your users do not have access to the Start ➢ Run command. However, when you're logged in as the local administrator, you want the Run command. The JSI FAQ site has a tip (`www.jsiinc.com/subl/tip5600/rh5619.htm`) that tells you how admins (and other users) can override Local Group Policy for Windows 2000, XP, and Server 2003. Note that in Windows Vista, with the multiple local GPO feature, this tip is no longer required to segregate administrative policy from nonadministrative policy. However, this tip is valid only when the workstation isn't a domain member.

Tip #2: Reset Local Group Policy to the defaults.   If you've set up a Local Group Policy and want to restore it to its default configuration, there's no easy way. However, my good pal Mark Minasi has a newsletter (#32) on the subject. Track it down at `www.minasi.com/archive.htm`. Even Mark admits that this solution might not be totally complete.

Tip #3: Copy a Local GPO from one computer to another.   This tip works in all versions of Windows, including Windows Vista. If you have the need to replicate out a Local GPO from one machine to another, it's possible (but not advisable). In fact this tip is expressly untested, unverified, and unsupported by the Group Policy team. Anyway, if you choose to proceed, you could simply copy the files contained within `%systemroot%\system32\GroupPolicy` from the source machine to the target machine. But note that not everything will come over. Scripts and Administrative Templates will come over, but other stuff like security will not, because as I mentioned earlier, security policy settings on the Local GPO are not stored within the file system. In short, if you try this trick, be sure to test the results to make sure all the stuff you want to come across does come across.

As you're performing this tip, be sure that you also hand-modify the `gpt.ini` found in the root of this directory. In short, make sure the number present here is greater than the number found in the `gpt.ini` of your target machines. As you'll learn later, the `gpt.ini` houses the *version number* of a GPO. If you don't set the version number higher than what is already present on the target computer, the Local GPO engine doesn't know anything has changed, and hence you won't see the updated settings. And it's not just a matter of setting the version number to the same number plus 1. Version numbers are a bit more complicated than that. So, before you run off and try this tip, you'll also need to learn more about how version numbers work. See the sidebar later in the chapter entitled "Understanding Group Policy Version Numbers," which should give you the data you need.

Inside Active Directory Group Policy Objects

Here's the strange part about Group Policy (as if it weren't already strange enough). Chapter 1 discussed how creating a GPO really involves two steps. First, the GPO is written in the Group Policy Objects container, and then it is *linked* to a level—site, domain, or OU. So, we know that GPOs don't really "live" at the level where they're linked. Specifically, all GPOs live inside the Group Policy Objects container in the domain. That is, they're always kept nestled inside this container yet are logically linked (but not stored) to the other levels to which they point. I referred to the GPOs we created as swimming around in a virtual pool within the domain.

So far in our journey, we created four new GPOs which affect our storyline:

- "Hide Screen Saver Option," which we applied to the Default-First-Site-Name site

- "Hide Desktop Settings Option," which we applied to the Corp.com domain

- "Hide Display Settings Option/Restore Screen Saver Option," which we applied to the **Human Resources Users** OU

- "Auto-Launch Calc.exe," which we applied to the **Human Resources Computers** OU

We can check in with our concept of these GPOs as floating in a swimming pool within the Group Policy Objects container as shown here.

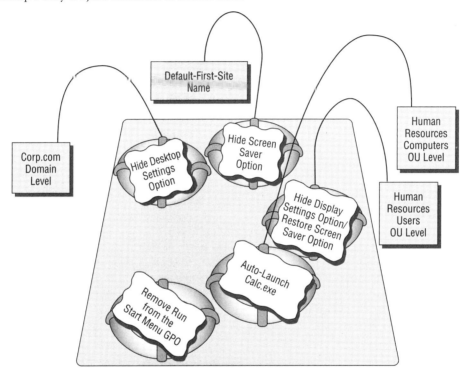

The Corp.com GPO Swimming Pool

As you can see, the GPOs never "live" at any level in Active Directory. They aren't really stored at any particular level, although it might appear (using the old-school interface) that they are.

To reiterate, if you leverage a GPO that is supposed to affect a site, an OU, or even a domain, the GPO itself is not stored directly at that level. Rather, the GPO is simply linked to the level in Active Directory. When a GPO is called to be used, it has to request a Domain Controller to fetch it from the Group Policy Objects container (and from its parts in SYSVOL) and pull the information out.

Each time you create a new GPO, it's born and placed into the swimming pool within the domain—ready for action if linked to a level in Active Directory. You can reuse a GPO at multiple levels in Active Directory simply by linking it to another level of Active Directory.

So, when GPOs are created for use at the site, domain, or OU level, they're always created within the domain swimming pool, the Group Policy Objects container, where we just link to the GPOs we need when we need them.

We're going to continue this discussion a littttle out of order here. We'll be talking about domain-linked GPOs, OU-linked GPOs, then round out with Site-linked GPOs. Yes, yes, we all know the "right" order is site, domain, OU—so bear with me here (I think you'll understand why we're going out of order by the time this little section is complete).

Group Policy Objects from a Domain Perspective

Since we know that all GPOs are just hanging out in the Group Policy Objects container waiting to be used, we can take this one step further. That is, even those GPOs linked to the domain level aren't exempt from having to be "fetched." When clients use domain-linked GPOs, they have to make the same requests and "ask" the Domain Controller for the GPOs that apply to them.

This is usually not a problem; the Domain Controller doesn't have far to go to get the GPO in the swimming pool to apply it to the domain. But this is precisely why doing *cross-domain* GPO linking is so slow and painful.

For instance, in an environment with multiple domains, it might appear to be easier to recycle an existing GPO that lives in another domain. But when it comes time to grab the information inside the GPO, it needs to be brought back all the way from Domain Controllers in the originating domain. Again, this cross-domain GPO linking is very, very painful and should be avoided at all costs. In the Appendix, I describe how to copy GPOs from one domain to another. This avoids the problem altogether because there's no "penalty" for creating a copy from a source domain and then having the copy live in your domain. Sure, it takes up a wee bit of storage in the new domain's swimming pool. But it's better than cross-domain linking.

Group Policy Objects from an OU Perspective

Since GPOs live in the Group Policy Objects container at the domain level, a distinct advantage is associated with the way Group Policy does its thing: it's tremendously easy to move, link, and unlink GPOs to the domain and/or its OUs. You could, if you desired, simply unlink a GPO in the domain or OU and link it back to some other OU. Or you could link one GPO to the domain and/or multiple OUs.

It's typical and usual that you'll use OUs to apply most of your GPOs. If GPOs live in the Group Policy Objects container swimming pool, it's easy for multiple, unrelated OUs to reuse the same GPOs and just create new links to existing GPOs.

Group Policy Objects from a Site Perspective

Site-level GPOs are a bit unique. If you used (or continue to use) the old-school interface via Active Directory Sites and Services to dictate a site-based GPO, you might be in for a world of pain. By default, all site-level GPOs created using the old-school interface will live in the Group Policy Objects container of the Domain Controllers of the *root* domain—and only the root domain, that is, the first Active Directory domain brought online. Then, every time a GPO meant for a site is called for use by a client system, a Domain Controller from the root domain must fetch that information. If the closest Domain Controller from the root domain is in Singapore, so be it. You can see where the pain could get severe.

The GPMC basically forces us to create site-based GPOs in a thoughtful way. Specifically, you need to create the GPO in the domain swimming pool of your choice. Then, you need to link the GPO from the domain to the site you want. As you saw in Chapter 1, we first create the GPO in the Group Policy Objects container.

The idea is to create the GPO in the domain that makes sense and is closest to where the site-linked GPO will be used. Then, once we expose the site, we just add a link to our existing GPO, which is already in the domain swimming pool. In short, we get the site GPO to leverage the closest domain's swimming pool. Sure, it takes a little extra planning to think about which swimming pool is closest to the users and computers in the site—but it's worth it. That way, we're not asking some Domain Controller in Singapore to serve our New York users.

Remember, by default, only members of the Enterprise Administrators group (or members of the Domain Admins group in the root domain) can create new site-level GPOs or link to existing GPOs from the site level. Optionally, this right can be delegated.

The Birth, Life, and Death of a GPO

Now that you understand where GPOs actually live, we can take the next step: understanding the "journey" of a GPO. Specifically, a GPO is born and must stay healthy if it's going to stay alive. If its usefulness becomes depleted, you can call in the Sopranos boys to whack it—never to be seen again.

How Group Policy Objects Are "Born"

Before you can give birth to GPOs, you need rights to do so, and you can get these rights in two ways. First, you can be a member of the Group Policy Creator Owners or Domain Admins Security groups.

If you're a member of the Group Policy Creator Owners group you have rights to create but not link GPOs. Domain Administrators can create GPOs and link them to where they want.

You can also be granted explicit rights via the Delegation tab in the Group Policy Objects container via the GPMC (as you saw in Chapter 2).

A new Group Policy Object is born when you right-click the Group Policy Objects container and choose "New." Now you're setting into motion a specific chain of events.

First, by default, the PDC Emulator is contacted to see if it's available for writing. If not, the user is prompted about how to proceed, as shown in Figure 4.2.

GPOs are initially born in the PDC Emulator, and then, a bit later, they are replicated to the other Domain Controllers within the site and then between sites. Assuming the PDC Emulator is available, you can give your GPO a friendly name, say "Hide Display Settings Option/Restore Screen Saver Option," as we did in Chapter 1.

FIGURE 4.2   If the PDC Emulator is not available for writing, the user is prompted for an alternate location.

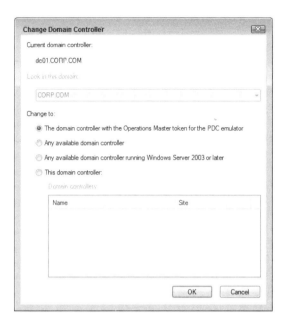

Once that happens, your GPO is officially "born." The PDC Emulator has already performed certain functions on your behalf:

- The GPO was given a unique ID that takes its form as a globally unique identifier (GUID).

- It created a *Group Policy Container (GPC)* object in the `Policies` folder of the system container in the Active Directory domain partition. Think of this as a reference in Active Directory for your new GPO.

- It created a *Group Policy Template (GPT)* folder in the SYSVOL Policies directory of the PDC Emulator. This is where the real files that make up your GPO live. They're replicated to every Domain Controller for quicker retrieval.

- Additionally, if "Create a GPO in this domain, and Link it here" is used when focused on the domain or OU level (or the old-school interface is used), the new GPO you just created is automatically *linked* to the current level you were focused at—domain or OU.

When you inspect the properties of any new GPO, you'll see the unique ID it is automatically given, as shown in Figure 4.3.

So, every GPO is made up of two components (the GPC and GPT), and those components are split between two places on that Domain Controller. The good news, though, is it all ties back to the GPO's GUID. We'll explore each of these components in the next two sections.

FIGURE 4.3 **FIGURE 4.3**   Every GPO gets a unique name.

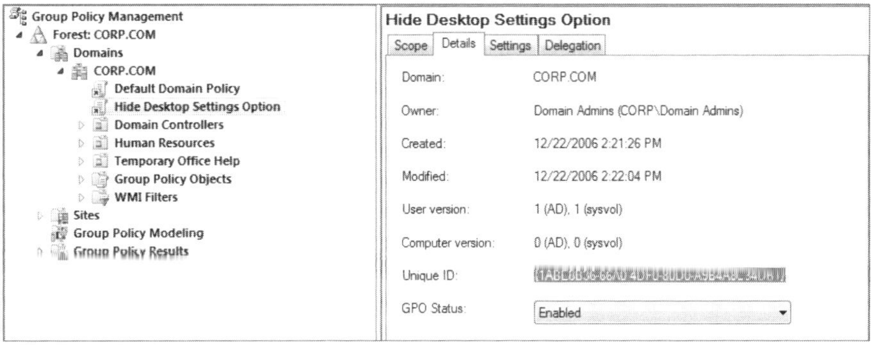

How a GPO "Lives"

A GPO in Active Directory is made up of two constituent parts. One part isn't enough, and the GPO cannot live without both parts. Both parts are required in order to communicate the GPO message.

As you'll see in a bit, the GPO derives its life from these two parts.

Group Policy Containers (GPCs)

The Active Directory database contains the first half of a GPO. Not to get too geeky, but these are just objects (of class `groupPolicyContainer`), which we refer to as the Group Policy Containers, or GPCs. Each GPO defined in a domain has exactly one GPC object defined for it. Then, it's this GPC object which can hold multiple properties related to the Group Policy Object—for instance, version and display information and some policy settings. A GPC has a unique name that takes the format of a globally unique identifier (GUID)—see the sidebar "GPC Attributes." The GUID is *not* the friendly name we use when administering the GPO. The friendly name is stored as an attribute—called `displayName`–on that GPC object in Active Directory.

You can see the GPCs for every Group Policy you create by diving into the Active Directory Users And Computers console.

To view the GPCs and their GUIDs, follow these steps:

1. Log on to the server DC01 as Administrator of the domain.

2. Choose Start ➢ Programs ➢ Administrative Tools ➢ Active Directory Users And Computers.

3. Choose View ➢ Advanced Features, as shown in Figure 4.4, to display the `Policies` folder.

4. Expand the `System` folder to display the `Policies` folder along with the GPCs, as shown in Figure 4.5.

FIGURE 4.4   Turn on the "Advanced Features" setting to see the Policies folder (and a whole lot more).

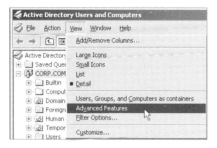

FIGURE 4.5   Expand the Policies folder to expose the underlying GPC objects.

GPC Attributes

When a GPC object is created, it is given several attributes:

Common Name (CN)   In Active Directory, you'll see attribute is really called cn. An LDAP (Lightweight Directory Access Protocol) designation for the name is assigned to an object. GPC names use the GUID format to ensure uniqueness throughout a forest. For example, CN=2C53BFD6-A2DB-44AF-9476-130492934271.

Distinguished Name (DN)   In Active Directory, you'll see an attribute called distinguishedName. This is the object's common name plus the path to the object from the root of the LDAP tree. For example, CN=2C53BFD6-A2DB-44AF-9476-130492934271, CN=Policies, CN=System, DC=corp, DC=com.

Display Name   In Active Directory, you'll see an attribute called displayName. This is the friendly name assigned to the Group Policy in the user interface, for example, the Hide Screen Saver Tab GPO.

Version   In Active Directory, you'll see an attribute called versionNumber. This is a counter that keeps track of updates to a GPC object (more on this topic a little later).

GUID   In Active Directory, you'll see an attribute called objectGUID. This is the GUID assigned to the object itself.

You might find it a little confusing for the GPC object to have a GUID that refers to the object itself and a name that uses a GUID format. For an important reason, Microsoft needed a way to make the underlying, real name of GPOs unique, independent of their friendly names. Suppose two administrators create two (or more) GPOs with the same friendly name on their own Domain Controllers. When these GPC objects replicate, one of them has to be discarded, over-written, or renamed, depending on the exact circumstances of the replication collision. That could be a bad thing. Therefore, Microsoft solves this problem by using underlying unique names formatted with the GUID format. There is a negligible chance of identical GUIDs being created, not only within one Active Directory but also across the entire world, should the need arise to coexist with GPOs in other forests (such as with cross-forest trusts).

To see the major attributes for the GPC objects in your domain, take a look at Chapter 7. You'll find a Visual Basic (.vbs) script that lets you see (and document) these objects.

Up until this point, we've been using the GPMC interface to create GPOs. When we use the GPMC to create GPOs, we've made reference to the Group Policy Objects container within the GPMC as representation of the swimming pool. But the GPMC isn't showing you the real swimming pool—it's showing you a *representation* of the swimming pool. What it's showing you is the GPC part of the swimming pool. The other "half" of the swimming pool is the GPT (which we'll talk about next), the files that live in the replicated SYSVOL folder that exists on every domain controller in an Active Directory domain. The exact path to the GPT is \\<domain name>\sysvol\<domain name>\policies.

When you drill into a GPC container in Active Directory, you should see one GUID-named folder for every GPO you have created, plus two more for the two default GPOs—the Default Domain Policy and the Default Domain Controllers Policy (which we'll explore in Chapter 6).

In Figure 4.5, I have lots of GPOs already created; therefore, I have lots of containers. You might have fewer.

Those two default GPOs, in fact, have what are referred to as "well-known GUIDs." That is, the GUID for each of those two GPOs will be the same no matter what AD domain you look at. They are same in your AD domain as mine! That makes it easy to find them. When you're used to seeing those two GUIDs time and again, you will know right away which GPOs they represent.

When you try to drill down into the subcontainers, some will and some will not expand past the `{GUID}\Machine` and `{GUID}\User levels`. Those that do expand do so because you have set up policy settings in that specific GPO that Active Directory needs to maintain information on, such as when you Publish or Assign applications. We'll look at where each policy area stores its settings after the section on the GPT. We'll explore Publishing and Assigning applications in great detail in Chapter 10.

Don't be surprised if, at this stage in working through the book, you do not have any fully expandable subfolders as shown in Figure 4.5. The subfolders that don't expand simply don't have any Group Policy settings stored within them. Most everything else the GPO needs to be useful is stored in the GPT, which is explored in the next section.

Who Really Has Permissions to Do What?

In Chapter 2, we applied various permissions on the GPO, including who had "Read" and "Apply Group Policy" permissions, as well as who could see the settings or edit the stuff inside the GPO. The locking mechanism for "Who really has what permissions" on a specific GPO is found right here, at the `Policies` folder:

- On the one hand, the locking mechanism on the `Policies` folder itself dictates who can and cannot create GPOs. However, it should be noted that these permissions are not inherited to the GUID-named GPT folder itself. See the Note following Figure 4.8 for specific information on how to change the default permissions.

- On the other hand, the locking mechanism on the GUID-named GPT folders underneath the `Policies` folder dictates which users have access to "Read" and "Apply Group Policy," or can change the GPO itself.

In reality, the permissions that you see in GPMC for a given GPO reflect the permissions of *both* the GPC and GPT. While the permissions that you can grant to an Active Directory object do not map one-to-one to the permissions that you can grant to a file system folder like those found in SYSVOL, they roughly translate into the same permissions. For this reason, it's very important that you *not* try to directly modify the permissions on a GPO by simply modifying the permissions on either the GPC or the GPT independently. The best tool for this task is the GPMC's security filtering and delegation features.

However, in my GPanswers.com newsletter #13, (found at www.GPanswers .com/newsletter) you will find a tip which does walk through how to expressly change the underlying permissions in an emergency. Note that in that article, it's a special case, and, again, should only be performed as described in that particular emergency.

Who Can Create New Group Policy Objects?

Right-click the Policies container, select Properties, then click the Security tab to display several names, some of which should be familiar, including the Group Policy Creator Owners and the Domain Administrators group. Additionally present will be anyone you explicitly added via the Delegation tab upon the Group Policy Objects container in GPMC. You saw how to do this in Chapter 2. At that time, we added a user named Joe User from our domain.

If you examine the properties of the Policies container (as shown in Figure 4.6), you'll see the Group Policy Creator Owners group. Joe is also listed (because he was expressly granted permission via the GPMC). Note also that the Domain Admins and Enterprise Admins groups are also present, but those names are at the top of the list, so you can't see them in Figure 4.6.

FIGURE 4.6   Expand the Policies folder to expose the underlying GPC objects.

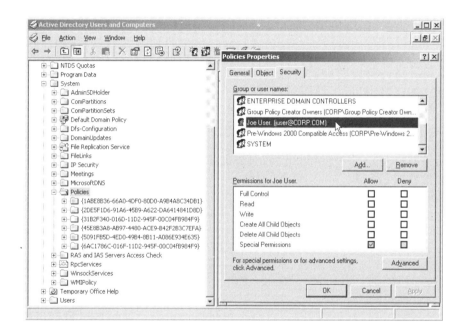

You can click the Advanced button to display Joe's precise "Special Permissions." Indeed, Joe has only one permission, and it's called "Create groupPolicyContainer Objects." Once he has this right, the system permits him to create GPC folders and populate them with Group Policy information when he creates a new GPO.

The Group Policy Creator Owners group has many, many more unnecessary permissions on the Policies folder, including "Create all child objects," "Create User Objects," and a whole lot of stuff that, really, doesn't have anything to do with Group Policy. Indeed, if you log on as someone in the Group Policy Creator Owners group and right-click the Policies folder, you can do some things you really shouldn't do, as you can see in Figure 4.7.

The system (thankfully) won't let you do *all* the functions listed here, but it does let you do *some* of them. And, again, you really shouldn't be poking around like this. Of course, the "right" thing to do is to only set permissions via the GPMC. However, I show you these things for demonstration purposes so you can get a better feeling for what is different between someone in the Group Policy Creator Owners Group versus someone who has been explicitly delegated rights via the Delegation tab upon the Group Policy Objects container in GPMC.

FIGURE 4.7 For the love of Pete, please don't do this.

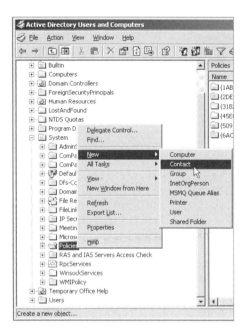

The Domain Administrators group and the Enterprise Administrators group also have explicit permissions here. When they create new GPOs, they do so because of their explicit permissions, not because they are members of the Group Policy Creator Owners group.

Who Can Manipulate and Edit Existing Group Policy Objects?

Right-click a GPO folder (with the name of a GUID) under the Policies folder and choose Properties to display the Security tab (see Figure 4.8), which will show the same information as when, in Chapter 2, you used the "Deny" attribute to pass over certain Security groups. That is, the same information is shown here as when we clicked the "Advanced" button in the Delegation tab when focused on the GPO (or GPO link, because it's using the same information taken from the actual GPO).

FIGURE 4.8   Each GPC can display the underlying permissions of the GPO.

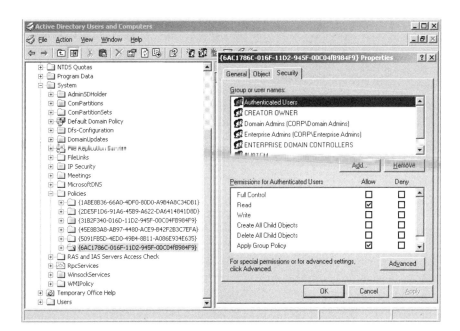

Unless otherwise delegated, the person or group who created the GPO is the only one other than Domain Admins and Enterprise Admins who can modify or delete the GPO. However, this may be a particularly sensitive issue if you have many Domain Administrators—as they all have "joint ownership" of the GPOs they create. There is a serious potential risk in one administrator taking the reins and modifying another administrator's GPOs.

> The permissions that a new GPO gets when it's created are controlled by the `DefaultSecurityDescriptor` attribute on the `groupPolicyContainer` class within the Active Directory schema. If you want your GPOs to get different default permissions when they're created, you can modify the schema instance of this attribute. The Microsoft Knowledge Base article at `http://support.microsoft.com/kb/321476/en-us` describes how to do that.

However, as you saw in Chapter 2, you can also grant someone explicit rights via the Delegation tab upon the GPOs container via the GPMC. In this example, I have done this for Joe. Figure 4.9 shows the properties of a GPO that Joe has created.

Since Joe has explicit permissions to create GPOs, he becomes the owner of the GPOs he creates. You can clearly see that Joe created it, and now he owns it. Hence, Joe doesn't have to worry about other explicitly anointed users or groups changing the GPOs he creates and owns. Note, however, that the Domain Administrators and Enterprise Administrators group will, in fact, be able to change any GPOs that Joe creates. Additionally, note that other users within Group Policy Creator Owners cannot dive in and edit Joe's GPOs. Again—Joe owns it; it's his.

FIGURE 4.9 If Joe creates a GPO, he owns the GPO. No one else (other than Domain Admins or Enterprise Admins) can edit it.

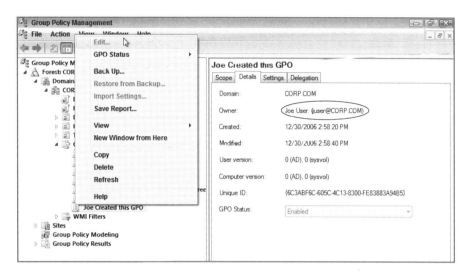

Using LDP to See the Guts of a GPC

The GPC object itself holds even more critical attributes for GPOs:

gPCFileSysPath The physical path to the associated Policies folder, or GPT, stored in SYSVOL. The Policies folder has the same name as the GPC, which is another reason that uniqueness is so important. The GPT is discussed in the next section.

gPCMachineExtensionNames This is a list of GUIDs of the computer-related CSEs (*client-side extensions*)—and the MMC snap-in that manages them—that will be called for this particular GPO. For instance, if a GPO has policy set on the Administrative Templates node under the Computer Configuration node in the Group Policy Object Editor, the gPCMachineExtensionNames list includes the GUID of the Registry client-side extension and the GUID of the MMC snap-in for the Administrative Templates node. CSEs are discussed later in this chapter in the "How Client Systems Get Group Policy Objects" section.

gPCUserExtensionNames This is a list of the GUIDs of the CSEs and their MMC snap-ins, called by a user-related Group Policy. Again, I'll discuss CSEs a bit later in this chapter.

When you try to dive in and view these attributes using Active Directory Users And Computers, you cannot see them. The only way to see them is to use either the ADSIEdit MMC snap-in, or the LDP tool, which is an LDAP browser tool. Both tools are found by loading the support tools from the SUPPORT\TOOLS folder on the Windows Server 2003 CD.

LDP lets you perform LDAP queries right into the actual guts of Active Directory. Using LDP, you can see these attributes. Normally, you wouldn't want or need to go poking around in here, but taking the time to learn just where attributes are can help in your understanding of what constitutes a GPO.

To query a specific GPO to see its underlying attributes, follow these steps:

1. After loading the Support tools on the Domain Controller, choose Start ➢ Run to open the Run dialog box, and in the Open field, type **LDP** and press Enter to select the domain of your choice.

2. Choose Connection ➢ Bind and in the dialog box type the administrative credentials to the domain. In the Domain field, you'll need to type the DNS name of the domain, for example, **Corp.com**. If you successfully connect, you'll see your first query results in the right pane of the LDP window.

3. Choose View ➢ Tree to open up a dialog that lets you specify the distinguished name of the domain. If your domain is Corp.com, enter **dc=corp, dc=com**. If you do that correctly, your left pane will show the domain name with a plus (+) sign. You should be able to double-click the plus sign and expand the contents within the domain.

4. Find the System container and double-click it to expand it.

5. Find the Policies container and double-click it to expand it.

6. Find the unique name of the GPO you want to inspect and double-click it to expand it. (For information about how to find a specific unique name of a GPO, see the earlier section "How Group Policy Objects Are 'Born.'") In the following illustration, the attributes are highlighted.

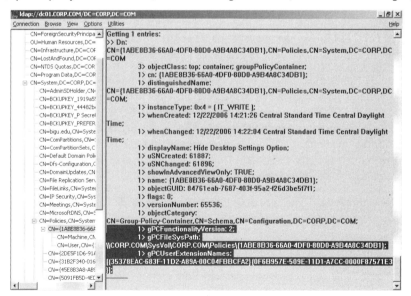

Once you find the unique name, the resultant LDP query will show you the properties on that GPO.

There is one more important attribute to inspect by using LDP: gPLink. Recall that a GPO can be linked by one level, multiple levels, or no levels. If a GPO is to be linked to a site, a domain, or an OU, that level needs to have a *pointer* or *link* to the GPO. When clients log on (computer and user), they use LDAP to query to each level they are a part of (site, domain, OUs) to find out if the level has the gPLink attribute set. If so, the client makes an LDAP query to find out what GPOs are meant for it. With the information in hand, it determines what files to download from the SYSVOL share on its logon server. (You can see these queries happening for yourself, when you inspect Userenv.log, explored later in the section "Turning On Verbose Logging.")

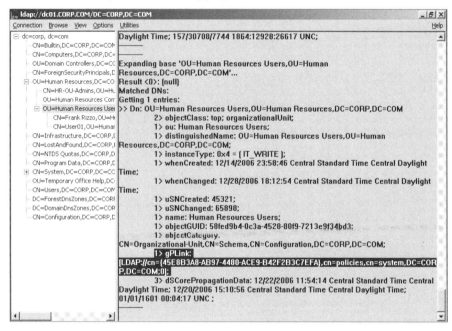

To see the gPLink attribute, you can simply click the level you want to inspect. In this case, click the **Human Resources Users** OU you created in Chapter 1.

In the right pane, find LDP's query results. The gPLink attribute has LDAP pointers to the unique names of the GPOs. In this case, the **Human Resources Users** OU has links to the "Hide Display Settings Option/Restore Screen Saver Option" GPO, in my case, 45E8B3A8-AB97-4480-ACE9-B42F2B3C7EFA. If you clicked the **Human Resources Computers** OU, you should see the "Disable Task Scheduler" GPO, again, in my case {965BAA1A-C60B-4C55-ADA0-D79598D668B6}.

Group Policy Templates

As we just learned, GPCs are stored in the Active Directory database and replicated via normal Active Directory replication. A Group Policy Template (GPT) on the other hand, is stored as a set of files in the SYSVOL share of each Domain Controller. Each GPT is replicated to each Domain Controller through FRS (File Replication Service).

When we used the Properties tab of the GPO, we were able to find its unique name (as we did earlier in Figure 4.3). We can use the unique name to locate the GPC in Active Directory, and it's the same unique name we can use to locate the GPT in the SYSVOL.

To see the GPTs in SYSVOL, follow these steps:

1. On a Domain Controller in the domain, open Windows Explorer.

2. Change the directory to the SYSVOL container. Its usual location is `C:\Windows\SYSVOL\SYSVOL\{domain name}` (in this case, `C:\Windows\SYSVOL\SYSVOL\corp.com`).

3. Change into the `Policies` folder. You'll see a list of folders. The folder names match the GPC GUID names stored in Active Directory (seen in the previous exercise). Figure 4.10 shows a `Policies` folder containing many GPOs.

FIGURE 4.10 The unique names of the GPOs are found as folder names in SYSVOL. This is the unique name for the "Hide Display Settings Option/Restore Screen Saver Option" you saw in Figure 4.4 earlier.

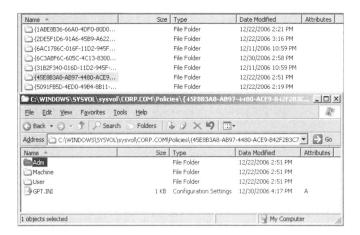

Double-clicking a `Policies` folder inside SYSVOL displays the contents of the GPT. Inside, you'll see several subfolders and a file. The first entry on this list is the file (`gpt.ini`) the rest are subfolders.

gpt.ini   The one file you will always find under the GUID folder. It holds the version number of the GPT as well as the equivalent information to the `gpcMachineExtensionName` and `gpcUserExtensionName` attributes found on the GPC object in Active Directory. Namely, these two keys within the `gpt.ini` list the GUIDs of the Client Side Extensions and their associated MMC snap-in extensions that have been implemented within the GPO. This lets the client know which CSEs need to be called when GPOs are processed. (You'll read about version numbers in the next section.) You'll also see a little text snippet in every `gpt.ini` which says "displayName=New Group Policy Object". This snippet of text is the same for every GPO and is currently unused at this time.

\Adm   If you create your GPOs using a Windows Vista management station (as we discussed in Chapter 1 and we'll drive home in Chapter 5), you won't see an ADM directory in any of your newly created GPOs. However, if you create GPOs from pre-Vista machines, this directory is created to house policy settings called Administrative Template files. In short, when you create or edit a GPO from a pre-Vista machine, the Administrative Templates (`.adm` files) are copied from the `\Windows\INF` folder. Again, this happens from the machine where you're editing that GPO, into the GPT's `\Adm` folder.

By default, those `.adm` files are `Conf.adm`, `Inetres.adm`, `System.adm`, `wmplayer.adm`, and `wuau.adm`.

Hang tight. You'll find more info about this as you hit Chapter 5. Double-clicking the `\Adm` folder displays the templates. Note that the `\Adm` folder will not exist until the GPO is opened for the first time from a pre-Vista machine and you click either the Computer or the User Administrative Template node.

Note, that the presence of the `\Adm` folder in the GPT is an artifact of pre-Windows Vista operating systems. When you create and edit a new GPO using Vista, no `\Adm` folder is created because Vista no longer copies the ADM files up to the GPT—they are held locally in `C:\windows\policydefinitions` or in the "Central Store." However, if you edit a GPO that was created with Vista using a "down-level" operating system (for example, XP, 2003, and so on), the `\Adm` folder will get created and populated in the GPT. Note that this behavior— editing a Vista GPO from a down-level version of Windows—is generally not a good idea. Once you've gone Vista from a GP perspective, it's best to edit those GPOs using Vista from then on. The next chapter describes the Central Store and ADMX files in great detail.

\Machine   This folder contains the settings for the computer side of the GPO, including startup and shutdown scripts (though there's nothing requiring them to live here; they could be located in other places as well), pointers to applications that are assigned, and Registry settings (among other settings). The actual contents of the `\Machine` folder depend on the computer options specified in the GPO. The potential contents include the following:

The *Registry.pol* File   Holds the Registry settings set in Computer Configuration ➢ Administrative Templates as well as settings for Software Restriction Policy under Computer Configuration ➢ Windows Settings ➢ Security Settings ➢ Software Restriction Policies.

The *\Applications* Folder   Stores pointer files called Application Advertisement Scripts, or AAS files. These files are used in conjunction with Group Policy Software Deployment.

These are the instructions that the client computers use to process Software Installation. Software Installation is further discussed in its own chapter, Chapter 11, but AAS files are described further in the sidebar entitled "Inside AAS Files."

Inside .aas Files

The .aas file serves a specific role in the context of Software Installation policy. This file is created when you first deploy an MSI package. It contains information related to the advertisement of the package.

Advertisement is an MSI feature that allows you to deploy part of an application (you can think of it like a shortcut or file extension association) to a computer or user. The whole application is not installed right away, but instead, when the user first clicks the shortcut or activates a file extension associated with the advertised package, the installation proceeds at that time. This feature is known as *Install-On-First-Use*.

The .aas file holds that advertisement information specific to the package you've deployed. It also contains the hard-coded path to the package you've specified. This is why you cannot easily change the path to a package once you've deployed it via Software Installation policy. This .aas file must be regenerated and the path to the package that is referenced in the GPC portion of the GPO must also be updated.

The \Microsoft\Windows NT\Secedit Folder   Stores a file called Gpttmpl.inf. This file holds various computer security settings, defined under the Computer Configuration ➢ Windows Settings ➢ Security Settings portion of the GPO. You can also set up these settings in advance and deploy them *en masse* using the techniques described in Chapter 6.

The \Scripts\Shutdown Folder   Contains the instructions for which shutdown scripts to run and, optionally, the actual files used for computer shutdown scripts. The instructions as to which scripts will run and where the scripts are stored are held in a file called scripts.ini, within this folder. Can be of any scripting file type (that the ShellExecute process can run), including .bat, .cmd, .vbs, .js, and others. You'll see how to use this in Chapter 6.

The \Scripts\Startup Folder   Contains the instructions for which startup scripts to run and, optionally, the actual files used for computer startup scripts. The instructions as to which scripts will run and where the scripts are stored are held in a file called scripts.ini, within this folder. Can be of any scripting file type, type (that the ShellExecute process can run), including .bat, .cmd, .vbs, .js, and others. You'll see how to use this in Chapter 6.

\User   This folder contains the settings for the user side of the Group Policy coin, including logon and logoff scripts, pointers to applications that are published or assigned, and Registry settings. Depending on the options used on each GPO, it represents what is in the \User folder under the computer side of the GPT.

The *Registry.pol* File   Holds the Registry settings set in User Configuration ➢ Administrative Templates as well as settings for Software Restriction Policy under User Configuration ➢ Windows Settings ➢ Security Settings ➢ Software Restriction Policies.

The *\Applications* Folder   Stores pointer files called AAS files for applications deployed with Group Policy Software Installation.

The *\Documents and Settings* Folder   Contains a file called `Fdeploy.ini`, which stores applicable Folder Redirection settings. Set up Folder Redirection as described in Chapter 9.

The *\Microsoft\IEAK* Folder   Stores files to represent the changes made in User Configuration ➢ Windows Settings ➢ Internet Explorer Maintenance.

The *\Microsoft\RemoteInstall* Folder   Stores `Oscfilter.ini`, which specifies Group Policy Remote Installation Services settings. See Chapter 11 for how to set up Remote Installation Services and manage it with Group Policy.

The *\Scripts\Logon* Folder   Contains the instructions for which logon scripts to run and, optionally, the actual files used for user logon scripts. The instructions as to which scripts will run and where the scripts are stored are held in a file called `scripts.ini`, within this folder. Can be of any acceptable file type, including `.bat`, `.vbs`, `.js`, and others. You'll see how to use this in Chapter 6.

The *\Scripts\Logoff* Folder   Contains the instructions for which logoff scripts to run and, optionally, the actual files used for user logoff scripts. The instructions as to which scripts will run and where the scripts are stored are held in a file called `scripts.ini`, within this folder. Can be of any acceptable file type, including `.bat`, `.vbs`, `.js`, and others. You'll see how to use this in Chapter 6.

Group Policy Settings Storage

As I've indicated, Group Policy settings, the things that you set when you're editing a GPO, are stored within one half of the GPO—either the GPC or GPT. The decision as to which is used to store a given setting varies with the size of the data being stored. Typically, because Active Directory is not designed for storing large blocks of data, those settings that require big chunks of stuff are stored in the GPT instead of the GPC.

But it really does vary by each Client Side Extension. Table 4.1 indicates where each Client Side Extension, up to and including Windows Vista, stores its settings.

Verifying That GPCs and GPTs Are in Sync

The two pieces of information that make up a GPO are GPCs and GPTs:

- GPCs are stored in the Active Directory database and are replicated via normal Active Directory replication.

- GPTs are stored in the SYSVOL folders of every Domain Controller and are replicated using FRS replication.

TABLE 4.1 Client Side Extensions and their Storage Locations

Client Side Extension	Storage Location	Comments
Wireless	Stored in AD, under the GPC container for a given GPO, within the path CN=wireless,CN=Windows, CN=Microsoft,CN=Machine	Wireless policies are stored in AD as objects of class msieee80211-Policy. This class is only supported in Active Directory domains of Windows Server 2003 and newer AD domains. So, even though this CSE is on Windows XP, the policy must still be defined in domains which have that minimum schema level. Note there is also a required schema update to support the enhanced Wireless policy that's only supported on Windows Vista clients. This is further explained in Chapter 7.
Folder Redirection	Stored in SYSVOL, under the GPT container for a given GPO. Folder Redirection policy is stored in a file called fdeploy.ini in the subfolder User\Documents and Settings within the GPT.	
Administrative Template Policy	Stored in SYSVOL, under the GPT container for a given GPO. Administrative Templates policy is stored in a file called registry.pol, which can be defined per user and per computer. Within a given GPT, if you've defined both user and computer Administrative Templates policy, you will see a registry.pol file under both the user and machine subfolders.	ADM files that are in use by a given GPO are stored with the GPO in the GPT. You'll find them in a folder called ADM, off the root of the GPT for a given GPO. Thus, each GPO that sets Administrative Templates policy will store its own copy of the ADM files used to edit it, even if they are the same as another GPO. Again, this has particular ramifications when adding your own ADM templates or using operating systems earlier than Windows Vista. See the next chapter for all the gory details.
Disk Quota	Stored in SYSVOL, under the GPT container for a given GPO. Disk quota policy is also stored in registry.pol, however, you'll only find it in the copy of registry.pol stored under the machine folder, as this is a per-machine policy only.	

TABLE 4.1   Client Side Extensions and their Storage Locations *(continued)*

Client Side Extension	Storage Location	Comments
QoS Packet Scheduler	Stored in SYSVOL, under the GPT container for a given GPO. QoS policy is also stored in `registry.pol`, however, you'll only find it in the copy of `registry.pol` stored under the machine folder, as this is a per-machine policy only.	
Startup/Shutdown & Logon/Logoff Scripts	Stored in SYSVOL under the GPT container for a given GPO. Machine-specific scripts are stored in the `machine\scripts\startup`; `machine\scripts\shutdown` folders. User-specific scripts are stored in the `user\logon` and `user\logoff` folders.	Note that script files themselves do not have to be stored in SYSVOL. You can reference scripts located anywhere on your network, as long as they are accessible to the computer or user. The `scripts.ini` file found in the `computer\scripts` folder and `user\scripts` folder in SYSVOL contains the actual references to any scripts that you've defined.
Internet Explorer Maintenance and Zonemapping	Stored in SYSVOL under the GPT container for a given GPO. Specifically IE Maintenance settings are stored in the GPT under the `\User\Microsoft\IEAK` folder.	Basic "branding" settings are stored in a file under this folder called `install.ins`. Security zone settings are stored in a subfolder called `Branding`, and are stored as `.inf` files.
Security Settings	Stored in SYSVOL under the GPT container for a given GPO. Security settings are stored in the `Machine\Microsoft\Windows NT\SecEdit` folder in a file called `GptTmpl.inf`.	The format of this file is identical to those created when you use the MMC security templates editor to create a security template. The exception to this is Software Restriction policy, which is stored in the `registry.pol` file.
Software Installation	Stored in both the GPC and GPT. Within the GPT, deployed package information is stored under the container machine (or user) `\Applications`, within an "Application Advertisement File" or AAS file. Within the GPC, a special object of class `packageRegistration` is created for each application deployed. This object can be found in the GPC for a GPO under `machine` (or `user)\Class Store\Packages`.	`packageRegistration` objects found in the GPC contain information such as the path to the MSI file, any transforms (modifications) that have been selected, and whether the application is published or assigned. (See Chapter 11 for more details.)

TABLE 4.1   Client Side Extensions and their Storage Locations *(continued)*

Client Side Extension	Storage Location	Comments
IP Security	IPsec policy is a special case. Settings are stored as special objects strictly in Active Directory but *not* within the GPC. Namely IPsec policy settings are stored under the CN=IP Security, CN=System container within a domain. Therefore, IP Security settings are stored domain wide and can be referenced by any GPO in the domain. When you *assign* a particular IPsec policy to a GPO, an additional object is created within the GPC of the GPO—specifically, an *ipsecPolicy* object is created under the Machine\Microsoft\Windows container under the GPO. This object stores the association between the available IPsec policies in the domain and that GPO.	
Windows Search (Vista only)	Stored in SYSVOL, under the GPT container for a given GPO. Windows Search policy is also stored in registry.pol, however, you'll only find it in the copy of registry.pol stored under the machine folder, as this is a per-machine policy only.	
Offline Files (Vista only)	Stored in SYSVOL, under the GPT container for a given GPO. Offline Files policy is also stored in registry.pol, within both the machine and user folders, depending upon which side is being set.	
Deployed Printer Connections (Vista Only)	Stored in AD, under the GPC container for a given GPO, within the path CN=PushedPrinterConnections, CN=Machine (or CN=User)	Deployed Printer Connection policies are stored in Active Directory as objects of class msPrint-ConnectionPolicy. This class is only supported in Windows Server 2003 R2 (and Longhorn Server) domains. Therefore, this feature, Deployed Printer Connection policy, can only be defined in such domains which have that minimum schema level.

TABLE 4.1   Client Side Extensions and their Storage Locations *(continued)*

Client Side Extension	Storage Location	Comments
Enterprise QoS Policy (Vista Only)	Stored in SYSVOL, under the GPT container for a given GPO. Enterprise QoS policy is also stored in `registry.pol`, within both the machine and user folders, depending upon which side is being set.	
802.3 & Vista Wireless Policy (Vista Only)	Both of these policy areas are stored in AD in the GPC but require a schema update.	See Chapter 8 for the required schema update to support both Wired and Wireless schema policy.

Understanding Group Policy Version Numbers

If you take a peek at any GPO's `gpt.ini`, you'll see its version number. You can see the same number if you dive in to the GPC using the directions found in the sidebar (in this chapter) entitled "Using LDP to See the Guts of a GPC."

So, how is that version number constructed? Here's the formula:

Version = (Number of user section changes * 65536) + (Number of computer section changes)

So, when you create a new GPO, the version number is 0. Click Edit over a GPO and start editing, and then the numbers start going up. Enable a policy on the computer side and click OK. Then set it back to "Not Configured." That'll add 2 to the version number. Edit a policy on the user side and click OK. That'll add 65536. Change it back to "Not Configured" and it'll add another 65536. The version number's largess isn't super important here. That is, it doesn't matter how huge the number gets.

So, how do we, in our daily lives see the version number? In the Details tab of any Group Policy, as seen here.

In this example, we can see the User side has been modified twice (2 * 65536) and the computer version has been modified 3 times (add 3 to that). So, if we peek in the gpt.ini of this GPO, the version number should be 131075.

Again, both the GPC and the GPT store the version number for the GPO. Buuut, as we've described, there could be situations where replication hasn't finished and the GPC and GPT version numbers don't agree. With that case, the GPMC (which shows the version numbers via the "Details" tab of a GPO) will *always* use the GPC version number as the final reference but will give you a message if these are not in sync.

Here's the trick: for Windows 2000, for Group Policy to be applied, both the GPC and the corresponding GPT need to be synchronized. *Synchronization* simply means that the versionNumber attribute on the GPC object for a given GPO needs to be the same as the versionNumber key found in the GPT's gpt.ini file for that same GPO.

For all versions of Windows after Windows 2000, the GPC and GPT no longer need to have the same version for Group Policy processing of that GPO to proceed.

Recall that both the GPC and GPT are originally written to the PDC Emulator by default. Once they're written, the goal is to replicate the GPC and GPT to other Domain Controllers. With just one Domain Controller in a domain, there are no replication issues, because there are no other Domain Controllers to replicate to; it's all happening on one system. But when multiple Domain Controllers in a domain enter the picture, things get a little hairier. This is because normal Active Directory replication and FRS replication are on completely independent schedules (though under normal circumstances, they take the same path).

An administrator can create or modify a GPO, and the GPC might not replicate in lockstep with the files in the GPT. This isn't normally a problem because, over time, all Domain Controllers end up with exactly the same information in their replicas of the Active Directory database and in their SYSVOL folders. But during a given replication cycle, there may be intervals when the GPC and GPT *don't* match on a particular Domain Controller.

Additionally, the GPC and GPT share a *version number* for each half of the GPO—computer and user. The version numbers are incremented each time the GPO is modified and are included in the list of attributes that are replicated to other Domain Controllers. Remember in Chapter 1 I stated that if a specific GPO doesn't change, the default for the client is to not process the GPO. After all, if nothing's changed, why should the client bother? The client uses these version numbers to figure out if something has changed. The client keeps a cache of the GPOs it last applied along with the version number within the Registry. Then, if the GPO has been touched, say, by the modification of a particular policy setting or the addition of a policy setting, the version number of the GPO in Active Directory changes. The next time the client tries to process GPOs, it will see the change, and the client will download the entire GPO again and embrace the revised instruction set! So, version numbers are important for clients to recognize that new instructions are waiting for them.

So far, so good. Now, there's a bit more to fully understanding version numbers. According to Microsoft, here's the secret to figuring out whether a GPO is going to process on a workstation:

- Both the GPC and GPT parts of the GPO must be present on the Domain Controller the workstation uses to log on.

- If the client processing Group Policy is Windows 2000, then the GPC and GPT must have the same version number.

- If it's XP, Server 2003, or Vista, then the GPC and GPT can have different version numbers and Group Policy processing will still occur.

- In all cases, if the version number held in the GPC or GPT is different than the version number held in the Registry from the last time that GPO was processed, then Windows considers that a change has occurred and goes ahead and processes policy.

The main point here is that for early versions of Windows (Windows 2000), Group Policy processing would fail if the version numbers didn't match up. It's still important for the two pieces to synchronize at some point. If they aren't synchronized at some point, this implies one piece doesn't have the latest information for settings. At some point, the replication should complete and all Domain Controllers will have the same Group Policy data; then, machines and users will get the latest version of Group Policy settings. If this *never* happens then you have a problem with your domain and should follow up with the tools and techniques in this section.

 Version numbers aren't the only thing that would constitute a "change." A change could also be a removed GPO (or added GPO), a change in Security group membership, and a new or removed WMI filter. Also, it's important to point out that if one GPO changes, the CSEs that process that GPO must re-process *all* GPOs in the list, not just the one that changes.

Changing the Default Domain Controller for the Initial Write of Group Policy Objects

GPOs are, by default, created and edited using the Domain Controller that houses the PDC Emulator. Of course, over time, those new and modified GPOs make it to all other Domain Controllers using replication. However, sometimes in large Active Directories, you may not want to leverage the PDC Emulator as the "go to" place when creating and editing Group Policy.

Imagine this scenario: there is one domain but two sites—the United States and China. The U.S. site holds the Domain Controller designated as the PDC Emulator. Therefore, whenever an administrator in China writes a GPO, they must connect across the WAN to write the GPO and then wait for the entire GPO (both the GPC half and the GPT half) to replicate to their local Domain Controllers.

You can, however, specify which Domain Controller to write the GPO to, which is a two-step process:

1. Select a Domain Controller to be *active*. Open the GPMC, right-click the domain name, select "Change Domain Controller," and select the Domain Controller to which you want the Group Policy to apply.

2. Create your GPO and edit it. At the root node of the Group Policy snap-in, choose View ➢ DC Options. Now you have the following three choices:

   - "The one with the Operations Master token for the PDC Emulator." The default behavior, this option finds the PDC Emulator in the domain and writes the GPO there. Replication then occurs, starting from the PDC Emulator.

   - "The one used by the Active Directory snap-ins." Since you just selected the *active* Domain Controller, this is your best bet, as you know exactly which Domain Controller you selected in the first step.

   - "Any available Domain Controller." The odds are good that you will get a local Domain Controller to write to (based on Active Directory site information), but not always.

Therefore, the best course of action is to select the Domain Controller you want to initially write to and then select "The one used by the Active Directory snap-ins" to guarantee it.

Sound like too much work for each GPO? Alternatively, you can create a GPO that affects those accounts that can create GPOs. Use the policy setting located at User Configuration ➢ Administrative Templates ➢ System ➢ Group Policy named "Group Policy Domain Controller Selection." You'll get the same three choices listed earlier. Set it, and forget it.

Here's one more parting tip for this sidebar. Often, GPOs are created with the additional intent to use Security groups to filter them. After creating a GPO with the GPMC, an administrator will also create some Security groups using Active Directory Users And Computers to filter them. However, after creating the GPO and the Security groups, many admins are surprised that the Security groups they want to add "now" are not immediately available. This is because the GPMC is using one Domain Controller, and the Active Directory Users And Computers tool is using another Domain Controller. Therefore, replication of the group has not yet reached the Domain Controller the GPMC is using! So the tip is to manually focus both the Active Directory Users And Computers and/or GPMCs explicitly on the same Domain Controller (or just the PDC Emulator) before creating GPOs where you'll also want to filter using groups.

Using *Gpotool.exe*

If you suspect you're having problems with keeping your GPTs and GPCs in sync, you can use Gpotool.exe, a tool included with the Windows 2000 and Windows 2003 Resource Kits. You can run Gpotool.exe on any Domain Controller to verify that both the GPCs and GPTs are in sync and have consistent data among all Domain Controllers in the domain. At last check the `Gpotool.exe` (and other Group Policy–related tools) can be downloaded from `http://tinyurl.com/ydjmm3`.

Running `Gpotool` without any parameters verifies that all GPCs and GPTs are synchronized across all Domain Controllers in the domain. If you are having trouble with only one GPO, however, you might not want to go through the intense process required to check every GPO's GPC and GPT on every Domain Controller. Instead, however, you can use the `/gpo:` switch, which allows you to specify a friendly name or GUID of a GPO you are having problems with. For instance, if you suspect that you are having problems with any of the "Hide Screen Saver Option" or "Hide Display Settings Option/Restore Screen Saver Option" GPOs we created in Chapter 1, you can run `Gpotool /gpo:Hide` to search for all GPOs starting with the word *Hide*, as shown in Figure 4.11.

 To specifically verify the "Hide Display Settings Option/Restore Screen Saver Option" setting, you can also run `Gpotool /gpo:"Hide Settings Tab / Restore Screen Saver Tab"` as seen in Figure 4.11. Note that the `/gpo:` switch is case sensitive. For instance, running `Gpotool /gpo:Hide` is different from running `GPOTOOL /gpo:hide`.

This example shows when things are going right. This next example (see Figure 4.12) shows when things might be wrong.

FIGURE 4.11 Use Gpotool to see if your GPCs and GPTs are synchronized across your Domain Controllers.

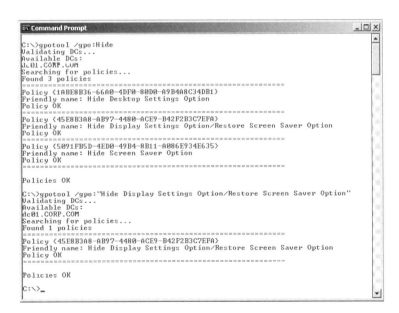

FIGURE 4.12 Gpotool has found trouble in paradise.

In this example, we are verifying the synchronization of the GPO named "Broken2." In this case, the versions between the GPC and GPT do not match. You can see this when comparing what the tool calls the DS version with the SYSVOL version. The DS version represents the GPC, and the SYSVOL version represents the GPT.

Before panicking, recall that this "problem" might not actually be a problem. Remember, the GPC and GPT replicate independently. The DC our clients are currently using might have simply received the SYSVOL (GPT) changes before the Active Directory changes (GPC) or vice versa. Wait a little while, and the two versions might converge. If they do not converge, this problem could indicate either Active Directory or FRS replication issues.

Here are some additional tips about using Gpotool:

- Running Gpotool on a large domain with lots of GPOs can take a looooong time and really bog down your Domain Controller performance. If possible, run Gpotool only after hours, when the fewest number of people will be affected.

- If you must run it during working hours, you might want to specify the /dc: option and specify to check only the GPOs on the PDC-Emulator (the place where GPOs are initially born and initially modified). If you're going to have a problem, it's quite likely to be initially pinpointed on this key Domain Controller.

- Gpotool has one extra super-power. That is, it can also verify the underlying ACLs of the GPT part of a GPO. Recall, that the GPT is the part of the GPO that lives in SYSVOL. To perform this extra check, you need to specifically specify it on the command line of Gpotool as Gpotool /checkacl. By default, this test is not run because it is additionally time- and resource-intensive. There is one key point about the /checkacl switch: it only checks the ACL inheritance flag on the SYSVOL Policies folder itself, not the ACLs on the individual folders which contain the guts of the GPO. So, if you have a specific permissions problem on the folder containing a GPO, the /checkacl switch won't really help you ferret that out.

- One caveat about `Gpotool`—it only checks to see if the version numbers are the same between the GPC and GPT. It does not check to see if all of the files that are supposed to be in the GPT are there, for example. If you're having FRS replication problems for example, then only some of the GPT files may have replicated to a given DC, and `Gpotool` won't tell you that if it finds that the gpt.ini file has the information it needs.

Using *Replmon* to See the Version Numbers

The `Replmon` (Replication Monitor) tool is available as part of the Support tools on the Windows 2003 (or Windows 2000) Server CD. `Replmon` is one of the most useful free tools Microsoft has ever created.

For our purposes, we'll use it in a fashion similar to how we used `Gpotool`; that is, `Replmon` can tell us if a GPO's GPC and GPT are in agreement with the version numbers.

First, load the Support tools in the `\SUPPORT\TOOLS` folder. Then, `choose` Start ➢ Run to open the Run dialog box, and type **Replmon** in the Open box. Right-click the Monitored Servers icon and choose "Add Monitored Server." For now, just add the PDC Emulator. In my case, I'll add DC01. Once the server is being monitored, right-click it and choose "Show Group Policy Object Status" to display a screen like that shown in Figure 4.13.

In Figure 4.13, you can see that the GPO named "Broken2" has an X in the Sync Status column. The version numbers are dissimilar in the GPC and GPT. Again, this might not be a real "problem" because the GPC and GPT are being independently replicated. Perhaps this Domain Controller did not yet get the latest updates.

FIGURE 4.13   Replmon can show you the version numbers of all your GPOs.

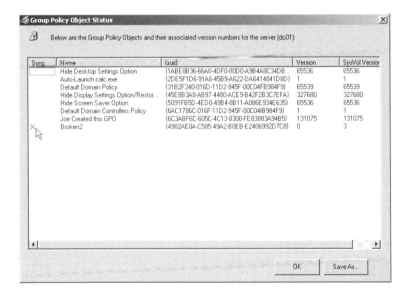

Isolating Replication Problems

You can try to see if Active Directory replication is working (and, hence, if GPC replication is working) by performing several "litmus tests." Here are some examples:

- Create a new GPO in the Group Policy Objects container. Just create it with no policy settings, and don't link it anywhere.

- Create a new OU in Active Directory Users And Computers or the GPMC.

- Add a new user in Active Directory.

In each case, you want to see if these objects are replicated to other DCs. After creating your objects on one Domain Controller, use the Active Directory Users And Computers and/or GPMC to check other Domain Controllers. Simply right-click the domain and choose another Domain Controller.

If these litmus tests fail, you can try to force replication using Active Directory Sites And Services. If you need extra-strength replication, Replmon can help force replication in multiple ways.

You can try to see if SYSVOL replication is working via FRS (and, hence, if GPT replication is working) by simply throwing any file—say, a Readme.txt file—into the SYSVOL share of any Domain Controller, and seeing if it is replicated to the other Domain Controllers' SYSVOL shares. If it is not automatically copied to the other Domain Controllers, test each machine's connectivity using the ping command.

Here are some additional tips for troubleshooting FRS replication:

- Microsoft TechNet has an excellent feature-length article, "Troubleshooting FRS," at the TechNet home page at http://tinyurl.com/7mlt5.

- Microsoft has a tool, SONAR (part of the Windows 2003 Resource Kit), that can dramatically help with FRS troubleshooting.

- Microsoft has another tool, ULTRASOUND, which surpasses SONAR's ability to help troubleshoot FRS.

ULTRASOUND and SONAR are available on the Microsoft website. At last check, SONAR can be found at http://tinyurl.com/5ouk9, and Ultrasound can be found at http://tinyurl.com/odgu. General FRS and troubleshooting and information can be found at www.microsoft.com/frs as of this writing.

The Microsoft Knowledge Base articles Q221112, Q221111, Q272279, and Q229928 are good starting points to learn more about FRS and how to troubleshoot SYSVOL replication problems by debugging FRS. See Q229896 and Q249256 for details on how to debug Active Directory replication.

Death of a GPO

As you saw in Chapter 2, there are two ways to stop using a GPO at a level in Active Directory. One way is to "Delete the link" to the GPO at the level being used in Active Directory. In the swimming pool analogy, we're simply removing the tether to our child in the pool, but we're leaving the object swimming in the pool should other levels want to use it.

The other way to stop using a GPO is to delete it. With the GMPC, you can delete a GPO only by traversing to the Group Policy Objects node, right-clicking it, and choosing Delete, as you saw back in Figure 2.7. But, again, be careful; other levels of Active Directory (including those in other domains and forests) might be using this GPO you're about to whack.

 As we've discussed in previous chapters, cross-domain linking of GPOs is a no-no. And, if you whack the GPO in the source domain, it won't clean up links to *other* (target) domains.

How Client Systems Get Group Policy Objects

The items stored on the server make up only half the story. The real magic happens when the GPO is applied at the client, usually a workstation, although certainly servers behave in the same way. Half of Group Policy's usefulness is that it can apply equally to servers as well as desktops and laptops. Indeed, with the advent of Windows 2003 and, of course, Windows Vista , the new policy settings they bring to the table mean you can control and configure more stuff than ever. So the details in this section are for all clients—servers and workstations.

When Group Policy is deployed from upon high to client systems, the clients always do the requesting. This is why, when the chips are down and things aren't going right, you'll need to trot out to the system and crack open the Event Log (among other troubleshooting areas) to help uncover why the client isn't picking up your desires.

Microsoft doesn't provide a way to instantaneously "push" the policy settings inside GPOs to clients, even if you think they should get a new change right now. Out of the box, there's no "push the big red button and force the latest Group Policy to all my clients" command to make sure every client gets your will. This can be a little disappointing, especially if you need a security setting, such as a Software Restriction Policy propagated to all your clients right now. There are two ways, however, to make this a reality:

- In Chapter 7, I'll show you a little scripting magic to forcefully push Group Policy out the door. Note, however, that this script needs to be "prepared" on the client machine before you can leverage it.

- In the Third-Party Group Policy Solutions Guide on www.GPanswers.com is a link to a free tool, called RGPrefresh, which also performs this function. (Alternatively, you can download that tool right from my fellow MVP Darren Mar-Elia's website at http://www.gpoguy.com/rgprefresh.htm.)

- Also in the Third-Party Group Policy Solutions Guide on www.GPanswers.com is a link to another free tool called SpecOps GPrefresh, which also performs this function. This tool is graphical and hooks in to Active Directory Users and Computer and allows you to perform four functions upon your client machines: Group Policy Refresh, reboot, shutdown, or startup (if the client machine has a wake-on-LAN card).

But, without these "tricks," unfortunately, Group Policy is processed only when the computer starts up, the user logs on, at periodic intervals in the background, as discussed in Chapter 3. In that chapter, you learned "when" Group Policy is processed; in this section, you'll learn both "how" and "why" Group Policy is processed.

The Steps to Group Policy Processing

Group Policy processing on the client is broken down into roughly two parts. The first part is called "core" or "infrastructure" processing. We'll break it down for Windows Vista and pre-Vista machines here, the two types of computers you're likely to have.

Core Processing for Pre-Windows Vista Machines

During the core processing stage of Group Policy processing, Windows tries to accomplish a number of tasks. Chief among those is to:

- Determine if the connection to the Domain Controller is over a slow link
- Discover all of the GPOs that apply to the computer or user
- Discover which Client Side Extensions have to be called
- Discover whether anything has changed (GPOs, Security group memberships, WMI filters) since the last processing cycle
- Create the final list of GPOs that need to be applied

In order to perform these tasks, Windows requires a number of network protocols be successfully passed between the client and the DC that it's paired with. These protocols, and their usage, is listed here:

- ICMP for slow link detection
- RPC (TCP port 135 and some random port that's greater than port 1024) for authentication to AD
- LDAP (TCP port 389) for querying AD to determine the list of GPOs, group membership, WMI filters, and so on
- SMB (TCP port 445) for querying the GPT in SYSVOL

If the client tries to get to the server and any of the protocols listed above are blocked (usually by a firewall), then all Group Policy processing will fail. Thus it's important that Windows clients have unimpeded access to all potential domain controllers that will respond to authentication and Group Policy requests for these protocols. Again, it's not super-common in the Windows world (yet) to turn the firewalls on for Domain Controllers and servers.

Another point to note is that Group Policy processing in Windows versions prior to Windows Vista ran within the privileged Winlogon process. Winlogon is a system service, and thus has the highest level of privilege within Windows. For that reason, poorly behaved CSEs could potentially crash Windows. This didn't happen often (or ever, to my knowledge, but it was certainly possible). As we'll see in the next section, the inner workings of Group Policy changes in Windows Vista, as we'll see with the *Group Policy service*.

Once the core steps are complete, each CSE DLL is called by the Winlogon process, in the order that they are registered in the Registry under HKLM\Software\Microsoft\ Windows NT\CurrentVersion\Winlogon\GPExtensions (with the exception of Administrative Templates policy, which always runs first), and each CSE processes the GPOs that have been discovered during the core processing cycle.

Core Processing for Windows Vista

So, Microsoft has made a significant change to the Group Policy processing engine in Windows Vista. They have moved the engine from Winlogon into a separate service, called the **Group Policy Client** service. This service is "hardened" so that even an administrator cannot easily stop it.

This is probably a good thing because there are not too many situations where you'd want to disable Group Policy processing completely. As I mentioned, a normal administrator cannot easily stop the Group Policy Client service. If you go into the Services MMC snap-in, and highlight the service, you'll notice that the options to stop and start the service are grayed out. It takes a bit of work to stop the service and when you do, it will automatically restart itself after a short period of time. However, if you want to see this in motion, here is the general process.

If you want to try this out (just for fun) you'll need to start the Windows Task Manager and select the Services tab. Locate the service called gpsvc, and note the process ID listed next to it, as shown in Figure 4.14. Next, move to the Processes tab in Task Manager and locate the svchost process with the same process ID as the gpsvc entry. Highlight that svchost process and press the End Process button to end the service.

That's all there is to it!

FIGURE 4.14   Viewing the Group Policy Client service process

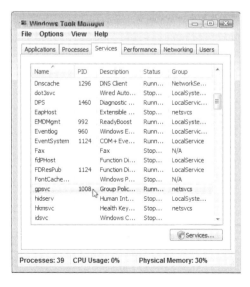

Now, the main difference between core processing for Windows Vista vs. the older operating systems is the ICMP slow link detection process. Even though, underneath the hood, there's lots of new stuff for Vista, it acts pretty much like XP. Except in one big respect, and that's the slow link detection process. This is described next.

Windows Vista and Slow Link Detection

Windows Vista uses a completely different mechanism to detect a slow link. Instead of using ICMP pings, Vista relies on the Network Location Awareness (NLA) service that is part of the operating system. The NLA service uses a series of higher level communications with Domain Controllers to determine when a Domain Controller is available and at what link speed it is available. The NLA process is more dynamic and thus is able to inform the Group Policy engine when a Domain Controller becomes available (where the previous mechanism was not). Because of this, it's important to understand under what scenarios GP processing occurs when NLA detects that a DC is available. We'll discuss this later in the chapter in the section on "Troubleshooting NLA in Windows Vista"

Client-Side Extensions

When a Group Policy "clock" strikes, the Group Policy engine springs into action to start processing your wishes. The GPOs that are meant for the client are downloaded from Active Directory, and then the client pretty much does the rest.

When GPOs are set from upon high, usually not all policy setting categories are used. For instance, you might set up an Administrative Template policy, but not an Internet Explorer Maintenance policy. The client is smart enough to know which policy setting groups affect it.

The client knows which settings group affect it specifically because it asks each GPO which extensions have been set within it through the gpcMachineExtensionName and gpcUserExtensionName attributes in the GPC that we introduced earlier.

This happens during the "core" processing part of Group Policy. During this core processing cycle the client queries Active Directory to get its list of GPOs, figures out which ones actually apply to it, and makes a list of the CSE that will need to run for the GPOs found. Once all that core work is done, then each CSE is called in turn to do its thing.

CSEs are really DLLs (Dynamic Link Libraries) that perform the Group Policy processing. These DLLs are called by the system Winlogon process (or the Group Policy Client Service in Windows Vista) and are shipped, out-of-the-box in clients capable of processing Group Policy: Windows 2000, Windows XP, Windows 2003, and Windows Vista. These CSEs are automatically registered in the operating system and are identified in the Registry by their GUIDs.

Additional CSEs can be created by third-party programmers who want to control their own aspects of the operating system or their own software. See the Sidebar "Group Policy Software Vendors with their own CSEs" for a sampling.

Group Policy Software Vendors with their own CSEs

The whole idea of Client-Side Extensions (CSEs) is that if you have a great idea, and you want to make that idea happen via Group Policy, you can do it. Several vendors have stepped up and created their own CSEs which implement their ideas. Come to www.GPanswers.com for a latest look on products that have their own CSEs. As of this writing, the following companies have the following products with their own CSEs.

- Quest

    Quest Group Policy Extensions for Desktops

    Found here: http://www.quest.com/group_policy_extensions_for_desktops/

    This product helps you craft policies in ways that were previously difficult. For instance, you can leverage an existing machine's GPO settings and make it a "template" to zap down to other systems. This also has configurations which manipulate Microsoft Outlook, control the Registry, manage files and folders, and more.

- NetIQ

    IntelliPolicy for Clients

    Found here: http://www.netiq.com/products/ipol/default.asp

    This product contains a wide variety of ways to control your systems including manipulating Scheduled Tasks, locking down hardware (like USB and serial ports), and enforcing power management on desktops.

- Special Operations Software

    SpecsOps Deploy

    Found here: http://www.specopssoft.com/products/specopsdeploy/Default.asp

    This CSE enables you to perform several Group Policy Software Installation tasks (discussed in Chapter 10) that you can't natively perform. For instance, you can distribute software to users and computers that are already logged on as well as get a detailed log of which computers received software.

    Specops Inventory

    Found here: http://www.specopssoft.com/products/specopsinventory/Default.asp

    This product performs hardware and software inventory via the Group Policy engine and provides detailed reports of what software and hardware your enterprise is using.

- PolicyPak Software

  PolicyPak family of tools

  Found here: www.PolicyPak.com

  This is a set of specific CSEs which control applications which aren't natively Group Policy enabled. So, if you wanted to manage Adobe Acrobat Reader or WinZip or the Norton Antivirus client via Group Policy, check out PolicyPak.com.

In Windows 2000, the OS shipped with 9 CSEs. In Windows XP and 2003, Microsoft added 2 more, for a total of 11 CSEs. Vista adds an additional 4 for a total of 15.

The three Windows XP, SP2 and Windows 2003, SP1 CSEs are Internet Explorer Zonemapping, 802.11x Wireless policies, and Quality of Service Packet Scheduler policies. Vista adds the Enterprise QoS, 802.3, Offline Files, Deployed Printer Connections, and Windows Search CSEs. Some additional policy functionality, such as Software Restriction Policies, was added in XP and Windows 2003 but was implemented within an existing CSE.

To take a look at the CSEs on a Windows 2000, Windows XP, or Windows Vista workstation, follow these steps:

1. On Windows XPPRO1 or VISTA1, log on as Administrator.

2. For Windows XP, choose Start ➢ Run (for Windows Vista just type `regedit` into the Search dialog box) to open the Run dialog box, in the Open box type **Run Regedit**, and press Enter to open the Registry Editor, as shown in Figure 4.15.

FIGURE 4.15   The client-side extension DLLs actually perform the GPO processing.

3. Drill down into HKLM ➤ Software ➤ Microsoft ➤ Windows NT ➤ Current Version ➤ Winlogon ➤ GPExtensions. Here you will find a list of GUIDs, each representing a CSE.

    Let's take a look at the next sections to understand precisely what we're looking at.

CSEs for Pre-Windows Vista Machines

Figure 4.15 shows a sample CSE and the settings for disk quotas. See Table 4.2 for the CSEs listed by Class ID, the functions they perform, and the associated DLLs. Note that a particular DLL can be responsible for more than one function.

TABLE 4.2   GUIDs, Their Functions, and Their Corresponding DLLs for pre-Windows Vista Machines

Class ID	Function	DLL
{C6DC5466-785A-11D2-84D0-00C04FB169F7}	Software deployment	appmgmts.dll
{3610EDA5-77EF-11D2-8DC5-00C04FA31A66}	Disk quotas	dskquota.dll
{B1BE8D72-6EAC-11D2-A4EA-00C04F79F83A}	EFS recovery	scecli.dll
{25537BA6-77A8-11D2-9B6C-0000F8080861}	Folder redirection	fdeploy.dll
{A2E30F80-D7DE-11d2-BBDE-00C04F86AE3B}	Internet Explorer settings	iedkcs32.dll
{e437bc1c-aa7d-11d2-a382-00c04f991e27}	IP security	gptext.dll
{35378EAC-683F-11D2-A89A-00C04FBBCFA2}	Registry settings (Administrative Templates)	userenv.dll
{42B5FAAE-6536-11D2-AE5A-0000F87571E3}	Scripts	gptext.dll
{827D319E-6EAC-11D2-A4EA-00C04F79F83A}	Security	scecli.dll
{0ACDD40C-75AC-47ab-BAA0-BF6DE7E7FE63}	Wireless (802.11x) (Windows XP only)	gptext.dll
{426031c0-0b47-4852-b0ca-ac3d37bfcb39}	Quality of Service Packet Scheduler (Windows XP only)	gptext.dll
None	Software Restriction (Windows XP only)	None
None	Remote Installation Services (RIS)	None

Why Don't All CSEs Have DLLs? Neither Remote Installation Services (RIS) nor Software Restriction polices require CSEs to be associated with DLLs. RIS is active *before* the operating system is. Software Restriction policies don't require CSEs because they "tag along" on the functionality of another CSE.

 When creating custom ADM or ADMX templates (see "ADM/ADMX Template Syntax" on this book's website), the CLIENTEXT keyword specifies which client-side extension is needed to process particular settings on the client computer. This is required for some policy features, such as Software Restriction and Disk Quota policy, that use the same file to store their settings as does Administrative Template policy.

CSEs for Windows Vista Machines

See Table 4.3 for the Windows Vista CSEs listed by Class ID, the functions they perform, and the associated DLLs. Note that a particular DLL can be responsible for more than one function.

TABLE 4.3 GUIDs, Their Functions, and Their Corresponding DLLs for Windows Vista Machines

Class ID	Function	DLL
{C6DC5466-785A-11D2-84D0-00C04FB169F7}	Software Installation	appmgmts.dll
{3610EDA5-77EF-11D2-8DC5-00C04FA31A66}	Disk quotas	dskquota.dll
{B1BE8D72-6EAC-11D2-A4EA-00C04F79F83A}	EFS recovery	scecli.dll
{25537BA6-77A8-11D2-9B6C-0000F8080861}	Folder redirection	fdeploy.dll
{A2E30F80-D7DE-11d2-BBDE-00C04F86AE3B}	Internet Explorer branding	iedkcs32.dll
{e437bc1c-aa7d-11d2-a382-00c04f991e27}	IP security	polstore.dll
{35378EAC-683F-11D2-A89A-00C04FBBCFA2}	Registry settings (Administrative Templates)	userenv.dll
{42B5FAAE-6536-11D2-AE5A-0000F87571E3}	Scripts	gpscript.dll
{827D319E-6EAC-11D2-A4EA-00C04F79F83A}	Security	scecli.dll
{0ACDD40C-75AC-47ab-BAA0-BF6DE7E7FE63}	Wireless (802.11x) (Windows XP only)	wlgpclnt.dll

TABLE 4.3 GUIDs, Their Functions, and Their Corresponding DLLs for Windows Vista Machines *(continued)*

Class ID	Function	DLL
{426031c0-0b47-4852-b0ca-ac3d37bfcb39}	Quality of Service Packet Scheduler (Windows XP only)	gptext.dll
{4CFB60C1-FAA6-47f1-89AA-0B18730C9FD3}	Internet Explorer Zonemapping	iedkcs32.dll
{7933F41E-56F8-41d6-A31C-4148A711EE93}	Windows Search	srchadmin.dll
{7B983727-8072-47ea-83A4-39C6CE25BAE6}	Offline Files	cscobj.dll
{8A28E2C5-8D06-49A4-A08C-632DAA493E17}	Deployed Printer Connections	gpprnext.dll
{B587E2B1-4D59-4e7e-AED9-22B9DF11D053}	802.3 Policy	dot3gpclnt.dll
{FB2CA36D-0B40-4307-821B-A13B252DE56C}	Enterprise QoS	gptext.dll

Inside CSE Values

For each CSE, several values can be set or not. Not all CSEs use these values. Indeed, Microsoft does not support modifying them in any way. They are presented in Table 4.4 for your own edification, but in most circumstances, you should not be modifying them unless explicitly directed to do so by Microsoft Product Support Services (PSS).

 Remember, the CSE sets these values—you don't, unless you're directed by Microsoft PSS to help make sure the CSE is working the way it's supposed to.

TABLE 4.4 Client-Side Extension Values

Registry Value	Data Type	Function	Data	Default
DLLName	REG_EXPAND_SZ	Contains the DLL name	CSE DLL	Per CSE
ProcessGroupPolicy	REG_SZ	The name of the callback function within the CSE that processes policy	The function name	Per CSE
NoMachinePolicy	REG_DWORD	Indicates whether this CSE supports per-computer settings	0=Does Not; 1=Does	0

TABLE 4.4　Client-Side Extension Values *(continued)*

Registry Value	Data Type	Function	Data	Default
NoUserPolicy	REG_DWORD	Indicates whether this CSE supports per-user settings	0=Does Not; 1=Does	0
NoSlowLink	REG_DWORD	Enable/disable over slow link	0=Process; 1=Don't process	0
NoBackgroundPolicy	REG_DWORD	Enable/disable background GPO processing	0=Process; 1=Don't process	0
NoGPOListChanges	REG_DWORD	Process if changed or not	0=Always process; 1=Do not process unless changes	0
PerUserLocalSettings	REG_DWORD	Caches policies for user in the machine section of the Registry	0=Don't cache; 1=Cache	0
RequiresSuccessful-Registry	REG_DWORD	Forces CSE DLLs to be registered with the operating system	0=Don't care; 1=CSEs must be registered	0
EnableAsynchronous-Processing	REG_DWORD	Enable/disable asynchronous GPO processing	0=Synchronous; 1=Asynchronous	Depends on the CSE

Note that many of the options listed in Table 4.4 (for example, NoSlowLink, NoBackgroundPolicy, NoGPOListChanges) can be set within the Computer Configuration ➢ Administrative Templates ➢ System ➢ Group Policy section of a GPO. When they are set through policy, then the values shown in the Registry value column listed in the table are ignored.

I hope you won't have to spend too much time in here. But I present this information so that if you need to debug a certain CSE, you can go right to the source and see how a setting might not be what you want.

Remember that most of these settings are established either by the system default or can be changed. You can change the settings yourself—such as the ability to process over slow links, the ability to be disabled, or the ability to be processed in the background—using the techniques described near the end of Chapter 3.

Where Are Administrative Templates Registry Settings Stored?

Because one of the most commonly applied policy settings is the Administrative Templates, let's take a minute to analyze specifically how Administrative Templates are processed when the client processes them.

Here, we're just talking about proper "policies" and not "preferences" (which are discussed in Chapter 5).

I've already discussed how Group Policy is more evolved than old NT 4–style policies. Specifically, one of the most compelling features is that most policy settings do not tattoo the Registry anymore. That is, once a setting is applied, it applies only for that computer or user. When the user or computer leaves the scope of the GPO (for example, when you move the user from the **Human Resources Users** OU to the **Accounting Users** OU), the Registry settings that did apply to them are removed, and the new Registry settings then apply.

When an NT 4–style policy was written, the writer could choose to modify any portion of the Registry. Now, as you've seen, when the settings specified in the Administrative Templates section of Group Policy no longer apply (for example, when a new user logs on or the computer is moved to another OU), the settings are removed or applied appropriately for the next user.

Administrative Templates Group Policy settings are usually stored in the following locations:

User Settings   HKEY_CURRENT_USER\Software\Policies

Computer Settings   HKEY_LOCAL_MACHINE\Software\Policies

Alternatively, some applications may choose the following locations:

User Settings   HKEY_CURRENT_USER\Software\Microsoft\Windows\CurrentVersion\Policies

Computer Settings   HKEY_LOCAL_MACHINE\Software\Microsoft\Windows\Currentversion\Policies

Microsoft is encouraging third-party developers to write their applications so that they look in the first set.

Knowing how this works helps us understand why Windows XP has about 200 more Administrative Templates policy settings that can apply to it. It's quite simple: the specific program that's targeted for the policy setting looks for settings at these two Registry locations. Sometimes that application is one we overlook a lot—Explorer.Exe! For Windows XP, Explorer.exe has been "smartened up" and now knows to look in these Registry keys for about 200 new items. Windows XP/SP2's Firewall has been smartened up to look for about 20 new items. You get the idea.

This also answers the question of why Windows 2000 machines seem to "overlook" policy settings that are designed only for Windows XP or Windows 2003. In short, "older" operating systems (which are really applications) simply don't know to "look" for new policy settings (even though those settings are written into the target machine's Registry). So, all operating systems (which, again, are really applications) that can download the policy settings *do*. But, who cares? If an older system applies a policy setting, the Registry is modified and then it's generally ignored by the applications running on it. Windows 2000 just doesn't know to look for the new Registry changes that Windows XP, Windows Vista, or Windows 2003 policy settings change. Occasionally, with the release of a service pack, the application in question might get a new lease on life and understand some new policy settings—because the application has now been updated to look for them in the Registry. This has already happened for Explorer, Software Update Services, Windows Media Player, and Office to name a few.

 If you have a mixture of Windows 2000 desktops and member servers and Windows XP, Windows Vista, or Windows 2003 member servers, you might need to keep track of policy settings that affect only XP, for example. It's likely a good idea to create GPOs with names specific to which operating system they apply to: Windows 2000, Windows XP, Windows 2003, and/or Windows Vista.

Because the settings inside Administrative Templates are written to only these four locations, we are free from the bonds of having our Registries tattooed. The Administrative Templates CSE (Userenv.Dll) applies the settings placed in any of these four locations to the current mix of user and system.

As you move users in and out of OUs, or change group membership, then the settings that apply to them change as well. Under the covers, this process is a bit more subtle. The way the nontattooing behavior works is that when Registry settings are first applied, they are merged into files that are stored on the computer in per-computer and per-user areas—each file is called ntuser.pol. The next time that the Administrative Templates CSE runs, it looks into these stored files and makes a list of all of the policy settings that exist in the four "special" keys I mentioned previously (in the "Where Are Administrative Templates Registry Settings Stored?" section). It then deletes all of those settings, as specified by that file. Then, the CSE re-creates that file with all the new Administrative Template settings that currently apply to the computer or user. Finally, it applies those values to the computer or user portions of the Registry.

Any settings that are outside the four "special" locations are *not* covered by this removal process and thus, you have the tattooing behavior.

 For information on how to use other Administrative Templates, see Chapter 5, and for information on how to create your own Administrative Templates, see "ADM/ADMX Template Syntax" on this book's website.

Why Isn't Group Policy Applying?

At times, you set up Group Policy from up on high, and your users or workstations do not receive the changes. Why might that be the case?

First, remember how Group Policy is processed:

- The GPO "lives" in the swimming pool in the domain.

- The client requests Group Policy at various times throughout the day.

- The client connects to a Domain Controller to get the latest batch of GPOs. (Group Policy isn't somehow "pushed" from up on high.)

- If it's status-quo, that is:

  - Nothing has changed inside the GPO (based on changed version number)

  - The location of the user or computer hasn't changed in Active Directory

  - The user or computer hasn't changed group memberships

  - Any WMI filters set on the GPO haven't changed.

  …the default behavior is to not reprocess the GPOs (though this can be changed as explored in Chapter 3).

- If there is a change (with respect to any of these previous bullet points), then all applicable CSEs reprocess all applicable GPOs.

That's the long and the short of it.

Now, if you think all this is happening properly, try to answer the following questions to find out what could be damming the proper flow of your Group Policy process.

Reviewing the Basics

Sometimes, it's the small, day-to-day things that prevent a GPO from applying. By testing a simple application that has normal features, you can often find problems and eliminate them, which allows Group Policy to behave the way you expect.

Is the Group Policy Object or Link Disabled?

Recall from Chapter 1 that there are two halves of the Group Policy coin: a computer half and a user half. Also recall that either portion or both can be disabled. Indeed, a GPO itself can be fully disabled (see Figure 4.16).

Check the GPO itself or any related GPO links. Click the Details tab and check the GPO Status setting. If it is anything other than "Enabled," you might be in trouble.

If you change the status of the GPO, that status changes on all links that use this GPO.

Are You Sure about the Inheritance?

Recall that Group Policy flows downward from each level—site, domain, and each nested OU—and is cumulative. Also recall that in all versions of Windows prior to Vista, there is only one Local Group Policy for a computer, which is applied first.

And, in Vista there are three levels of MLGPOs. See Chapter 1 for the full rundown. Remember, in MLGPOs it's a "last written wins" policy.

FIGURE 4.16 You can disable the entire GPO if desired.

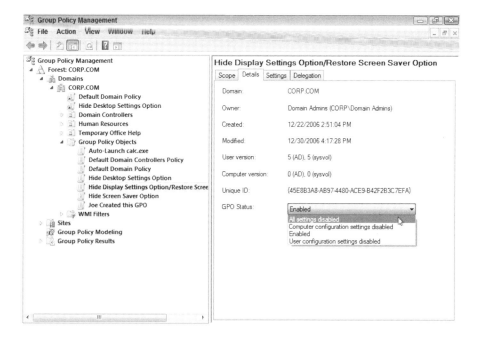

Are You Trying to Apply Policy to a Group inside an OU?

This bears repeating: You can't just plunk an NT-style/Active Directory group that contains users into an OU and expect them to get Group Policy. Group Policy doesn't work that way; you can only apply Group Policy directly to users or computers in an OU. Not a group.

Multiple Group Policy Objects at a Level

Also recall that there can be many GPOs at any level, which are applied in the reverse order— that is, from bottom to top, as described in Chapter 2. Since any two (or more) GPOs can contain the same or even conflicting settings, the last-applied GPO wins. If you mean for one GPO to have higher precedence, use the Up and Down buttons to manipulate the order. Remember, the GPO with the *lowest* number gets the *highest* priority. Confusing, I know, but that's the deal.

Examining Your Block Inheritance Usage

The GPMC gives you a quick view of all instances of Block Inheritance with the Blue Exclamation point (!). Remember: once you select to block inheritance, *all GPOs* from higher levels are considered null and void—not just the one policy setting or GPO you had in mind to block. It's as if you were starting from a totally blank slate. Therefore, whenever you block inheritance, you must start from scratch—either creating and linking new GPOs or simply linking to existing GPOs already swimming in the GPOs container.

Examining Your "Enforced" Usage

Conversely, be aware of all of your "Enforce" directives. The Enforce icon is a little lock next to the GPO link. "Enforce" specifies that the policy settings selected and contained within in a *specific* GPO cannot be avoided at any inherited level from this point forward. Note that "Block Inheritance" applies to a container in Active Directory (for example, a domain or an OU), while "Enforced" applies to a GPO link. So if you have a GPO linked to four containers in Active Directory, you could have only one of those links "Enforced," two of them or all of them (or none!). When "Block Policy Inheritance" and "Enforce" are seemingly in conflict, "Enforced" always wins. Recall that "Enforced" was previously known as "No Override" in the old-school parlance.

Are Your Permissions Set Correctly?

Recall from Chapter 2 that two permissions—"Read" and "Apply Group Policy"—must be set so that the affected user processes a specific GPO. By default, Authenticated Users have these two rights, but you can remove this group and set your own filtering via the "Security Filtering" section on the Scope tab of a GPO link.

In Chapter 2, I showed you two ways to filter:

- Round up only the users, computers, or Security groups who *should* get the GPO applied to them.

- Figure out who you *do not* want to get the GPO applied to them, and use the "Deny" attribute over the "Apply Group Policy" right.

When all is said and done, users will need both "Read" and "Apply Group Policy" permissions on the GPO itself to apply GPOs. And, you can prevent a GPO from applying by simply setting "Deny" access on one or the other of these two rights. Though, if you're going to use this technique, best practices dictate to always try to deny access on "Apply Group Policy" and not "Read."

 We try to always deny "Apply Group Policy" (and not "Read") because later, that user might need to be able to modify the GPO. And, without read access, they cannot modify it.

Having only one of those permissions means that Group Policy will not apply when processing is supposed to occur. Additionally, make sure to remember that the "Deny" attribute always trumps all other permissions. If an explicit "Deny" attribute is encountered, it is as if it were the only bit in the world that matters. Therefore, if a specific GPO is not being applied to a user or a group, make sure that "Deny" isn't somehow getting into the picture along the way.

Any use of the "Deny" bit is not displayed in the "Security Filtering" section of the Scope tab; so you really have no notification if it's being used. I predict this will be a common reason for Group Policy not applying; the old-school way to perform Group Policy filtering involved heavy use of the "Deny" bit, and now the GPMC will not easily display this fact unless you use the Group Policy Results Wizard (or gpresult.exe).

Advanced Inspection

If you've gone through the basics, and nothing is overtly wrong, perhaps a more subtle interaction is occurring. See if any of the following questions and solutions fit the bill.

Is Windows XP/Windows Vista Fast Boot On?

The default behavior of Windows XP and Windows Vista is different from that of Windows 2000. The default behavior of Windows 2000 is to process GPOs in the foreground (at computer startup or user logon) synchronously. That is, for the policy settings that affect a Windows 2000 computer (which will take effect at startup), every GPO is applied—local, site, domain, and each nested OU—even before the user has the ability to press Ctrl+Alt+Del to log on. Once the user logs on, the policy settings that affect the user side are applied—local, site, domain, and each nested OU—before the user's Desktop is finally displayed and they can start working.

This usually isn't too much of a problem for the policy settings within GPOs that affect computers, but it can seriously affect your user's experience if enabled for user policy processing. Even *after* a user is logged on, GPOs can suddenly be downloaded and policy settings start popping up and changing the user's environment.

Moreover, as I stated in Chapter 3, by default, several key items in Windows XP take between two and three reboots to become effective. To that end, I suggest you modify the default behavior. The strongest advice I can give you is to create and link a new GPO at the domain level. Name your new GPO something like "Force Windows XP and Vista machines to act like Windows 2000," and enable the **Always wait for the network at computer startup and logon** policy setting. Then, select "Enforced" so it cannot be blocked.

To find this policy setting, drill down through Computer Configuration ➢ Administrative Templates ➢ System ➢ Logon branch of Group Policy. (For more information, see Chapter 3.)

Therefore, if you have erratic Group Policy application (especially for Software Installation, Folder Redirection, or Profile settings), see if the Windows XP and Windows Vista default of Fast Boot is still active.

Is Asynchronous Processing Turned On in Windows 2000?

Windows 2000 was born with a way to try to act like Windows XP and Vista and process GPOs asynchronously. However, doing so is not recommended, as amazingly unpredictable results can occur. Windows XP was built from the ground up to do asynchronous processing; Windows 2000 really wasn't. So, in a nutshell, don't turn on Asynchronous processing for Windows 2000 machines. It's a bad idea.

 Asynchronous Processing is independent for both the computer and the user sides.

Are Both the GPC and GPT Replicated Correctly?

As stated in the first part of this chapter, Group Policy is made up of two halves:

- The GPC, which is found in Active Directory and replicated via normal Active Directory replication
- The GPT, which is found in the SYSVOL share of one Domain Controller and replicated via FRS to other Domain Controllers

Both the GPC and GPT are replicated independently and can be on different schedules before converging.

Use the techniques described earlier in conjunction with Gpotool and Replmon to diagnose issues with replicating the GPC and GPT.

Did You Check the DNS Configuration of the Server and Client?

In order for the GPC and GPT to actually replicate correctly, the DNS structure must be 100 percent kosher at all times—both on the server and at the client. If you suspect that the GPC and GPT are not being replicated correctly, you might try to see if the DNS structure is the way you intend. If it is, I don't specifically recommend you rip it all up and reconfigure it if everything else is working. The Microsoft Knowledge Base article at http://support.microsoft.com/kb/291382/en-us provides a good foundation for understanding how to create a healthy DNS infrastructure.

In some cases, one Domain Controller might not be providing Group Policy to your clients. In the next section, I'll show you how to find out if your clients are really logged on and, if so, what Domain Controller the computer and user are using for logon.

Are You Really Logged On?

Windows 2000 doesn't perform the logon process precisely the same way that Windows XP or Windows Vista does. Specifically, when a user logs on to a Windows XP or Vista machine, Windows XP or Vista might or might not have really made contact with a Domain Controller to validate that user and give them a Kerberos ticket to the network. Kerberos is the newer authentication mechanism that has supplanted NTLM. Windows XP and Windows Vista will try its darndest to speed things up (again) and log on with cached credentials. Windows XP and Windows Vista will then try to contact a Domain Controller and get the Kerberos ticket for the user.

In Windows 2000, it is easy to identify the Domain Controller where the local Desktop authenticated. You issue a set command at a command prompt and look for the contents of the *LOGONSERVER* variable, as shown in Figure 4.17.

FIGURE 4.17 The LOGONSERVER variable shows the Domain Controller where this Windows 2000 client is picking up its Group Policy settings.

```
C:\WINNT\system32\cmd.exe                                    _ □ X
C:\>set
ALLUSERSPROFILE=C:\Documents and Settings\All Users
APPDATA=C:\Documents and Settings\User01\Application Data
CommonProgramFiles=C:\Program Files\Common Files
COMPUTERNAME=W2KPRO
ComSpec=C:\WINNT\system32\cmd.exe
HOMEDRIVE=C:
HOMEPATH=\
LOGONSERVER=\\DC01
NUMBER_OF_PROCESSORS=1
OS=Windows_NT
Os2LibPath=C:\WINNT\system32\os2\dll;
Path=C:\WINNT\system32;C:\WINNT;C:\WINNT\System32\Wbem
PATHEXT=.COM;.EXE;.BAT;.CMD;.UBS;.UBE;.JS;.JSE;.WSF;.WSH
PROCESSOR_ARCHITECTURE=x86
PROCESSOR_IDENTIFIER=x86 Family 6 Model 14 Stepping 8, GenuineIntel
PROCESSOR_LEVEL=6
PROCESSOR_REVISION=0e08
ProgramFiles=C:\Program Files
PROMPT=$P$G
SystemDrive=C:
SystemRoot=C:\WINNT
TEMP=C:\DOCUME~1\User01\LOCALS~1\Temp
TMP=C:\DOCUME~1\User01\LOCALS~1\Temp
USERDNSDOMAIN=CORP.COM
USERDOMAIN=CORP
USERNAME=User01
USERPROFILE=C:\Documents and Settings\User01
windir=C:\WINNT
```

In Windows 2000, if you aren't logged on to a Domain Controller, you see the variable set to the local computer name.

WARNING In Windows XP and Windows Vista, you simply cannot trust this *LOGONSERVER* variable to tell you the truth. Additionally, you cannot trust the Windows XP or Windows Vista SYSTEMINFO utility either, which claims to provide this data.

Just based on the way Windows XP and Windows Vista does its logon thing, you cannot use these aforementioned methods. XP will simply do a bald-faced lie and say that you are logged on (via the *LOGONSERVER* variable, with the information from the last Domain Controller it contacted).

With Windows XP and Windows Vista, to ensure your user and computer are really logged on the network, you can count on just one tool—Kerbtray (or the command-line equivalent, klist.exe). Kerbtray and klist are found in the Windows 2003 Resource Kit and are small enough to be put on a floppy and run on a suspect machine. When you run Kerbtray, it puts a little icon in the notification area. If the computer and user have Kerberos tickets, the icon turns green, and you know you're really logged on. However, if the Kerbtray returns a graphic of a bunch of loose keys (that, in my opinion, look like question marks), as shown in Figure 4.18, you know you're not actually logged on and, hence, not downloading the most recent GPOs. Again, if you were really logged on, the graphic would be a green ticket.

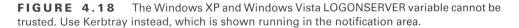

FIGURE 4.18   The Windows XP and Windows Vista LOGONSERVER variable cannot be trusted. Use Kerbtray instead, which is shown running in the notification area.

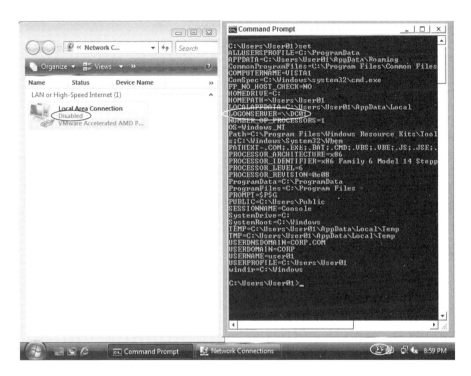

In Figure 4.18, you can see several things:

- The computer's network card is disabled (as shown in the Network Connections window).

- The *LOGONSERVER* variable is set to a Domain Controller (as shown in the CMD prompt window). Feel free to simply say out loud, "If the network card is off, this is bloody impossible."

- Kerbtray, thankfully, returns that icon of a bunch of loose keys verifying that we're not really logged on.

So, to find out if you're really logged on when using a Windows XP or Windows Vista computer, it's "Kerbtray or the highway." Once you've validated with Kerbtray that the computer has really logged on, you can *then* use the *LOGONSERVER* variable to make sure which Domain Controller the Windows XP or Windows Vista machine has used. Because, you'll know the truth: whether or not you're really logged on.

Did Something Recently Move?

If a computer account or a user account is moved from one OU to another, Windows (all versions) can wait as long as 30 minutes to realize this fact. Once they do, it might or might not apply background Group Policy processing for another 90 or more minutes! Running GPUpdate (or SECEDIT for Windows 2000 machines) will not help.

However, if you're expecting a specific setting to take effect on a user or computer that has moved more than 150 minutes ago, you'll then need to figure out if the move has been embraced by the Domain Controller the workstation used to authenticate. (See the previous section for information about how to determine the Domain Controller via the *LOGONSERVER* variable, but make sure you're really logged on!)

You can then fire up Active Directory Users And Computers and connect to the Domain Controller in question, as shown in Figure 4.19.

If the target computer's local Domain Controller does not know about the move, you might want to manually kick off replication using Active Directory Sites And Services. If the target computer's local Domain Controller *does* know about the move, you might want to try logging the user off and back on or restarting the computer. Although using SECEDIT (for Windows 2000 machines) or GPUpdate (for Windows XP, Windows Vista and Windows 2003 machines) to refresh the GPO is a good option, it's best to log off and/or reboot the machine to guarantee the computer will perform the initial policy processing as described in Chapter 3.

> I've seen Microsoft documentation which states that running GPUpdate /force on a Windows XP/SP2 machine will "jump start" the machine and/or user account into recognizing that it has moved around in Active Directory. I've done extensive testing but get inconsistent results. Sometimes it seems to work, other times it doesn't. In short, when a user or computer is moved around in Active Directory, I always re-login as the user, or reboot the computer. It's slightly better with Windows Vista, but even then, I've seen it work and not work.

FIGURE 4.19 You can always manually connect to a Domain Controller to see if Active Directory has performed replication.

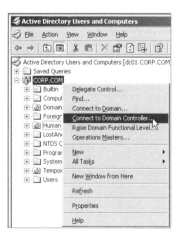

Is the Machine Properly Joined to the Domain?

With Windows 2000, if a device is moved from one OU to another and then the device is rebooted *before* DC replication occurs, sometimes the device can be bumped out of being a domain member because the "computer trust," also known as a "secure channel," is broken. To see if the computer trust (secure channel) to the domain is damaged, you can use NLTEST, which is in the Windows 2000 Support Tools on the Windows 2000 CD. The verification syntax is `nltest /sc_query:domain_name`. If the test passes, then you're kosher. If not, you might need to disjoin and rejoin the device to the domain.

Is Loopback Policy Enabled?

Enabling loopback policy will turn Group Policy on its ear: loopback forces the same user policy settings for everyone who logs on to a specific computer. If you're seeing user policy settings apply but not computer polices, or if things are applying without rhyme or reason, chances are loopback policy is enabled. Review Chapter 3 to see in depth how it works, when you should use it, and how to turn it off.

In Windows XP, determining you are in loopback mode is difficult.

In Windows Vista, it's a little easier. Look for Event ID 5311 in the Windows Vista "GroupPolicy" Event Logs. In the event directly, you'll see if loopback policy processing mode is set to Replace, Merge, or not enabled. We show this a little later in Figure 4.31.

How Are Slow Links Being Defined, and How Are Slow Links Handled?

If you notice that Group Policy is not applied to users coming in over a slow link, remember the rules for slow links:

- Registry and security settings are always applied over slow (and fast) links.

- EFS (Encrypting File System) and IPsec (IP Security) policies are *always* applied over slow links. You cannot turn this behavior off, even though settings found under Computer Configuration ➢ Administrative Templates ➢ System ➢ Group Policy branch imply that you can. This is a bug in the interface as described in Chapter 3.

- By default, Disk Quotas, Folder Redirection, Internet Explorer settings, and Software Deployment are not applied over slow links. Updated and new logon scripts are also not downloaded over slow links. You can change this default behavior under Computer Configuration ➢ Administrative Templates ➢ System ➢ Group Policy, as described in Chapter 3. Note that there is a difference between processing scripts policy and running scripts. Scripts themselves only run during a foreground processing cycle (computer startup or user logon), but the *updating* of the list of scripts that need to run can be done in the background. That updating is what I'm referring to here.

Additionally, you can change the definition of what equals a slow link. By default, a slow link is 500Kb or less. You can change the definition for the user settings in User Configuration ➢ Administrative Templates ➢ System ➢ Group Policy ➢ **Group Policy Slow Link Detection** and for the computer settings in Computer Configuration ➢ Administrative Templates ➢ System ➢ Group Policy ➢ **Group Policy Slow Link Detection**. Figure 4.20 shows the user settings. If Group Policy is not being applied to your slow-linked clients, be sure to inspect the slow-link definition to make sure they fit.

Last, don't forget about your broadband users on DSL or cable modem. Those speeds are sometimes faster than 500Kb and sometimes slower than 500Kb. This could mean that your broadband users might get GPOs on weekends but not when logged on during peak usage times. Therefore, if this happens, set the definition of slow link up or down as necessary.

FIGURE 4.20   Make sure you haven't raised the bar too high for your slower-connected users to receive Group Policy.

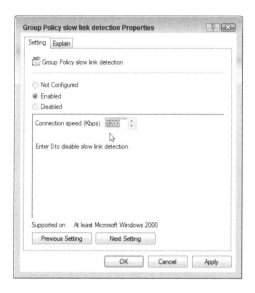

Finally, it should be noted that if you set the Slow Link Threshold to 0, the client will always assume it's on a fast link.

Troubleshooting NLA in Windows Vista

If you're working on a Windows Vista client, then you may need to determine if an NLA refresh has occurred. As I mentioned earlier, NLA is the service that replaces ICMP slow link detection when determining link speed and Domain Controller availability in Windows Vista.

If the Domain Controller is not available to the client, either because the client is remote and not connected to the company network, or the Domain Controller is simply not available, then Group Policy processing will fail.

When the Domain Controller becomes available again, NLA will detect its presence and trigger an immediate request to perform a background refresh of Group Policy. But, here's the trick: NLA will *only* actually perform this refresh if the previous refresh of Group Policy has failed. If the previous Group Policy refresh succeeded, and *then* the Domain Controller becomes unavailable and *then* available again (before the next Group Policy processing cycle), then NLA will not trigger a background refresh. You will be able to see NLA-based Group Policy refresh by looking at the Group Policy Operational Log, described in the section entitled, "Verbose Logging in Windows Vista." The event will look identical to that shown in Figure 4.21.

FIGURE 4.21   Viewing an event indicating an NLA-based Group Policy refresh

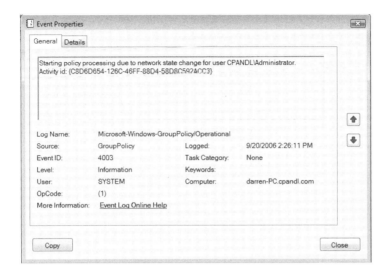

Note that it took as much as ten minutes for NLA to complete its detection of the Domain Controller and trigger a background Group Policy processing cycle in my testing. So, don't expect an NLA-based Group Policy refresh to happen immediately after your DC becomes available. Depending upon your system and network, your mileage may vary.

Is the Date and Time Correct on the Client System?

Time differences greater than five minutes between the client system and the validating Domain Controller will cause Kerberos to simply not permit the logon. If you don't have Kerberos, you've got a logon problem, and that's going to yield a Group Policy problem.

Are Your Active Directory Sites Configured Correctly?

Sometimes Group Policy won't apply if your client isn't in a properly defined Active Directory site (that has IP information associated with it). With that in mind, check the subnet the client is on, and verify that it is correctly associated to an Active Directory site and that the site has Domain Controller coverage.

Did You Check the DNS Configuration of the Client?

One of the most frequently encountered problems with Windows 2000 and above is that things just "stop working" when DNS gets out of whack. Specifically, if you're not seeing Group Policy apply to your client machines, make sure their DNS client is pointing to a Domain Controller or other authoritative source for the domain. If it's pointing to the wrong place or not pointing anywhere, Group Policy will simply not be downloaded. As a colleague of mine likes to say, "Healthy DNS equals a healthy Active Directory."

Moreover, in the age of Windows 2003 with its multiple forests with cross-forest trusts, Group Policy could be applying from just about anywhere and everywhere. It's more important than ever to verify that all DNS server pointers are designed properly and working as they should. For instance, if clients cannot access their "home" Domain Controllers while leveraging a cross-forest trust, they won't get Group Policy.

Finally, to put a fine point on it, Group Policy leverages *only* the fully qualified name. It's not enough to verify that you can resolve a computer named `xppro1` as opposed to `xppro1.corp.com`. The first is actually the NetBIOS name and *not* the fully qualified domain name. The second is the fully qualified domain name. If you find yourself in a DNS resolution situation where resolving the NetBIOS name will work, but the fully qualified name will not work, then you have a DNS problem that needs to be addressed.

Are You Trying to Set Password or Account Policy on an OU?

As you'll see in Chapter 6, certain Group Policy items, namely password and account policy, cannot be set at the OU level. Rather, these policy settings are only domain wide. The GUI lets you set these policy settings at the OU level, but they don't affect users or machines. Well, that's not really true, as you'll see in Chapter 6, but, for the purposes of troubleshooting, just remember that you can't have, say, six-character passwords in the **Sales** OU and 12-character passwords in the **Engineering** OU. It won't work. (You will see in Chapter 6 where password policy affects local accounts in an OU. Stay tuned for that later.)

Did Someone Muck with Security Behind the Group Policy Engine's Back?

As you saw in Chapter 3, there are a number of ways to "go around" the back of the Group Policy engine. Remember, though, that these exploits require local administrative access. However, this implies that users with local administrative access can manually hack the Registry and return their systems to just about however they want. Then, as I've described, Group Policy will not reapply upon background refresh, logon, or reboot. It reapplies changes only when something related to Group Policy has changed, as previously mentioned.

Windows 2000 uses the `SECEDIT` command to refresh Group Policy, but, as I've stated, it still won't forcefully reapply all the settings—even if the `/enforce` switch is used (which just forcefully reapplies security settings). Windows XP's and Windows Vista's `GPUpdate` command will refresh changed Group Policy as well, but its `/force` switch is quite powerful and will reapply all settings—even those that have not changed.

Is the Target Computer in the Correct OU? Is the Target User in the Correct OU?

This is my personal sore point. This is the one I usually check last, and it's usually what's at fault. That is, I've simply forgotten to place the user object or the computer object into the OU to which I want the GPO to apply. Therefore, the object isn't in the "scope" of where Group Policy will apply.

You can configure all the user or computer policy settings on an OU that you like, but, quite obviously, unless that user or computer object is actually *in* the OU, the target computer will simply not receive the message you're sending. And, no, you cannot just move a Security group that contains the user or computer objects and plunk it in the desired OU. Group Policy doesn't work that way. That actual user or computer object needs to be in the site, domain, or OU that the GPO applies! And since no two objects can be in any two OUs at the same time, this can be a challenge.

 Security groups are irrelevant—except for filtering.

Is There a Firewall On (or Between) Your Domain Controllers?

Windows XP/SP2 and Windows Vista get a lot of press because they ship with the firewall turned on. But Windows 2003 (with and without SP1) *also* has a firewall. It's just that Windows 2003's firewall isn't turned *on* by default.

So, if your Domain Controllers are Windows 2003, and, someone inadvertently turned on the built-in firewall, your clients will not be able to make contact to then download the Group Policy Objects.

Likewise, if someone has put up a firewall between your client and your Domain Controllers and it's blocking some of the core protocols required by the client to communicate with a Domain Controller, you simply won't be able to get the Domain Controller's attention, and hence you can't download Group Policy.

Did You Disable ICMP (Ping) from Your Clients to Your Domain Controllers? (for Pre-Vista Machines)

Once a client system makes contact with a Domain Controller to download its Group Policy Objects, it then immediately does a quick "speed test" to see whether it's on a fast network or a slow network. It does this by the ICMP protocol, more commonly described as "Ping."

Before we get into what happens when clients cannot ping Domain Controllers, let's first examine why they might not be able to ping Domain Controllers:

- There's a firewall between the client and Domain Controller that prevents ICMP.

- There's a firewall on the Domain Controller itself (such as Windows 2003's firewall that prevents ICMP).

- You have a router between the client and the Domain Controller that doesn't like the size of the ICMP test packets the client is using (2048 bytes is the default ICMP packet size used by slow link detection). Therefore, the ICMP test packets are being discarded, and it's as if they're never reaching the Domain Controller at all. Microsoft has a Knowledge Base article about this specific problem and its resolution at http://tinyurl.com/df9bx.

Let's examine the first two issues (which are really the same thing). That is, what if ICMP simply cannot be passed along to the Domain Controller? Perhaps a corporate decision to squash ICMP packets has been passed down, and now you just have to "handle it."

If ICMP is disabled, and slow link detection has not been disabled on the client, then no Group Policy processing will occur. It simply fails. You either have to disable slow link detection or you need to allow ICMP to pass unrestricted between the client and the Domain Controller. Note that when slow link detection is disabled, a "fast link" is *always* assumed. With that in mind, be sure to consider the impact when software installation and folder redirection comes into play.

 You can disable slow link detection by following the instructions in the Microsoft Knowledge Base article at `http://support.microsoft.com/kb/227260/en-us`.

Did Someone Muck with the ACLs of the GPT Part of the GPO in SYSVOL?

There is very, very little reason to ever need to manually dig into the guts of the GPO within SYS-VOL (that's the GPT part) and manually manipulate the file ACLs. However, uninitiated administrators will sometimes play—to nasty consequences. And, as stated earlier, `Gpotool /checkacl` won't actually validate the file ACLs on the GPO's GPT parts. In other words, if the ACLs on the GPT are damaged, your best bet is to whack the GPO and restore from backup. The restore process should create the GPO with the correct ACLs upon its recreation. You can also try using the GPMC to simply make a modification to a damaged GPO's ACLs. Any change will do. By doing so, this can sometimes "re-synchronize" the ACLs on the GPC and GPT, though it depends upon how badly the GPT's ACLs have been modified as to whether this method will work.

Client-Side Troubleshooting

One of the most important skills to master is the ability to determine what's going on at the client. By and large, the Group Policy Results tool, which you run from the GPMC, should give you what you need. However, occasionally, only trotting out to the client can truly determine what is happening on your client systems.

You could be roaming the halls, just trying to get the last Krispy Kreme glazed doughnut from the break room, when someone snags you and plops you in their seat for a little impromptu troubleshooting session. They want you to figure out why Group Policy isn't the same today as it was yesterday or why they're suddenly getting new or different settings.

This section will describe the various means for determining the RSoP (Resultant Set of Policy) while sitting at a client or using some remote-control mechanism such as Microsoft SMS (Systems Management Server), VNC (Virtual Networking Client), or even, in the case of Windows XP or Windows Vista, Remote Desktop. As you saw in the last chapter, the GPMC has two tools to help you tap into this data: Group Policy Results and Group Policy Modeling. However, there are other client-side tools at your disposal. Additionally, I'll describe how to leverage a function in Windows XP, Windows 2003, and Windows Vista to determine a target user's and computer's RSoP remotely!

Let me add a word about Group Policy troubleshooting technique before you run off and try to troubleshoot things. There is a good progression to things that is worth following:

- The first step you should take is to use the RSoP capabilities I describe in the next sections to make sure you know what's happening—which GPOs are applying, which aren't, and why.

- Once you've got that under your belt and still can't find the problem, the next step is to dive into the logs—starting with the Application Event Log on the problem client.

- Then proceed to the `userenv.log` file for Windows XP (described in the "Advanced Group Policy Troubleshooting with Log Files" section) or the Group Policy Event Logs for Windows Vista (also described in the "Leveraging Vista Admin Logs for Troubleshooting" section later).

- If `userenv.log` doesn't yield results, and you still can't find the problem, progress to CSE-specific logs.

This approach will minimize the time you spend solving a problem and leaves the most complex troubleshooting tasks as a last resort.

RSoP for Windows 2000

If you're sitting at a Windows 2000 machine, there aren't a lot of options to help you determine the RSoP. However, one particular tool can really bring home the bacon—`GPResult.exe`. This is one of the most important tools for Group Policy troubleshooting. When the going gets tough and I can't figure out what's going on, I look to `GPResult` to help tell me the score. You'll find `GPResult` in the Windows 2000 Server Resource Kit, but it is also built into the Windows 2000 Service Pack 4 and is in `C:\Windows\system32`.

The main goal of `GPResult` is to expose which GPOs are applied from where and the settings. The Achilles heel of `GPResult` on Windows 2000 is that it *must* be run on the client experiencing the problem.

WARNING `GPResult` appears only on Windows 2000 installations on which Service Pack 4 was installed *after* the machine was installed. `GPResult` will not appear if a slipstreamed Windows 2000 with SP4 was used to create a machine fresh. This is a bug in the definition of the service pack and is subject to change in future service packs. You can just expand `GPResult.exe` from the service pack files and plunk it in the `C:\windows\system32` folder without any penalty.

TIP If you can set up a Telnet server on a client system, you can `telnet` to the client and then run `GPResult` as if you were at the client. This could save you a hike or two. However, you'll need to log on with the credentials of the user (not of the local administrator) to get the same results. Note that Telnet passwords are usually cleartext, which can be a bad, bad thing if someone sniffs the wire.

GPResult has three modes—normal, verbose, and super-verbose—and can expose the user settings, the computer settings, or, by default, both. If you don't have Windows 2000 SP4 loaded, you can copy GPResult onto a floppy (from an SP4 installation or from the resource kit) or run it over the network.

Although GPResult is powerful, it has a limited set of options:

- /v displays verbose output. In the next section, you'll see an example of verbose output.

- /s displays super-verbose output. This equates to the new /z option in GPResult for Windows XP, Windows Server 2003 and Windows Vista. Again, I'll discuss how you might use this in the next section.

- /c limits the output to the computer-side policy settings.

- /u limits the output to the user-side policy settings.

You can mix and match the options. For instance, to display verbose output for the computer section, you can run GPResult /v /c.

We'll explore GPResult in depth in the next section, but, due to space concerns, I'll describe it mostly from a Windows XP and Windows Vista perspective.

> **NOTE**   The Windows 2000 GPResult isn't nearly as feature rich as its Windows XP, Windows Vista or Windows 2003 counterpart (for example, it will not show you detailed security policy results), but, as you'll soon see, there is still life in the Windows 2000 version.

RSoP for Windows Vista, Windows 2003, and Windows XP

Windows Vista, Windows XP, and Windows 2003 greatly expand our capacity to determine the RSoP of client machines and users on those machines. In this section, we'll explore several options. The first stop is a grown-up GPResult to help us get to the bottom of what's happening on our client machines. It should be noted that GPResult provides the same information as the GPMC's Group Policy Results Wizard, which can be used to generate the same data if a graphical tool is desired over the GPResult command-line variety.

GPResult for Windows 2003, Windows Vista, and Windows XP

GPResult for Windows Vista, Windows 2003, and Windows XP is more advanced than its Windows 2000 counterpart because it relies on the WMI-based RSoP infrastructure that was added in these newer operating systems. Indeed, you can run GPResult when you're sitting at a user's desktop or at your own desktop, or you can run it remotely and pretend to be that user. If you're running it while sitting at someone's desktop, you'll likely use the following options:

- /v is for verbose mode. It presents the most meaningful information.

- /z is for zuper, er, super-verbose mode. Based on the types of policy settings that affect the user or computer, it displays way more information than you'll likely ever want to see, based on the types of policy settings that affect the user or computer.

- /scope:user limits the output to the user-side policy settings, and /scope:computer limits the output to the computer-side policy settings.

There was a change in GPResult.exe for Windows Vista. Namely, as a regular, nonelevated user running GPResult.exe in Vista, you will only get user-side results from the tool. If you attempt to report on computer-side settings, you will get an access denied error until you run the command in an elevated context. Note, you could delegate specific users or groups the right to read this data using the GPMC.

You can mix and match the options. For instance, to display verbose output for the user section, you can run GPResult /v /scope:user.

GPResult in a Windows Vista World

There is one special note about running GPResult for Windows Vista. That is, if you try to run it as a regular user to get your RSoP data, you'll only be able to see the user side settings. Why? Because that's all you have access to in this more-secure Windows Vista world. To address this, you have two choices.

Choice 1   Run GPResult twice: once as the user in question, and again as an admin. (You run GPResult as an admin by running a command prompt as an administrative user.) This way, you take the user-side RSoP (that you just ran as the user) and the computer-side RSoP (that you just ran as an administrative user). Then, both of those halves make up the genuine RSoP. Frustrating, but necessary with the way Windows Vista security prevents regular users from seeing this. What makes this more frustrating is that if you've never logged in to a particular client machine as that administrator, you get an error from GPResult which expresses that there is no RSoP data for that admin. So, in the following shot, we're logged in as Joe User trying to get his RSoP data (top window). As stated, the computer side is inaccessible to him by default. So, we perform the runas command to get our own command-line window as the Administrator (bottom window). To counter, we then run GPResult /scope:computer we still get an error about the *user* side not having data (bottom window), even though we simply want the *computer* side of the equation. Frustrating to the max.

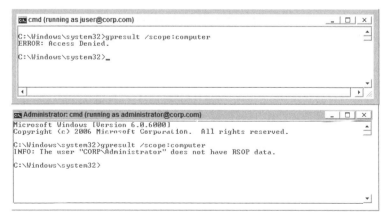

Choice 2   Use the GPMC to delegate users the ability to see their own computer-side RSoP data. Again, this isn't permitted by default in a Vista world. This works just fine for pre-Vista machine. So, in my opinion, there's very little reason not to just permit the user to see it. Assuming you wanted to permit everyone in the domain to see their own RSoP data, we need to review how to perform delegation (discussed in the last chapter). If we wanted to perform this delegation, we would use the GPMC, click the domain level, click the Delegation tab. In the Permission drop-down, we would select "Read Group Policy Results data," then add in "Authenticated Users"(or modify the rights over the Domain Users group, which is always already listed) and select to apply to "This container and all child containers."
You can see a screenshot of this here.

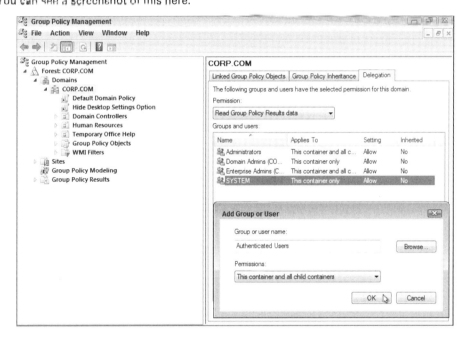

In this little sidebar we talked about what it takes to get the RSoP of a machine if we're physically sitting down at it. It's a totally different story if you're looking to get this data remotely, from another machine. And the equation gets even more intense if you're looking to delegate rights to a nonadministrative user (like someone on the help desk). A little later in this chapter, we review how to successfully retrieve Group Policy Results and Group Policy Modeling data as a nonadmin user. Be sure to read those sections to get the full picture, or you'll be left out in the cold wondering why you're getting "Access Denied" messages.

Those sections are "Remotely Calculating a Client's RSoP (When You've Delegated Permissions to Someone Who's Not a Local Administrator of the Target Machine)" and "Remotely Calculating a Client's Group Policy Modeling Analysis Data (When You've Delegated Permissions to Someone Who's Not a Local Administrator of the Target Machine)."

Here's the result of running **GPResult** with no arguments while logged on to the XPPRO1 workstation (which is in the **Human Resources Computers** OU) as Frank Rizzo (who is in the **Human Resources Users** OU). I have slightly modified the output for formatting purposes. Note that some of the display might be somewhat different from yours.

```
Microsoft (R) Windows (R) XP Operating System Group Policy Result tool v2.0
Copyright (C) Microsoft Corp. 1981-2001


Created On 12/30/2006 at 10:00:40 PM



RSOP results for CORP\frizzo on XPPRO1 : Logging Mode
------------------------------------------------------


OS Type:                    Microsoft Windows XP Professional
OS Configuration:           Member Workstation
OS Version:                 5.1.2600
Domain Name:                CORP
Domain Type:                Windows 2000
Site Name:                  Default-First-Site-Name
Roaming Profile:
Local Profile:              C:\Documents and Settings\frizzo
Connected over a slow link?: No



COMPUTER SETTINGS
------------------
    CN=XPPRO1,OU=Human Resources Computers,OU=Human Resources,DC=CORP,DC=COM
    Last time Group Policy was applied: 12/30/2006 at 9:58:06 PM
    Group Policy was applied from:      dc01.CORP.COM
    Group Policy slow link threshold:   500 kbps


    Applied Group Policy Objects
    ----------------------------
        Auto-Launch calc.exe
        Default Domain Policy


    The following GPOs were not applied because they were filtered out
    ----------------------------------------------------------------
        Hide Desktop Settings Option
            Filtering:  Not Applied (Empty)
```

Hide Screen Saver Option
    Filtering: Not Applied (Empty)

Local Group Policy
    Filtering: Not Applied (Empty)

The computer is a part of the following security groups:

BUILTIN\Administrators
Everyone
BUILTIN\Users
XPPRO1$
Computers-That-Get-the-Auto-Launch Calc.exe-GPO
Domain Computers
NT AUTHORITY\NETWORK
NT AUTHORITY\Authenticated Users

USER SETTINGS

CN=Frank Rizzo,OU=Human Resources Users,OU=Human Resources,DC=CORP,DC=COM
Last time Group Policy was applied: 12/30/2006 at 9:59:44 PM
Group Policy was applied from: dc01.CORP.COM
Group Policy slow link threshold: 500 kbps

Applied Group Policy Objects

    Hide Display Settings Option/Restore Screen Saver Option
    Default Domain Policy
    Hide Desktop Settings Option
    Hide Screen Saver Option
    Local Group Policy

The user is a part of the following security groups:

Domain Users
Everyone
BUILTIN\Users
LOCAL
NT AUTHORITY\INTERACTIVE
NT AUTHORITY\Authenticated Users

You can redirect the output to a text file with GPResult > filename.txt.

You can glean all sorts of juicy tidbits from GPResult. Here are the key areas to inspect when troubleshooting client RSoP:

- Find the "Applied Group Policy Objects" entries for both the user and computer. Remember that Group Policy is applied from the local computer first, then the site level, then the domain level, and then each nested OU. If a setting is unexpected on the client, simply use the provided information along with the Group Policy Object Editor to start tracking the errant GPO.

- Use the "Last time Group Policy was applied:" entry to check to see the last time the GPO was applied—via either initial or background refresh processing. Use GPUpdate to refresh this, and then ensure that the value is updated when you re-run GPResult.

- Use the spelled-out distinguished name of the computer and user objects (for example, CN=Frank Rizzo, OU=Human Resources Users, DC=corp, and DC=com) to verify that the user and computer objects are located where you think they should be in Active Directory. If they are not, verify the location of the user and computer accounts using Active Directory Users And Computers. You might need to reboot this client machine if the location in Active Directory doesn't check out.

- Use "The user is a part of the following security groups" and "The computer is a part of the following security groups" sections to verify that the user or computer is in the groups you expect. Perhaps your user or computer object is inside a group that is denied access to either the "Read" or "Apply Group Policy" permissions on the GPO you were expecting. Note that if you make a change to a computer's Security group membership, Group Policy will not pick up that change unless you reboot the computer. There is no way around this, unfortunately. The same holds true for user group changes—the user will need to re-logon before the Security group changes take.

- Find the "Connected over a slow link?" entry for the log and the "Group Policy slow link threshold" entries for both the user and computer. Remember that the various areas of Group Policy are processed differently when coming over slow links. (See Chapters 3 and 10.)

- Find the "The following GPOs were not applied because they were filtered out" section for both the user and the computer section. If you have GPOs listed here, the user or computer was, in fact, in the site, domain, or OU that the GPO was supposed to apply to. However, the GPOs listed here have not applied this user or computer for a variety of reasons. GPResult can tell you why this has happened. Here are some of the common reasons:

Denied (Security)   The user or computer has been explicitly denied "Read" and "Apply Group Policy" rights to process the GPO. For instance, in the previous example, the "Auto-Launch Calc.exe" doesn't apply to XPPRO1 because in Chapter 2, we explicitly denied the XPPRO1 computer object the ability to process the "Apply Group Policy" attribute.

Not Applied (Empty)   This GPO doesn't have any policy settings set in the user or computer half. For instance, in the previous example, the "Hide Desktop Settings Option" GPO doesn't have any computer-side policy settings. Hence, this GPO doesn't apply to Frank's computer object. Specifically, here the Group Policy engine is seeing that the number of revisions for either the user or computer half is 0. This is tied to the version number of the GPO so if the version number is not updated correctly when a GPO change is made, the GPO could be mistakenly viewed as empty.

Not Applied (Unknown Reason)   Usually Block Inheritance has been used, or the user doesn't have rights to read the GPO (though other, truly "unknown reasons" could also be valid). In the previous example, the "Hide Screen Saver Option," which is set at the site level, won't apply to Frank because we've blocked inheritance at the **Human Resources** OU.

Three Different *GPResults*—Three Different Outputs!

If you want to take GPResult to the next level, use it with the /v switch. You can then see which Registry settings are specifically being altered by the GPOs. This could be useful if you want to manually dive into the Registry and perform the same punch the policy setting is doing on a machine that isn't connected to Active Directory and see if you get the same results.

However, running GPResult /v on Windows 2000, Windows XP, Windows 2003, and Windows Vista returns totally different results. For the sake of brevity, here are three comparison snippets to illustrate some additional information possible with GPResult /v. This output has been taken out to show you some specific details and also formatted slightly for readability.

GPResult /v for Windows XP SP1 is the least useful. When you run it, you'll get output similar to the following.

```
Administrative Templates
GPO: Hide Desktop Settings Option
Setting: Software\Microsoft\Windows\CurrentVersion\Policies\System
State:   Enabled
```

This output merely tells you that the GPO "Hide Desktop Settings Option" manipulates a Registry key somewhere in the path specified in the Setting field. Whoopie.

When you run the command on a Windows 2003 or Windows Vista computer, you get the following:

```
Administrative Templates
-----------------------
GPO: Hide Desktop Settings Option
KeyName: Software\Microsoft\Windows\CurrentVersion\Policies\
System\NoDispBackgroundPage
Value: 1, 0, 0, 0
State: Enabled
```

This output is more useful, because it shows you that it's the "NoDispBackroundPage" Registry entry with the value of 1 in the Registry that is performing the function. I'm guessing the difference in output between Windows XP and Windows 2003 and Windows Vista is just a GPResult bug, but as of Windows XP+SP1 (and the beta of SP2), the output displayed is, in fact, different.

However, the most useful GPResult /v output comes from the GPResult in the Windows 2000 Resource Kit! (Yes! Windows 2000!)

```
The user received "Registry" settings from these GPOs:
    Hide Desktop Settings Option
        Revision Number:   3
        Unique Name:    {1ABE8B36-66A0-4DF0-80D0-A9B4A8C34DB1}
        Domain Name:    corp.com
        Linked to:     Domain (DC=corp,DC=com)
    The following settings were applied from: Hide Desktop Settings Option
        KeyName:    Software\Microsoft\Windows\CurrentVersion\Policies\System
        ValueName:    NoDispBackgroundPage
        ValueType:    REG_DWORD
        Value:    0x00000001
```

The Windows 2000 GPResult /v shows you the ValueName (like the Windows 2003 version), but also shows you the ValueType (REG_DWORD). Additionally, it can also easily show you the association between the GPO friendly name (say, "Hide Desktop Settings Option") and the GUID (in my case, "{1ABE8B36-66A0-4DF0-80D0-A9B4A8C34DB1}"). You might need this information later with other tools such as the Event Viewer, which may or may not use the friendly name.

So my advice? The GPResult built into Windows XP, Windows 2003, and Windows Vista is much better for basic troubleshooting. Its output describing *why* specific GPOs are not being processed is excellent. However, keep a copy of the Windows 2000 version of GPResult handy. It runs just fine on Windows XP and Windows 2003 and Windows Vista machines, and, because of its additional functions in displaying both the Registry and the GPO GUID, you can get a lot closer to knowing *what* has been changed.

Remotely Calculating a Client's RSoP Using Windows XP, Windows Vista, or Windows 2003 *GPResult*

The Windows 2000 version of GPResult doesn't work the way the Windows XP, Windows Vista, and Windows 2003 version does. The Windows XP, Windows Vista, and Windows 2003 version of GPResult has a secret weapon tucked up its sleeve. You can almost hear it say, "Are you talkin' to me?"

Its weapon is that it can tap into the WMI provider built in to Windows XP, Windows Vista, and Windows 2003. GPResult is like the GPMC's Group Policy Results Wizard. That is, it can be run from any Windows XP, Windows Vista, or Windows 2003 machine and, provided the target machine is turned on, the system can collect information about any particular user who has ever logged on locally. It's then a simple matter of displaying the results. You simply run GPresult, point it to a system, and provide the name of the user whose RSoP data you wish to collect.

This magic only works on Windows XP, Windows Vista, and Windows 2003 as both source computers and target computers. Windows 2000 computers don't have a tap into this WMI magic; so they can't play.

There are two more important cautions here (which I talked about in the "*GPResult* for Windows 2003, Windows Vista, and Windows XP" section, but they bear repeating). That is, this magic only works if the target user has ever logged on to the target machine. They only need to have logged on just once, and they don't even need to be logged on while you run the test. But if the target user has *never* logged on to the target machine, remotely calculating GPResult for that user will fail. Additionally, remotely trying to get a Windows XP/Service Pack 2 or Windows Vista computer's RSoP via GPResult will fail if the Windows Firewall is enabled.

As described in Chapter 2, either turn off the Windows Firewall or enable the Windows XP/ Service Pack 2 policy setting titled **Windows Firewall: Allow Inbound Remote Administration Exception,** which can be located in Computer Configuration ➢ Administrative Templates ➢ Network ➢ Network Connections ➢ Windows Firewall ➢ Domain (or Standard) Profile. This setting does affect both Windows XP/SP2 and Windows Vista machines.

Or, for your Windows Vista clients, you can really be gung-ho and use the new Windows Firewall with Advanced Security (which you'll learn about in Chapter 7), which of course has an alternate method only for Windows Vista. This would be found under Computer Configuration ➢ Windows Settings ➢ Security Settings ➢ Windows Firewall with Advanced Security ➢ Windows Firewall with Advanced Security ➢Inbound Rules.

With that in mind, here are your additional Windows XP, Windows Vista, and Windows 2003 GPResult options:

- /s <*target system name or IP address*> points to the target system.

- /user <*optional domain\username*> collects RSoP data for the target user.

You can combine any of the aforementioned GPResult switches as well. If you log on to DC01 and want to see only the user-side policy settings when Frank Rizzo logs on to XPPRO1, type the following:

```
gpresult /user frizzo /s xppro1 /scope:user
```

Again, this command only succeeds if Frank has ever logged on to XPPRO1 (which he has).

GPResult is much better at telling you *why* a GPO is applying rather than *what* specific policy settings are contained with a GPO. For instance, notice that at no time did GPResult tell us what policy settings were contained in the local GPO. And, even when we performed a GPResult /v, we only found out the Registry keys that were modified—not the proper name of the specific policy setting that is doing the work. For these tasks, we'll need to use the GPMC (as seen in Chapter 3) or the RSoP snap-in (described in a bit in the "The RSoP MMC Snap-in" section).

Remotely Calculating a Client's RSoP (When You've Delegated Permissions to Someone Who's Not a Local Administrator of the Target Machine)

In Chapter 2 (and, to a lesser extent in this chapter) we talked about the idea of opening up the Windows XP or Windows Vista firewall to **Windows Firewall: Allow Inbound Remote Administration Exception**. Again, this policy setting is located in Computer Configuration ➢ Windows Firewall ➢ Domain Profile.

The idea is that you can't remotely grab an RSoP using either GPResult.exe or the GPMC's Group Policy Results Wizard without being able to communicate to the WMI provider on the target machine. To do this, at minimum, you need to open up ports 135 and 445, which is precisely what this particular policy setting will do on a computer.

But, there's a little twist (which we've already discussed). That is, you need rights to view the RSoP data. Now, if you're a local administrator on the target machine, you already have all the rights you need. You just needed to open up that firewall enough to get that data.

But, if you want to delegate rights to, say, the help desk (or another nonadministrative group) you do, in fact, need an extra boost to ensure they can read the RSoP data. (If you need a refresher on how to delegate the permission in the first place, be sure to read Chapter 2's section entitled "Special Group Policy Operation Delegations.") Again, this area is located in the Delegation tab on the OU (or Domain or Site) you want to delegate rights to.

Once you've performed the delegation of the "Read Group Policy Results Data" right upon the user and/or computer you want, you also need to perform these very important additional delegation steps. (Again, these steps are only required if you've delegated this ability to a non-administrator of the target machine.)

For instance, let's assume that Tom User (from the help desk) needs access to read Group Policy Results data from a computer that Brett Wier is using (Vista1.corp.com). First, you delegate rights over that OU that Vista1.corp.com is in such that Tom can "Read Group Policy Results Data." Then, you create and link a GPO which affects the target computer's OU. Then, make sure the following policy settings are enabled within that GPO:

1. Computer Configuration ➢ Administrative Templates ➢ Network Connections ➢ Windows Firewall ➢ Domain Profile ➢ **Windows Firewall: Allow Inbound Remote Administration Exception**. Choose which subnets to allow inbound requests from (or specify * to allow all subnets).

2. Computer Configuration ➢ Windows Settings ➢ Security Settings ➢ Local Policies ➢ Security Options ➢ **DCOM: Machine Access Restriction in SDDL syntax**. When you edit the policy setting, you'll first "Define this policy setting" then click Edit Security, add in Tom User and specify to allow Remote Access. When you do this, a Security Descriptor is (thankfully) automatically built, like O:BAG:BAD:(A;;CDCLC;;;) and is usually quite long. You can see a screenshot of this in Figure 4.22 (though the security descriptor isn't in the screenshot, because I haven't hit OK yet).

3. Computer Configuration ➢ Windows Settings ➢ Security Settings ➢ Local Policies ➢ Security Options ➢ **DCOM: Machine Launch Restriction in SDDL syntax**. Again, be sure to click "Define this policy setting." Then, add in the same person (Tom User) and grant the "Remote Launch:Allow" and "Remote Activation:Allow" rights.

Since you've changed the computer-side settings, be sure to run `gpupdate /force` on the target machine (or just reboot it).

When you do, you'll have the ability for a nonadministrative user to have the ability to read another computer's RSoP data using the GPMC's Group Policy Results Wizard.

FIGURE 4.22   For each DCOM permission, add in the delegated user and specify they have Remote Access: Allow permissions.

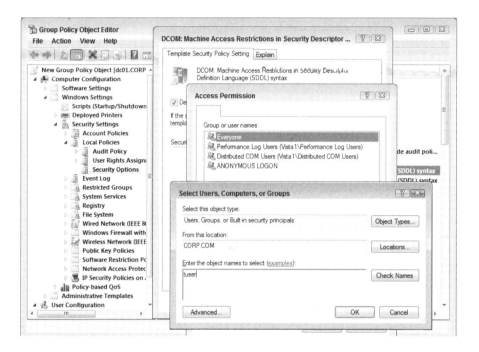

After these steps are performed, you've delegated a user (or group, like the Help Desk) and have now enabled the ability to "reach out" and see what's going on at other machines—even if they're not a local admin. Don't forget about the golden rule here, though: If the target machine's firewall is blocking your incoming request, even though you've now delegated the permission, it still ain't gonna work.

Remotely Calculating a Client's Group Policy Modeling Analysis Data (When You've Delegated Permissions to Someone Who's Not a Local Administrator of the Target Machine)

This is a similar situation to what we encountered before. Imagine you've given Tom User from the help desk the rights to "Perform Group Policy Modeling analyses." If you need a refresher on how to delegate the permission in the first place, be sure to read Chapter 2's section entitled "Special Group Policy Operation Delegations." Be sure to delegate the permission upon both the OUs which contain the user and computer accounts, or you'll be stuck with seeing only half the results data. However, just performing the delegation steps aren't enough—you'll still get an Access Denied message from the Group Policy Modeling Wizard as soon as you try to pick the Windows Server 2003 Domain Controller on which to perform the calculations.

So, since Windows Server 2003/SP1, the default security for DCOM permissions has changed, requiring changes akin to what you saw in the previous section. But, here's the trick: you're not modifying the target computer's DCOM settings, you're modifying the Windows Server 2003/SP1's Domain Controller settings. To do this, create and link a GPO on the **Domain Controllers** OU. I suggest you *don't* modify the default Domain Controller for this purpose, though it would work just fine. Then, modify the GPO as follows:

1. Computer Configuration ➤ Windows Settings ➤ Security Settings ➤ Local Policies ➤ Security Options ➤ **DCOM: Machine Access Restriction in SDDL syntax**. When you edit the policy setting, you'll first "Define this policy setting" then click Edit Security, add in Tom User, and specify to allow Remote Access. When you do this, a Security Descriptor is (thankfully) automatically built, like O:BAG:BAD:(A;;CDCLC;;;) and is usually quite long. You can see a screenshot of this in Figure 4.22.

2. Computer Configuration ➤ Windows Settings ➤ Security Settings ➤ Local Policies ➤ Security Options ➤ **DCOM: Machine Launch Restriction in SDDL syntax**. Again, be sure to click "Define this policy setting." Then, add in the same person (Tom User) and grant the "Remote Launch:Allow" and "Remote Activation:Allow" rights.

Now, Tom User from the help desk can see Brett Wier (and Brett's Computer) Group Policy Analysis data using the Group Policy Modeling Wizard.

Windows XP's Group Policy "Help and Support System" RSoP Tool

If wading through a mountain of text-based GPResult output isn't your cup of tea, I've got some good news for you: you can view RSoP information graphically in Windows XP, Windows Vista, and Windows 2003. If a user has problems, you cannot find a Windows 2003, Windows Vista, or Windows XP machine to log on to (to remotely perform the tests), and you still want the user to tell you what their RSoP is, this tool is handy. You can get what you need over the phone and have the user just click-click-click to get you the results you want to hear (instead of asking them to dive into the scary world of command-line tools).

To launch the Windows XP Group Policy "Help and Support System" RSoP tool, otherwise just known as the "GUI RSoP tool," choose Start ➤ Help and Support to open Help and Support Center. Then click "Get support, or find information in Windows XP newsgroups." Next, click "Advanced System Information." Finally, select "View Group Policy settings applied." Figure 4.23 shows the results.

You'll see the many sections of user and computer Group Policy in the GUI RSoP tool. On Windows XP, this tool is, in some ways, superior to GPResult because you can see which Registry keys are being modified by Active Directory GPOs and also what's going on inside the Local GPO. Although this tool does provide the names of the GPOs that apply, it doesn't address "why" GPOs are or are not applying, as GPResult does. So, a yin and yang approach with both the GPResult and the GUI RSoP tools may be needed to get the whole story.

FIGURE 4.23   The RSoP tool in the Help and Support Center is useful when you're asking users to help you help them.

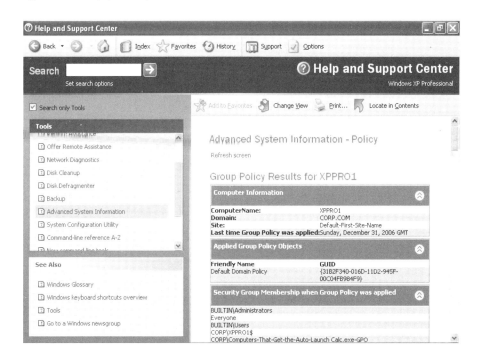

 WARNING   At the bottom of the GUI RSoP, you'll see an option to save the report to an HTML file. The default location is C:\, but nonadministrators cannot save files here. If users save to an HTML file, be sure they have permission for the folder.

The RSoP MMC Snap-in

Yet another tool can help you determine the RSoP of the client. Technically, this tool is named the RSoP MMC snap-in. This tool has, more or less, been rendered obsolete by the reports you get from the GPMC, and the tool has been deprecated in Windows Vista.

 WARNING   I'm showing you how to use the tool here only for reference and completeness. Again, in Vista, this tool is not to be used; it won't work properly and the results you get from it could be bogus.

RSoP Generation from Help and Support Center

In Figure 4.23, you can see the "Save this report to an .htm file" option. Just below that (not shown) is the "Run the Resultant Set of Policy tool" option. This option launches this tool (again, technically, the RSoP MMC snap-in), which will show you only the policy settings that are set and which GPOs they are coming from: local, site, domain, or OU, as shown in Figure 4.24. You can also simply run `rsop.msc` from Start ➢ Run.

FIGURE 4.24   The RSoP MMC snap-in tool shows you only the policy settings that are configured.

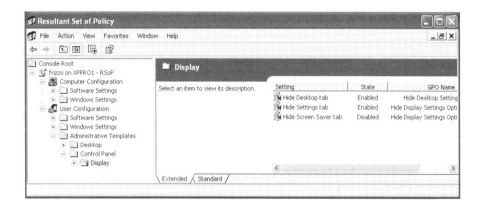

The bad news is that you still need to drill down a bit into each folder to get to the end. The good news is that the list is prefiltered and will only show you the policy setting name, the state, and the GPO from whence it came.

RSoP Generation from the True RSoP MMC Snap-in

Instead of launching the RSoP MMC snap-in tool from within the Help and Support Center, you can do just what its name implies. That is, run it directly as its own MMC snap-in. To do so, follow these steps:

1. Choose Start ➢ Run to open the Run dialog box. In the Open box, enter **MMC** and press Enter to open the MMC.

2. Choose File ➢ Add/Remove Snap-in.

3. Click Add to see the list of snap-ins and select "Resultant Set of Policy" to start the Resultant Set of Policy Wizard.

4. Click Next to open the Mode Selection screen. If you're running Windows XP, or Windows Vista only Logging is available. If you've got at least one Windows 2003 domain controller in your forest, Planning mode is also listed.

5. You'll then specify to perform the calculation on this computer or another Windows XP, Windows Vista, or Windows 2003 computer.

6. Next, you'll select the user; you can pretend to log on as any user who has logged on to the machine at least one time before. Note that you won't be able to "pretend" to log on as just anyone unless you're *really* logged in as someone with Administrator rights on the target machine.

7. Once the parameters are plugged in, you can press Next as seen in Figure 4.25.

The RSoP MMC snap-in tool does have one goodie that its bigger brother, the GPMC, does not have. That is, besides showing the "winning" GPO, it also lets you know the "losing" GPOs. After you complete the wizard and close the open screens, the RSoP you just calculated will appear in its own window, similar to what is seen in Figure 4.24.

FIGURE 4.25 The RSoP MMC snap-in tool calculates the reaction between the specified user and computer.

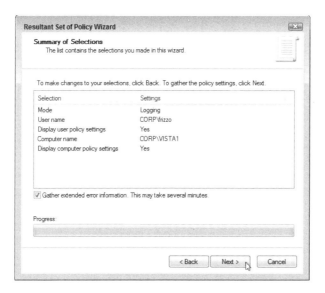

Advanced Group Policy Troubleshooting with Log Files

We've already explored some of the techniques to troubleshoot Group Policy application. You can enable some underlying operating system troubleshooting tools to help diagnose just what the heck is going on when the unexpected occurs.

Using the Event Viewer

Quite possibly, the most overlooked and underutilized tool in Windows is the Event Viewer. The client's Event Viewer logs both the successful and unsuccessful application of Group Policy (see Figure 4.26).

Before beating your head against the wall, check the client's Event Log for relevant Group Policy records. The Event Log in Windows XP and Windows 2003 spits out much more information and many more warnings than did the Event Log in Windows 2000—so take advantage of it.

In Windows Vista, the Event Log takes on a whole new importance with respect to Group Policy troubleshooting. In fact, as we talk in this section about logs that are useful in troubleshooting, we'll talk about how this all changes in a Windows Vista world.

In Figure 4.26, the Event Log returned an error code of 1053. Doing a quick search in Microsoft TechNet, you can find a related Windows 2000 article, Q261007, which shows that the client is pointing to an incorrect DNS server. Again, search the Knowledge Base when you find an event that might be at fault. You might find a hidden gem there—just perfectly ready to solve your problem.

FIGURE 4.26   The Event Viewer is a terrific place to start your troubleshooting journey.

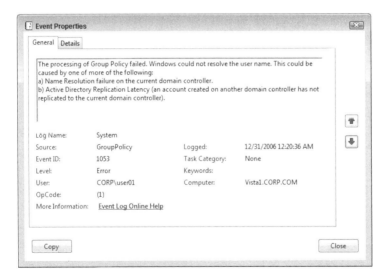

Diagnostic Event Logging (for Pre-Vista Machines Only)

If you really want to go bananas, you can enable *diagnostic logging* to supercharge your Event Log in Windows 2000, Windows XP, and Windows 2003. To do so, a Registry key to the client machine must be created. Traverse to `HKEY_Local_Machine\Software\Microsoft\Windows NT\CurrentVersion`. Create a Diagnostics key, but leave the Class entry empty. You can specify logging types by creating one of two `REG_DWORD` keys:

RunDiagnosticLoggingGroupPolicy   Create this REG_DWORD to log only Group Policy events. To enable logging, set the data value to 1. Log entries appear in the Application Log.

AppMgmtDebugLevel   Create this REG_DWORD, but do so with a data value of 4b in hexadecimal. At the next targeted software deployment, you'll find a log in the local \windows\debug\usermode folder named appmgmt.log, which can also aid in trouble-shooting why applications fail to load.

Some older Microsoft documentation also shows RunDiagnosticLogging-IntelliMirror and RunDiagnosticLoggingAppDeploy keys as viable options for the "Diagnostics" key. These entries are apparently documentation bugs and do absolutely nothing in Windows.

When you've finished debugging, delete the Diagnostic keys so your Event Logs don't fill up.

Diagnostic Event Logging (for Vista)

In Windows Vista, Event Logs entries related to Group Policy have changed significantly. First of all, Group Policy related events have moved from the Application to the System Log. The system generates Group Policy events with an event source of (who woulda guessed?) "Group-Policy", as shown in Figure 4.27.

FIGURE 4.27   Viewing the Windows Vista System log and Group Policy Events

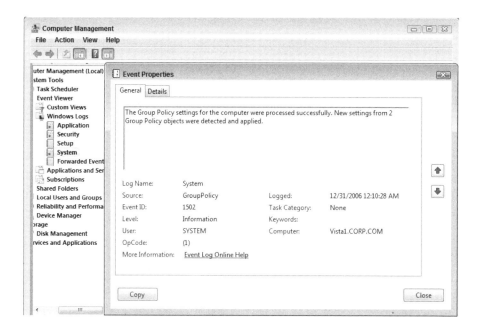

The logging of Group Policy events in Vista is on by default, so you don't need to enable anything specifically. You can simply filter events in this log with a source of Group Policy and get a snapshot of GP Processing. The events recorded in this log related to Group Policy are really a summary of each processing event—they tell you things like whether Group Policy processing proceeded successfully, which Domain Controller was used to process policy, and how many GPOs were processed. They do not provide deep levels of detail. In the next section, we'll talk about how you can get that detail out of the Event Log in Windows Vista.

Turning On Verbose Logging

Sometimes, all the server pieces are working perfectly, but the end result on the client is cock-eyed. You can examine Group Policy step by step by turning on *verbose logging*, which goes beyond the diagnostic Event Log Registry hacks.

Verbose Logging (for Pre-Vista Machines)

When you enable verbose logging by editing the Registry at the client, you are telling the system to generate extra events in a file called USERENV.LOG in the \windows\debug\usermode folder (or \winnt\debug\usermode for Windows 2000). By default, this file is enabled in Windows XP and Server 2003 but is not set to verbose mode. You can then examine the file to see what the client thinks is really happening.

To enable verbose logging, follow these steps:

1. Log on locally to the client system as the Administrator.

2. Run REGEDIT.

3. In the Registry Editor, traverse to HKEY_Local_Machine\Software\Microsoft\ Windows NT\CurrentVersion\Winlogon.

4. In the Edit DWORD Value dialog box, add a REG_DWORD value by entering **UserEnvDebugLevel** in the Value Name box, and in the Value Data box, enter the hex value of **10002**, as shown in Figure 4.28. Click OK.

5. Close the Registry Editor.

The hex value 10002 signifies verbose logging. The hex value 10001 signifies to log only errors and warnings. The hex value 10000 doesn't log anything.

Note that after making this entry in Windows XP or Windows 2003, verbose logging is enabled right away, but Windows 2000 often requires a reboot for the logging change to take effect. After you modify the entry, log off as the local Administrator, and log on as someone with many GPOs that would affect their user object—say, Frank Rizzo in the **Human Resources Users** OU. After logging on as Frank, you can immediately log off and back on as the Administrator for the workstation and then read the log file.

FIGURE 4.28   Verbose logging requires a hack to the Registry.

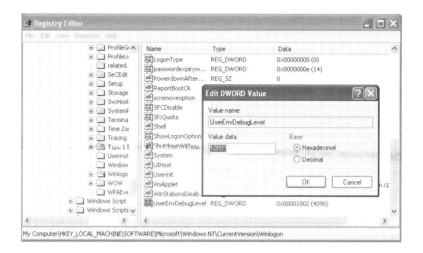

 You can also hack the Registry at a command prompt. You can use the RUNAS command to run the command prompt as the Administrator. For this system, type **runas /user:XPPro1\administrator cmd**, and type the password to log on as the Administrator.

In the Userenv.log file in the \windows\debug\usermode folder, you should come across the following snippet. The output here has been truncated and formatted for better reading and for the sake of example. Additionally, line headers such as ProcessGPOs, AddGPO, and SearchDSObject have all been removed.

```
Starting user Group Policy (Background) processing...
Starting computer Group Policy (Background) processing...
User name is:  CN=Frank Rizzo,OU=Human Resources Users,OU=Human
Resources,DC=corp,DC=com, Domain name is:  CORP
Domain controller is: \\DC01.corp.com  Domain DN is corp.com
network name is 192.168.2.0

User name is:  CN=XPPRO1,OU=Human Resources Computers,OU=Human
Resources,DC=corp,DC=com, Domain name is:  CORP

Domain controller is: \\DC01.corp.com  Domain DN is corp.com
Calling GetGPOInfo for normal policy mode
```

```
No site name defined.  Skipping site policy.

Searching <OU=Human Resources Users,OU=Human Resources,DC=corp,DC=com>
Found GPO(s):  <[LDAP://cn={45E8B3A8-AB97-4480-ACE9-
B42F2B3C7EFA},cn=policies,cn-system,DC=corp,DC=com;0]>

Searching <OU=Human Resources,DC=corp,DC=com>
Found GPO(s):  < >
<OU=Human Resources,DC=corp,DC=com> has the Block From Above attribute set
Searching <DC=corp,DC=com>

Found GPO(s):
<[LDAP://cn={45E8B3A8-AB97-4480-ACE9-B42F2B3C7EFA}
},cn=policies,cn=system,DC=corp,DC=com;0][LDAP://CN={31B2F340-016D-11D2-945F-
00C04FB984F9},CN=Policies,CN=System,DC=corp,DC=com;0]>
GPO will not be added to the list since the Block flag is set and this GPO is
not in enforce mode.


Searching <CN={45E8B3A8-AB97-4480-ACE9-
B42F2B3C7EFA},CN=Policies,CN=System,DC=corp,DC=com>
User does not have access to the GPO and so will not be applied.
Found functionality version of:  2
Found file system path of:  <\\corp.com\SysVol\corp.com\Policies{45E8B3A8-AB97-
4480-ACE9-B42F2B3C7EFA} >
Sysvol access skipped because GPO is not getting applied.
Found common name of:  < {45E8B3A8-AB97-4480-ACE9-B42F2B3C7EFA} >
Found display name of:  <Hide Display Settings Option / Restore Screen Saver
Option >
Found user version of:  GPC is 2, GPT is 65535
Found flags of:  0
Found extensions:  [{35378EAC-683F-11D2-A89A-00C04FBBCFA2}{0F6B957E-509E-11D1-
    A7CC-0000F87571E3}]
```

You can learn a lot quickly by doing a little sleuthing inside the results. First, the computer is processing in Normal mode (as opposed to Loopback mode). And, while you're here, you can sniff out two back-to-back "errors" that I've detailed below.

The first error occurred due to some Active Directory site misconfiguration error. The text is clear: "No site name defined. Skipping site policy."

The second error occurred when the GPO represented by GUID {45E8B3A8-AB97-4480-ACE9-B42F2B3C7EFA} wasn't applied. This is the "Hide Desktop Settings Option" GPO we created and linked to the domain. The report states that the "GPO will not be added to the list since the Block flag is set and this GPO is not in enforce mode." This indicates that the GPO isn't being enforced while the OU level (**Human Resources**) is blocking inheritance.

The last error occurred when the GPO with the {45E8B3A8-AB97-4480-ACE9-B42F2B3C7EFA} was not applied due to "User does not have access to the GPO." In my case, the GUID matched with the "Hide Display Settings Option/Restore Screen Saver Option" GPO. Back in Chapter 2, one example denied the HR-OU-Admins Security group the access to read that GPO, so it would not apply to them. Frank Rizzo is a member of the HR OU-Admins group and, hence, does not get the GPO.

> You might also want to check out a free tool that can make the job of parsing this log a bit easier. The guys at SysProSoft have a free tool that does the hard work. Check it out at http://www.sysprosoft.com/policyreporter.shtml. It's also listed on GPanswers.com in the "Third-Party Solutions" guide.

Some other information you can glean from this file includes the timestamp when the event occurred. Each line of the userenv.log file includes some text that looks like the following:

USERENV(2b8.2bc) 09:09:57:250

The meaning of this is relatively straightforward. Userenv is the process under which these events are occurring. (2b8.2bc) indicates, in hexadecimal form, the process and thread ID of this particular event, and then time shown indicates the time that this event is occurring. The time is broken down as hour:minute:second:hundreths-of-a-second. The process and thread ID tag is useful if, for example, you are troubleshooting Group Policy processing after issuing a GPUpdate command. Because GPUpdate runs both computer and user processing at roughly the same time, each of these will have unique thread IDs but events will be intertwined with each other. So, you can use the thread ID to distinguish a user processing event from a computer processing one.

Additionally, the one piece of information that userenv.log will tell you (that you can't get elsewhere very easily) is the time interval until the *next* background processing update. This usually comes at the end of a given processing cycle and looks something like this:

USERENV(2b8.908) 09:15:41:062 GPOThread: Next refresh will happen in 105 minutes

The downside to userenv.log is that it also logs user profile activity, which can really muddy up your Group Policy troubleshooting. Because of this, I usually just delete or rename the existing userenv.log file in the C:\windows\debug\usermode folder. Then, I'll run GPUpdate. When it's finished, my userenv.log file contains *only* the data from that last Group Policy processing cycle. In short, this process makes it much easier to troubleshoot.

Other Types of Verbose Logging

In addition to userenv.log, some of the individual CSEs provide their own verbose log files that you can enable with Registry tweaks. When you can't get the information you need from the Event Log or userenv.log, your next step is to try and track down the problem with one of these CSE-specific logs. While not every CSE creates its own log file, most of the important ones do, and you can use these logs to get more detailed information about a particular Group Policy area that has gone awry. The following table lists all available CSE-specific logs and Registry values needed to enable them.

Component	Location of Log	Location in Registry	Value
Security CSE	%windir%\Security\ Logs\WinLogon.log	HKLM\Software\ Microsoft\Windows NT\CurrentVersion\Win logon\GPExtensions\{82 7d319e-6eac-11d2-a4ea-00c04f79f83a}	ExtensionDebugLevel DWORD 2
Folder Redirection CSE	%windir%\Debug\ UserMode\FDeploy.log	HKLM\Software\Micros oft\Windows NT\CurrentVersion\Dia gnostics	FDeployDebugLevel DWORD 0x0B
Software Installation CSE	%windir%\Debug\User Mode\AppMgmt.log	HKLM\Software\Micros oft\Windows NT\CurrentVersion\Dia gnostics	AppMgmtDebugLevel DWORD 0x9b

 See Darren Mar-Elia's website www.GPOguy.com for a great ADM template to help automate these Registry punches, if needed, on your client machines.

Verbose Logging in Windows Vista

Windows Vista introduces major changes to the information that the Group Policy engine provides for you to troubleshoot problems. This is great news! But in order to best leverage that new data, you're going to need to know where and how to find that data. This section is devoted to that task.

Windows Vista no longer keeps verbose Group Policy logging information in userenv.log. Instead this type of detailed logging has moved to the System Event Log—which in the context of Group Policy is referred to as the *Admin Log*—and into a new place called the *Group Policy Operational Log*.

Both of these logs leverage the new features in the code-named "Crimson" Event Log system. This is a good thing because the events logged here are now clearer and more easily collected than they were in the userenv.log file. Crimson also has some neat features, such as subscription, that I'll introduce here, that can further help with your Group Policy troubleshooting tasks. The Group Policy logs are also enabled as verbose by default, so you don't need to bother with turning on and off Event Logs with Registry hacks.

To find the Group Policy Operational Log, simply open the Event Viewer and drill into Applications and Services Logs ≻ Microsoft ≻ Windows ≻ Group Policy ≻ Operational. What you'll get is a set of events similar to those found in Figure 4.29.

FIGURE 4.29   Viewing the Group Policy Operational Log in Windows Vista

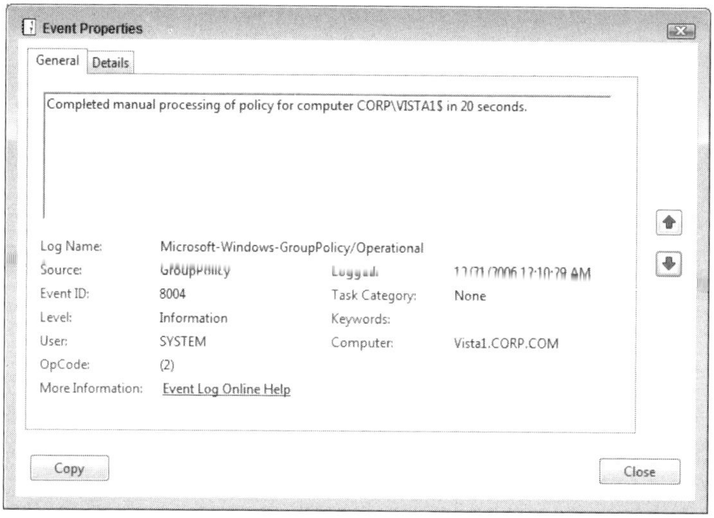

As you can see from the figure, the Group Policy Operational Log has more detailed and useful information than the userenv.log, such as the amount of time it took to process Group Policy for a user. If you're using Windows Vista, then the Operational Log is going to be your best Group Policy friend and will provide almost all the information you need to track down Group Policy problems. I say "almost" because while Vista made great strides in consolidating the userenv.log file into the Event Logs, the CSE-specific logs that I mentioned earlier for previous versions of Windows still exist in Windows Vista and are still stored in separate text files that must be explicitly enabled.

Leveraging Vista Admin Logs for Troubleshooting

Let's look at how you might use the Vista Admin log for troubleshooting a Group Policy problem.

The System log is designed to give you high level information about the state of the Group Policy Engine. So it will tell you things such as it computer Group Policy processing succeeded or failed, but it won't necessarily tell you what happened or why (see Figure 4.30).

One other useful piece of information the Admin log will give you is the time it took for Group Policy processing to occur. You can see this in the event in Figure 4.30 by clicking the Details tab in the lower preview pane of the event viewer, as shown in Figure 4.31.

Note that in Figure 4.31, the "ProcessingTimeinMilliseconds" field shows 3059 milliseconds, or 3.059 seconds. That is how long it took for computer processing to occur. Also note that the "ProcessingMode" is listed as 0. That indicates that the computer is working in normal processing mode, as opposed to loopback processing. If the value were 1 or 2, that would indicate that loopback merge mode, or replace mode, respectively, was enabled. And, of course, the "DCName" field indicates which DC serviced the Group Policy engine's request for Group Policy processing during the last cycle.

FIGURE 4.30 Viewing a Group Policy Admin Log event

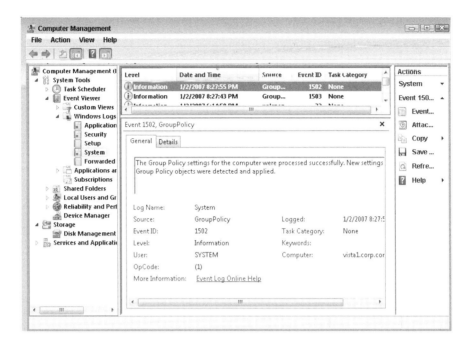

FIGURE 4.31 Viewing the Group Policy Processing time

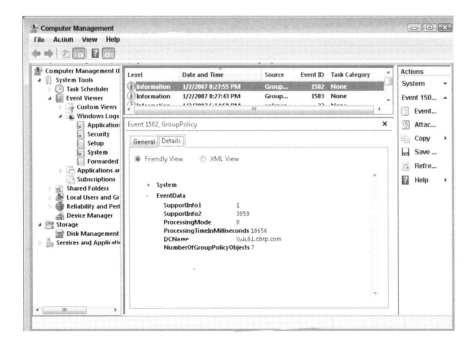

In addition to telling you when things are good with Group Policy, the System log will also tell you when things aren't so good. And, new to Vista, the failure logs will also try to give you some hints as to why things aren't working. For example, check out the event in Figure 4.32.

FIGURE 4.32   Viewing a Group Policy failure event

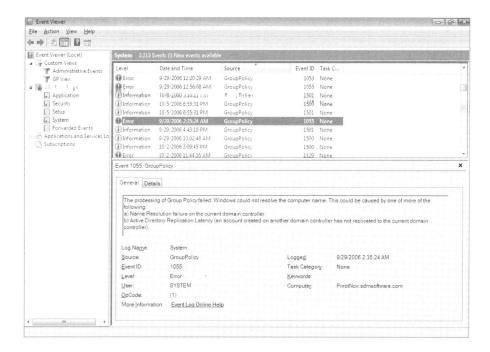

As you can see from Figure 4.32, not only does the event tell you that Group Policy processing has failed because it couldn't resolve the computer name, but it also gives you several possible reasons why that failure occurred. Additionally, if you were to click the hyperlinked "Event Log Online Help" link at the bottom of the page, you would be taken to a Microsoft website that contains more detailed information about this event ID.

Leveraging Vista Operational Logs for Troubleshooting

Assuming that the Vista Admin Logs don't help you track down the problem, the next step would be the Group Policy Operational Logs. As I mentioned, these logs provide the same level of detail that the userenv.log file provided in prior Windows version, but in a nice Event Log format.

This is great, but how can you really use this data to troubleshoot a problem when there are so many events generated in a given processing cycle? For example, a given Group Policy processing cycle could generate 20–30 Operational Log events, and the Operational Log itself could contain hundreds of these events. The goal is to narrow in on *one* Group Policy processing cycle and walk through the steps that it took to either succeed or fail. You can accomplish this task using a custom view, a feature of the Crimson Event Log system.

Each instance of a Group Policy processing cycle is uniquely identified by a field in the event called a *Correlation Activity ID*. This is akin to the thread ID I mentioned earlier when discussing the userenv.log file. By creating a custom view that filters events by this ActivityID, you can get a listing of only those Group Policy Operational events related to a given processing cycle. Let's walk through how to do that.

To filter the Operational Event Logs by a specific Group Policy Activity ID:

1. Start the Event Viewer utility.

2. The first thing you need to do is find the activity ID for the Group Policy processing cycle you're interested in. You can do that by going into the Operational Log, finding an event that is part of the cycle in question, clicking the Details tab in the lower Preview Pane, and selecting the XML View button, as shown in Figure 4.33. Copy this activity ID someplace safe—we'll need it in a second.

FIGURE 4.33   Locating the Correlation ActivityID in a Group Policy Event

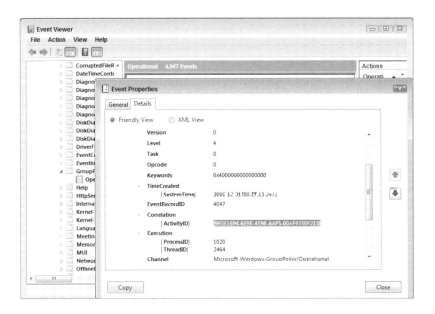

3. On the left-hand pane of the Event Viewer, right-click the Custom Views node and choose "Create Custom View."

4. The "Create Custom View" dialog appears on the Filter pane, but for this exercise, we're going to enter the XML filter directly, rather than using the check boxes. So, click the XML tab and check the box that says "Edit query manually."

5. Paste the following XML query string into the filter query box:

```
<QueryList><Query Id="0" Path="Application"><Select Path="Microsoft-Windows-
GroupPolicy/Operational">*[System/Correlation/@ActivityID='{INSERT ACTIVITY
ID HERE}']</Select></Query></QueryList>
```

6. Replace the Activity ID you found in step 2 in the spot that says, "INSERT ACTIVITY ID HERE." Once you do that, press OK twice and the upper right results pane of the Event Viewer will show only a filtered view of your Group Policy events.

GPLogView

Now that we've filtered the events down to a single Group Policy cycle, you might be saying to yourself, "Gee, that's pretty hard to see what's really going on given that I have to scroll through each event without getting to see them all in a single view." Well, for that reason, Microsoft has created a tool called GPLogView.

This command-line utility lets you output the events of a Group Policy Operational Log to a variety of easy-to-read formats, including straight text and HTML. You can download the tool at `http://go.microsoft.com/fwlink/?LinkId=75004`.

Here is a taste of what it can do. You can use it to do the exact same thing we did in the previous custom view description—output the events associated with a single Activity ID. To do that you would run the `gplogview.exe` command using the following syntax:

```
Gplogview -a 9A867233-04FF-4625-B7D1-6DEB763E2DCA -o ouput.txt
```

This generates a step-by-step listing of all events with the activity ID I've supplied to an output file called `output.txt`. If I open `output.txt` in Notepad, I see a nice listing, similar to what I got in `userenv.log` but without the clutter and unintelligible references to APIs! Figure 4.34 shows a small sample of the output.

FIGURE 4.34 Viewing the output from GPLogView

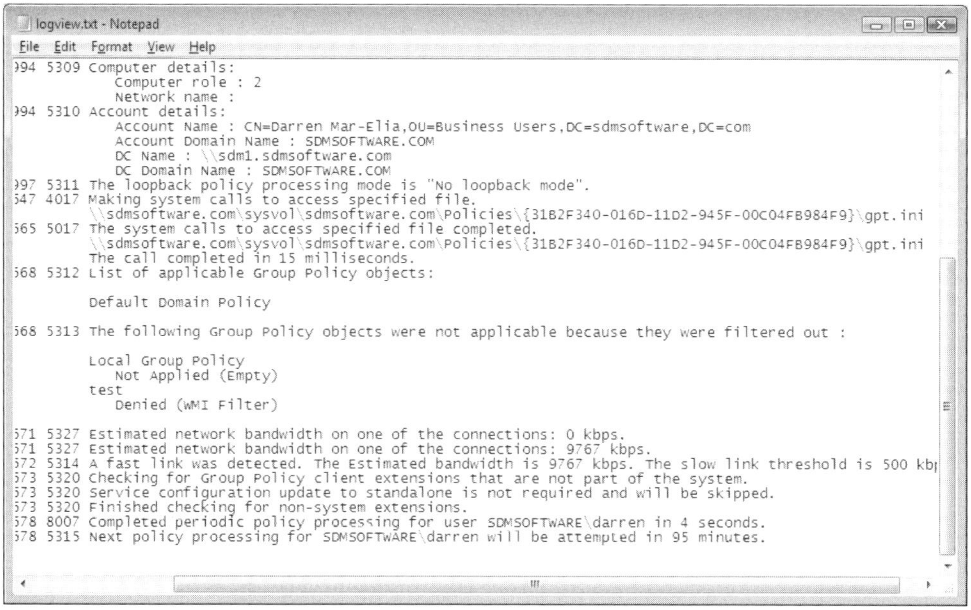

```
logview.txt - Notepad
File Edit Format View Help
)94 5309 Computer details:
         Computer role : 2
         Network name :
)94 5310 Account details:
         Account Name : CN=Darren Mar-Elia,OU=Business Users,DC=sdmsoftware,DC=com
         Account Domain Name : SDMSOFTWARE.COM
         DC Name : \\sdm1.sdmsoftware.com
         DC Domain Name : SDMSOFTWARE.COM
)97 5311 The loopback policy processing mode is "No loopback mode".
547 4017 Making system calls to access specified file.
         \\sdmsoftware.com\sysvol\sdmsoftware.com\Policies\{31B2F340-016D-11D2-945F-00C04FB984F9}\gpt.ini
565 5017 The system calls to access specified file completed.
         \\sdmsoftware.com\sysvol\sdmsoftware.com\Policies\{31B2F340-016D-11D2-945F-00C04FB984F9}\gpt.ini
         The call completed in 15 milliseconds.
568 5312 List of applicable Group Policy objects:

         Default Domain Policy

568 5313 The following Group Policy objects were not applicable because they were filtered out :

         Local Group Policy
            Not Applied (Empty)
         test
            Denied (WMI Filter)

571 5327 Estimated network bandwidth on one of the connections: 0 kbps.
571 5327 Estimated network bandwidth on one of the connections: 9767 kbps.
572 5314 A fast link was detected. The Estimated bandwidth is 9767 kbps. The slow link threshold is 500 kb
573 5320 Checking for Group Policy client extensions that are not part of the system.
573 5320 Service configuration update to standalone is not required and will be skipped.
573 5320 Finished checking for non-system extensions.
578 8007 Completed periodic policy processing for user SDMSOFTWARE\darren in 4 seconds.
578 5315 Next policy processing for SDMSOFTWARE\darren will be attempted in 95 minutes.
```

Note that it provides useful information such as the bandwidth detected during slow link detection, the time until the next processing cycle, which GPOs were applied and denied, and why.

Additionally, if you look at the actual events in Event viewer that correspond to each of the events listed in the output from GPLogView, you can get some additionally useful information. For example, at the start of every policy processing cycle, some useful summary flags are included in each event under the Details tab, such as show in Figure 4.35.

FIGURE 4.35   Viewing summary flags for a Group Policy Operational event

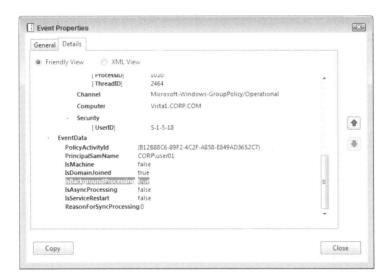

The flags you see in this figure can provide a glimpse into the kind of processing that is occurring. For example, the *isBackgroundProcessing* = true flag indicates that this is a background processing cycle, rather than a foreground one. This is important because certain CSEs, such as Software Installation and Folder Redirection, don't run during background processing. This summary view also provides useful information such as whether processing occurred asynchronously (IsAsyncProcessing) and whether it's machine or user processing that is being logged (IsMachine).

Overall, the Group Policy Operational Log is the place to be when it comes to troubleshooting Group Policy problems in Windows Vista.

Microsoft has an indispensable document on Group Policy troubleshooting and the Event Logs for Windows Vista. It's called (cleverly enough) "Troubleshooting Group Policy with Event Logs." You should be able to find it on GPanswers.com in the Microsoft Resources section. Or, just Google for the name of the whitepaper.

Group Policy Processing Performance

I often hear the question, "Is it better to have fewer, bigger GPOs or more GPOs with fewer settings?" The answer to that question is the basis for this section.

The bottom line around Group Policy processing performance is that the time it takes to process Group Policy is highly dependent upon what you're doing within a given set of GPOs and the state of your environment. If you think about all the things we've discussed in this chapter about how Group Policy is stored and processed, then you have probably discovered that there is a lot of variability in the process. For example, setting Administrative Template policy is a lot less time-consuming than repermissioning a large file tree using File Security policy. Likewise, installing Microsoft Office using Software Installation policy is going to take more time than setting users rights on a given system.

Additionally, the time that Group Policy processing spends during the core processing phase, where the client communicates with AD to determine which GPOs to apply, is typically a small percentage of the overall processing time as compared to the CSE processing part of the cycle. Thus having to enumerate more GPOs or less GPOs will have a negligible effect on the overall processing time as compared to having to perform the more time-intensive CSE processing. And, it's also important to remember that Group Policy processing only occurs if something changes in the Group Policy infrastructure for a given computer or user. So, in most environments, days may go by in between true processing events. Given that, the question of performance really gets down to what's acceptable in your environment.

The best thing you can do to optimize processing performance is measure and understand where time is being spent during a given processing cycle. You can do this using any number of the tools we've mentioned in this chapter. For example, the `userenv.log` file in pre-Windows Vista versions of the OS will timestamp each step of the processing cycle, letting you see where time is being spent. Similarly the Group Policy Operational Log will do the same thing in Vista. In addition, you can download a free command-line utility called `gptime.exe` at `www.gpoguy.com/tools.htm` that outputs the time spent processing Group Policy for either a local or remote computer.

There are a number of factors that can affect Group Policy processing performance more than just the number of GPOs you have applied to a given user or computer. Some of these are highlighted here:

- Keep the number of Security groups applied to a GPO to a minimum. The more Security groups a client has to read and process to determine if a GPO applies or does not apply, the more time is spent during the core processing phase.

- Make sure that you are not forcing policy application for a given CSE (by enabling the relevant policy under `Computer Configuration\Administrative Templates\System\Group Policy`) during every refresh cycle unless you absolutely have to.

- Make sure that you minimize the amount of "expensive" operations that your GPOs do. Expensive operations include Folder Redirection of large amounts of user data, Software Installation of large applications over the network and repermissioning of large file or Registry trees. Additionally, Scripts policy can be problematic if the scripts are performing complex tasks that can hang. The default script timeout in Group Policy is ten minutes.

That means a script could hang there for up to ten minutes, with your users waiting, until it finally times out.

- WMI Filters (discussed in Chapter 10) also take a biggish chunk of processing time to figure out if the condition is "true" or not. You should use WMI filters if you need them, but not to excess.

So, in the end, the question of whether fewer, bigger GPOs perform better than more, smaller GPOs is probably not the right question to ask. The better question is which configuration is easier to manage. Once you answer that question, then you can optimize for performance using the tips I've relayed in this section.

Final Thoughts

You want to be a better troubleshooter for Group Policy issues? You're well on the way.

In the last chapter, you learned when Group Policy is supposed to apply. It doesn't just happen when it wants to, it happens according to a set of precise timings. In this chapter, you learned two more key items to help on your troubleshooting journey. First, you learned the real story about what's going on under the hood. Then, you learned how to take that knowledge and troubleshoot Group Policy. Hopefully, every page in this chapter will help you further troubleshoot Group Policy should something go awry. However, here are some parting tips when troubleshooting Group Policy:

Check the basics.   When troubleshooting, first check the basics. Make sure you're not using "Block Inheritance" or "Enforced" where you shouldn't.

Check permissions.   Users need both "Read" and "Apply Group Policy" permissions to the GPOs. Computers do too. If a user (or group the user is in) is "Denied" access to either of these permissions, then the GPO will not apply.

Leverage the built-in tools.   Use the built-in debugging tools, such as the Event Viewer, supercharged with the Diagnostics key to help troubleshoot even tougher problems.

Leverage additional tools.   There are lots of additional troubleshooting tools at your disposal. Be sure to check out the Appendix, in which we introduce WinPolicies, GPMonitor, GPInventory, and more.

Verify replication is working.   If a client isn't getting the GPOs you think they should, it just may be that normal replication hasn't finished yet. GPCs replicate via Active Directory replication. GPTs replicate via FRS replication. They are supposed to take the same path, but sometimes they don't. Use `Gpotool` and `Replmon` to troubleshoot.

Check out Microsoft's troubleshooting documentation.   There are two official white papers on Group Policy troubleshooting from Microsoft. One can be found at `http://go.microsoft.com/fwlink/?LinkId=14949`.

There's also another, more modern version at http://tinyurl.com/8ld5p. I was one of the reviewers who provided input into this later document.

Remember all the log files at your disposal. In this chapter, we've discussed a few log files. However, there are many more available. As we'll see in other chapters along our journey, there are log files for many processes related to Group Policy. We've just seen UserEnv.log, but additionally, there is FDeploy.log (examined in Chapter 9, in the "Folder Redirection" section), Appmgmt.log (examined in Chapter 10, in the "Software Installation" section), and others. Reference the two aforementioned Microsoft documents on Group Policy trouble-shooting for the additional logs, in areas such as troubleshooting "internal" GPMC or Group Policy Object editor workings via the Gpmgmt.log and GPedit.log, respectively.

5

ADM and ADMX
Template Management

You might occasionally wonder, "Where do all those bazillions of policy settings come from?" They're not a magical gift from the Group Policy Fairy Godmother—they're encoded inside files within Windows which allow you to do the stuff you want to do. Group Policy has lots of nooks and crannies in which many options can be set. It's likely you'll spend most of your time manipulating the Administrative Templates section. Consequently, you need to know where all these settings come from.

In Windows XP, the Administrative Templates section comes from ADM files. In Windows Vista, that same section comes from ADMX files.

These templates hold the key to a large chunk of what makes Group Policy great. These settings are so important and powerful because they alter the Registry on the target computer. These ADM and ADMX files describe the Registry settings that can be toggled on or off through the Group Policy Object Editor.

That's where the duality of this chapter comes in. It's not only going to be really important to understand the "under the hood" goings on of both ADM and ADMX files, but also where Windows Vista brings new features to the table when ADMX files are used.

And, while not strictly necessary, if you want to take your Group Policy game to the next level, you might want to invest some time in understanding the language used to create ADMX files. After you understand the syntax, you can create, modify, and troubleshoot almost any Registry change that is implemented by the Administrative Templates in the Group Policy Object Editor.

Finally, a little later in the chapter, we'll explore a new tool from Microsoft and FullArmor which can take existing ADM files you might already have and convert them into ADMX files.

You'll find the complete reference for creating your own ADMX templates in the "ADMX Template Syntax" download on this book's website. If you still feel you need to create ADM files after reading this chapter, the previous edition's download of a similar reference, "ADM Template Syntax," should still be available on GPanswers.com as well.

Policies vs. Preferences

One of the most heralded benefits of moving away from your old Windows NT 4–based System Policy is the nonpersistence of the Registry changes using Group Policy. Every Windows NT 4 System Policy change was *persistent*. When you enabled a System Policy, it stayed turned on until you set an explicit policy to turn it off. You couldn't just delete the policy and have the setting go away, as is the case with today's Group Policy engine. If you used Windows NT System Policy, you had to fight the same problem over and over.

Versions of Windows since Windows 2000 utilize a new model for policies. Microsoft created special locations in the Registry for Windows 2000, aptly named *Policies*. Microsoft documentation states that four Registry areas are considered the approved places to create policies out of Registry hacks:

- `HKLM\Software\Policies` (computer settings, the preferred location)

- `HKLM\Software\Microsoft\Windows\CurrentVersion\Policies` (computer settings, an alternative location)

- `HKCU\Software\Policies` (user settings, the preferred location)

- `HKCU\Software\Microsoft\Windows\CurrentVersion\Policies` (user settings, an alternative location)

These locations are preferred because they have security permissions that do not allow a regular user to modify these keys. Again, the preferred locations are noted above, if any software developers are reading this book (and you know who you are).

When a policy setting is set to "Enabled" and the client embraces the Group Policy directives, a Registry entry is set in one of these keys. When the GPO that applied the keys is removed, the Registry values associated with it are also removed. However, it should be noted that the application (or operating system component) needs to look for changes to these keys in order for it to take effect. That is, the Group Policy engine doesn't "notify" the application—the application has to do its own checking. So, with this in mind, if an older operating system receives a policy setting for a newer operating system, nothing "bad" happens. It just gets ignored.

 WARNING It should be noted that local administrators have security permissions to these keys and could maliciously modify delivered GPO settings because of rights within this portion of the Registry.

This is the magic that makes Group Policy shine over old-style NT 4 System Policy; that is, Group Policy won't tattoo because it's being directed to go in a nonsticking place in the Registry. Old-style NT 4 System Policy had no such facility. Today, Microsoft calls these NT-style policies that tattoo *preferences*.

You might want to control a pet application that you have deployed in-house, say, DogFood-Maker 6.1. Great—you've decided you want more control. Now, you need to determine which Registry values and data DogFoodMaker 6.1 understands. That could take some time; you might be able to ask the manufacturer for the valid Registry values, or you might have some manual labor in front of you to determine what can be controlled via the Registry. You'll then be able to begin to create your own templates.

However, after you've determined how DogFoodMaker 6.1 can be controlled via the Registry, you'll find you have two categories of Registry tweaks:

- Values that fit neatly into the new Policies keys listed earlier

- Values that are anywhere else

You'll have some good news and some bad news. If DogFoodMaker 6.1 can accept control via the Registry, you can still create template files and control the application. The bad news is that if the Registry punches it accepts are not inside the Policies keys listed earlier, you will not have proper Policies. Rather, they become old-style tattooing preferences.

To reiterate, the target applications must be programmed to look for values in the Policies keys. Some applications, such as Word 2000, check the Policies keys (specifically HKEY_CURRENT_USER\Software\Policies\Microsoft\Office\9.0\Word\).

Other applications, such as WordPad, do not "understand" the Policies keys. (WordPad looks in HKEY_CURRENT_USER\Software\Microsoft\Windows\CurrentVersion\Applets\Wordpad). Hence, WordPad wouldn't be a candidate to hand-create a template file for the purpose of coding for true policies settings. You could, however, still create your own *preferences* for WordPad that modify and tattoo the Registry. Therefore, you will have to do the legwork to figure out if your applications are compatible with the new Profiles keys.

Because preferences and policies act so differently, you will need to quickly identify them within the Group Policy Object Editor interface. You will want to note whether you're pushing an actual new-style policy to them or a persistent old-style policy. You'll see both cases in this chapter.

When viewed on Windows Vista, new-style policies are designated by little "paper" icons. When viewed on Windows XP, new-style policies are designated by little blue dots. Again, these are "proper" because they modify the Policies Registry keys.

Policies that represent Registry punches in places *other* than the preferred Microsoft policies are designated another way. On Windows Vista, they're represented by paper icons with a down arrow. On Windows XP, they're designated by red dots.

Again, you'll see this distinction a bit later as you work through the examples.

Since this is an important distinction in the rest of this chapter, let's recap:

- New-style policies are temporary Registry changes that are downloaded at logon and startup (and periodically in the background). They don't tattoo the Registry (though they are maintained and stay persistent should the user log on while offline). These are set to modify the Registry in specific Microsoft-blessed Policies keys. Applications need to be coded to recognize the presence of the keys in order to take advantage of the magic of policies. In the Vista Group Policy interface, these look like little paper icons.

- New-style policies also don't overwrite user preferences if they exist. For instance, if a program like Microsoft Word is policy-enabled, and a user specifies to enable "Correct two initial capitals," but later the administrator chooses to disable this setting with a GPO, the original user's desires will just magically "come back." So, when you remove a true policy setting from a GPO (that is, set to "Not Configured"), the original user preference will be "returned."

- Old-style preferences are persistent Registry changes sent from on high using the Group Policy Object Editor. These typically tattoo the Registry until they're specifically removed. In the Vista Group Policy Object Editor interface, they look like paper icons with a little down-arrow. Unlike new-style policies, if you remove the GPO, you "orphan" the settings on the target computer (no fun at all). They work like old-style NT System Policy. These can be set to modify the Registry anywhere.

Hang tight, dear reader. The differences between preferences and policies will be underscored a bit later when we add in additional templates and you create your own settings to manipulate your clients later in this chapter.

ADM vs. ADMX File Distinction

Because Windows XP and Windows Vista have such radically different ways of presenting (what appears to be) the same stuff to you via the Group Policy Object Editor, it might be helpful to get a brief rundown of each technology. It's likely you have a mixed environment—of Windows XP and Windows Vista. So, as we proceed in the chapter, you'll have a feel for what's going on under the hood.

Again, many settings are available in both the Computer and the User Administrative Template sections of the Group Policy Object Editor. How these settings are displayed depends on what is inside the default ADM templates. Therefore, when you create any new GPO, you start with baseline policy settings.

Windows XP ADM File Introduction

The default templates are stored in the `%systemroot%\inf` folder, which is usually `C:\windows\inf`, and you'll find the following templates are installed by default on Windows XP+SP2 machines:

- `Conf.adm`
- `Inetres.adm`
- `System.adm`
- `Wmplayer.adm`
- `Wuau.adm`

These five ADM templates create both the Computer and User portion within Administrative Templates of a default Group Policy. Table 5.1 provides information about what each default template is and what lives inside it.

inetcorp.adm and inetset.adm are two ADM templates which can alternatively be used to manipulate Internet Explorer settings. However, it is not advised, as they don't work well for newer versions of Internet Explorer.

TABLE 5.1   Default ADM Templates

ADM Template	Features	Where to Find in Interface
Conf.adm	NetMeeting settings.	Computer Configuration/User Configuration ➢ Administrative Templates ➢ Windows Components ➢ NetMeeting
Inetres.adm	Internet Explorer settings, including security, advanced options, and toolbar settings. It is equivalent to the options that are available when using the Internet Options menu inside Internet Explorer.	Computer Configuration/User Configuration ➢ Administrative Templates ➢ Windows Components ➢ Internet Explorer
Inetcorp.adm (not used in a GPO by default)	Used for Internet Explorer Maintenance preference mode settings.	User Configuration ➢ Windows Settings ➢ Internet Explorer Maintenance. We won't be exploring this particular ADM template much. If you want more information on its ins and outs, read http://tinyurl.com/z3cae. It is not suggested to use this unless especially directed by a specific Microsoft document or PSS person.
Inetset.adm (not used in a GPO by default)	Internet Explorer "Advanced Settings" for Internet Explorer 6.	User Configuration ➢ Windows Settings ➢ Internet Explorer Maintenance ➢ Advanced. Only visible in Internet Explorer Maintenance Preference mode (see Chapter 6's "Internet Explorer Maintenance Policies" section). It is not suggested to use this unless especially directed by a specific Microsoft document or PSS person.
System.adm	Operating system changes and settings. Most of the Computer and User Administrative Template settings are in this ADM template.	Everything else under Computer Configuration/User Configuration ➢ Administrative Templates
Wmplayer.adm	Windows Media Player 9 settings.	User Configuration ➢ Administrative Templates ➢ Windows Components ➢ Windows Media Player
Wuau.adm	Controls client's access to Software Update Services servers.	Computer Configuration ➢ Administrative Templates ➢ Windows Components ➢ Windows Update

Windows Vista ADMX File Introduction

As we saw with Windows XP, there's a mere handful of ADM files which make up the bulk of our settings. In Windows Vista, things change from ADM files to ADMX files, and what was once a handful is now an entire growler-full.

NOTE What's a growler? `http://tinyurl.com/jos6c`.

Windows Vista ADMX files are stored in the `%systemroot%\PolicyDefinitions` folder, which is usually `C:\windows\PolicyDefinitions`.

There are now about 132 ADMX files which roughly cover the same settings found in Windows XP. They're generally component specific. For instance, you'll find things like `WindowsMediaPlayer.admx` and `EventLog.admx`, amongst others.

Here's something neat about ADMX files—they're language neutral. That is, the definitions for the Registry values that are controlled are inside the ADMX file. However, the text strings describing the policy and the Explaintext are contained within a *separate* file called an ADML file. These ADML files are located in specific sub-directories for each language within the `c:\windows\PolicyDefinitions` folder. For instance, U.S. English is contained within the en-US directory, which can be seen in Figure 5.1.

TIP en-US is for US English. For other locales, visit `http://tinyurl.com/qpomo`. For instance, HE is for Hebrew, RU is for Russian, DE is for German, AR is for Arabic.

On GPanswers.com in the "Book Resources" section, I'll have a table with the names of all the ADMX and ADML files, what they do, and more.

FIGURE 5.1 A quick list of some ADMX files. Note the language-specific directory here for English (en-US).

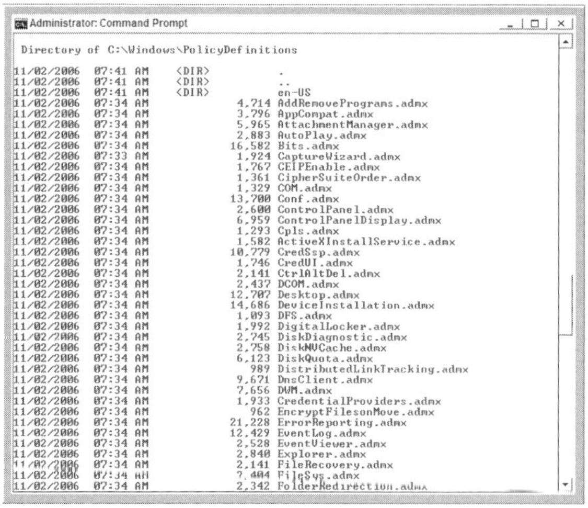

ADM vs. ADMX files—At a Glance

Our goal for the rest of the chapter is to give you an in-depth look at both ADM and ADMX files and for you to understand the differences between them. However, before we get going, here's a quick little reference table so you can see where we're going and also utilize this table as an ongoing reference.

ADM Files	ADMX Files
Lots and lots of definitions are packed into several large-ish files. The biggest one is SYSTEM.ADM.	Definitions are split logically into much smaller ADMX files, generally by Windows feature area.
Each ADM file contains settings in one specific language.	ADMX files are language neutral. Language-specific information is contained within a corresponding ADML file. Language-specific files live in hard-coded directories. For example, U.S. English language files live in %systemroot%\PolicyDefinitions\en-us.
Live on each Windows XP machine in %systemroot%\inf.	Live on each Windows Vista machine in %systemroot%\PolicyDefinitions
Every time a GPO is "born" it costs about 3–5MB on each Domain Controller because the ADM files are placed inside the GPO.	GPOs created from ADMX files never have big space requirements. That's because the ADMX files are never pushed into the GPO themselves (regardless if the Central Store is used or not). We'll discuss the Central Store a bit later.
Use their own proprietary ADM syntax for describing Registry policy.	Use standard XML as the syntax for describing Registry policy.

Creating and Editing GPOs in a Mixed Environment

As I noted in Chapter 1, Windows XP and Windows 2003 have about 200 more policy settings available to them than their Windows 2000 pals do. And Vista has about 700 more policy settings than Windows XP.

The good news (as I've previously stated) is that Windows 2000 clients ignore policy settings meant for Windows XP or Windows 2003. And Windows XP clients ignore policy settings meant for Windows Vista. This makes sense: older clients don't have the "moving parts" required to do anything if these policy settings are set.

You're likely to have a mix of client and server systems. It's likely you'll have:

- Domain Controllers: Windows 2000, Windows Server 2003, and/or Longhorn Servers
- Member servers: Windows 2000, Windows Server 2003, and/or Longhorn Server
- Client machines (your users' machines): Windows 2000, Windows XP, Windows Vista
- Management stations (your machines, the ones you manage Group Policy from): Windows XP, Windows Vista

Figure 5.2 shows a typical Active Directory domain that could be representative of what you might have.

The question is: With all these types of client systems, how do we ensure we've got the maximum power to control them all?

That's what we're going to explore in this next section.

FIGURE 5.2 A typical Active Directory domain with administrative systems, client systems, Domain Controllers and servers

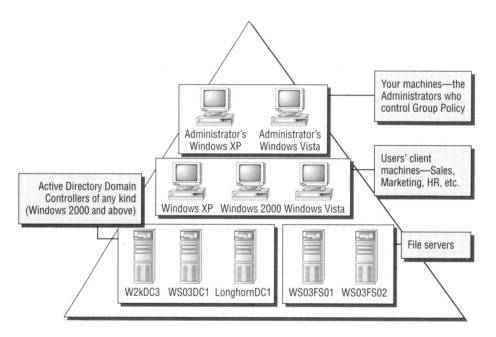

How Do You Currently Manage Your Group Policy Objects?

Before we proceed, you need to answer this question: How do you currently manage, create, and modify your GPOs?

- Do you walk up to a Domain Controller (or use Terminal Services to connect directly to a Domain Controller) to create or modify your GPOs?

- Do you use any machine you happen to be working on that day to create or modify your GPOs? (This could be a Windows 2000, Windows XP, server—whatever.)
- Do you use a specific machine to manipulate all the GPOs over which you have control? That is, do you have a *management station* you use when you need to manage your GPOs?

If you use either the first or second option, you're likely going to want to change your habits and start working with a strategy that gets you toward a *management station*.

Here's why. Every time a new operating system is released (and again each time a new service pack is released), there's more power to behold. Here's a brief history of increased power and what you can control:

Windows Version	Number of Policy Settings	What Can You Control?
Windows 2000	About 300 policy settings	Windows 2000
Windows 2000 + SP1	About 20 additional policy settings	Windows 2000, Windows 2000 + SP1
Windows 2000 + SP4	5 additional policy settings	All version of Windows 2000
Windows XP	About 150 additional policy settings	Windows XP and all versions of Windows 2000
Windows Server 2003	About 24 additional policy settings	Windows Server 2003, Windows XP, and all versions of Windows 2000
Windows XP + SP1	About 10 additional policy settings	Windows XP + SP1, Windows XP, and all versions of Windows 2000
Windows XP + SP2	About 600 additional policy settings	Windows XP + SP2, Windows XP + SP1, Windows XP, and all versions of Windows 2000
Windows Server 2003 + SP1	About 5 additional policy settings	Windows Server 2003 + SP1, Windows Server 2003, Windows XP + SP2, Windows XP + SP1, Windows XP, and all versions of Windows 2000
Windows Vista	About 700 additional policy settings	Windows Vista, Windows Server 2003 + SP1 , Windows Server 2003, Windows XP + SP2, Windows XP + SP1, Windows XP, and all versions of Windows 2000

Windows Version	Number of Policy Settings	What Can You Control?
Longhorn Server	Even more additional policy settings (not yet known at this time)	Longhorn Server, Windows Vista, Windows XP + SP2, Windows XP + SP1, Windows XP, Windows Vista, Windows Server 2003 + SP1, Windows Server 2003, and all versions of Windows 2000

> Additionally, when service packs come out, Microsoft has been known to update the wording of policy settings and the Explaintext for clarity (though its underlying actions are usually the same).

So, Microsoft makes updates; you have more power, right? Sure. But the message is clear: if you want to control every client and server machine in your environment using Group Policy—use the latest version of the OS—Windows Vista.

What Happens When You Create a New GPO?

Windows XP uses ADM files and Windows Vista uses ADMX files (for editing GPOs)—and different things happen when GPOs are created using these management stations types. Figure 5.3 shows the "Reader's Digest" version of what we'll be discussing here, and after that will be the in-depth analysis of what's going on.

Creating and Editing a New GPO While Using a Pre-Vista Management Station

In order for us to create GPOs using a Windows XP machine, we need to have the GPMC console loaded (downloadable at `http://tinyurl.com/q77wx`). Note that the GPMC requires the .NET Framework files (downloadable at `http://tinyurl.com/758p8`).

> Note the GPMC requires .NET Framework 1.1. If you *only* have 2.0, the GPMC won't install.

Recall from Chapter 4 that when you use any ADM templates, these templates are added to the file-based Group Policy Template (found in SYSVOL) of the GPO. Unfortunately, there's no master update location where you can just drop the latest ADM files from Microsoft (or other vendors) and universally update the ADM files of existing GPOs and any future GPO that will be created. Indeed, you'll need to understand where new GPOs get their ADM templates from when you create new GPOs or modify existing GPOs.

In all cases, the editor you use (either Active Directory Users And Computers or GPMC) really uses the GPEDIT MMC snap-in (really the GPEDIT.DLL) when actually poking around or creating new GPOs. GPEDIT pulls the ADM template files from the computer it is running on. And it yanks these ADM template files from %systemroot% \inf—usually c:\windows\inf—directly into the GPO. Each time you do this, you're burning about 3–5MB of disk space—on every Domain Controller. This is because all material inside the GPO is replicated to every Domain Controller.

If you've created 100 GPOs using pre-Vista machines (like Windows XP or Windows 2000), you're using about 300–500MB of disk space—on every Domain Controller to store these ADM files. This problem is called SYSVOL bloat. In Figure 5.4, you can see a sample SYSVOL with several GPOs. Recall that GPOs live on every Domain Controller in the sysvol\corp.com\ Policies directory underneath their GUID. Each GPO has an ADM directory each containing the same ADM templates at about 3–5MB each directory.

FIGURE 5.3   What's copied into the GPO when using which type of management station

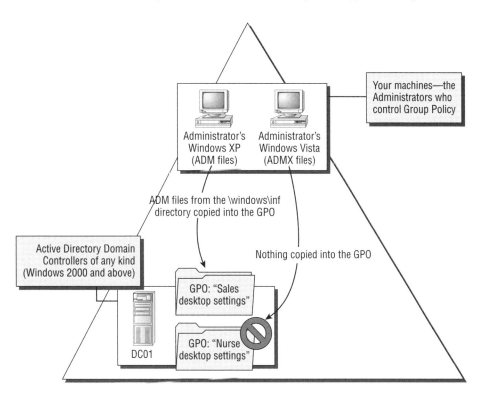

FIGURE 5.4 Every GPO created with a pre-Vista management station pushes about 3.3MB into SYSVOL.

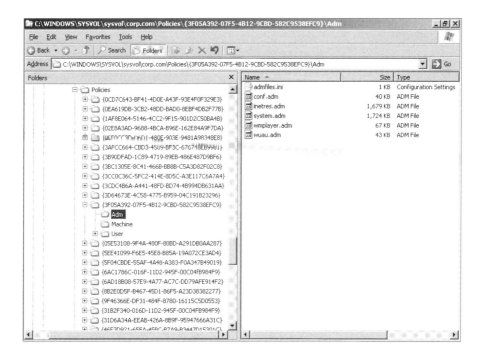

How to Prevent SYSVOL Bloat If You're Still Using Pre-Vista Management Stations

There is a way to avoid copying up the ADM files into the GPO, hence wasting the 3–5MB on each Domain Controller per GPO. The trick is to use a policy setting entitled **Always use local ADM files for Group Policy Object Editor** (located in Computer Configuration ➢ Administrative Templates ➢ System ➢ Group Policy) and have it affect your management station.

By enabling this policy, you're telling your management station: "I'm not going to push ADM files into the SYSVOL folder." Sounds great, right?

The downside, however, is that if you try to edit the GPO on a machine that doesn't have the same ADM templates as the GPO (or worse, the local machine is just plain missing an ADM template), you simply won't be able to edit the GPO the way you want. You'll have to track down the original machine that had the full complement of ADM templates to properly manage the GPO.

Because of the downsides, this workaround is only suggested for very large environments that have lots of GPOs which are taking a long time to replicate because of all the ADM template data being pushed into the GPO.

Here's the big ol' scary warning about the policy setting: it only works if the management station is Windows Server 2003 (not Windows XP). Why? I have no idea. So, if you want to prevent SYS-VOL bloat from ADM files, and you want to utilize this sneaky way to do it, you absolutely must make your management station Windows Server 2003 (and not Windows XP).

Microsoft talks a bit more about this in Knowledge Base article 816662.

Creating a New GPO While Using a Windows Vista Management Station

In order for us to create GPOs using a Windows Vista management station, we don't need to do much. The GPMC is already loaded and waiting for us. We can just type **gpmc.msc** at the command prompt to fire it up.

Once we create a GPO using our Windows Vista management station, we can also take a look at what's generated inside SYSVOL. In Figure 5.5, you can see the top Window was created using a Windows Vista management station. You know this because there's no ADM directory.

And, because there's no ADM directory (and no ADM files inside it) there's no wasted space (SYSVOL bloat) from ADM files.

FIGURE 5.5 The top window shows a GPO's contents when created using a Windows Vista management station. The middle window shows a GPO's contents when created using a Windows XP management station. The bottom window shows the contents of the ADM directory for the GPO created using the Windows XP management station.

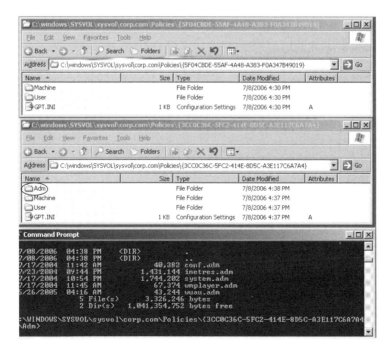

What Happens When You Edit an Existing GPO?

Here's where things get complicated. That is, you could have the four following situations:

- Scenario 1: Start out by creating and editing GPO on a pre-Vista management station (like Windows 2000, Windows XP, Windows Server 2003, and so on). Edit using another pre-Vista management station. In this scenario, no Windows Vista is involved.

- Scenario 2: Start out by creating and editing GPO on a pre-Vista management station. Edit using a Windows Vista station.

- Scenario 3: Start out by creating and editing GPO on a Windows Vista management station. Edit using another Windows Vista station.

- Scenario 4: Start out by creating and editing GPO on a Windows Vista management station. Edit using a Windows XP management station.

Scenario 1: Start Out by Creating and Editing GPO on Pre-Vista Management Station. Edit Using Another Pre-Vista Management Station.

Again, here, Windows Vista isn't involved. In this scenario, it's all about pre-Vista machines using old-school ADM templates and ADM template behavior. And, of course, note that by creating a GPO using a Windows XP machine, you won't be able to get to any of the Vista goodies—that's because all the Windows Vista goodies are only available when you use a Windows Vista management station.

So, let's imagine that you've created 128 GPOs using an old-and-crusty Windows 2000 machine. Of course, all 128 GPOs have the Windows 2000 versions of those ADM templates (yes, old and crusty).

Now, you learn about a policy setting in Windows XP that requires the corresponding Windows XP templates. What are you going to do?

Easy! Jump on a Windows XP machine and edit the GPO using the GPMC!

This is because, as we already understand, the ADM template files used to modify and update a GPO are always copied from your management station. Older ADM templates inside GPOs are automatically updated when you re-edit a GPO on a machine that has new ADM templates.

When you edit the GPO on your Windows XP management station and merely look at the policy settings in the Administrative Templates section, the editor will say: "Ah-ha! I've got Windows XP templates available to me! This specific GPO's ADM templates are only Windows 2000! I can tell because the date is sooo old. I'll update the underlying ADM templates automatically from c:\windows\inf in Windows XP—without even saying a word. That's because I have newer ones!"

And it then proceeds. And it proceeds because the time/date stamp for Windows XP ADM templates your editor has access to is more recent than the time/date stamp for Windows 2000 ADM templates. It's doing you a favor behind your back. You must repeat for every old GPO you want to update. If you want to update all your GPOs with Windows XP ADMs, you simply have to open each old GPO and look at the policy settings in the Administrative Templates section. But again, you need to do this from a Windows XP management station. Then they'll be updated.

Again, there's no universal master update location where you can just "drop in" your latest ADM templates and be done. However, with a script, you can update all your GPOs at one time (see the sidebar "Automatically Updating All Your Existing GPOs at Once with the Latest ADM Templates.")

Automatically Updating All Your Existing GPOs at Once with the Latest ADM Templates

In Chapter 7, you'll get a grip on all the myriad of things you can do with scripting and Group Policy. However, one thing that we won't tackle there (but we do want to tackle here) is how to automatically update all your existing GPOs with the latest ADM templates. As of this writing, the latest ADM templates are Windows 2003/SP1, but you could use this same tip to update all your GPOs with the ADM templates from, say, Windows XP/SP2 or earlier (not that you would really want to). Or, use this tip when XP/SP3 comes out.

To update all your GPOs (or just some of them), Microsoft has a downloadable script that will do this for you at `http://tinyurl.com/7v4s2`. It runs as a command line (as opposed to a GUI-based script). When you're ready to give the script a try, be sure to run it from the command line as `cscript admupdate.vbs` so it continues to use the command line for output (and not try to push data to the graphical output).

Here's what you need to tell the script:

- You need to tell it which GPOs to update. You can update using the /GUID switch, the /GPOfriendlyname switch, or the very powerful /ALL switch.

- You need to tell it where the latest ADM files reside. You do this with the /ADMSRC switch.

- You need to tell it what domain to update. You do this with the /DNSDOM:*<domain>* switch.

There are other switches available.

But, if you tell it just this much information, it performs a *simulation* of what it will do.

When you're actually ready for the script to do the deed and perform the upgrade, you need to add the /FILECOPY:ON switch (not shown in the preceding example). This actually performs the work. Note that this could take a *long* time and cause a *lot* of replication traffic. So, be sure to do it in the off-hours if possible.

Again, running this script isn't expressly necessary—for two reasons. First, because, as we've discussed, anytime you specifically touch an old GPO with an updated management station, the GPO will be automatically updated. Use this script to simply guarantee that the latest ADM files are pushed to every GPO. Second, by the time this chapter is over, I'm going to have convinced you to use a Windows Vista management station. And, then the GPOs themselves won't care about ADM files at all.

But, if you're still in a Windows XP-only environment, where you don't even have one Windows Vista management station, then this tip is still useful for you.

Scenario 2: Start Out by Creating and Editing a GPO on a Pre-Vista Management Station. Edit Using a Windows Vista Station.

This will be the common "upgrade" scenario. That is, you've already got your gaggle of GPOs created. You created them using Windows 2000, Windows XP, or Windows Server 2003 with Active Directory Users and Computers or the GPMC. Now, Vista comes along, and you're ready to use it. What happens?

Not much! If you start to use a Vista management station and edit an existing GPO created by a pre-Vista operating system, nothing happens in SYSVOL. No Vista ADMX files are copied anywhere, and very little happens overall.

However, while you're editing the GPO, you'll have access to all the latest-greatest Vista policy settings, one of which is seen in Figure 5.6.

For argument's sake, let's say you decided to enable "Turn off Windows HotStart"—a Windows Vista-only feature.

Now, what happens if you try to edit and/or report on those settings using Windows XP? Short answer: It's not good. That's because Windows XP doesn't know how to interpret the Vista-only settings you've set within the GPO. If you try to edit the GPO on a Windows XP machine, you simply won't see the newly available Windows Vista policy setting.

And, if you try to look at it using the GPMC's "Settings Report" feature, the Vista-only settings show up as "Extra Registry Settings" as seen in Figure 5.7.

In Figure 5.7 you can see the Settings tab from GPMC running on an XP machine, which is a report of what's going on inside the GPO.

FIGURE 5.6   Editing an existing GPO with Vista gives you the ability to see updated settings.

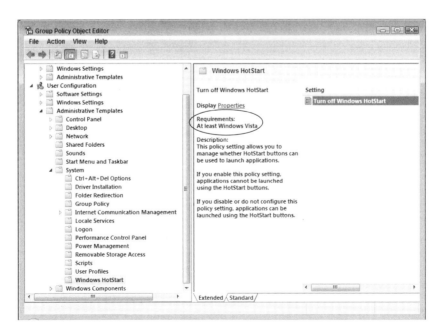

FIGURE 5.7   Windows XP doesn't know how to interpret Vista-only settings within a GPO. These settings show up as "Extra Registry Settings."

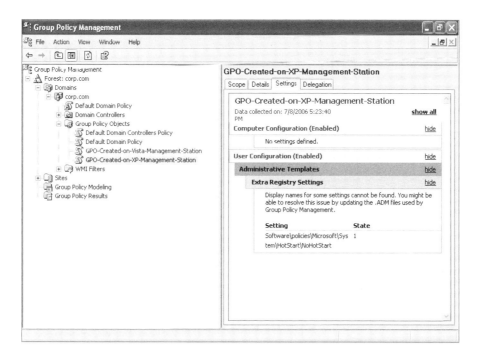

Again, if you were to continue to use your Windows XP management station to *edit* the GPO, you'd find that you simply wouldn't be able to find the "Turn off Windows Hotstart" policy setting   or any other Windows Vista-specific policy setting for that matter.

While it's clearly not a good idea, there is nothing that technically that prevents you from using Windows XP to make a change to a GPO that was edited by Vista. In short, you simply can't see the Vista settings.

If a custom ADM file has been added to the GPO (yes, ADM) then Vista will utilize it and present it.

Scenario 3: Start Out by Creating and Editing a GPO on a Windows Vista Management Station. Edit Using Another Windows Vista Station.

This is the scenario you want to strive for. That is, always use Windows Vista to create and edit your GPOs. When Windows Vista + SP1 comes out (with its additional policy settings), you'll be all set. You won't have to do a thing (except use a Windows Vista + SP1 management station) to be "latest and greatest."

If you backtrack to a Windows Vista (no service pack) machine, you won't have access to the latest and greatest Vista + SP1 settings (and the GPMC won't accurately report what's Enabled or Disabled, either because it simply cannot "know" about those updated policies).

So, it sounds like the message is. "Always use the latest-greatest operating system and service pack as my management station." But what if you're not ready to personally upgrade your management station to the latest and greatest? Or, what if you had 20 administrators, each with their own management station?

If *only* there were a way to ensure that all your administrators always used the latest and greatest ADMX files, you'd have no issues. That way, even older version of Windows Vista would be able to determine the latest and greatest settings.

Sounds like a dream, right? Good news: It's a dream that we'll make a reality in the next big section, with the "Central Store." so stay tuned!

Scenario 4: Start Out by Creating and Editing a GPO on a Windows Vista Management Station. Edit Using a Windows XP Management Station.

Avoid this scenario whenever possible. This is the worst of all worlds because when you originally created the GPO on your Windows Vista management station, you did so without copying the 3–5MB of ADM files up (remember: Windows Vista doesn't use ADM files). So, you did good here!

However, by merely viewing the GPO using Windows XP, you end up pushing up the 3–5MB of ADM files into the GPO. So, every time you do this, you'll see an ADM directory inside the GPO because they were pushed up from your Windows XP machine. And it's done "invisibly."

Vista Management Stations and the Central Store

As we discussed, the ideal world is to use only Windows Vista as your management stations. Remember: if you have even one Windows Vista client machine out there in sales, marketing, Human Resources, and so on, you'll need to manage it *from* a Windows Vista machine, because Windows XP won't have the definitions of the policy settings that Windows Vista clients have.

So, we'll assume from here on that you'll only be using Windows Vista as your management station, eschewing Windows XP management stations. If you want the best practices for Windows XP management stations (again, only if you have zero Windows Vista clients, right?), then you'll have to pick up the previous edition of this book (same chapter, Chapter 5) which has lots of tips, tricks, gotchas, bugs, trials, and tribulations about Windows XP management stations.

As you're reading this right now, Vista is pretty darned new. But let's fast forward a bit and assume, oh, that we're up to Windows Vista + SP3. Yep, Windows Vista Service Pack 3 has just been released and you need to control the new whiz-bang features that only come with Windows Vista + SP3 client computers. (Again, I'm dreaming a little into the future here; new whiz-bang features might or might not come in service packs or other delivery vehicles, but stay with me through this example anyway).

"No problem!" you say, "I'll just create a Windows Vista management station." And you'd be right! Except that you already have a Windows Vista management station. So you wouldn't want to run out and create a whole new machine just for this. You'd want to leverage the Windows Vista management station you already have, right?

Sure!

This is easy! You're a diligent administrator (you bought this book, after all), and you know you have two ways to update your current management station:

- Apply SP3 to your Windows Vista management station. That would update the ADMX files which live in c:\windows\PolicyDefinitions.

- Or, you could forgo applying SP3 to your Windows Vista management station and simply copy the ADMX (and associated ADML files) from another Windows Vista + SP3 machine to your management station. Again, you'll plunk them in the c:\windows\ PolicyDefinitions directory.

So, the message again sounds simple: whenever Microsoft has new ADMX/ADML files, get them into your management station.

Simple, yes—until you realize you have 20 administrators in your company, each with their own Windows Vista management station. Or you remember those administrators who love to bounce from machine to machine because they have three sites to run. Yikes! How are you going to guarantee that all of these administrators will use the updated ADMX files?

Let's assume you've successfully upgraded *your* Windows Vista management station to SP3, but only some of your 20 administrators successfully upgrade to Windows Vista + SP3 (or have created custom ADMX files) (or jam in the ADMX files into c:\windows\PolicyDefinitions).

This becomes a big problem—fast. Here's why: If you create a new GPO, that GPO will have the definitions for all the whiz-bang stuff Windows Vista + SP3 has to offer. However, when another administrator (who doesn't have the latest ADMX files) tries to edit or report on that GPO, they simply won't see the policy settings for Windows Vista + SP3 available.

 GPMC reports about this newly created GPO would show them as "Extra Registry Settings," but actually trying to edit the GPO itself will not show the new whiz-bang features.

What you need is a way to ensure that all administrators who are using Windows Vista management stations have a one-stop-shop way to ensure they're getting the latest ADMX files. That way, everyone will be on the same page, and there will be no challenges when one administrator creates a GPO and another tries to edit it.

Windows Vista Central Store

Windows Vista management stations have a trick up their sleeve. That is, they can use a "central store" for ADMX and ADML files. Recall that the ADMX files are the definitions themselves, and the ADML files are the language-specific files for each ADMX file.

The idea is that the central store lives on every Domain Controller. So, after the central store is created, your Windows Vista management station simply looks for it—every time it tries to create or edit a GPO—and it will automatically use the definitions contained within the ADMX files inside the central store.

This means you don't have to worry about running around to each of your 20 management stations to update them whenever new ADMX files come out. You simply plop them in the central store and you're done. You don't even have to tell the Windows Vista management stations you did anything; they'll just automatically look and use the latest definitions!

Here's the best part: it doesn't matter what kind of Domain Controllers you have. Doesn't matter if you have Windows 2000, Windows Server 2003, Longhorn Server or a mix of all three. It's the Windows Vista management station which is doing the work to look for the central store in the place upon the Domain Controller.

Wait, I'm going to stop here, and take a big deep breath and say it one more time. Because I know you're reading fast and want to get to the good stuff. So, say it out loud if you have to: **It doesn't matter if you have Windows 2000, Windows Server 2003, Longhorn Server, or a mix of all three. It's the Windows Vista management station which is doing the work to look for the central store in the place upon the Domain Controller.**

Got it? You don't have to "sell" your boss into upgrading the whole server back-end just to get this cool Central Store stuff.

So, let's read on and make it happen.

Creating the Central Store

Creating the central store must be done by a Domain Administrator, because only a Domain Administrator has the ability to write to the location we need in SYSVOL. You can do this operation on any Domain Controller, because all Domain Controllers will automatically replicate the changes we do here to all other Domain Controllers via normal Active Directory/SYSVOL replication. However, it's likely best to perform this on the PDC Emulator, because that's the default location the GPMC and Group Policy Object Editor use by default.

To create the central store:

1. On the PDC emulator, use explorer or the command line to create a directory within `%systemroot%\sysvol\sysvol\`*domain name*`\policies`. You want to create a directory called `PolicyDefinitions` as seen in Figure 5.8.

2. We need a location to store our language-specific ADML files. Within `PolicyDefinitions` you'll create a directory for each locale. Again, U.S. English is US-EN. For other locales, visit `http://tinyurl.com/qpomo`.

WARNING   Note that the directory name must be the same as specified in the locale reference page. If it's not, the ADMX file will not find its corresponding ADML file for that language.

FIGURE 5.8 Create a new directory called PolicyDefinitions in the Policies folder of SYSVOL

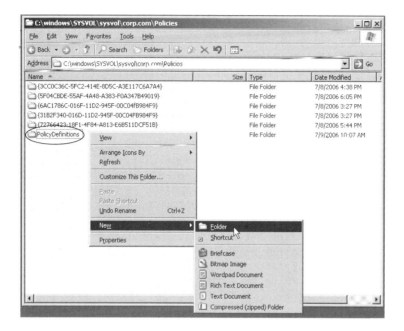

Populating the Central Store

Now, you simply have to get the ADMX and ADML files from your Windows Vista machine into the central store. There are a zillion possible ways to copy the files there. But, the steps are most easily done with two **xcopy** commands. This will work if your Windows Vista management station has access to the Domain Controller and that you have write rights.

To copy in the ADMX files into the central store from your Windows Vista management station:

```
xcopy %systemroot%\PolicyDefinitions\*
%logonserver%\sysvol\%userdnsdomain%\policies\PolicyDefinitions
```

To copy in the ADML files into, say, the U.S. English directory we created earlier:

```
xcopy %systemroot%\PolicyDefinitions\EN-US\*
%logonserver%\sysvol\%userdnsdomain%\policies\POlicyDefinitions\EN-US\
```

 You can also use a free graphical utility for creating and populating the central store automatically at www.gpoguy.com/tools.htm.

Verifying You're Using the Central Store

Once you've created the central store directories in SYSVOL and copied the ADMX and ADML files to their proper location, you're ready to try it out! Start out by closing the GPMC if already open on your Windows Vista management station then re-opening it. You can fire up the GPMC by clicking Start and in the Run box typing **gpmc.msc**.

And, then just create and edit a GPO.

However, can you be sure you're really using the central store? Even if you miscopied the files or misnamed a directory, it would likely still look like it was working. That's because you'll simply "fall back" to using your local c:\windows\PolicyDefinitions directory which holds your ADMX files.

So, on one of your Windows Vista management stations, I suggest a little test. That is, rename the PolicyDefinitions directory within c:\windows. If you rename it to something like zzz_PolicyDefinitions, and you can continue to use the GPMC to create and edit GPOs—you therefore *must* be using the central store to pull those ADMX and ADML files.

There is a secondary test as well to help you verify that you're using the central store. That is, when you create and edit a GPO, then click the Settings tab inside the GPMC, you'll see a line under either Computer Configuration or User Configuration which says "Policy definitions (ADMX files) retrieved from the central store." You can see this in Figure 5.9.

FIGURE 5.9 Any time you click the Settings tab, the impromptu report will demonstrate if you are using the Central Store for your ADMX files.

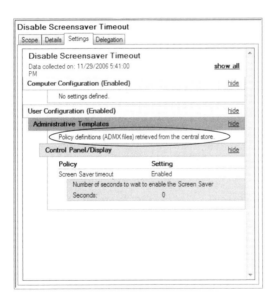

Updating the Central Store

ADMX and ADML files will be updated. When Longhorn Server comes out, they'll be newer than the ones in the "out of the box" Windows Vista. Likewise, when Windows Vista's SP1, SP2, and so on comes out, those will be newer still, and so on.

When this happens, you'll need to update the central store, which couldn't be easier. Simply copy the latest and greatest ADMX files to the `PolicyDefinitions` directory you created in SYSVOL, and copy the latest and greatest ADML files to the language-specific directory within `PolicyDefinitions`.

Then you're done.

Additionally, other products, like Office 2007 will have ADMX and ADML files. If you wish to make those available to all administrators, just do the same thing. Drop them into the central store and you're done. (More about Office 2007 ADMX files a bit later.)

Office 2007 has, confusingly, both ADM templates and ADMX templates. As of this writing, ADMX templates are not available for download, but the ADM templates are. You can find the ADM templates here, www.tinyurl.com/hzfcr, but don't bother putting them in the Central Store, because ADM templates and the Central Store don't mix.

ADM and ADMX Templates from Other Sources

The templates Microsoft provides with Windows are just the beginning of possibilities when it comes to Administrative Templates. The idea behind additional templates is that you or third-party software vendors can create them to restrict or enhance features of either the operating system or applications.

If you know what to control, you're in business. Just code it up in an ADM or ADMX file and utilize it. If you're starting from scratch and have a choice, of course you'll want to use ADMX files instead of ADM files. That's because you can leverage the central store for ADMX files instead of remembering to copy ADM files to every management station.

However, it should be noted that you might already be using an ADM file or three. If you are, how do you get them to the ADMX "promised land"? A free tool, of course. Before we get into that, I will say that's the best option: get those custom and additional ADM files into ADMX format and leverage the central store. However, for completeness, I do want to explain what happens if you try to introduce an ADM file directly into a Windows Vista management station.

Using ADM Templates from Other Sources

Recall that ADM templates are the pre-Vista way to make definitions of what we can control. And, recall that there are both true *policies* and *preferences* which can be defined within an ADM file (or, ADMX file too).

Policies write to the "correct" place in the target computer's Registry. And, when the user or computer falls out of the "scope of management" of the GPO (that is, it doesn't apply to them anymore), the setting should revert back to the default.

Preferences write anywhere in the Registry that the application might be looking for it. Preferences tattoo the Registry. So, when the user or computer falls out of the scope of management of the GPO, the setting just sticks around.

You have the ability to get some ADM files from various sources. These ADM files sometimes have definitions for true policies. Other ADM files have definitions for preferences. How do you know which are which? The good news is, the Group Policy Object Editor interface shows you a difference between the two.

In Windows XP (and earlier) it shows blue for policies and red for preferences. In Windows Vista, it shows a little paper icon for Policies and a paper icon with a down arrow for preferences. That way, you can make an informed decision on whether or not you want to implement a preference.

Indeed, on GPanswers.com (`http://www.gpanswers.com/faq/` in the "Tips and Tricks" section halfway down the page), we have a gaggle of downloadable ADM templates that people have created to control various aspects of applications and of their systems.

Leveraging ADM Templates from Your Windows Vista Management Station

If you want to leverage and load one of these ADM templates into an existing GPO, simply edit it using the GPMC and bringing up the Group Policy Object Editor as seen in Figure 5.10. Then, choose either User Configuration ➢ Administrative Templates or Computer Configuration ➢ Administrative Templates, right-click over either instance of Administrative Templates, and choose Add/Remove Templates to open the Add/Remove Templates dialog box.

Click the Add button to open up the file requester, and select to load the ADM template you want. I'll show you in the next section or two where to track down more ADM files, but I wanted to show you this first so you'd know how to use them.

The original (pre-Vista) default location to start looking for ADM files is from `\windows\inf`; however, in practice you could store your ADM files anywhere. Just remember that every time you use an ADM template, you're copying that file directly into the GPO within SYSVOL.

When adding an Administrative Template, the interface suggests that you can choose to add it from either the Computer Configuration or the User Configuration node. In actuality, you can add the ADM template from either section, and the appropriate policy settings appear under whichever node the ADM template was designed for.

FIGURE 5.10   You can still Add/Remove Templates from a GPO you create with Windows Vista.

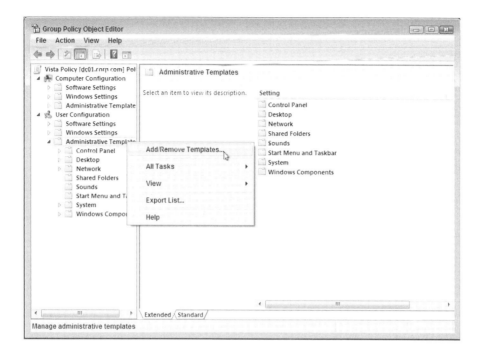

Once ADM templates are added using a Windows Vista management station, ADM templates show up under a special node within the Group Policy Object Editor, called "Classic Administrative Templates (ADM)" as seen in Figure 5.11. In Figure 5.11, I've loaded an ADM template for Word 2003 (again, I'll show you where to get these templates in a minute so you can experiment, too).

Viewing Old-Style Preferences

Again, ADM files can have definitions for true policies or for old-style preferences. If you load additional ADM templates into the Group Policy Object Editor (as shown in Figures 5.12), that contain old-style preferences, you simply won't see them as available in the Group Policy Object Editor.

A little later, I'll show you how to "create your own" ADM file which controls the Windows XP start sound. However, that trick won't produce a proper policy; rather, it produces an old-style preference.

Once you have the ADM file in hand, you'll load it into the GPO the same way. Choose either User Configuration ➢ Administrative Templates or Computer Configuration ➢ Administrative Templates, right-click over either instance of Administrative Templates, and choose Add/Remove Templates (see Figure 5.10) to open the Add/Remove Templates dialog box.

FIGURE 5.11 ADM templates are permitted in GPOs created from Windows Vista management stations. True policy settings are automatically available for use.

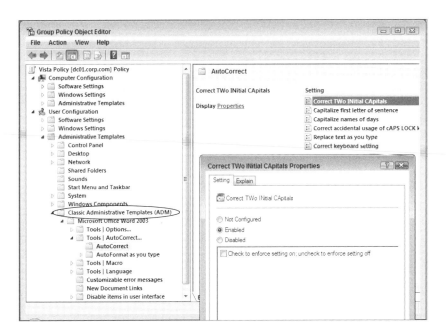

Click the Add button to open up the file requester, and select to load the ADM template you want. I'll show you in the next section or two where to track down more ADM files, but I wanted to show you this first so you'd know how to use them.

Once loaded, you'll see the same Classic Administrative Templates (ADM) node and the list of categories contained within the ADM file containing preferences (as seen in Figure 5.12). But, you won't see any settings. Again, that's because the Group Policy Object Editor automatically prevents you from seeing preferences—you need to turn on that ability inside the GPO.

To see the preference settings contained within the ADM file, use the menu at the top and select View ➤ Filtering to open the Filtering dialog box, as shown in Figure 5.13.

By default, the "Only show policy settings that can be fully managed" check box is checked. This is a safety mechanism that prevents old-style tattooing policies from being visible. Uncheck the check box, and you'll be in business.

After you turn on the ability to see the preferences within the interface, you'll notice that icons for old-style preferences have paper icon with a down arrow on them. This is to indicate that this is a preference and not a true policy, and these values will stick around even after the policy no longer applies to the user or computer.

Indeed, the Windows Vista Group Policy Object Editor is nice enough to even tell you this fact, as seen in Figure 5.14. You can see the little "down arrow" icon for any tattooing "preference."

FIGURE 5.12   ADM files containing preferences will show the categories available, but not the actual preferences until you enable that feature for the GPO.

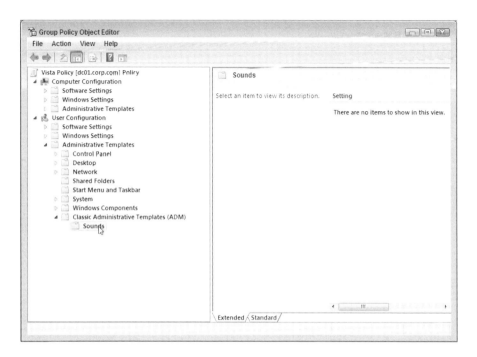

FIGURE 5.13   To see old-style preferences, clear the "Only show policy settings that can be fully managed" check box. This check box is checked by default to prevent you from seeing old-school preferences.

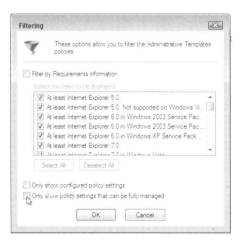

FIGURE 5.14 Windows Vista's Group Policy Object Editor warns you about the issues when leveraging preferences and not policies.

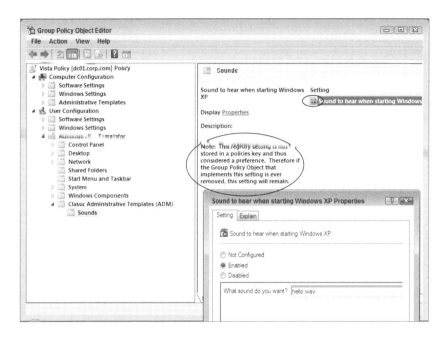

Microsoft Office ADM Templates

If you are also interested in deploying Office 2000, Office XP, or Office 2003, you'll be happy to know that they each come with a slew of customized ADM templates for you to import and use to your advantage.

- For Office 2000, download the Office 2000 Resource Kit tools at www.microsoft.com/office/ork/2000/appndx/toolbox.htm.

- For Office XP, download the Office XP Resource Kit tools at www.microsoft.com/office/ork/xp/appndx/appa18.htm.

- Office 2003 templates are located in the Office 2003 Resource Kit. Check www.microsoft.com/office. At last check, some even newer templates are available in the Office 2003/SP2 Resource Kit at http://tinyurl.com/4wxxn.

- Office 2007 templates are located at http://tinyurl.com/2w9qs7. However, Office 2007 is the first to also ship with ADMX templates (discussed a little later).

For information on how to automatically deploy Office 2000, XP, or 2003 (with patches and personalized customizations) to your users, see Chapter 10.

The file you're looking for (with either Office 2000 or XP) is called `Orktools.exe` (for Office 2003, it's `Ork.exe`), and it's about 9MB. After you install the corresponding Resource Kit on your management station, the following files are automatically placed in the `\windows\inf` folder for importation like the other ADM files.

Office 2000, Office XP, Office 2003, and Office 2007 ADM Templates

Here is a list of the ADM templates available for Office 2000, Office XP, Office 2003 and Office 207.

Office 2000 Templates	Office XP Templates	Office 2003 Templates	Office 2007 Templates	Description
access9.adm	access10.adm	access11.adm	access12.adm	Access settings
clipgal5.adm	gal10.adm	gaal11.adm	N/A	Restrict access to media clips
excel9.adm	excel10.adm	excel11.adm	excel12.adm	Excel settings
frontpg4.adm	fp10.adm	fp11.adm	N/A	FrontPage settings
instlr1.adm	instalr11.adm	instalr11.adm	N/A	Windows Installer settings
office9.adm	office10.adm	office11.adm	office12.adm	Common Office settings
outlk9.adm	outlk10.adm	outlk11.adm	outlk12.adm	Outlook 2000 settings
ppoint9.adm	ppt10.adm	ppt11.adm	ppt12.adm	PowerPoint settings
pub9.adm	pub10.adm	pub11.adm	pub12.adm	Publisher settings
word9.adm	word10.adm	word11.adm	word12.adm	Word settings
N/A	N/A	N/A	visio12.adm	Visio Settings
N/A	N/A	aer.adm	N/A	Corporate Windows Error Reporting (see the "Microsoft Corporate Error Reporting" section later in this chapter)

Office 2000 Templates	Office XP Templates	Office 2003 Templates	Office 2007 Templates	Description
N/A	N/A	rm11.adm	N/A	Microsoft Relationship Manager File location
N/A	N/A	scrib11.adm	onent12.adm	Microsoft OneNote 2003 settings
N/A	N/A	N/A	cpao12.adm	Calendar Printing Assistant for Outlook 2007
N/A	N/A	N/A	groove12.adm	Groove 2007
N/A	N/A	N/A	ic12.adm	Office InterConnect 2007
N/A	N/A	N/A	inf12.adm	InfoPath 2007
N/A	N/A	N/A	proj12.adm	Project 2007
N/A	N/A	N/A	spd12.adm	Sharepoint Designer 2007

Implementing a Customized Office Policy

After the Office templates are on the server, you can simply load them alongside the currently loaded templates. You can load all, some, or none—it's up to you.

In this example, we'll make believe we need to set up a custom Word 2000 policy for a collection of users. Normally, as in this example, Office template settings are meant for users, not computers. However, Office does include computer-side settings that you can use to override user-side settings if you want.

 If you don't want to use the Office 2000 ADM templates in this example, you can substitute Office XP or Office 2003 templates. Just make sure you also have the corresponding Office suite installed on the target machine!

Here, you'll see how to use an additional template. We'll load the WORD9.ADM template alongside our current default templates. Then, we'll change the default behavior of our Human Resources users for Word 2000 as follows:

- The grammar checker is turned off while we type in Word.
- The spell checker is turned off while we type in Word.
- Word will ignore words in uppercase during spell check.
- Word will ignore words with numbers during spell check.

To change Word's default behavior for the **Human Resources Users** OU, follow these steps:

1. Log on to your Windows Vista management station as the Domain Administrator.

2. Download the Office 2000 Resource Kit tools and make sure the ADM templates are properly installed in the \windows\inf folder.

3. Fire up the GPMC.

4. Right-click **Human Resources Users** OU and select "Create and link a GPO here."

5. Create a new GPO called "Word 2000 Settings."

6. Edit the "Word 2000 Settings" GPO.

7. Choose either User Configuration ➤ Administrative Templates or Computer Configuration ➤ Administrative Templates, right-click over either instance of Administrative Templates, and choose Add/Remove Templates to open the Add/Remove Templates dialog box.

When adding an Administrative Template, the interface suggests that you can choose to add it from either the Computer Configuration or the User Configuration node. In actuality, you can add the ADM template from either section, and the appropriate policy settings appear under whichever node the ADM template was designed for.

8. Click the Add button to open up the file requester, and select to load the Word9.adm template from the \windows\inf folder. Click Close to close the Add/Remove Templates dialog box to return to the Group Policy Object Editor.

9. To turn off the "Check Grammar As You Type" feature, drill down to User Configuration ➤ Administrative Templates ➤ Microsoft Word 2000 ➤ Tools ➤ Options ➤ Spelling & Grammar ➤ Check Grammar As You Type. Then, enable the setting, but do *not* select the check box. This forces the policy on the user, but clearing the check box forces it off.

10. Repeat step 9 for "Check Spelling As You Type," "Ignore Words in Upper case," and "Ignore Words with Numbers."

You can try this exercise with the other Office 2000–supplied templates listed earlier. These will affect Excel, PowerPoint, Access, and the like.

To test your new policy on the **Human Resources Users** OU, simply log on to any Windows 2000 or Windows XP machine loaded with Word 2000 as a user who would be affected by the new policy. For instance, log on to XPPRO1 as Frank Rizzo, our old HR pal from Chapter 1 (assuming you have Word 2000 loaded).

Then in Word, choose Tools ➤ Options to open the Options dialog box, and make sure the settings reflect the policy settings you dictated.

Now, in this example we just explored, we were using the raw ADM files. Again, you can (as you'll discover a little later) take these ADM files and covert them—lock, stock, and barrel, into ADMX files to be used in the central store.

Also note that Office 2007 will have available downloadable ADMX files—no need to convert or do anything fancy. Just plop 'em in your Central Store and start using them. We'll talk more about the Office 2007 ADMX files a little later. Check it out in the upcoming section "Using ADMX Templates from Other Sources."

Other Microsoft ADM Templates

Microsoft has two additional applications outside the Office family of products that leverage the Group Policy infrastructure by using ADM templates.

Microsoft Software Update Services (SUS) and Windows Server Update Services (WSUS)

The job of Microsoft's Software Update Services (SUS) and the newer Windows Server Update Services (WSUS) is to ensure that patches are deployed to your Windows 2000, Windows XP, and Windows 2003 client systems. After a server is set up to deploy the patches, the client system learns about the server by way of a custom ADM template.

The template is built in to Windows 2003 and Windows 2000 + SP4 as Wuau.adm. However, the template is not built in to Windows 2000 + SP3.

You can learn more about SUS, how to deploy it, and how to use the rather complex ADM templates from two articles I wrote for *MCP Magazine*, which you can find at http://tinyurl.com/86sbj and http://tinyurl.com/5gfuk. These articles form a two-part series about installation and troubleshooting. The latter's main focus is on understanding the ADM template. Lastly, Microsoft has an excellent guide to the policy settings with regard to WSUS available at http://tinyurl.com/8nalu.

Microsoft Corporate Error Reporting

Microsoft has a service that lets corporate IT administrators "trap" error messages to a central server, instead of being sent directly to Microsoft, which is called Corporate Error Reporting (CER). CER can help track systems that frequently crash and can provide an easier way to connect with Microsoft if a system does fail often. It can trap information for a lot of Microsoft's most popular applications including Office XP, Windows XP, Windows 2003, Project 2002, and Sharepoint Portal Server.

Microsoft CER uses the ADM file Cer2.adm. You can get more information on CER at www.microsoft.com/resources/satech/cer/. You'll find the ADM file in the "toolbox" section of the web page.

ADM Templates You Shouldn't Use with Windows 2000, Windows XP, or 2003

Both the Office 2000 Resource Kit and Windows 2003 Server itself come with additional ADM templates that are not truly meant for the Group Policy Object Editor. Make a note of them so that you don't use them by mistake.

Office 2000 NT/95 Templates

Additional settings to configure Internet Explorer 5 are included in the Office 2000 Resource Kit, but they are not automatically copied to the \windows\inf folder. These are found, after the Office 2000 Resource Kit is installed, in the \Program Files\IEAK\policies\EN folder. The ADM policies in the ADM templates (located in the following table) are *not* meant for the Group Policy Object Editor. Rather, these are for the old-style Windows NT/95 Poledit.exe program.

Internet Explorer 5 Templates	Description
Aaxa.adm	Data binding settings.
Chat.adm	Microsoft Chat settings.
Conf.adm	NetMeeting settings.
Inetcorp.adm	Dial-up, language and temporary Internet files settings.
Inetres.adm	Internet properties, including connections, toolbars, and toolbar settings. Equivalent to the Tools ➤ Internet Options command.
Inetset.adm	Additional Internet properties: AutoComplete, display, and some advanced settings.
Oe.adm	Outlook Express Identity Manager settings. Use this to prevent users from changing or configuring identities.
Sp1shell.adm	Active Desktop settings.
Subs.adm	Offline Pages settings.

Some of these templates *can* be loaded into Windows 2000, but you probably wouldn't want to do so; some settings included in these templates include actual policies (nontattooing), and some include only preferences (only tattoo). To review the difference between policies and preferences, see the opening section of this chapter. You can just use the included Internet Explorer template settings found in Windows 2000's `inetres.adm`, instead of loading these templates that include both policies and preferences.

Windows NT Templates

Additionally included with a Windows 2000 computer are even more ADM templates. These are not for use within the Windows 2000 Group Policy Object Editor either; rather, they are for use with the old-style NT `Poledit.exe` program. This feature set includes the following:

Windows NT Template	Function
Common.adm	User interface options common to Windows NT 4 and Windows 9x. For use with System Policy Object Editor (`Poledit.exe`).
Inetcorp.adm	Dial-up, language, and temporary Internet files settings. For use with System Policy Object Editor (`Poledit.exe`).
Inetset.adm	Additional Internet properties: AutoComplete, display, and some advanced settings. For use with System Policy Object Editor (`Poledit.exe`).
Windows.adm	User interface options specific to Windows 95 and Windows 98. For use with System Policy Object Editor (`Poledit.exe`).
Winnt.adm	User interface options specific to Windows NT 4. For use with System Policy Object Editor (`Poledit.exe`).

These templates are really not 100 percent compatible with the Group Policy Administrative Template interface if imported directly. Some will indicate that they are unsupported, as shown here.

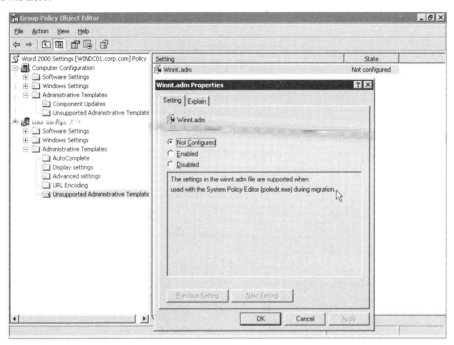

These are to be used with the old System Policy Object Editor (`Poledit.exe`). For instance, if you do end up loading, say, the `Winnt.adm` into the Windows 2003 Group Policy Object Editor, you are informed that it won't work, and the settings will not be displayed.

Using ADMX Templates from Other Sources

You'll get ADMX files the same way you got ADM files: companies like Microsoft will make them available to control the products they support, and enterprising geeks will produce ADMX files which control other parts of the operating system and third-party applications.

The same basic note and warning applies though: ADMX files can contain both (or either) true policies or old-school preferences. And, if they do contain preferences, you'll need to explicitly show them in the Group Policy Object Editor as seen in Figure 5.14.

ADMX Templates for Office 2007

As of right now, Office 2007 has been released, but the ADMX files for it have not been released.

But, when they are, you already know what to do. Just chuck 'em in the Central Store (both ADMX and ADML files in the appropriate places) and you'll be golden. Then all the new GPOs that you create will be able to control Office 2007!

ADMX Templates from Other Sources

Will other Microsoft products have ADMX files? We hope so. So, while I have nothing specific to report now, check in every so often on GPanswers.com (especially the newsletters, where I'll try to let you know about any new ones that pop up).

Darren Mar-Elia, who runs GPOguy.com and is the technical editor of this book's edition has an ADMX version of his troubleshooting tool, called GPOLOG.adm at www.gpoguy.com/gpolog.htm.

Deciding How to Use ADMX Templates

Once you have the ADMX templates, you need to decide how to use them. If you've already created the central store—terrific. Just plop them into the central store and you're done. However, note that this means that all administrators who have access to create GPOs using Windows Vista management stations will be able to leverage this ADMX file.

You might not want to enable all administrators to leverage this ADMX template.

If that's the case, you only have one option: put the ADMX files you want to use on the Windows Vista management station you use. The downside, however, is that if another Group Policy administrator (on his Windows Vista management station) tries to edit the GPO or report on it, he won't get the same view of all the settings that you do. That's because his Windows Vista management station doesn't contain the ADMX file you're using.

So, best practice is to use the ADMX file central store whenever possible.

ADMX Migrator and ADMX Editor Tools

Since leveraging ADM files directly inside GPOs which also use ADMX files can be fraught with peril, wouldn't it be a better idea to just utilize ADMX files everywhere? That way, you can just plop 'em all in the central store and be done. If you already have custom ADM files and need to get them to ADMX land, there's a free utility which was written by FullArmor Corporation and licensed by Microsoft to give to you for free.

It's got a silly name: the ADMX Migrator tool. Doesn't it sound like it migrates ADMX files? Well, it doesn't. Maybe it should have been called ADM2ADMX or something, but, regardless of the name, it's a cool tool. You can download the tool from Microsoft here: http://tinyurl.com/ydb6ub. (Believe me when I tell you the non-Tiny-Url would choke a horse.) Note that it first requires the .NET Framework 2.0 to be previously installed.

Additionally, inside the ADMX Migrator tool package is a neat ADMX editor as well to help you hand-craft your own ADMX files from scratch. The idea is that you don't have to "learn" a new language and hand-code it using, say, Notepad. Just use the tool to create your own ADMX files and you're in business.

For these examples, I'm running the tools on my Windows Vista management station, but they'll work just fine on a Windows XP which has the .NET Framework 2.0 loaded as well.

ADMX Migrator

There are lots of places you can get pre-made ADM files. You might try leveraging some right now—some are at GPanswers.com, others are found online from various other websites. Here's an example of a simple ADM file if you want to follow along. Just take this text, and copy it into Notepad and save it as Sounds.ADM.

```
CLASS USER

CATEGORY "Sounds"
    POLICY "Sound to hear when starting Windows XP"
        KEYNAME "Appevents\Schemes\Apps\.Default\SystemStart\.Current"
        PART "What sound do you want?" EDITTEXT REQUIRED
        VALUENAME ".default"
        END PART
    END POLICY

END CATEGORY
```

Then run the tool named faAdmxConv.exe against the ADM file you have. It can be as simple as just pointing to the file, but there are more switches if you have specific requirements. Once run, it will create an ADMX and ADML file for the ADM, which is then ready to be put in the central store (or, if you're not using the central store, then with individual Windows Vista management stations). You can see the program run and its output in Figure 5.15.

FIGURE 5.15 The faAdmxConv.exe tool will take your ADM and convert it into an ADMX and ADML file.

Then, if you want to leverage these in the central store, put the ADMX file in the \PolicyDefinitions directory within the SYSVOL and the ADML file in the language directory (en-US for English).

ADMX Editor

In the previous example, we leveraged an existing ADM file which modified Windows XP's startup sound. What if you wanted to create the ADMX file from scratch?

Creating an ADMX template can sometimes be difficult. The hardest part can be figuring out which Registry setting you need to modify on the client system. You can use several tools to help you. One such tool is ProcessMonitor from Microsoft's Sysinternals tools. You can find it at http://tinyurl.com/y45pu7. This tool can help point out what's changing on the client.

Then, armed with that information, you can triumphantly create your own custom ADM or ADMX template and try it. That's where the ADMX editor, also in the ADMX Migrator download comes in.

Once you fire it up, you'll be able to create a new ADMX file and add categories, like "Misc XP Sounds" as seen in Figure 5.16. Note that it's not easy (at all) to realize you need to click to the right of Display Name to get that field to turn on. Once you do, you can enter in the name.

Then, right-click over your new category and enter in your first policy setting. Here, we're only entering one: "Sound to hear when starting Windows XP." We then give it the Registry key (seen in the previous ADM listing) and the Registry value name (also seen in the previous ADM listing) and finally specify that it's a User-side setting with the pull-down menu next to Class. You can see these all entered in Figure 5.17.

Then, you can add different "Elements," such as a Dropdown List, ComboBox, and more as seen in Figure 5.18. You can also enter in your own Explaintext and Supported On text.

FIGURE 5.16 Once you create a new ADMX file, you can create your first category, such as "Misc XP Sounds."

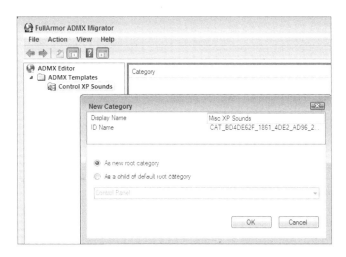

FIGURE 5.17   You can create your own policy settings within the categories you previously created

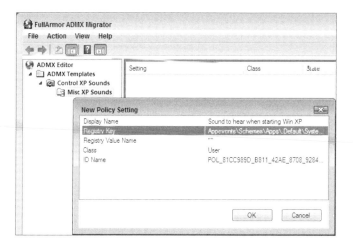

FIGURE 5.18   You can add various elements like TextBox requesters, DropdownLists and more.

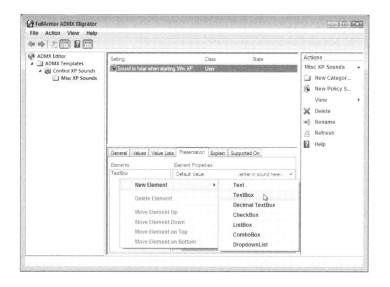

When ready, you can right-click over the ADMX file (in my example the node labeled "Control XP Sounds") and click Save As. This will create an ADMX and ADML file. Be sure to (again) move the ADMX into the central store and the ADML file into the language directory (en-US) for English.

I really wish there was some kind of "preview mode" to see if you got it right before you went through the motion of copying the ADMX and ADML files to their final location. Because there's potentially a lot of trial and error involved before you get it just right.

When you do get it right, however, and fire up the GPO editor you'll notice that the category is there (in my example it's called Misc XP Sounds), but the settings within it are absent. That's because the keys we're dictating aren't part of the proper Policies keys, and hence won't show by default. If you want to expose them, you'll need to select View ➤ Filtering from the Group Policy Object Editor window, and in the Filtering dialog, *uncheck* "Only show policy settings that can be fully managed." When you do this, you'll see the setting show up, with a little down-arrow designating that it's not a true Policy setting, as seen in Figure 5.14.

Finding the Policy Settings You Need and Cracking the ADM/ADMX Files

I get about ten e-mails a day which ask me, "Hey Jeremy, how do you 'X' with Group Policy?" (where X is some policy or trick I've never personally tried to do before).

My standard answer is: "I don't know" because I simply don't have all 1800 Windows XP and certainly not all 2400 Windows Vista policy settings memorized. So, I immediately follow up my "I don't know" with "But we can find out!"

Microsoft's *Policy Settings Spreadsheets* for Windows XP and Windows Vista

Microsoft has created two wonderful documents: one for Windows XP and one for Windows Vista.

In short, you can download a Microsoft Excel spreadsheet detailing the following:

- Every policy setting
- Every path to every policy setting (User or Computer, Administrative Templates ➤ etc.)
- Every security setting
- Every Explaintext entry for each policy setting
- Every Registry punch for every policy setting

I always keep an updated pointer from my GPanswers.com website in the Microsoft resources to this spreadsheet. Again, at this time, Microsoft has one for Windows XP management stations and one for Windows Vista management stations. I don't know how much longer they plan on keeping the Windows XP version around. You can see what this looks like in Figure 5.19.

Additionally, since it's just Excel, you can perform quick sorts. For instance, by using column E (Supported on), you can limit the view to show you, say, only Windows XP+SP2 settings.

This is super handy.

FIGURE 5.19 The PolicySettings.xls settings reference spreadsheet

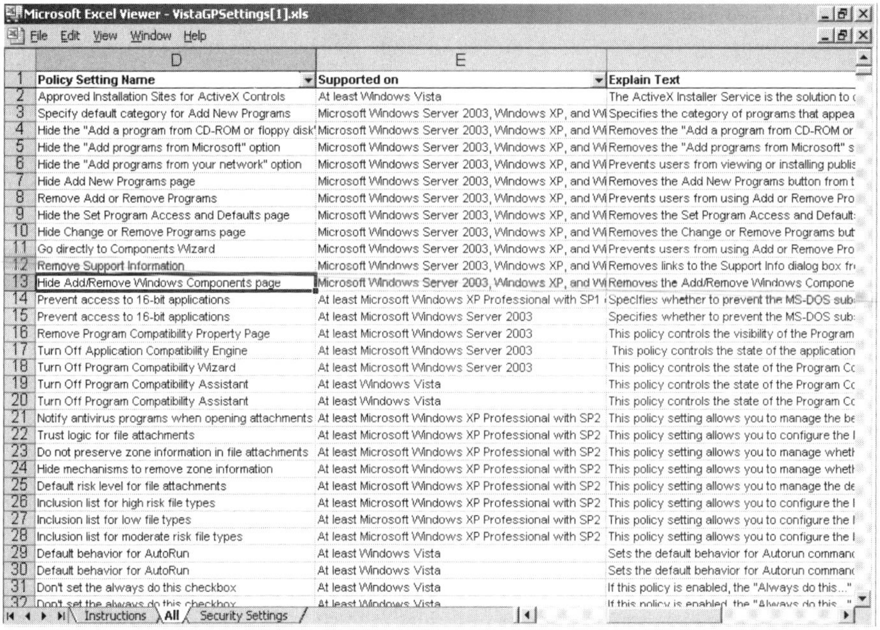

	Policy Setting Name	Supported on	Explain Text
2	Approved Installation Sites for ActiveX Controls	At least Windows Vista	The ActiveX Installer Service is the solution to (
3	Specify default category for Add New Programs	Microsoft Windows Server 2003, Windows XP, and Wi	Specifies the category of programs that appea
4	Hide the "Add a program from CD-ROM or floppy disk'	Microsoft Windows Server 2003, Windows XP, and Wi	Removes the "Add a program from CD-ROM or
5	Hide the "Add programs from Microsoft" option	Microsoft Windows Server 2003, Windows XP, and Wi	Removes the "Add programs from Microsoft" s
6	Hide the "Add programs from your network" option	Microsoft Windows Server 2003, Windows XP, and Wi	Prevents users from viewing or installing publis
7	Hide Add New Programs page	Microsoft Windows Server 2003, Windows XP, and Wi	Removes the Add New Programs button from t
8	Remove Add or Remove Programs	Microsoft Windows Server 2003, Windows XP, and Wi	Prevents users from using Add or Remove Pro
9	Hide the Set Program Access and Defaults page	Microsoft Windows Server 2003, Windows XP, and Wi	Removes the Set Program Access and Default:
10	Hide Change or Remove Programs page	Microsoft Windows Server 2003, Windows XP, and Wi	Removes the Change or Remove Programs but
11	Go directly to Components Wizard	Microsoft Windows Server 2003, Windows XP, and Wi	Prevents users from using Add or Remove Pro
12	Remove Support Information	Microsoft Windows Server 2003, Windows XP, and Wi	Removes links to the Support Info dialog box fr
13	Hide Add/Remove Windows Components page	Microsoft Windows Server 2003, Windows XP, and Wi	Removes the Add/Remove Windows Compone
14	Prevent access to 16-bit applications	At least Microsoft Windows XP Professional with SP1	Specifies whether to prevent the MS-DOS sub:
15	Prevent access to 16-bit applications	At least Microsoft Windows Server 2003	Specifies whether to prevent the MS-DOS sub:
16	Remove Program Compatibility Property Page	At least Microsoft Windows Server 2003	This policy controls the visibility of the Program
17	Turn Off Application Compatibility Engine	At least Microsoft Windows Server 2003	This policy controls the state of the application
18	Turn Off Program Compatibility Wizard	At least Microsoft Windows Server 2003	This policy controls the state of the Program Cc
19	Turn Off Program Compatibility Assistant	At least Windows Vista	This policy controls the state of the Program Cc
20	Turn Off Program Compatibility Assistant	At least Windows Vista	This policy controls the state of the Program Cc
21	Notify antivirus programs when opening attachments	At least Microsoft Windows XP Professional with SP2	This policy setting allows you to manage the be
22	Trust logic for file attachments	At least Microsoft Windows XP Professional with SP2	This policy setting allows you to configure the l
23	Do not preserve zone information in file attachments	At least Microsoft Windows XP Professional with SP2	This policy setting allows you to manage wheth
24	Hide mechanisms to remove zone information	At least Microsoft Windows XP Professional with SP2	This policy setting allows you to manage wheth
25	Default risk level for file attachments	At least Microsoft Windows XP Professional with SP2	This policy setting allows you to manage the de
26	Inclusion list for high risk file types	At least Microsoft Windows XP Professional with SP2	This policy setting allows you to configure the l
27	Inclusion list for low file types	At least Microsoft Windows XP Professional with SP2	This policy setting allows you to configure the l
28	Inclusion list for moderate risk file types	At least Microsoft Windows XP Professional with SP2	This policy setting allows you to configure the l
29	Default behavior for AutoRun	At least Windows Vista	Sets the default behavior for Autorun comman
30	Default behavior for AutoRun	At least Windows Vista	Sets the default behavior for Autorun comman
31	Don't set the always do this checkbox	At least Windows Vista	If this policy is enabled, the "Always do this..."
32	Don't set the always do this checkbox	At least Windows Vista	If this policy is enabled, the "Always do this..."

Last Ditch Effort Troubleshooting via Registry Punch

Chapter 4 discussed many ways to troubleshoot if Group Policy doesn't seem to be applying. However, if you've verified that you're getting the policy setting via GPRESULT or the Group Policy Results Wizard and you're certain you should be getting a specific policy you set, perhaps the problem is elsewhere.

Occasionally, there are bugs in the help text definitions of some policy settings in the ADM/ADMX templates. Sometimes the policy setting states that "Enable" does one thing and "Disable" does another—and, really, it doesn't work that way at all. Other times, the actual underlying definition of the policy setting is incorrect, and the Registry location it's set to modify doesn't really do anything. In all honesty, these problems are few and far between, but it is precisely what service pack updates to existing ADM files try to correct.

So, if you're 1000 percent convinced you're getting the GPO laid down on the client system, yet you're still not seeing the result of a specific policy setting, take it to the next step. That is, crack open the spreadsheet (or ADM/ADMX file itself), locate the policy definition, find the portion of the Registry that the policy will be setting, and manually enter that hack into your client system. After you do, verify it against what the policy setting says it's supposed to do.

Is it actually doing what it says it's supposed to do? For instance, if you suspected that the **Force Classic Control Panel View** policy setting wasn't doing what it says it was going to do, simply crack open `ControlPanel.admx` using Notepad, and locate the **Do not display Manage Your Server Page** policy setting (as shown in Figure 5.20).

FIGURE 5.20 Open the ADMX template to locate the policy and the corresponding Registry hack.

As you can see, the policy setting modifies `Software\Microsoft\Windows\CurrentVersion\Policies\Explorer`. It adds a value of `ForceClassicControlPanel` and sets it to 1 to force the XP Control Panel to revert back to the older Windows 2000 style.

You can plunk this into the Registry yourself and see this actually happen; you don't need to set a GPO to try it. After you verify the results, you're closer to knowing precisely what's going on.

Final Thoughts

Managing ADM and ADMX files can be a little tricky. The key message to take away is always use a Windows Vista management station to do your editing. If you bounce around using various operating system types, you'll be back in "SYSVOL bloat" hell again.

It's easy to use Microsoft and third-party, vendor-supplied ADM templates to control your applications or to make your own ADM modifications. But remember—only applications coded to read Registry settings from the Policy keys will be true Policies. They will be applied and removed when different users log on or off. They will not tattoo. They will appear with a paper icon (in Windows Vista) or a blue dot (in pre-Windows Vista versions) in the Group Policy Object Editor. Most applications are not yet Policy key–aware, which means if you want to create your own modifications, you'll likely need to make them preferences. Preferences do not modify the Policy keys. They tattoo the Registry. They will appear with a down-arrow (in Windows Vista) or a red dot (in pre-Windows Vista versions) in the Group Policy Object Editor.

If you want an application which can truly policy-enable your existing applications, check out PolicyPak.com.

Be wary of download ADM templates you find online. They'll usually work as advertised, but the problem, again, is that they're likely chock full of irritating tattooing preferences, not lovely nontattooing policies. One site that's full of such ADM templates is `http://worldofasp .com/ts/download.cfm`. Of course, I have some free ADM templates to download at `www .GPanswers.com/faq`.

If you have an ADM file you want to use in the central store, you'll have to convert it to ADMX first. Use the downloadable ADMX Migrator tool to perform that magic. Additionally, use the ADMX Editor (part of the ADMX Migrator download) to hand-create your own ADMX files if you like.

If you're interested in hand-creating ADMX files, we will have tips and tricks and a forum on `GPanswers.com`. We will also maintain the previous edition's "ADM Template Syntax" section if you need that as well. Lastly, check out Microsoft's document to "Step-by-Step Guide to Managing Group Policy ADMX Files" at `http://go.microsoft.com/fwlink/ ?LinkId=55414`. And for the truly geeky, you can check out the ADMX schema, located at `http://tinyurl.com/28k56v`.

6

Implementing Security with Group Policy

You could say that the first half of this book is finished. If you think about it, we've definitely discussed just about everything with regard to the Group Policy engine, how things work under the hood and lots of best practices to take with you on your Group Policy journey.

But being an Active Directory/Group Policy administrator has two facets. One facet is the healthy care and feeding of your Active Directory and Group Policy infrastructure—that is, doing all the stuff we've already talked about correctly. The other half of your job is to *do stuff* with this Group Policy knowledge. And, a good place to start is here—by securing your systems with this new knowledge. But, Group Policy is a big, big place and we simply don't have room to go over *all* the stuff you can do with Group Policy. So, I'm picking the most important things to show you in the next remaining chapters with the amount of room I have.

 Because we won't have time to explore every new Group Policy nook and cranny in the rest of the book, I strongly encourage you to look at http://tinyurl.com/ffelo, which is housed on Microsoft's website and has a really nice chart of all the Windows Vista-updated Group Policy areas.

So, in this security chapter we've got just an enormous amount to cover. Here's the list.

Default GPOs   We'll first look at the two default GPOs: the "Default Domain Policy" GPO and the "Default Domain Controllers Policy" GPO and how they help tighten security.

Local vs. Effective Permissions   Why do security settings sometimes show up differently on our client machines? You'll find out.

Auditing Servers and Group Policy Usage   Who is using our clients and servers? You'll find out how to find out.

User and Computer Scripts   Old-school logon scripts were never like this. Find out why.

Internet Explorer Settings   With the advent of Internet Explorer 7, things get a little confusing. There are several different areas to control Internet Explorer, and we'll check out where those are.

Restricted Groups   You'll find out how to force group membership and nested group membership.

Software Restriction Policies   Put the smackdown and allow/disallow specific applications to run.

Last, but certainly not least, we'll harness and focus our Group Policy power.

Often, you'll want to find a way to tie down a specific machine so it will be nigh invulnerable to outside forces. You might want to do this in public computing environments, such as libraries or nursing stations, or if you have machines in open areas that you feel are specifically vulnerable to attack. You'll learn all about that in this chapter in the "Securing Workstations with Templates" section.

The last thing we'll talk about is a way to secure your servers using Group Policy. This technique came with Windows 2003/SP1 and it's called the Security Configuration Wizard, or SCW for short. Don't let the fact that it's a "wizard" fool you into thinking it's got limited power. It's a superstar, and you'll see how to use it and how to make your Group Policy world rock with new power.

While we'll mention some Windows Vista-specific tidbits here, the new Windows Vista-only goodies are in the next chapter. Note that you'll still see our screenshots from Windows Vista—because, as we've already discussed, to get the most out of Group Policy, you'll want to use a Windows Vista management station.

Combined, these two chapters on Group Policy and Security are biiig. So don't try to read them both at once. Watch a ballgame and get a beer about halfway through each chapter.

Then come back, ready to rock. I'll be here for you.

> Windows 2003/SP1 and Windows Vista bring some new additions to the table. As you're plunking around some of the special security policy settings, newer operating systems give you a "heads up" pop-up style message if you're about to modify a security setting that could do some harm. Microsoft calls these "soft barriers" because they don't prevent you from shooting yourself in the foot, but they do warn you first. You can check out MSKB 823659 for specific security policy settings that are affected. The pop-ups warn about anything that could be considered a risky configuration and alert you to known compatibility problems.

The Two Default Group Policy Objects

Whenever you create a new domain, three things automatically happen:

- The initial (and only) OU, named **Domain Controllers**, is created automatically by the DCPROMO process.

- A default GPO is created and linked to the domain level, called "Default Domain Policy."

- A default GPO is created for the **Domain Controllers** OU, called "Default Domain Controllers Policy."

This section helps answer the question, "Why are these GPOs different from all other GPOs?"

These two GPOs are special. First, you cannot easily delete them (though you can rename them). Next, it's a best practice to modify these GPOs only for the security settings that we'll describe in this section. Too often, people will modify the "Default Domain Controller Policy" GPO or "Default Domain Policy" GPO—only to mess it up beyond recognition. So, these special default GPOs systems shouldn't be modified with the "normal stuff" you do, day to day. In general, stay clear of them, and modify them only when a setting prescribed for them is actually required.

Instead of modifying the "Default Domain Controller Policy" GPO or "Default Domain Policy" GPO for normal stuff, you should create a new GPO and link it at the level you want, then implement your policy settings inside that new GPO. And, it's a best-practice to always be sure that the defaults are highest in the link order (that means they're the most powerful if anything should conflict in another GPO at the same level).

 The "Default Domain Policy" GPO and "Default Domain Controllers Policy" GPO can actually be deleted, but I strongly recommend that you DON'T EVER DELETE THESE. If you truly want to delete either of the default policies, you'll need to add back in the "Delete" Access Control entry to a group you belong to, Domain Administrators, for instance. Even then, I can't see why you would want to delete them. If you want to disable their link for some reason (again, I can't imagine why), do that, but leave the actual GPOs in place. If you do run into a situation where these are deleted, then use the command dcgpofix.exe (described in detail later) to get them back.

It's not that the GPOs themselves are really all that different, but rather that the location of these GPOs is special, as you'll see later in this chapter. The locations in question are the domain level and the **Domain Controllers** OU.

GPOs Linked at the Domain Level

If you take a look inside the domain level, you'll see one GPO that was created by default: the "Default Domain Policy." The purpose of this GPO is to set the default configurations for the "Account Policies" branch in the Group Policy Object Editor. These Account Policies encompass three important domain-wide security settings:

- Password policy
- Account Lockout policy
- Kerberos policy

Again, the default policy settings are set inside the "Default Domain Policy" GPO and linked to the domain level. However, you can change the defaults of the Account Policies in one of several ways:

- By modifying the "Default Domain Policy" GPO directly
- By creating your own GPO linked to the domain level and changing the precedence order within the domain level

You'll see how shortly.

Again, the special part about the domain level of Group Policy is that this is the only place these three policy settings can be set for the domain. And the default settings for the domain are prespecified in the "Default Domain Policy" GPO.

If you try to set Password policy, Account Lockout policy, or Kerberos policy anywhere else in the domain, (say, at any OU or on any site), the settings are ignored when users log on to the domain; they don't matter, and only those linked to the domain level take effect.

Microsoft has taken a lot of heat for the fact that Account Policies must agree for all the accounts in the domain. This means that if two administrators of two OUs can't agree on Account Policies (usually things like password length), they'll need to split into two domains—a major administrative overhead and nightmare.

Check out Special Operations Software's Specops Password Policy (located at www.gpanswers.com/solutions/?id=48) to solve the problem of having different password lengths for domain accounts within a single domain. But the point of the story is, in the box, Active Directory doesn't natively let you do magic like this.

Special Policy Settings for the Domain Level

In addition to Password policy, Account Lockout policy, and Kerberos policy, three additional policy settings take effect only when a GPO is linked to the domain level. They are located under Computer ➤ Windows Settings ➤ Security Settings ➤ Local Policies ➤ Security Options:

Network Security: Force logoff when logon hours expire (was "Automatically Log Off Users When Logon Time Expires" in Windows 2000)   You can set up accounts so that users logged on to Active Directory must log off when they exceed the hours available to them.

Accounts: Rename administrator account (was "Rename administrator account" in Windows 2000)   You can use this policy setting to forcefully rename the Administrator account. This works only for the Domain Administrator account when set at the domain level. This is useful as a level of "extra protection" so that no matter what the Administrator account is renamed to in Active Directory Users And Computers, it will "snap back" to this name after Group Policy refreshes. The "display name" in Active Directory Users And Computers won't actually change, but the underlying "real" name of the account will be changed.

Accounts: Rename guest Account (was "Rename guest account" in Windows 2000)   You can rename the domain Guest account using this policy setting. This works only for the Guest account when set at the domain level.

Accounts: Administrator account status   This setting is only valid for Windows 2003 domains (and presumably, Longhorn server). You can forcefully disable the Administrator account using this setting. See this tech note for more information: http://tinyurl.com/y36ths.

Accounts: Guest account status   This setting is only valid for Windows 2003 domains (and presumably, Longhorn server). You can forcefully disable the Guest account using this setting. See this tech note for more information: http://tinyurl.com/y39kqp.

Setting these three special security settings at any other level has no effect on domain accounts contained within Active Directory. However, if you linked a GPO containing these settings to an OU, the local computer would certainly respond accordingly.

 Again, these policies cannot affect domain accounts when a GPO containing those settings is linked to, say, the Sales OU or Marketing OU. This is because these policies must specifically affect the Domain Controllers computer objects.

Modifying the "Default Domain Policy" GPO Directly

You can dive into the "Default Domain Policy" GPO in two ways. Use the Group Policy Management Console (GPMC) and click the domain name. You'll see the "Default Domain Policy" GPO linked to the domain level. If you try to edit the GPO at this level, you'll see the standard set of policy settings you've come to know and love while inside the Group Policy Object Editor. (Though again, as I've stated, you won't want to add "normal stuff" to this GPO.)

However, since the "Default Domain Policy" GPO is "special," Microsoft provides an alternate way to get right into the Security settings of the "Default Domain Policy." Follow these steps:

1. Log on to the Domain Controller DC01 as a Domain Administrator.

2. Choose Start ➤ Programs ➤ Administrative Tools ➤ Domain Security Policy.

You will be immediately placed into the "Default Domain Policy" GPO focused on the Security settings, as seen in Figure 6.1. These two methods are identical and modify the exact same location; however, the second method is a special "limited view" and shows *only* the security settings within the GPO.

For instance, you can specify (among other settings) that the password length is 10 characters, the user is locked out after the third password attempt, and Kerberos ticket expiration time is 600 minutes. But these values are only valid for the entire domain.

 Again, if you want to add more policy settings at the domain level (which would affect all users or computers in the domain)—great! But try to leave the "Default Domain Policy" GPO alone, except when you need to change the "special" policy settings as described in this section.

Creating Your Own Group Policy Object Linked to the Domain Level and Changing the Precedence

Recall that at any level (site, domain or OU), all the policy settings within all the GPOs linked to a level are merged unless there is a conflict. Then, the GPO with the highest precedence "wins" at a level. I talked about this in Chapter 2. The same is true regarding the settings special to the domain level: Password policy, Account Lockout policy, and Kerberos policy.

The defaults for these three policies are set within the "Default Domain Policy" GPO, but you could certainly create and link more GPOs to the domain level that would override the defaults. That doesn't necessarily mean that you should. Take a look at the example in Figure 6.2.

FIGURE 6.1 The "Default Domain Policy" GPO (linked to the domain level) sets the domain's default Account Policies, Kerberos policy, and Password policy. If you link GPOs containing these policy settings anywhere else, they are essentially ignored when Active Directory is being used.

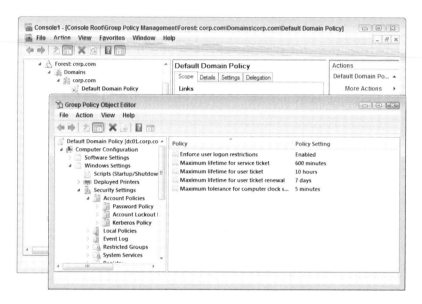

FIGURE 6.2 If you have a GPO with a higher precedence than the "Default Domain Policy" GPO, it will "win" if there's a conflict.

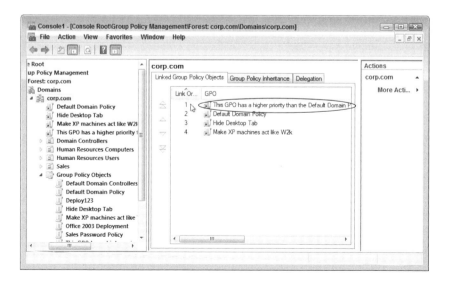

Here, a GPO is higher in priority than the "Default Domain Policy." If you do this, you better know precisely what you are doing! Again, this is because any policy setting within any GPO with a higher priority than the "Default Domain Policy" GPO will "win."

Which Approach Do You Take?

As you've seen, you can either modify the "Default Domain Policy" GPO or create your own GPO and ensure that the precedence is higher than the "Default Domain Policy" GPO. If you need to modify a special domain-wide account policy setting, which approach do you take? Here are the two schools of thought:

School of Thought #1   Modify only the Account Policies settings in the "Default Domain Policy" GPO. Then, ensure that it has the highest precedence at the domain level. This guarantees that if anyone does link other GPOs to the domain level, this one always wins.

School of Thought #2   Leave the defaults in the "Default Domain Policy" GPO. Never modify the "Default Domain Policy" GPO—ever. Create a new GPO for any special settings you want to override in the "Default Domain Policy" GPO. Then, link the GPO to the domain level, and ensure that it has higher precedence than the "Default Domain Policy" GPO (as seen in Figure 6.2).

Various Microsoft insiders have given me different (sometimes conflicting) advice about which to use. So what do I think?

If you want to modify any special domain-wide security settings, use School of Thought #1. This is the simplest and cleanest way. If you do it this way, you'll always treat the "Default Domain Policy" GPO with kid gloves and know it has a special use. And you can check in on it from time to time to make sure no one has lowered the precedence on it. Additionally, some applications, such as Microsoft SMS, will specifically modify the Default Domain Policy GPO. Hence, if you want that application to run smoothly, it's best to let it do what it wants to do.

School of Thought #2 has its merits. Leave the "Default Domain Policy" GPO clean as a whistle, and then create your own GPOs with higher precedence settings. However, I don't think this is a great idea, because you might forget that you set something important inside this new GPO.

Either way works, but my preference is for School of Thought #1.

Group Policy Objects Linked to the Domain Controllers OU

How is the **Domain Controllers** OU different? You can see there is also a default GPO linked, named the "Default Domain Controllers Policy" GPO. But, before we dive into it, let's take a step back. First, it's important to think of all the Domain Controllers as essentially equal. If one Domain Controller gets a policy setting (Security setting or otherwise), they should all really be getting the exact same policy settings. On logon, users choose a Domain Controller for validation at random; however, you want the experience they receive to be consistent, not random. Moreover, when you, as the Domain Administrator, log on to a Domain Controller at the console, you also want your experience to be consistent.

Oh, and did I mention that when servers are finished being promoted into Domain Controllers via DCPROMO, they automatically end up in the **Domain Controllers** OU? So, that's where the "Default Domain Controllers Policy" GPO comes into play. Again, it's easy to find the "Default Domain Controllers Policy" GPO. It's linked to the **Domain Controllers** OU.

You can also get right into the Security settings of the "Default Domain Controllers Policy" GPO by following these steps:

1. Log on to the Domain Controller DC01 as a Domain Administrator.

2. Choose Start ➢ Programs ➢ Administrative Tools ➢ Domain Controller Security Policy.

You will be immediately placed into the "Default Domain Controllers Policy" GPO focused solely on the Security settings.

These two methods are essentially identical and modify the exact same location; however, the second method shows only the available *security* settings within the GPO. Since all Domain Controllers are, by default, nestled within the **Domain Controllers** OU, all Domain Controllers are affected by all the aspects inside the "Default Domain Controllers Policy" GPO. Of specific note are the Security Settings, as shown in Figure 6.3.

For instance, you'll want the same Event Log settings for all Domain Controllers. You'll want to set it once, inside a GPO linked to the **Domain Controllers** OU, and have it affect all Domain Controllers. By default, the "Default Domain Controllers Policy" GPO has the following set to specific defaults, which should remain consistent among all Domain Controllers.

FIGURE 6.3   The "Default Domain Controllers Policy" GPO affects every Domain Controller in the Domain Controllers OU.

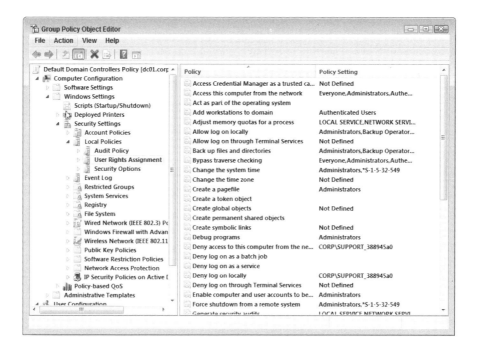

Right-click any node and choose "Export List" from the shortcut menu to export to a text file for an easy way to document complex settings, such as User Rights Assignments.

Audit Policies   Located in Computer Configuration ➤ Windows Settings ➤ Security Settings ➤ Local Policies ➤ Audit Policy. Here you can change the default auditing policies of Windows 2000 or Windows 2003. Windows 2000 is a little light for my taste, and Windows 2003 is a little strong. We talk about auditing later in this chapter in the "Auditing with Group Policy" section.

User Rights Assignment   Located in Computer Configuration ➤ Windows Settings ➤ Security Settings ➤ Local Policies ➤User Rights Assignment. Here you can configure which accounts you will "Allow log on locally" or "Log on as a service" among other specific rights.

Domain Controller Event Log Settings   Located in Computer Configuration ➤ Windows Settings ➤ Security Settings ➤ Event Log. Set them here, and all Domain Controllers in the Domain Controllers OU will obey. Settings such as the maximum size of logs are contained here. Note, however, that decreasing the size of an Event Log will not take effect on the DCs; you can enforce a log size increase, but not a decrease.

Various Security Options   Located in Computer Configuration ➤ Windows Settings ➤ Security Settings ➤ Local Policies ➤ Security Options. Here you'll find settings such as "Interactive logon: Do not display last user name," which will affect the behavior of clients, servers, and/or Domain Controllers. Windows 2000 domains have different names for these settings. Note that GPOs created on Windows Vista machines will have more Windows Vista-specific security options available. The Group Policy spreadsheet (found at GPanswers.com in the Microsoft Resources Section) has a list of all the security options and what target machines can be affected.

The same rules apply to the **Domain Controllers** OU as they do for the domain level. That is, you can put a GPO in at a higher precedence than the "Default Domain Controllers Policy" GPO. However, my recommendation is to use the "Default Domain Controllers Policy" GPO for the "special" things that you set at this level, and ensure that it's got the highest precedence when being processed within the OU.

Oops, the "Default Domain Policy" GPO and/or "Default Domain Controllers Policy" GPO Got Screwed Up!

If you modify the "Default Domain Policy" GPO or "Default Domain Controllers Policy" GPO such that you want to return it back to the defaults, you might just have a shot. The procedure is different for Windows 2000 domains or those with Windows 2003 Domain Controllers. First, you'll need to determine which default GPO got screwed up; then you need to take the appropriate steps. These procedures are among the most popular requests for

Microsoft Product Support Services. However, these tools should be performed only as an absolute last resort because it will restore your defaults as if the installation were done "out of the box." So, be careful. If you have a backup of your defaults, you should try to perform a restore first—before using these "emergency-only" tools.

Repairing the Defaults for Windows 2003 Domains

As long as you have even one Windows 2003 Domain Controller, you have it made in the shade. Well, not too made, as you might already be in the doghouse if the default GPOs are screwed up. However, Windows 2003 domains with their Windows 2003 Domain Controllers come with a command-line tool, DCGPOFIX, to make it easy to restore back to the defaults. You can tell DCGPOFIX to restore the "Default Domain Policy" GPO (with the /Target:Domain switch) or the "Default Domain Controllers Policy" GPO (with the /Target:DC switch). Or you can restore both with the /Target:BOTH switch, as in Figure 6.4.

FIGURE 6.4   Use DCGPOFIX with Windows 2003 Domain Controllers to restore the defaults if necessary.

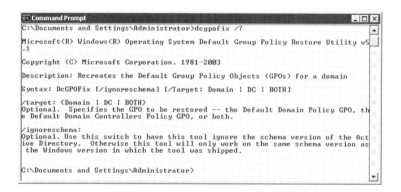

Optionally, you can simply reset the User Rights Assignment for Windows 2003 instead of plowing back the entire "Default Domain Controllers" GPO. To do so, see the Knowledge Base article "HOW TO: Reset User Rights in the Default Domain Group Policy in Windows Server 2003" (KB 324800).

Repairing the Defaults for Windows 2000 Domains

If the "Default Domain Policy" GPO or "Default Domain Controller Policy" GPO for a Windows 2000 domain get irreparably damaged, you can download and run a tool that was previously available only to customers when they called Microsoft Product Support Services. That is, Windows 2000 now has an equivalent to Windows 2003's DCGPOFIX. Its name is RecreateDefPol, and you have to download it. Here's a (shortened) link to the tool: www.tinyurl.com/3yyr3.

Understanding Local and Effective Security Permissions

The whole point of Group Policy is that when you make a wish from upon high, your client machines will embrace your wish. I've already discussed that Group Policy can be set, if you like, on the local machine. However, GPOs from Active Directory that contain policy settings that conflict with those on the local machine will "win" and override those set at the local machine.

If a local security policy is set on a machine and then a GPO in the domain "wins" you'll want to know, at a glance, which changes are coming from upon high within Active Directory Group Policy. This is the difference between "local" policies and "effective" policies.

 With Windows 2000 clients, it was sometimes difficult to tell that your security wishes were being embraced. Windows 2000 local policy has a Local Setting and Effective Setting column to assist; but it wasn't always accurate. An older KB article (Q257922) described this as "Local Security Policy May Not Accurately Reflect Actual System Settings." However, that KB article is no longer available.

The user interface in Windows Vista, Windows XP, and Windows 2003 member servers has changed a bit since Windows 2000. Specifically, it now clearly distinguishes between security policies that can be changed locally versus security policies that are coming from upon high.

Figure 6.5 shows the local machine policy via GPEDIT.MSC. Many Security Option settings are not being enforced from an Active Directory GPO (say, at the domain level or in an OU that contains the client machine). However, in Figure 6.5, I set up one policy setting, the **Devices: Restrict CD-ROM access to locally logged in user,** set to Enabled within a GPO linked to the OU that contains the computer. Because Active Directory GPOs trump local computer policy, this security policy setting therefore cannot be adjusted locally.

Setting this security policy setting locally (once it's set from a GPO linked to the OU) is not permitted. Indeed, the icon changes within GPEDIT.MSC to show you that the security policy is set within Active Directory:

- The security policies that are being dictated from a GPO in Active Directory have a little scroll icon flanked with two computers.
- The security policies that can still be set locally have "1/0" icons.

This same "effective setting" icon theme is valid throughout other security settings categories: Account Policy (including Password policy), Audit Policy, User Rights Assignment, and Security options.

The Strange Life of Password Policy

If you create a new GPO, link it to any OU, and then edit your new GPO, it certainly appears as if you *could* set the Password policy and Account Lockout policy.

For example, I have a **Sales** OU in which I recently placed VISTA1. As you can see in Figure 6.6, I created and linked a GPO, called "Sales Password policy," to the **Sales** OU. I am setting the Password policy such that the minimum password length is 10 characters.

FIGURE 6.5   Active Directory GPOs restrict the modification of local computer policy. Windows XP and Windows Vista have a better way than Windows 2000 to display effective permissions. The icon within the local computer policy has changed from "1/0" icons to a scroll and computer icon.

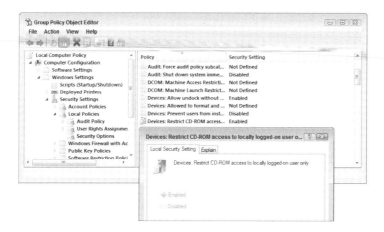

FIGURE 6.6   It might seem counterproductive to set the Password policy at any level but the domain.

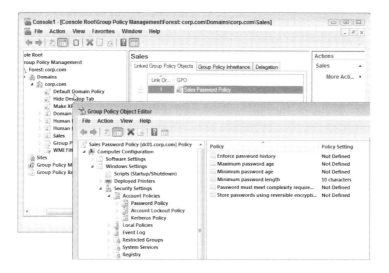

At first glance this would seem to be counterproductive, because, as already stated, these policy settings only take hold of the accounts in the domain via the "Default Domain Policy" GPO. But administrators might actually want to perform this seemingly contradictory action. That is, when the user logs on locally to the Windows workstation, the account policy settings contained in the GPO linked to the OU will have been magically planted on their machine to take effect for *local* accounts. In Figure 6.7, I have logged in as the local administrator account on the workstation.

FIGURE 6.7   Setting a Password policy in the domain (other than at the domain level) will affect passwords used for local accounts upon member machines.

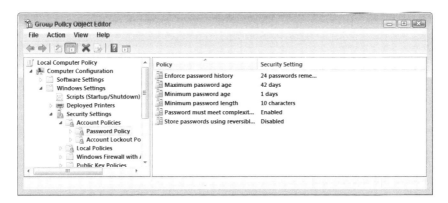

Again, this won't affect users' accounts when users are logging on to the domain; rather, it affects only the local accounts on the targeted computers. This could be helpful if you grant local administrator rights to users upon their workstations or laptops and want to set a baseline.

If you are still using Windows 2000 machines, Figure 6.7 would show both "Local" and "Effective" settings for Windows 2000 Professional machines. However, because of the behavior described here, the effective settings might not be accurate. Again, this is noted in the old KB 257922: "Local Security Policy May Not Accurately Reflect Actual System Settings."

Auditing with Group Policy

Auditing is a powerful tool. It can help you determine when people are doing things they shouldn't, as well as help you determine when people are doing things they should. Either way, you'll use Group Policy to turn on your auditable events. Certain aspects of auditing you'll turn on at the **Domain Controller** OU level, inside the "Default Domain Controllers Policy" GPO. Other aspects of auditing you'll typically turn on at other OU levels (via a GPO linked to the OU containing the systems you want to audit).

In Figure 6.8, you can see the default auditing settings contained within the "Default Domain Controllers Policy" GPO.

FIGURE 6.8 Windows 2003 enables lots of auditable events by default.

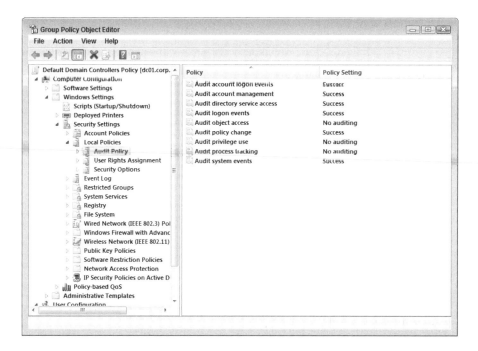

The list of possibilities for auditing are numerous and confusing. Table 6.1 shows what can be audited, along with where you should perform the audit.

No matter how much you audit, it does you no good unless you're actually reviewing the logs! There is no way out of the box to centralize the collection of logs from your Domain Controllers, servers, or workstations. Consider a third-party tool, such as Microsoft MOM or Event Log Sentry from www.engagent.com.

TABLE 6.1 Auditable Events

Auditing Right	What It Does	Where You Should Set It	Is It On by Default in Windows 2003 Active Directory?	Notes
Audit account logon events	Enters events when someone attempts to log on to Active Directory.	In the "Default Domain Controllers Policy" GPO to monitor when anyone tries to log on to Active Directory.	Yes.	By default, only successes generate events. Settings can be changed to record logon failures as well.

TABLE 6.1   Auditable Events *(continued)*

Auditing Right	What It Does	Where You Should Set It	Is It On by Default in Windows 2003 Active Directory?	Notes
Audit account management	Enters events when someone attempts to create, delete, rename, enable, or disable users, computers, groups, and so on.	In the "Default Domain Controllers Policy" GPO to generate events for when users, computers, and so on are created in Active Directory. Set at the OU level to generate events on file servers or workstations for when users and groups are created on member machines.	Yes. Enabled on Domain Controllers, which log Active Directory events only. Not enabled on member servers.	By default, only successful object manipulations generate events. Settings can be changed to record failures as well.
Audit directory service access	Enters events when Active Directory objects are specified to be audited.	In the "Default Domain Controllers Policy" GPO.	Yes. In the "Default Domain Controllers Policy" GPO, which will log Active Directory access and GPO creation, deletion, and modification. See the "Auditing Group Policy Object Changes" section. Not enabled on member servers.	Works in conjunction with the actual attribute in Active Directory that has auditing for users or computers enabled. Can be used to audit other aspects of Active Directory. See the "Auditing Group Policy Changes" section.
Audit logon events	Enters events for interactive logon (Local logon) and network logon (Kerberos).	Set at OU level to generate logon events on servers you want to track access for.	Yes. In "Default Domain Controller Policy" GPO, which affects only Active Directory logons.	Set this setting to determine if UserA touches a shared folder on ServerA. This will constitute an auditable event for "Audit logon events."

TABLE 6.1   Auditable Events *(continued)*

Auditing Right	What It Does	Where You Should Set It	Is It On by Default in Windows 2003 Active Directory?	Notes
Audit object access	Enters events when file objects are specified to be audited.	If you store files on your Domain Controllers, you can set this at the "Default Domain Controllers Policy" GPO. Else, set it at the OU level to monitor specific files within member machines.	No.	Works in conjunction with the actual file on the file server having auditing enabled. See the "Auditing File Access" section.
Audit policy change	Enters events when changes are made to user rights, auditing policies, or trust relationships.	In the "Default Domain Controllers" GPO to monitor when changes are made within Active Directory. Set at OU level to monitor when changes are made on member machines.	Yes. In "Default Domain Controllers Policy" GPO, which affects only Active Directory events.	
Audit privilege use	Enters events when any user right is used, such as backup and restore.	In the "Default Domain Controllers Policy" GPO to generate events for when accounts in Active Directory are used. Set at the OU level to generate events on file servers when accounts on member machines are used.	No.	

TABLE 6.1 Auditable Events *(continued)*

Auditing Right	What It Does	Where You Should Set It	Is It On by Default in Windows 2003 Active Directory?	Notes
Audit process tracking	Enters events when specific programs or processes are running.	In the "Default Domain Controllers Policy" GPO to affect Domain Controllers. Set at the OU level to monitor processes on specific servers within the OU.	No.	This is an advanced auditing feature that can generate a lot of events once turned on. Only turn this on at the behest of Microsoft PSS or another troubleshooting authority.
Audit system events	Enters events when the system starts up, shuts down, or any time the security or system logs have been modified.	In the "Default Domain Controllers Policy" GPO to determine when Domain Controllers are rebooted or logs have been modified. Set at an OU level to monitor when member machines are rebooted or logs have been modified.	Yes. In "Default Domain Controllers Policy" GPO, which affects only Domain Controllers.	

Auditing Group Policy Object Changes

You might be asked to determine who created a specific Group Policy and when it was created. To that end, you can leverage Active Directory's auditing capability and use Group Policy to audit Group Policy! Whenever a new Group Policy is born, deleted, or modified, various events such as the event in Figure 6.9 are generated.

These events are generated in Windows 2003 because two things are automatically set up by default in Windows 2003 Active Directory:

- **Audit directory service access** is enabled in the "Default Domain Controllers Policy" GPO. You can see this in Figure 6.8, earlier in this chapter.

- Auditing is turned on for the "Policies" object container within Active Directory. The Policies folder is where the GPC (Group Policy Container) for a given GPO is stored in Active Directory. Auditing is turned on so that events are generated when anyone creates, destroys, or modifies any objects inside the folder.

FIGURE 6.9   This type of event is generated when GPOs are modified.

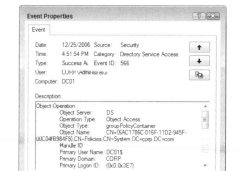

To view the Policies container, follow these steps:

1. Launch Active Directory Users And Computers.

2. Choose View ➤ Advanced Features. This enables you to see some normally hidden folders and security rights within Active Directory Users And Computers.

3. Drill down into Domain ➤ System ➤ Policies.

4. Right-click the Policies folder, and choose the Properties from the shortcut menu to open the Properties dialog box.

5. Click the Security tab.

6. Click the Advanced button to open the "Advanced Security Settings for Policies" window.

7. Click the Auditing tab, which is shown in Figure 6.10.

If you drill down even deeper, you'll discover that the "Everyone" group will trigger events when new GPOs are modified or created. It is this interaction that generates events, such as what is seen in Figure 6.9.

 If you wanted to hone in on who triggered events (as opposed to the Everyone group) you could remove the Everyone group from being audited (shown in Figure 6.10) and plunk in just the users or groups you wanted to monitor.

Clearly, you can do a lot when creating or modifying a GPO. As you saw in Figure 6.9, the Event ID for GPO Auditing is Event ID number 566. However, there are numerous instances of Event 566, each with information that depends on precisely what you do to the GPO. The bad news is that the audit doesn't show you the GPO's "friendly name"; rather, it shows only the GUID, which is a little disappointing and makes things difficult to track down.

FIGURE 6.10   Auditing for GPO changes is set on the Policies folder within Active Directory Users And Computers.

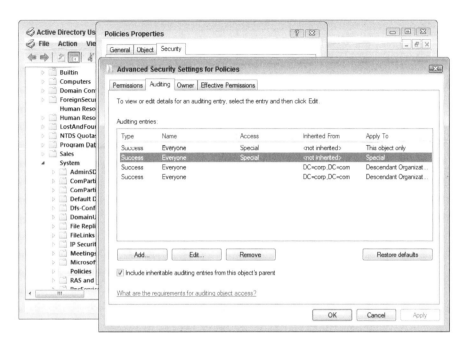

Table 6.2 shows what to expect when looking within Event 566.

TABLE 6.2   The Contents of Event 566

Action that Occurred	Field to Look For	What It Shows in the Field
Create a new GPO	Accesses	Create Child groupPolicyContainer
Modify a GPO	Properties	Write Property—Default property set version-Number gPCMachineExtensionNames group-PolicyContainer
Remove a GPO	Access	WRITE_DAC
	Properties	WRITE_DAC groupPolicyContainer
Change GPO status	Properties	Write Property—Default property set flags groupPolicyContainer

TABLE 6.2 The Contents of Event 566 *(continued)*

Action that Occurred	Field to Look For	What It Shows in the Field
Remove the "Link Enabled" status or remove the link from an OU	Properties	Write Property—Default property set gPLink organizationalUnit
Enforce/unenforce a GPO link	Properties	Write Property—Default property set gPLink organizationalUnit (or domainDNS if done at the domain level)
Block/unblock inheritance on an OU	Object Type	OrganizationalUnit
	Properties	Default property set gPOptions organizationalUnit
Change permissions	Properties	WRITE_DAC groupPolicyContainer

Windows 2000 shows these as Event 565, whereas Windows 2003 shows these as Event 566. The "Field to Look For" column and the "What It Shows" column may not be precisely the same for Windows 2000 domains.

Windows 2000 will also pop up Event 643 whenever the "Default Domain Policy" GPO is processed (whether changed or unchanged). You might see a lot of these, and you can safely ignore them.

Auditing File Access

If you want to enable auditing when users attempt to access files on file servers, you could run around to each server and turn on file auditing. Or (insert fanfare music here), you could use Group Policy to do it in one fell swoop.

So, to leverage file auditing on a wide scale, you need to do the following within Active Directory:

- Create an OU.
- Move the accounts of those file servers in the OU.
- Create a GPO linked to the OU.
- Enable the **Audit object access** policy setting inside the GPO linked to the OU.

Once you do this, you then specify which files or folders on the target file server you wish to audit. To do so, follow these steps:

1. At the target file server itself, use Explorer to drill down into the drive letter and directory that you want to audit. Right-click the folder (or just one specific file), and choose Properties from the shortcut menu to open the Properties dialog box.

2. Click the Security tab, and then click the Advanced button to open the "Advanced Security Settings" for the share.

3. Click the Auditing tab.

4. Click Add, to pop up the "Auditing Entry" dialog as seen in Figure 6.11. This dialog will allow you to add users to the Auditing entries.

The simplest and most effective entry you can add is the "Everyone" group, as shown in Figure 6.11. When anyone tries to touch the file, you can audit for certain triggers, such as the "Read" permission.

FIGURE 6.11   Set auditing for files on the file or folder on the target system.

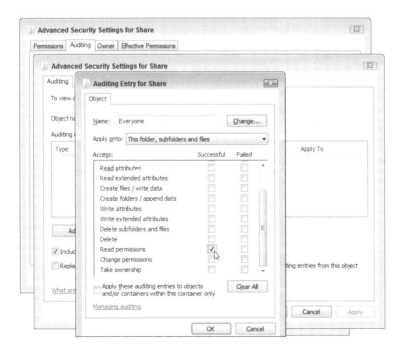

Logon, Logoff, Startup, and Shutdown Scripts

Users have always been able to get logon scripts. NT 4 used User Manager For Domains to assign logon scripts, and Windows 2000 and 2003 domains may use Active Directory Users And Computers to assign logon scripts. However, you can step up to the next level using Group Policy and get more than just logon scripts:

- Users can get logon and logoff scripts.

- Computers can get startup and/or shutdown scripts.

And, the best part is, you're not limited to old DOS-style batch files. Scripts deployed via Group Policy can use DOS-style .BAT or .CMD scripts, VBScript (.VBS files), or JavaScript (.JS files), or even executables.

Although logon and startup scripts might be useful to map to network drives and automatically fire up Excel, the scripts can be equally useful when logging off or shutting down. Imagine automatically scripting the clean up of the Temp folder or the ability to kick off a full-drive sweep of your virus scanner.

To use scripts with Group Policy, users must be in the site, domain, or OU linked to a GPO that contains a logon or logoff script. As the name of the script implies, users execute the script only at logon or logoff. Computers must also be in the site, domain, or OU linked to a GPO that contains a startup or shutdown script, which they run only at startup or shutdown.

> **WARNING**   User and computer scripts delivered via Group Policy do not run "visible" to the user, which prevents users from canceling the script. To that end, scripts run silently in the background unless there is a problem. At that point, you have to wait until the script times out (10 minutes by default). I'll show you a bit later how to expose the scripts to run visible.

In these examples, I'll use basic DOS-style .BAT commands to explain the concept. Here is an example of a script that displays "Hello World" and then pauses for a key press, before removing the files from the *%temp%* folder. In Notepad, create the following file:

```
Echo "Hello World."
Pause
Del /Q /S %temp%
Pause
```

> **WARNING**   Only your Windows XP, Windows 2000, and Windows 2003 clients receive scripts from GPOs. If you have down-level clients (such as Windows NT), they can run only old-style logon scripts. The old-style logon script is located as a "Logon Script" field in the user's Profile tab inside "Active Directory Users And Computers."

Startup and Shutdown Scripts

The Startup and Shutdown script settings are found under the Computer Configuration node in the Windows Settings ➢ Scripts branch. You can get your proposed script into the proper GPO in many ways; however, I think I have found the ideal way as follows:

1. Once you're in the Group Policy Object Editor, drill down to Computer Node ➢ Startup Scripts and double-click it. The Startup Properties dialog box will appear.

2. Click the Add button to open the Add a Script dialog box.

3. In the Script Name field, you can enter a filename or click Browse to open the Browse dialog box, as shown in Figure 6.12.

FIGURE 6.12   You can create .BAT or .VBS files on the fly with this little trick.

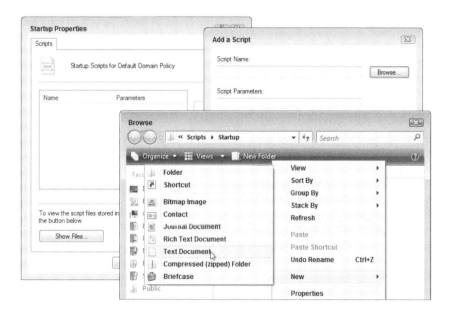

4. To create a new file, right-click in the Browse dialog box, and choose New ➢ Text Document, for example.

5. Enter a name for the file, for example, `myscript.bat`.

6. When asked if you want to change the file extension, click Yes, right-click the file, and choose Edit from the shortcut menu to open Notepad.

7. Type your script, and save the file.

8. Select the new file as the proposed script.

Again, the computer account must be in an OU with a linked GPO that contains a script. However, don't reboot yet. By default, you won't see the script run. And, since our script contains a Pause statement, your users will wait a really long time before the script times out. To allow the script to be visible (and enable you to press any key at the pause), enable a policy setting that also affects the machine. Traverse to Computer Configuration ➤ Administrative Templates ➤ System ➤ Scripts, and select either **Run startup scripts visible** or **Run shutdown scripts visible,** or select both options.

Last, it's important to understand the context in which Startup and Shutdown scripts run. Specifically, they run in the LocalSystem context. If you want to connect to resources across the network, you'll need to ensure that those resources allow for computer access across the network (not just user access) because the script will run in the context of the computer account when it accesses network resources.

Logon and Logoff Scripts

The Logon and Logoff script settings are under the User Configuration node in the Windows Settings ➤ Scripts tree. If you're implementing new logon scripts, I suggest you follow the steps in the previous section. Again, the user must be in an OU with a linked GPO with a script. However, don't log off and log back on yet. By default, you won't see the script run. To allow the script to be visible (and enable you to press any key at the pause), you need to enable a Group Policy. Traverse to User Configuration ➤ Administrative Templates ➤ System ➤ Scripts, and select either **Run logon scripts visible** or **Run logoff scripts visible**, or select both options.

Logon and Logoff scripts run in the user's context. Remember that a user is just a mere mortal and might not be able to manipulate Registry keys that you might want to run in a logon or logoff script.

Script Processing Defaults (and Changing Them)

One final note about scripts before we move on. Different scripting types run either synchronously or asynchronously. Here's the deal:

Logon Scripts Run Asynchronously by Default By default, logon scripts run asynchronously. That is, all scripts at a level will basically fire off at the same time. There is no precedence order for scripts at the same level, and there is no knowing which script will finish before another. If you want to change this behavior to help "link" one script after another, you have to tell the client computer to run the scripts *synchronously*. If you want to change this (and many times you'll want to), set enable Computer Configuration ➤ Administrative Templates ➤ System ➤ Scripts, and Enable **Run logon scripts synchronously.**

Bizarrely, there is also a setting that does the exact same thing located on the User Settings ➤ Administrative Templates ➤ System ➤ Scripts ➤ **Run logon scripts synchronously.** Again, recall that if there's a conflict between these settings, the ones that affect the computer will "win."

Startup Scripts Run Synchronously by Default By default, startup scripts run synchronously. That is, all scripts are processed from lowest to highest priority order. Then, each script is run—consecutively—until they're finished. This usually makes the most sense, so I tend to leave it as is. However, if you want to change it, enable Computer Configuration ➤ Administrative Templates ➤ System ➤ Scripts, and enable **Run startup scripts asynchronously.**

Group Policy Scripts Time Out in Ten Minutes   As stated, if a script just hangs there, you'll have to wait a whopping ten minutes for it to time out. You can change this with the policy setting found at Computer Configuration ➢ Administrative Templates ➢ System ➢ Scripts called **Maximum wait time for Group Policy scripts.**

Old-School Logon Scripts Run "Visible"   If you use Active Directory Users and Computers to assign a user a logon script, those scripts will be visible to the user. If you want to hide old-school logon scripts from users while they run, you can change this with the policy setting found at User Settings ➢Administrative Templates ➢ System ➢ Scripts ➢ **Run legacy logon scripts visible.**

Before we move on, let's take a second to talk about "perceived slow" performance when scripts are used with Group Policy. In previous chapters, I suggested you might want to make your Windows XP and Windows Vista machines act like Windows 2000. That is, use the **Always wait for the network at Startup and Logon** policy setting which throws Windows XP and Windows Vista into "synchronous" processing mode. There can be one problem with this. This can affect you if you have laptops which are not always "on the network" at bootup. This *can* cause slower performance. Imagine you have users on traveling laptops with startup and login scripts. By default, the scripts are stored on the Domain Controller. So, during bootup or login time, the laptop tries to connect to the Domain Controller for the script. You may want to dictate to the client to use a local path (like `c:\scripts\blah.vbs`) instead of the default which will go to the server.

Don't Panic: What to Do If Login Scripts with Network Drive Mappings Aren't Working as Expected with Windows Vista

Let's assume you have a share called "share" on DC01. Now, let's assume you have a simple login script within a GPO linked to, say, **Human Resources Users** OU. And this simple script simply

- Cleared out any mapped drives
- Said "Hello World"
- And mapped a letter (s:) as a network drive to \\dc01\share and
- Paused for a keypress before finishing.
- It would look like this:

```
net use * /d /y
Echo "Hello World."
net use s: \\dc01\share
pause
```

Try this script as a logon script for a user using a pre-Vista machine, and it works great. The drive letter maps at logon time, and the user can use it as long as they want.

Try this script as a logon-script for a user using a Windows Vista machine, and, well, you're going to have some issues, as shown in Figure 6.13.

Wait—this gets even weirder. During my testing of the shipping version of Windows Vista, I tried logging out and logging in again, and it totally worked (as seen in Figure 6.14). Here's the thing: The correct behavior is that it's not *supposed* to succeed at all, and I can't explain why it does sometimes succeed the second login.

FIGURE 6.13 Login scripts run file on Windows Vista, but a mapped network drive will be inaccessible to the user

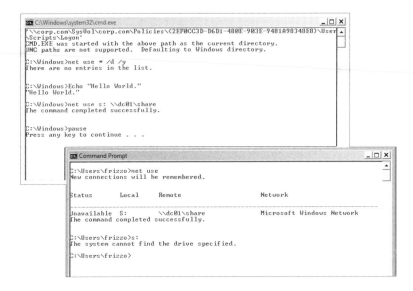

FIGURE 6.14 Second time's a charm when logging in with login scripts.

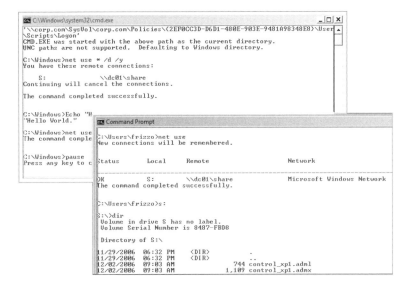

It's not supposed to succeed because User Account Control (described in detail in the next chapter) is kicking in. So drive mappings from a higher-privilege user shouldn't be able to be leveraged from mere mortal user accounts. (Again, I'm not sure why it succeeds on the second try sometimes. It's not supposed to.)

In short, I'm guessing that you won't ever want it so that the user can't have access to mapped drives. And with these two tips, you can make the behavior act like Windows XP.

Remediation #1

You can set a Registry value on your Windows Vista machines so that it doesn't matter how the network drives are mapped. They'll be accessible by every user. Again, this has to be done on the target machine. Set HKLM ➢ Software ➢ Microsoft ➢ Windows ➢ CurrentVersion ➢ Policies ➢ System ➢ `EnableLinkedConncctions (REG_DWORD)` to 1.

Adding this Registry value or changing its value back to 0 requires a reboot. By default, the Registry value doesn't exist on the system and, therefore, the linked connections are NOT added.

Note that creating `EnableLinkedConnections` and setting it to a 1 is not officially supported in Windows Vista. Only the second method (described next) is fully supported.

Remediation #2

We've referenced the Microsoft document entitled "Deploying Group Policy Using Windows Vista" before. It can be found here: `http://tinyurl.com/yenok6`.

Inside, there's a section titled "Group Policy Scripts can fail due to User Account Control." There's a script located in the Appendix which you run. This script then calls your login script and in doing so, will bypass this issue.

But it does so in a, well, not very pretty way. It submits your login script to be run as a scheduled task. So, in short, it'll take a bit (maybe more) for your login script to run. Note that you could edit the script to remove the information messages that the script is being sent to the Task Scheduler.

When I tried to use this method (using the exact provided steps) there was a problem. That's because the document didn't specify to type in the whole path of your login script as a parameter. Therefore, when the task scheduler tried to run it, it simply failed. The documentation sample and script should be changed by the time you read this.

Restricted Groups

With a special security-related Group Policy function, you can use Restricted Groups to strictly control the following tasks:

- The membership of security groups that you create in Active Directory
- The security group membership on groups created on member machines (workstations or servers)
- The security groups that are nested within each other

You might want to strictly control these security groups or nestings to make sure that users in other areas of Active Directory, say, other domain administrators, don't inadvertently add someone to a group that shouldn't be there. Here are some practical uses of this technology:

- Ensure that the domain's Backup Operators group contains only Sally and Joe.

- Ensure that the local Administrators group on all desktops contains the user accounts of the help desk and desktop support personnel.

- Ensure that the domain's Sales global group contains the domain's East Sales, West Sales, North Sales, and South Sales local groups.

You set up these Restricted Groups' wishes via a GPO. You might be thinking to yourself that if the domain administrator creates the GPO, can't any domain administrator just delete the GPO and work around the point of the Restricted Groups settings? Yes, but the point of Restricted Groups is additional protection, not ultimate protection.

 An analogy might be "museum putty." The idea behind museum putty is that you attach it to your precious objects as extra protection in case an object gets bumped from the shelf. You can see museum putty here: `http://tinyurl.com/ycxc78`. The idea is that if someone tries to "bump" users in or out of the group, this will keep just the users you want in place.

My pal Darren Mar-Elia, the Technical Editor for this book, suggests that this could cause problems in Windows 2000 domains because they don't support link-value replication (a feature to help control group membership changes via replication). If you want to read his take on why this feature might not be such a hot idea, check out his blog here: `http://tinyurl.com/yar653`.

Strictly Controlling Active Directory Groups

The ideal way to strictly control Active Directory groups with specific Active Directory users is to create a new GPO and link it to the **Domain Controllers** OU.

You *could* modify the "Default Domain Controllers Policy" GPO directly, but, as stated earlier, it's better to create a new GPO when dealing with "normal" settings such as this one. This keeps the "Default Domain Controllers Policy" GPO as clean as possible. Likewise, you *could* modify the "Default Domain Policy" GPO. But, again, keeping away from the defaults for other than their special uses (as previously discussed) is preferred.

 If you set up Restricted Groups policies at multiple levels in Active Directory, there is no "merging" between Restricted Groups policy settings. The "last applied" policy wins. For example, if you set up a Restricted Groups policy, link it to the domain level and create another Restricted Groups policy, and link it to the **Domain Controllers** OU, the one linked to the **Domain Controllers** OU "wins."

1. Open the GPO and traverse to Computer Configuration ➢ Windows Settings ➢ Security Settings ➢ **Restricted Groups**.

2. Right-click Restricted Groups, and choose Add Group from the shortcut menu, which opens the Add Group dialog box.

3. Click Browse to open the Browse dialog box, and browse for a group, say, the domain's Backup Operators, then click OK.

4. When you do, the Backup Operator Properties dialog box, as shown in Figure 6.15, appears.

You can now choose domain members to place in the "Members of this group" list. In Figure 6.15, I have already added Sally User's account, which is in the domain, and I'm about to add Joe User's domain account.

FIGURE 6.15 You can specify which users you want to ensure are in specific groups.

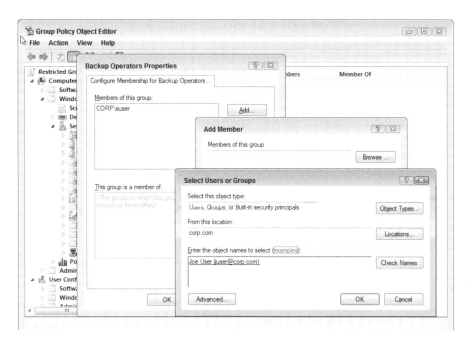

 Be careful about just typing in the user account names without either browsing the domain or manually entering the domain with the DOMAIN\user syntax. Restricted Groups in Active Directory will not apply correctly unless you do this.

When Restricted Groups Settings Take Effect

After you enter the users in the "Members of this group" and click OK, you can sit back and wait for all Domain Controllers to get the change and process Group Policy. However, if you have only one Domain Controller in your test lab, this change should occur quickly. You can run GPUpdate to make it occur even faster in this case. This happens because any new GPO you create and link to the **Domain Controllers** OU should get picked up and applied right away—about five minutes after replication occurs.

Now, take a look inside the Backup Operators group using Active Directory Users And Computers. Sally and Joe's accounts should be forced inside Backup Operators.

When Restricted Groups Settings Get Refreshed

If someone were to *remove* Sally and Joe from Backup Operators in Active Directory Users And Computers, their accounts would be repopulated during the Background Security Refresh, which is every 16 hours.

As described in Chapter 3, you have two choices if you don't want to wait 16 hours for the Background Security Refresh:

- Link a GPO to the **Domain Controllers** OU level, with the **Security policy processing** policy setting with the "Process even if the Group Policy objects have not changed" flag set. Then, the Background Security Refresh will process with the normal background refresh (every five minutes).

- Force a manual refresh by running GPUpdate /FORCE on your Domain Controller. Recall that GPUpdate /FORCE may be used when the underlying GPO hasn't changed and you want your changes reflected immediately.

The users removed from Backup Operators will pop right back in!

There is one caveat with the "Members of this group" section of Restricted Groups. That is, this is an explicit list. If you then add more users using Active Directory Users And Computers, they will also be removed when the Restricted Groups policy is refreshed! Only the users listed in the "Members of this group" section will return.

Strictly Controlling Local Group Membership

You can ensure that specific users are members of specific groups on local machines—workstations or servers. For instance, you can guarantee that Joe and Sally are members of the local Administrators group on all the machines in the **Nurses** OU.

To do this, follow these steps:

1. Create a new GPO, and link it to the **Nurses** OU. Make sure the Nurses computer accounts are in the **Nurses** OU.

2. Dive in to Computer Configuration ➢ Windows Settings ➢ Security Settings ➢ **Restricted Groups**.

3. Right-click **Restricted Groups**, and select the "Add Group" option from the shortcut menu to open the "Add Group" dialog.

4. These initial steps are nearly identical to the previous exercise where we wanted to restrict an Active Directory group. In the last exercise, we clicked the "Browse" button to locate a security group in Active Directory. However, to signify a local group, we'll just type in the word **Administrators**; *don't click Browse.*

5. You'll then see a similar Properties dialog box as seen in Figure 6.15.

6. At this point, you can populate the "Members of this group" in the same way you did before. Simply click "Add," and choose the domain members of Sally and Joe, similar to what is seen in Figure 6.15.

When the machine is rebooted or the background policy is refreshed, the local Administrators group is populated with Sally and Joe.

The caveat of the "Members of this group" still applies. That is, this is an explicit list. By default, all workstations have the "DOMAIN\Domain Admins" listed as members within their local Administrators group. If you don't add "DOMAIN\ Domain Admins" while creating a Restricted Group, they won't be there on the next background refresh.

Strictly Applying Group Nesting

Another trick Restricted Groups can perform is that it can ensure that one domain group is nested inside another. Like the "Strictly Controlling Active Directory Groups" trick, you need a GPO linked to the **Domain Controllers** OU.

The interface is a bit counterintuitive; the idea is that you name a group (say, HR-OU-Admins) and then specify the group of which it will be a member.

To nest one group within another:

1. Open the GPO and traverse to Computer Configuration ➢ Windows Settings ➢ Security Settings ➢ **Restricted Groups**.

2. Right-click Restricted Groups, and choose "Add Group" from the shortcut menu, which opens the Add Group dialog box.

3. Click Browse to open the Browse dialog box, and locate the first group.

4. When you do, the Properties dialog box appears, as shown earlier in Figure 6.15.

5. Then, you'll click the "Add" button in the "This group is a member of" section of the Properties dialog box. You'll then be able to specify the second group name.

When you're finished, and the Group Policy applies, the result will be that the first group will be forcefully nested within the second group. In order for this to really work well, it helps to remember that different domain modes allow for different levels of group nesting. Here's the Cliffs Notes version:

- Windows 2000 mixed mode domains and Windows 2003 interim mode domains can nest global groups only into domain local groups.

- Windows 2000 and Windows 2003 native mode domains can nest global groups into domain local groups. Additionally, global groups can be nested into global groups.

WARNING While you are creating a Restricted Groups policy, take care. Results can be unpredictable when you mix the "This group is a member of" and "Members of this group" sections. If you have ensured a group's membership using the "Members of this group" setting, don't attempt to further modify that group's membership by feeding the "This group is a member of" users (by lying to it) to extend the original group's membership! On occasion, the "This group is a member of" and "Members of this group" will conflict if you try to add users to both headings.

Tricking Restricted Groups So It's Not "Rip and Replace"

Let's assume you have the following scenario: before you ever even heard of this "Restricted Groups" thing, someone on your desktop design team declared that Fred and Alice would be local admins on all machines. Just add Fred and Alice as local administrators on all desktop machines.

Well, that's great for a small office. But when Fred or Alice leaves—you've got a problem. Sure, you wouldn't mind if Alice was still a local administrator on these machines, but it might even be smarter to keep whoever is a local admin on the machine right now and add in a domain-based group to all computers' administrators group so you can dictate via Active Directory who is a local admin.

It *is* possible to trick the Restricted Groups function into allowing you to simply add members to a group (and not rip and replace them). As we saw earlier, anytime we try to use "Members of this group" it becomes a "rip and replace" for the members of that group. So, that's precisely *not* what we're going to do.

Instead, if you want to trick Restricted Groups into adding a domain-based group into a local Group Policy (and not rip and replace what's already there) perform the following steps:

1. In Active Directory, pre-create the group you know you'll want to add to the existing local administrators. In my example, I'll use a group called **DesktopAdmins**.

2. Open the GPO and traverse to Computer Configuration ➢ Windows Settings ➢ Security Settings ➢ **Restricted Groups**.

3. Right-click Restricted Groups, and choose "Add Group" from the shortcut menu, which opens the Add Group dialog box.

4. Click Browse to open the Browse dialog box, and locate **CORP\DesktopAdmins**.

5. Then, you'll click the "Add" button in the "This group is a member of" section of the Properties dialog box. You'll then be able to specify "administrators" in the second group name. Again, since we're talking about the local administrators group, you simply *type it in*. Don't "browse" for it.

Once you're done, you can wait for the Group Policy refresh cycle (or, type gpupdate.exe on your target machine) and see the results. In Figure 6.16, you can see two test users (tuser1 and tuser2) added using Restricted Groups.

FIGURE 6.16 You can fool Restricted Groups into specifically adding domain-based groups into your local groups (instead of ripping and replacing). In this example, several local administrators (tuser1 and tuser2) are not removed when this policy is applied.

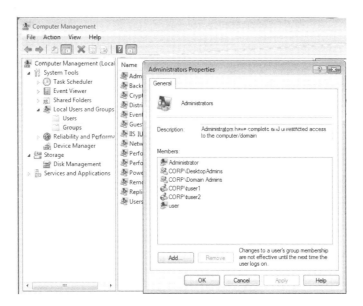

Which Groups Can Go into Which Other Groups via Restricted Groups?

The processing of Restricted Groups can sometimes be picky depending on the scenario. (This is officially documented in the MSKB article 810076.) And the "out of the box" processing changes a little bit and becomes more standardized for the most up-to-date clients: Windows 2003, Windows 2000 with SP4, and Windows XP with SP2.

MSKB 810076 now has several tables to help you out during your testing of this feature. Again, to ensure that the tables work for you, you need Windows 2003, Windows 2000 with SP4, or Windows XP with SP2, or you need the hotfix in the Knowledge Base article 810076 applied to machines that will receive the forced users or groups.

Windows Vista isn't represented in this table yet, but hopefully it will be. While I haven't tested every combination, I'm told it's supposed to act like Windows XP/SP2.

Software Restriction Policy

Windows XP and newer machines have a CSE (Client Side Extension) that Windows 2000 doesn't have: Software Restriction Policies. Software Restriction Policies enable you, the administrator, to precisely dictate what software will and will not run on your Windows XP desktops.

Many viruses show up in your users' inboxes as either executables or .VBS scripting files. Just one launch within your confines, and you're cleaning up for a week. Additionally, users will bring in unknown software from home or download junk off the Internet, and then, when the computer blows up, they turn around and blame you. What an injustice!

To that end, Microsoft developed Software Restriction Policies, which can put the kibosh on software that shouldn't be there in the first place. You can restrict software for specific users or for all users on a specific machine. You'll find Software Restriction Policies in Computer Configuration ➢ Windows Settings ➢ Security Settings ➢ **Software Restriction Policies**. Just right-click over the Software Restriction Policies node, and select "New Software Restriction Policies," as shown in 6.17, to get started.

FIGURE 6.17 Software Restriction Policies are available in both the Computer and User nodes.

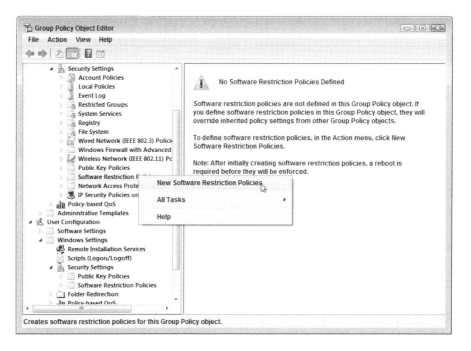

Software Restriction Policies is also available as a node under User Configuration ➢ Windows Settings ➢ Security Settings ➢ **Software Restriction Policies**, which can also be seen in Figure 6.17.

Like other policies that affect users or computers, you'll need an OU containing the user or computer accounts you want to restrict, and you'll need a GPO linked to that OU. Or you can set a GPO linked to the domain level, which affects all Windows XP and Windows 2003 machines (or, alternatively, users). Typically, you'll use the Computer side branch of Software Restriction Policies. That way, all users on a specific machine are restricted from using specific "known bad" applications.

Software Restriction Policies are also valid when set upon a local computer within a local policy (via GPEdit.msc). This can be particularly useful for a Windows 2003 acting as a Terminal Server. Software Restriction Policies are meant to replace the APPSec.exe tool.

GPOs containing Software Restriction Policies might be common in environments that include Windows XP, Windows 2003, and Windows 2000 machines. However, Windows 2000 machines that are affected by GPOs containing Software Restriction Policies will simply ignore the settings and restrictions contained within.

Software Restriction Policies' "Philosophies"

Using Software Restriction Policies with your Windows XP users involves three primary philosophies. You can choose your philosophy by selecting the "Security Levels" branch of Software Restriction Policies, as shown in Figure 6.18.

FIGURE 6.18 The Security Levels branch of Software Restriction Policies sets your default level of protection.

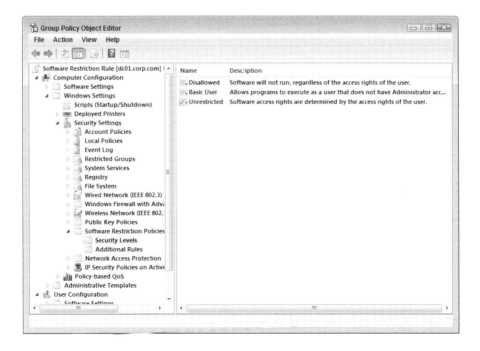

Philosophy #1 (aka "The Black List") *Allow everything to run except specifically named items.* Here, we've chosen the default that the "Unrestricted" option is selected. Windows XP and Windows Vista allow all programs to run, like normal. However, if the administrator names certain applications, such as a virus or a game, it will be prevented from running. It's as if you're putting the things you don't want on the "black list" but allowing everything else to run.

Philosophy #2 (aka "The Doggie Door") *Don't allow programs of a certain type to run.* Allow only specifically named items of that type to pass. I nickname this one "Doggie Door." The "Unrestricted" option is selected. You can choose to squelch all files of a certain type, say, all .VBS files. However, you can instruct Windows XP and Windows Vista to allow .VBS files that are digitally signed from your IT department to run.

Philosophy #3 (aka "The White List") *Nothing is allowed to run but the operating system and explicitly named items.* This is the "Full Lockdown" approach. The "Disallowed" option is selected. This is the most heavy-handed approach but the safest. Only operating system components will run, unless you specifically open up ways for programs to be run. Be careful when using this method; it can get you into a lot of trouble quickly.

Within these philosophies, you have one extra super-power if you use Windows Vista as your target machine. That is, you can specify that specific software can only be run with "Basic User" credentials. So, that is, if you decide that you want to run a specific application but are concerned that in doing so it might run with too many rights, you can specify it to run as a "Basic User."

You cannot select "Basic User" security level for a Certificate Rule (described next).

Software Restriction Policies' Rules

Once you've chosen your philosophy, you can choose how wide the door is for other stuff. There are four rules to either allow or deny specific software:

- Hash
- Path
- Certificate
- Network zone (or Internet Zone on pre-Vista management stations)

To create a new rule, select the "Additional Rules" folder, and right-click in the right pane to see your choices, as shown in Figure 6.19.

By default, four Path rules are set that enable access to critical portions of the Registry. These are enabled so that the operating system can write to the Registry even if the "Disallowed" option is set in the "Security Levels" branch.

FIGURE 6.19   The Security Levels branch of Software Restriction Policies sets your default level of protection.

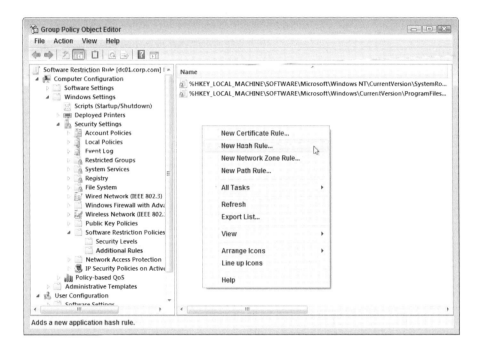

Hash Rule   In computer science terms, a "hash value" is a numeric representation, or fingerprint, that can uniquely identify a file should it be renamed. It's sort of like a "checksum" value. For instance, if I rename Doom.exe to Gloom.exe, the actual bits, the 1s and 0s, contained within the .exe file are the same. Therefore, the hash value is the same. However, if any changes are made to the file (even if one bit is changed), the hash value is different. Hash rules are quite useful in containing any application that's an .EXE or a .DLL.

Sure, it's true that a user could use a hex editor (such as FRHED from www.kibria.de/frhed.html) and change just one bit in an .EXE or .DLL file to get a new hash value, but it's bloody unlikely. And that's reasonably good protection for most of us. A little review/tutorial of FHRED can be found here: www.geocities.com/thestarman3/tool/frhed/FRHED.htm.

Path Rule   You can specify to open (or restrict) certain applications based on where they reside on the hard drive. You can set up a Path rule to specify a specific folder or full path to a program. Most environment variables are valid such as *%HOMEDRIVE%*, *%HOMEPATH%*, *%USERPROFILE%*, *%WINDIR%*, *%APPDATA%*, *%PROGRAMFILES%*, and *%TEMP%*. Additionally, Path rules can stomp out the running of any file type you desire, say, Visual Basic files. For example, if you set up a Path rule to disallow files named *.vb*, all Visual Basic file variants will be unable to execute.

Certificate Rule   Certificate rules use digitally signed certificates. You can use certificate rules to sign your own applications or scripts and then use a certificate rule to specify your IT department as a "Trusted Publisher." Users, admins, or Enterprise Admins can be specified as trusted publishers. Be sure to read the sidebar entitled "Software Restriction Policies and Digital Signatures" before rolling out Certificate Rules. Note that this rule is unable to specify the "Basic User" security level as previously described.

Network Zone Rule (on Windows Vista Management Stations) or Internet Zone Rule (on Pre- Vista Management Stations)   Users will download crap off the Internet. This is a fact of life. However, you can specify which Internet Explorer zones are allowed for download. You can specify Internet, Intranet, Restricted Sites, Trusted Sites, and My Computer. The bad news about Zone rules, however, is that they simply aren't all that useful. They prevent downloads of applications with the MSI format but nothing else. So, in my opinion, they're not quite ready for primetime use. (Note that we talk more about MSI files in Chapter 10.)

Setting Up a Software Restriction Policy with a Rule

As stated, you can craft your Software Restriction Policies in myriad ways. Space doesn't permit explaining all of them, so I'll just give you one example. We'll test our Software Restriction Policies by locking down a nefarious application that has caused countless distress to innumerable, hapless people: Solitaire for Windows XP!

To restrict Solitaire from your environment, follow these steps:

1. Create a new hash rule as seen in Figure 6.19 earlier in this chapter.

2. Click Browse and locate Sol.exe.

You might have to type \\XPPRO1\c$\windows\system32\sol.exe to point to a copy of Solitaire on one of your Windows XP machines if you're logged on at a domain controller (because Solitaire isn't present on Windows 2003 servers). If you have Windows XP/Service Pack 2 loaded on your client system, you can't do this until the SP2 firewall is turned off.

In Windows XP, the "File hash" entry is filled in with the file hash value of Sol.exe from the machine, as shown in Figure 6.20.

In Windows Vista, there isn't a file hash that's shown, but it's still doing the work.

Underneath the hood Windows Vista actually created *two* file hashes. One hash is an MD5 hash (for older Windows XP and Windows Server 2003 clients) and another is an SHA-256 hash for newer XP, Windows Server 2003, and Windows Vista clients. Windows Vista still reads MD5 hashes created using older Windows XP management stations.

FIGURE 6.20   Once you specify the file, the hash value is filled in.

Testing Your Software Restriction Policies on Windows XP or Windows Vista

In the previous example, you could create a Software Restriction Policy that affects users or computers. If your policy is for users, for this very first test, log off. If your policy is for computers, reboot the machine. Follow these steps to immediately demonstrate the desired behavior of Software Restriction Policies:

1. Log on the machine that should get the Software Restriction Policies.

2. Choose Start ➢ Run to open the Run dialog box.

3. In the Open box, type **Sol.exe**. You'll see the message shown in Figure 6.21.

If you were to open a command prompt and then type **Sol.exe**, you would also be restricted. You'd see the message "The system cannot execute the specified program" which is what you might expect.

FIGURE 6.21   On Windows XP machines, Solitaire is prevented from running.

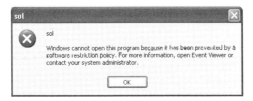

Software Restriction Policies and Digital Signatures

Note that there is a security policy setting named **System settings: Use Certificate Rules on Windows Executables for Software Restriction Policies** located in Computer Configuration ➤ Windows Settings ➤ Security Settings ➤ Local Policies ➤ Security Options.

You'll need to enable this policy setting if you create a Certificate rule on a *digitally signed* .EXE. You can tell if a file is digitally signed by checking out its properties and looking for a Digital Signatures tab, as seen here in the file's properties. WINWORD.EXE has a Digital Signatures tab, while Sol.exe has none.

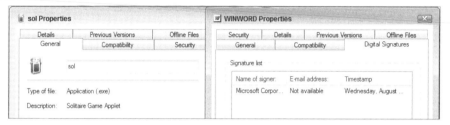

If you were to restrict a digitally signed .EXE, such as WINWORD.EXE, this policy setting would be necessary for the Certificate rule to be embraced by your client systems.

As stated, this policy setting is only necessary for digitally signed .EXEs. However, if you only deal with digitally signed .VBS or .MSI files, you don't have to worry about this setting at all.

Understanding When Software Restriction Policies Apply

As you just saw, Software Restriction Policies appear to apply at the initial policy processing time, that is, when the user logs on to the machine. However, Group Policy's "Initial policy processing" isn't the mechanism that enforces the Software Restriction Policies. This is a little confusing, so stay with me.

When you log on to a machine, you're running a shell program that launches other programs. This is sometimes called a "launching process." That shell program (or launching process) is familiar—Explorer.exe. Whenever Explorer.exe (or other launching processes) launch restricted software, they check a portion of the Registry for any restrictions. How does this help determine when Software Restriction Policies apply?

Software Restriction Policies are housed in KEY_LOCAL_MACHINE\SOFTWARE\Policies\Microsoft\Windows\Safer\CodeIdentifiers.

When Windows XP (pre-SP2) Applies Software Restriction Policies

Let's imagine that we haven't deployed any Software Restriction Policies to our computers or users and walk through a basic scenario:

Sally the nurse is already logged on to XPPRO1 (her workstation) in the **Nurses** OU. She likes to play Solitaire—a lot. We want to prevent the computers in the **Nurses** OU from running Solitaire (Sol.exe). We create a new GPO called "Computer Side Software Restriction" and link it to the **Nurses** OU. We drill down into Computer Configuration ➤ Windows Settings ➤ Security Settings ➤ **Software Restriction Policies**. Our new Software Restriction Policy contains a Hash rule to restrict Solitaire. Group Policy applies in the background (maximally 120 minutes later), or you ask Sally to run GPUpdate /FORCE. This guarantees that the GPO containing the Software Restriction Policy is received.

Now, you want to see how Sally (who is already logged on) will embrace the Software Restriction Policy.

If Sally is running Sol.exe, it will continue to run until she closes it. You can understand how this makes sense. However, after she closes it, things get strange.

- If Sally chooses Start ➤ Run to open the Run dialog box, then enters **CMD** in the Open box (to spawn a new shell), types **Sol.exe**, and then presses Enter, Solitaire will be restricted.

- If Sally chooses Start ➤ All Programs ➤ Games ➤ Solitaire (or chooses Start ➤ Run to open the Run dialog box, types **Sol.exe** in the Open box, and then presses Enter) Solitaire will run!

You can see this interaction in Figure 6.22. Again, this is only for Windows XP (pre-SP2).

Looking at Figure 6.22, we see in number 1 that the topmost command prompt was opened first. In this command prompt, GPUpdate /FORCE was run to make sure the computer received the GPO containing the Software Restriction Policy. In number 2, Sally then opened a new command prompt and tried to run Sol.exe. It is restricted. You can see the command prompt respond with "The system cannot execute the specified program." Yet, when Sally then ran Sol.exe via Explorer (that is, from the Start Menu), in number 3, Solitaire ran, as seen in number 4.

Why does this happen?

Because the "Launching programs" (either CMD or Explorer) control which software is restricted. And it's the launching program that needs to get the "signal" from the Software Restriction Policies—not the actual application! The launching program only checks Software Restriction Policies when it's first initialized. For Explorer, that's when the user logs on.

So, when Sally logs off and logs back on—she again uses the Start Menu and locates and starts Solitaire (or uses the Run dialog box)—Solitaire is restricted. This is because Explorer (the launching program) has been refreshed and checks the Software Restriction Policies entries in the Registry.

When Windows XP/SP2, Windows 2003 (any SP), or Windows Vista Applies Software Restriction Policies

If you place Software Restriction Policies on Windows XP/SP2, Windows 2003 (any SP), or Windows Vista, the Software Restriction Policies apply a bit more rationally. That is, as soon as the Software Restriction Policies are downloaded via Active Directory Group Policy, no new instances of that application are possible.

FIGURE 6.22 On Windows XP (pre-SP2), a logoff and logon will be required for all "Launching Programs" to get the signal to restrict software.

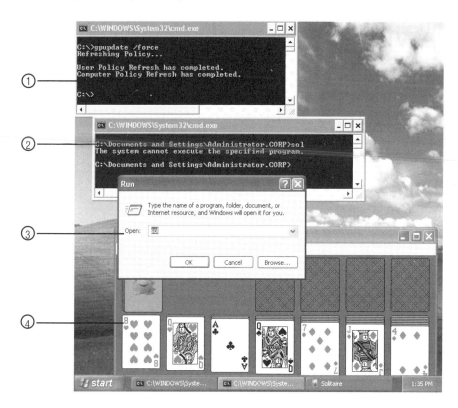

It doesn't matter if the launching program (i.e., Explorer) has already been started; it doesn't need a refresh. It just restricts the software as specified in the Software Restriction Policies as soon as the Group Policy containing the Software Restriction Policies is applied. This is good. Very good.

And Windows Vista and Windows XP/SP2 now act just like Windows 2003. As soon as a GPO that has Software Restriction Policies meant for either the user or computer is embraced by the client machine, the rule takes effect immediately. Thank goodness! Note, however, that programs *already* running don't magically stop running. This will only prevent future instances of the specified application from running.

However, one Windows 2003 Software Restriction Policy anomaly should be noted. Specifically, if you log on locally to a standalone or member server and create a Software Restriction Policy, the Software Restriction Policy acts like Windows XP. That is, the "launching program" must be reset in order for the Software Restriction Policy to take effect. Again, this is only when local GPOs are set upon Windows 2003 standalone or member machines.

Troubleshooting Software Restriction Policies

You can troubleshoot Software Restriction Policies in two primary ways:

- Inspect the Registry to see if the Software Restriction Policies are embraced.
- Enable advanced logging.

Inspecting the Software Restriction Policies Location in the Registry

If Software Restriction Policies aren't being applied, and you logged off and back on, log on again as the administrator at the target machine and check KEY_LOCAL_MACHINE or HKEY_CURRENT_USER\SOFTWARE\Policies\Microsoft\Windows\Safer\CodeIdentifiers. Inside, you'll see numbered branches containing the rules. In Figure 6.23, you can see Sol.exe being restricted by a hash rule.

Do note that operating system files change with service packs—sometimes even innocuous things like Sol.exe! If, after a service pack, your client isn't restricting applications as you expect, make sure the version number of the restricted application matches the version actually located on the client. More specifically, make sure the hash values match.

FIGURE 6.23   The Registry lays out what will be restricted.

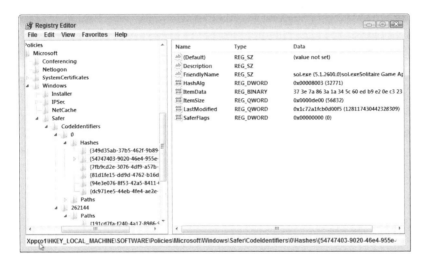

Software Restriction Policies Advanced Logging

You can troubleshoot Software Restriction Policies via a log file. To do so, follow these steps:

1. In the Registry, traverse to KEY_LOCAL_MACHINE\SOFTWARE\Policies\Microsoft\Windows\Safer\CodeIdentifiers.
2. Create a new string value named LogFileName.
3. In the Data field of the new Registry key, enter the full path and name of a log file, for example, **c:\srplog.txt**.

Now, whenever an application runs, a line is written to the log file explaining why it can or cannot run. Here are two lines from that log file: the first when I run Notepad (which is free to run), and the second when I run the Sol.exe (which is restricted).

```
cmd.exe (PID = 1576) identified C:\WINDOWS\system32\notepad.exe as Unrestricted
    using path rule, Guid = {191cd7fa-f240-4a17-8986-94d480a6c8ca}
```

```
cmd.exe (PID = 1576) identified C:\WINDOWS\system32\sol.exe as Disallowed using
    hash rule, Guid = {e669efa3-96d8-4c16-b506-2fec88fbee33}
```

 You'll find a great article on Software Restriction Policies in TechNet. Just search for an article named "Using Software Restriction Policies to Protect Against Unauthorized Software."

Oops, I Locked Myself Out of My Machine with Software Restriction Policies

If you make a Software Restriction Policy too tight, you can lock yourself right out of the system! Don't panic. If the policy is a GPO in Active Directory, remove the policy setting or disable the GPO. After Group Policy processes on the client, log on again as the user, and you should be cleared up.

However, if you make a Software Restriction Policy using the local policy editor (GPEdit.msc) and you lock yourself out, you have a slightly longer road to recovery. Follow these steps:

1. Reboot the machine, and press F8 upon startup to open the Advanced Options menu at boot time.

2. Select SAFE MODE and allow the computer to continue to finish booting.

3. Log on as the machine's local administrator.

4. Dive in to HKLM\Software\Policies\Microsoft\Windows\Safer\CodeIdentifiers. Delete everything below the "CodeIdentifiers" key.

5. Reboot the machine.

You should be out of the woods now.

However, if the policies were set on a given user, the steps are a bit different. Just drill down to that user's HKCU hive file and nuke them there.

More Software Restriction Policies resources can be found at:

http://www.microsoft.com/technet/windowsvista/security/rstrplcy.mspx (http://tinyurl.com/hsthc)

http://www.microsoft.com/technet/security/prodtech/windowsxp/secwinxp/xpsgch06.mspx (http://tinyurl.com/mx96v)

Securing Workstations with Templates

In many environments, it's important to ensure that collections of workstations have the same level of security. What good is it if one machine is locked down tight when the bad guys can simply move along to another machine to get on to your network? The "out of the box" security on Windows machines may or may not be adequate for your environment.

You'll need tools to ensure environment-wide security. The Security Templates MMC snap-in and the Security Configuration and Analysis tool are your partners for generating a baseline of security. You can use these tools to "tattoo" the Registry of the computer to make it more difficult to attack—both on and off your network. After you define your security goals with these tools, you can use Group Policy to easily ensure that all affected machines embrace the same baseline for security.

For our examples here, we'll be using Windows XP and not Windows Vista. Why, you ask? Not for any specific reason other than Windows Vista doesn't come with any "starter" templates. Using Windows XP just makes this particular set of examples easier. That way, we're not creating a whole new template from scratch using Windows Vista.

To get started, we'll load the appropriate snap-ins. In this exercise, we'll use one MMC and load the two snap-ins on a Windows XP Professional machine while logged on as a local administrator. After we load the MMC snap-ins, we'll use the tools to become familiar with the predefined templates and start locking down some of our machines.

Before we get too far along in this section, here's the scoop: You'll be using these exercises to lock down your Windows XP (and/or Windows Vista or Windows 2000) machines. Although you *can* perform these procedures for Windows 2003, I advise against using this procedure to lock down your Windows 2003 machines. That's because in the next major section, "The Security Configuration Wizard for Windows 2003/SP1," I'll show you a technique that is faster and works specifically for Windows 2003 servers. That is, the procedure in that section won't work for Windows Vista, Windows XP, or Windows 2000 machines, so use the information in this section for them.

 This exercise assumes you're loading the snap-ins at a Windows XP Professional machine, though you can certainly perform a similar exercise at a Windows 2000 machine.

1. Choose Start ➢ Run to open the Run dialog box, and in the Open box, enter **MMC** and press Enter to fire up a "naked" MMC.

2. Choose Console ➢ Add/Remove Snap-in to open the Add/Remove Snap-in dialog box.

3. Click Add to open the Add Standalone Snap-in dialog box.

4. Locate and add the Security Configuration and Analysis and Security Templates snap-ins by scrolling through the list and clicking "Add." Add each snap-in individually, so they'll both be on your MMC palette.

5.   Click Close to close the Add Standalone Snap-in dialog box.

6.   Click OK to close the Add/Remove Snap-In dialog box.

When finished, your MMC should look like that in Figure 6.24.

FIGURE 6.24   The Security Configuration and Analysis and Security Templates nodes are loaded in the MMC. The available security templates are listed here.

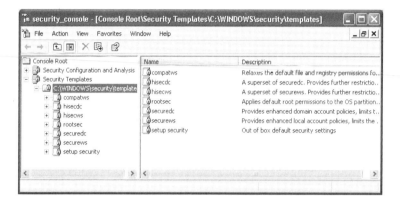

 As, I noted earlier, this section demonstrates these techniques with Windows XP and not Windows Vista, and that's because while Windows Vista is perfectly capable of leveraging the examples here, Windows Vista doesn't ship with any templates. So, I suggest you try this out on your Windows XP machine and if you love them, create new templates for Windows Vista. Additionally, note that creating fresh templates on Windows XP and leveraging them on Windows Vista could be problematic because not all the security goodies for Windows Vista are present on Windows XP. Again, we're using Windows XP as the examples here so you can get a feel for the interface—then do this when ready for Windows Vista.

Security Templates

To get multiple machines to embrace a collection of security settings, you'll roll your proposed settings into what is called a security template. A security template is nothing more than a collection of security settings wrapped up in an easy-to-deploy, text-based `.INF` file. Once you have the `.INF` file locked and loaded the way you want, you can leverage Group Policy to assert your will across your enterprise.

You leverage security templates that come from many sources:

▪   Some templates are built into Windows. These predefined templates exist for workstations, servers, and domain controllers, and they range in intensity from "default security" to "highly secure." Again, note that Vista has no templates included in the box.

- You can create your own security templates from scratch or use the predefined templates as a jumping-off point to create your own.
- Microsoft and other noted third parties have their own collection of security templates for your use. More on third-party templates in a bit.

In these next sections, we'll take a look at the predefined templates and see what they can offer us. We'll then plan a lockdown of our own machines by customizing a template (leveraging one of the predefined templates). Once we actually lock down our machines by applying our templates, we'll see if our lockdown was successful—using both the graphically provided MMC snap-in tools and the command-line interface.

Finally, in the last section, we'll use the template we customized to lock down multiple machines at once using the broad stroke of Group Policy.

Security templates are supposed to help you set a baseline of security upon a gaggle of systems. Let's take a quick look at the available templates within Windows.

I encourage you to not actually do anything with these templates until you read all the way through this section.

Default Security for Windows 2003 and Windows XP

If a machine is a "fresh install," three templates define the default "out of the box" security for a Windows XP or Windows 2003 Domain Controller or a Windows 2003 member server. On Windows XP, you'll find `delftwk.inf` in the `c:\windows\inf` folder. The system used this file when it was being born to set the out-of-the-box settings.

On Windows 2003, you'll find `defltdc.inf` and `defltsv.inf` in the `c:\windows\inf` folder. These templates define the baseline security for Windows 2003 Domain Controllers and Windows 2000 servers. The `DCFirst.inf` template is used to populate the first Windows 2003 Domain Controller with the default Account Policies (Password policy, Account Lockout policy, and Kerberos policy).

Additionally, if a Domain Controller is upgraded from NT 4 or Windows 2000, a different set of security templates is placed on that machine. The templates used by an NT 4 system are called `DCup.inf`, and the templates used by Windows 2000 are called `DCup5.inf`. An NT 4 Terminal Server Edition or Windows 2000 machine with Terminal Services/Application mode will run `Dsupt.inf` to write its default configuration settings. The system automatically uses these files, which are discussed here only for reference. You shouldn't need to touch them again after the system uses them.

Incremental Security Templates

You can use several predefined security `.INF` template files as a jumping-off point. Rather than use them as is, you can modify them to suit your specific requirements. Indeed, you'll see how to leverage an existing template a bit later in this chapter.

The supplied templates tighten or loosen a workstation, server, or DC (whichever the specific case may be), using the Security Configuration and Analysis MMC snap-in or the secedit command-line tool. (Both are described in detail later in this chapter.) You can see the provided incremental security templates listed in the Security Templates node as seen in Figure 6.24 earlier in this chapter.

Before we look at how to apply these .INF files to workstations, let's briefly examine each template (based on machine type) and see what it's supposed to do.

This information in this section is specific to Windows 2003 and Windows XP and is not compatible with Windows 2000. When upgraded from NT 4, Windows 2000 machines need to be enhanced with "Basic" templates that are not listed here. For more information on Windows 2000 and security templates, see the previous edition of this book. Other helpful resources are on TechNet at http://support.microsoft.com/?kbid=234926. An additional reference to Windows 2000 templates is at the end of this chapter in the "Final Thoughts" section.

Domain Controller *.INF* Template Files

These .INF settings apply to Windows 2003 Domain Controllers.

securedc   Increases the security required in the Password policy and Account Policy, bumps up the amount of auditing that occurs on the Domain Controller, and increases some Event Log settings, such as the size. This template doesn't modify any file or Registry ACLs (Access Control Lists).

hisecdc   Chokes off all communications with down-level machines by turning off NTLM communication. Only those machines that use NTLM v2 or Kerberos will be able to communicate with any machines to which this template is applied.

You can find certification guidelines for applications at www.microsoft.com/windowsserver2003/partners/isvs/cfw.mspx.

Applying the Hisecdc.inf template to Domain Controllers is dangerous and can prevent clients from authenticating to your Domain Controllers.

XP Professional *.INF* Template Files

These settings apply to Windows XP Professional machines.

compatws   Applications must pass certification guidelines to be considered "Windows Logo"–compliant. Sometimes, an older application does not follow the new rules once it's up and running. Use this template to allow some older applications (such as Office 97), which are not Windows Logo–certified, to run properly when mere mortals in the Users group run them.

This template elevates the permissions of the Users group by modifying common Registry keys, files, and folders. Often, administrators will give in and grant users who complain about incompatible applications admission into the Power Users group. Applying this template should satisfy their needs without putting them in the Power Users group. Because of this, this template removes all users and groups from the Power Users group.

You can see this behavior for yourself. As an administrator, load Word 97 with the Office 97 spelling check feature onto an NTFS volume on a Windows 2000 or Windows XP machine. Then, log back on as a regular user and, using that Word 97 installation, try to run the spelling utility. As a regular user, you cannot because certain files must be read/writeable to the installation point of Office 97 (usually under Program Files). Apply this template, and your woes disappear. The compatws.inf template modifies NTFS permissions on the Program Files folder so that mere mortals can modify the settings.

securews   These settings increase the security required in the Password policy and the Account Policy, bump up the amount of auditing that occurs on the workstation, and increase some Event Log settings such as the size. This template doesn't modify any file or Registry ACLs.

hisecws   This template turns off NTLM communication and allows only communication with other machines that are running NTLM v2 or Kerberos. NTLM v2 is available on Windows 2000, Windows 2003, and Windows XP machines and on Windows 9x machines and Windows NT 4 machines that have the Directory Services client installed. Kerberos is available only on Widows 2000 machines (and higher). Like the compatsw template, all users and groups are flushed from the Power Users group. A note of caution here: The hisecws.inf template turns off NTLM authentication and allows communication only with other machines that are running NTLM v2 or Kerberos.

Microsoft gives you a nitty-gritty look at the provided templates at http://tinyurl.com/47e5u and in KB 816585 (for Windows 2003) and KB 309689 (for Windows 2000).

Other Security Template Sources

There are several places that you locate additional templates to use on your systems.

Security Templates from Uncle Bill   On Microsoft's website, you'll find two publications that work in tandem to help administrators secure both Windows 2003 and Windows XP: "Windows Server 2003 Security Guide" and "Threats and Countermeasures: Security Settings in Windows Server 2003 and Windows XP." At last check, it can be found here: http://tinyurl.com/dkbu. The download includes several ready-to-use security templates that will go a long way to help you secure your environment. You'll find new templates for Domain Controllers, IIS, IAS, member server, print servers, client systems, and more! Just three words say it all: Great job, Microsoft.

An older work from Microsoft, the "Windows 2000 Hardening Guide," contains tips as well as security templates. You can find it at http://tinyurl.com/anm1.

Special Microsoft Templates

Depending on how a machine was born or upgraded, two templates will be different from machine to machine: DC security.inf and setup security.inf. The contents of DC security.inf are created "on the fly" when you upgrade or create a Domain Controller from scratch. During DCPROMO, a combination of defltdc.inf, dcfirst.inf, and defdcgpo.inf are used to configure the system; then DC security.inf is generated. The setup security.inf template is created on the fly when you upgrade or create a member machine from scratch.

These templates contain a snapshot of some of the security that was configured on the system just prior to performing an upgrade or running DCPROMO. (They'll contain default settings if you performed a fresh install.) This can be particularly helpful if something fails to work after an upgrade or DCPROMO. You can look inside these files to determine what the previously set security was on that system and try to adjust it on the new system.

The templates listed in the previous section won't affect User Rights Assignments that were specifically added to your machine. However, applying the setup security.inf and DC security.inf templates resets the changed User Rights Assignments to the defaults (or your previous configuration). If you want to do this, my advice is to restore only the specific area you want; don't apply the whole template lock, stock, and barrel. You can see how to do this via the secedit command's /areas switch (described later in this chapter in Table 6.3). Usually, you don't want to roll back your entire security to the defaults. Rather, you can pick and choose which sections you want to restore.

Security Templates from Uncle Sam   Two U.S. governmental agencies have each provided their take on some proper security templates:

- The National Security Agency has free advice and templates for securing Windows XP and Windows 2000 and even some NT, Cisco, and e-mail server advice at http://www.nsa.gov/snac/.

- The National Institute of Standards and Technology (NIST) has some templates to help secure Windows 2000 and Windows XP at http://csrc.nist.gov/itsec/guidance_W2Kpro.htm and http://csrc.nist.gov/itsec/guidance_WinXP.html.

Your Own Security Templates

Now that you know which built-in templates perform which functions, you have three options:

- Apply a built-in template as is to a workstation.

- Create your own template from scratch, and apply it to a workstation.

- Modify a built-in template that is already close to what you want to suit your needs, and then apply it to a workstation.

In this section, we'll primarily explore the third option, which essentially covers the skills required to utilize the other two options as well.

You might want to copy the default templates for safekeeping. You can copy them from the `%windir%\security\templates` folder to a floppy, another folder, a partition, or a computer. However, other Windows XP machines in your environment probably hold the default versions of these files as well, so it is relatively easy to get them back.

Creating a Fresh Template from Scratch

To create your own template, in the Console Root folder just right-click the default folder under Security Templates and choose "New Template" from the shortcut menu, as shown in Figure 6.25. Then give your new template a name.

FIGURE 6.25 You can create your own security templates if desired.

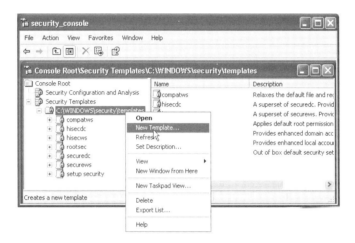

When you do this, no security features are defined. This could mean a lot of manual labor handcrafting the template to your heart's desire. The rewards are great, however, as you'll know exactly what is and what is not defined. When you define your own templates, you can either specify a setting on the target or keep the default setting on the target.

Reusing an Existing Template

Instead of going through the laborious task of handcrafting every Account Policy, Event Log setting, and Registry setting (to name a few), you can use one of the existing templates and modify it to suit your needs.

For instance, you might want to increase the security above and beyond what the `hisecws.inf` provides as follows:

- Turn off the Indexing Service. (Only administrators can turn it on.)

- Place the `Repair` folder (where the Registry backup lives) under stronger lock and key.

In this example, we'll modify the `hisecws.inf` template. To use that template as a jumping-off point, right-click it and save it under a different name, for example, `hisecws_plus.inf`. Your `hisecws_plus.inf` template should show up as an additional entry in the list next to the other templates seen in Figure 6.22.

Modification 1: Stop the Indexing Service

First, we'll disable the Indexing Service at startup. When disabled, this process won't kick off unless an administrator manually turns it on or a process running in the system context turns it on. Follow these steps (which you can also use to disable other services):

1.   From the Security Templates MMC snap-in, drill down into hisecws_plus ➢ System Services ➢ Indexing Service.

2.   Double-click Indexing Service to open the "Indexing Service Properties."

3.   Click the "Define this Policy Setting in the Template" check box.

4.   You can optionally select the "Edit Security" button to modify the security settings. You don't really have to change anything to enforce this policy. Though, for completeness, you could add the Domain Administrators group to ensure that they always have Full Control. If you want, add the Domain Administrators group, then select "Full Control" from the list of properties, and click OK.

5.   Click the "Disabled" radio button if it is not already selected.

6.   Click OK to close the Template Security Policy Setting dialog box.

The Indexing Service is now set to be disabled, as shown in Figure 6.26.

Modification 2: Tweak the Repair Folder

The Repair folder within Windows contains a backup of your Registry data. The files in this folder need to be well protected to ensure that password-cracking programs and the like are not run against the files, exposing the sensitive passwords.

FIGURE 6.26   The Indexing Service has been set to be disabled.

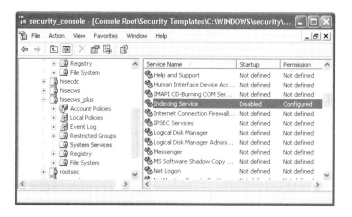

To protect the Repair folder from prying eyes, follow these steps:

1. Drill down into `hisecws_plus` ➢ File System. Right-click File System and choose Add File from the shortcut menu to open the Security dialog box.

2. Locate the *%systemroot%*\Repair folder (usually `c:\windows\repair`).

3. You'll be prompted to edit security for this folder.

4. You can deny local users and add the HR-OU-ADMINS group, as shown in Figure 6.27.

FIGURE 6.27 Use the Security dialog box to allow or deny access to specific folders.

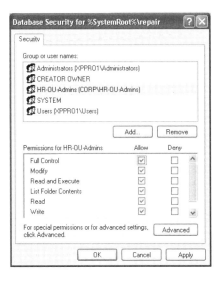

For this example, we want to ensure that the members of our own HR-OU-ADMINS group can access the files at any time. When you click OK in the Security dialog box, you are presented with several choices:

- If you choose "Propagate Inheritable Permissions to all Subfolders and Files," any files or subfolders will receive these NTFS permissions by inheritance only. If there are explicit ACLs on the files or folder, they will not be overwritten.

- If you choose "Replace Existing Permission on All Subfolders and Files with Inheritable Permissions," all current permissions on all affected files and folders are wiped out and replaced with what you have here. This is the default setting.

- If you choose "Do Not Allow Permissions on this File or Folder to Be Replaced," you're asking the operating system not to allow normal inheritance to flow from upper-level folders down to this folder. This option is not valid if an upper-level folder has the "Replace Existing Permission on All Subfolders and Files with Inheritable Permissions" setting.

In this instance, we'll choose the defaults, and click OK to exit the Template Security Policy Setting dialog box.

Now that you've created your templates, you can leverage them to create a safer, tighter, more secure computing environment. The next section will show you how to apply your template to a workstation.

> Be sure, at this point, to right-click the `hisecws_plus.inf` template and select Save. If you don't, your settings could be lost.

The Security Configuration and Analysis Snap-In

The Security Configuration and Analysis snap-in has one purpose: to compare a template with the currently defined settings on a target machine. If the security doesn't match, the Security Configuration and Analysis snap-in can force the settings defined inside the template to be thrust upon the target computer.

The Security Configuration and Analysis snap-in performs an apples-to-apples comparison between the guidelines you set up in the template and what's currently running on the target machine. If there are holes in the target machine, you have two choices: live with the holes, or plug up those holes with the template.

Creating a Baseline

The first step in creating a baseline is to create a database to hold the results of your comparison. You've already loaded the Security Configuration snap-in alongside the Security Templates snap-in on a sample workstation in your domain at the beginning of this chapter, so we're ready to proceed. If you didn't load the two snap-ins on a sample workstation in your domain, do so now.

To create our database, follow these steps:

1. Right-click Security Configuration And Analysis snap-in, and choose "Open Database" from the shortcut menu to open the Open Database dialog box.

2. Since we're using the `hisecws_plus.inf` template, you might want to be consistent and enter **hisecws_plus.sdb** in the "File Name" field, though you're certainly not obligated to. Additionally, it's usually best to house the `.SDB` file in the same location as the `.INF` file so you can find it more easily later. Click "Open" when you've entered in a name.

3. The Import Template dialog box appears. Select your `hisecws_plus.inf` template file.

> You will get inconsistent baseline results if you try to run the templates meant for workstations against a server or domain controller. Remember, the templates are geared toward specific types of machines.

Once the database is generated, the right pane changes to show you the path of the database, as shown in Figure 6.28.

FIGURE 6.28   The right pane changes to reflect your database path.

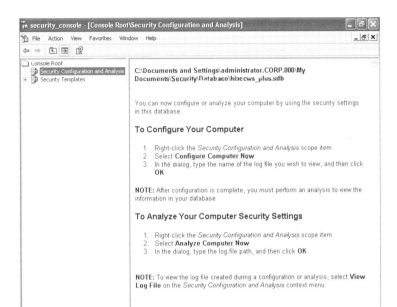

You are now ready to analyze the current computer.

Run the Analysis on the Current Machine

Once you've got your database that houses the sum of the security settings set up, you are ready to analyze the machine against a template. Follow these steps:

1. Right-click the Security And Configuration Analysis snap-in, and choose "Analyze Computer Now" from the shortcut menu to open the Perform Analysis dialog box. When you do, you'll see what is shown in Figure 6.29 where the analysis will span the six categories of security.

2. A default temporary log location is specified in the Perform Analysis dialog box. It really doesn't matter what the name is. Click OK to run the analysis.

FIGURE 6.29   The security analysis checks out the six categories of security.

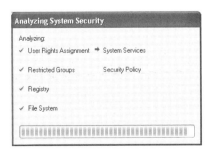

When the analysis is complete, the right pane in the Security Configuration And Analysis snap-in changes to a style similar to that of the Security Templates snap-in.

Analyzing the Results

You can analyze the results in two ways:

- You can use the graphic user interface of the Security Configuration and Analysis tool to drill down and double-check that the settings you specified in the template are, indeed, being applied or not being applied to the current workstation.

- You can paw through the log file by hand and see what it came up with.

The former is much less painful, but there are reasons, described in the "Using the Log File to Find Differences" section, that you might want to paw through the log files.

You can check for the changes that were present in the original hisecws.inf template or the modifications you made, such as the NTFS restrictions in the *%systemroot%*\repair folder.

Graphically Displaying Differences

Lots of settings are configured within the hisecws_plus.inf template. For example, in the Security Configuration and Analysis snap-in, drill down to Local Policies ➤ Security Options. You'll see the following possibilities when graphically analyzing the results:

- If the setting has a green check mark, the template you used has a definition, and the computer has a setting that already matches. In other words, this computer is compliant with your guidelines for this setting.

- If the results have a big red X, the template has a definition, but the computer you're analyzing either doesn't have a setting or the setting doesn't match.

- If the results don't have either a green check mark or a big red X (only the little 1s and 0s icon), the computer has a setting, but nothing is defined in the template—so there's technically no "problem."

- If the results have a big red exclamation mark, the setting wasn't analyzed. This can happen for one of two reasons:

  - The item was not originally defined in the baseline policy.

  - An error (for example, Access Denied) occurred when querying the item.

As Figure 6.30 shows, many Security Options have a big red X, meaning that they were defined in the template but the test machine is not compliant.

Using the Log File to Find Differences

You might want to rerun the analysis, but save the log file in an easy-to-get-to location, such as the c:\temp folder. You can then open and read the log in any text editor, such as Notepad or WordPad. You can, if you're feeling adventurous, paw through the file and manually locate the changes—though this is messy and cumbersome. If you want to go the nongraphical route, you can sometimes speed things up by using your text editor's search feature to find all instances of "Mismatch."

If you're particularly command-line savvy, use the FINDSTR.EXE command to sift through the hisecws_plus.log and output just those lines that contain the word "Mismatch."

FIGURE 6.30 A big red X indicates that the machine is not complying with specific settings in the template.

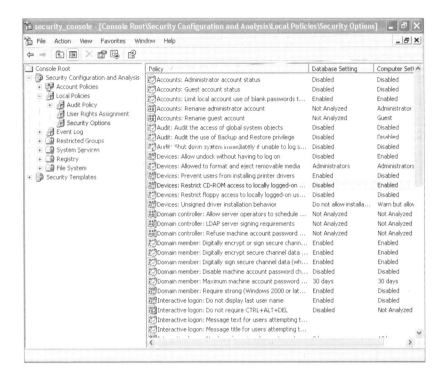

Applying the Template

Now that you know which attributes your target machine does and does not subscribe to, you're ready to apply the template. You can do so in two ways: graphically, via the Security Configuration and Analysis snap-in tool, or via the command-line tool, `secedit`.

If you want to heavily armor your test machine, go ahead and apply the template. Else, cancel out now.

Graphically Applying the Template

After you perform the baseline analysis using the Security Configuration and Analysis snap-in tool, you can apply the settings to your test machine. To do so, right-click the Security Configuration and Analysis snap-in tool and choose "Configure Computer Now" from the shortcut menu. An analysis is not technically required before applying the template, but it's highly recommended so that you know where you currently stand. You'll be prompted for a location to save the log file.

At this point, the computer is configured to the settings you specified in the template. You could, if desired, rerun the analysis phase to see if the application took place. When you see the red Xs change to green check marks, you'll know the application was successful.

Using *secedit* to Analyze and Apply the Template

You can use `secedit` in Windows 2003, Windows XP, and Windows 2000 if you want to write batch files that analyze or apply the policy as we did with the graphical Security Configuration and Analysis tool.

You can use `secedit` to analyze the template against the computer's database at any time. To start `secedit` in analyze mode, you'll need to know the parameters it takes. The following is a sample command line (to be typed all on one line):

```
secedit /analyze /db c:\temp\hisecws_plus.sdb
        /cfg
    c:\windows\security\templates\hisecws_plus.inf
         /log
     c:\temp\hisecws_plus.log
        /verbose
```

Let's break this command into bite-sized chunks.

The `secedit /analyze` chunk requires a /DB parameter, which you must point toward an existing .SDB database. If no database exists, `secedit` creates a new one on the fly. In this case, we're specifying /DB to use the file and path of `c:\temp\hisecws_plus.sdb`. This assumes that `c:\temp` exists. (It may not.)

If you want to generate a new database on the fly, you'll need to specify the /CFG parameter to point toward your .INF template file, say `c:\windows\security\templates\hisecws_plus.inf`. Use the /log flag to specify a location and name for your log, for instance, `c:\temp\hisecws_plus.log`.

Optional parameters are /verbose, which spells out in detail the status, or /quiet, which spits out nothing. The verbose parameter can be useful in debugging situations, and quiet can be useful in batch files when you don't want anyone to know anything is happening.

Now that you understand the command and its parameters, open a command shell and type the **secedit** command, as shown in Figure 6.31.

FIGURE 6.31   Use the secedit command to perform batch analysis.

You can analyze the data in two ways, as discussed earlier. You can do so graphically, using the Security Configuration and Analysis tool, or you can use the log at `c:\temp\hisecws_plus.log`. To analyze the data graphically, right-click the Security Configuration and Analysis tool, and choose Open Database from the shortcut menu. To analyze the data using Notepad or another text editor, open `c:\temp\hisecws_plus.log`.

Using *secedit* to Generate a Rollback Template

The Windows 2003 and Vista versions of the `secedit` command can do something that the Windows XP and Windows 2000 `secedit` command cannot. It can create a new template that can be used if you want to roll back after a botched template application. Here's the trick though: you must do this *before* you actually apply the template (next step).

To run `secedit` in this mode, you'll need to know the appropriate parameters. A sample command line using `secedit` to generate a rollback template on a Domain Controller might be:

```
secedit /generaterollback /db c:\temp\anyname.sdb
        /cfg
    c:\windows\security\templates\securedc.inf
        /rbk
    c:\save_my_bacon
```

In this example, we use the `/cfg` command that we're about to apply the `securedc.inf` template. And, should we need to roll back, it will create the file `rollback_before_securedc.inf` to roll back to the state before we applied the `securedc.inf` template (again, you'll see how to apply templates in the next step).

Here's the big warning though (first of two): if you later decide to apply *another* security template, you'll need to run this command *again*. If you need to perform a rollback, simply apply the security templates back in order such that the most recently created is applied first, and so on back to the first one that was created.

The second big warning is that the resulting template will not have data sufficient to roll back file or Registry ACLs. These templates will roll back everything else though.

Again, note however, that Windows XP doesn't have the `/generaterollback` switch, so, unfortunately, you can't use it here, before the next step.

Using *secedit* to Configure

You can use `secedit` to configure the machine using the template you defined. To run `secedit` in configure mode, you'll need to know the appropriate parameters. The following is a sample command line:

```
secedit /configure /db c:\temp\hisecws_plus.sdb
        /cfg
    c:\windows\security\templates\hisecws_plus.inf
        /log
    c:\temp\hisecws_plus.log
        /verbose
```

Again, let's break the command into bite-sized chunks. The secedit /configure chunk requires a /DB parameter, which you must point toward an existing .SDB database, say, c:\templatecopy\hisecws_plus.sdb.

Use the /CFG parameter to point to your .INF template file, c:\templatecopy\ hisecws_plus.inf. If you don't specify a /CFG entry, secedit applies the currently stored template in the database specified in the /DB parameter.

Use the /log flag to specify a location and name for your log, for example, c:\temp\ hisecws_plus.log.

Use the /overwrite switch to overwrite the current information in the database with the information in the security template.

The secedit can also surgically replace a specific area in the template to the target machine. Use the /areas switch to isolate and specify one or several areas, as shown in Table 6.3.

TABLE 6.3   Valid Keywords for *secedit*'s /areas Switch

Area	Where to Find
SECURITYPOLICY	Sets all security settings inside the template, except for the Restricted Groups, User Rights Assignment, Registry Keys, File Services, or System Services
GROUP_MGMT	The Restricted Groups branch in the template
USER_RIGHTS	The Local Policy ➢ User Rights Assignment in the template
REGKEYS	The Registry branch in the template
FILESTORE	The File System branch in the template
SERVICES	The System Services branch in the template

To specify multiple areas, you can simply string them together (with a single space between each one), such as /areas REGKEYS SERVICES. To apply all areas, don't specify the /areas switch, since they'll all apply by default. Optional parameters are /verbose, which spells out in detail the status, or /quiet, which spits out nothing at all.

The use of the parameter /cfg c:\temp\hisecws_plus.inf is optional because we already used that .INF file to create our .SDB database in the last step.

Once this process is complete, your system is as secure as the template file dictates.

If you get an "Access is Denied" error, try closing the MMC snap-in in order to close the file lock on the .SDB database.

You can learn more about the secedit command by opening a command shell and typing **secedit /?.**

Applying Security Templates with Group Policy

You could schlep around to each workstation or server and run secedit with the /configure switch. This works reasonably well in stand-alone environments, if you only need to tie down a handful of machines, or if you're still in an NT 4 domain or a Novell environment and haven't yet upgraded to Active Directory. But a much more common scenario occurs when you want to enforce the same required security setting on multiple machines simultaneously. This requirement is typical at call centers, nursing stations, and public kiosks.

Group Policy's mission is to make broad-stroke enforcement a piece of cake, and this instance certainly qualifies.

Let's say you want to deploy the hisecws_plus.inf template on all the computers in an OU named **Nurses Computers** OU. Follow these steps:

1. Ensure that the **Nurses Computers** OU exists. (We're making it up for the sake of example here.)

2. Move all machines to be affected by this security edict into the **Nurses Computers** OU.

3. Copy the hisecws_plus.inf template from the workstation to a location accessible to the server. You can do this in several ways. The goal is to get the hisecws_plus.inf template that you generated on the workstation over to the server. You can use a network share, e-mail, or even a floppy! When you transfer the file, simply place it into any folder on the server you desire. The best location is the Domain Controller's c:\windows\ security\templates folder.

4. Create a new GPO and link it to the **Nurses Computers** OU. This GPO will be used to import the settings inside the hisecws_plus.inf template you created. Give the GPO a descriptive name, such as "Force hisecws_plus.inf."

Once you're editing the GPO, drill down to Computer Configuration ➤ Windows Settings ➤ Security Settings. To utilize any security .inf template, simply right-click Security Settings (as shown in Figure 6.32) and choose "Import Policy" from the shortcut menu.

1. Select the policy you want to use by pointing the file requester toward the hisecws_plus.inf file and selecting it. You'll also notice a "Clear this Database Before Importing" check box:

   - When this check box is checked, the current Security settings are replaced with those that you defined in the custom .INF template.

   - When this check box is unchecked, only the attributes you specifically modified are changed. In other words, the state is maintained in those attributes that have no definition.

FIGURE 6.32   Drill down into the Security Settings, right-click, and then import a template.

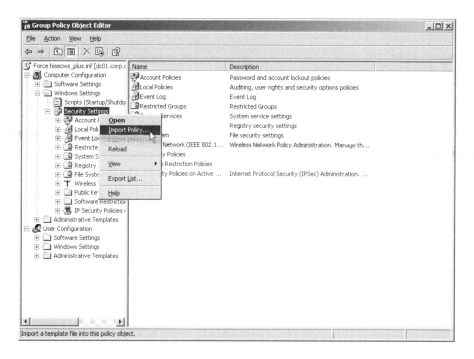

2.   You can ensure that the template was imported correctly by verifying that the changes you modified in the hisecws_plus.inf template are reflected. For instance, when modifying the hisecws_plus.inf template, make sure the %*systemroot*%\repair folder is listed. You can even dive in and inspect the settings.

3.   When ready, close the Group Policy Object Editor.

Now, you are ready to reboot the machines affected by the **Nurses Computers** OU, or you can wait until the machines embrace the new security settings you specified in the GPO. Afterward, you can verify that the settings you specified in the hisecws_plus.inf template are indeed being reflected and locked down across all machines in the OU.

If you get really gung-ho and want to hack the security templates yourself to add your own security settings, it's difficult and ornery but possible. You'll find two excellent references, "How to Customize Security Settings within Templates," at http://tinyurl.com/3n72j and "How to Add Custom Registry Settings to Security Configuration Editor" at http://tinyurl.com/49p6m. Note that this later technique is really about modifying the Local Security Options section in the GPeditor and has nothing to do with Security Templates per se.

The Security Configuration Wizard for Windows 2003/SP1

The biggest addition to Windows 2003/SP1 (as far as Group Policy is concerned) is the Security Configuration Wizard, or SCW. I know, I know. You hate wizards. But this one is really super powerful. So powerful, in fact, that it has its own home page at Microsoft.com at www.microsoft.com/scw. Wow!

In the last section, you learned how to leverage security templates and secure your workstations. You then linked a GPO, slurped in the security template and secured a gaggle of workstations all in one goal.

In this section, the goal is similar. You'll run the SCW on one of your Windows 2003 machines, say, your Domain Controller. You'll tell the SCW which "roles" the Domain Controller has. For instance, perhaps in addition to being a Domain Controller, it's also a print server and a file server and also maybe a DHCP server. Once you've told it what the machine will be used for, it will pop out a security policy that describes how to secure this Windows 2003 server. Next, you'll convert the policy into a GPO. Finally, you'll link the GPO to an OU in Active Directory, which contains the collection of Windows 2003 servers you want to secure! Hence, all servers in the OU will have the same security policy.

The true goal of the SCW is to "reduce the attack surface." That's the common phrase used when we want to stop all unused services and close up any remaining unused doors. We won't be able to go over all the ins and outs of the SCW. But we will go through a simple example. And, as icing on the security cake, put a Group Policy cherry on top at the end. It'll be sweet.

One note before we get going here: The tasks you perform with the SCW are strictly to secure your Windows 2003/SP1 machines. The output produced by the SCW is not—NOT—meant to secure your Windows Vista, Windows XP, or Windows 2000 machines. Doing so could render your Windows Vista, Windows XP, or Windows 2000 machines wounded and perhaps unrecoverable.

Installing the SCW

As stated, the SCW is available only on Windows 2003 machines after SP1 is loaded. Once it's been loaded, the SCW's help icon should automatically appear on the desktop. However, this does not mean that the SCW is actually installed. To install the SCW, you need to sojourn to Add/Remove Programs and specifically add it. Let's do that now. To install the SCW:

1. Log on to your Windows 2003/SP1 Domain Controller as Administrator.

2. Click Start ➢ Programs ➢ Control Panel ➢ Add or Remove Programs.

3. Click the Add/Remove Windows Components button.

4. In the Components list, locate and select Security Configuration Wizard, as seen in Figure 6.33.

5. Click Next to load the component and close Add/Remove Programs.

FIGURE 6.33 The Security Configuration Wizard's help file automatically appears on the desktop after SP1 is loaded. However, you need to specifically add in the SCW components via Add/Remove Programs.

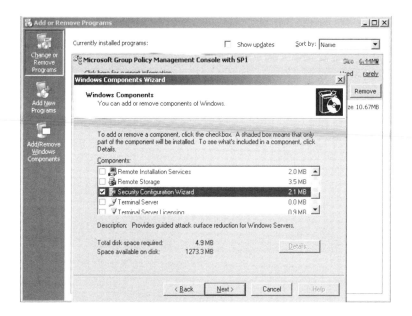

Once the SWC is loaded, you're ready to rock.

A Practical SWC Example

In this example, we'll produce an SCW policy that turns off all unnecessary services for our Domain Controller. And, we'll additionally leverage this policy for additional Domain Controllers (later) if more come aboard. To create a SCW policy, you'll run the wizard in several big-ish steps.

Initial SCW Kickoff

1. Start the SCW by clicking Start ➢ Programs ➢ Administrative Tools ➢ Security Configuration Wizard.

2. At the first screen of the wizard, click Next.

3. At the "Configuration Action" screen ensure that "Create a new security policy" is selected and click Next, as seen in Figure 6.34.

4. At the "Select Server" screen, ensure that the DC01 server is selected and click Next. This is the machine that we'll leverage as the baseline machine. That is, the SCW will inspect this machine and see what's running on it so it can make some determinations about which services and such you might want to secure. When you do, the SCW will inspect this machine and try to determine what its current roles are.

5. After the SCW checks out your system, you'll receive a "Processing Complete" message and be given the opportunity to "View Configuration Database." The Configuration Database is simply a list of all possible roles the server might play. So, at this time, just click Next.

FIGURE 6.34   Kick off the SCW by creating a new security policy.

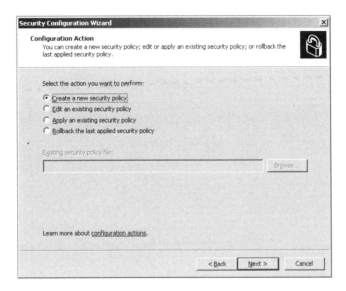

Role-Based Configuration Section

1. Now, you'll be at the first screen of the "Role-Based Service Configuration." This section of the wizard helps you add or remove roles this server might be playing. Again, as a Domain Controller, you might also have plans for it to be a print server. Click Next to continue.

2. When you do, you'll be at the "Select Server Roles" screen, where you are viewing a list of "Installed Roles," as seen in Figure 6.35. The SCW takes a "best guess" about what it thinks this server is already trying to do, and selects those as "Installed Roles." If you have future plans for this machine (or for others later, as you add to the OU) and want to add a role, go ahead at this point. You can select from the list presented here or use the "View" drop-down list and select to see "All Roles." Perhaps some day you'll also use certificate services on this machine. In that case, you would need to locate "Certificate Server" from the list and check it. When you've selected the services you want, click Next.

3. Now, you'll be at the "Select Client Features" screen. Here, you'll specify which client components your server runs. Again, by default, it chooses which components it thinks are already in use. Note that for some reason, the "Group Policy Administrative Client" isn't selected, even though the GPMC is detected. I'm not sure why this is overlooked and unselected by default. But, in short, if you plan on running the GPMC on the servers that will get this policy, be sure to also select "Group Policy Administrative Client."

4.   Choose any additional features you know you are using or want to eventually use and click Next.

5.   You'll be at the "Select Administration and Other Options" page. Like the pages before it, it makes a best guess about which options you want to use. Choose any additional features you know you are using or want to eventually use and click Next.

FIGURE 6.35   The SCW shows you the roles it thinks are currently running on your server.

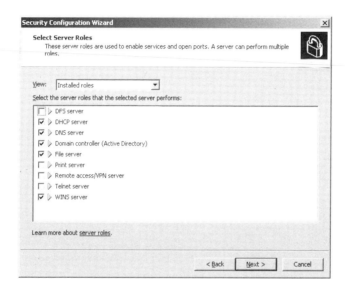

6.   At the "Select Additional Services" page, the SCW looks to see if there are any services you might have also loaded. By default, those are checked to continue to run. Click Next to continue.

7.   At the "Handling Unspecified Services" page, you're asked how to handle the services you loaded on the Windows 2003 machine. Select "Do not change the startup mode of the service" and click Next.

8.   At the "Confirm Service Changes" page, you can see what will happen to the myriad of services running on your Domain Controller. In Figure 6.36, you can see that many services, currently set to "Automatic," will now be configured to "Disabled."

9.   When you click Next, you'll proceed to the Network Configuration Section.

Network Security Section

This part of the wizard is optional. And that's a good thing.

Right on this opening page of this section, you can click the "Skip this section" check box and click Next to proceed to the next section.

FIGURE 6.36 The SCW will make your system less vulnerable to attack by disabling unused services.

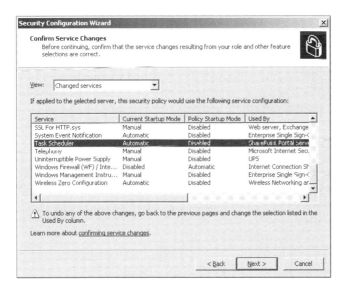

If you choose to continue with this section, you'll encounter the following pages (which are similar in idea to the already-examined pages). That is, the wizard tries to determine what you're already doing on this system and keeps those parts enabled and available for use; it will also close off sections that it thinks are not being used.

However, if you zip through this section, you're basically telling the SCW to turn on the Windows firewall for servers that this security policy will affect. That's a risky game because if you fail to open a port, your clients won't be able to access a program running on your server. So, proceed down this section with caution.

For our examples, we'll select to "Skip this section" and proceed.

Registry Settings Section

Like the previous section, this section is optional. Here you can make decisions about SMB signing, which operating systems can connect to this server, LDAP signing, Outbound and Inbound Authentication Methods, and more.

If you're interested in the materials in this section, be sure to read the materials on www.microsoft.com/scw.

For our examples, we're going to skip the Registry Settings Section by selecting "Skip this section" and clicking Next.

Audit Policy Section

Again, this section is optional. And I think you'll likely want to skip it. We examined Audit Policy earlier in this chapter, and it's likely you've already manually configured your audit policy and set it upon the OUs containing the servers you already want to audit.

Moreover, as the warning on this page describes, after these settings are set, they are permanently tattooed.

For our purposes, we'll select "Skip this section" and click Next.

Save Security Policy Section

At this point, you're ready to save your policy. But it doesn't get saved as a GPO. No, no! That would be too easy! Instead, it is saved as an XML file! On the "Security policy file name" line, enter in a legal path on this server and a name for the file, say, **c:\OurSecureDCPolicy.xml**. In the Description field, enter in something useful as well, as seen in Figure 6.37.

However, before you click Next, note that you can also, optionally, choose to "Include Security Templates." Yes! These are the same security templates you could have created in the previous section. Here's the idea: The SCW is easy to use and lets you manipulate a lot of stuff but not everything. Security templates are hard to use but let you manipulate (just about) everything. So, if you created any security templates for that additionally increased security for your Windows 2003 servers, you can add them here. Note, however, that if there's a settings conflict between a security template and the SCW, the "winner" will be the SCW—not the setting contained within the security template.

When ready, click Next.

You'll be asked if you want to apply the policy now or later. At this point, choose "Apply later" and click Next.

At the final page of the wizard, click Finish.

FIGURE 6.37   Here you can add in additional security templates or just save your SCW policy out as an XML file.

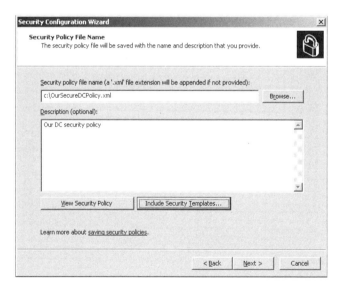

Converting Your SCW Policy to a GPO

At this point, you've got a nice XML file that you, well, can't do a lot with in its current form. However, the goal is to convert this XML file to a bona-fide GPO that you can then link to an OU of your choosing. In this case, you will link it to your **Domain Controllers** OU.

You can covert the GPO with the scwcmd.exe command. The syntax of the command line is as follows:

```
scwcmd transform /p:name_of_xml_file_ /g:name_of_GPO_we_want_to_create
```

So, because you saved the XML file as c:\OurSecureDCPolicy.xml, and you arbitrarily call the GPO OurSecureDCGPO, the syntax will be:

```
scwcmd transform /p:c:\ourSecureDCPolicy.xml /g:OurSecureDCGPO
```

Once performed, you should get a "Command completed successfully" message. A GPO is now created with the name you've provided after the /g (in this case, OurSecureDCGPO).

IIS configuration that is defined in the SCW policy is not parlayed into a transformed GPO. It is lost.

Viewing and Applying Your Transformed GPO

At this point, fire up the GPMC to see if the GPO you just created by transforming the XML file is there. It should be in the Group Policy Objects node but not linked to any site, domain, or OU. Note that you might have to refresh the list of GPOs in the Group Policy Objects node to see the new GPO.

When ready, link the GPO you created to the final destination. In our working example, you would link the GPO to the **Domain Controllers** OU. You don't really need to do this now, but you can do so if you so choose. Again, the GPO will just sit there in the Group Policy Objects node swimming pool—doing nothing—unless it's actually linked to a GPO.

One quick word of warning about the resulting GPO that is created. That is, if you click the Settings tab inside the GPMC to see the resulting GPO that is created, you might not see anything! However, if you edit the GPO, you'll be able to see the settings that are actually contained within the GPO (see Figure 6.38). This is a micro-bug that I'm sure will be fixed with a hotfix. Stay tuned on GPanswers.com because I'll update you with a newsletter as soon as I know of an update.

Note that if you change any settings within the GPO, the problem magically fixes itself, and then you can see the settings contained within the GPO by clicking the Settings tab. Something about editing the GPO inside the Group Policy Object editor fixes the converted GPO and makes it viewable. Again, this is a bug that I'll try to keep an eye on for an update.

FIGURE 6.38 The Settings tab might not show any settings from the transformed GPO. However, editing the GPO will show that the settings are, indeed, changed inside the GPO.

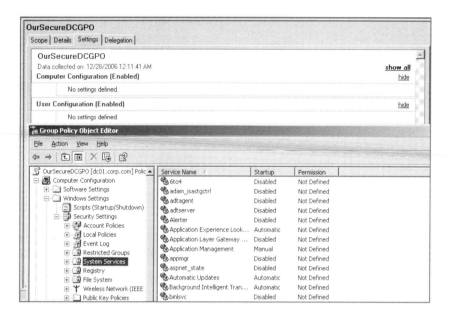

SCW Caveats

There are two additional warnings when using the SCW to create XML policies and then convert them to GPOs.

Don't use the SCW (and corresponding GPOs) to apply settings to machines other than Windows 2003/SP1 That's the official word from Microsoft. The SCW is simply not meant to be used to deploy settings to Windows 2000, Windows XP, or even Windows 2003 without SP1. That's right, so don't do it! Microsoft did not test the SCW with these operating systems, so applying GPOs transformed from SCW's XML files could be very, very dangerous if not applied to Windows 2003/SP1.

Don't expect file and Registry ACLs to be able to "roll back" After you lay down file or Registry ACLs using GPOs (either transformed from SCW's XML files, via security templates, or by hand), you cannot roll these settings back. They are always permanently tattooed on the target system.

Final Thoughts

To know security, you need to know Group Policy. To that end, we've toured some of the major sights along the Group Policy security highway. From the "Default Domain Controllers Policy" and "Default Domain Policy" GPOs to Windows XP and Windows 2003 Software Restriction Policies to Security Templates—a lot can be accomplished in there.

Walking up to a specific machine and applying local security sounds like a great, straight-forward idea—until you have so many machines you couldn't possibly walk up to them all. This chapter covered some alternate methods for asserting your will across the network.

Use security templates for all types of machines. But if you're configuring Windows 2003/SP1 machines, the new SCW is your new best friend.

Remember that items in the security branch of a GPO will take effect, maximally, every 16 hours—even if the Group Policy doesn't change in Active Directory. This ensures that if a nefarious local administrator changed the policies on his workstation, they'll eventually be refreshed. However, recall that this "Security Background Refresh" will not affect other areas of Group Policy by default. If you want similar behavior, be sure to read Chapter 3 where we discuss the implications of the setting named "Process even if the Group Policy objects have not changed." You can enable different sections of Group Policy to do this by drilling down in the Group Policy Object Editor within Computer Configuration ➢ Administrative Templates ➢ System ➢ Group Policy. Again, this was covered in Chapter 3. So, for fullest security and protection, re-read that chapter to understand why and how to enable those settings.

What I Didn't Cover

Unfortunately, space limitations restrict me from delving into *all* security functions of Group Policy. Of note, two categories are missing from this Group Policy security roundup which can affect all computers (pre-Vista and Windows Vista):

- Certificate Services and Public Key Infrastructure (PKI)
- EFS and the EFS Recovery Policy

For More on Certificate Services and PKI   For getting a grip on Certificate Services and PKI, check out "Best Practices for Implementing a Microsoft Windows Server 2003 Public Key Infrastructure" at http://www.microsoft.com/pki

For More on EFS and the EFS Recovery Policy   You'll find information on the Encrypting File System in Windows XP and Windows Server 2003 at http://tinyurl.com/576kx.

Additionally, see the Knowledge Base articles "HOW TO: Configure a Domain EFS Recovery Policy in Windows 2000" (KB313376) and "Best Practices for the Encrypting File System" (KB 223316).

Designing vs. Implementing

This chapter is titled "Implementing Security with Group Policy" because that's what we did. However, an equally challenging project is the *design* of your security policy battle plans *before* you march headlong into implementation. One excellent Microsoft resource, made specifically for the task of working through some examples to design security with GPOs, is the "Common Scenarios" white paper at http://tinyurl.com/4oaks. You can also just search for "Group Policy Common Scenarios Using GPMC" on Microsoft's website.

The "Common Scenarios" white paper includes several "canned" GPOs that help you learn how to design a security policy and includes situations where computers should be Lightly Managed, Mobile, and Kiosk. Once you play with each scenario, you can decide which features you want to keep in your own environment. These GPOs aren't really meant to be deployed as-is (you should modify them to suit your own business), but you'll get a better handle on some security design options. A white paper is included to help you work though the scenarios. In all, I think it's an excellent follow-up once you've been through the exercises in this chapter.

7

Windows Vista Security Enhancements with Group Policy

In the last chapter, we touched upon lots of security goodies. Some were about Vista systems, but most were about pre-Vista systems. In this chapter, it's "The All Vista Channel." *All Vista, All the Time*. WVST FM!

Okay, I'm done playing around.

So, the stuff you'll learn here is (mostly) specifically for Windows Vista (and presumably Server Longhorn). Here's a foretaste of what we're going to cover:

Vista's Enhanced Wireless and New Wired Ethernet Policy Windows XP already has Wireless policy. Windows Vista's is better. And it also has a new Wired Ethernet policy which we will check out.

Internet Explorer 7 It's big. It's new. It's Internet Explorer 7. And it's got Group Policy control.

User Account Control (UAC) Or, more specifically, we'll be talking about *controlling* User Account Control.

Vista's updated Windows Firewall with Enhanced Security Windows XP /SP2 already had a pretty good Windows Firewall, and it was controllable using Group Policy. Windows Vista's is better and more controllable via Group Policy.

Device Installation Restrictions This lets us take control and limit access of what hardware is being installed on our client machines.

So, let's roll up those sleeves and get started.

Wireless (802.3) and Wired Network (802.11) Policies

Built-in support for wireless networks was new for Windows XP and Windows 2003 and is now enhanced for Windows Vista. Additionally, Windows Vista has a Wired policy which is new and neat.

You can see two new nodes in Computer Configuration ➤ Windows Settings ➤ Security Settings ➤ **Wired Network (IEEE 802.3) Policies** and **Wireless Network (IEEE 802.11 Policies)**, as seen in Figure 7.1.

FIGURE 7.1   New nodes for Wired and Wireless Policies are now available.

Here's the trick though: to actually make the examples in this section work, you're going to have to stop what you're doing, take a big deep breath and read this:

www.microsoft.com/technet/itsolutions/network/wifi/vista_ad_ext.mspx (shortened to http://tinyurl.com/yd7hyy)

It's entitled "Active Directory Schema Extensions for Windows Vista Wireless and Wired Group Policy Enhancements" and you *need to do this now*. That is, you need to update your Windows Server 2003/Active Directory schema to support these new features. And, sorry to say, this procedure is a little cumbersome. There's no runme.exe to make the magic happen. And you must be an Active Directory Schema Admin to make these changes.

So, instead of reproducing all the steps here, just go there, take the time to do this in your test lab (or get permission to do this in your real world) then come back here when you're finished. Don't forget that there are two scripts you must run: one for Wired and one for Wireless policy.

Note that if you try to create new Wireless Network (IEEE 802.11) Policies for Windows XP *without* updating the schema, these policies will succeed, because Windows XP doesn't require the updated schema. Do note, however, this still requires the Windows Server 2003 Active Directory schema; the Windows 2000 Active Directory schema won't work.

However, if you don't have the schema update, and you attempted to create a new Wireless Policy for Windows Vista or new Wired Policy (which is Windows Vista–only anyway) you'll encounter what you see in Figure 7.2.

FIGURE 7.2   What happens if you try to create a new Wired or Wireless policy for Windows Vista without the schema update

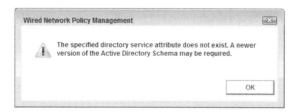

Assuming you've modified the schema as required, you're ready to move on.

802.11 Wireless Policy for Windows XP

When you right-click **Wireless Network (IEEE 802.11) Policies** you can select to "Create a New Windows Vista Policy" or "Create a New Windows XP Policy." For XP, you know which one to pick.

You can set all sorts of wireless parameters for your Windows XP or Windows 2003 computers (though it's unlikely you'll have many Windows 2003 computers with wireless cards). The policy settings themselves are beyond the scope of this book and include options such as WEP, EAP/Smartcard usage, and other scary-sounding wireless settings. However, you can learn about the controllable settings in Chapter 6 of the "Windows Server 2003 Planning Guide." Just search TechNet for "Planning Guide 6—Designing Wireless LAN Security Using 802.1X." At last check it was found here: `http://tinyurl.com/yzm3tv`.

Note that your users need to be connected to the hard-wired network at least one time and download Group Policy from a Domain Controller to get the appropriate certificates for Wireless policy.

802.11 Wireless Policy and 802.3 Wired Policy for Windows Vista

Windows Vista's Wireless policy adds some new bells and whistles, and the Wired policy is brand-spankin' new.

In the new goodies for Wireless you get things like "Mixed Security Mode" (where you can configure several settings to single SSID) and "Allow and Deny Lists" (where you can dictate specifically which SSIDs they can connect and not connect to).

At last check a good starting point for leveraging these policies can be found here:

`www.microsoft.com/technet/windowsvista/network/default.mspx`

(shortened to `http://tinyurl.com/yb7rn`)

Like the Windows XP version of this policy, your users need to make contact with a Domain Controller to download Group Policy over the wired Ethernet at least one time before this policy can kick in.

The wired policies don't look all that exciting at first blush. But, they're the backbone for Network Access Protection (NAP)—an upcoming feature for Longhorn (with Windows XP or Windows Vista as clients) that will prevent rogue machines from getting on your network. You can learn more about NAP here: www.microsoft.com/technet/network/nap/default.mspx and get a Step-by-Step guide to NAP in a test lab here: http://tinyurl.com/yks6dg.

You can also use this if your Cisco switch enforces 802.1x authentication. This is common in high-security environments where you want to prevent unauthorized users from plugging laptops into hot network drops.

Managing Internet Explorer with Group Policy

There's Internet Explorer 6 and now Internet Explorer 7. And you need to know how to control them. And that's where it get a little confusing because there's lots of areas in Group Policy which look like they can do the job. In this section we'll explore the places you can control Internet Explorer via Group Policy.

Internet Explorer 7 comes included with Windows Vista. However, it should be noted that Internet Explorer 7 is technically labeled by Microsoft as a "required" upgrade for your existing Windows XP machines. So, this tip might be too late for you. That is, if you want to "block" Internet Explorer 7 from being laid down upon your existing Windows XP machines, you can "block" it. It's called the "Toolkit to Disable Automatic Delivery of Internet Explorer 7" and is found here: http://tinyurl.com/fh3bv.

The three big things we'll talk about are

- Internet Explorer Maintenance Policy (which mostly controls Internet Explorer 6)

- Internet Explorer 7's built-in control from Windows Vista management station

and

- Internet Explorer 7's ADM for Windows XP management stations

Internet Explorer Maintenance (IEM)

The point of Internet Explorer Maintenance (IEM) settings is to set preferences for things. The definition here for preferences is "suggestions for how a user should use Internet Explorer."

You set Internet Explorer Maintenance settings for users by traversing down to User Configuration ➤ Windows Settings ➤ **Internet Explorer Maintenance**.

So, if you set a preference for the Internet Explorer Home Page to be www.GPanswers.com, that's great! You can see IEM settings in Figure 7.3 where I've set the Home Page URL to www.GPanswers.com.

FIGURE 7.3   You can set preferences using Internet Explorer Maintenance.

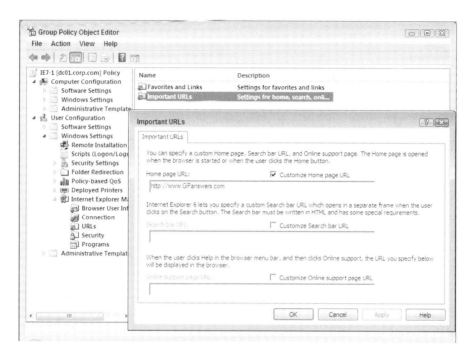

But here's the trick about IEM settings: There's nothing specifically saying the user can't open up Internet Explorer, go into the options of the browser and set whatever settings they want *in place* of your preferences. In Figure 7.4, a user affected by this policy can just fire up Internet Explorer 7 on Windows Vista and change the home page to whatever they want! (Not that anyone would want to change from GPanswers.com!)

How about this lovely scenario: You spend Friday night at the office putting together a new Internet proxy server. You have 10,000 clients, and now you have to update them. You *could* walk around to each of them to tell Internet Explorer the name of the new proxy server. However, if you use Group Policy with Internet Explorer Maintenance policies, you simply set the name of the new proxy server from upon high and go home for the night.

Again, you'll find all sorts of gizmos to play with that control Internet Explorer: home page settings, proxy settings, security zone settings, favorites, and so on. However, it should be noted that not all IEM settings will affect Internet Explorer 7, as shown in Figure 7.5.

Again, a complete rundown of all the Internet Explorer Maintenance Mode settings is beyond the scope of this book; however, there is one "not so obvious" element to this branch of Group Policy: the two modes you can use to deploy Internet Explorer Maintenance settings.

FIGURE 7.4 Users can change the preferences set in Internet Explorer Maintenance to whatever they want.

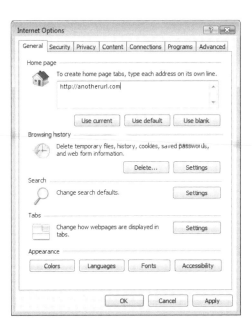

FIGURE 7.5 Some Internet Explorer Maintenance settings are not going to work for Internet Explorer 7.

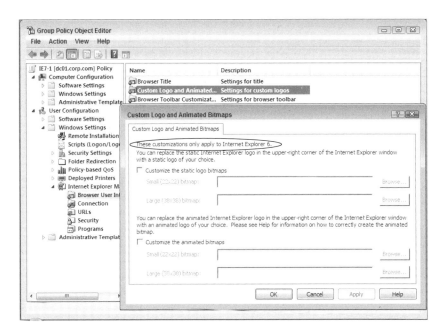

Mandatory Mode   Acts like other Group Policy settings; that is, your desires are forced upon your client machines. If users change them, the settings are restored. Using this mode is helpful when you want to guarantee important options such as security settings and proxy settings. Additionally, you'll need to locate the **Internet Explorer Maintenance Policy Processing** policy setting (located in Computer Configuration ➤ Administrative Templates ➤ Group Policy). Inside that setting there's a check box labeled "Process even if Group Policy Objects have not changed." Again, nothing specifically prevents them from changing these values, but, once that setting is selected, when a foreground or background refresh is triggered, the values should be returned.

Preference Mode   This is the default and what we just saw. That is, once you make a setting for a user, the change is reflected upon the client. But, it allows users to change them if they desire. This mode is good for users whom you want to give some degree of liberty (for example, developers) but want to encourage them to use your preferred settings.

If the two modes are confusing, here's the cheat sheet: Preference mode only applies once and then never again, while mandatory mode will always reapply (like normal policy, but on steroids, because it won't care if the version has changed).

The Internet Explorer Maintenance interface is a little goofy. For some items (such as customized program settings), you'll import the settings from the machine on which the Group Policy Object Editor is actually running. Additionally goofy is that once you make a change to Preference mode, you cannot return to Mandatory mode without wiping out all your settings (via the Reset Browser Settings option).

Windows 2003 allows for what is known as "Internet Explorer Hardening," which is meant to prevent rogue Active X controls and the like from applying. Active X controls are little pieces of code that enhance the Internet Explorer experience, but could be used maliciously. Microsoft has two great references on the subject: http://tinyurl.com/54wwd and http://tinyurl.com/cf7pt. You can also search Microsoft's website for "Internet Explorer Enhanced Security Configuration."

Internet Explorer Settings Warning

As stated, setting up the Internet Explorer settings can be a bit wacky. There's one more wacky piece that makes them sometimes very difficult to work with. Setting some policy settings within Internet Explorer are "sticky." That is, they don't act like regular policy settings that just revert to some default when they don't apply.

If you set up Internet Explorer Maintenance policies at multiple levels in Active Directory, you'll want to test to see the "merging" of your policy settings. Some Internet Explorer Maintenance policy settings "merge," and others do not—it depends on what you are setting up. Proxy settings, for instance, do not merge; the last applied policy "wins." However, this is not true for the "Trusted Sites" configuration settings. These policy settings *will* merge. Again, be sure to test your GPOs with Internet Explorer Maintenance policies to verify whether your specific policy settings merge or not.

The one that comes to mind is the Internet Explorer Maintenance proxy server setting (mentioned previously). If you later choose to work without a proxy server and kill the GPO, the proxy setting you set sticks with all your clients. It doesn't—does not—peel off the setting. This is a major hassle and one that has no great answer to fix.

I retested this with Windows Vista's Internet Explorer 7, and, sure enough, they fixed it. But previous versions of the operating system aren't so fortunate.

I've heard reports of other Internet Explorer settings being sticky; but in my testing, the proxy setting is the only one I've witnessed being sticky. In short, before rolling out Internet Explorer settings (of any kind), you should also ensure that the settings you roll out are nonsticky. Or, if they are sticky, be sure to have a back-out plan to remediate the stickiness if you need to.

Internet Explorer's Group Policy Settings

You're using a Windows Vista management station, right? Of course right, because you read Chapters 1, 2, and 5. But, if for some reason you're not (and you're using, say, a Windows XP or Windows Server 2003 management station), you might need to control the new goodies in Internet Explorer 7. If you need to do that, you'll need to get the ADM Files for Internet Explorer 7 to load upon your management station. You would go to `http://tinyurl.com/ynjyry` (expands to a Microsoft download) to get them. Then, use the information in Chapter 5 to import an ADM template.

But wait. You say you are using a Windows Vista management station? Then good news for you—the work is already done. The controls for Internet Explorer 7 are already in the box. Nothing to download, nothing to worry about.

The point of the Group Policy settings, found in (User and Computer Configuration) ➢ Administrative templates ➢ Windows Components ➢ Internet Explorer ➢ Internet Settings and (User and Computer Configuration) Administrative templates ➢ Windows Components ➢ Internet Explorer are to guarantee settings.

In other words, preferences (what we just saw earlier) "suggest" a setting; the Group Policy settings "guarantee it." Be sure to read the Explaintext for each Group Policy setting as well as read the requirements. Not every setting is valid for both Internet Explorer 6 and 7, so be sure to read and test.

Do You Know about the Internet Explorer IEAK?

The IEAK is used to set preferences or just to configure a standalone Internet Explorer machine. Sure, you'll usually want to use Group Policy in an Active Directory environment to set true policies (and lock down settings). But the IEAK uses a file type called .INS to set preferences. The IEAK can be downloaded here.

`www.microsoft.com/technet/prodtechnol/ie/ieak/default.mspx`

Once your `.INS` file is created, you can package it in a custom `ie7setup.exe`, which can be used for deployment. Again, you'll usually not want to use the IEAK for domain-joined machines, as you've got the power of Group Policy to do that for you.

It's true, however, that the IEAK settings and Group Policy settings are darn close in similarity. But, there are a few things that can be done *only* using IEAK that cannot be done through Group Policy. Two examples are the ability to set default feeds and the default search provider which are only available in the IEAK.

But you might be asking yourself: "Which would 'win' if both applied?" The short answer is "which ever technology gets applied last."

So, if you start off with IEAK settings, those settings are applied.

If you later change to using Group Policy settings, those are applied.

In short the advice is as follows:

- If you want to guarantee settings, and *can* use Group Policy to do so, you should strive to use Group Policy.

- If you must set preferences, try to do it using Group Policy first, try the IEAK second.

For more information on the IEAK, check out this swell article in Technet Magazine: `http://tinyurl.com/ytuwnt`.

Finding Internet Explorer ADM Policy Settings

Windows XP/SP2 and Windows 2003/SP1 added 619 possible Internet Explorer policy settings. Windows Vista adds even more.

Again, you'll find most of these settings at Administrative Templates ➤ Windows Components ➤ Internet Explorer ➤ Internet Control Panel ➤ Security Page. These settings are under both User Configuration *and* Computer Configuration nodes.

In Chapter 2, we discussed how Microsoft has an Excel spreadsheet with every policy setting available for download. To get a grip on all that's new here, I suggest you download it (track it down via `GPanswers.com` in the "Microsoft Resources" section) and then click the "Inetresx.admx" column of the spreadsheet. Here you can isolate and check out just the Internet Explorer settings, select to see only the new policy settings for "at least Internet Explorer v6.0 in Windows XP Service Pack 2 or Windows Server 2003 Service Pack 1," and get a feel for what's new and what you might choose to use in your environment.

Additionally, remember you can filter inside the Group Policy Object while you're editing it. Just click View ➤ Filtering and select to "Filter by Requirements information." Then, select only "At least Internet Explorer 7.0" and you'll *only* see the new settings as seen here.

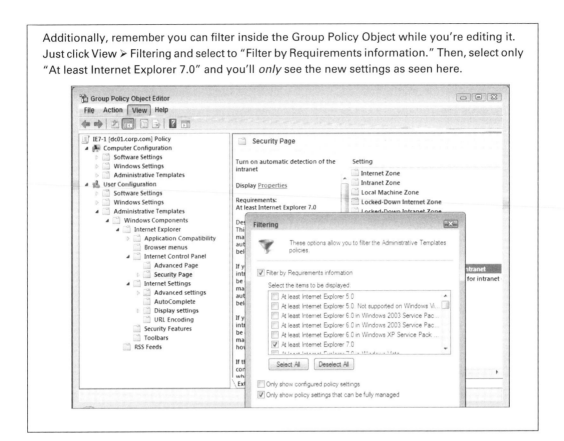

Controlling User Account Control (UAC) with Group Policy

UAC is the "User Accounts Control" feature for Windows Vista. You might see it as the "annoying extra pop-up box I need to click in order to do anything useful in Vista!" Well, sometimes it might seem that way. But that's not exactly accurate. What's really happening is that you're seeing a prompt for anything that requires administrator rights (that is, that affects the entire computer and all users on that computer) in Windows Vista. So, in reality, it's not that bad; UAC is designed to put a (small) roadblock in front of administrative tasks and applications.

An example of a UAC dialog box that can pop up based on the types of actions and programs you want to run is shown in Figure 7.6, where a mere-mortal user is trying to "Allow a program through Windows Firewall" and is prompted for local administrator credentials.

FIGURE 7.6 Anytime a user clicks on an action with a "shield" icon, they are prompted for credentials.

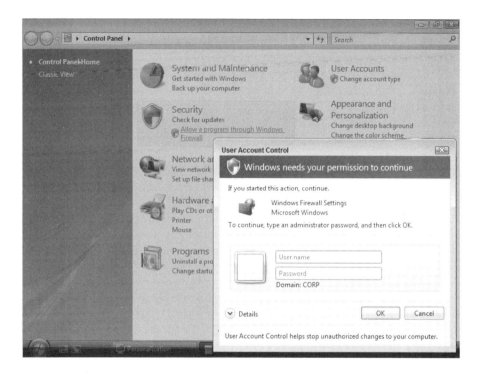

In UAC parlance, a mere-mortal, or regular user, is officially called a *Standard User*. There are three types of prompts you might get when UAC is active:

- Teal bar plus a shield: This program is a part of Windows Vista.

- Gray plus a shield with an exclamation mark: This is signed and trusted by Windows Vista. Trusted means that the certificate used to sign the application "chains" to a certificate in the computer's "Trusted Root Certification Store." Note: the Trusted Root Certificate Store can also be managed via Group Policy.

- Orange plus a shield with an exclamation mark: This program isn't part of Windows Vista and is either unsigned or Signed but not yet Trusted.

And, at first blush, you might be right. It might be annoying to provide that one extra click or provide alternate credentials. But, the underlying idea of UAC is a really good one.

In the short term, you might see the UAC prompts a lot. That's because when you're first configuring Windows Vista, there will be a lot of "system wide" changes you'll want to make. But over time, how often are you really making those kinds of changes? Once the computer is configured for your specific environment and the bulk of the software is installed, you will rarely ever see a UAC dialog again.

That is, for regular users, they need permissions to do the more privileged operations on a Windows Vista machine.

Additionally, when you log on as an Administrator (local or Domain Administrator), you get "stripped" of your admin rights until you click to say you want to leverage them. UAC's goal is to implement the "Principle of Least Privilege": only use privileged user rights when needed.

The UAC prompts leverage of a technology called UIPI (UI Process Isolation) and another called MIC (Mandatory Integrity Levels). The idea is that the operating system is protected from nonprivileged processes. Only certain types of Windows messages and input are permitted to interact with this dialog. Therefore, previous attacks where the malware would simply click the security dialog before the user ever saw the prompt are thwarted—only privileged processes can interact with the UAC dialogs. This helps prevent what is known as "process injection" and "shatter attacks."

What's the upshot? Sure, it's one extra click (as an admin) or a user must provide credentials. But what's the benefit? In short, even for admins you get the benefit of not doing something potentially harmful because there's one extra click in the way. (How many times have you wished you could have taken an extra "beat" before doing something potentially harmful?)

The other big goodness is that all applications run without admin privilege by default; therefore, scenarios like web browsing and e-mail become much more secure without any changes to the applications. You cannot have "Protected Mode IE" without UAC.

So, I encourage you to find it in your heart to try and love this feature. Here's the idea: you want all your users to run as "Standard User" (those who have heard me speak will know I refer to these folks as "mere-mortals"). That is, they are in the local Users group of the workstation or in the Domain Users group and not in the local Administrators group of the workstation or the Domain Admins group in the domain. In short: they're just users. Additionally, if you want to throw some numbers at the managers in your corporations, the Gartner Group states that running your enterprise Desktops as a Standard user can reduce TCO by as much as 40 percent versus running that same Desktop with administrative credentials. The idea is that if the user, I mean, administrator of that local machine could just stop making all those darned changes, you would be at their desk fixing their computer a whole lot less. Get it?

Take a quick gander at the general UAC document on Microsoft's website here:

www.microsoft.com/technet/windowsvista/security/uac.mspx

then come back and learn about the nine different Group Policy controls you have at your disposal to configure it the way you want it to work.

Finally, we'll wrap up our talk on UAC with some prescriptive guidance for certain scenarios to help you configure users based on what they're trying to accomplish.

 If you're starting to develop for Windows Vista, here's a tip. In the past versions of Windows, we ran by default as admin and therefore developed and tested as admin, the manifestation being applications developed this way tended to not work for the Standard User. Now, the idea is that your developers will be developing and testing as Standard User by default.

Just Who Will See the UAC Prompts, Anyway?

The point of UAC is to have "administrative" type users run as mere-mortals until they need to use their super-powers. To that end, you'll likely want to get a handle on just who is going to be affected by UAC prompts and have to run as mere-mortals on Windows Vista (until they elevate their credentials and use that super-power).

There are two categories of folks: anyone who's a member of some special Active Directory or SAM groups and anyone who has one of eight special rights.

Which Groups Are Affected by UAC

The 15 accounts and related SIDs which are affected by UAC are

- Built-in Administrators
- Power Users
- Account Operators
- Server Operators
- Print Operators
- Backup Operators
- RAS Servers Group
- NT 4 Application Compatibility Group
- Network Configuration Operators
- Cryptographic Operators
- Domain Administrators
- Domain Controllers
- Certificate Publishers
- Schema Administrators
- Enterprise Administrators
- Group Policy Administrators

UAC sometimes call these users "Split Token Users or Hybrid Users" as they have two user tokens (nonadmin and admin). See the sidebar "How Token Filtering/Split Token Works."

Elevated Rights and SE Privileges

If the user does not belong to any of the groups listed in the preceding section but has any of the privileges listed in Table 7.1, a filtered token will be created for the user with these privileges removed. These privileges are found in the Group Policy Object Editor in Computer Configuration ➤ Windows Settings ➤ Security Settings ➤ Local Policies ➤ User Rights Assignment.

You can get these rights from any level: Local, Site, Domain, or OU. Additionally, many rights are predefined in the default Group Policy Objects (discussed in the previous chapter).

T A B L E   7 . 1   Rights and SE names which generate a filtered token user experience

Right	"SE" name
Create a token object	SeCreateTokenPrivilege
Act as part of the operating system	SeTcbPrivilege
Take ownership of files or other objects	SeTakeOwnershipPrivilege
Back up files and directories	SeBackupPrivilege
Restore files and directories	SeRestorePrivilege
Debug programs	SeDebugPrivilege
Impersonate a client after authentication	SeImpersonatePrivilege
Modify an object label	SeRelabelPrivilege
Load and unload device drivers	SeLoadDriverPrivilege

You can check to see if a currently logged in user has one of these privileges by typing `whoami /priv` at a command prompt.

How Token Filtering/Split Token Works

If you log in with Domain Administrator rights to a Windows XP machine, you can "do" just about anything you want, including shooting your foot off, easily. This is because if you're assigned rights at some level of Active Directory or SAM, Windows XP just lets you use them. Sounds good, until you start making a mistake while web surfing or using e-mail.

In Windows Vista, things get a little more cautious. Again, the idea in Windows Vista is that if you're a member of one of the special groups, listed in Table 7.1, you will get a "split token." That means that in your daily life, you're running around as a mere-mortal. When you need to rip off your shirt and become Superman, you can do that too—but you have to find a close phone booth, er, UAC prompt to help you with that.

So, for instance, if a user is a member of the Administrators group, the filtered token will have the Administrators group membership set to DENY ONLY. Yep, you read that right. As they're running around as a mere-mortal, anything they try to do on the system is expressly Denied.

Meanwhile, a second protection mechanism kicks in. All the machine-impacting privileges are removed from the token. Therefore, as the Domain Administrator is going about his daily life on a Windows Vista machine, when he starts up things like `explorer.exe`, it's using a nonelevated process token.

You can look at this token using whomai.exe, which is included in Windows Vista. First run whoami /groups in a Command window when logged in as Domain Administrator, as shown here.

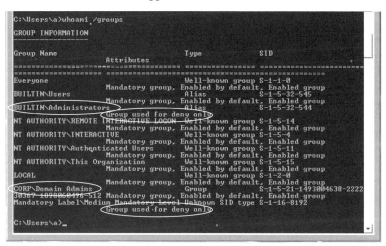

If you look closely you'll see the BUILTIN\Administrators and the CORP\Domain Admins group both have a special "Deny" token—just for them. Kooky! Again, this is reinstated once UAC prompts are satisfied.

Additionally, you can see what privileges are being used at any time with whoami /priv, as shown here.

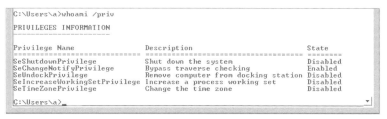

Compare this to the whoami /priv command when run on a Windows XP machine shown here:

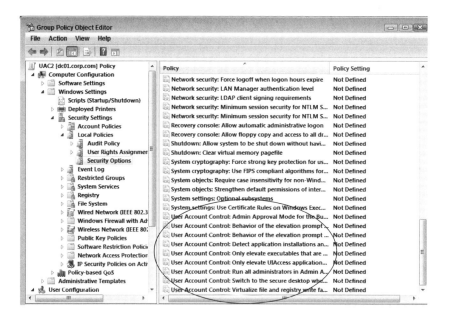

So, Windows XP doesn't "filter" anything. Windows Vista goes the extra mile to strip out unused rights until you actually need them. Note the whoami tool isn't built into Windows XP like it is in Windows Vista. You can load the whoami tool from the Windows XP support tools here: http://tinyurl.com/4uhnu.

Understanding the Group Policy Controls for UAC

There are nine Group Policy controls for UAC. They are all found within Computer Configuration ➤ Windows Settings ➤ Security Settings ➤ Local Policies ➤ Security Options and all start with the words "**User Account Control:**" as seen in Figure 7.7.

Let's examine each policy setting so you can decide if you want to change the default behavior.

FIGURE 7.7 The User Account Control entries are all found under Security Options.

What?? No Usable Local Administrator Account on Windows Vista?

By default, the Windows Vista built-in Administrator account is disabled. Yep, you read that right—there is no usable built-in Administrator account on Windows Vista. It's there, it's just disabled. Indeed, check out the following figure, where I'm simply typing net user administrator at a Windows Vista command prompt. Note that the "Account active" flag is set to "No."

However, if you create a new Windows Vista machine (that isn't joined to the domain), the first user you create by default has the equivalent permissions to a local administrator and all subsequent users are Standard Users—see the following figure where my first user on this fresh Windows Vista installation is named "User." Confusing, right?

So, be careful to whom you give that first local user account's name and password to. That first user account really has administrator rights! Yikes!

However, if, during setup, you join the domain directly, you won't have any local user accounts created, and hence, you won't have any accounts you can log on to as a local administrator. Of course, you could always log on to the Enterprise or Domain Administrator accounts (but we're talking about local accounts here).

So, what about that disabled local Administrator account? Well, again, you need to ask yourself: do you really need it? In a domain environment, you could always just log in a Domain Administrator. And, if the machine wasn't joined to the domain during setup, you could log in with that first user. So, all bases are covered.

But, if you really felt like you wanted to bring back that local Administrator account, you could do so. Historically, this account has been used for pure maintenance. That's why, by default, it's not enabled and has special behavior once enabled. So, before I tell you how to enable the local Administrator account, I want to explain a big ol' cautionary note: that is, the local Administrator account is exempt (by default) to all UAC prompts. Yep, all of them. So, if you enable this account and romp around within Windows Vista while using it, there are absolutely no safety checks. If you wanted to change this behavior, you would manipulate the User Account Control: Admin Approval Mode for the Built-in Administrator account policy setting.

Again, it's not recommended that you enable the local Administrator account, but if you wanted to, the command line you would type is:

```
net user administrator complexp@ssw0rd /active:yes
```

Again, I'm not suggesting you run out and enable all your local Administrator accounts. But, if you do have some "corporate wide" reason to do this, it would be wise to set a complex password during machine creation time (with an answer file).

But there's another way to enable the local Administrator account. Assuming the password is set on the local Administrator account (say, via the answer file at machine creation time), you can use Group Policy to just "turn it on." You'll find the setting to turn this on in Computer Configuration ➢ Windows Settings ➢ Security Settings ➢ Local Policies ➢ Security Options ➢ **Accounts: Administrator account status**.

By the way, you might be wondering what happens if your Windows XP machine is upgraded to Windows Vista? The short answer: if you have no other enabled accounts except Administrator, it will leave the Administrator account there but force it to use UAC prompting like all other accounts.

Before we finish off talking about the local Administrator account, there is one more local Administrator–related change you need to be aware of. In pre-Windows Vista, you could, if you wanted to, boot into Safe Mode logon with the *disabled* built-in Administrator account. Don't know why you'd want to, but it was possible.

Because Windows Vista is trying to encourage Standard Users on desktops (in businesses) and engaging Parental Controls (in the home), Safe Mode had to go under some security changes:

On Workgroup or Nondomain Joined Computers

If there is at least one active local Administrator account, Safe Mode will not allow logon via the disabled built-in Administrator account. But, there's no issue logging in with any active Administrator account. If there are no other local Administrator accounts that are active, Safe Mode will allow the disabled built-in Administrator account to logon for disaster recovery. From that point, it is suggested that a new Administrator account is created before rebooting the computer.

On Domain Joined Computers

The disabled built-in Administrator account cannot log on in Safe Mode under any circumstances. Here's where it gets tricky: if a user whose account is also in the Domain Administrators account has ever logged in to that machine before, they can log in again, no problem, using Safe Mode. But what if no one from the Domain Administrators group has ever logged on to that machine? Then, the computer must be started in "Safe Mode with Networking" since the credentials will not have been cached. Hopefully, Windows Vista will not be "so broken" that networking support won't work in this case. If the machine is disjoined from the domain, it reverts back to the nondomain joined behavior.

User Account Control: Admin Approval Mode for the Built-in Administrator account

As we've already discussed, both users and administrators have to "say yes" or provide administrator credentials.

 Only admins can say "yes." Standard users must obtain administrator credentials. Standard users cannot just say "yes."

This prevents them from doing things that could be potentially harmful to the machine. So, this setting dictates the "Admin Approval mode" for the Built-in Administrator account. What built-in Administrator account? Check out the sidebar titled "What?? No Usable Local Administrator Account on Windows Vista?"

If you choose to enable this built-in Administrator account, this policy setting affects this account.

Enabled   By enabling this setting, the built-in Administrator will be forced to honor UAC prompts.

Disabled (Default)   By default if you choose to leave this feature disabled (the default) and log in with the local Administrator account, then that account is exempt from UAC prompts.

User Account Control: Behavior of the Elevation Prompt for Administrators in Admin Approval Mode

As stated, even if you log on as a domain Admin to a local Windows Vista box, you're still going to get UAC prompts.

Actually, if you log on with any of 15 different privileged SIDs or 8 user rights, you'll get UAC prompts as an Admin. Or, if you log in with any of 8 user rights, you're also going to see the prompts.

We saw these accounts in a list earlier in this chapter and the user rights in Table 7.1.

This policy setting controls how, when logging in as a member of one of those groups or with one of those rights, you'll see prompts.

If you're an admin, the system already knows you're an admin. It won't (by default) re-ask you to supply credentials. It will, however, ask you (essentially) to acknowledge you're about to do a potentially harmful or impactful thing, like installation of an application or creating a new user.

Prompt for consent (default)   Because you're already an admin, by default you don't need to resupply your username and password.

Prompt for credentials   This requires an admin to re-enter their username and password or provide the username and password of any other Administrator account.

Elevate without prompting   Use with caution: this will silently say "yes" to any prompt if you're logged in as an admin. Microsoft suggests that this only be used in the most secure (they call it *constrained*) environments.

User Account Control: Behavior of the Elevation Prompt for Standard Users

As expected, mere-mortals have to supply some additional credentials to perform administrative tasks. When will mere-mortals be asked for administrative credentials?

Prompt for credentials (default)   Users logging in to nondomain joined machines will always be prompted for administrative credentials. If the user enters valid administrative credentials, the user will be permitted to perform. Note the policy setting Explaintext says "Default for home," but it's really default for everyone.

Automatically deny elevation requests   If users shouldn't access stuff that they shouldn't, why even prompt for credentials? If you set this policy setting to "Automatically deny elevation requests" the user will simply get an "Access Denied" anytime they try to do something privileged. We discuss this a bit later in our "UAC Policy Setting Suggestions" section.

This setting's Explaintext says "Default for enterprise," but it's really a "strong suggestion" for the enterprise. See the scenarios a little later for more information about why this is recommended.

User Account Control: Detect Application Installations and Prompt for Elevation

This security setting determines the behavior of application installation detection for the entire system.

Enabled (default)   Applications that start with the words "setu" (yes, that's right, "setu," as in `setup.exe`, `setupnow.exe`, and others), "instal" (yes, again, it's "instal"), or "update" will be automatically detected by UAC and prompted for credentials. Note the policy setting Explaintext says "Default for home," but it's really default for everyone.

Disabled   If you're using GPSI or SMS to deploy your software, this feature isn't needed. It's really only required when Junior or Grandma tries to run `setup.exe` for EvilApp6. GPSI and SMS automatically work around this, so you can safely set this to "Disabled" here if you want to.

This policy setting says "Default for enterprise," but it's really a "strong suggestion" for the enterprise. See the scenarios a little later for more information about why this is recommended.

User Account Control: Only Elevate Executables that are Signed and Validated

You can set up UAC such that applications only run if they are digitally signed via a PKI (Public Key Infrastructure) and Trusted. Enterprise administrators can control the allowed applications list by populating certificates in the local computer's Trusted Root Store.

    Population of this store is supported by Group Policy.

Enabled   Only applications signed by a trusted PKI certificate are permitted to run.

Disabled (default)   Doesn't matter if the application is signed via PKI.

User Account Control: Only Elevate UIAccess Applications that are Installed in Secure Locations

IL (Integrity Level) or MIC (Mandatory Integrity Control Infrastructure) is a whole new concept in Windows Vista (and one that's simply too deep to go into here). In short, it lets certain users and programs have certain rights to files based on their "trust level." An ever-so-brief overview of MIC can be found here: `http://tinyurl.com/y8753w`, though decent online information on this subject is kind of hard to come by. (One such decent, but not online place, is Mark Minasi's new book *Administering Vista Security: The Big Surprises*, also by Sybex.)

Enabled (default)   Specifies that an application will only launch with "UIAccess integrity" if it resides in a secure location in the file system. The secure locations in Windows Vista are limited to the following directories:

- `\Program Files\`, including subdirectories
- `\Windows\system32\`
- `\Program Files (x86)\`, including subdirectories for 64-bit versions of Windows

Windows enforces a PKI signature check on any interactive application that requests execution with UIAccess integrity level regardless of the state of this security setting.

Disabled   An application will start with "UIAccess integrity" *even if it does not* reside in one of the three secure locations in the file system.

User Account Control: Run All Administrators in Admin Approval Mode

This is the "master switch" for UAC.

Enabled (default) If this setting is Enabled, all UAC prompts are possible (although they might not all happen based on other things you set). However, at least this switch needs to be Enabled. Changing this setting requires a system reboot.

Disabled If you Disable this policy, UAC and all of its supporting functionality just goes away. Not suggested.

The Security Center feature in Windows Vista will demonstrate that the overall security of the operating system has been reduced.

User Account Control: Switch to the Secure Desktop When Prompting for Elevation

When you try to perform any administrative task, including taking remote control of a PC, you are prompted for authorization. This security setting determines whether the elevation request will prompt for the interactive users desktop or the Secure Desktop.

You might be wondering what the difference is between prompting for the *Secure Desktop* versus the *Interactive Desktop*. The Secure Desktop only allows trusted SYSTEM processes to run on it, which means that an application must have already been approved by an Administrator to be installed and run with SYSTEM privilege. The Interactive Desktop allows USER processes to run, which doesn't require such high-level approval to install and run. The interesting part of all this is that it only requires USER-level privilege to spoof the user into believing he or she is seeing and/or clicking on something that really is being generated, legitimately, from Windows Vista. Therefore, by placing the elevation dialog on the Secure Desktop, only a highly-privileged process can hope to run there, which means that the dialog the user is seeing and interacting with is a genuine dialog that Windows Vista has generated (not some bad guy hoping you'll press OK).

 The Secure Desktop protects against input and output spoofing when a user interacts with the UAC elevation dialog.

Enabled (default) All elevation requests by default will go to the Secure Desktop. The Secure Desktop is used here as an "anti-spoofing" technology, so it is recommended that you leave this on.

Disabled All elevation requests will go to the interactive users desktop. In some specific cases (e.g., an enterprise that leverages Remote Assistance and doesn't allow their Standard Users the ability to approve an elevation request), it may be alright to disable this policy.

Virtualize File and Registry Write Failures to Per-User Locations

In Chapter 9, you'll learn about a new Windows Vista feature which "redirects" File and Registry changes so applications stop writing to "protected" Windows applications but just keep on working. The idea is that some applications might try to write to profile and Registry locations they really don't have access to.

So a Windows Vista system will redirect (or, as Microsoft calls them *Virtualize*) these writes to writable places in the profile and Registry. So, if an application tries to write application data to %ProgramFiles%, %Windir%, %Windir%\system32, or HKLM\Software\, this Virtualization feature kicks in and gently places the data into the kosher places in the file system and Registry.

This will happen automatically as a Standard User.

An administrator may choose to disable this feature—if she's sure she's running all Windows Vista–compliant applications. But how would you really be sure?

Enabled (default)   Facilitates the runtime redirection of application write failures to defined user locations for both the file system and registry.

Disabled   Applications that write data to protected locations will simply fail as they did in previous versions of Windows.

While virtualization is fully configurable, it is not usually required to change the defaults. The default settings for virtualization handles most applications' behaviors correctly. For more information see: http://tinyurl.com/hqmh5.

UAC Policy Setting Suggestions

There are nine UAC settings, which we just explored. That means you've got a lot of power to control UAC. As we stated, you really don't want to just "turn it off." You want to tune it based on your situation.

Let's examine some cases, the default behavior and some suggested remediations.

Case 1: Enterprise Desktop: Standard User (Who Gets Help Remotely When Needed)

This is the type of user who will never need to perform an elevated or privileged administrative task. This is the majority of users. If you need to help them, how will you? Likely, you'll simply use Remote Desktops and perform desktop management remotely.

Suggestion 1: Set UAC: Behavior of the elevation prompt for Standard Users to Disabled
If the user should never perform an administrative task, then why present them with the opportunity? By performing this simple change, they simply won't see the UAC prompts, and it will be denied. By performing this step, you're reducing the overall "attack surface."

Additionally, if users see the credential dialog, it can motivate the user to call the help desk and beg, beg, beg for a valid Administrator account. You don't want to get caught in this trap. You can eliminate this type of support call.

Suggestion 2: Set UAC: Switch to the Secure Desktop when prompting for elevation to Disabled   The Secure Desktop can be disabled if the logged on Standard User never elevates. The technology is designed to protect elevations; if the logged on user never elevates, the Secure Desktop protection is not needed.

Case 2: Enterprise Desktop: Standard User (Who Gets "Over the Shoulder Help" When Needed)

Some environments are such where the user puts in a request, the administrator walks over to the desk and, while the user is logged in, helps adjust or install applications. This is sometimes called "Over the Shoulder" (OTS) assistance. This can be in places like doctor and lawyer offices and other smaller places that occasionally need tuning.

Main Suggestion: UAC: Behavior of the elevation prompt for Standard Users set to Prompt for credentials   In smaller organizations it may be preferable to leave this policy enabled to facilitate administrative help without requiring the administrator to perform a Fast User Switch and log on as himself.

Case 3: Enterprise Desktop: Protected Administrator

This is the case where you've been just forced into giving Sally local administrative privileges on her own machine. You don't want to do it, but you have to for some reason. This can happen if Sally is already an administrator of her Windows XP machine before you upgrade it to Windows Vista.

In UAC parlance, Sally would be called a *Protected Administrator* because she is a user who is either directly or indirectly a member of the local administrators group of the client workstation.

Main Suggestion: All UAC policies at default   Windows Vista UAC policy defaults are optimized for the Protected Administrator user account type. Simply upgrade Sally's XP Desktop to Windows Vista, and the default UAC policies will enforce that the applications the previously ran on XP with administrative privileges now run with the equivalent privilege of a Standard User.

So now, your e-mail editor and web browser will no longer run with administrative privileges unnecessarily. Rejoice in attack surface reduction!

Case 4: Enterprise Desktop (Running Only Windows Vista "logo'd" Software)

I'm not holding my breath for this one in the near or mid term, because I know you're going to have lots of old and crusty software that isn't "Ready for Windows Vista."

Suggestions: Set **UAC: Behavior of the elevation prompt for Standard Users** to **Automatically deny elevation requests** to Disabled

Set **UAC: Switch to the secure desktop when prompting for elevation** to Disabled

Set **Virtualize file and registry write failures to per-user locations** to Disabled

If you are running applications that are designed for the Standard User you will not use nor require the virtualization feature. This feature was designed as legacy application compatibility mitigation but comes with a price.

Applications that leverage virtualization perform a "double read" when accessing data that could potentially be in a virtualized location.

So, if the application was installed to %ProgramFiles%\ApplicationX\ and under that folder is FileX and FileY, if during runtime ApplicationX modifies and saves FileY, this forces FileY to be virtualized to %userprofile%\..\..\VirtualStore\Program Files\ApplicationX\FileY.

The next time ApplicationX tries to access FileX it must first look in the user "VirtualStore" as FileX could have potentially been virtualized. If FileX is not found, it will then query the "real" %ProgramFiles%\ApplicationX\FileX.

That's going to be a performance hit. But with these settings, you would increase performance. Again, only a good idea if all the applications are Windows Vista-ized.

Case 5: Enterprise Desktop: Protected Administrator (All Applications Are Signed)

Again, this is more of a long term goal for you to reach in your environment. The goal is that all applications are signed by the organization and only a restricted set of "Application signing certificates" are trusted by the client computer.

Main Suggestion: Set Only elevate executables that are signed and validated to Enabled This configuration will ensure that only those applications that either ship with Windows Vista or are explicitly signed and trusted by the organization will be allowed to run with administrative rights.

 WARNING If you invoke an elevated cmd.exe "command host," you can then launch most applications from within the command host environment, thus bypassing this policy check.

Case 6: Power User–Style User Who Shares Computers with Standard Users

In this case, you would want the power user to be prompted when they do an administrative action. Give the right credentials, then, poof! They're in. But you also want to silently deny the regular user. Don't let them even see what they shouldn't play with.

Main Suggestion: Set Behavior of the elevation prompt for administrators in Admin Approval Mode set to Elevate without prompting If the user wants to gain the benefits of the "Split Token" but never see a UAC elevation dialog, then this configuration is better than disabling UAC all together.

Remember that when UAC is disabled, all of its supporting technologies are also disabled. In almost all cases this is not desirable.

There are rumors that some of the UAC functionality may change with Windows Vista + SP1. Additionally, there may be updates to some UAC Group Policy functionality, or perhaps even more Group Policy control for UAC. When this is all available, I'll have updates in my newsletter. So, be sure you're signed up at www.GPanswers.com/newsletter.

Configuring Windows Firewall with Group Policy

Windows XP, Windows Server 2003, and Windows Vista all have a firewall that you can enable if you want to. Actually, Windows XP and Windows Vista already have that firewall enabled.

But really, what's the point? The point of a firewall on your machine (whatever kind it is) is to allow certain kinds of traffic to pass through and certain kinds of traffic to be prevented. That's it. Nothing mysterious here about a firewall.

Windows XP/SP2 and Windows Vista turn on their respective firewall by default, filtering inbound communication. We saw this phenomenon in Chapter 2 when we tried to perform a "Group Policy Results" to our Windows XP or Windows Vista client system and got an RPC error (which is the same error we'd get if the machine were off). Note that Windows Server 2003/SP1 and Windows XP/SP2's firewall are functionally equivalent. However, Windows Server 2003/SP1's firewall is not turned on by default when the system is running. (It is, however, turned on by default, initially, if you're performing an integrated Windows Server 2003/SP1 installation, but that's another story.)

Windows Vista has a brand-spankin' new firewall and a killer updated way via Group Policy to control it. Let me jump to the end of the story and just declare right now that it's simply not possible for us to go into every possible thing you can do with the Windows Vista firewall with Group Policy. That's (at least) a whole book in and of itself.

My goal here is to get you acquainted with both the Windows XP and Windows Vista versions of the firewall vis-à-vis Group Policy. That way, when you know the underlying geeky firewall technology, protocols, encryption, certificates, etc., you'll be ready to implement it all because your Group Policy knowledge will be solid enough to allow you to do what you want.

The other big part is helping you understand precedence order. With a lot of things in Group Policy–land, understanding why a policy (Group Policy or IPsec policy or Connection Rule Policy, and so on) takes effect is paramount to being a master troubleshooter.

Again, the Windows Firewall is a big, big topic, and you should read everything you can get your hands on here: www.microsoft.com/windowsfirewall.

Before you go headlong into manipulating and changing the default firewall settings for Windows XP or Windows Vista, I recommend that you use caution. In other words, the firewall is, in fact, turned on by default for Windows XP/SP2 and Windows Vista (and off for Windows Server 2003/SP1). This is done for a reason.

It provides the most protection from the bad guys trying to infect and hack your Windows desktop machines, but keeps the traffic flowing to your server machines, which, presumably, you're paying attention to. So, if you're going to start opening up ports on your desktop machines (or kill the firewall altogether), please use these policy settings with caution. Know what you're changing and why you're changing it.

Again, the defaults are there for a reason!!!

Everything Old Is New Again: The Windows XP and Windows Vista Firewall Controls

Before we get too far down the pike here, do let me describe one potential pitfall about what's happened here in Windows Vista. That is, because Windows XP (and Windows Server 2003 for that matter) already had a firewall (with one set of Group Policy controls), and now that Windows Vista has an updated firewall (with an updated set of Group Policy controls), it can sometimes be a little confusing just what you're controlling and where you're supposed to go in the Group Policy Object Editor in order to control it.

Now there are two sets of firewall settings:

- The "older" Windows XP firewall settings (where both Windows XP and Windows Vista machines can embrace most of these settings)

- The "newer" Windows Vista firewall settings (where Windows XP may not know what to do).

Indeed, in Chapter 2, we used the policy named **Windows Firewall: Allow inbound remote administrative exception** when we wanted to allow the required ports on both Windows XP and Windows Vista to open up so we could perform a Group Policy Results analysis.

Yep, that one worked! But, I haven't tested all the Windows XP policy settings against a Windows Vista firewall. And, indeed, there's a more specific, targeted way to achieve the same goals with Windows Vista's new firewall.

So, my humble suggestion, before you start creating lots and lots of Group Policy Objects with Windows Firewall policies in them, is to name them as such based on what operating system they're supposed to target. Then, you have a very clearly named GPO which you can link to proper places in your hierarchy.

Therefore, I suggest you keep your GPOs separate. Have GPOs which only affect the Windows XP firewall and GPOs which only affect the Windows Vista firewall. In this example, you can see two GPOs linked to two OUs. We have "Sales Windows XP Firewall Policy" and "Sales Windows Vista Firewall Policy," and they're only affecting the specific type of computers inside the OUs. I think, in the long run, this is the cleanest and least-confusing path.

This might not always be possible, but it is by far the cleanest implementation

The other way to specify which GPOs affect which machines is via WMI filtering (explored in detail in Chapter 11). With WMI filters you can "target" a machine based on various characteristics. Once you've read that chapter and are comfortable, then come back here when ready. Here are the WMI queries you'll need to target a specific GPO to a specific machine type.

For Vista `Select * from Win32_OperatingSystem Where BuildNumber=6000`

For Windows XP `Select * from Win32_OperatingSystem Where BuildNumber =2600`

Manipulating the Windows XP and Windows Server 2003 Firewall

Most of the discussions in this particular section will revolve around trying to manipulate the Windows XP firewall (or Windows Server 2003 firewall, if you've enabled it). Again, as stated, most of the techniques we'll perform here should work just fine if the target machine is a Windows Vista. However, we'll explore the ins and outs of manipulating the Windows Vista firewall in the next section.

Domain vs. Standard Profiles for Windows XP and Windows Server 2003

If you dive down into the new firewall policy settings, contained within Computer Configuration ➢ Administrative Templates ➢ Network ➢ Network Connections ➢ Windows Firewall, you'll notice two branches: Domain Profile and Standard Profile. You can see this in Figure 7.8.

FIGURE 7.8 The Domain Profile is used when the machine can make contact to a Domain Controller. The Standard Profile is used when the machine is in a hotel room or at Starbucks, etc.

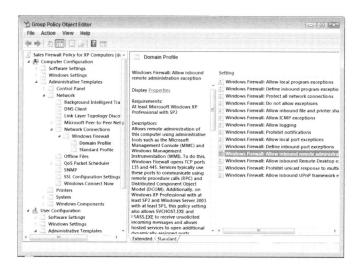

Inside each branch, you'll see a gaggle of settings that are exactly the same. So, what gives?

When policy settings within the Domain Profile are enabled, they affect the firewall when they make contact with Domain Controller. This is usually when a computer is at the central office and a normal logon occurs.

 In Windows XP the computer didn't actually need to authenticate to a Domain Controller for Domain Profile policy settings to kick in. In Windows Vista, authentication to a Domain Controller is required.

When policy settings within the "Standard Profile" are enabled, they affect the firewall when Windows *cannot* authenticate to a Domain Controller. This might happen when the user is in a hotel room, an Internet cafe, or other areas with public connectivity.

You might set up your Domain Profile settings to have additional port exceptions to be used by the central office administrative team for scanning and remote administration. And, you can leverage your "Standard Profile" settings to ensure the firewall is at its maximum enforcement. In short, you get to choose how strong the firewall will act in each of these circumstances.

Microsoft has a great little article on how the computer fundamentally determines if it should use the Domain Profile or the Standard Profile. Check it out here: http://tinyurl.com/cao73.

Again, these settings here are meant for the Windows XP/SP2 firewall, but should also work if a Windows Vista firewall gets these settings from a downloaded Group Policy. However, I haven't personally tested each and every one. Here are some tips if you choose to affect Windows Vista machines with Windows XP/SP2 settings:

- Standard Profile settings apply to both the private and public profiles for Windows Vista.

- If you configure the Windows Vista–specific firewall policy, then the Standard Profile settings will stop applying. The assumption is that if the computer is getting a new policy, you must have started using the new policy model.

- There's a known bug in the "allow local port" and "allow local program" settings when applied to Windows Vista. It might not always work when it should. There's a KB in progress. Stay tuned for an update on GPanswers.com.

Killing the Firewall for Windows XP and Windows Server 2003

There might be times when you just want to outright kill the Windows XP or Windows Vista firewall. Additionally, you can prevent an inadvertent mishap should someone try to enable it on Windows Server 2003/SP1!

In Chapter 2, I explained how to kill Windows XP's firewall (which works the same process for Windows Server 2003's firewall, though it isn't even on by default) or Windows Vista's firewall. Again, though, the recommended course for manipulating Windows Vista's firewall will be discussed later, even though this technique will, in fact, work.

To kill the XP/SP2 or Windows Vista firewall, drill down to Administrative Templates ➢ Network ➢ Network Connections ➢ Windows Firewall ➢ Domain Profile and select **Windows Firewall: Protect All Network Connections**. But here's the thing. You don't choose to

Enable this policy. No, no. You *Disable* it. Yes, you read that right—you Disable it. Read the Explaintext help inside the policy for more information on specific usage examples.

Before you up and do this though, do remember it's a better idea to leave it on and just filter based on the traffic you know you want. Only kill the firewall as a last resort.

Opening Specific Ports, Managing Exceptions, and More for Windows XP and Windows Server 2003

Microsoft did a lot of the hard work for me. That is, they've put together a stellar document in how to fully manage all aspects of your Windows XP/SP2 (and Windows Server 2003/SP1) firewall with Group Policy. By using the techniques Microsoft provides, you'll be able to have very granular control over how the firewall is used in your company (and when users are away from your company).

You can learn how to open specific ports, make specific program exceptions, turn on logging, and more.

For more information about deploying Windows Firewall, see "Deploying Windows Firewall Settings for Microsoft Windows XP with Service Pack 2" on the Microsoft Download Center website at `http://tinyurl.com/a8bfc`. An additionally excellent article can be found here: `www.microsoft.com/technet/community/columns/cableguy/cg0106.mspx` (shortened to `http://tinyurl.com/ujg25`).

Windows Firewall with Advanced Security (for Windows Vista)—WFAS

In this section we'll take a bite-sized tour of what we can do with the updated Windows Firewall with Advanced Security for Windows Vista, or just WFAS for short.

WFAS's two "prime directives" in life are to:

- Block all incoming traffic (unless it is requested or it matches a configured rule)

- Allow all outgoing traffic (unless it matches a configured rule to prevent it)

As you go along in these examples, you'll see UI references to "Location" type (which can be "Domain Location," "Public Location," and "Private Location." To help you understand Network Location Types, be sure to read this article: `www.microsoft.com/technet/community/columns/cableguy/cg0906` `.mspx` (`http://tinyurl.com/ykmp9r`). Because the Windows Vista machines we'll be manipulating are joined to the domain, they will be considered a part of the "Domain Location" where we can control the WFAS via Group Policy.

Additionally, the IP security (IPsec) function (discussed in more detail next) is also part of WFAS (where it was a separate node of the UI in the Group Policy Object Editor for pre-Vista management stations). We'll see how this all fits together as we work through this section.

Holy Cow! Three Ways to Set WFAS Settings!

There are actually three different *stores* for Windows Firewall for Advanced Security policies and four different ways to make that happen:

- The Active Directory–based Group Policy you know and love

- Local Group Policy accessible via gpedit.msc

and

- By running WF.MSC, which opens a GUI to the "local WSAF store"

Here's where it gets confusing, so stay with me here: the store hosting rules from WF.MSC and from Local Group Policy are in fact *separate*.

If you crack open WF.MSC, you'll see that there are a number of default rules in WF.MSC (as seen here).

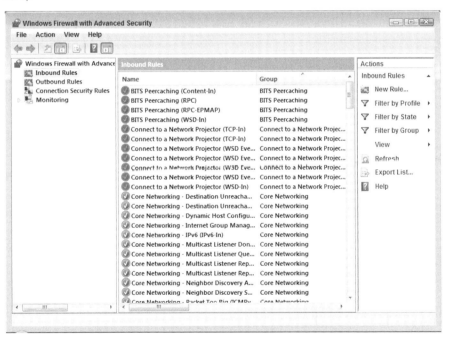

But open the Local Group Policy editor, and you won't see those rules at all!

You can also see this behavior via the command line. The command is: Netsh (then press Enter) advfirewall (then press Enter). Once inside, you can poke around. This is the command-line interface for all the goodies you're looking at in the Group Policy Editor.

By default you're poking around the "local Windows Firewall store" (the same thing you'd see when you use WF.MSC), but you can use the set store command to change focus to, say, the local GPO or even an Active Directory–based GPO. The idea is that once you've "set store" to another place, say a particular GPO, you can do everything via the command line you could do via the GUI.

Nice touch!

Getting Started with WFAS "Properties"

The first place you might want to check out on your WFAS journey is the "Properties" of the WFAS node. Now, I say "Properties" with quotes because there isn't a precise name for them. But, I'll call them "WFAS Properties" for our purposes. You find them by right-clicking over the "Windows Firewall with Advanced Security" node (with the little brick and the world icon) and selecting Properties as seen in Figure 7.9.

FIGURE 7.9   The Windows Firewall with Advanced Security has "Group Policy–like" properties inside.

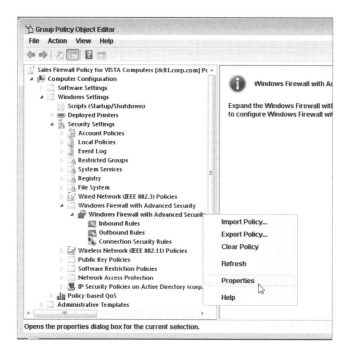

Once there, you'll have lots of settings to play with. These settings specify certain behavior types based on how the machine is connected and some IPsec Settings. You can see this in Figure 7.10. However, the trick about *all* of the WFAS Properties settings is that they act exactly like regular Administrative Templates policies. So, recall how in all Administrative Templates policy settings there is an "Enabled," "Not Configured," and "Disabled" ability? Well, all the settings contained here work exactly the same way across multiple GPOs if configured. You can see an example of a subproperties page in Figure 7.10 where it demonstrates "Yes," "No," and "Not Configured." Each setting also displays the default setting if you do nothing (which is a nice touch).

FIGURE 7.10 Imagine all the settings in the WFAS Properties are just like Administrative Templates settings in other areas of Group Policy.

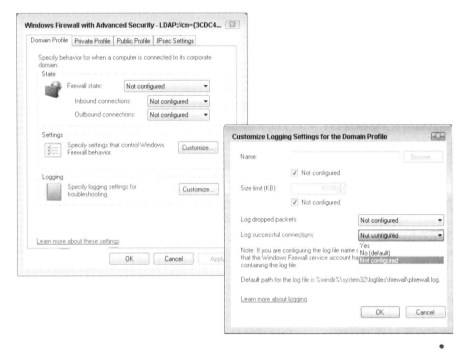

Again, the point is that all the settings contained at this level are just like normal, everyday, garden variety Group Policy. If stored at the Local or domain-based levels, the regular Group Policy precedence rules will apply.

What we'll learn about *next* is a little different, because, while it uses the Group Policy interface, it's not exactly got the same "Group Policy rule precedence" that you've come to know and love with the kinds of settings in here. Stay tuned, I'll try to explain it as we learn more and more, and then wrap up our discussion about WFAS with an overall cheat-sheet to help you get which rules come from where and what will win.

Creating New Inbound and Outbound Rules with the WFAS

WFAS is updated to support a neat-o keen new UI as well as some amazing under the hood features. Again, we simply don't have room to go over everything, so we'll have to make due with a brief tour. One important point to note is that WFAS has both inbound and outbound rules (where Windows XP's firewall only had inbound rules). You can see where to create rules in Figure 7.11 and simply right-click over the rule type to create a New Rule.

FIGURE 7.11   Once you locate the Inbound and Outbound Rules nodes, you can right-click to select "New Rule"

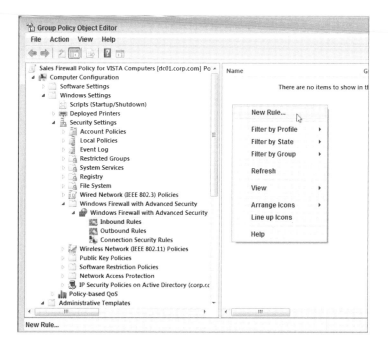

Inbound Rules   The goal of inbound rules is to prevent the bad stuff from reaching your machine and only allow traffic you request to reach you. This is the kind of thing most firewalls are used for.

Outbound Rules   At first blush, outbound rules seem counterintuitive. Why would you ever want to restrict outbound communication, right? Well, you might want to lock down a workstation from opening connections outbound to particular services. For example, you might have a specialty workstation which is only supposed to be used as a web-browser machine. Well, you can then lock out all outbound remote ports except port 80 (HTTP) and 443 (SSL/HTTPs). This would potentially allow you to squelch a virus or malware program that was trying to "phone home" or otherwise be a baddie. (Note this only works if you lock out remote ports. If you locked out the local ports, this trick won't work.)

Connection Security Rules   These rules dictate if this machine is going to be able to talk to other machines at all. You can create all kinds of rules here, including only being able to talk with machines that are on the same domain, or just enable specific machine-to-machine contact. This is the new way to perform IPsec rules, though there's little mention of the word "IPsec," actually. Additionally, there are settings here which work in conjunction with an advanced feature (which we cannot cover here) called "Network Access Protection" (or NAP). The idea is that if your machine doesn't meet certain criteria, then it shouldn't be allowed to talk with its other brothers and sisters. This is configured via the NAP MMC snap-in. Learn more about NAP at www.microsoft.com/nap.

The rules you create should be ignored by pre-Vista machines (such as Windows XP). Be sure to read the sidebar entitled "Everything Old Is New Again: The Windows XP and Windows Vista Firewall Controls."

Inbound and Outbound Rule Types

Once you've elected to create a rule, there are four kinds of rule types to choose from, as seen in Figure 7.12.

Program   You can actually dictate which programs (specified by path and executable name) you want to allow traffic to flow between. You need to also specify an action (Allow, Block, or "Allow the connection if it is secure"). Note that the "Allow the connection if it is secure" setting requires a valid connection security configuration as well as IPsec rules deployed to handle the IPsec portion of the enforcement.

Port   This is a specific rule based upon TCP or UDP ports. You must also specify which ports (separated by commas). Specific ranges, say, 80–100, won't work unless individually listed with commas separating them.

Predefined   This will likely be where most people spend their time. This is a collection of "well known" services and which ports to open up if you want traffic to flow.

Custom   This is the kitchen sink. If you want to go whole-hog and tweak until you're blue in the face, this is the place for you. If you couldn't configure the settings using one of the other three ways, this is where you do it.

If you want to try this out for a Windows Vista machine, select Predefined, then use the pull-down to see the various Predefined options as seen in Figure 7.13. If we want to parallel the example in Chapter 2 (which Allowed Remote Inbound Administration Exception), we could simply select "Remote Administration" as seen in Figure 7.13.

By clicking Next in the wizard, you'll zip past all the predefined rules this will achieve, saving you oodles of time. Once the wizard is complete, you'll see the new inbound rule and its name, as seen in Figure 7.14. To see what that rule is really doing, just check out the Properties for each line item.

FIGURE 7.12   After creating an inbound or outbound rule, you must select the type. Most often, you'll select Predefined.

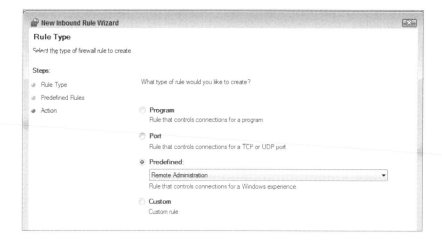

FIGURE 7.13   Use the Predefined rules to allow the kinds of "well known" traffic your people might need.

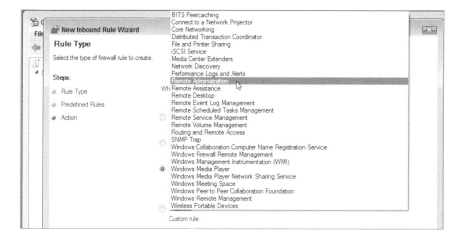

Connection Security Rules

In the previous example we leveraged an inbound rule to open up the Windows Vista firewall to allow a remote administration exception. And the procedure would be pretty similar if we wanted an outbound rule as well.

FIGURE 7.14   When the rule is complete, you'll see the results in the right pane.

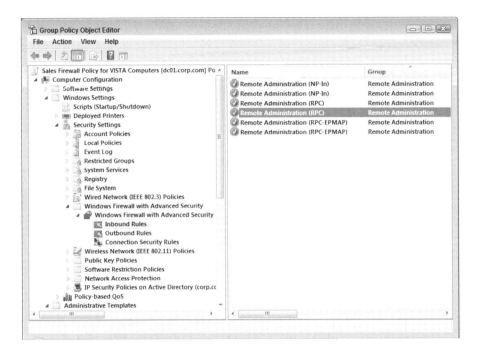

However, Connection Security rules are different. Connection Security rules define how and when computers authenticate using IPsec or Authenticated IP. Connection Security rules are used in establishing server and domain isolation, as well as in enforcing NAP policy.

These allow for you to specify which other computers you can talk with at all. Again, the idea here is to prevent your target machines from talking with the bad guys.

You can see the list of available Connection Security rule types in Figure 7.15.

More info on Authenticated IP at http://tinyurl.com/yelj7a. More information on rule types at http://tinyurl.com/yx4rkk.

Rule Precedence

What if you have multiple WFAS rules applying? Which WFAS rule is going "win" to restrict the traffic?

Additionally, what if you have multiple GPOs which affect this target machine with multiple rules? Turns out, it doesn't matter. All rules are simply "additive" amongst all GPOs—for the type of rule it is.

So, all Inbound Rules are all added up. All Outbound Rules are all added up, and so on. What you might care about is what if there's a conflict between, say, an Inbound Rule and an Outbound Rule. What will win there?

FIGURE 7.15 There is lots of flexibility in WFAS Security Rules.

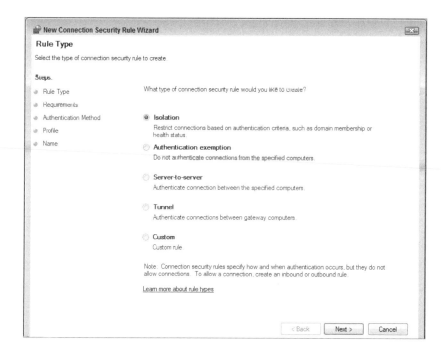

Again, the list of WFAS rules is merged from all sources and then processed in the order shown below from top to bottom. This rule process ordering is always enforced, regardless of the source of the rules:

1. **Windows Service Hardening.** This rule restricts services from establishing connections. These are generally automatically configured out-of-the-box so that Windows Services can only communicate in specific ways (that is, restricting allowable traffic through a specific port). However, until you create a firewall rule, traffic is not allowed.

2. **Connection security rules.** This type of rule defines how and when computers authenticate using IPsec. Connection security rules are used in establishing Server and Domain Isolation, as well as in enforcing NAP policy.

3. **Authenticated bypass rules.** This type of rule allows the connection of particular computers if the traffic is protected with IPsec, regardless of other inbound rules in place. Specified computers are allowed to bypass inbound rules that block traffic. For example, you could allow remote firewall administration from only *certain* computers by creating an "Authenticated bypass" rule for those computers. Or, you could enable support for Remote Assistance by the Help Desk *only* from the Help Desk computers.

4. **Block rules.** This type of rule explicitly blocks a particular type of incoming or outgoing traffic.

5. **Allow rules.** This type of rule explicitly allows a particular type of incoming or outgoing traffic.

IPsec (Now within Windows Vista's Firewall with Advanced Security)

The Internet Protocol security function, or IPsec for short, has a big job: secure the exchange of packets on your TCP/IP network. Its primary mission is host-to-host authentication. However, you can additionally choose to encrypt the traffic via Tunneling or Network Encryption so others can't "spy" on the data flying by.

Maybe you have one super-important Human Resources server. And you want to ensure that no one except the Human Resources people can talk with that server. That's IPsec's job: ensuring only the right people on the right computers can talk with the other computers you specify.

 IPsec is based on IKE. The RFCs on IKE only support the concept of Machine Authentication. Microsoft, however, has gone the extra mile and introduced an extension to IKE called Authenticated IP (AuthIP). This new ability introduces the ability to support *user* authentication *as well as* computer authentication. Additionally, the administrator can choose to use *both* user and computer authentication if desired.

IPsec General Resources

IPsec is a big, big topic, and not one we can cover in enormous detail here. However, my job for this section is to get you up to speed on Windows Vista's new implementation of IPsec and explain how "legacy" IPsec interacts with the "new" IPsec. So, if you're not familiar with IPsec and want to follow along, you'll have to spend some quality time at the following websites:

- `www.microsoft.com/ipsec` (`http://tinyurl.com/c7vuf`)

- `www.microsoft.com/sdisolation`

- A great document from Microsoft entitled "Introduction to Windows Firewall with Advanced Security" found at `http://tinyurl.com/yx4rkk`

- `www.microsoft.com/technet/itsolutions/network/evaluate/new_network.mspx` (`http://tinyurl.com/ydzhad`)

- `www.microsoft.com/windowsserver2003/techinfo/overview/netcomm.mspx` (`http://tinyurl.com/4x5y`)

I also recommend this excellent webcast from TechEd 2006 by Microsoft's Steve Riley which covers both the firewall and IPsec improvements: `http://tinyurl.com/yl4bw3`

Getting Started with IPsec in Windows Vista

Here's where it starts to get a little confusing. That's because there are two types of IPsec rules. I don't know if they have "proper" names, so we'll just call them "older" and "newer" rule types.

Older rule types are found in the node Computer Configuration ➤ Windows Settings ➤ Security Settings ➤ **IP Security Policies on Active Directory**.

Server and Domain Isolation with IPsec for Windows XP and Windows Vista

IPsec, at its core, restricts who is talking to whom. Okay, great. So, armed with that knowledge, you can take it to the next level and make sure that machines you know nothing about can't talk to machines you do.

For instance, imagine a consultant comes into your business with a laptop and plugs in. Chances are, with enough poking around, he could figure out your IP address scheme. Now he's able to ping servers and see what's going on over there on machines without a firewall. And, what if he brought a virus in with him from the cold, dark, outside world? Oops, you've got a problem.

To combat this, let's assume instead you want to create "rings of protection" amongst machines you trust and machines you really-really-trust. That's the idea of Server and Domain Isolation with IPsec. You can see the general idea here in this graphic.

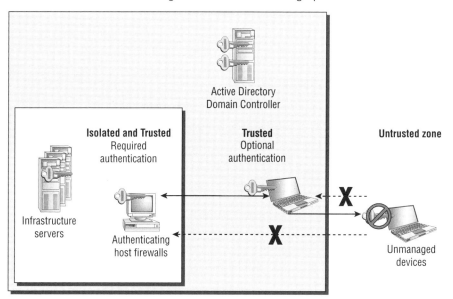

What sounds like a swell idea (and it is) can be a b-i-g project. Indeed, to protect your Windows XP, Windows 2000, and Windows Server 2003 machines from outside invaders (so they'll only talk with other machines you trust) takes about 300 pages of reading and implementing. You can find the big guide for this here:

www.microsoft.com/technet/security/guidance/architectureanddesign/ipsec/default.mspx (http://tinyurl.com/yywxas)

However, you can find a more general "clearinghouse" of Server and Domain Isolation goodies at Microsoft's website here: www.microsoft.com/sdisolation (http://tinyurl.com/zc74p).

> Again, it's something like 300 pages to do this for pre-Vista. But in Windows Vista it's going to be a lot simpler. Stay tuned from Microsoft for more Windows Vista–specific documentation to perform domain isolation.
>
> Finally, be sure to check out `http://support.microsoft.com/default.aspx/kb/914841`, where you'll find information on the Simple Policy Update which actually adds more Windows Server 2003 and Windows XP IPsec support—specifically to reduce the amount of IPsec filters you need to pull this off.

Newer rule types are found inside the new WFAS. Specifically, again, it's Computer Configuration ➢ Windows Settings ➢ Security Settings ➢ **Windows Firewall with Advanced Security**. You can see both nodes highlighted in Figure 7.16.

To configure "old" IPsec policies, you right-click **IP Security Policies on Active Directory** and select "Create IP Security Policy."

To configure "new" IPsec policies, you right-click **Connection Security rules** and just get started with "New Rule." If IPsec is required it will just automatically be part of that rule.

Note, advanced IPsec configurations may require some additional "global" settings. To do this, right-click **Windows Firewall with Advanced Security** and select Properties, then click the IPsec Settings as seen in Figure 7.16. Then, when you click the "Customize" button in the IPsec Settings tab, you'll have the range of additional IPsec options to play with as seen in Figure 7.17.

FIGURE 7.16   You can see both the "old" and "new" places to configure IPsec policies.

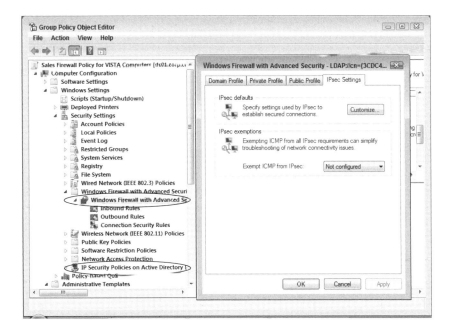

FIGURE 7.17 Some "base" IPsec settings for a GPO can be found in the "Windows Firewall with Advanced Security" properties.

Note that the "old" IPsec policies' "Default Response Rule" is not valid for Windows Vista machines. It will warn you of this if you try to create an IPsec policy using a Windows Vista management station. In short, don't mix old and new policies on the same computer.

Understanding how Windows Vista IPsec Rules work

There are now two types of IPsec rules that can be applied to a Windows Vista (and presumably a Windows Server Longhorn system). Again, we're calling these the "old" IPsec rules and the "new" IPsec rules here. The old IPsec rules are configured in the "IP Security Policy Management" MMC snap-in.

Old IPsec Rules These are IKE rules that only support machine-based Kerberos, x.509 certificates, and preshared key authentication. Old IKE-based rules are applied in the same way to Windows Vista as they were in pre-Windows Vista operating systems. That is, while multiple policies can be applied to a given machine, the last writer wins and there is no merging of IKE policy settings. So, if you had a policy set at the domain level and another set at the OU level, the OU level would "win" because there is no merging of any old IPsec rules.

New IPsec Rules Again, the new IPsec rules for Windows Vista (and Windows Server Longhorn) are found by using the WFAS. These rules are supported by an extension to IKE called "Authenticated IP" (AuthIP). As stated, a seriously good read on AuthIP can be found here: http://tinyurl.com/yelj7a. Here are some helpful tidbits as you explore the new Windows

Vista IPsec. These (really geeky) tidbits are coming (near-verbatim) from the IPsec team at Microsoft, so, thank them (not me) if you get a nice tip here.

- You can now leverage Interactive user, Kerberos/NTLMv2 credentials, User x.509 certificates, Machine X.509 certificates, NAP Health Certificates, and Anonymous Authentication (optional Authentication) for authenticating an IPsec connection.

- When configuring GPOs for connection security and firewall policies, you could disable the use of local firewall and connection security rules. That way, only the Group Policy linked to the site, domain, or OU GPOs could control the Windows Firewall behaviors. You can see where to do this in Figure 7.18 a bit later.

- Like other firewall and Group Policy rules, connection security rules are merged from all applicable GPOs (and processed according to the Rule Precedence list previously discussed).

- Connection Security policies can be configured to create both "old" (compatible) policies as well as Windows Vista and Windows Server Longhorn systems (see the sidebar entitled "Super-Geeky Note from the Microsoft IPsec Team #1: What's Going on Under the Hood").

- Only AuthIP policy is created for Windows Vista to Windows Vista (or Windows Vista to Windows Server Longhorn) because IKE doesn't support User Authentication. Again see the sidebar entitled "Super-Geeky Note from the Microsoft IPsec Team #1: What's Going on Under the Hood."

- As noted earlier, Connection Security rules are merged from all applicable GPOs. However there is a related group of settings for IPsec/Authenticated IP that manage the default IPsec behaviors that are not additive. The settings include the global authentication sets, Quick Mode and Key Exchange settings, and ICMP exemptions.

- On a Windows Vista client, Connection Security and IPsec rules can come from multiple GPOs. That is, all Connection Security rules on the client that make use of default auth/crypto sets will use the sets from the highest precedence GPO. If you need more flexibility, you have the three options: For authentication sets, configure the authentication through the Connection Security rule instead of using the default authentication. For Quick Mode crypto, use the command line `netsh advfirewall` to configure Quick Mode crypto settings on a per-Connection Security rule basis as needed. For Main Mode, only one set is supported per policy. In the case where multiple Main Mode crypto sets are received, the one from the highest precedence GPO will be applied to all Connection Security rules in the policy. There is unfortunately no way to customize the rules to use different Main Mode crypto sets.

> Honestly, these tips are more for the IPsec "superstars" out there than us normal people (me included), so don't panic if it's not 100 percent evident or relevant to your situation.

How Windows Firewall Rules Are Ultimately Calculated

Hopefully by now, you understand there are two categories of "things" that can be set by WFAS policy: properties and rules.

Super-Geeky Note from the Microsoft IPsec Team #1: What's Going on Under the Hood

On Vista, an admin can create IKE-based IPsec policies through the "IP Security Policy Management" snap-in. Additionally, on Vista, an admin can create Connection Security rules that will be compatible with down-level IKE-based policies.

So, when the policy is created, here's what's happening under the hood:

- If no Vista-specific features are required, the policy will be created with both a set of AuthIP (Vista) rules and a set of IKE rules for when the Vista system needs to connect to IKE-based 2000, XP, and 2003 systems.

- If there are Vista-specific features (like requiring the use of a second User Authentication), then the system will *not* create pre-Windows Vista IKE rules.

What? Why not?

Simple: Since IKE on XP can't do User Authentication, there's no need to create extra policies where only Windows Vista–specific features are used.

See! Told you this was geeky!

Super-Geeky Note from the Microsoft IPsec Team #2: Get the Right Certs to do the Right Job

There is a particular nuance with regard to certificates that you'll need to know about before you go headlong into using IPsec and AuthIP. Again, the IPsec/AuthIP policies which are created by WFAS will use AuthIP by preference.

- If both machines are Vista, then they'll use AuthIP to negotiate and authenticate

- If one of the two talking machines is pre-Windows Vista, then the system will use IKE-based functionality.

- AuthIP uses SSL certs with client and/or server authentication settings configured.

- SSL certs can be client authentication or client and server authentication certs. And, either should work.

What this means is that if you are constructing policies to use certificate authentication for Vista, you'll need certificates that will work with AuthIP. That means the certificates you deploy to the clients need to be SSL certs with client and/or server authentication (depending on if you want one-way or mutual authentication).

It should be noted that these certs differ from the standard digital certs used in Win XP/2003.

Precedence Order for Properties

Properties are found in three places:

- Running WF.MSC and right-clicking over the "Windows Firewall with Advanced Security" node (topmost node) and selecting Properties. This is the "local WFAS" store.

- Editing the local GPO of the machine and right-clicking over the "Windows Firewall Advanced Security Node" and selecting Properties.

- Creating a new Active Directory–based GPO, then right-clicking over the "Windows Firewall Advanced Security Node" and selecting Properties.

Again, these Properties all act like regular Group Policy Administrative Template settings.

Now, the one thing I waited to explain until now is this: you can "block" the local WFAS store from being added to the calculations. To do this, in any GPO that has Windows Firewall settings that apply to the computer, right-click the "Windows Firewall Advanced Security Node" and select Properties. Then, in, say, Domain Profile (or the other profiles), click Customize. Locate the "Rule Merging" section and select "No" as seen in Figure 7.18.

This will only block a rule merge. Or, additionally, you could choose "No" in the "Apply local connection security rules" to block those.

However, it should be noted that you could prevent a local admin from being able to control a property just by setting it in the GPO.

Again, the default is "Yes" that local WFAS store settings (and rules) would apply. Change this only if you do not want local rules to apply. However, do note that Windows Vista has a zillion built-in firewall rules. And, if you set this to "No" then all those rules suddenly—*poof*—turn off. And Windows Vista's default action would be to block all incoming traffic. And, to change this you would need to set specific rules (I suggest "Predefined rules") to allow which inbound traffic you would allow through.

FIGURE 7.18 You can block the application of the local WFAS firewall rules or local connection security rules by setting it in any Group Policy linked to the computer.

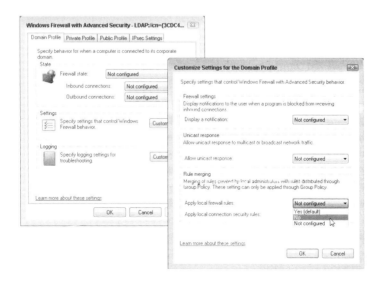

You could export the local WFAS store first, and then import it into a domain-based one if you so choose.

Precedence Order for Rules

We've already discussed "rule precedence" (see the "Rule Precedence" section earlier). Even though the specific "what rule will 'win'" aspect is pretty complicated, the overall Group Policy "rules" are pretty simple.

Basically, every Group Policy with any WFAS rules are simply added up. There isn't even really a concept of a "conflict" with WFAS rules, because the rules are just "separated" into buckets:

- So, all the Inbound Rules are added up from the local store, then all GPOs.
- Then, all the Outbound Rules are added up from the local store, then all GPOs.
- And all the Connection Security Rules are added up from the local store, then all GPOs.
- If there's a Deny/Block policy for *any* rule, that's always going to "win" for that rule type.

You can, if you want, disable the local WFAS store and ignore those rules. That way, you just guarantee that Group Policy is doing all the dirty work to configure everything. In my opinion, this seems like a good way to go, so you don't have to remember if there even is a local WFAS store.

Again, you can see how to kill the WFAS local store's rule application in Figure 7.18.

One final parting WFAS tip. If you check out the local WFAS editor by clicking Start and then typing **WF.MSC** in the "Start Search" dialog, you'll also have the ability to see the WFAS "monitor," which can be useful for troubleshooting.

Restricting Access to Hardware via Group Policy

You know it's true: those USB thumb-disk keys and removable media doo-dads make your personal life easier, but your professional life harder. You want a way to control which hardware devices can be installed and which can't.

Thank you, Group Policy, for coming to the rescue (as long as your target machine is a Windows Vista or Server Longhorn).

So, you could, if you wanted to, allow USB mice, but disallow USB disk-on-keys. You could allow CD-ROM readers, but not DVD-writers. You could allow Bluetooth but disallow PCMCIA.

You're in control, using Group Policy to secure your Windows Vista machines.

There are two sections in Group Policy to help you secure your hardware:

- Computer Configuration ➢ Administrative Templates ➢ System ➢ Removable Storage Access (seen in Figure 7.19)

and

- Computer Configuration ➢ Administrative Templates ➢ System ➢ Device Installation ➢ Device Installation Restriction (seen in Figure 7.20)

The first set (Removable Storage Access) is fairly self-explanatory: If you enable a policy setting for that kind of removable storage (CD/DVD, floppy, and so on), you can make it so that the whole device type cannot be read or written to. But it doesn't have the "superpower" the second set (Device Installation Restrictions) has.

FIGURE 7.19   There are some predefined hardware restrictions you can leverage in Group Policy.

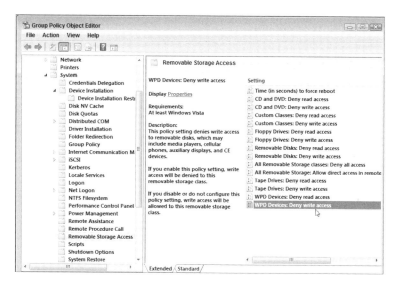

FIGURE 7.20   You can customize the kinds of hardware you want to restrict.

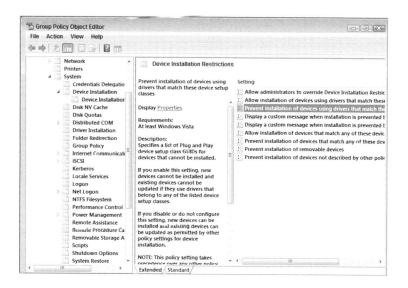

In the first set there is a policy setting group named **Custom Classes: Deny read access** and **Custom Classes: Deny write access.** It sounds like it has a similar ability to what we're about to explore. However, there is one difference. The Removable Storage Access policy set doesn't actually prevent the drivers from being installed. So, the driver for the class will be installed when the hardware is detected, but this policy prevents it from being read or written to. In the next section, when we explore the Device Installation Restrictions policy settings, we'll put the real smackdown on the driver itself.

Getting a Handle on Classes and IDs

First things first: you need to know what you want to restrict.

Think big.

Or small.

That's because you can restrict a specific "class" of devices or get super-specific and restrict a single hardware type. Or, you can do the converse, as well, and allow only specific device classes, like USB mice.

Here's the trick though: to really be effective you're going to need to track down the hardware you'll want to restrict.

So, if you want to say "No joystick drivers can be installed on my Windows Vista machines" and "Only USB mice can be installed on my Windows Vista machines," you'll likely need to get a hold of a joystick and a USB mouse. Now, this isn't always true. You can try to use the Internet to track down one of the following pieces of information:

- Hardware ID
- Compatible ID
- Device Class

But, it's much easier if you just have one of these devices in front of you. That way, you can introduce it to a Windows Vista machine and see for yourself what the Hardware ID, Compatible ID, or Device Class is. Once you know that, you'll know how to squash it (or leave it available).

In this example, we'll squash a specific sound card family: a "Creative AutoPCI ES1371/ ES1373." If you want to squash something else, (like specific USB devices, or even USB ports, and so on), just follow along and substitute the device you want.

To do this, fire up Device Manager on a machine that already has the hardware items installed. Then, when you find the device, right-click it and select Properties and select the Details tab. By default you'll see a "Device description." While interesting, it's not that useful. Select the Property drop-down and select "Hardware Ids" as seen in Figure 7.21.

The "Hardware Ids" page shows you from top to bottom the "most specific" to "least specific" device ID. If you look closely at the topmost item in the Hardware Ids value list, you'll see this sound card is specifically a "Rev 2" of the ES1371 sound board. That's pretty darned specific. As you go down the list, the description becomes less specific to encompass the whole family.

Additionally, you can also change the Property to "Compatible Ids." These also describe the hardware and are considered "less specific" than what you'll find in "Hardware Ids." You might choose to use the information found in "Compatible Ids" to try to corral more hardware that's similar into the "don't use" list—because it's less specific and might actually net you more results. Of course, the tradeoff is always that you might restrict something you didn't want to as you get less specific.

FIGURE 7.21 The Details tab of the device helps you determine how to squash it.

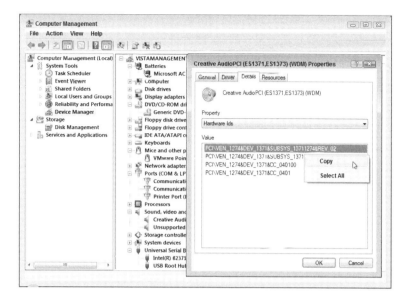

And, finally, the least specific category can be found by selecting "Device Class" from the Property drop-down. In my case, the sound card shows up as simply "Media." But lots of things could be considered Media, so, again, caution should be used the less specific you go.

Once you've decided on which value you want to leverage, right-click it, select Copy, and paste it into Notepad for safekeeping. Copying it directly as it's presented is important because in the next steps, the value must be entered exactly. If there are upper- and lowercase characters in the value, they must be transferred precisely.

 If you wanted to be a command-line commando instead of using the Device Manager to capture the Hardware Ids or Device Classes, check out the "Devcon" command-line utility at http://support.microsoft.com/kb/311272.

 Microsoft has a bunch of identifiers for common classes here which may be helpful if you don't have any physical access to the device: http://go.microsoft.com/fwlink/?LinkId=52665.

Restricting or Allowing Your Hardware via Group Policy

While we'll explore all the policy settings located in Computer Configuration ➢ Administrative Templates ➢ System ➢ Device Installation ➢ Device Installation Restriction (seen in Figure 7.22), there is really only one we'll need to complete this initial example.

FIGURE 7.22 Paste the device ID to ensure you've captured the device description exactly.

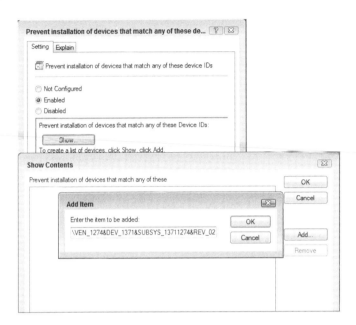

Create a GPO and link it to an OU (or domain, and so on) which contains the Windows Vista machines you want to control. Then edit the GPO and drive down into Computer Configuration ➤ Administrative Templates ➤ System ➤ Device Installation ➤ Device Installation Restriction ➤ **Prevent installation of devices that match any of these device IDs.** Select Enabled in the policy setting, click Show (also in the policy setting), and select Add in the "Show Contents" dialog. Then in the "Add Item" dialog box, paste in the information from the device you got before. All this can be seen in Figure 7.22.

Now, before we go on, here's the trick: if a machine already has the device installed, it doesn't magically uninstall and restrict access to the device. So, if you're going to restrict hardware, I suggest you do this early in your Windows Vista deployment.

When you turn on a machine which has never seen the hardware device before, you'll see the machine try to install the hardware device and provide pop-up balloon status information as to its progress. When completed, the goal is that the hardware is restricted, as seen in Figure 7.23.

Understanding the Remaining Policy Settings for Hardware Restrictions

In the example we just went though, we squashed the use of just one device. You could, if you wanted, go the opposite route, which is restrict *all* hardware by default and allow only *some*. This can be done using the policy settings described next. Again, you can see a list of these policy settings in Figure 7.20, which shows the Computer Configuration ➤ Administrative Templates ➤ Device Installation ➤ Device Installation Restrictions branch of Group Policy.

FIGURE 7.23 When implemented properly, the device driver will be prevented from installing.

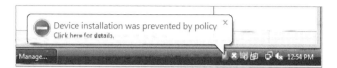

Allow Administrators to Override Device Installation Restrictions

By default, local administrators on the Windows Vista machine must honor the restrictions that are put in place. If you enable this setting, local administrators can install whatever hardware they want.

Allow Installation of Devices Using Drivers that Match These Setup Classes

By entering in device descriptions in this policy setting, you're expressly allowing these hardware devices as "allowed" into the system. Note this policy setting honors only setup classes and not device IDs (like those we used in the working example).

Prevent Installation of Devices Using Drivers that Match These Device Setup Classes

In the working example we used the Device Id to describe our hardware and used another policy setting, entitled **Prevent Installation of devices that match any of these device IDs.** It should be noted that the setting we used does not honor Class Id descriptions. To use Class ID descriptions you need to use this policy setting.

Display a Custom Message When Installation Is Prevented by Policy (Balloon Text) and (Balloon Title)

These are two policy settings to help you customize the message like what is seen in Figure 7.23.

Allow Installation of Devices that Match Any of These Device IDs

In the working example we used the Device Id to describe our hardware. However, I also stated that the least specific way to describe our hardware is based on hardware class. It should be noted that this policy setting does not honor Class ID descriptions. To use Class ID descriptions, use the policy settings **Allow installation of devices using drivers that match these device setup classes** or **Prevent installation of devices using drivers that match these device setup classes.**

This setting is best used with another setting entitled **Prevent installation of devices not described by other policy settings.** By preventing everything (by default) then using this setting you can specify precisely which devices you want to allow to be installed.

Prevent Installation of Devices that Match Any of These Device IDs

In the working example, this is the policy setting we used to restrict a specific type of hardware based on Device IDs. If we wanted to restrict using Device Classes, we would have to leverage other specific policy settings such as **Allow installation of devices using drivers that match these device setup classes** or **Prevent installation of devices using drivers that match these device setup classes.**

Prevent Installation of Removable Devices

This setting is a generic and quick way to restrict any hardware device which describes itself as "removable" including USB devices. I wouldn't count on this particular policy setting that often. Use the techniques described earlier to get moderately restrictive Device IDs and lock them down specifically. There's no telling what the hardware is telling Windows about itself to really be sure.

Prevent Installation of Devices not Described by Other Policy Settings

This is the "catch-all" policy setting to basically restrict all hardware, unless you've specifically dictated that something can install. This policy in conjunction with the various "Allow" policies (such as **Allow installation of devices that match any of these device IDs**) can make a really powerful combination to only allow the hardware you want in your environment.

Final Thoughts

Windows Vista brings a lot more new security goodies to the table. But it's Group Policy that's the delivery vehicle.

Let's review some fine points before we say *au revoir* to Group Policy and security:

- Windows XP has a wireless policy you can use right away. However, to use Windows Vista's wireless and wired policy, you need to upgrade the schema.

- Internet Explorer 7 has a lot of goodies to play with. And, they fixed my (least) favorite aspect of Internet Explorer. That is, when you clear out the proxy server setting, Internet Explorer 7 will recognize this and accommodate. Nice.

- User Accounts Control is a good thing. Don't turn it off entirely. However, use the information here to tweak it based on your situation so both you and your users can live with it.

- Windows XP and Windows Server 2003 have a built-in firewall. So does Windows Vista (and Server Longhorn). But the integration of both the firewall rules and IPsec together make a powerful combination and a real winner when it comes to setting up your networking rules.

- Restricting hardware is a good thing. But don't forget, just because you start to restrict hardware doesn't mean that users suddenly stop using hardware they've already installed. Again, the hardware restrictions we discussed only work for newly installed devices.

See you in the next chapter, where we talk about how to script your favorite Group Policy operations.

8

Scripting GPMC Operations

As you've seen in the preceding chapters, managing the daily operations of individual Group Policy Objects is simplified greatly through the Group Policy Management Console. However, we can make it even better. Through the magic of scripting, we can turn tasks that might take minutes into seconds. We can automate tasks and have them performed on a regular basis without us even showing up to work (even administrators have sick days, you know).

In this chapter, we're going to show you some of the nuts and bolts that make the GPMC work and how we can turn those bolts to meet our own needs. Once you get the hang of the GPMC objects and their methods, the sky is the limit to what you can script.

We are going to look at several time and labor saving options for the management of Group Policy through scripting. We'll start by explaining how the scripting model works with Group Policy and give you several functions that you can reuse in every Group Policy script. You'll find procedures for documenting your current Group Policy environment. You'll see how you can create and link GPOs to Active Directory containers. We'll even reveal how to automate the backing up and restoring of GPOs.

Many admins question the need for scripting in the modern GUI world. After all, why would I want to drop to a command prompt à la DOS when I can move my mouse around a pretty GUI interface and accomplish the same thing? The simple answer is that there is no single answer that applies to every administrator, so let's look at different reasons and find one that might apply to you.

Scripts give you repeatability in tasks. Regardless of who is running the script, it runs the same way every single time and the outcome is the same every time (barring unforeseen errors). Scripts also give you schedulability. (I don't know if that's really a word, but I'm going to use it anyway.) So, you can run a command-line script anytime, regardless of your normal work hours. If you need to perform a task and don't feel like coming in at midnight when no one else is on the system, you can schedule the script to run in your place.

Scripts can "remember" how to do the most esoteric task over and over again. Ever have "that problem" that needs to be addressed once in a blue moon? You know the one, you either have to look up how to fix it each time, or you have the KB articles tucked away in a folder whose name always escapes you. You can write a script that performs exactly the steps needed to perform the fix without any time wasted on looking up the solution for the umpteenth time.

Original information in this chapter by Bill Boswell. Revised and amended by Scott Fenstermacher.

And finally, one of my favorite rationales for scripting! Ever want to take a vacation but don't want to train someone in all your Group Policy knowledge for a two-week span? Scripts will let them hold down the fort while you slalom gracefully down a mountain of fresh powder (or work on your tan. To each his own, right?).

Most administrators find that once they start down the path of scripting, there's no looking back. There's no comparison between running a 30-second script and spending three to five minutes clicking around a GUI interface. A little work on the front end writing the script will save you hours of work on the back end.

To get the most out of this chapter, you'll want to be familiar with the VBScript scripting language. Due to space constraints, I can't present the full text of every script for you. I will show you the specifics of the script that perform the task at hand, but the full working scripts will be available for download from the publisher's website (`www.sybex.com`) as well as `www.GPanswers.com`.

Getting Started with GPMC Scripting

In this chapter, you're going to learn a little more than just vanilla VBScripts to do the job. To make you and your team more productive, I've added an extra cherry on top to our VBScript examples.

Normally, VBScripts are executed at the command line. But how about if we make it into a sexy web page? In short, you can create your own graphical applications using only scripts and HTML. The little gem to do this is called a HyperText Application, or HTA. You can have your graphical interface and scripts, too.

Inside HTA Scripts

HTA scripts are useful for a few reasons. First, you can double-click the HTA icon and go to work. None of this "open a command prompt and navigate to the right folder" drudgery. Second, it's graphical, which makes it easy for someone to simply fill in the blanks and get going without having to remember any esoteric command-line options. And finally, you can produce printed documents that are actually formatted and easy to read with one line of code!

In additional to command-line versions of our scripts, which are suitable for automation, we'll include an HTA that provides the same functionality. When you have a quick task to do, such as restoring a GPO from backup, you can jump into the HTA and accomplish the task quickly and efficiently.

The command-line scripts will use a format known as Windows Script Files (WSF). This is actually a format based on XML, with our primary script contained inside a script tag within the file. At first glance, you might think this will add more work to our script writing, but you'll see soon that it will actually make our new scripts shorter!

> **But I've Never Written an HTA Before!**
>
> HyperText applications are easier to write than you think. All you need to know is a little HTML and a little about Dynamic HTML. An HTA is really nothing more than an web page, formatted with the standard HTML tags such as <input> and <button>, plus a little VBScript on the side. Our HTAs will be short and sweet. We'll have a couple text boxes to enter the relevant information. Nearby, we'll have a button that starts the magic. That button will fire one of the VBScript functions embedded in the HTA. If any results are displayed, we'll simply format the output in some nice HTML and place it inside a <div> or <span> tag. No muss, no fuss, no strain, no pain.

The decision to present these scripts in both HTA and WSF formats can be summarized in one concept: the ability to include outside files. Both formats allow the script writer to take a file filled with functions and essentially "pull" those functions into a brand-new script. This is an invaluable tool for any programmer, regardless of their preferred language. First, we do not have to retype the same chunk of code over and over for every new script we write. Second, and perhaps most convincing, if we discover a flaw in one of those functions, we only have to fix it in *one* place rather than search for the flaw in several different scripts that might use that function. You will see this functionality in action in the coming pages.

> **What About PowerShell?**
>
> PowerShell, in case you've missed the hype, is a new scripting language from Microsoft, and a powerful beast of a scripting language it is. On the surface, PowerShell looks just like the shell scripting language employed by *nix systems. This is a good comparison because it uses the same principle of taking small utilities (in PowerShell, these are known as cmdlets) and piping them together to produce a result greater than the sum of its parts.
>
> These cmdlets are what put the power in PowerShell, but right now there isn't a series of cmdlets available for Group Policy management. Cmdlets will be shipping for each new server product shipping from Microsoft, such as Operations Manager and Configuration Manager. I'm sure Microsoft will see fit to release GP cmdlets soon. Until then, there isn't much synergy between Group Policy and PowerShell. But, stay tuned—the future looks bright.

Before Getting Started with GPMC Scripting

Jumping head first into scripting Group Policy objects is a dangerous proposition. We need to do a little looking before we leap. The GPMC object model runs deep, but there are some things it cannot do (at least by itself). So let's warm up with a look at the GPMC object model and scripting requirements.

The "Gotchas" of GPMC Scripting

First and foremost, you can only run these scripts on a machine that has the Group Policy Management Console installed. The GPMC application installs some libraries containing functions we are going to take advantage of. By this point in the book, we'll assume you already have that machine at hand with the GPMC installed.

GPMC scripts can manage Group Policy objects functions such as creating, deleting, and linking. One area of GPO management that is *missing* is the ability to actually manipulate the policy settings of the GPO itself. In other words, we can create the GPO via scripting, but you'll still need to dive into the Group Policy Editor and hand-edit (enable, disable, and configure) the policy settings themselves. One way to work around this limitation is to create your GPO in a test environment and import that GPO (after thoroughly testing it, obviously) into your production Active Directory network.

Scripting References

If you're new to scripting, this material might seem a little intimidating. You should not let that stop you though, as scripting is a skill more emphasized by the week by Microsoft. While I don't have the space to walk you through the basics of VBScript, I can give you some starting points for additional learning material. The following list will give you some books and websites to visit in your journey.

- *Microsoft Windows Scripting Self-Paced Learning Guide* (Microsoft Press) by Ed Wilson
- *VBScript Programmers Reference* (Wrox) by Adrian and Kathie Kingsley Hughes and Daniel Read
- *Microsoft WSH and VBScript Programming* (Premier Press) by Jerry Lee Ford
- *Learning VBScript* (O'Reilly) by Paul Lomax
- Microsoft Script Center, `www.microsoft.com/technet/scriptcenter`
- Scripting Answers, `www.scriptinganswers.com`

These will get you going down the path to VBScripting guru-hood, but they won't address how to work with the GPMC objects themselves. For that, you'll need other resources. The GPMC includes a compiled help file named `gpmc.chm`. This help file can be found on Windows XP or Windows 2003 in the folder `%Program Files%\GPMC\scripts` folder. While the GPMC included with Vista also contains this help file, it doesn't seem to include the scripts found in its XP cousin.

For a more concise view of the GPMC information, we can access the MSDN website for documentation. Visit `http://tinyurl.com/ouf8z` to start digging into the GPMC object model and the various capabilities of the GPMC objects.

One of the best resources for scripting the Windows universe is the Platform Software Development Kit (SDK). The Platform SDK Web Install can be downloaded at `http://tinyurl.com/cew8e`. However, before you jump to that link and start, be warned: this can result in a h-u-g-e download of information (depending on the options selected)—much more than you'll need for just the GPMC scripting information.

The Scripting Toolkit

To write scripts, all you need is Notepad. However, after a short period fixing fairly simple mistakes, you'll realize that the benefits of writing scripts in an Integrated Development Environment (IDE) will justify the cost. There are several good script editors available, each with different strengths, weaknesses, and price tags. Features to evaluate in a scripting editor include code coloring, automatic syntax completion, and drop-down object reference boxes.

In my opinion, the best script editor is PrimalScript from Sapien Technologies (`www.sapien.com`). It handles color-coding, syntax completion, and object references. It also includes a built-in wizard for building WMI queries and works with a number of scripting languages, including PowerShell. It also carries a price tag worthy of such a rich feature set.

Other editors for the more budget-conscious scripter include

- OnScript from XLNow (`www.onscript.com`)
- VbsEdit from Adersoft (`www.vbsedit.com`)

GPMC Object Model

Before we can discus scripting the GPMC objects, we have to know a little more about them. When the Group Policy Management Console was installed, it installed a set of COM object libraries on your machine. These libraries contain all the functionality used by the GPMC. These libraries also expose that functionality to languages such as VBScript and JavaScript through an automation object. Our plan is take advantage of those exposed functions for our own purposes.

The GPMC library is chock-full of functionality, more functionality than I have space to go into in a single chapter. Figure 8.1 shows an abbreviated hierarchy of GPMC objects available for our use.

FIGURE 8.1   The GPMC Object Model shows us the hierarchy of GPMC objects.

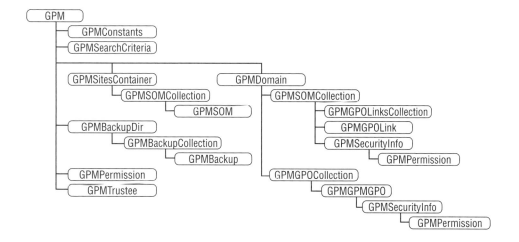

The main object we're going to work with in our scripts is the GPM (Group Policy Management) object. Through this object, we can create the other objects lower in the hierarchy, such as the GPMDomain object. As such, this will be the first GPMC object created in our scripts.

In the object model, the object GPMConstants deserves some special recognition. Constant values are used when we don't want to look up a particular integer value used as a flag by some function. Rather, a friendly name is assigned to that value, and that friendly name is used in our scripts to refer to the integer value. This object is going to supply a variety of constant values used by numerous other objects in the hierarchy, making our scripts not only easier to code, but also just plain easier to read.

You will also notice several objects identified as collections. A collection is a special object that contains a set of other objects, such as GPO or SOM objects. These objects are indexed by a sequence number. This collection object allows us to step through each individual object in the collection and process it according to our needs. In scripting, collection objects save us a lot of hassle when handling multiple objects.

Doing More by Scripting with the GPMC

In this book, you'll see some ways to perform various functions using the GPMC. But, in case you don't know the secret, the GPMC is really just built upon a big programming library. With enough elbow grease you could build the functions of the GPMC yourself (or, for that matter, build a whole GPMC-like tool of your own!).

To that end, we're going to show you some functions you could do in the GPMC by hand—but they'll be even better because they'll be automated.

The rest of the chapter will show you several different goodies you can do yourself to automate your various tasks around the GPMC.

So, let's check out the menu.

Common Group Policy Script Requirements

As you delve into the scripts in this chapter, you'll notice several recurring pieces of code. As previously mentioned, we will always need at least a GPM object in order to create the objects lower in the GPMC hierarchy. Along those lines, we'll use other objects with enough frequency to justify creating them right off the bat in our scripts.

In discussing the script formats earlier, I mentioned having the ability to pull outside script files into our new scripts. Since we are going to be creating these objects in each new GPMC script we write, it is now time to take advantage of that feature. We will take the following code and place it in a single VBScript file named GPMgmt.vbs, as shown here:

```
Dim gpm, gpmConstants, gpmDomain
Dim RootDSE, adsiDomain, dnsDomain
Dim adsiForestRoot, dnsForestRoot
```

```
' Global Subroutines and Functions
Sub CreateGPMObjects
Set gpm = CreateObject("gpmgmt.gpm")
Set gpmConstants = gpm.GetConstants
Set RootDSE = GetObject("LDAP://RootDSE")
adsiDomain = RootDSE.Get("defaultNamingContext")
dnsDomain = ConvertToDNS(adsiDomain)
adsiForestRoot = RootDSE.Get("rootDomainNamingContext")
dnsForestRoot = ConvertToDNS(adsiForestRoot)
Set gpmDomain = gpm.GetDomain(dnsDomain,"",gpmConstants.UsePDC)
End Sub
```

This code snippet gives us two things: first, it declares several variables right away, which makes them available throughout the entire scope of our script. Second, it gives us a single subroutine (CreateGPMObjects) to call when we are ready to start the Group Policy work in our scripts. In our scripts, we can make this code accessible by adding a single line to each file, as shown here:

For WSF files:

```
<script language="VBScript" src="GPMgmt.vbs" />
```

For HTA files:

```
<script language="VBScript" src="GPMgmt.vbs"></SCRIPT>
```

Virtually identical, aren't they? This makes it easier on us, which I'm definitely in favor of! The important part to note about both statements is the src attribute. Notice the lack of a path to the file? That means the GPMgmt.vbs file must reside in the same folder as our GPMC scripts. If you want to move the file to another location, you must change the path in the src attribute to point to the new location.

When you look inside the accompanying HTA files, you'll see an additional script included. This script is named HTA_Help.vbs and contains a few functions that make life easier when dealing with Dynamic HTML.

While we're working in the GPMgmt.vbs file, we should add a few additional functions as well. Occasionally, we're going to need to convert Active Directory paths (such as DC=corp,DC=com) into DNS names (corp.com). The ConvertToDNS function will do this for us:

```
Function ConvertToDNS (distinguishedName)
ConvertToDNS = Replace(Replace(distinguishedName,"DC=",""),",",".")
End Function
```

There are also a few types returned by GPMC functions that are associated with SOM types, trustee types, and access permissions, so I've added functions to convert these into something friendlier to read:

```
Function ConvertSOMType(SOMType)
Select Case SOMType
```

```
        Case gpmConstants.SOMDomain : ConvertSOMType = "Domain"
        Case gpmConstants.SOMOU :      ConvertSOMType = "OU"
        Case gpmConstants.SOMSite :    ConvertSOMType = "Site"
End Select
End Function


Function ConvertTrusteeType(trusteeValue)
Select Case trusteeValue
    Case 1 : ConvertTrusteeType = "User"
    Case 2 : ConvertTrusteeType = "Group"
    Case 3 : ConvertTrusteeType = "Domain"
    Case 4 : ConvertTrusteeType = "Domain Local Group"
    Case 5 : ConvertTrusteeType = "Well Known Group"
    Case 6 : ConvertTrusteeType = "Deleted Account"
    Case 7 : ConvertTrusteeType = "Invalid"
    Case 8 : ConvertTrusteeType = "Unknown"
    Case 9 : ConvertTrusteeType = "Computer"
End Select
End Function


Function ConvertAccessSetting(PermValue)
Select Case PermValue
    Case gpmConstants.PermGPOApply
        ConvertAccessSetting = "Apply"
    Case gpmConstants.PermGPOCustom
        ConvertAccessSetting = "Custom"
    Case gpmConstants.PermGPOEdit
        ConvertAccessSetting = "Edit"
    Case gpmConstants.PermGPOEditSecurityandDelete
        ConvertAccessSetting = "Edit and Delete"
    Case gpmConstants.PermGPORead
        ConvertAccessSetting = "Read"
End Select
End Function
```

Browsing through the GPMgmt.vbs file, you'll also see a few miscellaneous functions for dates and folder checks and the like but nothing groundbreaking. These are functions that we only want to write once and then use as needed. If you decide you want to customize these scripts, feel free to add your own functions to the script file or build your own and include it in your GPMC scripts.

Gathering Domain and Site Information

We're ready to do our first real "thing" with the GPMC scripting power.

To get our feet wet with the GPMC scripts, we'll tackle trying to discover some of the most basic information provided by the GPMDomain and GPMSitesContainer objects. This data can be gathered without any user input. You can use this data to be sure the system you are using is accessing the correct Active Directory domain and domain controller before proceeding with more advanced scripts. This script is our jumping off point for the rest of the scripts we'll explore in this chapter. The output will look something like this:

```
>cscript //nologo .\List_GPMC_Information.wsf


Here's a little information from the GPMDomain object:
This script uses PS1.corp.com in the corp.com domain to obtain its GPO
settings.


Here's a little information from the GPMSitesContainer object:
The forest root domain is corp.com.
This script obtains site settings from PS1.corp.com in the corp.com domain.
```

This output is from the command-line version of the script. The GPMDomain object is created by calling the CreateGPMObjects function. The GPMSitesContainer object is created through the GetSitesContainer function of the GPM object (also created when CreateGPMObjects is called). This function requires the DNS name of the container we want to examine, which in this case will be the forest root. A valid username and password can be supplied if the currently logged on Windows account does not have appropriate rights. With these two objects, we'll reference the properties that interest us and display them.

For this relatively short script, I'm going to include the entire WSF formatted script. Each script will begin and end with <job> tags (ending tags in XML will always have a forward slash preceding the tag name, such as </job>). WSF files can contain multiple jobs, but we'll stick with just one. The <comment> tags are optional but useful for easily adding update notes to the script file.

The main tags we are interested in are the <script> tags. The first <script> tag has two attributes, the first specifying the language of the script (VBScript) and the second specifying the location of the script (GPMgmt.vbs). This tag allows us to embed the GPMgmt.vbs script described earlier into our new scripts. Each script we create will use this same framework. We can even embed scripts written in a different language, such as JavaScript (as long as the scripting engine is installed on the client).

The second <script> tag is going to contain our new Group Policy script. This is where we're going to get down to the specific scripting details of each new task. So without further adieu, let's see how to extract information using the GPMC objects.

```
<job>
<comment>
```

```
Script : List_GPMC_Information.wsf
</comment>
<script language="VBScript" src="GPMgmt.vbs" />
<script language="VBScript">
CheckCScript
CreateGPMObjects

WScript.Echo "GPMDomain object information:"
With gpmDomain
    WScript.Echo "This script uses " & .DomainController _
        & " in the " & .Domain & " domain to obtain its GPO settings."
End With
WScript.Echo vbNL

Set gpmSitesContainer = gpm.GetSitesContainer(dnsForestRoot,"","",0)

WScript.Echo "GPMSitesContainer object information:"
With gpmSitesContainer
    WScript.Echo "The forest root domain is " & .forest & "."
    WScript.Echo "This script obtains site settings from " _
        & .DomainController & " in the " & .Domain & " domain."
End With
</script>
</job>
```

Starting at the top, the embedded script declares several variables and defines several functions that are going to be used in most of our GPMC scripts. The first of these functions, CheckCScript, simply looks at how the script is being executed. We want our scripts to execute using the CScript.exe engine. The CheckCScript function verifies this and halts the script if this is not the case. The next function, CreateGPMObjects, creates and instantiates the GPMC objects that will be used throughout the script.

With our basic GPMC objects created, we start by looking at a few of the GPMDomain object properties, such as the domain and domain controller currently being used. Next, a container object holding information about the GPM sites is created with the GetSitesContainer function of the GPM object. With those two objects in hand, all we need to do is pull the desired properties out of their respective objects and display them.

Taking this script functionality to the HTA format isn't a rough transition. The script stays the same, but we'll enclose it in a different set of clothes. This will be the same basic procedure followed for the rest of the HTA implementations. The resulting page looks something like Figure 8.2.

FIGURE 8.2   The List_GPMC_Information.hta file displays the general GPMC information.

Starting at the top, it will look just like a regular HTML document. But to obtain the behavior of an application, we have to add a special tag named <HTA:Application> and designate some properties to govern its behavior. Check out the following code:

```
<HTML>
<HEAD>
  <TITLE>List GPMC Information</TITLE>
  <HTA:APPLICATION ID="List_GPMC_Information"
    APPLICATIONNAME="List_GPMC_Information"
    BORDER="dialog"
    CAPTION="yes"
    CONTEXTMENU="yes"
    ICON="graphics/title.ico"
    INNERBORDER="yes"
    MINIMIZEBUTTON="yes"
    MAXIMIZEBUTTON="yes"
    SHOWINTASKBAR="yes"
    SCROLLABLE="yes"
    SINGLEINSTANCE="yes"
    SYSMENU="yes"
    WINDOWSTATE="maximize">
  <LINK href="GroupPolicy.css" rel="stylesheet" type="text/css">
  <SCRIPT src="GPMgmt.vbs" language="VBScript"></SCRIPT>
  <SCRIPT src="HTA_Help.vbs" language="VBScript"></SCRIPT>
</HEAD>
```

Most of the HTA tag properties deal with display issues—how we want the window to appear. The most important property, in my opinion, is the SINGLEINSTANCE property. Setting this to "yes" will allow only one instance of our HTA to run at a time. This will keep extra HTA instances running over each other trying to do the same job.

Along with the HTA tag are tags to incorporate a Cascading Style Sheet (CSS) page, which we can use to handle colors, fonts, and all those other HTML goodies that make a web page look good. There are also the two tags to include our outside helper scripts, GPMgmt.vbs and HTA_Help.vbs. Including these tags gives us access to our general GPMC functions and some additional functions to help with HTA coding, as you'll see soon. So let's look at some more code:

```
<BODY>
<SCRIPT language="VBScript">
Sub Window_OnLoad
self.resizeTo 500,400
Dim gpmSitesContainer
CreateGPMObjects
Set gpmSitesContainer = gpm.GetSitesContainer(dnsForestRoot,"","",0)
```

Getting into the <BODY> of our HTA, we start off with our script. Applications tend to run off events that happen during execution, and our HTA is no exception. In this case, since there are no buttons to push on our page, the only event we'll use is the Window_OnLoad event. If you guessed that this event fires when the window is loaded, you're right!

First, we set the window size with the self.resizeTo method. You can experiment with those values to find a size that works for you. Next, we invoke our global GPMC function CreateGPMObjects. That gives us our GPMC objects and we can get to work. As in the command script, we need a reference only to the gpmSitesContainer object to finish this script's job. The only job left is to display the results, so continue reading the following code:

```
gpmDomain_Domain_Span.innerHTML = gpmDomain.Domain
gpmDomain_DC_Span.innerHTML = gpmDomain.DomainController
gpmSC_Forest_Span.innerHTML = gpmSitesContainer.Forest
gpmSC_DC_Span.innerHTML = gpmSitesContainer.DomainController
gpmSC_Domain_Span.innerHTML = gpmSitesContainer.Domain
End Sub
</SCRIPT>

<div class="Title">List GPMC Information</div>
<button onclick="window.print()">Print</button>
<p>
<div class="Heading">GPMDomain Information:</div>
Domain Controller: <SPAN id="gpmDomain_DC_Span"></SPAN><br>
Domain:<SPAN id="gpmDomain_Domain_Span"></SPAN>
</p>
```

```
<p>
<div class="Heading">GPMSitesContainer information:</div>
Forest: <SPAN id="gpmSC_Forest_Span"></SPAN><br>
Domain Controller:<span id="gpmSC_DC_Span"></span><br>
Domain: <SPAN id="gpmSC_Domain_Span"></SPAN>
</p>
</BODY>
</HTML>
```

I've shown you the last bit of the <SCRIPT> block and the rest of the HTML code together because they go hand-in-hand. First, look at the ID values of the different <SPAN> tags. You'll see that they correlate to the object names in the last bit of the script. Using the <SPAN> tags allows you to mark a spot on the HTML page that you want to change the contents of by assigning the innerHTML property to some text value (which can include HTML tags). That is exactly what I did in the last piece of code.

That covers the code, but let's take a moment to talk about style (this is a web page, after all)! Check out the <DIV> tags, specifically the property called class. This refers to a formatting style that I've set up in the CSS page. Take a look at the contents of that file:

```
Body
{
    background-color: white;
    color: black;
    font-family: Tahoma,Arial;
    font-size: 100%;
    font-weight: normal;
    text-align: left;
    }
.Title
{
    background-color: gray;
    color: white;
    font-size: 200%;
    font-weight: bold;
    text-align: center;
    }
.Heading
{
    font-size: 120%;
    font-weight: bold;
    }
```

The first element, Body, refers to the page itself. I set the background color, the font color, and my preferences as far as the font style. The remaining elements, all prefixed with a period, refer to your own specific styles that you want to employ in the page. First I use .Title for the page heading. Then I use the .Heading style to give the section headings more emphasis. You can, of course, change these to suit your own tastes.

With that knowledge in hand, we'll move on to our remaining GPMC scripts. All the remaining scripts are simply variations on this same theme, the main difference being the code itself. In each script, the same basic GPMC code is used, but the order in which it is executed in the HTA might change. In the command-line scripts, arguments are used to provide necessary information to the script. In the HTA scripts, we can use text boxes to get the information and then give the user a button to click to invoke the script itself.

Documenting GPO Links and WMI Filter Links

Even with a good backup, documentation of your Group Policy universe is essential. Being able to hand over documentation in a hurry to other admins, regulators, or auditors can be a job-saving event.

To this end, we'll take a look at documenting your existing GPO links and WMI Filter Links.

The output of the scripts is fairly simple. For each GPO, it will list which containers are linked to that GPO. It will also describe what type of container it is in (OU, site, or domain) and the inheritance settings of the GPO. After listing through the GPO links, the WMI filters will be displayed. For each WMI filter, the script will list which (if any) GPOs are linked to the filter. The command-line script results will look similar to the following output:

```
>cscript //nologo .\List_GPOs_and_Links.wsf


The following list contains GPOs in the corp.com domain, the containers linked
to them, and their inheritance settings:

Office Policy
---------------------------------------
Offices (OU=Offices,DC=corp,DC=com)
 (Type - OU) (Inheritance Blocked? False)


International Policy
---------------------------------------
International (OU=International,DC=corp,DC=com)
 (Type - OU) (Inheritance Blocked? False)


Default Domain Policy
---------------------------------------
corp.com (DC=corp,DC=com)
 (Type - Domain) (Inheritance Blocked? False)
```

```
WUS
----------------------------------------
Domain Controllers (Type - OU) (Inheritance Blocked? False)
ImportOU (Type - OU) (Inheritance Blocked? False)
Offices (Type - OU) (Inheritance Blocked? False)


Completed GPO link search. Starting WMI Filter link search...
The corp.com domain has 3 WMI filters.


Windows XP Client (Windows XP Client)
-----------------------------------
Linked to: US Policy


Windows 2003 Servers (Windows 2003 Server WMI Filter)
-----------------------------------------------------
No GPOs are linked to this WMI Filter.


Windows 2000 Servers (Windows 2000 Servers)
-------------------------------------------
No GPOs are linked to this WMI Filter.
```

Of course, the HTA version of the script will display the information in a more friendly format and provide an easier method to print your results (just click the Print button!), as shown in Figure 8.3.

Getting into the code, we begin with the usual list of suspects we've seen in each of the previous scripts. We use our global `CreateGPMObjects` function to get the ball rolling. Next, we create a `GPMSitesContainer` object for the forest root. We also need to create two `GPMSearchCriteria` objects, one to search for Group Policy objects in the container and one to search for WMI filter links for each GPO.

 A GPMSearchCriteria object is a container of search rules used when examining a container. The container is always created first, and the rules are added later as needed. If you want to return everything associated with the container, you can forgo adding any search rules and just run the search with the blank container.

To get the entire list of GPO objects, we'll need to create the blank `GPMSearchCriteria` object and use it without any rules:

```
CreateGPMObjects
Set gpmSitesContainer = _
    gpm.GetSitesContainer(dnsForestRoot,"","",gpmConstants.UsePDC)
```

```
Set gpmSearchCriteria = gpm.CreateSearchCriteria()
Set somSearchCriteria = gpm.CreateSearchCriteria()

Set GPO_List = gpmDomain.SearchGPOs(gpmSearchCriteria)
```

FIGURE 8.3   List_GPO_and_Links.hta lists the GPOs and their linked containers, as well as WMI filters and their linked GPOs.

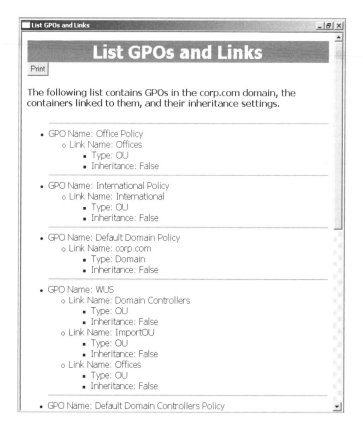

We'll iterate through each GPO, display its name, and search for any SOM links associated with it. Searching for SOMs is done with the SearchSOMs method of the GPMDomain object. First, we need to construct a SearchCriteria object that specifies we want to search SOM Links that contain the current GPO. This SearchCriteria object is then passed to the Search-SOMs method:

```
For Each GPO In GPO_List
    WScript.Echo GPO.DisplayName
    WScript.Echo String(40,"-")
    Set somSearchCriteria = gpm.CreateSearchCriteria()
```

```
    somSearchCriteria.Add _
        gpmConstants.SearchPropertySOMLinks, _
        gpmConstants.SearchOpContains, GPO

    Set SOM_List = gpmDomain.SearchSOMs(somSearchCriteria)
```

If any SOM links are found, we'll display information about each of them:

```
    If SOM_List.Count <> 0 Then
        For Each SOM In SOM_List
            WScript.Echo SOM.Name & " (" & SOM.Path & ")" & VbCrLf _
                & " (Type - " & ConvertSOMType(SOM.Type) & ")" _
                & " (Inheritance Blocked? " _
                & SOM.GPOInheritanceBlocked & ")"
        Next

        Set siteSOM_List = _
            gpmSitesContainer.SearchSites(somSearchCriteria)

        For Each SOM In siteSOM_List
            WScript.Echo SOM.Name & " (" & SOM.Path & ")" & VbCrLf _
                & " (Type = " & ConvertSOMType(SOM.Type) & ")" _
                & " (Inheritance Blocked? " _
                & SOM.GPOInheritanceBlocked & ")"
        Next

    Else
        WScript.Echo vbTab & "No links to this GPO."
    End If
Next
```

After searching for SOM Links, we'll look for WMI filter links. This is done again with a blank GPMSearchCriteria object using the SearchWMIFilters method of the GPMDomain object:

```
Set wmiSearchCriteria = gpm.CreateSearchCriteria()
Set wmi_Filter_List = gpmDomain.SearchWMIFilters(wmiSearchCriteria)

If wmi_Filter_List.Count <> 1 Then
    plural = "s"
Else
    plural = ""
End If
WScript.Echo "The " & gpmDomain.Domain & " domain has " _
    & wmi_Filter_List.Count & " WMI filter" & plural & "."
```

With a list of WMI filters in hand, we can iterate through the list and examine their properties individually. After displaying the filter description, we'll create another `GPMSearchCriteria` object to find the GPOs that are linked to each WMI filter:

```
For Each WMI_Filter In wmi_Filter_List
   With WMI_Filter
      WScript.Echo .Name & " (" & .Description & ")"
   End With

   Set gpoSearchCriteria = gpm.CreateSearchCriteria()
   gpoSearchCriteria.Add _
      gpmConstants.SearchPropertyGPOWMIFilter, _
      gpmConstants.SearchOPEquals, WMI_Filter

   Set Linked_GPO_List = gpmDomain.SearchGPOs(gpoSearchCriteria)
   If Linked_GPO_List.Count = 0 Then
      WScript.Echo "No GPOs are linked to this WMI Filter."
   Else
      For Each GPO In Linked_GPO_List
         WScript.Echo "Linked to: " & GPO.DisplayName
      Next
   End If
WScript.Echo vbNL
Next
```

With this script, we've gotten into some of the standard procedures in working with GPMC scripts and objects. Using the `GPMSearchCriteria` objects in conjunction with the different search methods available in the GPM objects is an essential skill in GPMC scripting. You will see this procedure used in almost every GPMC script that follows.

Documenting GPO Properties

Documenting GPO settings is a great way to get to know what GPOs exist on your production network, as well as generating a reference by which future GPOs should be configured.

The information retrieved from each GPO will look similar to the output shown next (only the first GPO is shown to save space; there were many more below it). We'll retrieve the basic GPO information such as name, GUID, Active Directory path, and domain, as well as examine its creation and last modification dates and computer and user version numbers. We can also verify that those versions are consistent between Active Directory and the information stored in SYSVOL. Here's what it'll look like when we're done:

```
>cscript //nologo .\List_GPO_Properties.wsf
====================
GPO Friendly Name: Office Policy
```

```
GPO GUID:{0979C03E-8AC5-4E96-8C03-D4DFCAE46CDC}
GPC Object Active Directory Path: cn={0979C03E-8AC5-4E96-8C03-
D4DFCAE46CDC},cn=policies,cn=system,DC=corp,DC=com
GPO Domain Name: corp.com
GPO Created: 10/12/2006 6:19:10 PM
GPO Last Modified: 10/12/2006 6:29:16 PM
Computer GPC Object Version: 9
Computer GPT File Version: 9
User GPC Object Version: 3
User GPT File Version: 3
The version assigned to Computer settings in this GPO are consistent between
Active Directory and Sysvol.
The version assigned to User settings in this GPO are consistent between Active
Directory and Sysvol.
The User settings in this GPO are enabled.
The Computer settings in this GPO are enabled.
```

Our HTA script covers the same bases, as shown in Figure 8.4,

FIGURE 8.4   List_GPO_Properties.hta displays information about your domain GPOs.

All we have to do to gather a list of the GPOs on our domain is search the forest room with a blank GPMSearchCriteria object. We can then iterate through our list and display all the properties of each GPO in turn. It starts by creating a SiteContainer object pointing to the forest root, then creating a blank SearchCriteria object. This blank object is passed to the Search-GPOs method of our gpmDomain object, which will return all the GPO objects in the domain.

```
CreateGPMObjects
Set gpmSitesContainer =
gpm.GetSitesContainer(dnsForestRoot,"","",gpmConstants.UsePDC)
Set gpmSearchCriteria = gpm.CreateSearchCriteria()
Set GPO_Domain_List = gpmDomain.SearchGPOs(gpmSearchCriteria)
```

With a list of GPOs in hand, we can iterate through the list and display the properties we want. To make the code a little easier to read, we use the With statement (and refer to the GPO object) to give us a shortcut to referring to the object's properties and methods. Inside a With block, any keyword beginning with a period is assumed to be referring to the With block's object.

```
For Each GPO In GPO_Domain_List
   With GPO
      WScript.Echo "GPO Friendly Name: " & .DisplayName
      WScript.Echo "GPO GUID:" & .ID
      WScript.Echo "GPC Object Active Directory Path: " & .Path
      WScript.Echo "GPO Domain Name: " & .DomainName
      WScript.Echo "GPO Created: " & .CreationTime
      WScript.Echo "GPO Last Modified: " & .ModificationTime
      WScript.Echo "Computer GPC Object Version: " _
         & .ComputerDSVersionNumber
      WScript.Echo "Computer GPT File Version: " _
         & .ComputerSysvolVersionNumber
      WScript.Echo "User GPC Object Version: " & .UserDSVersionNumber
      WScript.Echo "User GPT File Version: " & .UserSysvolVersionNumber
      WScript.Echo vbNL

      If .ComputerDSVersionNumber = .ComputerSysvolVersionNumber Then
         WScript.Echo "The version assigned to Computer settings " _
            & "in this GPO are consistent between AD and Sysvol."
      Else
         WScript.Echo "WARNING! The Computer settings in this GPO " _
            & "show a version mismatch between AD and Sysvol."
      End If
      If .UserDSVersionNumber = .UserSysvolVersionNumber Then
         WScript.Echo "The version assigned to User settings " _
            & "in this GPO are consistent between AD and Sysvol."
      Else
```

```
        WScript.Echo "WARNING! The User settings in this GPO " _
           & "show a version mismatch between AD and Sysvol."
     End If
     WScript.Echo vbNL


     If .isuserenabled Then
        WScript.Echo "The User settings in this GPO are enabled."
     Else
        WScript.Echo "The User settings in this GPO are disabled."
     End If


     If .iscomputerenabled Then
        WScript.Echo "The Computer settings in this GPO are enabled."
     Else
        WScript.Echo "The Computer settings in this GPO are disabled."
     End If
     WScript.Echo vbNL


   End With
Next
```

In this script, we looked at the basic properties of the existing GPOs in your domain. Now we turn our attention to the permissions assigned to a specified GPO.

Listing GPO Permissions

Just like other protected objects in Windows (files, AD objects, and so on), Group Policy Objects also have a security descriptor assigned to them. Through the GPMC, you can manage those permissions. Scripting security descriptors is historically not a fun prospect, and using the GPMC is your best option. What we can do, though, is create a script to look at the existing permission of a given Group Policy Object.

As you can see from the following output, I've specified that I want to view the properties of the GPO named WUS. It will provide the basic GPO information and list the security entries on the GPO's Access Control List. For brevity, I've narrowed down the full output on the command-line script:

```
>cscript //nologo .\List_GPO_Permissions.wsf /GPO:WUS


Here's information about the selected GPO:
==============================
GPO Friendly Name: WUS
Domain: corp.com
GPO GUID: {3D6C7676-D5E1-4EC8-8F02-D8A0EF2F0EA6}
```

```
Modification Timestamp: 10/12/2006 7:37:40 PM

The GPO has 5 security entries on the ACL.


========================================
Trustee Name: Domain Admins
Trustee Type: Group
Trustee Domain: CORP
Trustee DS Path: CN=Domain Admins,CN=Users,DC=corp,DC=com
Trustee SID: S-1-5 21-1553066526-2181830600-1936686154-512
ACE Mask: Edit and Delete
Denied? False
Inheritable? True
Inherited? False


========================================
Trustee Name: Enterprise Admins
Trustee Type: Group
Trustee Domain: CORP
Trustee DS Path: CN=Enterprise Admins,CN=Users,DC=corp,DC=com
Trustee SID: S-1-5-21-1553066526-2181830600-1936686154-519
ACE Mask: Edit and Delete
Denied? False
Inheritable? True
Inherited? False


. . .


Completed processing the security entries for WUS.
```

In the HTA script, the interface is a little friendlier. You can enter the name of the GPO in the GPO Name field and click the View Permissions button, as shown in Figure 8.5.

Using Command-line Arguments

Several of the command-line scripts that follow will use arguments. I personally despise scripts that force me to put command-line arguments in a specific order. It's much easier to use a named pair format, such as /GPO:WUS and let the script extract the argument using the name. To handle this in the scripts, we can use the WSH.Arguments.Named collection of VBScript. We can check the arguments, assign them to the internal variables as needed, and show the user a message if any of the required arguments are missing.

FIGURE 8.5   List_GPO_Permissions.hta displaying the security entries of the selected GPO.

To simplify matters, we'll get one GPO at a time. The HTA script allows you to enter the GPO name into a field and click the button. The command-line script allows you to either pass an argument named /GPO: or, if that argument is not found, it will prompt you for a GPO name:

```
If WSH.Arguments.Named.Exists("GPO") Then
    GPOName = WSH.Arguments.Named("GPO")
Else
    GPOName = InputBox("Enter the name of the GPO.","Enter GPO Name")
End If
```

With the GPO name in hand, we first need to verify it exists. We'll create a search criteria object which specifies the GPO name we want to examine and search for it. If the search fails to produce any items, meaning the GPO name doesn't exist, then the script will end.

```
CreateGPMObjects
Set gpmSearchCriteria = gpm.CreateSearchCriteria()
gpmSearchCriteria.Add _
    gpmConstants.SearchPropertyGPODisplayName, _
    gpmConstants.SearchOPcontains, GPOName
Set gpmGPO_List = gpmDomain.SearchGPOs(gpmSearchCriteria)
On Error Resume Next
set gpmGPO = gpmDomain.GetGPO(gpmGPO_List.item(1).ID)
If Err.Number <> 0 Then
```

```
    WScript.Echo "Sorry, that GPO name could not be found."
    WScript.Quit
End If
```

With a reference to the desired GPO, we start by showing a little friendly information about the GPO so the user can verify that this is indeed the GPO they want to view the permissions of.

```
WScript.Echo "Here's information about the selected GPO:"
WScript.Echo String(30,"=")
WScript.Echo "GPO Friendly Name: " & gpmGPO.DisplayName
WScript.Echo "Domain: " & gpmGPO.DomainName
WScript.Echo "GPO GUID: " & gpmGPO.ID
WScript.Echo "Modification Timestamp: " & gpmGPO.ModificationTime
```

Next, we get the security information from the GPO. The security information is contained in a collection object, obtained by calling the `GetSecurityInfo` method of the GPO object. Of course, collection objects mean we have iterate through each security object in the collection and list its respective properties. There are two groups of information we'll look at: the trustee information and the permission information.

Most of the trustee properties are self-explanatory. You'll notice a function named `ConvertTrusteeType` being called. This function is in our `GPMgmt.vbs` script and takes the `trusteeType` property of the security descriptor and returns a friendly name for the type, such as User, Group, and Domain.

```
Set gpmSecurityInfo = gpmGPO.GetSecurityInfo()
WScript.Echo "The GPO has " & gpmSecurityInfo.Count _
    & " security entries on the ACL."

For i=1 To gpmSecurityInfo.Count
    WScript.Echo vbCrLf & String(40,"=")
    Set gpmPermission = gpmSecurityInfo.item(i)

    With gpmPermission.trustee
        WScript.Echo "Trustee Name: " & .trusteeName
        WScript.Echo "Trustee Type: " _
            & ConvertTrusteeType(.trusteeType)
        WScript.Echo "Trustee Domain: " & .trusteeDomain
        WScript.Echo "Trustee DS Path: " & .trusteeDSPath
        WScript.Echo "Trustee SID: " & .trusteeSid
    End With
```

The information regarding the permission information is then displayed. We can see what type of access is granted by using the function `ConvertAccessSetting` to convert the `Permission` property into a friendly format, such as Apply, Edit, and Read. The script will also show if the permission denies (rather than grants) the access, if the permission is inherited, and whether the permission itself can be inherited.

```
    With gpmPermission
        WScript.Echo "ACF Mask: " & ConvertAccessSetting(.permission)
        WScript.Echo "Denied? " & .denied
        WScript.Echo "Inheritable? " & .inheritable
        WScript.Echo "Inherited? " & .inherited
    End With
Next
```

When you understand the permissions applied to a GPO, you can use the GPMC to change those permissions. This is known as Delegation. With a little additional scripting, you can modify the permissions of the GPO objects.

Creating and Linking New GPOs

The ability to create and link new GPO objects can be done through GPMC or through the scripting interface. For normal operations, I recommend using the GPMC since you will undoubtedly be editing its settings right away anyhow.

But let's say you already have a collection of GPOs baked and ready to go. It's getting late in the day and you'd rather not spend a lot of point-and-click time with your GPMC console. Instead, you can run a script that does the work for you while you spend some quality time in your favorite chair at home.

First, a quick look at the HTA script. The basic information necessary includes the name of your new GPO, the ADSI path to the OU to link the GPO to (the root path of your domain appears when the HTA is opened), and whether or not you want the new GPO to appear at the top of the precedence list. After entering this information into the HTA, click the Create Link button, as shown in Figure 8.6.

FIGURE 8.6   Create_And_Link_New_GPO.hta will create and link a new GPO to the specified OU.

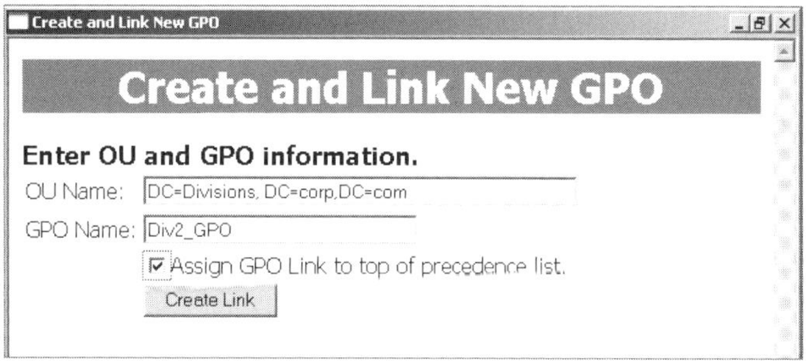

The command-line script needs some information to complete its task. It must know the name of our new GPO, the OU to link the new GPO to, and whether or not we would like the new GPO to appear on the top of the precedence list. These command-line arguments are /OU:{OU Name}, /GPO:{New GPO Name}, and /TOP, respectively.

```
>cscript //nologo .\Create_And_Link_New_GPO.wsf /OU:OU=Divisions,DC=corp,DC=com
/GPO:Div_GPO /TOP
Successfully linked Div_GPO to Divisions.
```

The OU must be the ADSI path (such as OU=Divisions,DC=corp,DC=com). The argument /TOP is optional; if it is omitted, we'll assume the new GPO should be placed at the bottom of the precedence list:

```
If WSH.Arguments.Count > 0 Then
    If WSH.Arguments.Named.Exists("OU") Then
        OUName = WSH.Arguments.Named("OU")
    Else
        ShowUsage
    End If
    If WSH.Arguments.Named.Exists("GPO") Then
        GPOName = WSH.Arguments.Named("GPO")
    Else
        ShowUsage
    End If
    If WSH.Arguments.Named.Exists("Top") Then
        LinkPrecedence = 1
    Else
        LinkPrecedence = -1
    End If
End If
```

Before we start doing anything to an Active Directory OU, especially one where the user has to manually type the path in, it's a good idea to make sure that the path actually points to a valid Active Directory object. The GetOU function is inside the GPMgmt.vbs script and simply handles the mechanics of binding to an AD object:

```
Set OU = GetOU(OUName)
If OU Is Nothing Then
    WScript.Echo "Unable to bind to OU " & OUName
    WScript.Quit
End If
```

Before the script tries to create the GPO, it will first check to verify that a GPO of the specified name does not already exist. If a GPO is found with the same name, a warning is displayed. While it is not a best practice to have GPOs with the same name, it is also not prohibited by Active Directory. The warning will give you the choice of stopping without creating the new GPO or continuing.

```
If GPOExists(GPOName) Then
    If MsgBox("A GPO named " & GPOName & " already exists!", _
        vbExclamation + vbYesNo) = vbNo Then
      WScript.Quit
    End If
End If
```

If everything checks out so far, we can get down to actually creating the GPO. To link to the OU, we'll need to retrieve its SOM list with the GetSOM function. Next, we call the CreateGPO function and receive an object associated with the new (but empty) Group Policy object. With that object, we assign its name and link it to the target OU. Creating a GPO link is done with the CreateGPOLink function of the SOM object, which we retrieved earlier from the OU object.

When using the CreateGPOLink function, two arguments are passed. The first specifies what order of precedence this GPO should have. Our script will either place the new GPO at the bottom of the list (by default) or at the top (when the script is run with the /TOP argument). If you glance back to the section of code that checks for the /TOP argument, you'll see the LinkPrecedence variable uses a value of 1 to put the new GPO at the top of the precedence list or −1 to put the GPO at the bottom.

```
Set NewGPO = gpmDomain.CreateGPO()
NewGPO.DisplayName = GPOName
Set SOM = gpmDomain.GetSOM(OU.distinguishedName)

On Error Resume Next
Set SOM_Link = SOM.CreateGPOLink(LinkPrecedence, NewGPO)
If Err.Number = 0 Then
    WScript.Echo "Successfully linked " & NewGPO.DisplayName _
        & " to " & SOM.Name & "."
Else
    WScript.Echo "An error occurred while linking to OU."
End If
```

You should now have a working Group Policy Object linked to an OU in your domain. Now you can switch into the GPMC, refresh the interface on the proper container, and begin modifying the GPO as needed.

Backing Up GPOs

In many networks, Group Policy objects tend to evolve over time. What started out as a simple GPO to manage desktop settings might grow into something that controls desktop, network, firewall, and even folder redirection settings. Eventually, one too many changes will take place to the GPO and you'll need to undo it. This is where GPO backups can provide not only recovery, but also a history of GPO changes over its lifetime.

In this script, all GPOs in the domain will be backed up. The HTA version of the backup script allows for impromptu backups. While you can always back up your GPOs through the GPMC, the HTA is targeted specifically for the task at hand. This is not only a bit quicker, but it also makes it easier to hand the backup task off to someone less familiar with the GPMC interface. You can enter the specified folder to place the backup in and click the Backup button, as shown in Figure 8.7. This is very useful when you have perfected the GPO of your dreams in your test domain and want to back it up for importing into your production domain.

See the Appendix for details about Backup and Import between domains.

FIGURE 8.7   Backing up GPOs through the Backup_All_GPOs.hta application

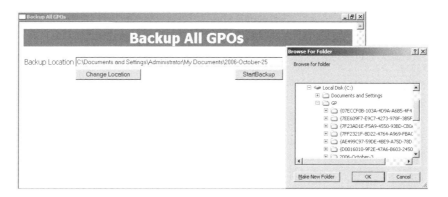

The design of the command-line script is suited for automation and scheduling (that's a hint, folks!). We will specify the backup location to the script. Optionally, we can tell the script to use the current date as the backup folder name through the switch /UseDate. This is an advantage over the BackupAllGPOs.wsf script included with the GPMC installation, because it will give you a history of GPO backups without changing the command-line arguments in a scheduled task.

```
>cscript //nologo .\Backup_All_GPOs.wsf /Folder:C:\GP /UseDate

Creating folder C:\GP\2006-October-17\
```

```
Backing up the Office Policy GPO.
GPO Backup successful.
Backing up the International Policy GPO.
GPO Backup successful.
Backing up the Default Domain Policy GPO.
GPO Backup successful.
Backing up the WUS GPO.
GPO Backup successful.
Backing up the Default Domain Controllers Policy GPO.
GPO Backup successful.
Backing up the Division Policy GPO.
GPO Backup successful.
Backing up the US Policy GPO.
GPO Backup successful.
Completed GPO backups.
```

Handling the arguments for this script is a fairly simple matter. In the following code, an additional check puts the folder name in the proper format to build a complete path to the backup folders.

```
If WSH.Arguments.Count > 0 Then
    If WSH.Arguments.Named.Exists("Folder") Then
        BackupFolder = WSH.Arguments.Named("Folder")
        If Not(Right(ReportFolder,1) = "\") Then
            BackupFolder = BackupFolder & "\"
        End If
    Else
        BackupFolder = WScript.Path
    End If
    If WSH.Arguments.Named.Exists("UseDate") Then
        BackupFolder = BackupFolder & GetDateName & "\"
    End If
End If
```

Before backing up our Group Policy objects, we need to verify that we are sending them to a valid place. We'll employ the `FileSystemObject` to check if the backup location exists; if not, it will attempt to create it for us.

```
Set FSO = CreateObject("Scripting.FileSystemObject")
If Not(FSO.FolderExists(BackupFolder)) Then
    WScript.Echo "Creating folder " & BackupFolder
    FSO.CreateFolder BackupFolder
End If
```

With the backup folder prepared, it's time to get to work. A blank GPMSearchCriteria object will return a list of all the GPOs in the domain. With each GPO object in the list, we simply call the Backup function and specify the backup location and a comment about the backup (in this case, we'll mention who performed the backup):

```
Set Network = CreateObject("WScript.Network")
Set gpmSearchCriteria = gpm.CreateSearchCriteria()
Set GPO_List = gpmDomain.SearchGPOs(gpmSearchCriteria)
For Each GPO In GPO_List
   WScript.Echo "Backing up the " & GPO.DisplayName & " GPO."
   Set gpmResult = GPO.Backup(BackupFolder,"Backup performed by " &
Network.UserName)
   Set gpmResult_Status = gpmResult.Status
   If gpmResult_Status.Count <> 0 Then
      For i=1 To gpmResult_Status.Count
         WScript.Echo gpmResult_Status.Item(i).Message
      Next
      gpmResult.OverallStatus()
   Else
      WScript.Echo "GPO Backup successful."
   End If
Next
LogFile.Close
WScript.Echo "Completed GPO backups."
```

Depending on the amount of GPO changes made in your organization, you can either manually run the backup script on an as-needed basis, or you can schedule the script through Task Scheduler. By specifying the /UseDate argument in the command-line script, you can maintain a history of GPO backups to refer to.

Restoring GPOs

Having a good backup of your GPOs is a start, but it doesn't do much good if you don't have some method to restore them. You can restore a GPO from GPMC, or you can use the scripting methods that we've been working with.

Restoring GPOs through an HTA script is simple and targets the task at hand. You can restore a GPO through the GPMC console, but you'll find that the HTA version is quicker. This simple, one-task approach makes it easier for someone less familiar with the GPMC interface to restore a GPO if need be. First, select the GPO backup folder (remember, you can click the Change Location button to use the standard Windows dialogs to select the folder). Click the List GPOs button to view the contents of the backup folder. If you don't see the GPO you want, change the location of the backup folder and list the GPOs again.

When you've found the GPO you want to restore, enter the number corresponding to the desired GPO in the GPO Number field. Then just click the Restore GPO button to start the restore process, as shown in Figure 8.8.

FIGURE 8.8   Restore_GPO.hta can be used to quickly restore a GPO to your domain.

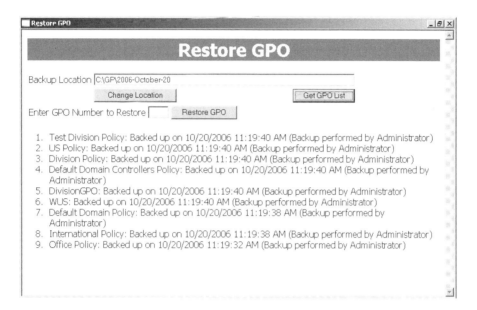

The command-line script uses the same arguments: /Folder to refer to the backup folder and /GPO to refer to the name of the GPO you wish to restore. In this script and the import script shown next, the /Folder argument may be combined with the /List argument to view the contents of the GPO backup folder. You can use this list to find the name of the GPO you wish to restore and pass it in the /GPO argument, as shown here:

```
>cscript //nologo .\Restore_GPO.wsf /Folder:C:\GP\2006-October-20 /GPO:WUS
```

After verifying the existence of the backup folder (the code for which you saw earlier), we'll continue with the restore process. First, we get a list of the GPO backups in the specified folder. With that list in hand, we'll look for the GPO that matches the name given by the user. When that name is found, we'll show the user a little useful information about the GPO to make sure that this is actually the GPO that they want to restore, and we'll ask the user to confirm that this is really the course of action that they want to take.

```
CreateGPMObjects
Set gpmBackup_List = GetGPOBackups(BackupFolder)
Set gpmRestoreGPO = Nothing
For i=1 To gpmBackup_List.Count
   With gpmBackup_List.Item(i)
       If .GPODisplayName = GPOToRestore Then
```

```
                Set gpmRestoreGPO = gpmBackupDir.GetBackup(.ID)
                With gpmRestoreGPO
                        WScript.Echo "GPO Friendly Name: " & .GPODisplayName
                        WScript.Echo "Domain: " & .GPODomain
                        WScript.Echo "Comment: " & .Comment
                        WScript.Echo "GPO GUID: " & .GPOID
                        WScript.Echo "GPO Backup GUID: " & .ID
                        WScript.Echo "Backup Timestamp: " & .Timestamp
                        WScript.Echo vbNL
                End With
            Exit For
        End If
    End With
Next


If gpmRestoreGPO Is Nothing Then
    WScript.Echo "Could not find specified GPO!"
    WScript.Quit
End If


WScript.StdOut.Write _
    "Are you sure you want to restore this GPO? (y or n) "
rs = WScript.StdIn.ReadLine
WScript.Echo VbCrLf
```

If the user agrees to the restore question, all we need to do is call the `RestoreGPO` method of the `GPMDomain` object. If any errors are encountered during the process, we'll show those to the user.

```
If StrComp(rs,"y",vbTextCompare) = 0 Then
    WScript.Echo "Restoring selected GPO..."
    Set gpmResult = gpmDomain.RestoreGPO(gpmRestoreGPO,0)
    Set gpmResult_Status = gpmResult.Status
    If gpmResult_Status.count <> 0 Then
        For i=1 To gpmResult_Status.Count
            WScript.Echo gpmResult_Status.Item(i).Message
        Next
        gpmResult.OverallStatus()
    Else
        WScript.Echo "Successfully restored GPO."
        WScript.Echo "This did not restore links from containers."
```

```
    End If
Else
    WScript.Echo "Operation aborted. No GPOs restored."
End If
```

After restoring the GPO, jump over to your trusty GPMC console and refresh the proper container. Verify that the restored GPO is indeed configured the way you were expecting it to be. If it isn't, return to your backups and try a different one.

Importing GPOs

Maintaining a separate testing environment is commonly regarded as a best practice in system administration. In Group Policy, a test environment allows you to verify that a new GPO setting is available and that it works as intended across different systems. It also allows you to make mistakes without harming your production network.

After spending hours creating and testing a new GPO, the easiest and more reliable way to put the new GPO into your production network is to copy or import the GPO from the test domain to the production domain. You can use the Copy feature in GPMC, but using a backup and import procedure allows you more control and maintains the current permissions and links on the existing GPOs.

 If you're unfamiliar with the idea of importing (a function that is only performed between domains), please read the Appendix at the end of this book for some examples, then come back here.

Importing a GPO through the HTA script is straightforward. First, select the GPO backup folder (remember, you can click the Change Location button to use the standard Windows dialogs to select the folder). Click the List GPOs button to view the contents of the backup folder. If you don't see the GPO you want, change the location of the backup folder and list the GPOs again.

When you've found the GPO you want to restore, enter the number corresponding to the desired GPO in the GPO Number field. You will also need to enter the ADSI path of the container you wish to link the newly imported GPO to. To remind you what an ADSI path looks like, the root ADSI path of the domain appears in the field when the HTA script starts.

With all the information in place, just click the Import GPO button to start the import process, as shown in Figure 8.9.

The command-line script uses the same arguments: /Folder to refer to the backup folder and /GPO to refer to the name of the GPO you wish to restore. You must also include the ADSI path to the container you wish to link the GPO to using the /OU: argument. If you want the new GPO to appear at the top of the precedence list, add the /TOP argument. You may also specify a migration table to associate with the imported GPO by adding the /MigrationTable argument.

FIGURE 8.9 Import_GPO.hta can be used to easily import a GPO to your production domain.

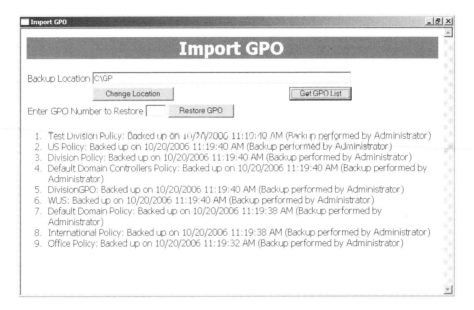

In this script and the restore script shown earlier, the /Folder argument may be combined with the /List argument to view the contents of the GPO backup folder. You can use this list to find the name of the GPO you wish to restore and pass it in the /GPO argument, as shown here:

```
>cscript //nologo .\Import_GPO.wsf /Folder:C:\GP\2006-October-20 /GPO:WUS /
OU:OU=Division,DC=corp,DC=com /TOP
```

The scripts need some information to do their job. First, they need to know the folder containing the GPO backups. Next, we need to specify the name of the GPO we want to import and the OU to link the imported GPO to. Optionally, we can use the /TOP argument to specify that the imported GPO should go on the top of the precedence list. The script also allows us to specify the backup folder and the argument /LIST to view the contents of the backup folder.

In addition to verifying that the backup folder exists (which we've looked at before), we should also verify that the OU we want to link the GPO to actually exists. The following code uses the GetOU function from the GPMgmt.vbs script to bind to the Active Directory object. If the bind fails, the script will end.

```
Set OU = GetOU(OUName)
If OU Is Nothing Then
    WScript.Echo "Unable to bind to OU " & OUName
    WScript.Quit
End If
```

Good! To import our GPO, we first have to create a blank GPO as a target. Next, we get the SOM for the target OU and link the new, blank GPO to the OU.

```
Set NewGPO = gpmDomain.CreateGPO()
NewGPO.DisplayName = GPOName
Set SOM = gpmDomain.GetSOM(OU.distinguishedName)

On Error Resume Next
Set SOM_Link = SOM.CreateGPOLink(LinkPrecedence, NewGPO)
If Err.Number = 0 Then
    WScript.Echo "Successfully linked " & NewGPO.DisplayName _
    & " to " & SOM.Name & "."
Else
    WScript.Echo "An error occurred while linking to OU."
End If
```

Moving right along, we get a reference to the backup folder and pull the list of GPOs it contains. We'll go through this list to find the ID of the GPO we want to import.

```
Set gpmBackupDir = gpm.GetBackupDir(BackupFolder)
Set gpmBackup_List = GetGPOBackups(BackupFolder)
For i=1 To gpmBackup_List.Count
    If gpmBackup_List.Item(i).GPODisplayName = GPOName Then
        GPO_ID = gpmBackup_List.item(i).ID
        Set GPOToImport = gpmBackupDir.GetBackup(GPO_ID)
        Exit For
    End If
Next
```

If a migration table was specified in the options, we need to get a reference to it in order to include it with our GPO import. The following code will check for a specified migration table and prepare it for use:

```
If Not(MigrationTableName = "") Then
   On Error Resume Next
   Set MigrationTable = GPM.GetMigrationTable(MigrationTableName)
   If Err.Number <> 0 Then
      WScript.Echo "Error loading the specified migration table."
      WScript.Quit
   End If
End If
```

We're almost ready to get to the real work, but first we should verify that the user really wants to perform this operation on the target domain, as a good safety measure:

```
WScript.StdOut.Write _
    "Are you sure you want to import this GPO? (y or n) "
rs = WScript.StdIn.ReadLine
WScript.Echo VbCrLf
```

If the user says yes, we call the Import method of the newly created GPO and check for error messages that might have occurred. If a migration table was specified, we have to alter the Import syntax just a bit to include the reference to the migration table:

```
If StrComp(rs,"y",vbTextCompare) = 0 Then
    WScript.Echo "Importing selected GPO..."
    If MigrationTable = vbNull Then
        Set GPMResult = NewGPO.Import(0, GPOToImport)
    Else
        Set GPMResult = NewGPO.Import(0, GPOToImport, MigrationTable)
    End If
    Set gpmResult = NewGPO.Import(0,GPOToImport)
    Set gpmResult_Status = gpmResult.Status
    If gpmResult_Status.count <> 0 Then
        For i=1 to gpmResult_Status.Count
            WScript.Echo gpmResult_Status.Item(i).Message
        Next
    gpmResult.OverallStatus()
    Else
        WScript.Echo "The GPO was successfully imported."
    End If
Else
    WScript.Echo "Operation aborted. No GPOs imported."
End If
```

With the GPO imported into your production domain, jump into your GPMC console, refresh the proper container, and verify that the imported GPO is configured as you expected. If it isn't, check the test domain GPO first to verify you've referenced the correct GPO. If the test domain GPO is configured properly, perform another backup on the GPO and attempt the restore again.

Final Thoughts

In this chapter, you've seen a handful of the capabilities scripting can add to your Group Policy management toolbox. While the Group Policy Management Console is an excellent tool, the use of scripts can take your domain management to the next level. Automating routine tasks such as backing up Group Policy Objects will not only solidify your domain, it will build up your reputation as a rock-solid administrator.

9

Profiles: Local, Roaming, and Mandatory

When a user logs on to a Windows machine, a profile is automatically generated. A *profile* is a collection of settings, specific to a user, that sticks with that user throughout the working experience. In this chapter, I'll talk about three types of profiles.

First is the *Local Profile*, which is created whenever a user logs on. Next is the *Roaming Profile*, which enables users to hop from machine to machine while maintaining the same configuration settings at each machine. Along our journey, I'll also discuss some configuration tweaks that you can set using specific policy settings—specifically for Roaming Profiles.

The third type of profile is the *Mandatory Profile*. Like Roaming Profiles, Mandatory Profiles allow the user to jump from machine to machine. But Mandatory Profiles force a user's Desktop and settings to remain exactly the same as they were when the administrator assigned the profile; the user cannot permanently change the settings.

Here's a little "cheat sheet" before we go much farther. That is, you need a guide to understand which operating system's profiles are compatible and which are not.

- Version 0: Windows NT
- Version 1: Windows 2000, Windows 2003, and Windows XP
- Version 2: Windows Vista and Longhorn Servers (as clients)

We'll barely be talking at all about Version 0 profiles here. But we will be getting into Version 1 and Version 2 profiles. So, before we get too far down the line, let's just break the bad news: if you're interested in setting up Roaming Profiles for both your Version 1 type machines and Version 2 type machines, you'll be setting up "separate but equal" profiles. That is, you'll set up two parallel Roaming Profile infrastructures and the two shall never meet.

If the two shall never meet, how will you share data for a user if he roams from a Windows XP to a Windows Vista machine and back again? That's the next chapter, where we take on redirected folders. So, stay tuned for that after you've successfully set up Roaming Profiles for Windows XP and Windows Vista.

In general, your users will use desktop machines when roaming. However, users could, of course, roam to a server, like Windows Server 2003 or Longhorn Server. Roaming Profiles will keep on working in those scenarios as well. Just remember that Windows Server 2003 is a Type 1 and Windows Longhorn Server is a Type 2.

What Is a User Profile?

As I stated, as soon as a user logs on to a machine, a Local Profile is generated. This profile is two things: a personal slice of the Registry (contained in a file), and a set of folders stored on a hard drive. Together, these components form what we might call the *user experience*—that is, what the Desktop looks like, what style and shape the icons are, what the background wallpaper looks like, and so on.

The *NTUSER.DAT* File

The Registry stores user and computer settings in a file called NTUSER.DAT, which can be loaded and unloaded into the current computer's Registry—taking over the HKEY_CURRENT_USER portion of the Registry when the user logs on.

In Figure 9.1, you can see a portion of a Windows XP's HKEY_CURRENT_USER, specifically, the Control Panel ➢ Desktop ➢ Wallpaper setting, which shows c:\WINDOWS\web\ wallpaper\Bliss.bmp in the Data column.

This portion of the Registry directly maps to a file in the user's profile—the NTUSER.DAT file. You'll find that many of a user's individual settings are stored in this file. Here are detailed descriptions for some of the settings inside NTUSER.DAT.

Accessories   Look-and-feel settings for applications such as Calculator, Clock, HyperTerminal, Notepad, and Paint.

Application   Settings for Office applications and most newer applications, such as toolbars.

Control Panel   The bulk of the settings in NTUSER.DAT. Settings found here include those for screen savers, display, sounds, and mouse.

Explorer   Remembers how specific files and folders are to be displayed.

Printer   Network printer and local printer definitions are found here.

Drive Mappings   Stored, persistent drive mappings are stored here.

Taskbar   Designates the look and feel of the taskbar.

FIGURE 9.1   A simple Registry setting shows the entry for the wallpaper.

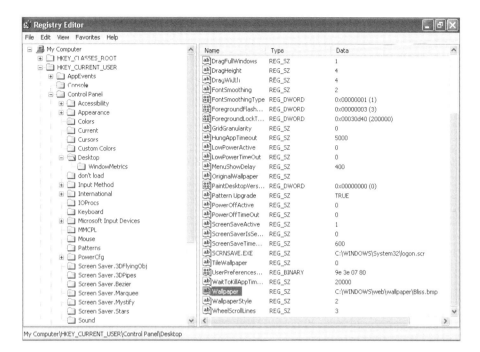

Profile Folders for Type 1 Computers (Windows 2000, Windows 2003, and Windows XP)

By default, Windows 2000, Windows 2003, and Windows XP profiles are stored in a folder underneath the C:\Documents and Settings folder.

Ultimately, what the user "sees" as their profile is an amalgam of two halves: their own personal profile and components from what is known as the "All Users" profile.

So, each user has a unique profile, and each user leverages a shared profile.

Understanding the Contents of a User's Profile (for Type 1 Computers)

Items in the profile folders can be stored in lots of nooks and crannies. As you can see in Figure 9.2, both visible and hidden folders store User Profile settings.

To show hidden files in an Explorer window, choose Tools ➢ Folder Options to open the Folder Options dialog box, and click the View tab. Click the Show Hidden Files and Folders radio button, and then click OK.

FIGURE 9.2   A look inside Frank Rizzo's profile reveals both visible and hidden folders.

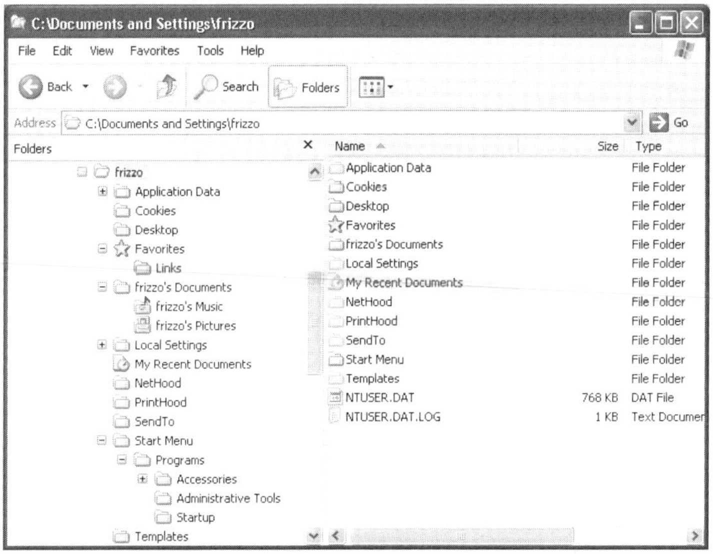

Here are the folders and a general description of what each contains:

Application Data   Used by many applications to store specific settings, such as the Office 2000 toolbar settings. Additionally, items such as Word's Custom Dictionary are stored here. MST files (Microsoft Transform Files) are stored here by default. MST files modify Windows Installer applications by providing customized application installation and runtime settings. (See Chapter 11 for more information on MST files.)

Cookies   Houses Internet Explorer cookies so that pages on the Internet can remember specific user settings.

Favorites   Houses Internet Explorer Favorites—the list of saved web page links.

Desktop   Contains only files that users store directly on the Desktop. Special icons such as My Network Places, My Computer, and the Recycle Bin are not part of the Desktop profile.

Local Settings   Contains application data specific to the user's machine, such as Internet Explorer History, temporary file storage, and other application data. This folder does not roam when Roaming Profiles are set up (see the "Roaming Profiles" section later in this chapter). Like the Application Data folder, this folder is to be used at an application vendor's discretion.

My Documents   Now, users of all sophistication levels can leverage this centralized repository for their data files. The My Documents folder has the advantage that it's easily understood by end users, instead of wondering about which file goes in which drive letter path. In fact, the default Office 2000, Office XP, and Office 2003 "Save as" path is to My Documents. This will come in handy, as you'll see in the next chapter. My Documents contains My Pictures, and Windows XP Profiles also contains My Music.

NetHood   Contains shortcuts to network drives. Even though the NT 4 Network Neighborhood was renamed to My Network Places, the NetHood folder is still around and still performs the same functions.

PrintHood   Contains shortcuts to network printers; similar to NetHood.

Recent   Contains a list of the most recently used application files and user data files like .TXT and .DOC files.

SendTo   Contains icons that applications can use to tie in to Explorer to allow file routing between applications such as Outlook and folders.

Start Menu   Contains the shortcuts and information that users see when they choose Start ➢ Programs. Each user's Start Menu folder is different. For example, if Joe installs DogFoodMaker 4 and Sally installs CatFoodMaker 8.1, neither will see the other's icons. To see each other's icons, the icons need to live in the All Users ➢ Start Menu folder (see next section). Note that if the application does a "per user" installation, then shortcuts will be present in the user's profile. If the application does a per machine installation then the shortcuts are in the All Users profile.

Templates   Contains the templates that some applications, such as Excel and Word, use to perform conversions. Like the Application Data folder, this folder is to be used at an application vendor's discretion.

The All Users profile (for Type 1 Computers) which is found at the variable location %ALLUSERSPROFILE% typically maps to C:\Documents and Settings\All Users.

Applications often add icons to the %ALLUSERSPROFILE%\Start Menu to ensure that all users can run them.

Again, users end up seeing the combination of their own profile plus whatever is presented in the All Users profile.

Profile Folders for Type 2 Computers (Windows Vista and Longhorn)

As I stated in the introduction to this chapter, the profiles for Windows XP and Windows Vista are basically incompatible. There might be some similarities between the two (and actually, Windows Vista goes the "extra mile" to try to help bridge the differences between the two). The items we'll be looking at here have moved from their original place in Windows XP to a new place in Windows Vista—the Users folder which is typically found hanging off of C:\. The \Users folder in Vista is the equivalent of the Documents and Settings directory in Windows XP.

Understanding the Contents of a User's Profile (for Type 2 Computers)

But inside the Windows Vista profile there are a lot of new folders, and some that simply look familiar. Let's take a quick look at what's inside the Windows Vista profile.

Contacts   This is new for Windows Vista. This stores what are known as "Windows Contacts."

Desktop   Similar in function to Windows XP's Desktop (see earlier).

Documents   Was My Documents in Windows XP. Same basic function. Stores basic documents such as word documents and such.

Downloads   This is new for Windows Vista. It becomes a storage spot for user's downloads.

Favorites   Similar in function to Windows XP's Favorites (see earlier).

Links   This is where Explorer's "Favorite Links" are stored. You'll see these down the left pane of Explorer.

Music   Was My Music in Windows XP.

Videos   Was My Videos in Windows XP (though not officially part of the Windows XP profile).

Pictures   Was My Pictures in Windows XP.

Saved Games   This is a new folder to save users' saved games into. I'm sure network administrators everywhere are just *thrilled* about this.

Searches   This is new for Windows Vista which will save stored searches for Explorer.

AppData   Was Application Data in Windows XP. Now in Windows Vista, AppData is bifurcated into two parts: local (to the computer only) and roaming (for the specific user). We'll be talking more about Roaming Profiles in a bit, but this part is important to understand for when we do tackle them.

The AppData\Roaming folder in Windows Vista performs the same function as the Documents and Settings\<*username*>\Application Data folder in Windows XP.

The AppData\Local folder is now meant to hold machine-specific application data that isn't supposed to roam with the user. This folder is to be the equivalent for Local Settings\ Application Data in Windows XP.

The AppData\LocalLow folder is a special directory with "low integrity" rights. So files that get stored here will have a lower integrity level than in other areas of the operating system. See the sidebar entitled "The *LocalLow* Folder within *AppData*" for more information.

In the next section, I talk about how several Windows XP holdovers are mapped to directories within AppData.

> ### The *LocalLow* Folder within *AppData*
>
> Within a user's AppData folder, there are two obvious entries: Local and Roaming. These make sense and are used when that corresponding condition is true. However, also note the presence of a "LocalLow" folder.
>
> Windows Vista has various ways applications can run. One way is Protected Mode, which guarantees a program will run with low rights. When running in this way, the application only has access to this portion of the User Profile. Windows Vista's Internet Explorer is one such application. Internet Explorer in Windows Vista runs in Protected Mode, so this prevents malware and other various "nasties" from infecting your computer, or possibly compromising user specific information.
>
> Protected Mode uses the LocalLow profile folder.
>
> Also note there are low integrity folders for Cookies, History, and Favorites.
>
> For more on integrity levels, check out Mark Minasi's book entitled *Administering Vista Security: The Big Surprises* from Sybex (2006).

Adjusting for Windows XP Holdovers

Even though we're exploring the Windows Vista profile, something interesting should be noted. That is, Windows Vista profiles are set up to automatically handle older applications which are still looking for Windows XP locations. For instance, if an application wanted to expressly save something in My Documents—it would have a problem. My Documents doesn't exist anymore, right? Now, it's just Documents for Windows Vista. To that end, the Windows Vista profile has what's called "Junction Points," so when an application visits My Documents it's really going to Windows Vista's Documents.

To see these pointers, we need to see the hidden files inside a Windows Vista profile. You can perform this by going to the user's profile and typing **dir /ah /og** (to show hidden files and to sort by directories first). You can see this in Figure 9.3.

Note that upon further inspection, the following folders appear at the top level of the profile, but really, they are placed into either AppData\Roaming or AppData\Local:

Windows XP Holdover	Linked to Windows Vista Folder	Directory path relative to c:\Users\{username}
My Documents	Documents	\Documents
Application Data	AppData	\AppData\Roaming
Cookies	AppData\Roaming	\AppData\Roaming\Microsoft\ Windows\Cookies
Local Settings	AppData\Local	\AppData\Local

Windows XP Holdover	Linked to Windows Vista Folder	Directory path relative to c:\Users\{username}
NetHood	AppData\Roaming	\AppData\Roaming\Microsoft\ Windows\Network Shortcuts
Start Menu	AppData\Roaming	\AppData\Roaming\Microsoft\ Windows\Start Menu
Recent	AppData\Roaming	\AppData\Roaming\Microsoft\ Windows\Recent
Templates	AppData\Roaming	\Appdata\Roaming\Microsoft\ Windows\Templates
Printhood	AppData\Roaming	\AppData\Roaming\Microsoft\ Windows\Printer Shortcuts
SendTo	AppData\Roaming	\AppData\Roaming\Microsoft\ Windows\SendTo

FIGURE 9.3   A view inside a Type 2 profile (dir /ah /og)

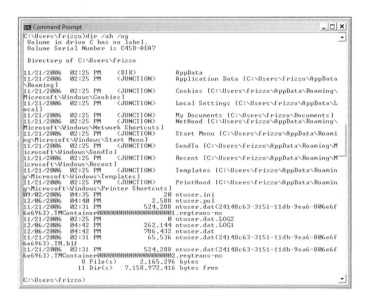

 Curious about what those "regtran-ms" files are? I was! According to my sources at Microsoft, these are the Kernel Transaction Manager (KTM) generated files. The Vista Registry uses KTM to avoid corruptions, so you should never see Registry corruption anymore. Let's hope anyway.

The Public Profile (for Type 2 Computers)

The Public profile in Windows Vista and Windows Longhorn replaces the "All Users" concept in Windows XP and previous machines. However, it provides the same basic function. That is, the end-user's experience becomes their own profile *plus* the contents of the Public profile. Again, categories like the Desktop and Start Menu become good candidates here, because the icons you place here affect everyone.

Virtualized Files and Registry for Programs

Some applications try to do bad, bad things. And Windows XP will (usually) let them. For instance, an application could try to write program data to c:\program files\dogfoodmaker5\ settings.ini.

This DogfoodMaker application really has no business writing settings there. In reality, settings should be in the user's profile, specifically in the Application Data (AppData) section (either user or machine based).

To that end, Windows Vista will "redirect" writes like this to a location where the application should be writing. Microsoft calls this redirection *virtualization*. Specifically *File Virtualization* and *Registry Virtualization*. Specifically, c:\users\<*username*>\AppData\Local\VirtualStore\ Program Files\dogfoodmaker5. And, because multiple users could be using the same machine, a separate copy of the virtualized file is created for each user that runs the application.

Indeed, if you wanted to see these redirected files right away, Windows Explorer has its own button to see these. If there is a virtualized version of a file related to the current directory, a Compatibility Files button appears that will take you to the virtual location to view that file. In this example, you can see that someone tried to put junk In the \Windows directory.

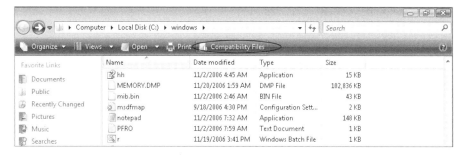

Writes to "incorrect" places to the Registry work the same way. "Bad" writes get redirected to HKEY_CLASSES_ROOT\VirtualStore\MACHINE or USER\SOFTWARE. This automatically takes effect if the application isn't UAC compliant. So, file virtualization doesn't affect applications that are run with a full administrative rights (when, say, someone elevates it to run as an admin).

This technology is, of course, a band-aid. It permits pre-Windows Vista applications to run in a predictable way. But, really, it should be considered a short-term fix rather than a long-term solution. The goal is to ensure that your application developers modify their applications such that they meet the guidelines of the Windows Vista Logo program instead of depending on file and Registry virtualization.

Note that file and Registry virtualization is disabled under some circumstances:

- File and Registry virtualization is simply not supported for Windows Vista 64-bit applications. These applications are expected to be UAC compliant and to write data to the correct locations.

- Virtualization is disabled for applications that include an application manifest with a desired execution level attribute. If you're a developer, you can learn more about application manifests here: `http://tinyurl.com/ftvn5`.

Additionally, note you can turn off virtual file and Registry abilities. That security policy is located in Computer Configuration ➢ Windows Settings ➢ Security Settings ➢ Local Policies ➢ Security Options ➢ **User Account Control: Virtualize file and registry write failures to per-user locations**. You need to click "Define this policy setting," then select Disabled to turn it off.

The Default Local User Profile

The Default Local User Profile folder contains many of the same folders as any user's own Local Profile. Indeed, the Default User Profile is the template that generates all new local User Profiles when a new user logs on.

When a new user logs on, a copy of the Default Local User Profile is copied for that user to C:\users\%*username*%. As will often happen, the user changes and personalizes settings through the normal course of business. Then, once the user logs off, the settings are preserved in a personal local folder in the C:\Users\%*username*% folder.

This Default Local User Profile is different from the Default Domain User Profile described later.

As an administrator, you can create your own ready-made standard shortcuts or stuff the folders with your own files. You can also introduce your own NTUSER.DAT Registry settings, such as a standard Desktop for all users who log on to a specific machine. In the following example, you can set up a background picture in the Default Local User Profile. Then, whenever a new user logs on locally to this machine, the background picture is displayed.

For Type 1 computers (Windows XP, Windows 2003, Windows 2000) the Default User Profile is stored in c:\Documents and Settings\Default User.

For Type 2 computers (Windows Vista and Longhorn) the Default User Profile is stored in c:\users\Default.

Changing the Profiles Folder for Windows XP Machines

Older applications sometimes balk at the new Local Profiles location, because they occasionally hard-coded information to the NT 4–style profile paths. This is probably why Microsoft chose to maintain the original profile location (`C:\WINNT\PROFILES`) when an NT 4 machine is upgraded to Windows 2000 or Windows XP.

If you come across any applications in your testing that prohibit you from using the new path, you can change the storage point for the Profiles folder. Although the storage point for the `Profiles` folder cannot be changed once a Windows 2000 (or Windows XP) machine is loaded, you can change it during an unattended setup. For instance, if you want to store the profiles under the old path of `C:\WINNT\PROFILES` or, say, under the `Profiles` folder on a large D: partition or hard drive, you can set up your answer file to contain the following:

```
[GUIUnattended]
Profilesdir="D:\PROFILES"
```

This technique works only for freshly installed systems, not for machines being upgraded from NT 4. Additionally, use this procedure when preparing servers for Terminal Services. This keeps users' profiles from choking the system partition with thousands of profile files and folders.

To set up your own Registry settings in `NTUSER.DAT`, follow these steps:

1. Choose Start ➢ Run to open the Run dialog box. In the Open box, type **regedt32.exe** and press Enter to open the Registry Editor.

2. Select `HKEY_USERS`, as shown in Figure 9.4.

3. Choose File ➢ Load Hive.

4. For Type 1 computers, browse to the `C:\Documents and Settings\Default User` folder, shown in Figure 9.4. For Type 2 computers, browse to `c:\Users\Default`. You might have to specifically type in the path, as the file requester may hide it from you if you are not displaying hidden files and folders.

5. Select `NTUSER.DAT`.

6. When prompted to enter a key name, anything will work, but for our example let's use **this is a dummy key name**, and click OK. Figure 9.5 shows an example. The key name is only temporary, so its name doesn't particularly matter.

7. Traverse to any Registry key and value. In this case, we'll change all future wallpaper to `Coffee Bean.bmp`. To do that, traverse to Dummy Key Name ➢ Control Panel ➢ Desktop and double-click "`Wallpaper.`" If you're using Windows XP, enter the value in this example, **C:\windows\coffee bean.jpg**, as shown in Figure 9.6. If you're using Windows Vista, enter **c:\windows\web\wallpaper\img35.jpg**. Note there might already be a default image set, but you're now changing it.

FIGURE 9.4 Load the NTUSER.DAT file into the Registry.

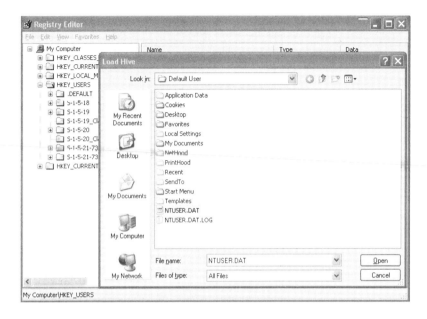

FIGURE 9.5 It doesn't matter what the temporary dummy key is called.

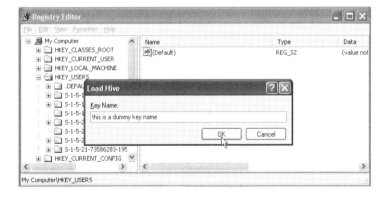

If the wallpaper file does not reside on the local system, you must alter the path to point to a server share. If the wallpaper is not present in the folder specified, no wallpaper will show up.

FIGURE 9.6   Enter the full path where the desired wallpaper is stored.

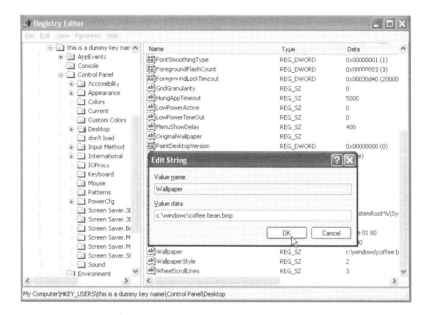

8. After you complete your changes, select your dummy key name, unload it by choosing File ➤ Unload Hive, and click OK to save the changes. Again, you must highlight your dummy key name to unload the hive.

Every time a new user generates a Local Profile, it pulls the settings from the Default Local Profile, which now has the coffee bean background picture. (Current users do not see the change because they've already generated Local Profiles before the coffee bean picture was set in the default Local Profile.)

Test your changes by creating a new local user and logging on. Since this user has never logged on before, this should create a new User Profile from the default profile. See if the new user gets the coffee bean background for Windows XP and the "waterdrop" background for Windows Vista.

The Default Domain User Profile

The Default Domain User Profile is similar to the Default Local User Profile, except that it's centralized. Once a Default Domain User Profile is set up, new users logging on to workstations in the domain will automatically download the centralized Default Domain User Profile instead of using any individual Default Local User Profile. This can be a way to make default centralized settings, such as the background or Desktop shortcuts, available for anyone whenever they first log on to a machine.

> **WARNING**   Don't create a Default Domain User Profile using Windows 2000, Windows XP, or Windows 2003 and expect your Windows NT clients to understand it. Remember: Windows NT is Type 0, Windows 2000, Windows XP and Windows Server 2003 are Type 1, and Windows Vista and Longhorn Server are Type 2. Exchanging material between the types can be unpredictable.

For these examples, we'll need you to create a new, mere-mortal user in the domain. In this example, we'll assume you created a user named Brett Wier.

Default Domain User Profiles for Type 1 Computers

It's easy to create a Default Domain User Profile for Type 1 computers. From any Type 1 computer, log on as Brett Wier and follow these steps:

1. Create a new, mere-mortal user in the domain. In this example, we'll create Brett Wier. From any workstation in your domain, log on as Brett.

2. Modify the Desktop as you wish. In this example, we'll use the Appearance tab in the Display Properties dialog box to change the color scheme to olive green. All you need to do is right-click the Desktop and select Properties. Then, select the Appearance tab. When you're done and back at the Desktop, create a text file, FILE1.txt.

3. Log off as Brett Wier.

4. Log back on to the workstation as the domain Administrator.

5. Click Start, and then right-click My Computer and choose Properties from the shortcut menu to open the System Properties dialog box.

6. Click the Advanced tab, and then click the Settings button in the User Profiles section to open the User Profiles dialog box.

7. Select bwier, as shown in Figure 9.7.

8. Click the Copy To button to open the Copy To dialog box, and in the "Copy profile to" field, enter the full path, plus the words **default user**, of the NETLOGON share of a Windows 2000 or Windows 2003 Domain Controller, as shown in Figure 9.8. In this example, it's \\dc01\netlogon\Default User. The Default User folder is automatically created.

9. Click the Change button in the Permitted to Use section, and change the default from the original user to Everyone, as shown in Figure 9.8. This lets everyone use the profile in the domain.

10. Click OK to actually copy the profile to the new folder and to close the Copy To dialog box.

11. Click OK to close the System Properties dialog box.

You can test your Default Domain Profile by creating a new user in the domain and logging on to any Windows XP or Windows 2000 machine. Verify that the Default Domain Profile is working by seeing if the olive green color scheme appears and that FILE1.TXT is present on the Desktop. Remember, you'll only see the magic for users who have no Local Profiles already on target machines.

FIGURE 9.7   Select Brett's entry in the User Profiles dialog box.

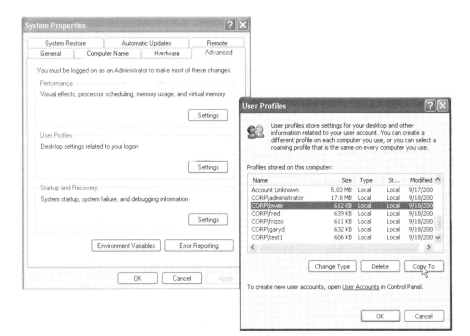

FIGURE 9.8   Copy the profile you just created to the NETLOGON share of a Domain Controller. Then, click Change to allow Everyone to use the profile.

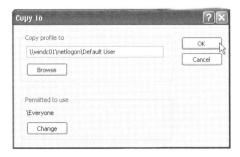

Default Domain User Profiles for Type 2 Computers

For Windows Vista and Longhorn, you can get the same control. But, here's the trick: remember how Windows XP (Type 1) and Windows Vista (Type 2) profiles are incompatible? Well, that's about to matter a whole lot, right here. To that end, we need to know a certain piece of Windows Vista magic. That is, Windows Vista will only read profile directories from the network if they end in a special moniker: .v2. That's right—the directory names must have a .v2 hanging off them for Windows Vista to read it. So, the steps we'll perform next will be almost like what we did for Windows XP earlier, except this time, we'll provide our name with the special `.v2` designation hanging off of it. Then, when users log on to Windows Vista machines for the first time, Windows Vista will recognize the special directory (Default User) with the extra-special `.v2` moniker and download the profile just for that operating system.

From any Type 2 computer, log on as Brett Wier and follow these steps:

1. Be sure you're logged in to a Windows Vista machine as Brett.

2. Modify the Desktop as you wish. In this example, go ahead and simply plop a new text file on the Desktop: `vistafile1.txt` and put some fake data in it.

3. Log off as Brett Wier.

4. Log back on to the workstation as the domain Administrator.

5. Click Start, and then right-click Computer and choose Properties from the shortcut menu to open the System Properties dialog box.

6. Click the Advanced System Settings task, and then click the Settings button in the User Profiles section to open the User Profiles dialog box.

7. Select bwier, as shown previously in Figure 9.7. Note this figure shows Windows XP, but it should look similar in Windows Vista.

8. Click the Copy To button to open the Copy To dialog box, and in the "Copy profile to" field, enter the full path plus the default user of the `NETLOGON` share of a Windows 2000 or Windows 2003 Domain Controller, as shown in Figure 9.8. In this example, it's `\\dc01\netlogon\Default User.v2`. Note that no quotes are needed, as seen in Figure 9.9. The `Default User.V2` folder is automatically created.

FIGURE 9.9 Be sure to put the .v2 extension in, because this is a Windows Vista (Type 2) profile

9. Click the Change button in the Permitted to Use section, and change the default from the original user to Everyone, as shown previously in Figure 9.8.

    This lets everyone use the profile in the domain.

10. Click OK to actually copy the profile to the new folder and to close the Copy To dialog box.

11. Click OK to close the System Properties dialog box.

You can test your Default Domain Profile by creating a new user in the domain and logging on to any Windows Vista machine. Verify that the Windows Vista ".v2" Default Domain Profile is working by seeing if the VISTAFILE1.TXT is present on the Desktop.

Remember, you'll only see the magic for users who have no Local Profiles already on target Windows Vista machines. Also remember that Windows XP users will have their own Default User profiles, so this can get a little confusing.

Roaming Profiles

Now that you're familiar with the files and folders that make up Local Profiles, you're ready to implement Roaming Profiles. Roaming Profiles are a logical extension to the Local Profiles concept. When users hop from machine to machine, the customized settings they created on one machine are automatically placed on and displayed at any machine they log on to.

For instance, you might have an organization in which 30 computers are at each site for general use by the sales team. If any member of the sales team comes into any office, they know they can log on to any machine and be confident that the settings from their last session are patiently waiting on the server.

Setting up Roaming Profiles for users in Active Directory is a straightforward process: share a folder to house the profiles, and then point each user's profile toward the single shared folder. By default, Roaming Profiles save a copy of the profile to the local hard drive. That way, if the network or server becomes unavailable, the user can use the last-used profile as a cached version. Additionally, if the user's Roaming Profile on the server is unavailable (and there is no locally cached copy of the Roaming Profile), the system downloads and uses a temporary Default User Profile as an emergency measure to get the user logged on with some profile.

As you'll see in the next chapter, another advantage associated with Roaming Profiles is that if a machine crashes, the most recent "set" of the user environment is on the server for quick restoration.

For those of you who threw up your hands and gave up using Roaming Profiles in Windows NT, I encourage you to try again with the newer operating systems.

From Windows 2000 onward, the Roaming Profile algorithm has been way improved since the NT 4 days. Specifically, there are three reasons why the improved algorithm is better than the old NT 4 counterpart:

Roaming Profiles Now Account for "Multiple Logins"   Most people had problems when a single user logged on to multiple machines at the same time. In NT 4, the profile was preserved only from the last computer the user logged off from—potentially losing important files in the profile. Modern Windows systems don't work that way. They do a file-by-file comparison of files *before* they get sent back to the server—sending only the latest time-stamped file to help quell this problem. So, give it another go if you despaired in the past.

However, one warning should be noted. All the user's settings are represented as one single file: NTUSER.DAT. Because the last writer wins, the NTUSER.DAT with the latest time stamp overwrites all others. If you make two independent changes to a setting on two different machines, you can lose one because only the NTUSER.DAT with the latest time stamp "wins."

Roaming Profiles Now Only Pull down and Push up Changed Files NT 4 Roaming Profiles were on the slow side—especially over slow links. The good news about profiles from modern systems is that only new and changed files are specifically moved around the network. So, if someone logs on to the same machine over and over again, the user is not waiting for the whole gamut of profile files to be downloaded. Logging in is now faster than ever.

Better Terminal Services Support for Roaming Profiles In Windows 2000, when the user logs off a session, the system tries 60 times—about once a second by default—to tidy up the NTUSER.DAT file and send it back to the server to be housed in the Roaming Profile. Usually, it only needs one try (and about one second) to do this task. This support has been increased since Windows 2000, so see the sidebar "A Brief History of the Unloading of NTUSER.DAT and UPHclean."

A Brief History of the Unloading of *NTUSER.DAT* and UPHclean

In Windows 2000, when a profile was ready to be unloaded, it simply waited for a little bit of time. If the handle was still not closed, Windows 2000 just gave up—nothing roams and the hive is still (uh-oh) loaded. This caused profile corruption a-go-go. To that end, a policy setting named "Maximum Retries to Unload and Update User Profile" can tell Windows 2000 to increase the number of tries. Bad news: there's a bug in the policy setting description which makes it seem like this policy is meant to affect Windows Server 2003 and Windows XP machines. But it doesn't. It's just for Windows 2000 machines.

In XP/WS03, the same unloading process occurs but with a little work-around. The current Registry is saved into another file, and then at logoff, roams that file to the server's NTUSER.DAT. But the problem is that the real NTUSER.DAT file on the local machine is still loaded. If, after a while, the handle is closed, then the hive will be unloaded. But if the handle is *not* closed, and if user logs on again, the hive will continue to be used.

Uh-oh again. Sounds like corruption city again, right?

In this case, Roaming Profiles will not be able to update this version of NTUSER.DAT even though the server's NTUSER.DAT might be newer. So, what's the solution?

So, Microsoft made a download available called "User Profile Hive Cleanup Service" (or UPH-Clean), to force the handle to be closed in just this situation. It solves this exact problem and is why it's suggested for Windows Server 2003 Terminal Services. You can locate the tool at `http://tinyurl.com/5of5r`.

In Vista, this "force unload" logic is already inside the profile service itself, so this problem simply won't be a problem anymore. Microsoft swears that it's a "guarantee" that the user hive will be unloaded and therefore roam it at logoff. It is doing the same thing as XP/WS03 UPHClean but in a much better way.

Setting Up Roaming Profiles

The first thing we need to do on our server, Dc01, is to create and share a folder in which to store our profiles. In this example, we'll choose a novel name—Profiles. Normally, you'd do this procedure on some file server somewhere—not on a Domain Controller. But we'll continue onward, because there's no harm here in our test lab. Again, I'll assume your server has two drives, C: and D:, and we'll perform these functions on our D: drive.

To create and share a folder in which to store Roaming Profiles, follow these steps:

1. Log on to Dc01 as Administrator.

2. From the Desktop, click My Computer to open the My Computer folder.

3. Find a place to create a users folder. In this example, we'll use D:\PROFILES. After entering the D: drive, right-click and select New ➤ Folder. Name your new folder **Profiles**.

 You can substitute any name for Profiles. Additionally, you can hide the share name by placing a $ after the name, such as Profiles$.

4. Right-click the newly created Profiles folder, and choose "Sharing and Security" from the shortcut menu to open Profiles Properties dialog box at the Sharing tab.

5. Click "Share this folder." Windows 2000 and Windows XP client computers require that the permissions on the share are at least set to "Change." The defaults on Windows 2003 servers are for Everyone to have Read rights, which isn't sufficient. Use the Permissions button to change the rights so that Authenticated Users have at least Change rights, as shown in Figure 9.10. Additionally read the sidebar on "Caching and Roaming Profiles" before continuing.

Now you need to specify which network user accounts can use Roaming Profiles. In this example, you'll specify Brett Wier. Brett will now be able to hop from workstation to workstation. When he logs off one workstation, the changes in the profile will be preserved on the server. He can then log on to any other workstation in the domain and maintain the same user experience.

FIGURE 9.10 Change the permissions on the Profiles share so that Authenticated Users have at least Change control.

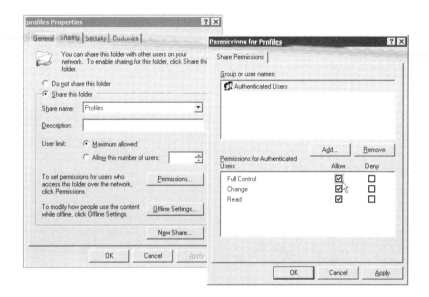

Caching and Roaming Profiles

Roaming Profiles are automatically cached with their own independent algorithm. In Figure 9.10, you can see the "Caching" button which controls caching on a share. We'll learn about offline files and caching in the next chapter. But, for now, we need to have a little side discussion about the Caching button.

Windows 2000 servers have caching turned off by default for all shares.

Windows 2003 severs have caching set up such that users can manually specify what files to keep offline.

A Windows XP machine tells you everything you need to know the first time you go to the event log when the default caching setting on a Windows Server 2003 is used in conjunction with a Roaming Profile share.

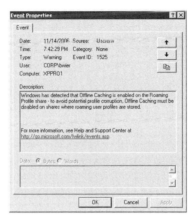

Windows XP explains that "…Offline Caching must be disabled on shares where roaming user profiles are stored." To do that, click the "Caching" button within the Profiles share and select "Files or programs from the share will not be available offline" as seen here.

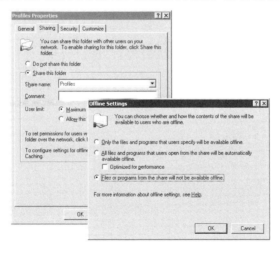

When you do, you'll see Windows XP and Windows Vista stop complaining. (Windows XP and Windows Vista complain with the same Event ID.)

For more information on this phenomenon, see the Knowledge Base article Q287566, "Offline File Caching Option Must Be Disabled on Roaming Profile." (For more on the Caching button, see Chapter 10.) Additionally, do not use the Encrypting File System (EFS) on shares containing Roaming Profiles. If you do so, roaming will not work.

To modify accounts to use Roaming Profiles, you'll leverage Active Directory Users and Computers as follows:

1. Choose Start ➤ Programs ➤ Administrative Tools ➤ Active Directory Users and Computers.

2. Expand Corp.com in the tree pane, and double-click Brett Wier's account to open the Brett Wier Properties dialog box; click his Profile tab.

3. In the Profile Path field, specify the server, the share name, and folder you want to use, such as **\\Dc01\profiles\%username%**. After you enter that, click OK. Then, just as a quick test, go back into the user account and look again at the Profile tab. When you do, you should see the username automatically filled in, as seen in Figure 9.11. For our purposes, you can leave all other fields blank.

The syntax of *%username%* is the secret sauce that allows the system to automatically create a Roaming Profiles folder underneath the share. The *%username%* variable is evaluated at first use, and Windows springs into action and creates the profile. Windows is smart too—it sets up the permissions on the folder with only the required NTFS permissions, such that only the user has access to read and modify the contents of the profile. If you want administrators to have access along with the user, see the information in the "Add the Administrators Security Group to Roaming User Profiles" section later in this chapter.

4. Click OK.

FIGURE 9.11   Point the user's profile path settings at the server and share name.

Modifying Multiple Users' Profile Paths

After you set up Roaming Profiles and get comfortable with their use, you'll likely want the rest of your users to start using Roaming Profiles as well. The Windows 2003 Active Directory Users and Computers tool allows you to modify the profile paths of multiple users simultaneously. To do so, follow these steps:

1. Select the users (hold down Ctrl to select discontiguous users).

2. Right-click the selection, and choose Properties from the shortcut menu to open the "Properties On Multiple Objects" dialog box:

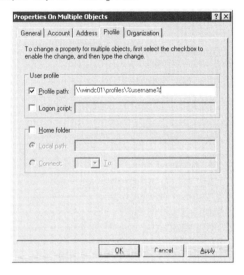

3. Click the Profile tab, if necessary.

4. Click the Profile path check box, and enter the path.

5. Click OK to give all the selected users the same path, making sure you use the %username% convention in the path you specify.

If you're running Windows 2000 (or just want to put on your coding hat), you can use the following sample VBScript code to run though all the users in the domain Corp.com in the Phoenix OU and change their profile path so that they have access only to their own profile folder. Upon first use by the user, the folder is automatically created, and the user is granted exclusive access to that folder.

```
Set UserContainer = getobject("LDAP://ou=Phoenix,dc=Corp,dc=com")
UserContainer.filter = array("User")
```

```
for each User in UserContainer
     Username = User.SamAccountName
     Userprofilepath = "\\Profile_server\Profiles\" & Username


     Wscript.Echo User.ProfilePath


     If User.ProfilePath = "" Then
          User.Put "ProfilePath" , UserProfilePath
          User.Setinfo
        Wscript.Echo "Profile for user " & Username & " has been set to " &
UserProfilePath & "."
     Else
          Wscript.Echo "Profile for user " & Username & " was already set to " &
UserProfilePath & "."
     End if


next
```

Testing Roaming Profiles

You can easily test Roaming Profiles if you have multiple workstation machines. I suggest you log on as Brett from both a Windows XP machine (Type 1) and a Windows Vista machine (Type 2). Make sure these workstations are members in your domain.

Roaming from Windows XP to Windows XP

Log on first to the Windows XP machine. Then, make two simple changes to the profile for testing:

1. In the My Documents folder, create XPFILE1.TXT and save some dummy data inside.

2. Change the color scheme to something different—like silver.

3. Log off as Brett Wier.

4. Log on to another workstation as Brett Wier and make sure that FILE1.TXT was properly sent to the second machine and that the background has changed.

Right-click the XPFILE1.TXT and choose Properties from the shortcut menu to see the file's properties. Take note of the path where the file is actually residing. You can compare that file's location now (the local hard drive) with the file's location after the next chapter is completed. Hopefully, by the time the next chapter is completed, the file will be magically transported to the server, and the display will demonstrate this.

Roaming from Windows Vista to Windows Vista

Now, log on as Brett to a Windows Vista machine.

Then, make two simple changes to the profile for testing:

1. In the My Documents folder, create VISTAFILE1.TXT and save some dummy data inside.

2. Change the color scheme to something different—like "Windows Classic."

3. Log off as Brett Wier.

4. Log on to another Windows Vista workstation as Brett Wier and make sure that VISTAFILE1.TXT was properly sent to the second machine and that the background has changed.

Right-click the VISTAFILE1.TXT and choose Properties from the shortcut menu to see the file's properties. Take note of the path where the file is actually residing. You can compare that file's location now (the local hard drive) with the file's location after the next chapter is completed. Hopefully, by the time you perform all the exercises in the next chapter, the file will be magically transported to the server and the display will demonstrate this.

Additionally, notice how XPFILE1.txt, the file created on the Windows XP machine is not present. Again, this is because Windows Vista (Type 2 profiles) and Windows XP (Type 1 profiles) don't "intermingle."

Back on the Server

If you check out what's transpired on the server, two unique directories are created for Brett, one for each type of computer he logs on to (Type 1 and Type 2), as seen in Figure 9.12.

Additionally, note that even if you're an administrator, you cannot dive in to Brett's profile folders. An example of this failure can be seen in Figure 9.13. This is a safety mechanism that gives Brett exclusive permissions over his own sensitive stuff. If you want administrators to have access along with the user, see the information in the "Add the Administrators Security Group to Roaming User Profiles" later in this chapter.

FIGURE 9.12 On the server, a folder for each computer type has been generated.

FIGURE 9.13 Administrators cannot poke around User Profiles (by default).

Upshot of Roaming Profiles in a Mixed Windows Vista and Windows XP World

It's bad news for mixed environments. Logging on to Windows XP and then to Windows Vista (or vice versa) does not "share" information in any way.

As we saw, XPFILE1.txt was created (and available) only in the Windows XP profile. And VISTAFILE1.TXT was created (and available) only in the Windows Vista profile. So, Windows XP and Windows Vista profile data can never be shared.

What a bummer (on the surface at least). But don't worry; we'll overcome it.

To that end, if we want a "one stop shop" place for our documents, Start Menu icons, and more, we'll have to leverage the Folder Redirection mechanism in the next chapter. Not to get too far ahead of ourselves, but Folder Redirection's goal is to make various items (like the Documents of Windows Vista and the My Documents of Windows XP) point to the *same place* on a network share. That way, regardless of the kind of machine you log in with (Windows XP or Windows Vista), your data will *always* be available.

So, stay tuned for that in the next chapter.

When Folder Redirection is used to maintain a "singe location" for XP and Vista clients, you get the added bonus! That is, your Vista machines see any changed data *instantly* and no longer have to logoff/logon for redirected data. This "split" scheme also helps logon/logoff performance as well.

The Impact of Users Latching on to *Documents*/*My Documents*

Because Documents (for Vista) and My Documents (pre-Vista) is part of the profile, there is the extra burden of lugging all the files in My Documents back and forth across the network each time a user logs on. This can have serious ramifications. Once users start using the My Documents folder, they generally don't want to stop. They place 50MB worth of PowerPoint files, 50MB of Word documents, and 50MB of Visio files in My Documents and then roam to another workstation, and they've just moved 150MB of data across the network at logon time! Ouch!

In any case, this pain can fortunately be mitigated in two ways. Windows 2000 and newer clients handle Roaming Profiles differently than their Windows NT cousin does.

Let's imagine that we have two users: one on Windows NT and another on Windows 2000, Windows XP, Windows Vista, or Windows 2003. Each user puts 300MB of files into the Roaming Profile. When a user on Windows NT does this, all files in the profile are copied up to the server—lock, stock, and barrel—up to the server and then back over to the target workstation every time a user logs on or off. Can you say "Painful"?

Windows 2000 and newer clients transfer *only* changed files up and back between the client and server. Thus, if a user transfers 60MB of data and then changes one file, only that file is sent back to be saved in the Roaming Profile. This feature is great news if a user uses the same machine day in and day out; only the changes are pushed up and back. But the usefulness of this feature breaks down any time a user roams to a computer they have never used before. In this case, the entire contents of the Roaming Profile (including Documents/My Documents) is brought down from the server.

That's why the real power comes with a key feature, Redirected Folders, which we'll explore in the next chapter.

Migrating Local Profiles to Roaming Profiles

In some situations, you might already have lots of machines with Local Profiles. That is, you didn't start off your network using Roaming Profiles, and now you have either many machines with Local Profiles or just pockets of machines with a combination of Roaming Profiles and Local Profiles. You can, if you want, maintain the user's Local Profile settings and transfer them to the spot on the server you set up earlier. You can convert a Local Profile to a Roaming Profile in two ways. Whichever option you choose, you first need to set up a share on a server.

Automatic Upload of Existing Local Profiles

In general, this step couldn't be easier. As we did earlier, on each user's Profile tab, point the profile path to \\servername\share\%username%, as seen in Figure 9.11. The next time the user logs on to a machine with a Local Profile (and then logs off), the Local Profile is automatically uploaded to the server to become their future Roaming Profile. For most users, this is the way to go.

And, remember, profiles are zapped up to their source on the server independently. If a user has used both a Windows XP or Windows Vista machine in the past, and then travels back to these Desktops, then each computer's profile is zapped up into their own directory. Those directories can be seen in Figure 9.12 as seen earlier.

But, what if the same filename exists, say, on the Desktop on three machines the user has logged on to in the past? The system will automatically figure out which is the "last written" file based on the file date. And, that file will end up being the only copy placed in the directory. In other words, you won't see three files with the same name in the profile directory—even if it exists on three local machines.

Manual Upload of Existing Local Profiles

If the user has logged on to multiple workstations and therefore has multiple Local Profiles, you might want to guarantee that one specific Local Profile becomes the Roaming Profile for that user. The procedure is nearly identical to the one you used to create the Default Domain

User Profile. To preserve a specific Local Profile and convert it to a Roaming Profile, follow these steps:

1. Log on as the Administrator to the workstation where the desired Local Profile resides.

2. Choose Start, right-click My Computer (for Windows XP) or Computer (for Windows Vista), and choose Properties from the shortcut menu to open the System Properties dialog box.

3. For Windows XP, click the Advanced tab, or for Windows Vista, click "Advanced system settings."

4. Then in the User Profiles section, click Settings to open the "User Profiles" dialog box.

5. Select the Local Profile you want to convert to a Roaming Profile, and then click the Copy To button to open the Copy To dialog box, as shown in Figure 9.14.

6. Enter the server name, shared folder name, and folder name of the profile storage path. In Figure 9.14, this is the path for a Type 1 computer (like Windows XP). If this were a Windows Vista machine, you would have to type **.v2** at the end, like \\dc01\profiles\ jkissel.v2, as shown in Figure 9.15.

7. Also, be sure to change the profile so that at least the user has access. It's generally okay to modify the profile permissions to Everyone.

8. Click OK.

When you do, the user's folder is automatically created in the shared folder.

FIGURE 9.14   In Windows XP, to move a specific profile to the server, use the Copy To dialog box.

FIGURE 9.15   If you want to zap up a Windows Vista profile, you need to add a ".v2" at the end, as seen here.

> ### Changing the Profile Type from Roaming to Local
>
> Mere-mortal users (those without administrative privileges) can go to the User Profiles dialog (as seen on Figure 9.7), choose their own profile, then change the profile type with the "Change Type" button. This will change their profile from Roaming to Local or back again and thus specify which copy of the profile (Local or Roaming) is to be used when they log on.
>
> If a user selects Local Profile, a Roaming Profile reverts to a Local Profile. The Roaming Profile on the server stays there, but the user doesn't use it when working at this local machine. The next time the user works at this specific workstation, the changes are only saved to the Local Profile.
>
> If the user selects Roaming Profile, and the Roaming Profile is on the server, the system determines which copy is newer. If the local copy is newer, the user is asked whether to keep or ditch the profile on the server.

Also, don't forget that for each specific user Local Profile you manually convert to a Roaming Profile, you'll need to modify the profile path (similar to that seen in Figure 9.11 earlier). Once you've done this, this user, Jimmy Kissel can now log on to any Windows 2000 or Windows XP machine as jkissel, and this specific profile (that you just pushed up) will follow him as a Roaming Profile.

Roaming and Nonroaming Folders

Oftentimes, you'll want to get a handle on specifically what, inside the Roaming Profile, is roaming and what isn't roaming. Things are different for Windows Vista and Longhorn Server (Type 2 computers) and Windows 2000, XP, and Windows 2003 (Type 1 computers). Let's check out those differences here.

Roaming and Nonroaming Folders for Type 1 Computers

Now that you have a grip on which folders constitute the profile and how to set up a Roaming Profile, it might be helpful to know a bit about what's going on behind the scenes. Remember that several folders make up our profile.

Type 1 Profile Directories That Do Not Roam

Local settings, including local machine-specific application folders and information, do not roam when Roaming Profiles are enabled. This is true for the local computer's `Application Data`. Some applications write information specific to the local computer here. The Application Data folder is located in `\Documents and Settings\<Username>\Local Settings`. Any subfolder below this folder also does not roam, including:

- `History`
- `Temp`
- `Temporary Internet Files`

Type 1 Profile Directories That Do Roam

All other folders do roam with the user:

There's an Application Data directory which does roam with the user. This Application Data folder is located in Documents and Settings\<*Username*>. This is typically a per-user store for application data, such as Office 2000/Windows XP/2003 Custom Dictionary. These are the kinds of things you would want to roam with the user.

- Cookies
- Desktop
- Favorites
- My Documents
- My Pictures
- NetHood
- PrintHood
- Recent
- Send To
- Start Menu
- Templates

Indeed, My Documents, My Pictures, Desktop, Start Menu, and Application Data have an additional property; they can each be redirected to a specific point on the server, as you'll see in the next chapter.

Roaming and Nonroaming Folders for Type 2 Computers

If we crack open a Windows Vista Roaming Profile, we can see some things are similar and some things are different compared to a Type 1 profile.

Figure 9.16 shows what the profiles look like when viewed from a pre-Vista machine. Note how the "My" prefix "magically" appears when viewed here, even though, under the hood there is no "My" prefix. You can see this in Figure 9.17 when viewed directly from a Windows Vista machine.

In order to see the contents in Figure 9.16, you need to be logged in as Brett Wier, or take ownership of the directory as the Administrator.

Let's get a grip on which directories roam and which don't roam.

Type 2 Profile Directories That Do Not Roam

Local settings, including local machine-specific application folders and information, do not roam, even when Roaming Profiles are enabled. The non-roaming directories will stay on each local computer in the \Users\<Username>\AppData\ directory. Inside \AppData are two directories which contain this non-roaming data: Local and LocalLow.

Any subfolders within Local or LocalLow do not roam, including:

- History
- Temp
- Temporary Internet Files

 See the sidebar entitled "The *LocalLow* Folder within *AppData*" for more information about LocalLow.

FIGURE 9.16   Some of the contents of a Type 2 computer are similar to a Type 1 computer. Note that when viewed on a pre-Vista machine, Type 2 profiles have the "My" prefix due to viewing them within a pre-Vista machine's Explorer.

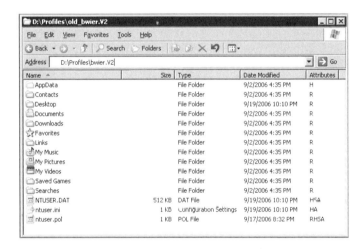

FIGURE 9.17   The same folder, when viewed directly from the command line. Note the absence of the "My" prefix for Music, Pictures and Videos.

Type 2 Profile Directories that Roam

All other folders do roam with the user. When a Roaming Profile is enabled, these directories are shot up to the server and stored within a user's own private directory with their <username>.v2:

- Contacts (new for Windows Vista)
- Desktop
- Favorites
- Documents (was My Documents in Windows XP)
- My Pictures (in Windows XP this was under My Documents and now, in Windows Vista, it's at the root of the profile).
- My Music (in Windows XP this was under My Documents and now, in Windows Vista, it's at the root of the profile).
- My Videos (new for Windows Vista)
- Under \Appdata\Roaming\Microsoft you will find:
  - Credentials
  - Crypto
  - Internet Explorer
  - Protect
  - SystemCertificates

Of course, your users will need their day-to-day goodies as they roam from machine to machine. This is known as Per-User Application Data. This stuff is stored within the Roaming Profile's \Appdata\Roaming\Microsoft\Windows directory. Here, you'll see lots of stuff you know and love, including the following Desktop attributes, as seen in Figure 9.18:

- Network Shortcuts
- Printer Shortcuts
- Recent
- SendTo
- Start Menu
- Templates
- Themes
- Cookies (hidden for some reason)

FIGURE 9.18   The AppData\Roaming directory in the Type 2 computer contains the only directories which will roam with the user.

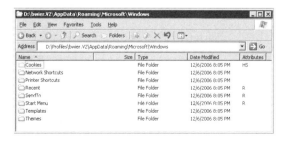

Additional System Profiles for Windows XP, Windows 2003, and Windows Vista (but Not Windows 2000)

Windows XP, Windows 2003, and Windows Vista contain two new profiles that are meant to be used by newly installed services: Local Service and Network Service.

Local Service   Meant to be used by services that are local to the computer but do not need intricate local privileges or network access. This is in contrast to the "System" account, which pretty much has total authority over the system. If a service runs as Local Service, it appears to be a member in the local users group. When a service runs as Local Service across the network, the service appears as an anonymous user.

Network Service   Similar to Local Service, but has elevated network access rights—similar to the System account. When a process runs under Network Service rights, it does so as the SID (Security ID) assigned to the computer.

Windows XP, Windows 2003, and Windows Vista automatically create these profiles, which are basically normal but still a little special. For instance, you will not see the Local Service or Network Service in the listing of Profiles in the System Properties dialog box. You can see them in the Documents and Settings folder; however, they're "super-hidden" so that mere-mortals cannot see them by default. You can see them in the top window here:

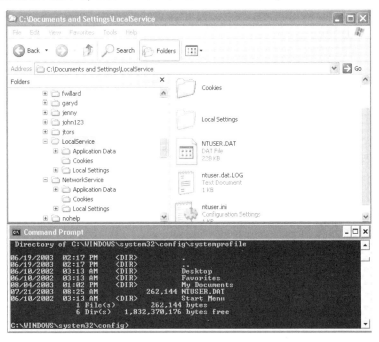

On Windows Vista, the LocalService and NetworkService profiles have moved to `%windir%\ServiceProfiles` directory. Windows can also load software, services, and its own profile when the computer starts up. Indeed, you see this profile in the "Log on to Windows" dialog box, in which you are prompted to press Ctl+Alt+Del. Basically, this is the profile for when no one is logged on.

When this happens, Windows loads what is called the .DEFAULT (pronounced "dot default") profile. In Windows 2000, the .DEFAULT profile was in `c:\winnt\%computername%`, in which *%computername%* is the name of the computer. But applications sometimes flipped out if services tried to load portions of this part of the profile's Registry. To adjust for this, Windows XP , Windows 2003, and Windows Vista plunked the .DEFAULT profile in `c:\windows\system32\config\SystemProfile`. Applications that leverage the .DEFAULT profile always use this Registry part, and troublesome application problems related to .DEFAULT should be quelled.

You can see the SystemProfile in the command prompt window in the lower half of the preceding graphic.

Managing Roaming Profiles

We've just been through how to set up and use Roaming Profiles. But don't leave home without these two parting words about managing them day to day.

Merging Local Profile and Roaming Profile

Once a Roaming Profile is established, users can hop from machine to machine confident that they'll get the same settings. However, if a user with a Roaming Profile hops to a Windows XP machine on which they once had a Local Profile, something special happens: the previous Local Profile and the existing Roaming Profile are merged (except for the NTUSER.DAT settings). This data is then saved to the Roaming Profile folder on the server at logoff time.

This is helpful should a user have just the one copy of a critical document stored in the My Documents folder of XPPRO2. The next time he logs on to XPPRO2, that missing document will now appear in his My Documents in his Roaming Profile. Oh, and you don't have to worry about overwriting existing files in the profile either; the latest time-stamped file is preserved.

Ditto for a Windows Vista machine and its profile. Just remember that these profiles are considered separate (because they are).

You can prevent this behavior on Windows XP and Windows Vista machines. For information on how to do this, see the "Prevent Roaming Profile Changes from Propagating to the Server" section later in this chapter.

Guest Account Profile

Who uses the Guest account anymore? Apparently someone, because Microsoft has slightly changed the behavior of the Guest account in Windows XP and onward. That is, the profile of a guest user is deleted at logoff—but only when the computer is joined to a domain. If the Windows XP or Windows 2003 machine is in a workgroup, no guest profiles (of users in the Guests group) are deleted at logoff.

If the Windows XP or Windows 2003 computer is in a domain, and a user is a member of both the Guests and the Local Administrators group, the profile is not deleted—quite an unlikely scenario.

Cross-Forest Trusts

Roaming Profiles, like GPOs, are affected by Cross-Forest Trusts. Whether a user gets a Roaming Profile depends on the client operating system they're logged on to. (This operating-specific variance is documented in Chapter 3.) When clients log on to computers that enforce the rule, you'll get the message shown in Figure 9.19.

You can use a policy setting to prevent this from affecting your client computers. To do this, locate the **Allow Cross-Forest User Policy and Roaming User Profiles** policy setting by drilling down in Computer ➢ Administrative Templates ➢ System ➢ Group Policy.

FIGURE 9.19   Users roaming within Cross-Forest scenarios receive this message.

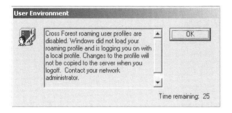

Affecting Roaming Profiles with Computer Group Policy Settings

Roaming Profiles are simple to set up and maintain, but sometimes you'll want to use certain policy settings to affect their behavior. The policies you'll be setting appear in the Computer Configuration section of Group Policy. Drill down into Administrative Templates ➢ System ➢ User Profiles, as shown in Figure 9.20. In Windows 2000, these User Profiles policies were not located under their own branch but in Administrative Templates ➢ System ➢ Logon.

Recall from Chapter 1 that computers must be in the OU that the GPO affects (or in a child OU that inherits the setting). Or the GPO could be linked to the root of the domain and scoped to a security group that the computer is a member of.

If a user is moved to a new OU then the user needs to logoff and back on. If a machine is moved to a new OU then the machine needs to reboot.

Before implementing any policy setting that affects Roaming Profiles, read through this section and determine if it adds value to your environment. Then, create a test OU and ensure that the behavior is as expected.

FIGURE 9.20 There are many policy settings that affect profiles.

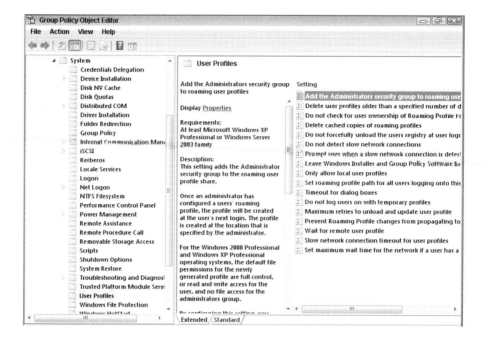

Do Not Check for User Ownership of Roaming Profile Folders

 This policy setting applies only to Windows 2003 computers, Windows XP (SP1 and later) computers, Windows 2000/SP4 computers, and Windows Vista computers.

Windows XP without a service pack and Windows 2000 with SP3 and earlier may have a potential security hole. If someone, such as a person in the Server Operators group, can pre-create the user's target profile subfolder on the server, that creator is also the owner of the sub-folder. When the user then pushes up their profile to the subfolder, the user isn't the only one with access to the profile; the creator/owner also has access. This could mean that the creator/owner can peer inside and get stuff they really shouldn't have.

If a client logs on to a Windows 2003, Windows XP (SP1 and later), Windows 2000/SP4 computer, or Windows Vista, the machine is smart enough to first check to see if the user is the only one with permissions on the folder (as seen earlier in Figure 9.13) before moving sensitive profile data up. If you enable this policy setting, you're telling newer machines to act like older machines and allow sensitive profile information to move up to the server, even if the user doesn't have exclusive access and ownership to the subfolder. Personally, I would leave this unconfigured. (You can read more about this in the Knowledge Base article 327259.)

Delete Cached Copies of Roaming Profiles

This is a space-saving and security mechanism that automatically deletes the user's locally cached profile when the user logs off. The default behavior is to allow files to be downloaded and pile up on each and every hard drive to which the user roams. You can enable this policy setting to (as the forest rangers say) "Leave only footprints and only take away memories at your campsite." Heck, you won't even be leaving any footprints.

This policy setting has two downsides, however; let's walk through two scenarios to examine these potential problems. And, we'll look at one really good use for this setting.

Scenario 1: Server Down at Login Time   This policy setting is set to delete cached copies of Roaming Profiles. The user logs on, makes some changes, and logs off. The profile is automatically sent back to the server, and the footprints are washed away on the local machine.

Now, let's say that the server that houses the Roaming Profiles goes down. By default, if the user tries to log on and the server is unavailable to deliver the Roaming Profile, the locally cached copy of the profile is summoned to take its place. Once you enable this policy setting, you're severing a potential lifeline to the user if the server that houses the Roaming Profile becomes unavailable. Enabling this policy setting sweeps up after the user on the local machine at logoff. If the server goes down, the user will not get their locally cached version of the Roaming Profile because there is no locally cached version of the profile. Rather, the only profile the user will get is a temporary Local Profile that is not saved anywhere when the user logs off.

Scenario 2: Up and Back and Up and Back   Again, by setting this policy setting, you're deleting all cached files. So, when the user logs back on to the same machine, all the Roaming Profile files need to get redownloaded from the Roaming Profile on the server, which means you're killing the caching inherent in the Roaming Profile system. In essence, you're making your machine act like NT 4, where the whole profile gets redownloaded at login. Note, however, that at logoff time, things should still be faster than NT 4 because you're pushing up only changes (where NT 4 would have pushed up *all* the files).

Using This Setting in a High-Security Environment   This policy setting is useful in high-security environments where you need to make sure that no trace of potentially sensitive data in the profile is left behind. Be careful when using it with laptops, however, because users frequently need to use their copy of the locally cached version of the profile to get their work done. Additionally, enabling this policy setting does prevent third-party tools from "resurrecting" deleted files inside the profile. It deletes the files but doesn't obliterate them to prevent industrious hackers from any possible recovery.

Once this policy setting is Enabled, the profile is erased only on logoff. And then it erases only profiles from machines on which users don't already have an existing cached copy! If you need to maintain a high-security environment, be sure to enable this policy setting early so that users don't have time to roam from machine to machine sprinkling copies of their profiles around (which won't get erased later by use of this policy setting).

To use this policy setting, you'll need to disable (or not configure) the **Do not detect slow network connection** policy setting, as described shortly. If a network connection is determined to be slow, it automatically tries to grab the locally cached copy of the profile, which doesn't exist if you've enabled this **Delete cached copies of roaming profiles** policy setting.

Delete User Profiles Older Than a Specified Number of Days

This policy setting applies only to Windows Vista computers (and, presumably, Longhorn Servers).

What happens when Sally User logs on to a Vista machine on the 4th floor—one time? All her profile junk gets downloaded on that machine and sits there—forever. Just eating up disk space, never to be reclaimed again. Until now.

If you set this policy setting and specify a certain number of days, the roaming (and local) profiles on that Vista machine will be wiped clean—automatically. The user doesn't have to do anything. The system will automatically flush them down the, er, wherever it flushes them.

Here's a huge warning: Be careful with this setting, however. As any data that is in, say, only in a Local Profile (like the Documents folder) will be gone once the profile is wiped clean. Note that the data stored in the server-side copy of a Roaming Profile, and also any data redirected using redirected folders, is not touched. See Figures 9.21 and 9.22 to see a before and after picture to see how drastic profile cleanup really is!

FIGURE 9.21 A typical Vista computer after multiple users have logged on to it over time.

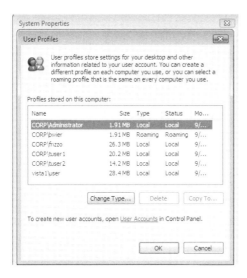

FIGURE 9.22   The same Vista computer this policy kicks in within 24 hours. Note even local User Profiles are gone.

Slow Network Connection Timeout for User Profiles

Enabling this entry performs a quick ping test to the profiles server. If the speed is greater than the minimum value, the Roaming Profile is downloaded. If, however, the speed is not fast enough, the locally cached profile is used unless you've enabled the previous entry (**Delete cached copy of local profiles**). In that case, the user ends up with a temporary profile as described earlier.

WARNING   Setting the **Do not detect slow network connection** policy setting, as described in the next section, forces anything set in this policy setting to be ignored.

This policy setting has two modes, which it uses automatically: IP and non-IP. If the computer housing the profiles is connected to a network using IP, the speed is measured in kilobits (Kb) per second. If the computer housing the profiles is not connected using IP, the speed is measured in milliseconds (ms).

This policy setting is a bit strange: even if it's not configured, it has a default. That default speed threshold for IP mode is 500KB; that is, if the ping test determines that the bandwidth to the machine that houses the profiles is greater than 500KB, the profile is downloaded. If the ping returns a bandwidth of less than 500KB, the Roaming Profile is skipped, and the locally cached profile is used.

That default speed threshold for non-IP mode is 120ms; that is, if a machine that houses the profiles responds in less than 120ms, the profile is downloaded. If the machine that houses the profiles does not respond to the test in 120ms, the profile is skipped, and the locally cached profile is used.

You might want to enable this policy setting and decrease the value thresholds if you want to increase the chances of a dial-up connection receiving the Roaming Profile instead of the locally cached profile. If you enable this policy setting, you'll need to manually specify both an IP ping time test and a non-IP ping millisecond test.

 Unrelated speed tests can verify the ability to apply GPOs for both the user and computer. They are in the Group Policy Editor under Computer or User Configuration ➤ Administrative Templates ➤ System ➤ Group Policy ➤ **Group Policy Slow Link Detection**.

Do Not Detect Slow Network Connections

Like the previous policy setting, this one is a little strange. If it's not configured, it still has a default; that is, the users affected by this policy setting check the **Slow network connection timeout for user profiles** setting to see what a "slow network" actually means. If you enable this policy setting, you're disabling slow network detection, and the values you place in the **Slow network connection timeout for user profiles** policy setting don't mean diddly, nor do the default values of 500KB or 120ms.

Wait for Remote User Profile

Again, even if this policy setting is not defined or disabled, there is still a default; if the speed is too slow, it will load the locally cached profile. If you enable this policy setting, the system waits until the Roaming Profile is downloaded—no matter how long it takes. You might turn this on if your users hop around a lot and the connection to the computer housing the Roaming Profiles is slow but not intolerable. That way, you'll still use the Roaming Profile stored on the server as opposed to the locally cached profile.

Prompt User When Slow Link Is Detected (in Vista, This Is Named "Prompt user when a slow network connection is detected")

When the ping test determines that the link speed is too slow, the user can be asked if they want to use the locally cached profile or grab the one from the server. If this policy setting is not configured or it's disabled, the user isn't even asked the question. If the **Wait for remote user profile** policy setting is enabled, the profile is downloaded from the server—however slowly.

For pre-Vista machines, if this policy setting is enabled, the user can determine whether they want to accept the profile from the server or utilize the locally cached profile.

For Windows Vista machines, if this policy setting is enabled, the user must determine before logon time (by using a check box at logon time) to use the local or remote profile, as seen in Figure 9.23.

If this setting is not configured or disabled, the system always uses the Local Profile instead of the Remote Profile when the link is slow.

FIGURE 9.23 You can specify to allow users to download their profile over a slow network connection before they actually log on using Windows Vista.

If you've enabled the **Delete cached copies of roaming profiles** policy setting, there won't be a local copy of the Roaming Profile, so the user will be forced to accept the Default User Profile. If the **Do not detect slow network connection properties** policy setting is enabled, this GPO is ignored.

Timeout for Dialog Boxes

This setting only applies to Windows 2000, Windows XP, and Windows Server 2003 clients (not Windows Vista).

If the **Prompt user when slow link is detected** policy setting is enabled, the user has a 30-second countdown to respond to whether they want to download their Roaming Profile anyway. Once this policy setting is enabled, the default value of 30 seconds can be changed. This dialog box timeout is also presented when the server that houses the Roaming Profile is unavailable, when the user logs off, or when the locally cached profile is newer than the Roaming Profile stored on the server. In all cases, the user can be prompted to determine what to do. The value you specify here is how many seconds to wait for an answer before the other policy settings make the decision for the user.

Do Not Log Users on with Temporary Profiles (Was Named "Log Users Off When Roaming Profile Fails")

This is the harshest sentence you can offer the user if things go wrong. By default, if the server is down (or the profile is corrupted), the user first tries to load a locally cached profile. If there is no locally cached profile, the system creates a TEMP profile from the Default User Profile.

However, if you choose to enable the setting, the behavior changes. If no Roaming Profile or locally cached profile is available (presumably because you've enabled the **Delete cached copies of roaming profile** policy setting), the user is not permitted to log on.

Maximum Retries to Unload and Update User Profile

As previously discussed, this policy setting is meant to assist Windows 2000 Terminal Services when trying to log users off and release their Roaming Profiles. Increase this value to increase the number of attempts made at unloading the pertinent Registry information and update the profile when users start to complain that things aren't the same as when the last logged off (especially on Terminal Services). The Explaintext states that this policy is valid for Windows XP and Windows 2003 machines. But it's not. Repeat: Does nothing for Windows XP or Windows Server 2003. Or Windows Vista machines for that matter. It's a Windows 2000–only policy setting.

Add the Administrators Security Group to Roaming User Profiles

As you saw in Figure 9.13 earlier in this chapter, only the user can dive in and poke around their own User Profile. However, you can specify that the administrator and the user have joint access to the folder.

Oddly, this policy setting is found under the computer side of the house—not the user. Therefore, it's somewhat difficult to implement this policy setting on a small scale, because it's sometimes a mystery as to which client machine users will log on to. If you want to use this policy setting, I recommend creating a GPO with this policy setting at the domain level to guarantee that any client computers that users log on to will be affected. Setting this policy setting such that it affects the file server housing the profiles doesn't do anything for you. It's the target client computers that need to get this policy setting.

This policy setting *only* takes effect when new users first log on to affected client computers. Once they're on, they'll make some changes that affect the profile, and then log off. When they log off, a signal is sent back to the directory housing the profile, which then finalizes the security on the directory so that both the user and the administrator can both plunk around in there.

To be especially clear, as I implied, this policy setting works only for new users—that is, those users who don't already have a Roaming Profile. Users who *already* have established Roaming Profiles are essentially left in the dark with regard to using this; but there is a ray of light. If you want the same effect, you can take ownership of a profile and manually establish administrative access for the administrator and the user, as described in the upcoming section "Mandatory Profiles from an Established Roaming Profile."

 This policy setting works with Windows 2000's Service Pack 2 and later, although the policy setting's Explaintext states that it's only applicable to Windows XP and Windows 2003. In Vista, the Explaintext states that it requires at least Windows XP or Windows Server 2003, and the policy is supported on Vista.

Prevent Roaming Profile Changes from Propagating to the Server

As previously discussed, when a user jumps from machine to machine and lands on one with an existing Local Profile, the system merges the Local Profile as a favor to the user. The idea is that if this Local Profile has a data file, say, RESUME.DOC, that's missing in the user's Roaming Profile, this is a perfect time to scoop it up and keep it in the Roaming Profile. You can dictate specific machines for which you don't want this to happen.

In general, you set this policy setting only on computers that you are sure you don't want the merge between Local Profiles and Roaming Profiles—perhaps because the Local Profiles contained many unneeded files. With the policy enabled, changes made to the profile are lost because the Roaming Profile is downloaded from the server logoff and not merged with the Local Profile.

In case you missed it, this policy makes the profile work like a Mandatory Profile, so don't save anything valuable in the profile because it is going to be lost!

This policy setting affects Windows XP, Windows 2003, and Windows Vista machines (even though Windows Vista isn't listed in the requirements). Windows 2000 machines cannot be affected by this policy setting (and hence, will always merge regardless if this policy setting is Enabled or not).

Only Allow Local User Profiles

This policy setting is useful when you have set up specialty machines, such as lab machines, library machines, kiosk machines, and so on. By setting this policy setting on the machines, you can ensure that a user's Roaming Profile doesn't "get in the mix" for what you designed this machine to be.

If trying to figure out all the ins and outs of Roaming Profile policies is giving you a headache, use the handy flowchart in Figure 9.24 to help figure out what each policy setting does and how it will affect your users.

Leave Windows Installer and Group Policy Software Installation Data

Earlier, we explored the **Delete cached copies of roaming profiles** policy setting. The idea was to "clean up" behind a user when he or she logged off. This is a great idea in theory, but had an unintended consequence.

FIGURE 9.24   Roaming Profile policy settings flowchart

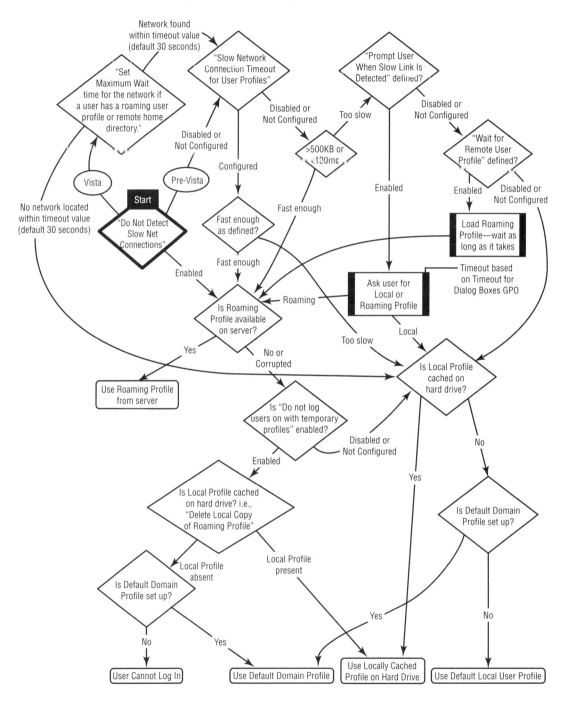

That is, if you opt to delete Roaming Profiles at logoff time, the information regarding applications deployed via Group Policy Software Installation (explored in Chapter 10) is also lost (by default). There is a new policy that affects users on Windows XP/SP2 (or Windows 2003/SP1) or newer (such as Windows Vista) called **Leave Windows Installer and Group Policy Software Installation Data.** Once enabled, the Group Policy Software Installation data remains on the hard drive, so subsequent logins for users are much faster.

So, if you're choosing to enable the **Delete cached copies of roaming Profiles** setting, also enabling this one is likely a good idea. This policy was created to deal with the scenario where applications are deployed via Group Policy Software Installation as a full install the application at logon time while **Delete cached copies of roaming profiles** policy is enabled. More information at `http://support.microsoft.com/kb/828452`.

Do Not Forcefully Unload the Users Registry at User Logoff

In versions of Windows previous to Vista, the logging off process sometimes just "hung" there. In Windows' defense it was usually a service or something which kept the user's profile open. To that end, UHPclean (described earlier) was developed to help correct that problem on Windows Server 2003 Terminal Services. (See the sidebar "A Brief History of the Unloading of `NTUSER.DAT` and UPHclean.")

Now, Windows Vista goes the extra mile and will automatically do this.

So, the only time to enable this policy is if you think something is getting broken by this automatic process. For instance, you log on a second or third time and notice your application didn't save settings which would normally be stored in the user's Registry hives doesn't seem to be there (or be there properly).

In other words, only enable this policy setting if you suspect some issue with the behavior of forcefully unloading the user's Registry at logoff.

This policy setting works with Windows Vista and, presumably, Longhorn Server.

Set Roaming Profile Path for All Users Logging on to This Computer

The policy setting enables you to establish a shared User Profile path for a specific computer. Think of it as "Everyone who logs on to this computer gets the same profile."

But just because you enable this policy setting, doesn't mean it's 100 percent guaranteed to be embraced. That's because other values might have precedence before this one takes effect.

Windows reads profile configurations in the following order and uses the first configured setting.

- The Roaming Profile path specified in the Terminal Services policy setting found at Computer Configuration ➢ Administrative Templates ➢ Windows Components ➢ Terminal Services ➢ Terminal Server ➢ Profiles ➢ **Set path for TS Roaming Profiles**

- The Roaming Profile path specific in the Terminal Server user object in Active Directory Users and Computers

- The per-computer Roaming Profile path specified (using this policy setting)

- The per-user Roaming Profile path specified in the user object in Active Directory Users and Computers

This policy setting works with Windows Vista and, presumably, Longhorn Server.

Set Maximum Wait Time for the Network if a User Has a Roaming User Profile or Remote Home Directory

This policy setting works with Windows Vista and, presumably, Longhorn Server.

This is a wordy policy setting, for sure, but what it does is simple. You can increase the network timeout if you know the computer may not find the network right away after a user chooses to log on. This can happen a lot in the cases where a wireless card is searching, searching, searching for the wireless access point, but, meanwhile, the user has already pressed Ctrl+Alt+Del to log on!

Ouch!

By setting this policy, the computer waits a bit first to see if the network suddenly becomes present.

If the network still isn't available (based upon this value, or 30 seconds by default) then the cached profile is used and the user won't have access to network home drive.

One More Policy Setting That You Might Like

This policy setting isn't specifically profile related, but it does relate to the logon experience.

Check out **Report when logon server was not available during user logon** found in Computer Configuration (and User Configuration) ➤ Windows Components ➤ Windows Logon Options. They both work the same way.

Once Enabled, this gives an informative dialog telling the user if, more or less, he's working online or offline. This can be a great first step in knowing what's going on and if there's really a problem or not.

Affecting Roaming Profiles with User Group Policy Settings

As you have just seen, most policy settings regarding Roaming Profiles are associated with the computer itself. Two policy settings, however, affect Roaming Profiles but are located on the user side of the fence: **Limit profile size** and **Excluding directories in roaming profile**. These policy settings are found under User Settings ➤ Administrative Templates ➤ System ➤ User Profiles, as shown in Figure 9.25.

Limit Profile Size

This setting limits how big the profile can grow. Remember, now the My Documents folder is part of the profile. If you limit the profile size, the profile can hit that limit awfully quickly.

It is recommended that you avoid using this setting unless you use the techniques described in the next chapter for redirecting folders for the My Documents folder. When that technique is applied, the redirected My Documents folder is no longer part of the profile, and the size can come back down to earth.

FIGURE 9.25 Some entries for profiles are found under the User Node in Group Policy.

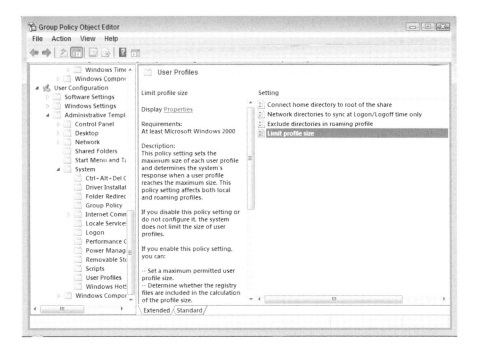

Once enabled, there are three other options:

"Show registry files in the file list" If selected, the user will see the NTUSER.DAT as part of the total calculations on space. I suggest you leave this unchecked because most users won't know what the NTUSER.DAT file is. And, by leaving it unchecked, the NTUSER.DAT file doesn't count toward the space used.

"Notify user when profile storage space is exceeded" box This notifies the user about size infractions.

"Remind user every *X* minutes" Use this setting so that it annoys the user every so often. This setting is only valid if the "Notify user when profile storage space is exceeded" box is checked, as shown in Figure 9.26.

Once this policy setting is configured, the affected users on Windows XP or Windows 2000 cannot log off until the files that compose their profile take up less than the limit. They are presented with a list of files in their profile, as shown in Figure 9.27, from which they must choose some to delete.

For Windows Vista machines, users get an extra notification in the notification area, as seen in Figure 9.28. To see the list of files, they have to double-click the X. (You might want to mention this in your custom message.)

FIGURE 9.26   You can limit the Roaming Profile size, if desired.

FIGURE 9.27   Once the Roaming Profile size is set, users can't log off until they delete some files.

FIGURE 9.28   Windows Vista allows for a custom message in the notification area.

Additionally, for Windows Vista, users can log off, but their changes aren't synchronized back to the server. At logoff, they get greeted with the message seen in Figure 9.29. It stays on the screen for a few seconds then goes away, allowing the next user to logon.

FIGURE 9.29 Users are notified their profile isn't completely synchronized.

> Your roaming user profile was not completely synchronized. See the
> event log for details or contact administrator.

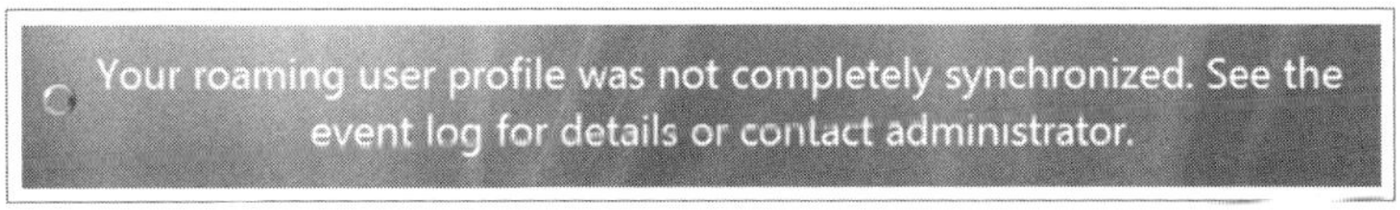

In general, this is a blunt instrument. The original use of this entry was for situations in which users stuffed lots of documents into their Windows NT Roaming Profile—onto the Desktop, for instance. Recall that Windows NT pushes the entire profile up and back causing major bandwidth headaches. Indeed, because users rely heavily on the My Documents folder (which is part of the profile), there's even more reason to be concerned.

WARNING Don't try to place disk quota restrictions on Roaming Profiles. Because applications sometimes put their own data inside the profile, users have a hard time tracking down files to delete if the quota prevented them from writing. Instead, use disk quotas on redirected folders, such as the My Documents folder. This is explored in the next chapter.

But instead of being forced to use this policy setting as your only weapon to fight disk space usage, you have an ace in the hole; in the next chapter, you'll learn how to use Folder Redirection to redirect My Documents. You can then place a disk quota on the redirected My Documents folder.

In Windows Vista this policy setting will automatically exclude \Appdata\Local and Appdata\LocalLow directories (and all their subdirectories).

Excluding Directories in Roaming Profile

As previously stated, several folders in the profile will not roam.

For pre-Vista machines, these folders are Documents and Settings*Username*\Local Settings\Application Data (and everything below it, including Local Settings, History, Temp, and Temporary Internet Files).

For Vista machines, these folders are \Appdata\Local and Appdata\LocalLow and all their subfolders (like \Temporary Internet Files).

You can add additional folders to the list of those that do not roam, if desired. You might do this if you want to fix a specific file to a Desktop (if you maintain locally cached profiles). For instance, you can exclude Desktop\LargeZipDownloads if you want to make sure those types of files do not roam with the profile.

TIP In Windows 2000, some, but not all, of the automatically excluded folders are presented in the Group Policy Editor. As far as I can tell, they're only there for show; deleting them produces no appreciable gain. (For example, you can't make the Temp, History, or other folders magically start roaming in the profile.) You can only add your own entries in addition to or in lieu of the presented entries. You will not see any of these folders listed when not using a Windows 2000 machine as your management station.

Enter additional entries relative to the root of the profiles. For instance, if you want to add the Desktop, simply add **Desktop** (not **c:\Documents and Settings\Desktop** or anything similar), because the Desktop folder is found directly off the root of each profile.

Connect Home Directory to Root of the Share

This setting is not supported in Windows Vista.

I'm pretty sure that by the time you get to the end of this book, you won't want to use old-style "Home Drives" anymore. That's because the changes in Roaming Profile behavior and redirected folders (see next chapter) present a better way for users to store their files. However, if you do end up using Home Drives for each user (located in the Account tab of each user's account's Properties), you can specify a location for users to store their stuff. Specific environment variables typically used when setting up home directories are defined differently in NT 4 and Windows 2000 (and later).

Those two environment variables, *%HOMEDRIVE%* and *%HOMEPATH%*, are automatically set when you set up, share, and assign a home directory for a user. NT 4 client computers aren't as smart as Windows 2000 computers, and they understand the "meaning" of the *%HOMEDRIVE%* and *%HOMEPATH%* shares a bit differently. To make a long story short, the fully qualified name path to the share isn't represented when those variables are evaluated on NT 4 clients; but it is for Windows 2000 and later clients. You can "dumb down" Windows 2000 and newer clients by applying this policy setting and making new clients act like old NT 4 clients.

This policy is not supported on Windows Vista. Vista always sets *%HOMEDRIVE%* and *%HOMEPATH%* in the new way.

Mandatory Profiles

Mandatory Profiles enable the administrator to assign a single user or multiple users the same, unchanging user experience regardless of where they log on and no matter what they do. In non–mumbo-jumbo terms, Mandatory Profiles ensure that users can't screw things up. When you use Mandatory Profiles to lock down your users, you guarantee that the Desktop, the files in the profile, and the Registry continue to look exactly as they did when they were set up.

Mandatory Profiles are great when you have a pesky user who keeps messing with the Desktop or when you have general populations of users—such as call centers, nurse's stations, or library kiosks—on whom you want to maintain security.

Once the Mandatory Profile is set for these people, you know you won't be running out there every 11 minutes trying to fix someone's machine when they've put the black text on the black background and clicked Apply. Actually, they can still put the black text on the black background and click Apply, and it does take effect. But when they log off or reboot (if they can figure out how to do that in the "dark"), the values aren't preserved. So, voilá! Back to work!

You can create a Mandatory Profile in two ways—either from a Local Profile (or locally cached profile) or from an existing Roaming Profile. I recommend creating your Mandatory Profile from a local (or locally cached) profile. By default, if you try to dive into an existing Roaming Profile folder on the server, you are denied access, as shown in Figure 9.13 earlier in this chapter. The system utilizes the *%username%* variable and automatically sets up permissions such that only the user specified can access that folder. To dive in, you have to take ownership of the entire subfolder structure first and then give yourself permission to access the folder.

In the next sections, you'll find the steps for both methods.

 If you previously set up the **Add the Administrators security group to roaming user profiles** policy setting, you won't need to worry about not being able to dive into the profile. However, the policy setting must be placed before the Roaming Profile is placed.

Establishing Mandatory Profiles from a Local Profile

The first thing to do when trying to establish the Mandatory Profile is to log on locally to any Windows 2000 or Windows XP machine as a mere-mortal user (without an existing Roaming Profile), make the modifications you want, and log off as that user.

Now that you have a local (or locally cached) profile that you want to use as your Mandatory Profile, follow these steps:

1. Log on as Administrator to the machine that houses the local (or locally cached) profile.

   For Windows XP and Windows 2000:

2. Click Start, and then right-click My Computer and choose Properties from the shortcut menu to open the System Properties dialog box.

   For Windows Vista:

2. Click Start, right-click Computer and select Properties from the shortcut menu.

3. Select "Advanced system settings" in the left pane.

   For both:

4. Click the Advanced tab, and then click the Settings button in the User Profiles section to open the User Profiles dialog box (as seen previously in Figure 9.7).

5. Click the "Copy To" button to open the "Copy To" dialog box, and then enter the full path plus a folder for the common users, as shown in Figure 9.30. This example has \\Dc01\profiles\allnurses. The allnurses folder is automatically created under the Profiles share.

FIGURE 9.30 For Windows XP (shown at left), use the Copy To dialog box to copy one profile for many users. If you want this profile to be used for Windows Vista (shown at right) computers, you need to specify a .v2 extension as seen here.

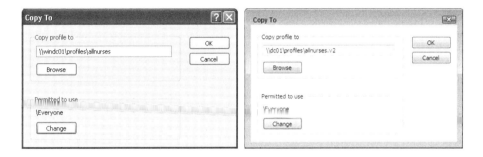

6. Click the Change button in the "Permitted to Use" section, to open the "Select User or Group" dialog box and change the default from the original user to Authenticated Users. This lets everyone use the profile in the domain.

7. Click OK to actually copy the profile and to close the "Copy To" dialog box.

8. Click OK to close the System Properties dialog box.

Next, use Explorer to locate the share we created earlier, named Profiles. Inside the Profiles directory, you should now see the `allnurses` (or `allnurses.v2` for Windows Vista) folder. Locate the `NTUSER.DAT` and rename it to `NTUSER.MAN`, as shown in Figure 9.31.

FIGURE 9.31 Change a Roaming Profile to a Mandatory Profile by renaming NTUSER.DAT to NTUSER.MAN.

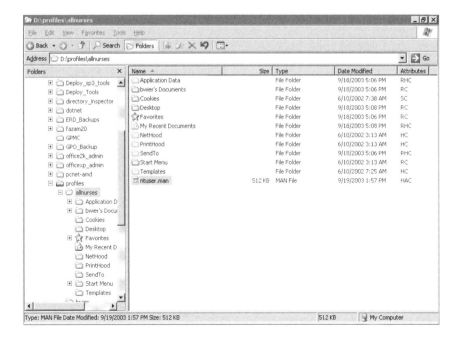

Because NTUSER.DAT is hidden by default, you might have to change the default view options. In Explorer, choose Tools ➤ Folder Options to open the Folder Options dialog box. Click the View tab, click the "Show Hidden Files and Folders" button, clear the "Hide File Extensions for Known File Types" check box, and click OK.

Finally, in the Properties dialog box, change the profile path of all the users who are to use the profile to \\Dc01\profiles\allnurses, as shown in Figure 9.32. Note that you do not need to specify the .v2 directory specifically for Vista users in the "Profile path" line. That is, just enter in \\Dc01\profiles\allnurses and Windows XP will use the non-.v2 directory and Windows Vista will automatically find and use the .v2 directory.

Since you copied the profile to the server with permissions for Authenticated User to use, you'll also want to modify the NTFS permissions of the allnurses folder under the Profiles share to make sure it's protected. You might choose to protect the allnurses folder by setting the Permissions as shown in Figure 9.33.

FIGURE 9.32 Point all similar users to the new Mandatory Profile.

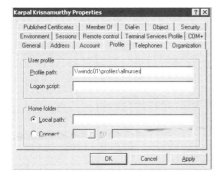

FIGURE 9.33 You can prevent people from inadvertently modifying the newly established profile.

Mandatory Profiles from an Established Roaming Profile

You might not be able to use a local (or locally cached) profile to generate the Mandatory Profile. This might be because you enabled the **Delete cached copies of roaming profiles** policy setting, and there are no locally cached profiles for you to use. In this case, you'll need to log in as Administrator on the server that houses the Roaming Profile, locate the profile folder, and take ownership of it. You can then copy the profile to another folder and have the user take back ownership of the folder. In this case, we'll take ownership of a profile for a user named garyd. To take ownership of a user's Roaming Profile, follow these steps:

1. Log on at the server as Administrator.

2. Locate the user's profile folder, right-click it, and choose Properties from the shortcut menu to open the User Properties dialog box.

3. Click the Security tab. You should get a message stating that the user is the only one with access to their own folder.

4. Click the Advanced button on the Security tab to get the "Advanced Security Settings" dialog box. Next, click the Owner tab.

5. Select Administrator (or Administrators) from the list, click the "Replace owner on subcontainers and objects" check box (as shown in Figure 9.34), and then click OK.

6. You will be prompted to confirm that you want to take ownership. Select Yes and wait until you have ownership.

FIGURE 9.34 Take ownership of the folder.

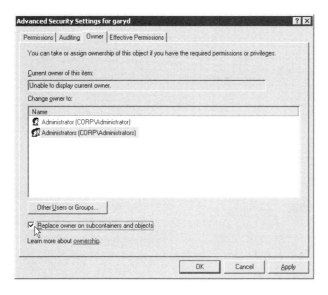

You can now rename the folder to a sensible name and then rename the NTUSER.DAT file to NTUSER.MAN. Last, point each user account to use this new profile, specifically pointing each account to the profile as shown in Figure 9.32 earlier in this chapter.

Since everyone now has Full Control (inherited from the parent), you might want to restrict access to the profile, similarly to that seen in Figure 9.33 earlier.

> You might need to add the Administrator account or the Administrators group to the ACL of the folder and let the permissions flow downward in order to be able to see the contents. In some extreme cases, you might also need to log off and back on as Administrator to get another access token.

Forced Mandatory Profiles (Super-Mandatory)

Mandatory Profiles might not always be so—if the server is down or a user unplugs their network cable, the Mandatory Profile does not load. Indeed, the user will get the Local Default User Profile. This could be a potential security problem and possibly a violation of your corporate policy.

In instances like this, you need to determine if it's more important that a user logs on (and gets the Default Local User Profile) or that, if they don't get the Mandatory Profile, they don't get to log on at all. Microsoft calls this type of profile "Super-Mandatory." In Figure 9.31 earlier in this chapter, we used a folder named allnurses as our Mandatory Profile folder. We can take this to the next step and ensure that no users using the allnurses folder can log on unless they can connect to the share on the server.

Don't forget: profiles are different for Type 1 (pre-Vista) and Type 2 (Windows Vista and Longhorn) computers. To that end, you'll need to set up Mandatory Profiles which "fit" for each type.

To force users who log on to Windows Vista to use a Mandatory Profile or lose logon capability, you need to first rename the allnurses.v2 folder such that it has .man.v2 instead. So, the final folder name will be allnurses.man.v2.

To force users to use the Mandatory Profile, or lose logon capability, simply follow these steps:

1. Create a Mandatory Profile as described earlier, including renaming the NTUSER.DAT to NTUSER.MAN.

2. For Windows XP machines, rename the entire folder from allnurses to allnurses.man. For Windows Vista machines, rename the entire folder from allnurses.v2 to allnurses.man.v2

3. Change the affected users' Profile tabs to point to the new location, such as \\Dc01\profiles\allnurses.man, as shown in Figure 9.35.

Once the forced Mandatory Profile is introduced onto a system, the system always checks to see if the Profile is available. If the forced Mandatory Profile is unavailable, the user is not permitted to log on.

FIGURE 9.35   You can force a Mandatory Profile if absolutely necessary.

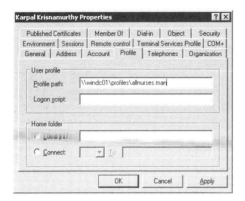

Technically, you can couple a Mandatory Profile with the **Log users off when roaming profile fails** policy setting to create the same effect. However, the method detailed here is preferred.

Final Thoughts

In this chapter, you learned about the three profile types: Local, Roaming, and Mandatory.

Local Profiles alone are great—for only the smallest of environments. However, remember that there's a lot you can do to get a similar look and feel for when new users show up on the job. You can craft a Default Local User Profile, or, even better, a Default Domain User Profile.

Step up to Roaming Profiles when you have even a handful of users and you want to allow them to bounce from machine to machine and keep their look and feel. Roaming Profiles have really grown up since the days of Windows NT. The algorithm to move the profiles up and back is much improved, and you should really give it another try if you once gave up in frustration.

Roaming Profiles are especially useful if you want to bring users' desktops and laptops back from the dead, as we'll explore in the next two chapters. Indeed, you can use Roaming Profiles as a handy way to upgrade users' machines while preserving their Desktops.

Remember that the Windows 2003 version of the Active Directory Users And Computers tool allows you to select multiple users at once and set their Roaming Profile path to a server. And, as stated earlier, there's no need to pre-create the folder underneath the shared directory— the system will automatically do that once the *%username%* variable is encountered.

Even though we set up Roaming Profiles for our Type 1 computers (pre-Vista) and our Type 2 computers (Windows Vista and Longhorn Server), we still have a problem. That is, we have no way to exchange data between the two. If someone logs on to Windows Vista and drops some music files in their profile, then they log on to an Windows XP machine, they simply won't see those music files. In the next chapter, we'll discuss Redirected Folders. The idea is that instead of saving critical data in our profile, we save it on a point on our server. That way, if we're on Windows Vista or Windows XP, we'll be able to just reach out and touch that data which lives on the server. We'll get there right around the corner.

As stated earlier, there are a lot of policy settings you can utilize to hone how profiles work. You can set up your environment to be moderately secure when using the **Delete cached copies of roaming profiles** policy setting. And you can allow joint ownership of the user's Roaming Profile directory on the server by utilizing the **Add the Administrators security group to roaming user profiles** policy setting.

Use Mandatory Profiles sparingly. With Group Policy settings available to tie down all sorts of settings, Mandatory Profiles are really only a last resort. And Forced Mandatory Profiles are a really, really last resort (if there's such a thing).

10

Implementing a Managed Desktop, Part 1: Redirected Folders, Offline Files, and Disk Quotas

You get Active Directory, you get Group Policy. That's the good news. The better news is how you can put your knowledge of Group Policy to use to keep your users happy. Here's the idea: easily create a consistent environment for your users no matter where they roam.

In the previous chapter, you used Roaming Profiles to kick off your journey to a consistent environment. But that only got you so far—especially if you had both Windows XP and Windows Vista machines. That's because when you roamed from Windows XP to Windows Vista (or vice versa) you didn't maintain the goodies, like the stuff you put in My Documents (for XP) and Documents (for Windows Vista). Each computer type became its own island.

Now, let's explore how to create a *managed desktop*. A managed desktop is one where you can create a predictable environment for your users to log in to and enjoy. It's not put together with wacky applications and icons all over the place. You know what to expect when your users log on, and so do they.

In this chapter, I'll give you an overview of what a managed desktop is and is not, and show you how to implement a slew of its features: Redirected Folders, Offline Files, Synchronization Manager, and setting Disk Quotas.

 In previous editions of this book, the idea of a managed desktop was called "Intelli-Mirror." But you have to look far and wide to find Microsoft using that term nowadays. I wasn't even sure Microsoft was using the term IntelliMirror anymore. But after a little poking around I found this URL: http://tinyurl.com/y9tesn, which is a Vista page, which clearly has the word IntelliMirror on it. But, we decided, after all to change the book's title because the term just isn't in regular use anymore. So, instead, we'll just refer to IntelliMirror as a "Managed Desktop."

In the next chapter, I'll wrap up creating a managed desktop with a discussion of software deployment via Group Policy. Finally, in Chapter 12, you'll see how the "circle of life" for a computer, so to speak, comes together with Shadow Copies and Windows Deployment Services.

Overview of Change and Configuration Management

Believe it or not, you're expensive. Your salary, the percentage of rent your office takes up, the software you use that helps the business run—it all costs money. Making those costs tangible is a difficult proposition. Some costs are hard to put into concrete numbers. How do you quantify the cost of sending a technician to a user's desktop when they've inadvertently set the background color, the foreground color, and the font color to black and hit the Apply button?

Accounting for these costs is a constant challenge, and bringing these costs under control is even more difficult. The Gartner Group, in the early 1990s, generated a new strategy to help with this predicament and proposed a new *TCO (Total Cost of Ownership)* model. This philosophical model essentially attempted to take the voodoo out of accounting for computing services. Simply account for every nickel and dime spent around computing, and voila! Instant accounting!

 You can find more info on Gartner Group's TCO model at www.gartnerweb.com/ 4_decision_tools/measurement/decision_tools/tco/tco.html (shortened to http://tinyurl.com/57f16).

Microsoft's first foray into aligning with the TCO philosophy was back in the NT 4 timeframe with their Zero Administration for Windows (ZAW) initiative. The first major technology set based on ZAW was called the Zero Administration for Windows Kit (ZAK).

Most organizations have two types of users: those who work on one application and one application only, and those who use a few apps (but seem to never stop playing with their Desktops). With those two types of users in mind, ZAK could be run in two modes: Taskstation, in which users were locked down to one (and only one) application, and Appstation, in which users could move between several strategically selected applications. ZAK's goal was noble: reduce the user's exposure to the Desktop and the operating system. Once that was reduced, less administration would be required to control the environment.

Although ZAK was a respectable first attempt, only a few organizations really used ZAK in the way it was intended. The adoption of ZAK never quite caught on due to the intricacy of implementation and lack of flexibility. Surprisingly, Microsoft still has ZAK available for NT 4 (a free download) at www.microsoft.com/windows/zak/.

With Active Directory as the backdrop to a new stage, a new paradigm of how administrators manage users and their Desktops could be created. Enter the Active Directory version of Zero Administration for Windows—now known as Change and Configuration Management (CCM) and the Microsoft term "IntelliMirror."

Again, recall that the Zero Administration for Windows program was an "initiative," not a specific technology. With Windows 2000, Microsoft renamed the ZAW initiative to Change and Configuration Management and introduced several new technologies in order to move closer to the TCO philosophy.

In accordance with the TCO philosophy, by creating a managed desktop, each step you implement tries to chip away at each of the sore points of administrating your network by implementing specific technologies. Figure 10.1 shows how Microsoft envisions the Change and Configuration Management initiative, and the Windows features and technologies therein.

Performing the steps in this chapter to create a managed desktop isn't an all-or-nothing proposition as ZAK had been. Administrators can pick and choose the features and functionality they want to deploy and when they want to deploy it. Although some features that I'll describe in detail here (such as Offline Files) are available when using Windows 2000 Professional or Windows XP workstation by itself, most features (such as Redirected Folders) are actuated only when you have the marriage between Active Directory and Windows 2000, Windows XP, Windows Vista, or Windows 2003 as clients.

Again, you built a bit of a foundation for your journey toward a managed desktop in the last chapter when you implemented Roaming Profiles. This enabled the basics of the "My documents follow me" and the "My settings follow me" philosophies. In this chapter, we'll explore the implementation of some of the other features needed to create a managed desktop: Redirected Folders, Offline Files, the synchronization capabilities (in both Windows XP and Windows Vista), and Disk Quotas.

FIGURE 10.1 This is Microsoft's picture of how to create a managed desktop (the concept formerly known as IntelliMirror).

		Features	Benefits	Technologies
Change and Configuration Management	Managed Desktop	User Data Management	Increased protection and availability of people's data "My documents follow me!"	Active Directory Group Policy Offline Folders Synchronization Manager Disk Quotas Redirected Folders
		User Settings Management	Centrally defined environment "My settings follow me!"	Active Directory Group Policy Offline Folders Roaming Profiles
		Software Installation and Maintenance	Centrally managed software "My software follows me!"	Active Directory Group Policy Windows Installer Service
		Remote OS Installation	Fast system configuration "Get Windows working on this machine"	Active Directory DNS DHCP Windows Deployment Services

Sometimes, in normal use, some people call Offline Files something else—
"Offline Folders" and also "CSC" for "Client Side Caching." In regular use,
they're all the same thing, but strictly, Microsoft documentation refers only to
Offline Files and not Offline Folders. So, to be consistent, we'll also try to call
the feature Offline Files.

Redirected Foldors

Redirected Folders allow the administrator to provide a centralized repository for certain
noteworthy folders from client systems and to have the data contained in them actually reside
on shared folders on servers. It's a beautiful thing. The administrator gets centralized control;
users get the same experience they always did. It's the best of both worlds.

Available Folders to Redirect

Windows XP and Windows Vista have different folders that are available for redirection.
In Windows XP you can set Redirected Folders for the following:

- My Documents
- My Pictures
- Start Menu
- Desktop
- Application Data

   In Windows Vista, you can Redirect the following folders:

- Contacts (not previously available in Windows XP)
- Start Menu (like Windows XP, but see note below)
- Desktop (like Windows XP)
- Documents (was called My Documents in Windows XP)
- Downloads (not previously available in Windows XP)
- Favorites (not previously "Redirectable" in Windows XP, but available in the roaming
  profile)
- Music (was called My Music in Windows XP)
- Videos (was called My Videos in Windows XP)
- Pictures (was called My Pictures in Windows XP)
- Searches (not previously available in Windows XP)
- Links (not previously available in Windows XP)

- AppData (Roaming) (was called simply Application Data in XP)
- And (Lord help us), Saved Games (not previously available in Windows XP)

 The Start Menu redirection support in Windows Vista is actually better than XP, because in XP you didn't have the ability to redirect each user's Start Menu folder to a different location. You could only do it to a shared location. It wasn't as flexible as My Documents.

For each of these settings, there is a Basic and an Advanced configuration.

The idea is to set up a GPO that contains a policy setting to redirect one or more of these folders for clients and "stick them" on a server. Usually the GPO is set at the OU level, and all users inside the OU are affected; however, there might occasionally be a reason to link the GPO with the policy setting to the domain or site level.

In the **Basic** configuration, every user who is affected by the policy setting is redirected to the same shared folder. Then, inside the shared folder, the system can automatically create individual, secure folders for each user to store their stuff.

In the **Advanced** configuration, Active Directory security group membership determines which users' folders get redirected to which shared folder. For instance, you could say, "All members of the **Graphic_Artists** Global security group will get their desktops redirected to the ga_Desktops shared folder on Server-6" or "All members of the Sales Universal security group will get their Application Data redirected to the Appdata share on Server Pineapple."

Note that any folders that lived under the My Documents folder (pre-Vista) now have an additional option as seen in Figure 10.2. That is, you can choose to let these documents just "Follow the Documents folder" which will maintain the legacy folder hierarchy of My Documents if need be. Again, this option is only for folders within Documents (Music, Videos, and Pictures.)

FIGURE 10.2   Music, Videos, and Pictures can all "Follow the Documents folder."

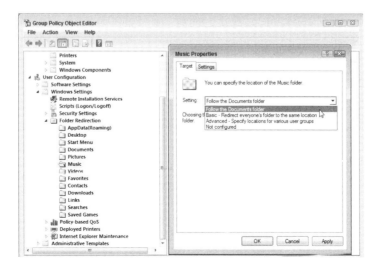

Redirected *Documents/My Documents*

For our journey through Redirected Folders, we'll work primarily inside the Documents folder. All the principles that work on the special Documents folder work equally well for the other special "redirectable" folders, unless otherwise noted. At the end of this section, I'll briefly discuss why you might want to redirect some other folders as well.

In the last chapter, we explored how to leverage Roaming Profiles to maintain a consistent state for users if they hop from machine to machine. Roaming Profiles are terrific, but one significant drawback is associated with using Roaming Profiles. Recall that My Documents (for Windows XP) and Documents (for Windows Vista) are now part of the profile. On the one hand, this frees you from the bondage of drive letters and home drives. No more, "Ursula, put it in your U: drive," or "Harry, save it to the H: drive."

On the other hand, once the user data is in Documents/My Documents, your network will be swamped with all the up-and-back movement of data within Documents/My Documents when users hop from machine to machine—20MB of Word docs here, 30MB of Excel docs there. Multiply this by the number of users, and it'll add up fast! Not to mention that (for XP at least) that data is synchronized at logon and logoff and hence, the user may have to wait until it's all completed. As we learned in the previous chapter, the Roaming Profiles algorithm does its best to mitigate that, but it's still got to move the changed files.

But with Redirected Folders, you can have the best of both worlds. Users can save their files to the place they know and love, My Documents (for Windows XP) and Documents (for Windows Vista), and anchor the data to a fixed location, so it *appears* as if the data is roaming with the users. But it really isn't; it's safe and secure on a file share of your choice. And, since the data is already on the server there's no long wait time when logging on or logging off.

There are two added bonuses to this scheme. Since all the Documents/My Documents files are being redirected to specific fixed-shared folders, you can easily back up all the user data in one fell swoop. Perhaps you can even make a separate backup job specifically for the user data that needs to be more closely monitored. Additionally, you can set up Shadow Copies for the disk volumes that house redirected Documents/My Documents files so users can restore their own files if necessary. The Shadow Copies function is explored in Chapter 11.

Basic Redirected Folders

Basic Redirected Folders works best in two situations:

- Smaller environments—such as a doctor's office or storefront—where all employees sit under one roof

- In an organization's OU structure that was designed such that similar people are not only in the same OU but are also in the same physical location

The reason these simple scenarios make a good fit with the basic option is that such situations let you redirect the users affected by the policy setting to a server that's close to them. That way, if they do roam within their location, the wait time is minimal to download and upload the data back and forth to the server and their workstation.

In the following example, I've created an OU called **LikeUsers** who are all using the same local server—DC01. Setting up a basic Redirected Folders for My Documents is a snap. It's a three-step process:

- Create a shared folder to store the data.
- Set the security on the shared folder.
- Create a new GPO and edit it to contain a policy setting to redirect the Documents/My Documents folder.

To create and share a folder to store redirected Documents/My Documents data, follow these steps:

1. Log on to DC01 as Administrator.
2. From the Desktop, double-click My Computer to open the My Computer folder.
3. Find a place to create a users folder. In this example, we'll use D:\DATA. Once you're inside the D: drive, right-click D:\ and select the Folder command from the New menu, then type in **Data** for the name.

You can substitute any name for Data. Some use DOCS, MYDOCS, or REDIRDOCS. Some administrators like to use hidden shares, such as Data$, MYDOCS$, or MYDOCUMENTS$. This works well, too.

4. Right-click the newly created Data folder, and choose "Sharing and Security," which opens the Properties of the folder, focused on the Sharing tab. Note that Windows Server 2003 will default such that the share is Everyone:Read. Click "Share This Folder," and ensure the share is set so that Authenticated Users have Full Control, as seen in Figure 10.3. Keep the rest of the defaults, and click OK.

FIGURE 10.3   Share the Data folder such that Authenticated Users have Full Control permissions.

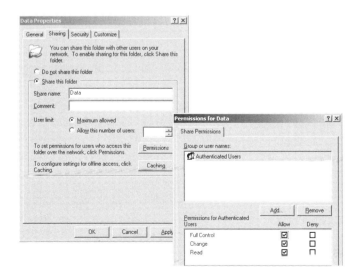

Be sure that the NTFS permissions allow write access for the users you want as well. In other words, both the Share level and NTFS permissions must allow the user to write in order for success.

Now that the share is created, we're ready to create a new GPO to do the magic. Again, you'll want to do this on your Windows Vista management station, VISTAMANGEMENT. To set up Redirected Folders for Documents/My Documents, follow these steps:

1. In the GPMC, right-click the OU on which you want to apply Folder Redirection (in my case, the LikeUsers OU), and choose "Create and link a new GPO here."

2. Name the GPO, say, "Documents Folder Redirection," as shown in Figure 10.4.

FIGURE 10.4 The LikeUsers OU has a GPO named "Documents Folder Redirection." After drilling down into the folder that you want to redirect, right-click and choose Properties.

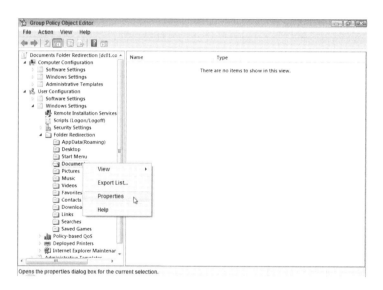

3. Right-click the new GPO, and choose Edit from the shortcut menu to open the Group Policy Object Editor.

4. Drill down to Folder Redirection by choosing User Configuration ➢ Windows Settings ➢ Folder Redirection. Right-click the **Documents** entry in the Group Policy Object Editor, and choose Properties to open the **Documents** Properties dialog box, as shown in Figure 10.5.

5. In the Setting drop-down list box, select "Basic—Redirect everyone's Folder to the same location."

 Don't click OK (or Apply) yet. There's more to do. If you do click OK or Apply, you're going to get a warning (which we'll talk about in the sidebar entitled "What Happens When You Edit a GPO from a Pre-Vista Management Station?").

Share Permissions: Full Control versus Change

In the last chapter, we set up a shared folder for our Roaming Profiles. We put Change control on the permissions, and this was enough. Interestingly, here, on the share that will house our Redirected Folders, we need Full Control permissions, or the Folder Redirection will fail.

So, is there a problem using Full Control? Is there a way to exploit an attack on a share with Full Control? Not really, unless the underlying NTFS permissions are open for an attack. Basically, as long as the root folder of the share is an NTFS folder with appropriate permissions, there is no reason to use anything other than Everyone:Full Control on the share; though there's certainly nothing wrong with Authenticated Users:Full Control either.

Some people used to insist on using share permissions, but it was often because they instituted the practice in the dark days of OS/2 and Microsoft LanManager and got used to it. The share permission is simply a security descriptor stored in the Registry entry for the share in the LanManServer entries on the server. Giving Everyone:Full Control doesn't change the permissions on the Registry entry itself, so it cannot be used as an exploit for getting a toehold on the server.

The moral of the story: have the correct NTFS permissions underneath the folder that contains the share. Indeed, share permissions aren't sufficient if someone gets physical access, or near-physical access, to the box; for example, via Terminal Services access.

FIGURE 10.5   The Basic settings redirect all users in the OU to the same location.

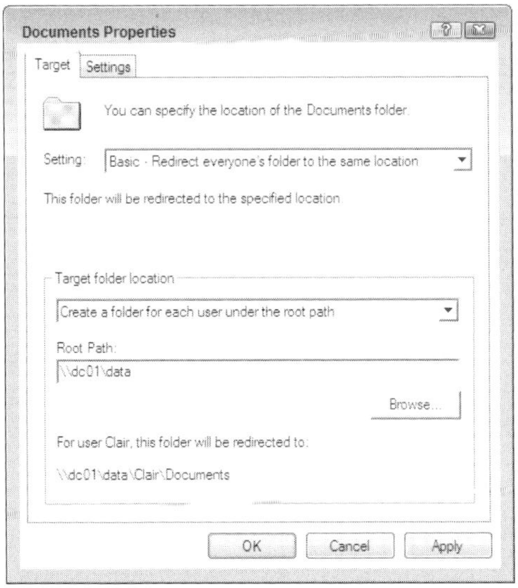

The Target Tab

The "Target folder location" drop-down list box has the following four options:

Redirect to the user's home directory. Many companies use home drives for each user and have the users store all their stuff there. To set a home drive for each user, in Active Directory Users And Computers, click the "Profile" tab for the user and enter a path in the "Home folder" section. The idea behind this setting is that it's an easy way to help users continue to use a drive letter they already know and love, say, H: (for Home directory) in addition to the Documents/My Documents redirection. If you choose this setting, both H: and Documents/My Documents point to the exact same place—the path you set in the Home folder section in Active Directory Users And Computers. In this book, we didn't set up home drives because Documents/My Documents redirection frees us from the need to do so. This setting is provided here only as a convenience for organizations that want to continue to use home folders. If you plan to eventually get rid of home drives in your company in lieu of just a redirected Documents/My Documents folder, my advice is not to use this setting; instead use the **Redirect to the following location** setting (explored shortly).

If the user has no home folder, this option is ignored, and the folder stays in its current location.

Create a folder for each user under the root path. If you plan to redirect more than just the Documents/My Documents folder (say, the Application Data or Desktop), you might want to select this option. This creates secure subfolders underneath the point you specify. As you can see in Figure 10.5 earlier in this chapter, entering \\DC01\data in the Root Path box shows an example of how all users affected by this policy setting are redirected.

This choice might be good if you don't want to have to remember what the specific environment variables point to.

In the example, you can see that Documents for a user Clair will be redirected to her own folder in the Data share. Go ahead and perform this now.

In our example, we're using DC01, a Domain Controller. You usually wouldn't do this; rather, you'd use a regular run-of-the mill file server (as a member, not a Domain Controller). We're doing that here simply for the sake of example.

Redirect to the following location. This option makes sense if you plan to redirect only Documents/My Documents or just one other redirectable folder.

It also makes sense if you want to leverage the maximum flexibility. This selection allows you to specifically dictate where you want the folder placed. That's because you can use environment variables here.

For instance, to use this setting, type **\\DC01\data\%*username*%** in the Target Folder Location text box. Then, a subfolder for the user is created directly under the Data shared folder. This is the selection to choose when none of the others are to your liking; that is, you have the most flexibility with this option.

> In advanced configurations, you can use this setting to (get this) share a Documents/My Documents folder. But you need to ensure you set the right ACLs on the folder as well as enable the policy named **Do not check for user ownership of Roaming Profiles** which is located in Computer Configuration ➢ Administrative Templates ➢ User Profiles.

Redirect to the local *userprofile* location.   With this option, you redirect the folder for the user back to their Local Profile. It's useful when you want to remove redirection for a particular folder without affecting the rest of the other Redirected Folders.

> Don't click OK (or Apply) yet. There's more to do. If you do click OK or Apply, you're going to get a warning (which we'll talk about in the sidebar entitled "What Happens When You Edit a GPO from a Pre-Vista Management Station?").

The Settings Tab

When you click the Settings tab, you have access to additional options for Folder Redirection. The Settings tab is the hidden gem of Folder Redirection; it activates a bit of magic. Figure 10.6 shows the Settings tab for Documents.

FIGURE 10.6   The Settings tab in Folder Redirection holds all sorts of magical powers!

By default, users have exclusive NTFS permissions to their directories, and the contents of their Documents/My Documents folders are automatically moved to the new directory. You can change this behavior, if desired, by making the appropriate choices on the Settings tab.

Because we're discussing My Documents (for Windows XP) and Documents (for Windows Vista) at this point, we'll dive into the Settings tab specifically for Documents for Windows Vista. However, each setting discussed here affects the other potentially Redirected Folders in exactly the same way. Let's take a look at some of the options available on this tab.

Grant the user exclusive rights to Documents.   By default, this check box is checked. You're instructing the system to create a secure directory underneath the redirection. This check box sets NTFS permissions on that directory such that only that user can enter the directory. This keeps prying eyes, even those of nosy administrators, out of people's personal business. If you want to change this setting, uncheck the box.

Unchecking the "Grant the user exclusive rights to Documents" check box sets no additional permissions, nor does it modify the target directory permissions in any way. When the folder gets created, it inherits its parent folder permissions instead of creating its own, exclusive, non-inherited permissions. The NTFS permissions are not modified. Because Windows 2000 and Windows 2003 use NTFS inheritance, newly created folders receive the same permissions as the parent folder.

If this box is checked, and you do need to dig into someone's personal directory, you'll have to take ownership of the directory, as described in the previous chapter. Or, if you set it up in advance (using the information in the "How to Grant Administrators Access to My Documents (or Other Redirected Folders)" sidebar), you'll be able to get in whenever you want! (Again, though, you need to set it up in advance.)

Move the contents of Documents to the new location.   By default, this check box is checked. When you start out on creating a managed desktop, Microsoft is betting that the first thing you do is to set up Roaming Profiles and then move on to setting up Redirected Folders. In between those two time periods, however, users have surely created their own documents and started putting them in their Documents folder in their Local or Roaming Profile. This check box magically moves (not copies) their documents from their profile (Roaming or Local) to the appointed place on the server the next time they log on.

If users have bounced from machine to machine and sprinkled data in the local Documents folder, the files in Documents will move them to the redirected location the next time the user logs on to that machine. The only time to worry is when two files have the same name—the latest time-stamped file "wins" and stays on the server.

Also apply redirection policy to Windows 2000, Windows 2000 Server, Windows XP, and Windows Server 2003 operating systems.   This setting gets the prize for most number of characters in a dialog box with just one check box. You'll only see this option when you create a GPO from a Vista management station.

You can see this highlighted in Figure 10.6. You'll only see this entry if you're creating this GPO from a Windows Vista management station. Here's what happens:

This check box turns on or off what is called (unofficially) "downlevel compatible" Folder Redirection mode. This addition helps bridge the differences between the pre-Vista and Vista system profile hierarchies.

If you enable this box (downlevel compatible):

- The target folder name for Documents folder will automatically be set to My Documents; of course, you can change it to whatever you like.

- The Music and Videos folders will also automatically be redirected to Follow the Documents folder, which means its target location will be <MyDocPath>\My Music and <MyDocPath>\My Videos. This is because pre-Vista Folder Redirection does not support individual redirection for these two folders.

- The Pictures folder, by default, will be set to follow the Documents folder. But there are some differences: since you can specify different locations in the pre-Vista system, you can do it on Vista as well. This means you can still change the Pictures folder to other places (including back to the local profile), as well.

If you disable this box (pure Vista mode):

- The target folder name will be Documents by default—you can still change it to other names.

- Pictures/Music/Videos will not automatically be placed within Documents as a parent. They remain where they are. You can configure them to redirect to any location you want, and the target folder name is also the new name without the "my" prefix.

The pure Vista mode gives the customer more flexibility, if you don't have pre-Vista systems in your environment, then it is better to use this mode.

Policy Removal   You must select one of the two settings under the Policy Removal heading. The point of having OUs is that you can move users easily in and out of them. If the user is moved out of an OU to which this policy applies, the following options help you determine what happens to their Redirected Folder contents.

> **Leave the folder in the new location when policy is removed.**   If this option is selected, and the user is moved out of the OU to which this policy applies, the data stays in the shared folder and directory you specified. This is the default. The user will continue to access the contents of the Redirected Folder. However, there is one potential pitfall when using this option. To get a grip on it, read the sidebar "Folder Redirection Pitfalls."

Redirect the folder back to the local userprofile location when policy is removed.   If this check box is selected, and the user moves (or the policy no longer applies), a copy of the data is sent to the profile.

If Roaming Profiles is not set up, a copy of the data is sent to every workstation the user logs on to. If you've set up Roaming Profiles, the data gets pushed back up to the server and shared folder that house the user's Roaming Profile when the user logs off.

This setting is useful if a user under your jurisdiction moves to another territory. Once this happens, you can eliminate their junk cluttering your servers (as long as you're not the administrator of the target OU). Use this option with care, though; since the user's data isn't anchored to a shared folder, the network traffic will increase when this data roams around the network.

It is recommended that you check with the target OU administrator to ensure that some Folder Redirection policy will apply to the user. This eliminates all the "up and back" problems associated with maintaining user data inside regular Roaming Profiles.

WARNING   Don't click OK (or Apply) yet. There's more to do. If you do click OK or Apply, you're going to get a warning (which we'll talk about in the sidebar entitled "What Happens When You Edit a GPO from a Pre-Vista Management Station?").

Folder Redirection Pitfalls

Earlier, you learned about the "Leave the folder in the new location when policy is removed" setting when redirecting folders. However, let's work through a quick example—we'll assume that the checkbox is checked, and a user is being asked to use two machines.

Let's imagine the following scenario:

- There is a user Fred in the Sales OU.

- Fred uses ComputerA

- There is a GPO linked to the Sales OU which contains a Folder Redirection policy. This policy redirects his Documents folder and has the "Leave the folder in the new location when policy is removed" setting enabled.

Fred logs on to ComputerA, and the Documents folder is redirected to \\server1\share1\Fred\docs. As expected, Folder Redirection is working fine and dandy.

Now, let's assume Fred gets transferred to another job in Marketing, say, and his account is moved from the Sales OU to the Marketing OU. Let's assume Marketing does not have Folder Redirection policy for Documents in place.

What happens the next time when Fred logs on to ComputerA?

Well, because the GPO doesn't apply to him, the policy for Folder Redirection will be removed. However, the Documents folder is still pointing to the server and he can see all of his data on the server. Fred clicks on his Documents folder and all is well. He sees the files on the server just fine. As far as the user is concerned, nothing "changes" because "Leave the folder in the new location when policy is removed" was selected.

A week later, ComputerA catches fire. Fred gets a brand new machine, ComputerB, on which he has never logged on before.

When Fred logs on to ComputerB his Documents folder will be pointing to c:\users\%username%\ Documents; not the server location like it was on ComputerA.

This makes sense: There isn't a Folder Redirection policy which affects Fred anymore. Remember—he's moved to Marketing, and they don't have a Folder Redirection policy. So, he never got the "signal" to use the server location he once did.

So, when Fred clicks on Documents on ComputerB, he sees … nothing. However, Fred still has *rights* to get his files. So, if he wanted access to his files on ComputerB, he would have to navigate to \\server1\share1\username\docs via Explorer window to be able to see his data.

How to Grant Administrators Access to *Documents/My Documents* (or Other Redirected Folders)

As you learned in the last chapter, it's possible to grant administrators access to the folders where users store their Roaming Profiles. In that chapter, you set up a policy setting that affects the client computers, and the first time the user jumps on the computer, the file permissions are set such that both the user and the administrator have joint access. However, that's not the case with Redirected Folders.

If you want both the user and the administrator to have joint access to a Redirected Folder such as Documents, you need to perform two major steps:

1. Clear the "Grant the user exclusive rights to Documents" setting (as seen in Figure 10.6).

2. Set security on the subfolder you are sharing that will contain the Redirected Folders.

In the Security Properties dialog box of the folder you shared, select Advanced. Uncheck the "Allow inheritable permissions from parent to propagate to this object" check box. Now, remove the permissions, and then add four groups, assign them permissions, and dictate where those permissions will flow. Here's the breakdown:

Administrators   Full Control, which applies to "This folder, subfolders, and files"

System Full Control, which applies to "This folder, subfolders, and files"

Creator Owner Full Control, which applies to "This folder, subfolders, and files"

Authenticated Users Create Folders/Append Data, Read Permissions, Read Extended Attributes, which apply to "This folder only" (as seen here).

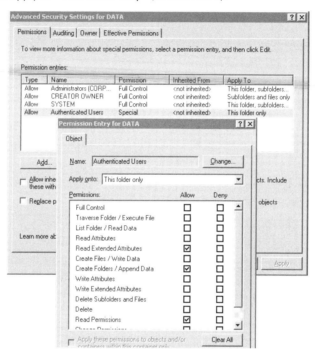

This information is valid for both Windows 2003 and Windows 2000 servers, and you can find more details in the Knowledge Base article Q288991. Adding these groups and assigning these permissions appears to remove the automatic synchronization of Redirected Folders, as you'll see a bit later. However, you can restore this functionality with the **Administratively Assigned Offline Files** policy setting—again, explored later.

In some circumstances when redirecting to Windows 2000 servers, I needed to grant the Authenticated Users the **List Folder/Read Data** access for this process to work fully.

But we have a problem. What if you've already set up Redirected Folders and users already have their own protected subfolders? How do you "go back in time" and fix the ones that already were created? In our example, our Redirected Folders are in D:\data. Follow these steps:

1. Start cmd.exe, and type **AT nn:nn /interactive cmd.exe** (nn:nn is a couple of minutes in the future) on the server where your share resides. This will get you access as the NT Authority\SYSTEM account which has the required permissions you'll need.

> **2.** Wait until the new command window opens. This can take up to a minute. In this window, you are acting as the SYSTEM account.
>
> **3.** Run `cacls "d:\data" /T /E /G DOMAIN\Administrator:F`.
>
> This command edits the ACL (`/E`) rather than replacing it. It grants the user DOMAIN\Administrator Full Control (`/G DOMAIN\Administrator:F`) and sets the permissions on all subfolders (`/T`). This should allow you to set all previously created folders to nearly the same standard.

Advanced Redirected Folders

Anything beyond the basics as previously described isn't required. However, you can set up some advanced options using the Setting drop-down list box, as shown in Figure 10.5 earlier in this chapter. Advanced Redirected Folders works best in two situations, both larger environments, for example:

- A campus with many buildings. You'll want to specify different Redirected Folders locations that are closest to the biggest groups of users.

- More likely, a specific department that is charged with purchasing its own server and storage. In this scenario, there's usually a battle over who can store what data on whose server. With this mechanism, everyone can have their own sandbox.

In either case, you can still have an OU that affects many similar users but that breaks up where folders are redirected, depending on the users' respective security groups. For example, we have an OU called **Sales** that contains two global security sales groups: East_Sales and West_Sales. Each Sales group needs their folders redirected to the server closest to them, either East_Server or West_Server. First, you'll want to create the shares on both the East_Server and West_Server as directed earlier. For this example, they're each shared out as Data. To perform an Advanced Folder Redirection, follow these steps:

1. If you're not already logged on to DC01 as Administrator of the domain using your station VISTAMANAGEMENT, do so now.

2. Start the GPMC.

3. Right-click the OU on which we want to apply folder redirection, in this case the **Sales** OU, and select "Create a GPO in the domain, and link it here."

4. Enter a descriptive name, such as "Advanced Folder Redirection for the **Sales** OU," for the GPO. Select it, and click Edit to open the Group Policy Object Editor.

5. The GPO for the OU appears. Drill down to Folder Redirection by choosing User Configuration ➢ Windows Settings ➢ Folder Redirection.

6. Right-click the Documents folder in the Group Policy Object Editor, and choose Properties from the shortcut menu to open the Documents Properties dialog box. In the Setting drop-down list box, select "Advanced—Specify Locations for Various User Groups." The dialog box changes so that you can now use the Add button to add security settings, as shown in Figure 10.7. Click OK.

7. Click the "Add" button in the My Documents Properties to open up the "Specify Group and Location" dialog box. Click Browse under Security Group Membership, and locate the **East_Sales** global security group.

8. In the Target Folder location, enter the UNC path of the Redirected Folder. In this case, it's \\east_server\data\%username%. Click OK to close the Specify Group and Location dialog box.

9. Repeat steps 7 and 8 for the **West_Sales** global security group.

 WARNING Don't click OK (or Apply) yet. There's more to do. If you do click OK or Apply, you're going to get a warning (which we'll talk about in the sidebar entitled "What Happens When You Edit a GPO from a Pre-Vista Management Station?").

FIGURE 10.7 Use the Advanced redirection function to choose different locations to move users' data.

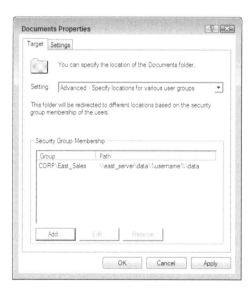

When finished, you should have both **East_Sales** and **West_Sales** listed.

The next time the user logs on, the settings specified in the Settings tab take effect; that is, by default, a new folder is generated specifically for each user, and the current documents in the user's Documents folder are transported to the newly Redirected Folder location.

What Happens When You Edit a GPO from a Pre-Vista Management Station?

If you've taken my advice thus far (in Chapter 2, and again in Chapter 5, and heck, for all the examples in this book), you done as I've suggested and you use a Windows Vista computer as your management station. Why? That's because you'll always have the "full ability" to edit whatever new goodies are in the Group Policy Object Editor.

And for Folder Redirection, this isn't any different. As you saw in Figure 10.4, Windows Vista has a lot more folders it can possibly redirect (like Links, Searches, and others listed above) and some that are more familiar (like Start Menu and Documents).

So, whenever you click OK after editing any Folder Redirection policies on Windows Vista, you'll always get a warning like this one.

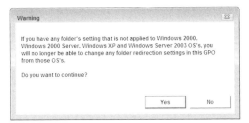

This warning is saying "You're editing this GPO on a Windows Vista management station. If you edit it on a pre-Vista management station, you're going to be in for a world of hurt."

Indeed, this is true. Take a look at the same GPO when viewed on a Windows Server 2003 management station if you had a policy for say, the Links folder. The GPMC on that older machine doesn't know how to interpret the settings. This makes sense: Vista is newer, older management stations don't know what to do with this information. Sometimes, it displays only the information it can. For instance, older GPMCs can still sometimes figure out what's going on in the Documents folder when it's redirected. But not always, as attested by this screenshot.

Then, if you decide to try and edit Folder Redirection policies of a GPO you created using Windows Vista by using a pre-Vista management station, again, it's a world of hurt. Take a look what happens when you try to make a change in, say, My Documents (if this was originally created on a Windows Vista management station). The system throws an "Access is denied" message. Which is pretty elegant considering the circumstances.

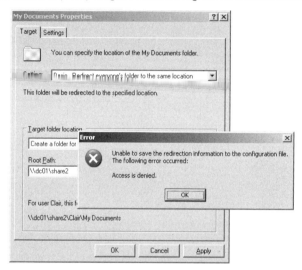

So, the message is clear: create and edit your GPOs using a Windows Vista management station. Don't create the GPOs using Windows Vista and then return to a pre-Vista management station.

In case you're interested, what's happening under the hood is this:

Vista Folder Redirection writes a new file into the GPT called fdeploy1.ini that doesn't overlap with the old one (called fdeploy.ini). However, it does populate fdeploy.ini when you select downward-compatible mode. But you see this message on a Windows XP management station because Vista sets the "old" fdeploy.ini file that it creates for downward compatibility as Read-only in the GPT, effectively preventing a down-level GPEditor from writing to it.

It's a pretty low-tech solution; but it works.

Testing Folder Redirection of *Documents/My Documents*

In the last chapter, you used Brett Wier's account to verify that Roaming Profiles were working properly. You did this by creating a test file, FILE1.TXT, in the My Documents folder and noting that the file properly roamed with the user when he hopped from machine to machine. Additionally, you noted that the file location was on the local hard drive—in his locally cached copy of his Roaming User Profile. To see whether My Documents is being redirected, move Brett's user account into an OU that has the My Documents folder redirected as specified in either the Basic or Advanced Folder Redirection settings.

You will need to log off and back on as Brett to see the changes take effect. Group Policy background refresh (as detailed in Chapter 3) does not affect Redirected Folders.

Let's first see what happens when we log onto a Windows 2000 machine as Brett Wier and open My Documents. Right-click FILE1.TXT and note its location, as shown in Figure 10.8.

FIGURE 10.8   Windows 2000 Folder Redirection in action

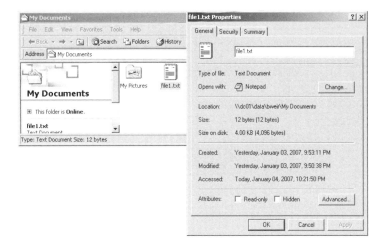

The file was automatically transported from the Roaming Profile and anchored to the fixed point on the server, in this case \\DC01\data\bwier\My Documents.

If you perform the same experiment on a Windows XP or Windows Vista machine, you'll see the same results, but notice the curious arrows on the files and folders (see Figure 10.9 for Windows XP and Figure 10.10 for Windows Vista).

The arrows signify that you're one step closer to having a managed desktop; a new feature is already working for you—Offline Files, which I'll talk about in the next major section. However, one point should be gleaned from these two figures. The behavior of Windows XP and Windows Vista is different from that of Windows 2000. That is, when a Windows Vista or Windows XP machine uses a Redirected Folder, the entire contents are automatically cached offline. Thus, when the network is offline, your users still have total access to the files they need.

Stay tuned for Offline Files, where we'll discuss how to actually put this knowledge to good use.

 You will not see the arrows if you performed the procedure in the "How to Grant Administrators Access to Documents/My Documents (or Other Redirected Folders)" sidebar earlier in this chapter. However, you will see these arrows if you follow these instructions in the "Administratively Assigned Offline Files" section later in this chapter.

FIGURE 10.9 Windows XP Folder Redirection in action

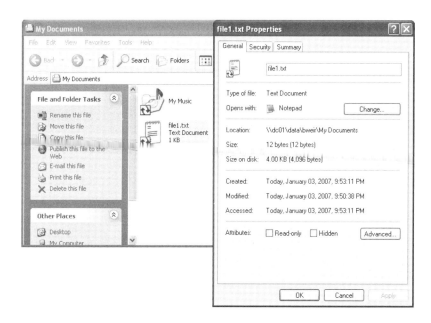

FIGURE 10.10 Windows Vista Folder Redirection in action

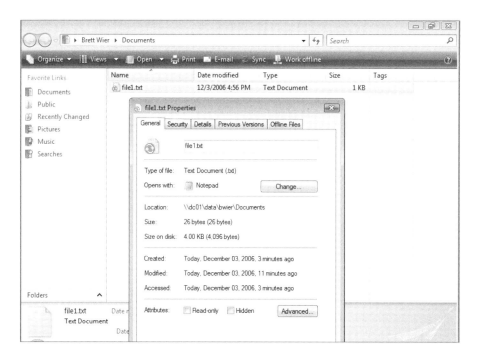

Redirecting the Start Menu and the Desktop

The Start Menu and Desktop might seem like weird items to redirect. However, there are some cases where you might want to.

One case is in a common computing environment—such as a nurse's station, library computer, or kiosk—where you want to make sure the same Start Menu and/or Desktop are always presented. Then, you can lock down the target location of the redirected items to ensure that they cannot be changed.

In cases like these, you specify a shared folder with Read-only access for the Security group who will use it and Full Control for just one person who can change the Start Menu or Desktop (such as a fake account that no one uses within that Security group). That way, no one in the affected group can normally change the common Start Menu or Desktop except for the administrative user of the bogus account you created, who has Full Control permissions over the share.

Instead of using the *%username%* variable, you fix the redirection to a specific shared folder and directory, as shown in Figure 10.11. Since all users are to use the same settings, there's no need to use *%username%*. Indeed, since you're locking the shared folder down as Read-only for the Security group, the username is moot.

You could also argue that redirecting the Desktop is a good for those who have users who think the Desktop is a good dumping ground for big documents. If you redirect the Desktop, you're reducing the size of the Roaming User Profile. It's up to you if you want to explore this option.

You'll find additional Group Policy settings regarding the configuration of the Start Menu in User Configuration ➢ Administrative Templates ➢ Start Menu & Taskbar.

FIGURE 10.11 Use one static path to ensure that all Desktops receive the same setting.

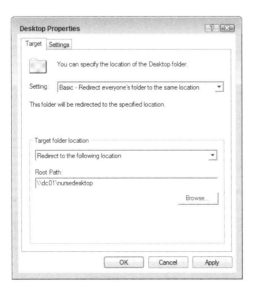

Redirecting the Application Data

Because application designers can decide what to put in the Application Data folder in the profile, an administrator never knows what size this folder could grow to. By redirecting the Application Data, files—such as custom dictionaries or databases—can be firmly planted on the server instead of having to go up and back with each logon with the Roaming Profile.

In Windows 2000 and XP, there were some potential downsides to redirecting Application Data. One potential downside is that this folder contains the user's private PKI (Public Key Infrastructure) keys. If you use Windows 2000 or Windows XP and redirect this folder to a server, the keys are available to anyone with access to those files on the server. This isn't necessarily a security breach, because the keys are encrypted with a hash of the user's password and other elements, but take special precautions just in case.

The real danger in redirecting Application Data for Windows 2000 and XP shows up when users need to decrypt EFS (Encrypting File System) files. To do so, they need access to their private PKI keys. If you've redirected Application Data to the server, and the server goes down or the user's computer goes offline, how will users get their keys to decrypt their EFS files?

- Well, in Windows 2000, this is a big problem by default. Because, remember, Windows 2000 machines don't automatically make Redirected Folders always available offline. So, in the case of Windows 2000 the keys are cached in memory until they are cleared out by reboot.

- If the client is a Windows XP, the EFS files are cached offline automatically. The only issue would be if someone turned off offline caching of files. If offline caching is turned off and the Application Data is redirected and the computer is off the network, the user most likely wouldn't be able to access their encrypted files.

- In Windows Vista, things have changed even further. In Windows Vista, when you redirect the `Appdata\Roaming` folder, the following folders are not redirected to the server: `Appdata\Roaming\Microsoft\` with subdirectories `Credentials`, `Crypto`, `Protect`, and `System Certificates`. So, previous worries about where the keys are and who has access to them are reduced.

The final note here is that because Microsoft applications use this directory to store their settings data, this folder is heavily accessed (for example, by Outlook). Redirecting this, especially if it's not cached, can be painful from a performance perspective. (Note however, that Windows XP and Windows Vista should automatically cache this folder when redirected.)

Group Policy Setting for Folder Redirection

There are only a handful of settings that control Folder Redirection. They're located in Computer *and* User Configuration ➢ Administrative Templates ➢ System ➢ Folder Redirection. If there's a conflict between the User and Computer side, the computer side will win.

Do Not Automatically Make Redirected Folders Available Offline (User Side Only)

As you're about to discover, Windows XP and Windows Vista go "the extra mile" and automatically cache every scrap of data you have in, say, Documents/My Documents (or any other

Redirected Folder). The idea is that if you're offline, you might need the data on the road. (Don't worry, we'll get to this in excruciating detail soon.)

This setting lets you disable that behavior. You might want to do this if you have laptops that travel to places with slowish links because all of the user's data will be downloaded over that slow link. See the section "Using Folder Redirection and Offline Files over Slow Links" a little later.

> In versions prior to Vista this was an Offline Files policy. It is now a Folder Redirection policy. Why the change? There was no Offline Files API prior to Vista, so a feature like Folder Redirection had no way to pin a folder into the CSC cache. Now that Offline Files has an API, Microsoft chose to move this "decision" to pin files over to Folder Redirection. Now Folder Redirection decides whether or not it should pin the Redirected Folder. It becomes a much cleaner solution under the hood.

Because this policy is a user-side policy, it becomes very difficult to implement on a "system wide" level. See the section "Do not Automatically Make Redirected Folders Available Offline."

Use Localized Subfolder Names When Redirecting *Start* and *My Documents* (Both User and Computer)

This setting is one that you might consider using in a multilingual corporate environment. However, it's very quirky.

The policy only actually affects legacy subfolders of Documents (My Music, My Pictures and My Videos) and the Start Menu subfolders. This policy *does not* affect the root Documents or Start Menu folders.

It supports the legacy scenario where users may be sharing data between a multi-lingual Vista machine and a localized Windows XP or Windows 2000 machine. In that scenario, the legacy folder structure is preserved. The subfolders like My Music also map correctly to the localized name on the localized downlevel OS. The supported scenario is only when the user goes across the same languages, i.e., Vista French to XP Localized French (but *not* across languages).

This policy setting only affects Windows Vista.

Troubleshooting Redirected Folders

Occasionally, Folder Redirection doesn't work as it should. Or, maybe it does. We'll check out some cases in which it appears not to be working but really is.

Windows XP/Windows Vista Fast Boot and Folder Redirection

If you see the message in Figure 10.12, you might initially think that Folder Redirection isn't working as it should. This event tells us that the default is that Fast Boot is enabled in Windows Vista and Windows XP, and Folder Redirection will not take affect until the next logon.

With the default (that Fast Boot is enabled), Basic Folder Redirection needs two logons to take effect and Advanced Folder Redirection needs three logons to take effect (see Chapter 3 for more information).

FIGURE 10.12 Fast Boot in Windows XP (and Windows Vista) can delay Folder Redirection until multiple reboots.

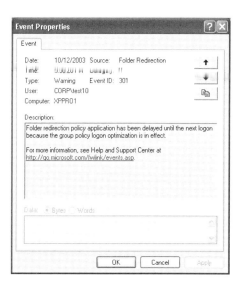

Permissions Problems

Be sure that the user has access to the folder; specifically, make sure that the share you use for Folder Redirection is set for Authenticated Users:Full Control. Without it, you might encounter EventID: 101s, as shown in Figure 10.13 (left) for Windows XP. Another common Windows XP event for security problems is Event 112: "The security descriptor structure is invalid." Again, the idea is that there are some permissions problems—usually share level permissions where Authenticated Users weren't set up properly for Full Control.

You can see a similar error for Windows Vista, but with event ID 502, as seen in Figure 10.13 (right).

Use *GPResult* for Verification

First, make sure the user is actually being affected by the GPO you set up that contains your Folder Redirection policy. Use the GPResult tool we explored in Chapter 3. Figure 10.14 shows a snippet from the output of GPResult /v on Windows XP when Folder Redirection is working.

FIGURE 10.13   Be sure the user has permissions to write to the share you set up. The Windows Vista event ID is different, but the results are the same.

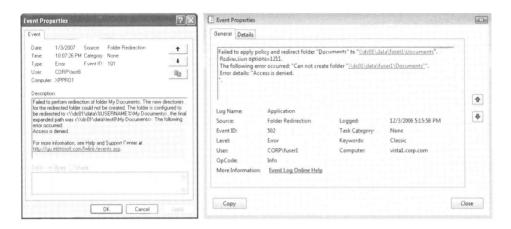

FIGURE 10.14   GPResult can help you determine if Folder Redirection is working.

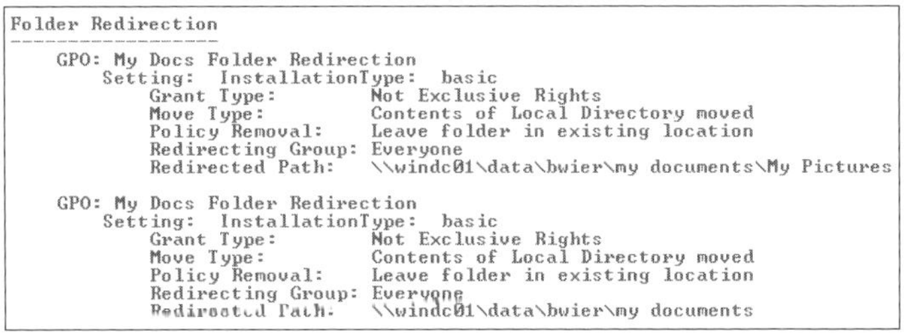

```
Folder Redirection
------------------
    GPO: My Docs Folder Redirection
        Setting:  InstallationType:  basic
            Grant Type:       Not Exclusive Rights
            Move Type:        Contents of Local Directory moved
            Policy Removal:   Leave folder in existing location
            Redirecting Group: Everyone
            Redirected Path:  \\windc01\data\bwier\my documents\My Pictures
    GPO: My Docs Folder Redirection
        Setting:  InstallationType:  basic
            Grant Type:       Not Exclusive Rights
            Move Type:        Contents of Local Directory moved
            Policy Removal:   Leave folder in existing location
            Redirecting Group: Everyone
            Redirected Path:  \\windc01\data\bwier\my documents
```

If no Folder Redirection policy displays in the output when you run GPResult /v, chances are the user is not being affected by the policy. Check to see if the user has permissions on the GPO for both Read and Apply Group Policy. If they are getting the GPO as indicated via GPResult /v, also make sure that the target server is still available, that the share is still shared, and that the users have rights to write to that share and folder. Last, make sure the user isn't hitting a disk quota on the volume on which the shared folder resides, as this can generate mixed results.

Enabling Advanced Folder Redirection Logging

Folder Redirection can provide a detailed log should the event log and GPResult not turn up what you're looking for. The procedure for this is different for pre-Vista and Windows Vista machines.

Turning on Advanced Folder Redirection Logging for Pre-Vista machines

For pre-Vista machines, you'll modify the registry which will create a log file for the Folder Redirection process. To do so, you need to modify the Registry as follows:

```
HKLM\Software\Microsoft\Windows NT\CurrentVersion\Diagnostics
```

If the Diagnostics key doesn't exist at the end of this Registry path, you'll need to create it. Then, add a new Reg_DWORD of FdeployDebugLevel and set it to 0f in hex or 15 in decimal.

Once you do this, you can find the log file at:

```
%windir%\debug\usermode\fdeploy.log
```

Only the administrator can read the log file, so you have two options. First, you can log out as the user and log back in as the local administrator to read the log file in action. Alternatively, you can use the runas command to view the log as an administrator while you're still logged in as the user.

Turning on Advanced Folder Redirection Logging for Vista Machines

You will essentially enable verbose logging the same way you did for pre-Vista machines, but you will have to do it with the elevated CMD.exe prompt. First, you'll need to click Start ➤ Accessories, right-click over the command prompt and select "Run As Administrator." Then, in the new command prompt, run the following command:

```
reg add "HKLM\Software\Microsoft\Windows NT\CurrentVersion\Diagnostics" /v
FdeployDebugLevel /t REG_DWORD /d "0xF" /f
```

Log off and log on and check out the Application log in Event Viewer.

Offline Files and Synchronization

We've mitigated the amount of traffic our network will have to bear from Roaming Profiles by implementing Redirected Folders—especially for My Documents (for Windows XP) and Documents (for Windows Vista). But we still have another hurdle. Now that we're anchoring our users' data to the server, what's to happen if the server goes down? What happens if our network cable is unplugged? What if our top executive is flying at 30,000 feet? How will any of our users get to their data? The answer, in fact, comes from another feature—Offline Files.

Offline Files seeks to make files within shares that are normally accessed online available offline! You can be sitting under a tree, on an airplane, in a submarine—anywhere—and still have your files with you.

Here's a brief overview of the magic: Once you enable a particular share to support the function, the client's Offline Files cache maintains files as they're used on the network. When users are online and connected to the network, nothing really magical happens. Users continue to write files upon the server as normal. However, in addition to the file writes at the server, the file writes additionally get reflected in the local cache too, as a protection to maintain the files in cache. Moreover, reads are satisfied from the client, thus saving bandwidth.

You can use Offline Files for any share you like and practically guarantee that the data users need is with them. As we've noticed, Windows Vista and Windows XP already seem to "know" about Redirected Folders. And, when they notice that you've redirected a folder, they automatically make that data available offline if you need it.

However, it's certainly possible to use Offline Files for public "common" shares. For example, an administrator can set up shares for customer data, and a server can have a "general repository" from which multiple users can access files. We'll see how this works around the bend (especially when two people change the same file). Sounds bad, but it's not crazy-bad.

We'll also understand the differences between Windows XP and Windows Vista's Offline Files engine. That's what we'll explore here.

So, for these examples, if you want to follow along, create a share called Sales on \\DC01. You wouldn't normally stick shares on your Domain Controller, but for our working example here, it'll be just fine. Additionally, stick 10 text files—`salesfile1.txt` through `salesfile10`
`.txt`—in there, so you can watch the reaction as various flavors of Windows try to touch these files. Finally, map a network drive over to \\DC01\\`sales` from your test machines (Windows 2000, Windows XP, and Windows Vista).

There are two shares that you should not place Offline Files upon. Don't use Offline Files with the SYSVOL share. Nor should you use Offline Files with the Profiles share you created in the last chapter (more on this later).

Making Offline Files Available

When you set up any shared folder on Windows 2000 Server or Windows Server 2003, you'll notice an "Offline Settings" button, as highlighted in Figure 10.15 (seen as the Caching button on Windows 2000). The Offline Settings dialog box is slightly different in Windows 2000 and Windows 2003. Figure 10.14 shows the Windows 2003 version, and the default in 2000 is "Manual Caching for Documents." The default named "Only the files and programs that users specify will be available online" setting may not really be the most efficient setting for this feature. The four settings are described in the following sections.

Only the Files and Programs that Users Specify Will Be Available Offline (or Windows 2000's "Manual Caching for Documents")

With this setting, users must specify which files they want to keep with them offline. They can do this in the Documents/My Documents folder by right-clicking a file (or more commonly, a folder) and choosing "Make Available Offline" (for Windows XP and 2000) or "Always available offline" (for Windows Vista) from the shortcut menu, as shown in Figure 10.16. The unofficial term for this is *pinning* a file, but you won't see that term in any official Microsoft documentation. Users can pin as many files as they like, the number of files is limited only by the size of their hard drive (in Windows XP) or, in Windows Vista, this can be imposed by a hard "max space" limit via Group Policy (explored a little later).

If a Windows 2000 or Windows XP user chooses to pin individual files manually (again, by right-clicking over a document and selecting "Make Available Offline" as seen in Figure 10.16A), the Offline Files Wizard asks them some simple questions. This wizard runs only the first time a user pins one or more files, and each user on a computer who pins files from that computer walks through the wizard once. Figure 10.17 shows a screen from the wizard.

As stated, in Windows Vista, the command is slightly different. It's called "Always Available Offline," and there is no wizard (see Figure 10.16B). It just does it—short and sweet.

FIGURE 10.15   Four offline settings for caching behavior are available in Windows 2003.

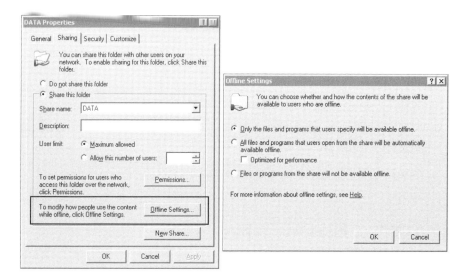

FIGURE 10.16A   Users can "pin" files by right-clicking them and making them available offline (Windows 2000 and XP).

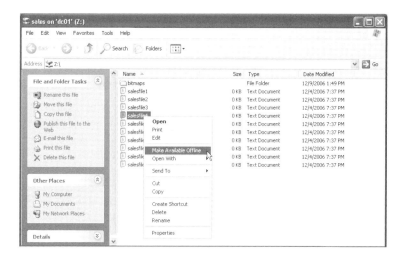

FIGURE 10.16B   Users can "pin" files by right-clicking them and making them available offline (Windows Vista).

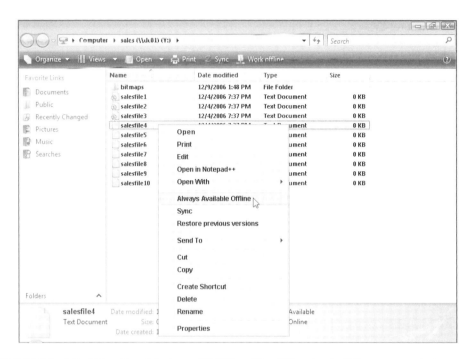

FIGURE 10.17   The Windows XP Offline Files Wizard asks if the user wants to synchronize upon logon and logoff (in Windows XP, usually a pretty good idea).

In pre-Vista systems, a balloon announces changes in Offline Files cache state, although a user who does not enable reminder balloons will still see the initial state change balloon tips. Once the wizard is finished, the pinned files are automatically brought down into the local cache. Users get a little graphical reminder attached to the pinned file's icon, as shown in Figure 10.18.

The reminder is an unobtrusive yin-yang icon symbolizing the harmony users will feel knowing their files are safe on the server and cached locally. Or maybe it's just two arrows showing the file can be "round-tripped." You can be the judge. You can see the round-tripped icon for Windows Vista and for Windows XP in Figure 10.18.

FIGURE 10.18 Pinned files can easily be recognized by their "round-trip" or yin-yang icon.

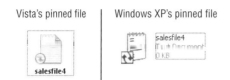

If you want, you can disconnect the network cable to your test client and still access any file that's now available offline.

As you saw in Figures 10.9 and Figure 10.10 earlier in this chapter, users logging on to Windows Vista and Windows XP machines with the redirected My Documents folder already have these yin-yang icons on their files and folders. Windows XP and Windows Vista do a little extra magic and guarantee that all files in important Redirected Folders (such as the redirected Documents/My Documents) are available wherever the user roams.

All Files and Programs that Users Open from the Share Will Be Automatically Available Offline (or "Automatic Caching for Documents" for Windows 2000)

If you plan to use Offline Files for more than just the user's private data, you typically select this option. When users access any files in a share with this setting, the files are copied and stored in a local cache on the workstation, where, by default, 10 percent of the C: hard drive space is used to maintain files in a first in/first out fashion.

Before turning this on for any share or shares, be sure to read "It's Not Offline Files—It's Explorer!" a bit later in this chapter to understand how turning this on could be a potential headache.

For Windows Vista, that default is changed to 25 percent of free disk space when the drive cache is first created. This could mean that if you have only a little space left when the drive cache is created, it won't be 25 percent of the drive.

Later in this chapter, in the "Manually Tweaking the Offline Files Interface for Vista Machines" section, you can see this "25% of available disk space" formula in action. In Figure 10.36, you'll see that my offline cache size is only 15.2%. This number was calculated because it was 25 percent of free disk space at that time.

For example, let's say you're using Windows XP and have a 1GB C: partition. In this case, 100MB of data flows in and out of your cache. Let's also say that you have 11 files, each 10MB in size, named FILE1.DOC through FILE11.DOC. You consecutively click each of them to open them and bring each into the cache. FILE1.DOC through FILE10.DOC are maintained in the cache until such time as FILE11.DOC is read. At that time, since FILE1.DOC was first in the cache, it is also the first to be flushed from the cache to make way for FILE11.DOC.

The files are ejected in a background thread called the "CSC Agent." The agent periodically makes a pass over the cache removing auto-cached files as necessary. If a Write operation grows the cache size beyond the established limit, it doesn't immediately evict the least recently used auto-cached file. The CSC Agent is only periodically brought into memory for execution.

Additionally, files can be pinned, as they were in the "Only the files and programs that users specify will be available online" (or Windows 2000's "Manual Caching for Documents") option. Pinned files don't count toward the cache percentage in Windows 2000 or Windows XP but *do* count towards pinned cache size in Vista.

In all cases though, pinned files are exempt from being flushed from the cache and are protected, hence, "always available" to your users when working offline.

While it's tempting, do not use "Automatic Caching for Documents" for the share that houses the Roaming Profiles you set up in Chapter 6. See the next section, "Files or Programs from the Share Will Not Be Available Offline (or 'Disallow Caching for Files of Any Type' on Windows 2000)" for the reasons.

Files or Programs from the Share Will Not Be Available Offline (or "Disallow Caching for Files of Any Type" for Windows 2000)

If you choose this option, no files are cached for offline use, nor can they be pinned. This doesn't prevent users from copying the files to any other place they might have access to locally or to another network share they have access to that does have caching enabled.

Another Option: "Optimized for Performance" (or "Automatic Caching for Programs" for Windows 2000)

This option's name is highly misleading. The idea is to use this setting for Read-only files that you want available offline and in the cache, such as executables. According to Microsoft, this setting does a "version check" instead of creating a handle on the server if the access is Read-only. Since there is no server handle, the system tries to use the local version first to save bandwidth when it can use either the locally cached version or the network version.

Upon performing a network trace of the interaction of "Optimized for Performance" (for Windows 2003) and "Automatic Caching for Programs" (in Windows 2000), there seems to be no discernible difference between it and Windows 2003's "All files and programs that users open from the share will be automatically available offline" (or "Automatic Caching for Documents" for Windows 2000). Therefore, use "All files and programs that users open from the share will be automatically available offline" (or "Automatic Caching for Documents") whenever possible.

Inside Windows XP Synchronization

Now, we want to spend a little time understanding what's going in synchronization land. Here, we'll explore Windows XP's synchronization engine. Then, we'll take some time and explore Windows Vista's synchronization engine.

Inside the Windows XP Offline Files and Synchronization Manager Interface

Most people would start out by exploring Tools ➢ Folder Option and selecting the "Offline Files" tab. You can see this in Figures 10.19 and 10.20.

FIGURE 10.19   The Folder Options item on the Tools menu is the first place to start your Offline Files configurations.

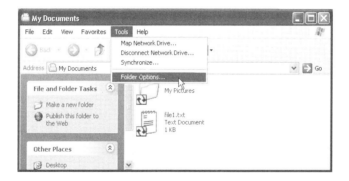

FIGURE 10.20   The default options for Offline Files on a Windows XP Professional machine. Only administrators can change all the options.

Indeed, this is where "Offline Files" live in Windows XP. But this is only half of where the synchronization magic in Windows XP *occurs*. That's because, in Windows XP, the Offline Files handler is used as a snap-in for a component called the Synchronization Manager. The Synchronization Manager is a framework for plug-ins such as Offline Files to use. The other half of the magic is in the Synchronization Manager itself.

You can open the Synchronization Manager (the Items to Synchronize dialog box, which is shown in Figure 10.21) in two ways:

- From the Desktop, choose Start ➢ Programs ➢ Accessories ➢ Synchronize.

- In Explorer, choose Tools ➢ Synchronize.

FIGURE 10.21 Users can select specific shares on which to synchronize items.

Users can specifically choose which plug-ins they want to use, such as "Offline Files" or "Offline Web Pages" as shown in Figure 10.21. For each plug-in, they can select which data (such as shares) they want the Synchronization Manager to handle. Additionally, the buttons in this dialog box perform the following functions:

Synchronize Forces the Synchronization Manager to pop into the foreground and start the synchronization process.

Properties Allows the user to open the Offline Files folder to view the files in the local cache. Same as the "View Files" button shown earlier in Figure 10.20.

Setup Allows you to refine how synchronization is controlled. You can see the result in Figure 10.22.

Here a user can specify which Synchronization Manager snap-ins to use. In this case, the "Offline Files" snap-in is selected (with one entry), and the "Offline Web Pages" is not selected. The other entries on the Logon/Logoff tab that need specific attention are the "When I log on to my computer" and "When I log off my computer." These entries co-interact with the Offline Files "Synchronize all offline files when logging on" and "Synchronize all offline files before logging off" as in Figure 10.20 earlier in this chapter. Now, we'll take some time to explore that interaction.

FIGURE 10.22   The Synchronization Manager is a framework for snap-ins such as "Offline Files" and "Offline Web Pages."

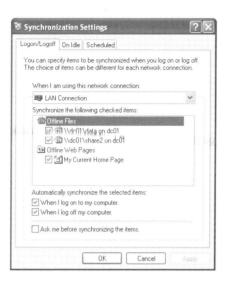

Understanding Offline Files and Synchronization Manager Interaction

Offline Files has two possible synchronization modes: Quick Sync and Full Sync. Here's how each works:

Quick Sync   At logon, the files that were modified in the local client cache are pushed up to the server. At logoff, only the files that the user actually opened on the server are brought down into the local cache.

Full Sync   At logon, *all* the files the user has in cache are synchronized with the copies on the server. Updated files on the server also come down into the cache. Also, if the user is caching an entire folder, those files come down into the cache. At logoff, the same occurs. That is, all the files the user has in cache and any new files on the server are synchronized in the cache.

For Full Sync, we're mainly concerned with the two options: "Synchronize all offline Files when logging on" and "Synchronize all offline files before logging off." The key word to focus on in these options is *all*. You can see these settings in Figure 10.20 earlier in this chapter. Checking either of these options (or both) directs the Offline Files handler to utilize the Synchronization Manager to synchronize *all* content.

The Synchronization Manager settings (seen in Figure 10.22) control how the Synchronization Manager responds to the "logon" and "logoff" conditions on the computer. If these check boxes are *not* checked, *no* Synchronization Manager activity occurs at the corresponding time. These settings apply equally to all handlers registered with Synchronization Manager—not just the Offline Files handler.

So that's how they work together: the two dialog boxes' settings are interdependent for how Offline Files will synchronize. Indeed, if the corresponding Synchronization Manager setting is *not* enabled, the Offline Files setting has no effect.

Table 10.1 describes the behavior at logon.

TABLE 10.3   Logon Behavior with Synchronization Manager Settings and Offline Files Settings

Synchronization Manager Setting "When I log on to my computer"	Offline Files "Synchronize all offline files when logging on"	Resulting Behavior
Off	Off	No sync activity at logon
Off	On	No sync activity at logon
On	Off	Quick Sync at logon
On	On	Full Sync at logon

Table 10.2 describes the behavior at logoff.

TABLE 10.4   Logoff Behavior with Synchronization Manager Settings and Offline Files Settings

Synchronization Manager Setting "When I log off my computer"	Offline Files "Synchronize all offline files before logging off"	Resulting Behavior
Off	Off	No sync activity at logoff
Off	On	No sync activity at logoff
On	Off	Quick Sync at logoff
On	On	Full Sync at logoff

Unfortunately, there is little coordination between the Synchronization Manager and Offline Files user interfaces. However, there is one small interaction: If you enable Offline Files' "Synchronize all offline files when logging on" or "Synchronize all offline files before logging off," Windows automatically enables the corresponding Synchronization Manager setting. The opposite is not true.

People often think there is more coordination between XP's Offline Files and Synchronization Manager than there really is. It's not uncommon for people to think that Synchronization Manager *is* Offline Files. Synchronization Manager is simply a place to host various synchronization plug-ins (such as Offline Files), a place where those plug-ins can display their items, and a place for users to select specific items for synchronization at specific times (and in response to specific events).

Inside Windows Vista File Synchronization

The Windows XP synchronization engine was good, but it could have been better. The Windows Vista File Synchronization was rewritten in several ways to try to address some of the shortcomings of the Windows XP version.

Better Handling of Downed Shares

If a user was using a Windows XP machine and was leveraging several offline-enabled shares and one network share went down, XP always thought the whole server went down. So, the upshot was that other shares (that you likely didn't set to be available offline) were then suddenly also not available. Again, that server itself really never went down, just one share on that server. While bad, it doesn't sound *that* bad on first blush. But, if you were using a domain-based DFS this could be a major problem. Especially if you put your redirected My Documents folder in a domain-based DFS. If even one share in the DFS went offline, XP would assume the whole caboodle wasn't available.

In Vista, things get smarter. If one share goes down, it doesn't assume (thankfully) that the whole server up and died. It just transitions that one share to offline and keeps trying the other shares. Same with domain-based DFS shares. If you can't access one, it doesn't assume the whole DFS up and died—it will make just the parts that appear offline to be available offline.

Better Handling of Synchronization

Synchronizing files gets much smarter in Vista. In Windows XP you had to close *all* your open files (handles, really) in order for synchronization to start. In Vista, it's supposed to be "absolutely seamless," to quote Microsoft. Now, in Vista, changes are just synchronized in the background, and the user doesn't really notice anything has happened. Of course, a file cannot be synchronized while it is held open for write. All files need to be closed, then they're automatically synchronized.

Also, modified files, or files currently in conflict, continue to stay offline while all other files and folders are transitioned online. The conflicting files are transitioned online after the conflict is resolved.

No More Logon/Logoff Syncing Files Dialog

On Windows XP, when you log off your machine, you'll see your files synchronizing (provided "sync at logoff" was turned on). This was often very confusing for a new user without any training about what was going on. In Windows Vista, there are no more synchronization dialogs during logoff (or logon, for that matter). In fact, there's actually no more synchronization at logoff. I make note of this in case you have some reliance that absolutely guarantees that your files need to be synchronized at logoff in Windows Vista as they were in Windows XP.

Better Transfer Technology

In Windows XP, the following file types cannot be cached:

- `.PST` (Outlook personal folder)
- `.SLM` (Source Library Management file)
- `.MDB` (Access database)
- `.LDB` (Access security)
- `.MDW` (Access workgroup)
- `.MDE` (Access compiled module)
- `.DB?` (everything that has the extension `.DB` plus anything else in the third character, such as `.DBF`, is never included in the cache)

In Windows Vista, those limitations are out the window. Not only is there a brand new algorithm to help determine which files and directories are different, but also this same technology sends over *just the changed data* in a file. So, previous limitations on the types of files are gone. The new technology is called "Bitmap Differential Transfer" or BDT for short. BDT is so amazing, it keeps track of what *disk pages* of the files have changed. So, if you change 2 bytes in a 2GB file, only that block of data is sent to the server, instead of the whole 2GB.

And, did you catch that Outlook `.PST` files are no longer unsupported? That is you can use Offline Files with 2GB `.PST` files, and Microsoft will support you.

In my opinion, that's worth the price of Windows Vista right there.

The BDT technology only works (right now) when you change a file on the *client* and want to sync it back to the *server*. This is fine, as this is the usual case. However, should someone work directly on a file on the server (and hence, your file on Windows Vista is out of date), sadly, the entire file is pulled down to the Windows Vista client. BDT can't send just the changed bytes. The other BDT limitation is that it isn't effective on *new* files. The entirety of new files are synchronized back to the server. And, this can be a pitfall, because some applications (like Microsoft Word) insist on creating new files sometimes—even though you're editing what "feels" like the same `.DOC` file.

Better User Interface Design and Experience

Vista doesn't show a pop-up and tell the client he's now offline. This is good. We don't need to scare the users any more than usual. Because the experience is now "seamless," there's nothing that needs to be said to the user. However, if you select an offline folder (such as the redirected `Documents`) you'll see a status in the bottom left as seen in Figure 10.23.

Additionally, a user can choose if they want to manually work offline (as also seen in Figure 10.23). A user might choose to do this if the connection to the server is slow, or maybe it's an expensive connection, or they just want to test the offline experience.

FIGURE 10.23   Windows Vista's Offline Files User Interface isn't as "in your face" as Windows XP.

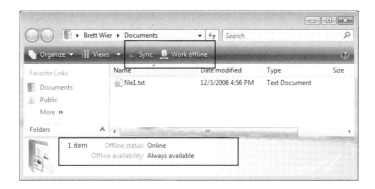

There's no pop-up window at logoff telling them anything about the offline synchronization—because there is no synchronization at logoff. Synchronization is just quietly happening in the background. The downside, as stated earlier, is that Windows Vista might not have all the files synchronized when a user logs off if a synchronization hasn't recently occurred.

What's Really Happening in the Background on Windows Vista?

The Offline Files service automatically synchronizes files in several scenarios:

- If the user is working online, every five minutes the service "fills" in any sparsely cached files. This helps reduce the chance of transitioning offline and sparse files becoming unavailable to the user.

- Approximately one minute after user logon, the Offline Files service performs a full two-way synchronization of all content cached by that user. This is essentially the "logon sync" that was prominent in XP.

- Whenever a share transitions from offline to online, the Offline Files service performs a full two-way synchronization of that scope for each logged-on user.

Because of these background activities, the need to sync at logoff is reduced (since Windows XP). Since sync-at-logoff is not officially exposed in either the Offline Files or Sync Center UI, a user must manually sync using Sync Center prior to logging off if they wish to ensure that they have (in their local cache) all of the latest content from the server(s).

Windows Vista also has a new "Sync Center" (reborn as the next generation of the Sync Manager from Windows 2000/XP). It's a complete redesign/rewrite but it serves the same function. This Sync Center can be found from the Control Panel or by clicking the little green arrows in the toolbar. The idea of the Sync Center is that it's a common User Interface where all files and devices can get synchronized. So, expect things like handheld devices and other synchronizing things to make their way here. I don't know if this will end up being a nice unified experience or kind of a "catchall" place for anything in Windows Vista-land that synchronizes. You can see the Sync Center in Figure 10.24.

FIGURE 10.24   The new Windows Vista Sync Center

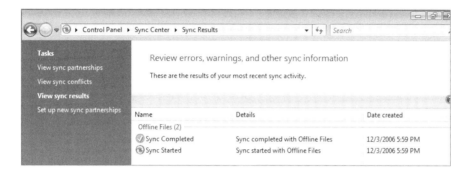

Better Offline Experience (Unified "Namespace" View)

Here's a common problem scenario with Windows XP: Let's assume Xavier had chosen to make three files out of ten available offline. When Xavier's computer goes offline, the three files Xavier had chosen to keep offline would, of course, still be there for Xavier to play with. However, the remaining seven files (which he didn't choose to make available offline) will simply—pop—disappear. This was oftentimes confusing for users who weren't sure what the heck was going on. Windows Vista now introduces "ghosting" (which has nothing whatsoever to do with a product by Symantec).

Let's take the same scenario for Victoria on her Windows Vista machine. If she chose to make those files "Always Available Offline," as in Figure 10.25, then she gets a different experience. Windows Vista's Offline Files Ghosting will show the seven files "ghosted" as seen in Figure 10.26. Ghosts are namespace holders; they are visually different and are grayed out, plus they have an X icon overlay showing that they're not really accessible. The files are on the server, but because they're only on the server, Victoria can't access the files until she reconnects and makes them available offline.

The "Offline Availability" status of "Not available" is an additional cue to the user that the file is not available for use. Note that these "Offline availability" and "Offline status" properties may be enabled as columns in the shell folder view. They're off by default because they take up valuable space, but some users may find them useful.

FIGURE 10.25   Before Victoria goes offline, she pins salesfile1.txt, salesfile2.txt, and salesfile3.txt.

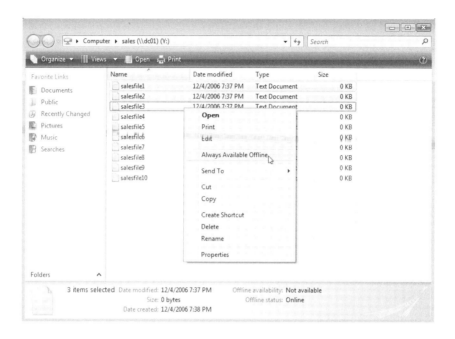

FIGURE 10.26   Files that are not available show a "ghosted" icon with a little "x."

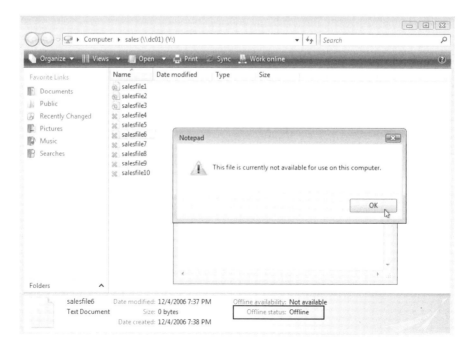

Better Cache Encryption

In Windows XP, offline files had the ability to be encrypted. This way if the laptop was stolen and the bad guy rooted around the file system, those offline files couldn't be seen in the clear. However, it wasn't long before it was realized that the encryption was based on the system account. Once you hijacked the system account, it was a trivial matter to see inside this encrypted cache. Just run a command prompt as the system account and, poof!, you're in!

In Windows Vista, offline files are now encrypted with the credentials of the first user who wants to encrypt a file. Using the user certificate is more secure (as hacking the system account is trivial), and this has a side benefit where multiple users of the same machine cannot see each other's encrypted cached files. However, this has a negative side detractor. What if Xavier and Victoria both have access to an encrypted file on a file server? Actually, this isn't a big deal if both Xavier and Victoria are both online using different systems. Both XP and Vista have provisions for multiple certificates to be inside a file allowing both users access to the file.

The problem comes in if Xavier or Victoria want to use that file while offline, and they both use the same Windows Vista laptop. Here's where it gets sticky. If you choose to enable Windows Vista's encrypted offline cache, you cannot share the same encrypted file with another user *on the same machine* (when that file transitions to offline). Only the user who initially encrypted the file can access that file when offline. The file is encrypted using only one certificate and that is the reason why multiple users cannot access them offline.

Again, this isn't a problem when Xavier or Victoria are online (and use the same Windows Vista laptop). When both users are online (and use the same Windows Vista laptop) it isn't a problem—both users can continue to access the server version from the same client and get in using their certificate.

Other Random New Goodies

Here's a smattering of additional goodies you get with Windows Vista's Offline Files:

- One of the key problems with Windows XP's Offline Files feature was that it was never quite sure if you were using a slow link or not. That is, if you had connectivity, but it was slow, it would still use the file over the network rather than just use the copy it had cached locally. This would get really, really bad if you had lots of files over the network and just even looked at a thumbnail view (in Windows XP). The whole file would be downloaded. In Windows Vista, this can change. It's not changed by default, but see the section a little later entitled "Using Folder Redirection and Offline Files over Slow Links."

- Windows Vista's Offline Files is much smarter about detecting a slow-link condition. And, during a slow link, it will simply transition to working offline. However, a user can, if desired, manually initiate a sync in the Sync Center. Finally, the user may force a transition to online mode if desired.

- You can, if you want, write your own scripts to manage the offline cache. Basically, all Offline Files functionality is scriptable and/or available via APIs. For instance, you could write a script to delete all files in cache, or initiate a sync, and other goodies as you wish. Documentation for these might be available by the time you read this (be sure to be subscribed to the GPanswers.com newsletter for updates). See note after the bullet points for some additional-geeky info about scripting.

- Windows XP had a 2GB maximum Offline Files limit. That limit is gone with Windows Vista.

- In case you missed it before, Windows Vista only sends the changed bits back to the server—not the whole file. This is via the Binary Differential Transfer (BDT) protocol. And, this new BDT magic works with (get this) any SMB server share back as far as Windows 2000. That's right. You don't need a Longhorn Server to take advantage of this. Your Windows Vista clients do all the magic on their own.

> Not to get too geeky, but the script support is implemented as a WMI provider. Inline documentation is available in the CIM repository on a Vista system and may be viewed using a tool such as CIM Studio. This documentation doesn't show how to use the classes and methods, but it does provide descriptions. Look for classes that are prefixed with `Win32_OfflineFiles`.

Roaming Profile Shares and Offline Cache Settings

You should not use any caching with shares for Roaming Profiles. If any caching is enabled for profiles, Roaming Profiles can fail to act normally. Roaming Profiles has its own "internal" caching that is incompatible with Offline Files caching.

The correct choice for Roaming Profile shares is to select "Files or programs from the share will not be available offline" for shares on Windows 2003 or "Disallow Caching for Files of Any Type" for shares on Windows 2000.

The Windows 2003 caching default is to select "Only the files and programs that users specify will be available online," and the Windows 2000 default is to select "Manual Caching for Documents." These settings are not ideal, as there might be a way for a user to get into the contents of their profile and make portions available offline.

If you did set up a profile share in the last chapter, go back to that share and ensure that the share is set to disallow all caching.

Handling Conflicts

But a potential problem lies in these public "common" shares: what if someone on the road and someone in the office change the same document? In that event, the Windows XP Synchronization Manager or Windows Vista Sync Center handles conflict resolution on behalf of the Offline Files component.

When conflicts occur on a Windows XP machine, a user sees what's seen in Figure 10.27. As you can see, the user can inspect the contents of each version of the file, although that's usually not much help because there's no "compare changes" component to this resolution engine, and there's no way to "merge" the documents. But you can paw through the file yourself if you can remember where the last change was. It's not much, but it's a start.

In general, the Offline Files handler is fairly smart. If a file is renamed on either side (network or local cache), the engine wipes out the other instance of the file (because it thinks it's been deleted) and creates a copy of the new one. Hence, it appears a rename has occurred.

In Windows Vista, if a file changes both on the server and on the client, you'll get a message like what's seen in Figure 10.28 when you start to work online again. Then, a similar conflict resolution experience can be seen in Figure 10.29 where the user can press the resolve button. Finally, the user can make a choice of how to deal with the conflict as seen in Figure 10.30.

FIGURE 10.27   The Windows 2000 and Windows XP conflict-resolution engine pops up when there's a conflict. It helps users decide which version of a file they want to keep.

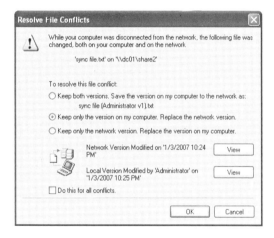

FIGURE 10.28   When Windows Vista connects up and recognizes a file has changed on both the server and the client, you'll get this message.

FIGURE 10.29   Use the Sync center's Resolve button to handle conflicts.

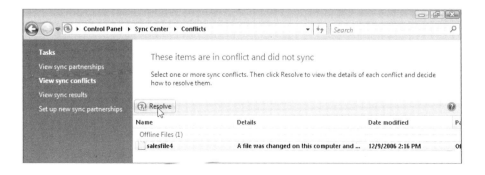

FIGURE 10.30 Vista shows you your options to resolve a conflict.

Client Configuration of Offline Files

In the previous editions of this book, I suggested that you might just want to default your shares to "All files and programs that users open from the share will be automatically available offline"—also known as Autocache. And, we're about to explore what happens if you leverage Autocache. But, before we dive into it, be sure to read the sidebar "Autocache vs. Administratively Assigned Offline Files."

Autocache vs. Administratively Assigned Offline Files

In previous editions, I suggested that you simply enable "All files and programs that users open from the share will be automatically available offline" for every share. In retrospect, I think I could have given you better advice.

Here's why.

Because once that setting is enabled on a share, *everyone* who connects to this share will Autocache the files. So, for instance, if you set Autocache on the Sales share, an errant Human Resources person just poking around and opening up that share will start to stream those Sales files into the cache—even if they don't plan on using them. Sure, eventually, those files will be ejected after nonuse, but why get the user into a situation where he's merely looking at a share and then downloading all the junk in it? (Of course, it isn't junk to the Sales guys— but the Human Resources person certainly doesn't care about it much.)

A better approach is to specify that Sales guys need to Autocache the Sales share. And you can't do that directly in the share. To do that, you'll need a policy setting named **Administratively Assigned Offline Files**. Now, before I get too far ahead of myself, I will say that enabling this policy setting takes work. That is, every time you create a new share for the sales guys, you'll have to edit the GPO and specify the additional share. That way, only the sales guys will Autocache the Sales shares. Ditto for Human Resources and other folks around your Active Directory.

So, setting Autocache on all your shares (except the Profiles share) sounds like a good thing; but it's a better thing (if you can keep on top of it) if you hone in on the focus of *who* Autocaches *which* shares with **Administratively Assigned Offline Files,** explored a bit later in the text.

If you do decide to use Autocache, you can configure clients to use Offline Files with the aforementioned setting in three ways:

- Take the "do nothing" approach.
- Run around to each client and manually specify settings.
- Use Group Policy (insert fanfare music here).

This section explores the options a client can set on their own computer (or with your assistance). Then, in two later sections, "Using Group Policy to Configure Offline Files (User and Computer Node)" and "Using Group Policy to Configure Offline Files (Exclusive to the Computer Node)," we'll explore the broader stroke pen of GPOs to see what sort of configuration we can do.

Another option is that you can script your changes via the Offline Files WMI provider described earlier. Of course, that only works for Windows Vista clients.

The "Do Nothing" Approach

If you do absolutely nothing at all, your clients will start to cache the files for offline use the first time they touch files in a share. This is called auto caching. The underlying Offline Files behavior is the same for Windows 2000 and for Windows XP. However, Windows XP and Windows Vista have a trick up their sleeves, depending on what settings you're using for Explorer.

Windows Server 2003 client computers are not enabled to cache files; this feature is specifically disabled in the operating system but can be turned on if really desired.

This difference will be important and should be noted if you plan to enable caching for your shares to use Offline Files. In the examples in this section, we have a share called SALES, which contains some important files for our sales users. For this example, again, ensure that the "All files and programs that users open from the share will be automatically available offline" caching option is set on the share on our server.

Windows 2000 Reaction to Enabling Caching on Shares

Wanda is using her Windows 2000 laptop. She maps a drive to the Sales share (which maps as E:, as shown in Figure 10.31). When she uses Explorer to view the files on E:, she sees one she needs (`customer1.doc`) and double-clicks it to open it (as you can see in the bottom right-most window in Figure 10.31). The file is now placed inside the Offline Files cache.

FIGURE 10.31   The files in the Offline Files folder cache are only those that Wanda (on her Windows 2000 laptop) has actually used.

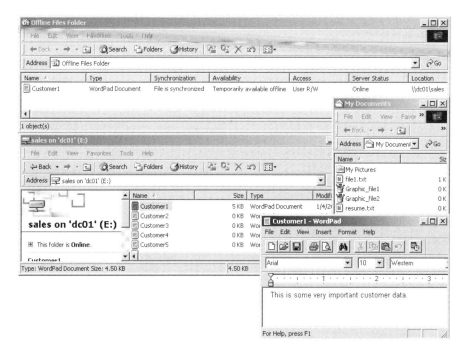

To see which files are within the file cache, Wanda chooses Tools ➢ Folder Options ➢ Offline Files ➢ View Files to open the topmost window in Figure 10.31. I'll discuss selecting View Files next, in the "Windows XP Reaction to Enabling Caching on Shares" section.

Wanda continues, using several documents in her redirected My Documents folder. Only the files she specifically opens will automatically be placed in the cache. She logs off and goes home.

Windows XP Reaction to Enabling Caching on Shares

Wanda's co-worker, Xena, is using a Windows XP laptop to do similar work. She maps a drive to the Sales share (which maps as Z:, as shown in Figure 10.32). When she uses Explorer to view the files on Z:, she sees one she needs (`hello1.doc`) and double-clicks it to open it (as shown in the bottom window in Figure 10.32). That file is immediately placed inside the Offline Files cache. It is now marked "Temporarily Available Offline."

FIGURE 10.32   An Offline Files folder in Windows XP shows much more activity than an Offline Files folder on a Windows 2000 machine.

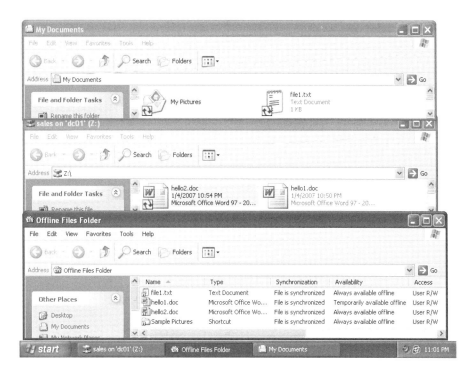

To see which files are in the file cache, Xena choose Tools ➢ Folder Options ➢ Offline Files ➢ View Files to open the topmost window (in Figure 10.32).

Additionally, as shown in Figures 10.9 and 10.10 earlier in this chapter, any files in redirected My Documents have the yin-yang round-trip icons. As I alluded to, this icon means that any file in a Redirected Folder is guaranteed to always be available offline (that is, pinned). What's interesting is that you can see the same icon demonstrating the file is round-tripped in two places. You can see the same icon in a document in My Documents (file1.txt) and also in the "Offline Files Folder" window. The file will be listed as "Always available offline." The other files within the redirected My Documents are present within the Offline Files Folder window but are simply not displayed in Figure 10.32 due to space constraints.

When Xena then uses Explorer to open Z: to see the Sales files, she sets into motion a flurry of events that are particular to Windows XP. That is, as soon as Explorer touches the rest of the files in the Sales share, they begin to download and are *automatically placed in the offline cache*. Again, Xena didn't click each of the files in the Sales share; rather, she only opened an Explorer window. This behavior is specific to Windows XP (and not to Windows 2000). The Explorer in Windows XP is different from that in Windows 2000. Specifically, Windows XP Explorer performs an actual "file touch" to retrieve additional information, such as the file's Summary information or, for instance, when it tries to create a mini-view of a graphic. This "file touch" occurs only in Explorer's Thumbnails view in Windows XP, not in List or Details view.

The Offline Files window may occasionally display that a particular file's status is listed as "Local copy is incomplete." This signals that the files are currently being downloaded into the cache. Once the files are fully downloaded and the window refreshed, the field changes to "File is synchronized" as seen next to the file `hello1.doc` in Figure 10.32.

Additionally, note that Xena can pin any file from the Sales share that she wants to guarantee to be available offline. She's done this with `hello2.txt` which is now marked "Always available offline."

Windows Vista Reaction to Enabling Caching on Shares

Windows Vista is similar to Windows XP (perhaps even more aggressive in what it caches). That's because just about every "View" in Explorer will trigger a touch to the file and make it zoom down into the cache.

After connecting to the share and looking at the files via Explorer, you can see which files it cached.

It's more than a little cumbersome to see the list of offline files. But, if you click the Control Panel, select "Classic View," and locate "Offline Files" you're almost there. Don't click "Sync Center" (which is something else entirely).

Control panel also has a search bar. You can type "offline" there and it will take you to offline files control panel applet.

Then you can click through and hit the button "View your offline files." You'll see a screenshot of this a bit later in Figure 10.35.

Then, click through the "Mapped Network Drives" and find Sales. Tucked away in the far right is a column labeled "Offline Availability" (though you might have to move around the columns a bit). However, in Figure 10.33 you can see the "Offline Availability" column.

FIGURE 10.33 The Windows Vista "Offline Availability" column shows you the status of your files.

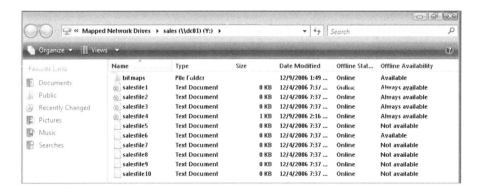

It's Not Offline Files—It's Explorer!

As you saw, Windows 2000 caches files differently than Windows XP, and Windows 2000 caches only files that are specifically pinned or files that are specifically used in shares that have caching enabled. Windows XP and Windows Vista cache files that are specifically pinned, files that are in Redirected Folders, and any file in a share that has caching enabled (once Explorer is used to touch the file).

But it's not really the offline cache that changes at all—it's Explorer! Because Explorer's Thumbnails view in Windows XP and Windows Vista is more rigorous than Windows 2000's counterpart, you're simply "more likely" to download stuff into the cache. Indeed, Explorer isn't the only possible program that works like this; any application that requires anything more than a basic touch to the file triggers a download of the file into the offline cache—regardless of whether the client is Windows 2000 or Windows XP! For instance, searching for files in network shares also plunks data into the cache. Basically, any time a file is opened for read, it's put in the cache.

On the surface, you might think this behavior of Windows XP's and Windows Vista's Explorer's Thumbnails view is a good thing. Sure, it's silently caching files! Indeed, how could this be a bad thing? Because if Wanda puts a 100MB file in the Sales share, Xena will be forced to download it. That's bad—especially if Xena comes in over a slow link. We'll explore at a detailed level what happens over a slow link in the "Using Folder Redirection and Offline Files over Slow Links" section coming right up.

But, for now, Table 10.3 has a sneak preview of what we're going to find. Table 10.3 shows specifically what happens with Windows 2000, Windows XP, and Windows Vista when Offline Files is used over fast and slow links.

TABLE 10.5   How Windows Explorer Reacts to Caching with Offline Files

Explorer View	Action for Windows 2000 (Slow or Fast Link)	Action for Windows XP (Slow or Fast Link)	Action for Windows Vista on Fast Link	Action for Windows Vista on Specified Servers And Shares Over specifically defined Slow Links
Thumbnails	Files are not downloaded into the cache when users open a window and are simply looking at the files. However, as soon as the file is clicked, it is downloaded into the cache.	As soon as you open a window in one of these views, all files begin downloading into the cache.	Not an option.	Not an option.

TABLE 10.5   How Windows Explorer Reacts to Caching with Offline Files *(continued)*

Explorer View	Action for Windows 2000 (Slow or Fast Link)	Action for Windows XP (Slow or Fast Link)	Action for Windows Vista on Fast Link	Action for Windows Vista on Specified Servers And Shares Over specifically defined Slow Links
Tiles	Not an option.	Files are not downloaded into the cache when a window is open and users are simply looking at the files. However, as soon as the file is clicked, the file is downloaded into the cache.	Not an option.	Not an option.
List	Files are not downloaded into the cache when a window is open and users are simply looking at the files. However, as soon as the file is clicked, the file is downloaded into the cache.	Files are not downloaded into the cache when a window is open and users are simply looking at the files. However, as soon as the file is clicked, the file is downloaded into the cache.	As soon as you open a window in one of these views, all files begin downloading into the cache.	Files are not downloaded into the cache unless specifically opened.
Details	Files are not downloaded into the cache when a window is open and users are simply looking at the files. However, as soon as the file is clicked, the file is downloaded into the cache.	Files are not downloaded into the cache when a window is open and users are simply looking at the files. However, as soon as the file is clicked, the file is downloaded into the cache.	As soon as you open a window in one of these views, all files begin downloading into the cache.	Files are not downloaded into the cache unless specifically opened.

TABLE 10.5 How Windows Explorer Reacts to Caching with Offline Files *(continued)*

Explorer View	Action for Windows 2000 (Slow or Fast Link)	Action for Windows XP (Slow or Fast Link)	Action for Windows Vista on Fast Link	Action for Windows Vista on Specified Servers And Shares Over specifically defined Slow Links
Large Icons (or Windows Vista Extra Large Icons, Large Icons, or Medium Icons)	Files are not downloaded into the cache when a window is open and users are simply looking at the files. However, as soon as the file is clicked, the file is downloaded into the cache.	Not an option.	As soon as you open a window in one of these views, all files begin downloading into the cache.	Files are not downloaded into the cache unless specifically opened.
Small Icons	Files are not downloaded into the cache when a window is open and users are simply looking at the files. However, as soon as the file is clicked, the file is downloaded into the cache.	Not an option.	As soon as you open a window in one of these views, all files begin downloading into the cache.	Files are not downloaded into the cache unless specifically opened.

Running Around to Each Client to Tweak Offline Files and the Synchronization Manager

If you wanted to, you could teach your users how to manage Offline Files themselves. (I'll wait a minute or two until the laughter stops.) Okay, maybe not, but if you ever needed to manage a computer that was using Offline Files, but not using Group Policy, here's how you'd do it.

Manually Tweaking the Offline Files Interface for Pre-Vista Machines

As you saw, Windows 2000 and Windows XP have a baseline interaction with the synchronization of files. Optionally, you can manually configure your clients for some additional features of Offline Files and the Synchronization Manager. Earlier I described the synchronization mechanism of Offline Files as a "plug-in" for the Synchronization Manager. When you want to change the client-side behavior of how Offline Files works, you need to fundamentally understand this concept.

Since Offline Files is one entity and the Synchronization Manager another, they have two separate interfaces. Since they're independent entities, some pieces work independently; however, since Offline Files has a plug-in to the Synchronization Manager, they are also interdependent. To get a unified idea of how these two components work separately and together, you first need to locate their interfaces and see what goodies each has. You then need to know how they interact.

To manually tweak the Offline Files behavior, you'll need to get to the Offline Files interface. This is different for pre-Vista and Windows Vista machines.

To tweak the settings for, say, a Windows XP machine, open the My Documents folder, and choose Tools ➢ Folder Options to open the "Folder Options" dialog box as seen previously in 10.19. In this case, we're using the My Documents folder, though any Explorer window returns the same results. As stated, 10 percent of the C: drive is configured to hold the cache as seen in Figure 10.20.

> The defaults are different for Windows 2000 Professional and Windows XP versus Windows 2000 and Windows Server 2003. In Windows XP and Windows 2000 Professional, the "Enable Offline Files" check box is checked, but it is unchecked for Windows 2000 Server and Windows Server 2003. The key here is "server." Offline Files is predominantly a client feature and is therefore disabled by default on server installations.

On the Offline Files tab, click the "Enable Offline Files" check box to display the other options (as follows), which the user can configure.

Synchronize All Offline Files When Logging On   This setting is available only for Windows XP, and the user can change it. This entry co-interacts with the Synchronization Manager's similar entries entitled "When I log on to my computer" and "When I log off my computer." I talked more about this in the section "Understanding Offline Files and Synchronization Manager Interaction."

Synchronize All Offline Files Before Logging Off   The user can change this option. This entry co-interacts with the Synchronization Manager's similar entries entitled "When I log on to my computer" and "When I log off my computer." I talked more about this in the section "Understanding Offline Files and Synchronization Manager Interaction."

Display a Reminder Every (or Enable Reminders for Windows 2000)   When this box is selected (and a number is entered), users get a little pop-up balloon explaining that the connection to the machine where the files are stored has been severed. This is another win-lose area. On the one hand, if this option is selected, your users are well informed that the network has gone down. On the other hand, your users are well informed that the network has gone down, and they will probably call you, complaining. (This is because every new dialog box a user encounters automatically means that you need to be called, but I digress.) You can leave this option on or off here or use Group Policy to turn it off (as you'll see a bit later). Figure 10.34 shows a special case for balloon reminders that cannot be turned off. This occurs when the state changes.

FIGURE 10.34 Pop-up balloons inform your users that they have lost connectivity to the network.

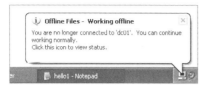

Create an Offline Files Shortcut on the Desktop (or Place Shortcut to Offline Files Folder on the Desktop for Windows 2000) Enabling this option displays a shortcut on the Desktop, the same as if you were to click the "View Files" button in the Folder Options dialog box. I'll discuss "View Files" in a moment.

Encrypt Offline Files to Secure Data Only administrators can choose this setting, which is available only for Windows XP and Windows 2003. Administrators everywhere should be running to enable this setting. This is one of the major benefits for putting Windows XP on desktops and especially on laptops. That is, if the user uses EFS (Encrypting File System), the files stored in the offline cache are also encrypted. In Windows 2000, this was a major security hole. Specifically, if the laptop were stolen, the bad guy wouldn't be able to get to the encrypted data files on the hard drive, except for those still preserved in the Offline Files cache! With just a little know-how, this was a major exploit. Did I mention how major this is? Be sure to select this check box (or use a GPO to ensure the policy setting gets delivered to all your Windows XP and Windows 2003 machines). The bad news is that even with this nice plug, an attack is still possible on EFS. See `www.sans.org/newsletters/hacking_efs1.htm` for more information.

Amount of Disk Space to Use for Temporary Offline Files This slider goes from 0 percent to 100 percent of your C: drive. The default is 10 percent. Again, only files set up to use "All files and programs that users open from the share will be automatically available offline" (or "Automatic Caching for Documents" for Windows 2000) use this setting. Files that are manually pinned are not counted toward the percentage specified here; they are always available. You can change this percentage using Group Policy, as you'll see a bit later. Due to a limitation in the way Windows 2000 and Windows XP were written, only 2GB of disk space can maximally be used.

The following three additional option buttons are certain to scare away even the most fearless of end users. You just click each of the following three buttons, which gives you more stuff to play with:

Delete Files This opens up the "Confirm File Delete" dialog box. Users run in terror when they see the word "Delete." Because of this, there's a good chance that they won't go poking around here. Indeed, nothing actually gets deleted other than the files in the local cache. Files on the server stay on the server.

Note if you Ctrl+Shift when clicking Delete, it completely reinitializes the offline cache, which might help with any specific corruption issues on your Windows XP (or Windows Vista machine, for that matter).

View Files This opens up the "Offline Files Folder" window. This button lets you peek into the local cache, as shown in Figures 10.31 and 10.32 earlier in this chapter. Files that are pinned are represented as "Always Available Offline." Those that are just in the cache for now are listed as "Temporarily Available Offline." This interface is similar to Explorer; it's really Explorer with rose-colored glasses on to make sure that the under-the-hood manipulations of the local cache are properly handled. The local cache is actually stored in the hidden directory C:\windows\CSC. Do not use Explorer or a command prompt to poke around there. The best way to manipulate locally cached files is through the View Files GUI.

Advanced This opens up the "Offline Files—Advanced Settings" dialog box. In this scary dialog box, you can specify what happens if a computer becomes unavailable. You can prevent the user of this workstation from accessing files in the local cache should the corresponding server go down. To be honest, I don't know why on earth you would ever do this, except for some wacky security concern. This is on a per-server, not per-share basis, so be especially careful if this user has many shares on one particular server.

Offline Files and Windows 2000 Server and Windows Server 2003

By default, Offline Files is enabled only on the workstation versions of the operating system, such as Windows XP and Windows 2000. On Windows 2000 servers and Windows 2003 servers, you specifically enable it (either via Group Policy or manually, as seen in the section "Offline Files Interface" and in Figure 10.20). The idea is that this function is largely used when mere-mortal users log on to their Desktop systems—not when administrators log on to servers. However, it can be manually enabled.

If you intend to use Offline Files when logged on to Windows 2003, you must disable Remote Desktops. To do so, right-click My Computer and choose Properties from the shortcut menu to open the System Properties dialog box. In the Remote tab, ensure that "Allow users to connect remotely to this computer" is cleared. Of course, this will disable Remote Desktop connections, but, indeed, it will allow you to utilize Offline Files while logged on at Windows 2003 systems.

Note that this problem between Terminal Services and Offline Files no longer exists in Vista. All of the interlock UI between the two features has been removed.

Manually Tweaking the Offline Files Interface for Vista Machines

Again, if you needed to manually tweak Offline Files for Windows Vista, here's how you'd do it. There's an "Offline Settings" icon hiding in the Control Panel. There are two ways to find it:

- In "regular" view, click under "Network and Internet" then select "Offline Files."
- In "Classic View" you can see Offline Files was just sitting there among the other icons.

Once selected, you'll note there are four tabs: General, Disk Usage, Encryption, and Network as seen in Figure 10.35.

General Tab   On the General tab, you can select "Disable Offline Files" which, when presented with local administrator credentials will do just that.

You can also open the Sync Center (previously discussed) or view all the files from all shares which are available offline.

FIGURE 10.35   You can manually turn off Offline files with local administrator credentials.

Disk Usage   The Disk Usage tab has two main items: changing the disk usage limits and flushing the cache with "Delete Temporary Files." This only deletes any unpinned files from the cache. You can see this in Figure 10.36.

In Windows XP, the space used by pinned files was excluded from the cache-space-usage calculation. This meant a user could pin files until he was out of hard drive space. In Windows Vista, both pinned files and automatically cached files must fit neatly into a container size you specify. The first slider (shown in Figure 10.36) is the total space that all offline files will use on this machine (including pinned files). The lower slider is just for automatically cached files. You can use Group Policy to guarantee these numbers via the Windows Vista–only policy setting titled **Limit disk space used by offline files**.

Encryption   This tab literally only has two buttons on it: Encrypt and Unencrypt. Here, in the User Interface, a user can do this manually. You'll also see later that Offline Files supports a Group Policy setting (named **Encrypt the Offline Files cache**) that causes the cache to become encrypted.

When that policy setting is enabled, or the Encrypt button is clicked, the Offline Files service performs the encryption automatically on behalf of the first user who logs on, shortly after he logs on. But what if multiple users use the same Windows Vista machine, say, as a traveling laptop?

FIGURE 10.36 You can use the sliders to manage your hard disk usage.

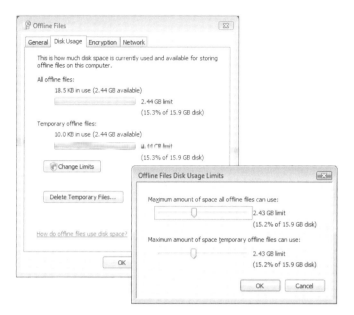

If it's desired to encrypt the redirected Documents folder, everything is hunky-dory for any user on a particular Windows Vista machine. However, if multiple users of a Windows Vista machine can access a given file (say, a share \\DC01\sales), the first user to log on and encrypt that file is the only user who can access that file while offline.

That's a subtle behavior but may be important if you share a specific laptop, encrypt the offline files which reside on a public share, and expect everyone to be able to read it when those users are offline.

Network The Network tab allows you to choose how often to verify you're working on a fast or slow connection. But, here's the trick about slow connections: you have to be ridiculously specific to Windows Vista and explain to it (like to a two-year old) exactly what servers and what shares and what speeds constitute a slow network connection.

So, even though Windows Vista automatically transitions to an offline state on a slow connection—you have to explain just what that slow connection is.

Not to put a fine point on it, but, as you're about to learn in the next big section, Windows Vista does not "believe" you're ever on a slow link by default. You'll have to teach it which servers and shares you consider slow. We'll see this a little later using Group Policy. The policy setting you'll use is entitled **Configure slow link mode** (which is a Windows Vista-only setting). I'm telling you this so you don't get confused with the unfortunately named **Configure Slow link speed** (which is a Windows XP-only setting).

Now, if you click the tab, you'll notice all the controls are grayed out.

So the check box in this tab is *only* available when the Windows Vista-specific policy setting **Configure slow link mode** is set. Once the check box is checked (by the policy being Enabled), the remainder of the controls will be enabled.

One more note here: this setting is a bit irregular. Once the policy setting is Enabled (which enables the controls), *any* user of the client is allowed to change that time value setting. And, that time value affects *all* users of the client computer. The rationale is that the setting must be per-machine to correspond with the per-machine cache, but any user of the client should be able to set it.

Power Admins Rejoice: *CSCCMD.exe* v. 1.1

I've got good news and bad news for you admins out there. That is, if you want to do a lot of ultra-geeky command-line-only stuff with Offline Files (properly known as Client-Side Caching) there's a great tool.

Good news: the tool is free.

Bad news: the tool only works with Windows XP (not Windows Vista yet) and is only available if you call Microsoft PSS.

Did I mention the tool is free? If you call PSS and reference MSKB article 884739 they'll just mail it to you—no questions asked. Check out all the geeky fun at http://support.microsoft.com/kb/884739.

There likely won't be a Windows Vista-version of the CSCCMD. And, even if there was, the scripting API provides much more flexibility (and capability) than CSCCMD. Microsoft's goal is to help you move toward using scripts. Stay tuned from Microsoft for a scripting guide including examples of how to control the Offline Files controls soon.

Using Folder Redirection and Offline Files over Slow Links

In Windows 2000 and Windows XP, Offline Files thinks a slow link is 64Kbps. Since no analog modem is going to achieve that speed, every normal dial-up user theoretically will be coming in over a slow link. When a user comes in over a slow link (less than 64Kbps), the system automatically uses their locally cached version of network files. Additionally, files will not sync when users log on.

Windows Vista handles things differently. It assumes every connection to a share is a fast link until told otherwise. You'll see how to change this behavior right around the bend if you want to manage users' experiences.

When using Offline Files over a slow link, you need to consider the consequences of, say, a private folder like a redirected Documents/My Documents as well as a public folder, like our Sales share. Then, we'll see how Windows 2000, Windows XP, and Windows Vista react over slow links.

Synchronizing over Slow Links with Redirected *My Documents*

The first place you can run into trouble is if the user has never synchronized on a particular machine. For example, Charles is a member of the Marketing group. He's given a generic "workgroup" laptop to take to an emergency meeting in China. But Charles doesn't synchronize with the fast LAN network before he runs out the door to catch his plane. Of course, he won't have any files while he's on the long flight to China; but worse, when he gets to China and dials in, he won't see any files in his My Documents folder either, although we know they're still safe and sound on the redirected network share set up for him.

Why does this happen for Charles in China? Because the default behavior for Charles's computer is that it won't process Folder Redirection over slow links. If you're planning to make redirected My Documents a reality over slow links (for users who haven't ever synchronized with the LAN), you'll need to set up a GPO that affects target computers; and, ideally, these target computers will receive this GPO before they leave for their trip. You'll need to set up a GPO that enables the policy under the **Computer Configuration ➢ Administrative Templates ➢ System ➢ Group Policy ➢ Folder Redirection policy processing** policy setting and, inside, set it to "Allow processing across a slow network connection." Again, if you don't do this, users won't see their files in My Documents when they dial up unless they already performed a synchronization with the Synchronization Manager before they left for the trip.

 WARNING Sync Center won't try to sync a folder if it does not yet exist in the Offline Files cache. Therefore, if the Documents folder has not yet been pinned by Folder Redirection, a specific Group Policy setting (described later), or the user (using Sync Center) won't cause the documents to become cached.

Now, you have to consider what operating system Charles is using. If you give Charles a Windows 2000 laptop, the logon time won't be too long. However, if you give Charles a Windows XP laptop, the logon time might be tremendously long. Why? Remember that Windows XP in conjunction with any Redirected Folder, such as My Documents, attempts to "Make Available offline" every file. If Charles has 300MB of files in his redirected My Documents folder, the system tries to automatically pin all 300MB of those files by copying the data from the server to the local system.

I hear you yelling at me now: "Jeremy, why on earth would I enable **Allow processing across a slow network connection** if I'm setting my Windows XP users up for torture?" My answer? In the upcoming section entitled, "Using Group Policy to Configure Offline Files (User and Computer Node)" see the Windows XP policy setting titled **Do not automatically make redirected folders available offline**, which will return Windows XP to the behavior of Windows 2000 and not pin all redirected files. That way, the bandwidth your Windows XP users utilize when dialing up won't get crushed when using slow connections with Redirected Folders.

Remember though, that unless the user copies the files he needs locally or manually pins them, the files in `My Documents` will not be available offline. This philosophy is a yin-yang thing, just like the icon.

Synchronizing over Slow Links with Public Shares

Let's look at another example. Harold, Walter, Xavier and Victoria are members of the Sales group.

- Harold stays put in the home office and works on a desktop machine.
- Walter has a Windows 2000 Professional laptop
- Xavier has a Windows XP laptop.
- Victoria has a Windows Vista laptop.

Walter, Xavier, and Victoria are sometimes in the office and sometimes on the road. When in the home office, all employees plunk files into the share `\\east_server\ salesfigures`, which is configured to use "All files and programs that users open from the share will be available offline." They all use the `Frankfurt.doc` file. Both Walter and Xavier normally synchronize their computers every time they log off, grabbing the latest version of `Frankfurt.doc`. And, because Victoria is using Windows Vista, her files are automatically synchronized in the background.

Walter, Xavier, and Victoria leave for Frankfurt, Germany, to woo a prospective account. During the time that Walter, Xavier and Victoria are on the plane, Harold (who's back in the office) modifies the `Frankfurt.doc` file with up-to-the-minute information on their prospective customer. Walter, Xavier, and Victoria all get drunk on the plane ride over and sleep the entire way. They don't even crack open their laptops to look at the `Frankfurt.doc` file on any of their laptops. In short, they don't modify their copies on the laptops; only Harold modifies a copy at the home office.

Walter, Xavier, and Victoria check in to the same hotel (different rooms) and dial the home office. They all want to ensure that the latest copy of `Frankfurt.doc` on the server is downloaded to their laptops to present to their client in the morning.

Windows 2000 Offline Files over Slow Links

When Walter connects, he's coming in over a slow link. Room service arrives just as he connects, and he forgets that he's logged on. An hour passes, and Walter remembers that he's dialed in! Frantically, Walter disconnects. Even with that hour-long connection, Walter does not receive any updated files via Quick Synchronization. Unfortunately, he will end up looking like a jerk in tomorrow's meeting.

Walter has four choices if he wants to get the latest copy of the file from the server:

- Manually copy the file from the share to a place on his local computer. (How quaint.)
- Right-click the file in the share and pin it with "Make Available Offline." The file is now permanently available offline.

- Double-click the file to open it. Then, the synchronization field changes to "Temporarily available offline" (though it should be already), and the "Modified" field is updated to the current time stamp from the server. The file is then updated in the cache.

- Manually force a synchronization over the slow connection to synchronize any pinned file or file already in the cache, including `Frankfurt.doc`.

Windows XP Synchronization Manager over Slow Links

Xavier dials the office as well. Room service arrives just as he connects, and, like Walter, he forgets that he's logged on. If Explorer in Windows XP is set up to display files in Thumbnails mode, Explorer is actually opening the files. Because `Frankfurt.doc` is actually opened, it naturally makes its way into the cache. You can see this by peering into the Offline Files folder (shown in Figure 10.37). You can see its status is changed to "Local copy is incomplete."

Some time later, the Synchronization column for `Frankfurt.doc` will change to "File is synchronized." Here's the upshot:

- Files aren't just automatically downloaded because it's Windows XP. They're downloaded because Explorer's Thumbnails view touches the files.

- All other files in the share that Xavier has used will try to update via Quick Synchronization (if Xavier hasn't updated the files himself on his laptop).

- As soon as Xavier uses Explorer to examine the files in the share with Windows XP's Thumbnails view, all the files in the share will try to be downloaded over the slow link. This could be painful.

FIGURE 10.37   Compared to Windows 2000, Windows XP's Explorer is more vigorous in actually touching and opening files; hence, they are downloaded into the cache.

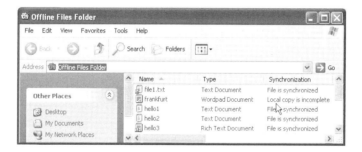

Xavier's computer is connected over a slow, expensive connection. And now he's downloading the `Frankfurt.doc` file (small) and any other (potentially very, very large) file that is now on the share. This could be a major problem if Xavier just wants that one file fast. Poor Xavier is after just the `Frankfurt.doc` file that Harold modified. Xavier has some options while using the slow connection:

- Wait long enough, and `Frankfurt.doc` will automatically download in the background. Again, this happens because in Windows XP Explorer opens the file in Thumbnails view.

- Wait long enough, and all files on the share will synchronize automatically. Windows 2000 will not do this. Again, this happens because in Windows XP Explorer opens the file in Tiles or Thumbnails view. However, files Xavier might not care about are also being synchronized.

- Double-click the file to open it. The Synchronization column then immediately changes from "Local copy is incomplete" to "File is synchronized."

- Manually copy the file from the share to a place on his local computer.

- Right-click the file in the share and pin it with "Make Available Offline."

- Manually synchronize `Frankfurt.doc` and all other files in the share. This spawns the Synchronization Manager to help ensure that Xavier has the latest file and also helps if any conflicts arise.

Windows XP's Synchronization Manager State Transitions

Mobile users access their locally cached versions of files. They then return to the office and dock their systems—without a new logon or logoff. This is called a *state transition*. When a state transition occurs, the system evaluates several criteria to decide if it should keep working offline (using the files in the local cache) or start working online (using the files on the network).

A successful transition to an online state requires the following:

- All offline files in the local cache must be closed.

- The connection must be greater than 64Kbps (by default).

If either of these requirements is not met, the user will still be using the locally cached version of the file—even if the network share is theoretically usable across the network.

Again, if this user wants to use a fast connection instead of the locally cached files, they can choose Start ➤ Programs ➤ Accessories ➤ Synchronize to kick-start the connection, or they can click the little computer icon in the notification area.

To get the latest files in the share, the user needs to synchronize again by choosing Start ➤ Programs ➤ Accessories ➤ Synchronize. If the connection is determined to be a fast connection, changed files are automatically added to the cache for recurring synchronization.

Sometimes an automatic state transition does not function as it should. In this case, users are advised to log off before docking. Once they are docked and network connectivity is established, logging on causes a normal synchronization cycle. Sometimes automatic state transition functions as it should but a little slower than expected. Don't forget that Microsoft Office isn't the only application that can keep files open. Other day-to-day productivity applications you deploy for users can keep files open, and, hence, a state transition does not occur.

Moving the Client-side Cache for Windows 2000, Windows XP, and Windows Vista

You might find a reason to change the original placement of the CSC folder. For instance, you might have some PCs with two (or more) physical hard drives. Perhaps you're running out of space on the C: drive, or maybe you just want to tune a machine's performance by splitting the duties over two hard drives.

You can use the Cachemov.exe utility in the Windows 2000 Server Resource Kit. Simply run Cachemov.exe on the workstation that has multiple hard drives. When you are done, you have a choice as to where to move the C:\%windir%\CSC, as shown here:

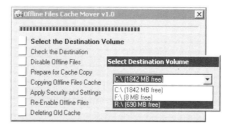

You can also use Cachemov.exe to execute batch-style in a logon script. If you want to affect multiple computers, you can run Cachemov.exe –unattend d:\, in which d is the drive to which the new CSC folder will move. Cchmvmsg.dll needs to be in the path when running cachemov.exe in unattended mode. This tool is not available in the Windows Server 2003 Resource Kit but seems to work fine with Windows XP. Use at your own risk.

Cachemov.exe won't work on Windows Vista. There is a procedure to move the cache for Windows Vista. As of this writing, it's not an MSKB yet, but you can find the steps here http://tinyurl.com/yngfu3.

Windows Vista's Synchronization Engine over Slow Links

Victoria dials up just like Walter and Xavier. Will Frankfurt.doc automatically come down over the slow link (and the other potentially large files in the share)? By default, yes if she looks at the share in any view which "touches the files." (See Table 10.3 earlier.)

But, here's the weird part about Windows Vista. It's much smarter about recognizing what a slow link is. Buuuut…by default Windows Vista will simply act like Windows XP and bring down every stinkin' file you even look at (even with a "File List" view in Explorer) over a slow link.

Ouch.

The good news is that you can control this. You simply have to tell Windows Vista which shares you want to throttle. The goal is to tell your Windows Vista clients which servers and shares should be cached over a slow link.

You tell the clients four things:

- The name of the server with the share(s)

- The name of the share(s)

- What constitutes a slow link (speed)

- What constitutes slow latency (wait time before the server responds)

Once your Windows Vista client "gets" this, it starts being *much* smarter about not downloading humongous files over slow links (like Windows XP would).

You do this with the **Configure slow-link mode** policy setting located in Computer Configuration ➤ Administrative Templates ➤ Network ➤ Offline Files, as seen in Figure 10.38A. In 10.38B you can see an example on how to precisely set up one server's characteristics. In 10.38B, you can see \\server1 and share1 being set to a slow link speed of 600Kbps and Latency of 50ms.

FIGURE 10.38A   You can specify a single lone * (star) to turn on slow-link mode for all shares on all servers.

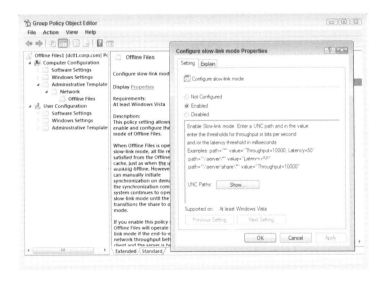

FIGURE 10.38B   Specify Throughput = 600000 for 600Kbps and Latency=50 for 50ms for instance to define your slow link threshold. Note, all paths should have an ending slash (\) and star (*) even if you're just specifying one server and one share.

So, when should you use throughput or latency thresholds?

Well, first thing's first: this policy can be set to use *either* throughput *and*/or latency thresholds. So, you can decide to use throughput, latency, or both.

About Throughput Estimates The throughput estimates are based on outbound traffic and can take some time to become available. That means, you may have to push some traffic to the server for the Windows Vista client to "wake up" and realize "Holy cow! This is slow!" The time taken to get throughput estimates depends on how long it takes for TCP/IP to "saturate" the outbound connection to the server. Offline Files checks this periodically and whenever it finds that the throughput is worse than the policy specified threshold, Files transitions the connection to slow-link mode.

About Latency Estimates Latency estimates, on the other hand are available more quickly. They do not have the outbound requirement either.

So, what should you use? Throughput, latency, or both? The short answer is, both. In our example, Victoria wasn't pushing anything up to the server. She merely viewed the share, and *blammo!* tons of stuff she wasn't really interested in came streaming down the slow link. But, take a moment to reread the above paragraph on throughput estimates. It only kicks in when stuff is pushed *to the server*. That's not happening here.

What is happening, however, is that the time for the server to respond over a dial-up connection (the latency) is going to be slow. A-ha! So, the right answer is both, because the check for latency doesn't care if you're pushing stuff up to, or pulling stuff down from the server. It should kick in quicker and take the share offline to prevent the deluge of stuff Victoria likely doesn't want.

So, can she at least get to the Frankfurt.doc file? I'm afraid to say the answer is maybe. During my testing, here's what I found (your mileage, as well as Victoria's mileage may vary):

- If Victoria was really connected to a \\server\share (that is, a specific server and a share upon that server), using a slow link (but, still connected nonetheless), in my testing I found that a user sometimes had access to the file, and sometimes the user was blocked from getting the file. This is because the file was changed on the server. Since the share has now transitioned to Offline, and I didn't have an up-to-date copy of the file, the user couldn't access the changed file.

- If Victoria really wanted to get that file, she would have to choose to "Work Online" for that particular share. Of course, the bad news is that all the goo on the share she doesn't particularly care about will come streaming down (slowly) over that slow link. But at least Victoria can get access to the file.

- If, however, a user like Victoria was really 100% offline (i.e., Victoria never got a chance to dial-in back to the office) then retains the last known copy of the file in cache (as might be expected).

So, the takeaway is that if a user like Victoria is connected, but slowly, she might not get access to the files she thinks she should have access to. That's going to be a tough one to explain to your users, I think. So, you may want to plan to show them how to transition shares to Online status if you choose to declare some shares eligible for slow link status. In Figure 10.39, you can see where the button is located that your users will need to learn to press. You can also see some files "ghosted" (with the little 'X' indicator) because they aren't in the cache (and hence, not available for use) and those files which are available for use (not ghosted).

FIGURE 10.39   When a slow connection transitions a share to Offline, only files already in the cache are accessible. To access files on the server over a slow link, select "Work online."

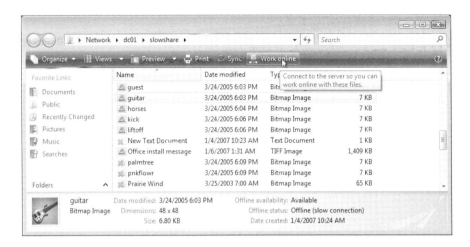

So, to use this policy setting, you add additional items for each server and share combination you needed to define individually. Or, you can also perform this operation "en masse" based on specific servers or, heck, have all Windows Vista clients react to all servers the same way.

Table 10.4 gives you some examples of some values you might want to specify using the **Configure slow-link mode** policy setting when entering in the "Enter the name of the item to be added" block, and the "Enter the value of the item to be added" block and what the result would be if you used these suggestions.

Once you're done clients will only download files into cache when actually opened up. This will speed up their normal day-to-day connection because they're not downloading files into cache that they don't need.

TABLE 10.4   Configuring the Configure slow-link mode policy setting examples. Note how no values require quotes, which can be confusing if you read the Explaintext in the policy setting.

"Enter the name of the item to be added" block	The "Enter the value of the item to be added"	Result of these settings
\\server1\share1*	Throughput=600000,Latency=50	Only \\server1\share1 would react for Windows Vista clients affected by this policy setting. The share will automatically transition to offline if the speed is less than 600Kbps **or** the Latency was less than 50ms.

TABLE 10.4 Configuring the Configure slow-link mode policy setting examples. Note how no values require quotes, which can be confusing if you read the Explaintext in the policy setting. *(continued)*

"Enter the name of the item to be added" block	The "Enter the value of the item to be added"	Result of these settings
\\server1*	Throughput=128000	All shares on \\server1 would react for Windows Vista clients affected by this policy setting. The share will automatically transition to offline if the speed is less than 128Kbps. Note that Windows Vista clients affected by this policy would not test for latency.
**	Throughput=400000,Latency=20	All shares on all servers would react for Windows Vista clients affected by this policy setting. All shares would automatically transition to offline if the speed was less than 400Kbps **or** the latency was less than 20 milliseconds. Note the trailing star (*) at the end of the expression to signify all shares.
**	Latency=30	All shares on all servers would react for Windows Vista clients affected by this policy setting. All shares would automatically transition to offline if the latency was 30 milliseconds. Note the trailing star (*) at the end of the expression to signify all shares.

Using Group Policy to Configure Offline Files (User and Computer Node)

Asking a user to configure their own Offline Files settings can be—to say the least—confusing. This isn't the fault of Microsoft—there's just a lot of options to play with. The good news is that most Offline Files settings can be delivered from up on high.

The policy settings for the Offline Files are found in two places in the Group Policy Object Editor. Some settings affect users specifically. To get to those settings, fire up the Group Policy Object Editor and traverse to Computer Configuration ➢ Administrative Templates ➢ Network ➢ Offline Files, as shown in Figure 10.40.

Nearly all the same settings are also found in the Computer side of the house, at User Configuration ➤ Administrative Templates ➤ Network ➤ Offline Files, as shown in Figure 10.41.

 There are no policy settings for the Windows XP Synchronization Manager or the Windows Vista Sync Center.

This gives you flexibility in how to configure Offline Files. You can mix and match—within the same GPO or from multiple GPOs. The general rule is that if both computer and user settings are specified on the target—the computer wins.

In this section, I'll briefly detail what each Offline Files policy setting does. Since most of the policies overlap in both User and Computer configuration nodes, I'll discuss all the User and Computer configuration settings and then discuss those that apply only to the Computer configuration settings.

FIGURE 10.40 You'll find a slew of Offline Files options under the Computer node.

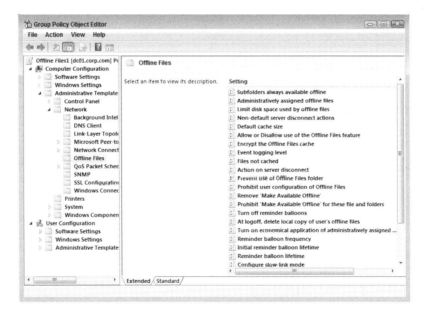

Prohibit User Configuration of Offline Files

If this policy setting is enabled, users on the target client computer embrace the default Offline Files settings and won't be able to change them. Indeed, this happens by the forceful removal of the Offline Files tab normally found in the Folder Options dialog box, as you saw in Figure 10.20 earlier in this chapter.

This policy setting does not apply to Windows Vista machines.

FIGURE 10.41 Many Offline Files options can also be found under the User node.

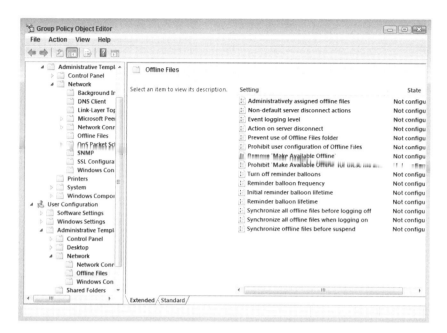

Synchronize All Offline Files When Logging On

Enabling this setting grays out the "Synchronize all offline when logging on" check box in the "Offline Files" tab in the Folder Options dialog box (as seen in Figure 10.20) on the target machine, so the user can't change it. Be sure to read the section "Understanding Offline Files and Synchronization Manager Interaction" earlier in this chapter to understand how this setting works.

This policy setting does not apply to Windows Vista machines.

Synchronize All Offline Files When Logging Off

Enabling this setting grays out the "Synchronize All Offline Files before Logging Off" check box in the "Offline Files" tab in the Folder Options dialog box (as seen in Figure 10.20) on the target machine, so the user can't change it. Be sure to read the section "Understanding Offline Files and Synchronization Manager Interaction" earlier in this chapter to understand how this setting works.

This policy setting does not apply to Windows Vista machines.

Synchronize All Offline Files Before Suspend

Enabling this setting ensures that a full synchronization occurs before the user suspends or hibernates the machine (which usually means they will undock it or otherwise take it offline). The operating system must know about the change, and this will not work if you just close the lid on a laptop.

This policy setting does not apply to Windows Vista machines.

Action on Server Disconnect

If this policy setting is enabled, you can select one of two options from the "Action" drop-down list box. This is analogous to the Advanced dialog box mentioned in the section, "Manually Tweaking the Offline Files Interface for Pre-Vista Machines." In a nutshell, you can allow normal operation of Offline Files or cease the use of Offline Files if the server goes offline. Again, avoid using this function, as it essentially defeats the whole purpose of Offline Files.

This policy setting does not apply to Windows Vista machines.

Nondefault Server Disconnect Actions

This is similar to the previous policy setting. It corresponds to the "Exception List," which is revealed after pressing the Advanced button—again, found in the Folder Options Offline Files tab. Whereas the previous policy setting specified the defaults for all servers, this policy setting specifies settings for specific servers.

Settings enabled here override those in the **Action on server disconnect** policy setting as well as any other policy settings set for the target systems. When this policy setting is enabled, the Exception list is removed to prevent users from making changes.

When you configure the Computer or User option of this policy setting, the box's radio buttons above the Exception list are gray, but the Exception list itself is not. You can add any computers you desire, but they will not take effect with the policy setting in place.

This policy setting is a bit wacky. That is, the policy setting will take effect on refresh, but the radio buttons don't show the actual setting until you reboot. My testing proved that a reboot was necessary for both Computer and User option settings to show in the interface. Also, when the User and Computer configurations conflict, the least restrictive setting takes precedence. If the Computer policy says you can't see the server when offline, but the User configuration says you can, you will be able to see the Offline Files when offline.

To configure this policy setting, choose Enable ➢ Show ➢ Add to open the Add Item dialog box. In the "Enter the Name of the Item to Be Added" field, type the name of the server that you want to have an explicit setting, such as **MysteryServer**. In the "Enter the Value of the Item to Be Added" field, enter either a **1** to keep the users offline or a **0** to keep them online, as shown in Figure 10.42. Click OK to add the server as an exception, click OK to close the Show Contents dialog box, and close the **Nondefault server disconnect actions** policy setting.

This policy setting does not apply to Windows Vista machines.

Remove "Make Available Offline"

Enabling this policy setting prevents users from pinning files by right-clicking them and selecting "Make Available Offline." Files are still cached normally as dictated through other policies or by the defaults. Additionally, enabling this policy setting will not unpin already pinned files. Therefore, if you think you might not want users pinning files, you'll need to turn this setting on early in the game, or you'll be forced to run around from machine to machine to unpin users' pinned files.

Enabling this setting does not interfere with either the "Automatic Caching for Documents" or the "Automatic Caching for Programs" setting on shared folders (as described earlier). Those files are not permanently cached (pinned).

FIGURE 10.42   Use this feature to prevent users from using a specific server's files when offline.

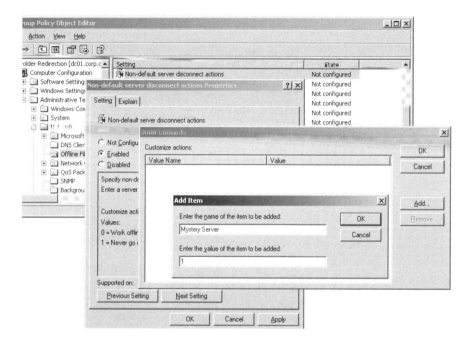

Prevent Use of Offline Files Folder

This setting prevents users from clicking the View Files button inside the Folder Options dialog box. Once this option is set, users may not know which files are currently available in the cache or always available in the cache.

This policy setting does not apply to Windows Vista machines.

Administratively Assigned Offline Files

This is arguably the most useful setting in the bunch. Recall that Windows XP and Windows Vista will automatically pin all files in Redirected Folders such as Documents (for Vista) or My Documents (for XP), which Windows 2000 will not do. However, with this policy setting, you can guarantee that your Windows 2000 users (especially laptop users) have all the files in their My Documents folder both on the local hard drive and safely synchronized to the server—not just redirected there. This ensures that the copy is both synchronized at the server and pinned to the local hard drive.

Remember, though, that in Windows 2000 (and Windows XP) since these files are pinned, they are exempt from the percentage cache used (10 percent by default). That is, all files that are pinned are guaranteed to be available on the hard drive if the user transitions to offline.

A side benefit is that the modest 10 percent cache for "temporarily available offline files" can be used for other network files as your users use them. To make Windows 2000 files always available offline, follow these steps:

1. Enable the setting.

2. Click the Show button next to Files and Folders.

3. In the Show Contents dialog box, click Add to open the Add Item dialog box.

4. Enter the server and share name. If you want to guarantee the redirection of `My Documents` (only necessary for Windows 2000), enter the server, share and folder for the user, or leverage the `%username%` variable, as shown in Figure 10.43.

5. Leave the "Enter the value of the item to be added" field blank.

6. Click OK to render the share Assigned Offline.

7. Click OK to close the Show Contents dialog box and the **Administratively assigned offline files** policy setting.

The next time your users get this policy setting assigned, all the files affected will be pinned. Every newly created file will be pinned as well, as shown in Figure 10.44.

Additionally, by enabling this setting, you can force a file or folder to be pinned for a user in any other share you like. For instance, you can force the vice president of sales to always have their sales figures available. This might be useful if they're on an airplane without a 30,000-foot network cable plugged back into the network on the ground. You can forcefully command that they receive certain files—even if they didn't pin them.

If you're using Windows Vista machines, be sure to check out the computer-side policy setting named **Turn on economical application of administrative assigned Offline Files** (which, isn't named correctly, so definitely be sure to read about this a little later).

Turn off Reminder Balloons

This corresponds to "Enable Reminders" in the Folders Options dialog box. Again, you might want to disable the balloons, because they may only serve to spook the herd. See Figure 10.34 earlier in this chapter for an example of a reminder balloon (though that particular balloon cannot be removed). Enabling this policy setting disables the balloons. Disabling this policy setting prevents users from disabling the balloons.

This policy setting does not apply to Windows Vista machines.

Reminder Balloon Frequency

By default, balloons pop up every 60 minutes to remind the user that they are working offline. Enabling this policy setting and setting a time in the spin box sets that frequency and prevents the user from changing it. Disabling the policy setting keeps the default (60 minutes) and prevents users from changing the defaults.

This policy setting does not apply to Windows Vista machines.

FIGURE 10.43 Use the Administratively assigned offline files policy setting to force specific files or folders to be pinned—like the *My Documents* folder!

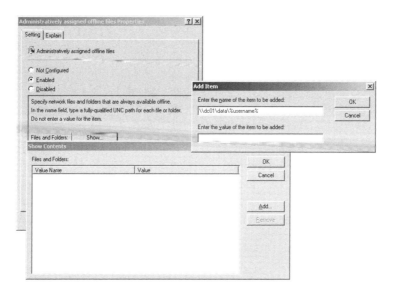

FIGURE 10.44 All files inside the *My Documents* folder on this Windows 2000 system are now pinned.

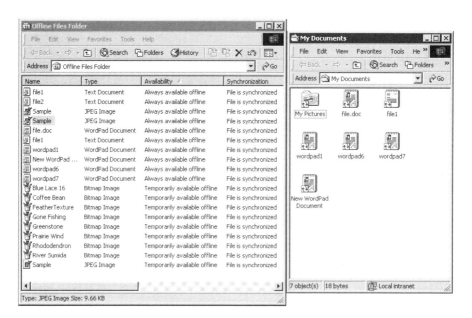

Initial Reminder Balloon Lifetime

The first balloon that pops up lasts 30 seconds. Use this setting to specify how long the first balloon stays up. Enabling this policy setting and entering a time in the spin box sets that duration and prevents the user from changing it. Disabling the policy setting keeps the default (30 seconds) and prevents users from changing the defaults.

This policy setting does not apply to Windows Vista machines.

Reminder Balloon Lifetime

After the first balloon pops up, consecutive balloons pop up every 60 minutes by default (or for whatever value is configured in the **Reminder Balloon Frequency** policy setting) for a total of 15 seconds each, as defined by this policy setting. Enabling this policy setting and entering a time in the spin box sets that duration and prevents the user from changing it. Disabling the policy setting keeps the default (15 seconds) and prevents users from changing the defaults.

This policy setting does not apply to Windows Vista machines.

FIGURE 10.45   The workstation log shows that the server is available.

Event Logging Level

 This policy setting does not affect Windows Vista. For Windows Vista "Sync Center" troubleshooting, see the section "Troubleshooting Sync Center."

This is a good debugging feature if users complain, er, report that their synchronizations are failing. Enable this policy setting, and enter a value of 0, 1, 2, or 3:

- Level 0 records an error to the Application Log when the local cache is corrupted.

- Level 1 logs the same as level 0, plus an event when the server that houses the offline file disconnects or goes down.

- Level 2 logs the same as level 1, plus an event when the computer affected by this policy setting disconnects.

- Level 3 logs the same as level 2, plus an event when the corresponding server gets back online.

Figures 10.45 and 10.46 show examples of notifications when a server becomes available again. Remember, these logs appear in the log at the workstation, not at the server.

FIGURE 10.46   The workstation log shows state transitions in relation to the server.

Prohibit "Make Available Offline" for These File and Folders

Okay, so there's a grammar problem in the name of this policy setting, but it's still useful. If you want to allow most users to pin files in a share but ensure that certain users can't pin files in a share, this is the policy setting for you. After you enable this setting, just add the full UNC (Universal Naming Convention) path to the share or share and file you want to block from being pinned. For instance, if you want to block \\DC01\sales from being pinned, enter it in this policy setting and then ensure that it applies to the appropriate users.

This policy setting applies only when users are using Windows XP.

Do Not Automatically Make Redirected Folders Available Offline

I get several e-mails a month asking me how to prevent Windows XP from pinning all files in Redirected Folders such as Documents. Here it is. Ensure that it affects all the users you want. Of course, this trick should work for Windows Vista as well.

Actually, this policy isn't found (anymore) in Computer Configuration ➢ Administrative Templates ➢ Network ➢ Offline Files. In Windows Vista, it's been moved to User Configuration ➢ Administrative Templates ➢ System ➢ Folder Redirection (and we discussed it earlier). But, I'm bringing it up again here because this policy does directly relate to Offline Files—even though it's been moved to the Folder Redirection section.

Because this policy is a user-side policy, it becomes very difficult to implement on a "system wide" level. See the upcoming section "Turning off Offline Files for Automatically Redirected Folders" which describes how to use the **Do not Automatically Make Redirected Folders Available Offline** policy setting by strapping on a set of fangs.

Using Group Policy to Configure Offline Files (Exclusive to the Computer Node)

As we just explored, most policy settings for Offline Files are duplicated in both the User and Computer halves of Group Policy. But several settings appear only on and apply only to the Computer half.

Allow or Disallow Use of the Offline Files Feature

This is the "master switch" for Offline Files. This policy can affect Windows XP and Windows Vista. Once a machine embraces this policy setting, a reboot is required. Disable (yes, disable) this policy setting and you effectively turn off Offline Files. Note that a restart is required.

In Windows XP, this policy setting is similar to the **Prohibit user configuration of Offline Files** setting discussed in the previous section. Once that policy setting is enabled, the Offline Files feature is active, and users cannot turn it off or change the settings. If *this* policy setting is enabled, Offline Files is enabled, but users can change the settings. If no additional GPOs are defined, the defaults are used. Once this policy setting is disabled, the target machine's Offline Files tab in the "Folder Options" dialog box (seen in Figure 10.20) has grayed-out check boxes, and Offline Files is disabled.

Recall that Offline Files is enabled only for Windows 2000 Professional and Windows XP. It's disabled for servers by default. You can use the **Allow or Disallow use of the offline files feature** policy setting to your advantage to turn on Offline Files on all your Windows 2000 Servers or Windows Server 2003 computers easily—not that you would need to, as it's highly unlikely your servers will often be offline. Note that Windows Server 2003 requires that Remote Desktop Connections be *disabled* in order for Offline Files to function. See the sidebar titled "Offline Files and Windows 2000 Server and Windows Server 2003" earlier.

> **WARNING** If you enable this feature, it should kick in right away (when the background refresh interval hits). However, disabling this feature is another story. If one or more files are open in the cache when you try to disable the feature, that disable operation will fail; a reboot is required. You can experience the same behavior when trying to disable the feature through the user interface.

Default Cache Size

> **NOTE** This policy setting applies to Windows 2000, Windows XP, and Windows 2003 computers only.

This corresponds to the "Amount of disk space to use for temporary online files" slider in the Offline Files tab in the Folder Options dialog box, as shown in Figure 10.20 earlier in this chapter. You can control what percentage of the C: partition is available for automatic caching.

If you enable this policy setting, you must enter a whole number that represents what percentage of the partition you will be using. If you want to use 31 percent, enter 3100. (The total range begins at 0 percent, then can be set to 100 or 1 percent, and ends at 10,000 or 100 percent.) This setting is then locked in, and users can't change it. If you disable this policy setting, the default of 10 percent is locked in, and users can't change it. Remember that this has a maximum size of only 2GB. Since this policy setting works with a percentage value, it can be difficult to know if that percentage exceeds 2GB on any target volume.

You might need to reboot the target machine for this policy setting to take effect. It does not always work when a background refresh is kicked off.

Files Not Cached

This policy setting applies to Windows 2000, Windows XP, and Windows 2003 computers only. This policy setting isn't necessary for Windows Vista, because all file types are cached.

By default, for Windows XP and Windows 2000 several file extensions cannot be cached, due to their sensitive nature. Microsoft is concerned that especially large files will be shuttled up and back with just 1 byte changed. Therefore, the synchronization is hard-coded not to cache certain file extensions, most notably databases. That is, for extra protection, Microsoft prevents databases from being cached. The following file types cannot be cached:

- .PST (Outlook personal folder)
- .SLM (Source Library Management file)
- .MDB (Access database)
- .LDB (Access security)
- .MDW (Access workgroup)
- .MDE (Access compiled module)
- .DB? (everything that has the extension .DB plus anything else in the third character, such as .DBF, is never included in the cache)

If you enable this policy setting, you can add to this list. For instance, you can add your own file types in the form of *.DOC, *.EXE, and *.JAM to also eliminate the caching of only .DOC, .EXE, and .JAM files. In my testing, there appears to be no way to allow the caching of the hard-coded database files listed earlier. If users try to synchronize any of these file types, the Synchronization Manager balks with a "Files of This Type Cannot Be Made Available Offline" message. Windows XP/Service Pack 2 adds the capability to turn off the error every time users log synchronize. Although it is basically a manual endeavor, the hacks are described in MSKB 811660 in the section titled "Exclusion Error Suppression."

Again, this isn't true for Windows Vista; all file types are supported.

At Logoff, Delete Local Copy of User's Offline Files

This policy setting sort of defeats the purpose of using Offline Files in the first place. Its main purpose is for logon use at a kiosk-style machine. That is, a user logs on for a bit and then logs off. You'll want to ensure their Offline Files are cleaned up behind them. Another reason I can see using this policy setting is to prevent files from being lifted off a user's hard drive. Theoretically, you can do this by digging around in the c:\windows\CSC folder. Even if the files are deleted at logoff, a good hacker could theoretically get the files back via an "undelete" program of some type.

Moreover, this policy setting doesn't guarantee a synchronization before it wipes the local cache clean upon logoff. Therefore, it is highly recommended that if you use this policy setting, you pair it with the "Synchronize all offline files before logging off" option (seen in Figure 10.21), which will save your users' bacon. Avoid using this option unless you have some workstation that needs extra security and is infrequently used, and you don't mind if the occasional file gets lost when using it.

If protection is what you're after, and you use EFS setup for your laptops users, a better option (for Windows XP machines only) is to use the "Encrypt the Offline Files cache" policy setting, discussed shortly.

This policy setting does not apply to Windows Vista machines.

Subfolders Always Available Offline

This policy setting is useful if you want to ensure that all subfolders are also available offline. Essentially, it prevents users from excluding the ability to cache subfolders and makes subfolders available offline whenever their parent folder is made available offline. Any new folder a user creates under cached subfolders is automatically cached and synchronized when the parent folder is scheduled for synchronization.

This policy setting applies only to Windows XP.

Encrypt the Offline Files Cache

If you have EFS set up for your laptop users, enabling this policy setting is a good idea. By default, even files stored in an encrypted format on shares are not protected in the Windows 2000 file cache. With Windows XP, they can and should be.

This policy setting applies only to Windows XP (regardless of all the notes in the policy setting's Explaintext "Requirements").

Configure Slow Link Speed

Recall that the Synchronization Manager in Windows 2000 and XP thinks a slow link is 64Kbps. When a user comes in over a slow link (less than 64Kbps), the system automatically uses their locally cached version of network files. Additionally, the foreground Synchronization Manager does not run. You can change the definition of the speed of a slow link, but only for Windows XP and Windows 2003 clients.

This policy setting applies only to Windows XP and Windows 2003 computers.

Synchronization Manager Limitations in Windows 2000 and Windows XP

You might see some weird behavior if a single computer is shared among multiple people. You can see this behavior in the following example:

Configure two GPOs that redirect My Documents to two different locations, \\WS03ServerA\UserDocs and \\WS03ServerB\UserDocs. Link the first GPO to OU-A and the second GPO to OU-B. OU-A contains Fred, and OU-B contains Robin.

Fred logs on and verifies that the My Documents redirection has taken effect by looking at the path in the Properties dialog box. If Fred opens the Synchronization Manager after creating or modifying a file in \\WS03ServerA\Data, he sees the \\WS03ServerA\UserDocs UNC in the synchronization list. When he logs off, he sees the synchronization happen for this UNC.

Now Robin logs on to the same Windows XP workstation and verifies that My Documents redirection has taken effect. When Robin opens Synchronization Manager, she sees the \\WS03ServerA\UserDocs UNC and the \\WS03ServerB\UserDocs UNC in the synchronization list. When she logs off, she sees both paths attempting to perform a synchronization.

You can take this to extremes, too. Try to configure five users in five different OUs with five different GPOs, each redirecting My Documents to one of five different servers. As each user logs on to a single Windows XP Desktop (or a Windows 2000 Desktop and chooses to manually cache the share), the UNC path for that user is added to the UNC paths for the other users in Synchronization Manager.

So what should you do? Allow only your laptop users to use offline caching. You can configure a GPO to prohibit offline caching for desktops and leave it enabled for laptops. Since laptop users don't tend to share their machines often, they don't build up many synchronization links. The workaround for those users is to open Synchronization Manager and uncheck all UNC paths except their own. But no user is going to do this.

After you have Windows XP/Service Pack 2 installed on the client, you have another option. You can leverage the tips in MSKB 811660, which explains how to perform several new feats of magic. One of the sections in the article describes how you can "Prevent admin pinning of files for nonprimary users." Hence, when logging out, the main user of the machine will no longer resync the other user's settings. Here's the bad news, though: there are no Windows XP/ Service Pack 2 policy settings to help you. This is basically, a manual endeavor to enter in the hacks described in MSKB 811660. Or, you can come to GPanswers.com for a downloadable ADM template that can perform this action on multiple clients at once.

The caching of permissions on directory entries in the Offline Files cache has improved this situation significantly in Vista.

Thanks to Bill Boswell for inspiration on this tip.

Configure Slow-Link Mode

We explored this earlier in the section entitled "Windows Vista's Synchronization Engine over Slow Links." Check out that section for detailed usage examples.

This policy setting applies only to Windows Vista machines.

Turn On Economical Application of Administrative Assigned Offline Files

Read the name of the policy setting again. Then forget it.

It should have been called **Turn** off **economical application of administrative assigned Offline Files**. Yes, off.

Here's the history of this setting. Recall that you can use the **Administratively assigned offline files** policy setting to guarantee a share be offline for a user. This is great, except that with Windows XP, people found that their servers were experiencing very high file loads when users would log on to their clients (that is, at 9 a.m.). What was happening was that each client was trying to process their **Administratively assigned offline files** policy. Windows XP/SP2 had a Registry punch (found in MSKB 830407) to ease this problem. It was called "economical administrative pinning." Once enabled, any client with this behavior enabled would perform the full pinning operation *only* if the top-level folder was not yet pinned in the Offline Files cache.

The result is that once the policy is processed once, subsequent logons to the server do not jam the server up.

This behavior was added and turned on, by default, in Vista. However, the policy title really should be **Turn** off **economical application of administratively assigned Offline Files**". Once this policy setting is Disabled (yes, Disabled), the policy setting reverts back to pre-Windows XP/SP2 behavior.

This policy setting applies only to Windows Vista.

Limit Disk Space Used by Offline Files

In Windows XP, files expressly pinned weren't counted toward Offline Files usage. In Windows Vista, with this policy setting, you can dictate how many megabytes you want to set aside for *all* Offline Files—those automatically cached and those pinned.

There are two settings here:

- One for total size of Offline Files (including those that are pinned) and
- One for the size of auto-cached files

The Group Policy interface allows you to set the second number higher than the first—but that setting isn't possible in real life. Indeed, if you go way back to Figure 10.36 you'll see the sliders for this setting in the interface. If you try it out, you'll notice you can't slide the second slider past the first. That's because you can't have a size bigger than the "Maximum amount of space all offline files can use." If you do that, the second number will automatically be set to the first number.

This policy setting applies only to Windows Vista machines.

Troubleshooting Sync Center

The Windows Vista event log is a deep and rich place. To that end, there are two places in particular to go when troubleshooting Sync Center problems.

Enabling the Offline Files Log

The Offline Files log file is located in Event Viewer ➢ Applications and Servers Logs ➢ Microsoft ➢ Windows ➢ Offline Files. Once there, dive one level deeper into the Operational log. By default, this log doesn't grab any data. You need to turn it on. Right-click over the Operational log and select "Enable Log" as seen in Figure 10.47.

The events you'll find here are mostly the successful or unsuccessful startup/shutdown of the Offline Files feature as well as online/offline transitions.

Enabling the Sync Log

There is also a "Sync Log," but you need the super-secret entry key to know it's there. The thing to know how to do is called "Show Analytic Channels," and here's how to do it.

In the Figure 10.47, in the rightmost pane, you'll see a "View" action. Click that View option and select "Show Analytic and Debug Logs." You can see "View" highlighted in 10.47 for quick reference. Once you do, you'll then be able to find the "Sync Log" hiding under Microsoft ➢ Windows ➢ Offline Files. Right click "Sync Log" and click the "Enable" item.

This is an analytic channel that reports sync activity *as it is happening* in the Offline Files service. It is not intended for use by end users but should prove useful to administrators (and could be asked of you by Microsoft PSS) to gather specific information about what's going on.

When that log is enabled, log entries appear for items that are being synchronized within the service. This means that any item synchronized by the service will be reported, not only items synchronized through Sync Center. You can see one of these events in Figure 10.48.

If you open one of these sync events to the "Details" page in the event viewer, you can see the XML format containing the details; then, you can buy your favorite scripting pal some lunch to make some killer reports for you based on the XML data!

Turning off Offline Files for Automatically Redirected Folders

I've never met a policy setting I didn't like. But I have met a few that "missed their calling." The policy setting **Do not Automatically Make Redirected Folders Available Offline** has missed its calling.

What on earth am I talking about?

Offline Files: Desktops vs. Laptops

Well, let's take a minute and analyze the normal function of Offline Files: its primary mission is to maintain files when you're not on the network so you can keep working. Super. So what kinds of computers are off the network a lot? Laptops, of course. And desktops generally *stay* on the network.

FIGURE 10.47   To get data in the OfflineFiles ➢ Operational Log, first enable it.

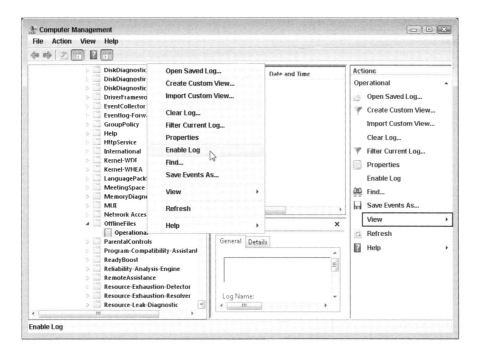

FIGURE 10.48   You can get blow-by-blow details of what is being synced via Offline Files.

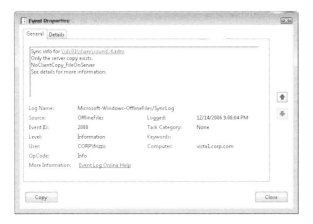

Assuming your laptops represent 10–30 percent of your workforce, do you need those files automatically cached on *every* machine in your enterprise? Like the remaining 70 percent of your desktops?

Why should you care about turning it off?

Because, depending on who you ask, it could be a security risk. Do you want cached copies of your precious documents on every machine to which your users roam? Likely not. Isn't putting your user's documents on every desktop they roam to a security risk? In a way, yes!

Sure, you could encrypt the Offline Files using EFS or Bitlocker, but, let's face it, most people simply don't use EFS today. And while Bitlocker looks really promising, I'm sure most enterprises will wait for it to be "battle tested" for a while before implementing.

Finally, let's not forget that every time a user roams to a desktop, they're really just wasting space on the local hard drive. Remember, desktops are *normally* connected to the network just fine. Do they really need *another* copy of our documents clogging up the local disk?

So, in my analysis (and I'm just one guy with an opinion here), Offline Files doesn't make sense on a well-running network where your desktops and servers are on a fast LAN. Let me be clear: it won't hurt anything either. But with files flying around everywhere, being sprinkled from desktop to desktop, it can be a security risk, waste space, and promote unnecessary synchronization and bandwidth.

Let me be a zillion percent clear: I positively love this feature for my *laptops*. I'm just not that wild about it for my *desktops*. However, I likely would keep it on my desktops if I was connected to servers on a slow WAN like a branch office (especially if that WAN link was flaky).

So, my first thought when I read the name of this policy setting (**Do not Automatically Make Redirected Folders Available Offline**) was "Aha! They're thinking what I'm thinking! There's a policy setting which enables me to turn it off for desktops!"

Except that's not how this policy setting works. This policy setting is not on the computer side; it's on the user side. So, inherently, it cannot simply be put in a GPO and linked to, say, the Desktops OU to turn it off.

With this policy setting, you can only say, "The users in Sales don't automatically make their Redirected Folders available offline." But that's not the point, is it? You want the Sales guys to cache their documents on their laptops but *not* cache them on the various desktops they roam to (especially if they're public computers).

Using WMI Filters to Forcefully Apply This Setting Specifically to Computers

Unfortunately, to teach you this solution would mean that you'd first have to read the next chapter. To implement the solution, you'll need to first understand how to create and apply WMI filters.

I'm not going to go into excruciating detail about that here; instead, I'm going to give you the short steps to the goal and the golden nugget you'll need to make the solution happen.

Then, once you're proficient with WMI filters (and have a full grasp on when and how to use them with caution), you'll be ready to come back here and implement them.

 Seriously: don't plod forth until you read all the warnings and such I have about WMI filters in the next chapter before coming back here to try this out.

Here are the short steps you'll need to forcefully disable Redirected Folders from automatically making the contents offline upon desktops:

1. Create a new GPO that sets the Enables the **Do not Automatically Make Redirected Folders Available Offline** policy. You don't need to configure any other settings in the GPO.

2. Link the GPO to OUs containing user accounts. Again, please, please read my warnings about how WMI filters can slow you down in the next chapter.

3. Create a WMI filter that determines if a machine meets certain criteria. My suggestion is to check to see if it's a desktop (and not a laptop).

   - If it's a desktop, then the users on those desktops will successfully embrace this GPO (and the synchronization behavior will stop).

   - If it's not a desktop, then the standard behavior to sync Redirected Folders will continue (this is what we want).

All you need is a sample WMI query (once you've learned the basics). This query will work a lot of the time (perhaps not all of the time).

```
select * from Win32_SystemEnclosure where ChassisTypes = 1 or ChassisTypes = 2
or ChassisTypes = 3 or ChassisTypes = 4 or ChassisTypes = 5 or ChassisTypes = 6 or
ChassisTypes = 7 or ChassisTypes = 13 or ChassisTypes = 15 or ChassisTypes = 16
or ChassisTypes = 17
```

This query checks to see what type of "Chassis" it is (and reports true if it's anything resembling a desktop).

How did I figure out this query? From the helpful folks at GPanswers.com, that's how. I found this tip on GPanswers.com community forums at http://tinyurl.com/yydhrt (on GPanswers.com) and a link to more information at http://tinyurl.com/7ukjc (on Microsoft.com).

Disk Quotas

Disk quotas restrict users' disk space—either on their local workstations or on your servers. Disk quotas are necessary because, without them, one user can monopolize an entire volume on a server by taking up all its disk space.

The underlying code for Windows NT disk quotas has been around since the Stone Age of the computer world—Windows NT 3.1 to be exact—but the interface never made its way out of Redmond. Until now.

 Don't take my word for it—check out the Knowledge Base article Q103657.

Microsoft's scheme for disk quotas in Windows 2003 is Per User/Per Volume—the same as it was for Windows 2000. Since a disk volume appears in Windows Explorer as a drive letter, you can just as easily think of it as Per User/Per Drive Letter. Quick Quotas in Windows 2003

entail but one improvement over Windows 2000. That is, Quick Quotas can charge disk quotas to users on files that are open as well as files that are closed. In Windows 2000, the files were only charged to the user when the files were closed.

This has several ramifications and limitations. First, there is no centralized "Quota Administrator" in Active Directory. You can't set up quotas centrally to say, "On every server in the Corp.com domain, Johnny Badguy gets 20MB." Nor can you say, "In total, on every server in the Corp.com domain, Johnny Badguy's total used disk space shall never be more than 200MB." Maybe someday, but not today. Some third-party independent software vendor is going to make a killing figuring out how to restrict a user's quota per domain or per forest. However, I made the challenge in the initial writing of this chapter some years ago, and today it's still not done.

Understanding File Ownership

The quota system figures out who is over quota based on the File Ownership attribute, which is only available under NTFS. Thus, only NTFS drives can be monitored for quotas.

At this point, you might be scratching your head and thinking that this is perhaps a good time to run the convert utility on any partitions housing user data. But beware: converted FAT to NTFS partitions do not automatically assign ownership to the user who seemingly owns the folder. Rather, the administrator becomes the owner of all files on the converted partition. In this case, the user who owns the file can actually take ownership of the file in two ways:

- Standard taking ownership

- Taking ownership the easy way

You can give the user's folder the Take Ownership right in the Permission Entry dialog box as shown here:

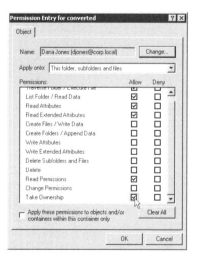

When a user logs on, they can then do the following:

1. Open Windows Explorer.

2. Right-click the folder and choose Properties from the shortcut menu to open the Properties dialog box.

3. Click the Security tab, and then click the Advanced button to open the Access Control Settings dialog box.

4. Click the Owner tab, select their username, click the "Replace owner on subcontainers and objects" check box, as shown here, and click OK.

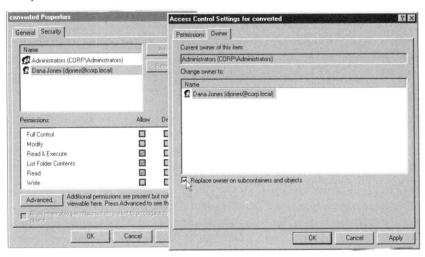

Between you and me, I bet there's a greater chance of the New York Mets winning the Super Bowl than any of your users figuring out that sequence!

A much better way to dictate ownership is through one of the following tools.

Chown.exe   You can get this tool, which is distributed by MKS Software, in three ways:

-   By accessing the APPS/POSIX subfolder on the Windows 2000 Resource Kit CD

-   By downloading the evaluation version at www.datafocus.com/eval/

-   By copying it from the Microsoft Services for Unix 3.5 download (www.microsoft.com/sfu)

The command syntax is as follows:

```
Chown.exe -R Djones d:\data\converted_directory
```

Here, -R signifies you are working on a directory, Djones is the username to be assigned ownership, and d:\data\converted_directory is a directory that is now on an NTFS drive.

Subinacl.exe You'll find Subinacl.exe on the Windows 2000 and Windows Server 2003 Resource Kit CD. This is the Swiss Army Knife of permissions altering. If you want to change the ownership of the d:\data\converted_directory directory, as we just did, the syntax is:

```
subinacl /file d:\data\converted_directory\*.* /setowner=CORP\Djones
```

You must specify the domain name in the short NetBIOS form of CORP, not the FQDN Windows 2000 DNS style name of, say, corp.com.

Ownership also plays another role when users print to the printing subsystem, they are essentially spooling an additional file embedded with their ownership information. If you restrict the partition that houses the print spooler too tightly with disk quotas, users might hit their limit and hence not be able to print. Usually, this isn't a problem because most configurations have the spooler on the C: drive and a user's data volume on the D: drive. Since Windows 2000 uses Per User/Per Volume criteria, affecting the D: drive with quotas, yet performing the print spooling from the C: drive, leaves printing functions unaffected.

However, if you use Group Policy to assign quotas, you could potentially restrict users from printing and other functions quite by accident. This could happen because the Group Policy actions affect all NTFS partitions on the affected system, as explored in the section "Enable Disk Quotas" later in this chapter.

Ownership information is also important if multiple users share the same file on a common share. For example, Frank and Harry both have Read and Write access to the Sales-Figures share on the D: volume. Frank's quota on the D: volume is 10MB, and Harry's quota is 30MB. Frank creates a new Excel worksheet, puts in three figures, and closes the file. The file size is 200Kb. Harry then opens the Excel worksheet, adds five million new figures, and closes it. Now the file is 9.98MB. That 9.98MB is charged to Frank's quota—because he created the file and is the owner.

Quotas and Groups

As previously stated, the quota scheme is Per User/Per Volume. There is no way to leverage Active Directory security groups to deny the writing disk data. In other words, you cannot say, "The engineers' share, which is on the D: volume, can only grow to 300MB." Frustratingly, it's only Per User/Per Volume.

To add insult to injury, the underlying code is there to verify against group quota checking. For instance, the Administrators group is exempt from quotas by default. You can change this default behavior (for administrators only), as in the example in the later section "Apply or Exempt Quotas for a Specific User."

It's sad that quotas are only Per User/Per Volume, but you can change this using third-party tools.

Writer Christa Anderson has a neat trick for (more or less) performing disk quotas on a per-group basis. The article is here: www.windowsitpro.com/ Windows/Article/ArticleID/43195/43195.html. *Windows IT Pro* magazine articles are read-only for subscribers.

Designing and Implementing a Quota Strategy

Setting up quotas on a volume is easy. First, you must decide on your strategy. You have three:

- Apply a default quota to anyone who owns any files on the volume.
- Apply specific quotas to specific users who own files on the volume.
- Apply a default quota to anyone who owns any files on the volume and apply or exempt a specific user to a quota on the volume.

To set up quotas on a volume, follow these steps:

1. Open Windows Explorer on a server.

2. Right-click the drive letter, and choose Properties from the shortcut menu to open the Properties dialog box.

3. Click the Quota tab, as shown in Figure 10.49.

4. Click the "Enable quota management" check box to display the other options.

Warn or Restrict?

There are two schools of thought regarding quotas. One school says that, once warned, users will actually remove some unwanted files once a line in the sand has been drawn with regard to space. The other school says that users never delete anything from the time they're born until the time they're dead, and no wimpy warning message is going to stop them from writing more data. With that in mind, you need to choose your school of thought.

FIGURE 10.49 You modify the options on the Quota tab for each drive letter.

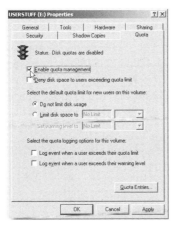

The options on the Quota tab are a little confusing. Let's take a look at them.

Do Not Limit Disk Usage   This disables a general warning level and hard limit for users on the server. You can still set limits for specific users on the server via the "Quota Entries" button (explored in the "Apply or Exempt Quotas for a Specific User" section).

Limit Disk Space To   Enabling this setting restricts the user to a certain amount of disk space.

Set Warning Level To   Instead of restricting the user right away, you can specify a warning limit. When the user hits the warning limit, they get a message. Usually, it's a good idea to set the warning at 80 percent of the actual hard quota.

The final two check box options are found under the "Select the quota logging options for this volume" section. They are "Log event when a user exceeds their warning level" and "Log event when a user exceeds their quota limit." Instead of enforcing a quota limit right away, you might want to monitor usage for a period of time, gathering a baseline of disk usage. It's true, however, that you'll have to spend some quality time with the server's log files to determine which users have gone over the set threshold.

Remember that, by default, the numbers you specify in the "Limit disk space to" and the "Set warning level to" entries affect all users who write any files to the volume. Once you've set up your defaults, click Apply to open the Disk Quota dialog box, as shown in Figure 10.50.

FIGURE 10.50   Once you apply Quota Defaults, the system looks for all users on that volume who own files.

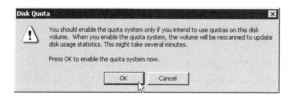

When you click OK, the quota system runs through the initial calculation of which users own which files on the volume and how much they own. The little traffic light symbol in the Quota Properties dialog box changes from red to yellow when performing this scan. When it's finished, it will change to green, and quotas will be activated.

Apply or Exempt Quotas for a Specific User

Usually, the needs of the many outweigh the needs of the few. But occasionally someone makes a legitimate request for exemption, such as your friend in the Accounting Department who promised you he'd burn more CDs of MP3 junk he downloaded from Kazaa for you on his lunch hour.

If you want to bump up or drop down a quota for a specific user or exempt them from quota analysis completely, start by clicking the "Quota Entries" button in the Quota tab of the Properties dialog box to open the "Quota Entries for Local Disk" dialog box. Now follow these steps:

1. To enter a specific quota for a user or group of users, choose Quota ➢ New Quota Entry. You'll then be prompted to enter the name of the user. Once you do, you'll see the "Add New Quota Entry" dialog box, as shown in Figure 10.51.

2. You can now set a specific quota or no quota for that user, as shown in Figure 10.51. To exempt the user from the quota, click the "Do not limit disk usage" button.

Once all users are entered, you can see which user is using how much disk space, as shown in Figure 10.52.

FIGURE 10.51   In the "Add New Quota Entry" dialog box, set a specific user's quota differently from the defaults.

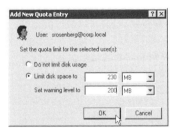

FIGURE 10.52   You can get a bird's-eye view of who's using how much disk space.

Quota Entries for Local Disk (D:)

Quota   Edit   View   Help

Status	Name	Logon Name	Amount Used	Quota Limit	Warning Level	Percent Used
OK	Sol Rosenberg	srosenberg@corp.local	277.87 KB	230 MB	200 MB	0
OK	Like User	luser1@corp.local	13.87 KB	20 MB	15 MB	0
OK	Jimmy Kissel	jkissel@corp.local	194.43 KB	25 MB	20 MB	0
OK	Dana Jones	djones@corp.local	257.9 KB	No Limit	No Limit	N/A
OK	Brett Wier	bwier@corp.local	730.31 KB	20 MB	15 MB	3
OK		NT AUTHORITY\SYSTEM	267.62 KB	20 MB	15 MB	1
OK		CORP\Administrator	381.6 KB	20 MB	15 MB	1
OK		CORP\Domain Admins	0 bytes	20 MB	15 MB	0
OK		BUILTIN\Administrators	2.82 GB	No Limit	No Limit	N/A

9 total item(s), 0 selected.

Import and Export Quota Entries

Although it's true that there's no way to set quotas so they apply over multiple servers, you can do the next best thing. You can export the list of users and quotas that you set up in the previous section to a file. You can then take that file to another server and import it. Voila! Instant disk quotas. There's no way to keep the two lists in sync. If you change one entry, the other server doesn't know about it. But this is a good way to move the exemptions list from one server to another quickly.

To export the list of quota entries, follow these steps:

1. In the Quota Entries dialog box, select the quota entries you want to export. (Click an entry, hold down the Control key, and select additional entries.)

2. Choose Quota ➢ Export.

3. In the "Export Quota Settings" dialog box, provide any filename you want (with or without an extension) and select Save.

4. On the server to receive the list, choose Quota ➢ Import and select the file.

That's it.

Using Group Policy to Affect Quotas

Certain aspects of the quota system can be embraced from edicts from upon high. However, I think it's better to use the fine-stroke quill of individual server settings rather than these settings, which are more like a two-inch-thick Magic Marker. You might find them useful, however.

You'll find the policy settings for Disk Quotas in Computer Settings ➢ Administrative Templates ➢ System ➢ Disk Quotas, as shown in Figure 10.53.

FIGURE 10.53   You can use policy settings to dictate quotas on specific machines.

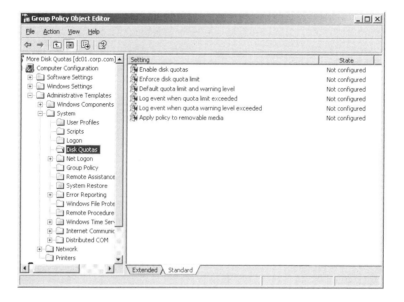

Enable Disk Quotas

This entry is analogous to "Enable Quota Management," as shown in Figure 10.48. Once this policy setting is enabled, all NTFS volumes on those computers that this policy setting affects will be part of the quota management system. Even administrators sitting at the local server will not be able to turn off the management once this policy setting is set. If this setting is disabled, disk quotas cannot be turned on, and even administrators sitting at the local server will not be able turn them on. By default, this setting is not configured, meaning that administrators can set up the quota system (or not) as they please.

Enforce Disk Quota Limit

This setting corresponds to the "Deny disk space to users exceeding quota limit" check box in the Quota tab in the Properties dialog box, as shown in Figure 10.48 earlier in this chapter. If this policy setting is enabled, users are denied space if the quota is reached. Administrators cannot clear the "Deny disk space to users exceeding quota limit" check box once this is set. If this policy setting is disabled, users can cross the "line in the sand" at will.

By default, this setting is not configured, meaning that administrators can choose to deny or not deny as they please.

Pair this policy setting with the next, **Default Quota Limit and Warning Level,** to set realistic warnings. Otherwise, the only limit is the physical space on the volume.

Default Quota Limit and Warning Level

This entry, as shown in Figure 10.54, corresponds to the "Limit disk space to" and "Set warning level to" entries as shown in Figure 10.49, earlier in this chapter.

FIGURE 10.54   You can set the default disk warning and disk limit of the affected computers.

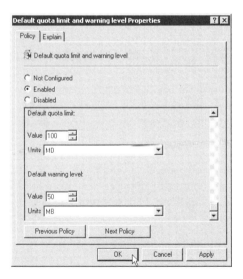

Simply enter the desired values in the "Default quota limit" and "Default warning level" fields. These entries apply for every NTFS volume on the affected computer.

In the event that this policy setting is applied after disk quotas are manually set up on a system, this policy setting overlooks current users (users who already own files on the volume) as well as users who explicitly have applied quotas or are exempt from them, as defined in the Quota Entries dialog box.

If this policy setting is not configured or is disabled, it is assumed that there is no limit to a user's space. Therefore, the warning and limit are ostensibly set to the maximum space available on the volume.

Log Event When Quota Limit Exceeded and Log Event When Quota Warning Level Exceeded

You might not be quite ready to put up the electric fence that prevents users from writing more files should their quotas be exceeded. You might want to simply log the actions for trend analysis. Enable this policy setting to generate the log entry; afterward, administrators cannot clear the corresponding check box. Disable the policy setting to guarantee no log entries.

Apply Policy to Removable Media

By default, JAZ, ZIP, CD drives and the like are exempt from quotas. Enable this policy setting to force the same compliance for removable media. Only NTFS-formatted media can be affected by this policy setting. Most USB devices can't be formatted NTFS, so they're automatically excluded from this policy anyway. Though, you may have a device that can be affected.

Final Thoughts

In the last chapter, you set up Roaming Profiles. But there was a problem. If you had both Windows Vista and Windows XP machines, you wouldn't "see" files, say, in the Documents folder in Windows Vista show up in the My Documents folder on Windows XP. Here, you set up Redirected Folders, which anchored My Documents (for Windows XP) and Documents (for Windows Vista) to the same place.

This gave you several key features: a centralized backup place for critical files, the ability for users' Documents contents to be available on any workstation, and the ability to mitigate the generated traffic caused by Documents being located within the profile. By default, the Documents folder is located within the profile.

You also set up Offline Files so that files work offline as though they were online. You used Group Policy to specify how your users and computers would use this function. Recall that Documents/My Documents is already automatically pinned if you use Windows XP and Windows Vista. But Windows Vista thinks everything is "fast" until you expressly tell it what servers (and optionally shares) it should check to see if it's slow. Oh yeah, you have to tell it what "slow" means too.

If you're still using Windows XP/Service Pack 2, you should note that there are some additional hacks you can perform to squelch some noise generated by Offline Files (see KB 811660) during logoff.

Last, you used quotas to mitigate how much disk space your users can eat on any given volume.

Creating a managed desktop isn't easy; there's a lot to configure. And you're well on your way to making your Windows life more livable. In the next chapter, we'll continue our desktop management story. We'll learn how to distribute software to our users and computers. So, turn the page and get started!

11

The Managed Desktop, Part 2: Software Deployment via Group Policy

Two chapters ago, I discussed and implemented the first big feature of getting your managed desktop story in gear—Roaming Profiles. Once Roaming Profiles are enabled, the user can roam from machine to machine, comfortable that their working environment will follow wherever they go.

In the last chapter, I discussed and implemented more features to get your managed desktop handled. First, we tackled Redirected Folders, which took Roaming Profiles one step further and anchored the user's Documents or My Documents folder to a share on a server. We then used the Group Policy settings on Offline Folders and the Synchronization Manager to ensure that certain files are always available in the cache if our connection to the server goes offline or if the server itself goes offline.

We're well on our way to implementing a fully managed desktop. That is, we want our users to roam freely across our entire environment and take all their stuff with them. But we're missing a fundamental piece of the equation: how can we guarantee that a specific application is ready and waiting for them on that machine? What good is having your user data follow you if an application needed to access the data isn't available? That's what we're going to handle in this chapter.

Group Policy Software Installation (GPSI) Overview

Without any third party software distribution mechanism (such as Microsoft's Systems Management Server (SMS) or Altiris), most environments require that you spend most of your time running from desktop to desktop. In a typical scenario, a user is hired and fills out the human resources paperwork, and a computer with the standard suite of software is dropped on their desk. Usually this machine comes from some sort of "deployment farm" in the back office, where scads of machines are imaged (a la Symantec *Ghost*) by the scores.

The user then starts to surf the Internet—er, I mean— get to work. Soon enough, it's discovered that the user needs a specific or special application, and a desktop technician is dispatched to fulfill the user's request for new software. When the desktop technician arrives, they either load the user's special software via the CD drive or connect to a network share to pull down the software.

Group Policy Software Installation, or GPSI for short, is the next big feature we'll set up. It's with this feature that users can automatically pull applications through the network, without needing anyone to be dispatched. This feature further chips away at the total cost of ownership (TCO) regarding workstation maintenance.

There are essentially four steps to going from zero to 60 when it comes to deploying software with GPSI features:

- Acquire a software setup package with an .MSI extension
- Share and secure a software distribution shared folder
- Set up a GPO to deliver the software
- Assign or Publish the software

We will approach each of these steps in our software configuration journey in the next few pages.

The good news is that GPSI can solve many of your software deployment woes. The bad news is that, like all other Group Policy features, the magic only happens with the marriage between Active Directory on the back end and Windows 2000 Professional, Windows XP, Windows Vista, or Windows 2003 on the client.

Before we get too far along, I want to clear up a terminology misnomer. Specifically, many people incorrectly refer to the Group Policy Software Installation mechanism as the lone word "IntelliMirror." As you might have noticed, we changed the book's title because IntelliMirror isn't being used very much; and I think this is why: IntelliMirror (the concept) was just one piece to the managed desktop story, where Group Policy Software Installation is only one of those pieces. Anyway, the term IntelliMirror has come and gone, but the idea of a managed desktop is here to stay.

Software installed this way—via Group Policy—is referred to in many Microsoft documents as "managed" software. Group Policy can perform what is generically known as an *advertisement* of software, and the Windows Installer Service picks it up and runs with it to perform the installation. Let's get started by understanding the Windows Installer Service.

Although it's true that Microsoft provides an "Active Directory Client" for Windows 9x and for Windows NT Workstation to be used with Active Directory, that "Active Directory Client" does not enable any Group Policy functionality. That client, by the way, is available on the Windows 2000 Server CD under the `clients\win9x` directory and provides additional features such as NTLMv2 authentication and some Active Directory searching. But it doesn't allow old clients to take advantage of Group Policy or GPSI.

The Windows Installer Service

A background service called the *Windows Installer Service* must be running on the client for the software deployment magic to happen. The Windows Installer Service can understand when Group Policy is being used to install or revoke an application and react accordingly. The Windows Installer Service has a secret super-power; it can run under "elevated" privileges. In other words, the user does not need to be a local administrator of the workstation to get software deployed via Group Policy.

So, the Windows Installer Service installs the software with administrative privileges. Once installed, however, the program is run under the user's context.

Windows Installer can install applications via *document invocation* or *auto-install*. That is, it is automatically started when you choose a specific extension or extensions. For instance, if you are emailed a file with a .PDF extension, and then double-click to open it (but don't yet have Acrobat Reader installed), the Windows Installer Service can be automatically invoked to bring down Adobe Acrobat Reader from one of your servers. This is described in more detail in the "Advanced Published or Assigned" section, later in this chapter. Additionally, Windows Installer can determine when an application is damaged and repair it automatically by downloading the required files from the source to fix the problem.

 To be clear, an Advertisement is a generic term which means that software is "offered" by Active Directory to the client machine. But, the client has three ways to accept that Advertisement. You'll see later that the shortcut can be selected, which will download the application (that's one way). Another way is to click a file extension that is registered for GPSI (we already mentioned this one), and finally, by invoking an advertised COM object (which we really won't be going into here).

Do note, however, that there are several versions of the Windows Installer Service. For our purposes, they'll all pretty much act alike, but it's good to know about the history.

- Windows 2000 had Windows Installer 1.

- Since Windows 2000 was released, Windows Installer 2 was released. It is integrated into Windows 2000 Service Pack 3 and higher. For your Windows 2000 machines, if you don't yet have Windows 2000 Service Pack 3 (and I can't imagine why you wouldn't), you can install the Windows Installer 2 Redistributable, which, at last check, is located at go.microsoft.com/fwlink/?LinkId=7613.

- However, before you go forth and deploy that update, note that Windows Installer 3 is available. This is already included in Windows XP/SP2.

- And, finally, Windows Vista brings us Windows Installer 4.

We discuss the ins and outs of Windows Installer 3 (and higher) in the "Inside the MSIEXEC Tool" section coming up.

Understanding *.MSI* Packages

About 99 percent of the magic in software deployment with Group Policy is wrapped in a file format called .MSI. The .MSI file has two goals: increase the flexibility of software distribution, and reduce the effort required to make new packages. Files in the .MSI format are becoming more and more "standard issue" when a software application is rolled out the door (though sometimes they are not). For instance, every edition of Office since Office 2000 has shipped as an .MSI distribution.

On the surface, .MSI files appear to act as self-expanding distribution files, like familiar, self-executing .ZIP files. But really, under the surface, .MSI files contain a database of "what goes where" and can contain either pointers to additional source files or all the files rolled up inside the .MSI itself. Additionally, .MSI files can "tier" the installation, for instance, you can specify "Don't bother loading the spell checker in Word, if I only want Excel." Sounds simple, but it's revolutionary.

Moreover, because .MSI files are themselves a database, an added feature is realized. The creator of the .MSI package (or sometimes the user) can designate which features are loaded to the hard drive upon initial installation, which features are loaded to the hard drive the first time they are used, which features are run from the CD or distribution point, and which features are never loaded. This lets administrators pare down installations to make efficient use of both disk space and network bandwidth.

With .MSI files, the bar is also raised when it comes to the overall management of applications. Indeed, two discreet .MSI operations really come in handy: Rollback and Uninstall. When .MSI files are being installed, the entire installation can be canceled and simply rolled back. Or, after an .MSI application is fully installed, it can be fully uninstalled. You are not guaranteed the exact same machine state from Uninstall as you are with Rollback, however. The GPSI features in Active Directory are designed mainly to integrate with the new .MSI file format. There is other legacy support, as you'll see later.

Utilizing an Existing *.MSI* Package

As stated, lots of applications come as .MSI files. Some are full-blown applications, such as Office 2000 and later. Others are smaller programs that you might use a lot, such as the GPMC (Group Policy Management Console) or the .NET Framework. All these aforementioned applications come as an .MSI. Be forewarned: just because an application comes as an .MSI doesn't necessarily mean it can always be deployed via GPSI; however, that's a pretty good indication. Yet even though versions of the Norton AntiVirus client shipped as an .MSI, it wasn't installable via GPSI until version 9. Ditto for Adobe Acrobat. Until Acrobat version 7, the Reader Program didn't ship as an .MSI, but the full "writer version" did. But even though earlier versions of Adobe Acrobat writer shipped as .MSI files, they simply weren't deployable via GPSI.

Additionally, some .MSI applications (such as Office 2000 and later) can be deployed to *either* users or computers. However, some applications, such as the GPMC.msi and the .NET Framework's .MSI can *only* be deployed successfully to computers.

You'll want to check with the manufacturer of the .MSI file to understand specifically how it needs to be installed. The .MSI files that can be deployed via GPSI usually come in three flavors:

- Some .MSI packages are just one solitary file, and they come ready to be deployed. The GPMC and the Windows Administration tools (Adminpak.msi) are examples in this category.

- Some .MSI packages have one file to "kick off" the installation. Then, there are a gaggle of other files behind it. The .NET Framework (netfx.msi) and service packs (update.msi) are examples in this category.

- Other .MSI files need to be "prepared" for installation. Usually, these applications are more complex. Office 2000, Office XP, Office 2003 (but not Office 2007), and Microsoft TechNet are examples in this category.

> The first edition of this text used an Adminpak.msi as its demonstration package for GPSI. The goal of Adminpak.msi is to plunk down all the administrative tools on your client systems for when you're performing system administration. If you don't have Adminpak.msi handy, you can read the previous edition to see how to distribute Adminpak.msi. Adminpak.msi is a bit special; however, there are versions specific for Windows 2000, Windows 2003, and Windows XP. As of this writing, there isn't yet one for Windows Vista, but I know they're working on it to coincide with the release of Longhorn Server. See the Knowledge Base article Q304718 for more details.

Many people want to deploy big applications, such as the Office suite. I'm going to help you understand how to deploy both Office 2003 and Office 2007. Each one is somewhat different in how it's deployed and configured for setup (not to mention tweaking), so we'll show both.

So, for these examples, I'll assume you have a copy of Office 2003 or Office 2007. Note that only the "Enterprise" versions of these applications are guaranteed to work using GPSI. Other editions, like "Home" and "School" may not work properly via GPSI.

Setting Up the Software Distribution Share

The first step is to set up the software distribution shared folder on a server. In this example, we'll use DC01 and create a shared folder with the name of **Apps**. We want all our users to be able to read the files inside this software distribution share because later we might choose to create multiple folders to house additional applications' sources. Later, we'll create our first application subfolder and feed Office XP into its own subfolder.

To set up the software distribution shared folder, follow these steps:

1. Log on to DC01 as Administrator.

2. From the Desktop, click My Computer to open the My Computer folder.

3. Find a place to create a Users folder. In this example, we'll use D:\APPS. Once you've opened the D: drive, right-click D: and select the Folder command from the New menu; then type in **Apps** as the name.

You can substitute any name for Apps.

4. Right-click the newly created Apps folder, and choose Sharing from the shortcut menu to open the Properties of the Apps folder focused on the Sharing tab. Click "Share this Folder." Windows 2003 servers should automatically have the Everyone group set to Read. While you're in the Permissions for the Apps dialog, additionally click the Add button and add the Administrators group to have Full Control permissions upon the share. Click OK to return to the Apps properties, and then click OK at the properties of the folder to share the folder.

You can use Share permissions, NTFS permissions, or both to restrict who can see which applications. The most restrictive permissions between Share level and NTFS level permissions are used. Here, at the Apps share, you want everyone to have access to the share. You'll then create subfolders to house each application and use NTFS permissions to specify, at each subfolder level, which groups or users can see which applications' subfolders.

Again, in this example, we're using a simple share on a simple server. Here, we'll be installing from a Domain Controller in our examples, which you wouldn't normally do in real life, but it's okay for our examples. Indeed, the best thing to do is to use DFS (Distributed File System) to ensure that users can get to this share from another server, even if this server is down. DFS is beyond the scope of this book, but do read the sidebar "Normal Shares versus DFS."

It's a really good idea to exclusively use DFS shares for package installation points. This is because if you move a package, you will likely cause a product reinstallation on your target machines. This happens whenever the original source location changes. By using DFS, you can avoid this problem.

Setting Up an Administrative Installation (for .*MSI* Files that Need Them)

As stated, not all .MSI files are "ready to go"; some need to be prepared. To prepare Office 2000, Office XP, and Office 2003 you must perform an *Administrative Installation* of its .MSI file. In this procedure, the system will rebuild and copy the .MSI package from your CD-ROM source to a destination folder for use by your clients. While the package is being rebuilt, it injects the serial number for your users and other customized data. Again, to be clear, not all .MSI packages must be prepared in this manner. Be sure to check your documentation.

Office 2007 does not require this Administrative Installation step (see the section "Creating an Administrative Share for an MSI (for .*MSI* files that Don't Need an "Administrative Installation") for Office 2007).

Again, we're using Office 2003 here, but substitute any package you want and be sure to discover beforehand if it requires an Administrative Installation.

To perform an Administrative Installation of Office 2000, Office XP, or Office 2003, you'll use the `msiexec` command built in to Windows 2000 and Windows 2003. The generic command is `msiexec /a whatever.msi`. For Office XP, the command is `msiexec /a PROPLUS .MSI`. For Office 2003, the command is `msiexec /a PRO11N.MSI`.

When you run this command, Office is not installed on your server (or wherever you're performing these commands). This can be confusing, as the Office Installation Wizard is kicked off, and it will write a bunch of data to your disk. Again, to be clear, an Administrative Installation simply *prepare*s a source installation folder for future software deployment.

The Office Installation Wizard will show that it's getting ready for an Administrative Installation, as shown in Figure 11.1.

Your next steps in the Installation Wizard are to specify the organization and the installation location and to enter the product key. For the installation location, choose a folder in the share you already created, say, `d:\apps\office2003distro`. Be sure to enter a valid product key, or you cannot continue. The next screen asks you to confirm the End User License Agreement. Finally, the Administrative Installation is kicked off, and files are copied to the share and the folder (as shown in Figure 11.2).

Creating an Administrative Share for an MSI (for *.MSI* Files that Don't Need an "Administrative Installation")

Office 2007 is different than its predecessors. It doesn't require any "preparation" from an Administrative Installation like Office 2003 or earlier. The only preparation you'll need to do is to create a subdirectory under APPS, perhaps `Office2007Source`, and copy the Office installation files to that directory.

FIGURE 11.1   You need to perform an Administrative Installation to prepare a source installation folder for Office.

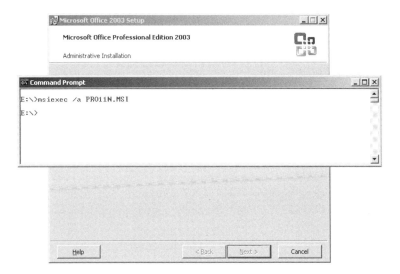

FIGURE 11.2 The files are simply copied to the share; Office isn't being installed (despite the notification that it is).

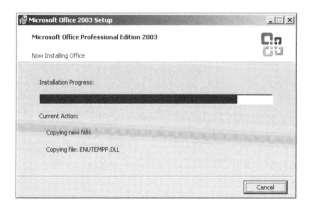

Normal Shares versus DFS

The GPSI features are like the postal service; they're a delivery mechanism. Their duty is to deliver the package and walk away. But it's something of a production before that package is delivered into your hands, and that's what we'll tackle in the next section.

Before we get there, however, you need to prepare for software distribution by setting up a *distribution point* to store the software. You can choose to create a shared folder on any server—hopefully one that's close to the users who will be pulling the software. The closer to the user you can get the server, the faster the download of the software and the less saturated your network in the long run.

In a nutshell, GPSI delivers a message to the client about the shared folder from which the software is available. However, if you are concerned that your users will often roam your distributed enterprise, you can additionally set up DFS. *DFS* is the *Distributed File System* that, when used in addition to Active Directory Site Topology definitions, can automatically direct users toward the share containing the software closest to them. The essence of DFS is to set up a front end for shared folders and then act as the traffic cop, directing users to the closest replica. To explore DFS, visit www.microsoft.com/dfs.

DFS has an extra huge benefit over using normal shares. If a normal share on a normal server goes down (and the client application needs a repair), the client can just find another node on the network which contains the software. Or, if you want to repurpose that server for something else, you don't have to worry about the gruesome problem of removing the software from everywhere, putting the share on the new server, and redeploying the application. With DFS you just add a server with the share contents and change a few pointers around on the back-end.

But what if you're in one of these two traps already? Is there hope to move from a "one server" GPSI deployment to something more robust? Yep! And that, my friends, is what my Newsletter #19 is all about on GPanswers.com. It's called the File Server Migration Toolkit (or FSMT for short). The FSMT can move files from an existing server to another server. And, here's the magic: it can tell the new server to take on the additional name of the old server. So, your clients never know anything has changed under the hood. Really, really neat stuff (and it uses DFS to do the magic). Again, check it out in Newsletter #19.

About Underlying Share Permissions

When you set up shared folders, also lock them down with NTFS permissions to prevent unauthorized users from accessing the installations. Even though GPSI can *target* specific users, it makes no provisions for security. Rather, if your users discover the distribution shared folder, they'll have the keys to the candy store unless you put security upon the shared folder or, even better, utilize NTFS permissions as a deadbolt on the lock.

You can expose or hide your shared folders; to hide them, add a $ (dollar sign) to the end of the share name. You can have one shared folder for each package or one shared folder for all your software with subfolders underneath, each with the appropriate NTFS permissions.

It is not recommended (or really possible) to dump all the installations in one shared folder without using subfolders. Using subfolders lets you differentiate between two applications that have the same name (for example, Setup.msi) or two versions of the same application (Office 2000 and Office XP).

Creating Your Own .*MSI* Package

It's great when applications such as Office 2003 come with their own .MSI packages, but not every vendor supplies .MSI packages. You can, however, create your own .MSI packages to wrap up and deploy the software you've already bought that doesn't come with an .MSI package.

WinINSTALL LE (for Light Edition) is included with the Windows 2000 Server CD. Up until recently, an updated version was available for free download at www.ondemandsoftware.com/ FREELE2003/. But as of recently, it seems it now costs about $50. You may also be eligible to use the FLEXnet AdminStudio SMS Edition. It's available for download here: http://tinyurl .com/yzb4wz, and might just be what the doctor ordered.

The general steps for using a repackaging tool are as follows:

1. Take a snapshot of a clean source machine.

2. Run the current setup program of whatever you want to wrap up.

3. Fully install and configure the application as desired.

4. Reboot the machine to ensure that changes are settled in.

5. Take a snapshot again, and scour the hard drive for changes.

Once the changes are discovered, they're wrapped up into an .MSI file of your choice, which you can then Assign or Publish!

Due to page count, I can't go into the ins and outs of creating your own .MSI files. However, I have two options for you. First, you can take a look at the first edition of this book (ISBN 0-7821-2881-5), which includes the step-by-step process. Or you can check out another resource that demonstrates this process with free and "pay" tools. *The Definitive Guide to Windows Installer Technology for System Administrators* (which is free and which I co-wrote) is available at http://desktopengineer.com/msiebook. The WinINSTALL LE tool I used in the first edition is good for light use, but if you want to deploy many applications across your enterprise, you'll start bumping heads with DLL conflicts and other nasties. To that end, you might have to check out some of the bigger, badder, third-party tools. Some of the more popular are InstallShield for Windows Installer (www.installshield.com) and Wise for Windows Installer (www.wise.com), which is now owned by Altiris.

The third-party tools have some fairly robust features to assist you in your .MSI package creation. As I stated, the .MSI format lets you detect a damaged component within a running application. This feature is called *keying* files for proper operation. For example, if your Ruff.dll gets deleted when you run DogFoodMaker 7, the Windows Installer springs into action and pulls the broken, but keyed, component back from the distribution point—all without user interaction.

Additionally, if you're looking for some heavy .MSI training, consider my pal Darwin Sanoy, who can be found at http://desktopengineer.com/windowsinstallertraining. (Let him know I sent you.)

Assigning and Publishing Applications

Once you have an .MSI package on a share, you can offer it to your client systems via Group Policy. GPSI is located under both Computer and User directories and then Software Settings ➤ GPSI. Before we set up our first package, it's important to understand the options and the rules for deployment. You, the administrator, can offer applications to clients in two ways: *Assigning* or *Publishing*.

Assigning Applications

The icons of Assigned applications appear in the user's Start Menu. More specifically, they appear when the user selects Start ➤ All Programs. However, colloquially, we just say that they appear on the Start Menu. You can Assign applications to users or computers.

What Happens When You Assign Applications to Users   If you Assign an application to users, the application itself isn't downloaded and installed from the source until its initial use. When the user first clicks the application's icon, the Windows Installer (which runs as a background process on the client machine) kicks into high gear, looks at the database of the .MSI package, locates the installation point, and determines which components are required.

Assigning an application saves on initial disk space requirements since only an application's entry points are actually installed on the client. Those entry points are shortcuts, CLSIDs (Class Identifiers), file extensions, and sometimes other application attributes that are considered .MSI entry points.

Once the icons are displayed, the rest of the application is pulled down only when necessary. Indeed, many applications are coded so that only portions of the application are brought down in chunks when needed, such as a help file that is only grabbed from the source when it's required the first time.

When portions of an application are installed, the necessary disk space is claimed. The point is that if users roam from machine to machine, they might *not* choose to install the Assigned application, and, hence, it would not use any disk space. If users are Assigned an application but never get around to using it, they won't use any extra disk space. Once the files are grabbed from the source, the application is installed onto the machine, and the application starts. If additional subcomponents within the application are required later (such as the Help files in Office XP's Word 2002, for example), those components are loaded on demand in a *just-in-time* fashion as the user attempts to use them.

What Happens When You Assign Applications to Computers   If the application is Assigned to computers, the application is *entirely* installed and available for all users who use the machine the next time the computer is rebooted. This won't save disk space but will save time because the users won't have to go back to the source for installation.

Publishing Applications

The icons of Published applications are placed in the "Add or Remove Programs" folder in Control Panel for Windows XP or "Install a program from the network" for Windows Vista. You can Publish to Users (but not computers). When you Publish applications to users, the application list is dynamically generated, depending on which applications are currently being Published. Users get no signals whatsoever that any applications are waiting for them in Control Panel.

Once the application is selected, all the components required to run that application are pulled from the distribution source and installed on the machine. The user can then close Control Panel and use the Start Menu to launch the newly installed application.

By default, the icons of Assigned applications are also placed in the "Add or Remove Programs" (or "Install a program from the network") folder for download. In other words, by default, all Assigned applications are also Published. The "Do Not Display this Package in the Add/Remove Programs Control Panel" option is unchecked by default; therefore, the application appears in both places by default upon Assignment. (I'll discuss this option in the "Advanced Published or Assigned" section.)

Published apps are also advertised to be run automatically via document invocation (again, also known as auto-install).

Rules of Deployment

Some rules constrain our use of GPSI, regardless of whether applications are Assigned through the Computer or User node of Group Policy. As just stated, the icons of Assigned applications appear on the Start Menu, whereas the icons of Published applications appear in the "Add or Remove Programs" folder (or "Install a program from the network" for Windows Vista) With that in mind, here are the deployment rules.

Rule #1   Assigning to computers means that anyone who can log on to machines affected by the GPO sees the Assigned application on the Start Menu. This is useful for situations such as nurses' stations. You can also Assign applications to users in the GPO, which means that whenever users roam, their applications follow them—no matter which machine they reside at physically.

Rule #2   You can't Publish to computers; you can only Assign to computers within a GPO.

Why the funky rules? Although I have no specific confirmation from Microsoft, I'll make an observation that might help you remember these rules: most users can use the Start Menu to launch applications. Therefore, Assigning applications to users makes sense.

Additionally, since applications Assigned to computers apply to *every* user who logs on to a targeted machine, the users in question can also surely use the Start Menu to launch the Assigned applications. But using Published applications takes a little more computer savvy. Users first need to know that applications are Published at all and then check the "Add or Remove Programs" folder (or "Install a program from the network" for Windows Vista) to see if any applications are targeted for them. A specific user might know that applications are waiting for them, but it's unlikely that all users using a computer would know that. Since this level of sophistication isn't really the norm, I bet Microsoft avoided providing Publishing capabilities for computers because there is no guaranteed level of sophistication for a specific user of a specific computer.

In any event, just remember the following rules:

- You can Assign to users.
- You can Assign to computers.
- You can Publish to users.
- You cannot Publish to computers.

Package-Targeting Strategy

So far, we've set up our software distribution shared folder, prepared the package to the point of distribution, and (optionally) tied it down with NTFS permissions. Now we need to target a group of users or computers for the software package. Here are some possible options:

- Leverage an OU for the users you want to get the package, move the accounts into this OU, and then Assign or Publish the application to that OU. Whenever members of the OU log on, the application is available for download. Each user can connect to the distribution source and acquire a copy of the installation. This is best for when your users are mostly using desktops. Because desktops are connected to the network, the "just-in-time" fashion of the download really makes sense here.

- Leverage an OU for the computers that you want to get the package, and then Assign the application to the computers in that OU. When the computer is rebooted, then, whenever any user logs on to the targeted machines, the application is fully downloaded and ready to go. This isn't true for every application (like Office 2007, shown later). But it is true for just about everything else. This is best if you have a gaggle of laptop users. You'll want to ensure that the entire application is loaded before users go on the road with their machines. This strategy is ideal for this scenario.

- Assign or Publish the application at the domain or OU level, and then use GPO Filtering with Security Groups (see Chapter 2). This is a more advanced technique but can be very useful when you want to give someone only the ability to modify group memberships, and (by modifying the group membership) also deploy software to a group of users.

- Assign or Publish the application at the domain or OU level, and then use WMI (Windows Management Instrumentation) Filtering based on specific information within machines. (See the section "GPO Targeting with WMI Filters" later in this chapter.) This is most useful if you want to strategically target machines based on very, very specific criteria. For instance, "Only deploy this software to users using Dell D600 laptops with revision 15 of the BIOS."

 There's also the ability to permission individual packages within a GPO for more fine-grained targeting. Check out the "Security" tab for each package.

We could use any of these methods to target our users. The first two options are the most straightforward and most common practice. In our first example, we'll leverage an OU and Assign the application to our computers. We'll use the **Human Resources Computers** OU and Assign them Office 2007.

Creating and Editing the GPO to Deploy Office

We are now ready to create our GPO and Assign our application to our users. In this example, we'll Assign Office 2007 to computers, but this procedure works to deploy Office 2003 as well.

WARNING Again, this performs the most basic of Office 2007 deployments. If you have a custom Office 2007 environment with bells and whistles and, like Burger King, want it "your way," there's a lot more that has to be done. Be sure to read the sidebar entitled "Installing and Customizing Office 2007 via GPSI" a bit later.

Open the GPMC, and then follow these steps:

1. To create a GPO that deploys Office 2007 to the **Human Resources Computers** OU, right-click the OU and choose "Create and link a GPO here" from the shortcut menu to open the "New GPO" dialog box. Enter a descriptive name, in the New GPO dialog box such as **Deploy Office 2007 (to computers)**. The GPO should now be linked to the **Human Resources Computers** OU.

2. Right-click the link to the GPO (or the GPO itself), and choose Edit from the shortcut menu to open the Group Policy Object Editor.

The software distribution settings are found in both Computer Configuration and User Configuration, as shown in Figure 11.3.

FIGURE 11.3   Right-click the GPSI settings to deploy a new package.

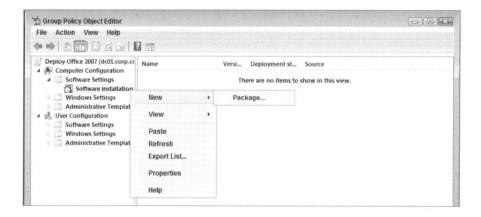

For this first package, we will Assign the application to the computers in the **Human Resources Computers** OU.

1. Choose Computer Configuration ➢ Software Settings.

2. Right-click Software Installation and choose New ➢ Package, as shown in Figure 11.3, to open the Open dialog box, which lets you specify the .MSI file.

You will need to specify the full UNC path on the shared folder for the application.

Back at Figure 11.1, we put our Office 2007 Administrative Installation inside the APPS share on the DC01 server inside the OFFICE2007SOURCE directory. If you take a look at the

Office 2007 media, you'll note there are lots of `.MSI` files which might work. However, there really is only one which is meant for GPSI distribution. The precise name will vary depending on the version of Office 2007 you've got. In my case, I've got Office 2007 Pro Plus. The file which I'll need to deliver using GPSI is named `ProPlusrWW.msi`. Therefore, the full UNC path to the application is `\\DC01\apps\OFFICE2007SOURCE\ProPlusr.WW\ProPlusrWW.msi`, as shown in Figure 11.4.

If you're deploying Office 2003, it is also based upon the version you have. For instance, the copy I have has an `.MSI` named `Pro11N.msi`.

Before You Ramp Up, Let's Talk about Licensing

A FAQ I get when I teach my Group Policy Intensive course is this: "If I use GPSI to deploy applications to my users, how does this affect my licensing agreements with Microsoft or other software vendors?" The next most frequently asked question about GPSI is this: "If I use GPSI to do mass rollouts, how can I keep track of licensing for reporting during audits?" Bad news on both fronts, friends.

Occasionally, the Microsoft technology doesn't work in lockstep with usable licensing agreements. Specifically, if you use GPSI as your mechanism to get software to the masses, you need to be especially careful with your Microsoft licensing agreements or any other licensing agreements. When you deploy any software via GPSI, you have the potential to load the software on a machine and make it available to any number of users who can log on to that machine. As I discussed, using GPSI to deploy to computers gives everyone who logs on to the machine (via the domain) access to the icons on the Start Menu. And, if you target users, whether the application is available only for that user depends on the application. For instance, a well-written `.MSI`, say Office XP, prevents users who aren't assigned the application from using it; but other `.MSI` applications (especially those you create with third-party tools) may not. And when you use GPSI to deploy an application to, say, users in an OU, you won't know how many users accept the offer and how many users don't end up using the application.

With that in mind, GPSI is a wonderful mechanism for deploying software. But in terms of licensing and auditing, you're on your own. My advice is that if you're planning to use GPSI for your installations, check with each vendor to find out their licensing requirements when you Assign to Users and Assign to Computers.

Remember: you have a large potential for exposure by doing a GPSI to users and/or computers; protect yourself by checking with your vendor before you do a mass deployment of any application in this fashion. Additionally, it's important to remember that there is no facility for counting or metering the number of accepted offers of software for auditing purposes.

That's where Microsoft's SMS is supposed to come into play to help you determine "who's using what." Additionally, if you're looking for an all-Group Policy solution to help mitigate these (and other) problems, check out Special Operations Software's Specops Deploy (`www.specopssoft.com`). But stay tuned—more on that later.

FIGURE 11.4 Always use the full UNC and never the local path when this dialog box requests the file.

WARNING

Do not—I repeat—do not use the Open dialog box's interface to click and browse for the file locally. Equally evil is specifying a local file path, such as d:\apps\office2003distro\pro11n.msi. Why is this? Because the location needs to be from a consistently available point, such as a UNC path. Entering a local file path prevents the Windows Installer at the client from finding the package on the server. Merely clicking the file doesn't guarantee that the package will be delivered to the client. Again—entering the full UNC path as shown in Figure 11.4 is the *only* guaranteed method to deliver the application to the client.

Once the full UNC path is entered, a dialog box will appear, asking which type of distribution method we'll be using: "Assigned" or "Advanced." "Published" will be grayed out because you cannot Publish to computers.

For now, choose "Assigned" and click OK. When you do, you'll see the application listed as shown in Figure 11.5. Note it might take a minute or two for the application to show up as seen in Figure 11.5. Hang tight—it'll show up.

FIGURE 11.5   The applications you assign are listed under the node you chose to use (Computer ➤ Software Installation or User ➤ Software Installation).

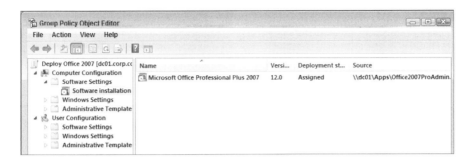

Understanding When Applications Will Be Installed

Once you've Assigned or Published an application, you'll need to test it to see if it's working properly. Here's how users and computers should react:

- Applications Published to users on any operating system should show up right away in Control Panel. No reboot or log out (and log back in) should be required, but you might have to refresh the "Add or Remove Programs" folder (or "Install a program from the network" for Windows Vista). An application isn't installed until a user specifically selects it or the application is launched via *Document Invocation* (also called *Install-On-First-Use* or *Advertisement*). Recall that document invocation allows the application to be installed as soon as a file associated with the application is opened.

- Applications Assigned to users on Windows 2000 or Windows 2003 computers should show up on next logon on the Start Menu. Applications Assigned to Windows 2000 or Windows 2003 computers should install upon next reboot. All users logging on to those computers will see the icons on the Start Menu.

- If you're deploying to users on Windows XP or Windows Vista computers or directly to Windows XP or Windows Vista computers themselves, you need to know whether Fast Boot is turned on. Recall from Chapter 3 that Fast Boot is enabled by default for Windows XP and Windows Vista machines, and you will need to explicitly turn it off. To review:

  - If Windows XP or Windows Vista Fast Boot is enabled and you Assign applications to users, it will take two logoffs and logons for the icons to appear on the Start Menu.

  - If Windows XP or Windows Vista Fast Boot is enabled and you Assign applications to computers, it will take two reboots before the Assignment is installed. Afterward, icons appear for all users on the Start Menu. If you want to turn off this behavior for Windows XP or Windows Vista, you can do so. Just check out Chapter 3.

  - Note, however, that Windows XP and Windows Vista Fast Boot is always off if a Roaming Profile is used.

> You'll need to adjust the deployment properties before certain applications will deploy properly to users. (More on this in the "Advanced Published or Assigned" section later in this chapter.)

Testing Assigned Applications

Before you go headlong and try to verify your deployment of Office 2007, first verify that a Windows 2000, Windows XP, or Windows Vista machine is in the **Human Resources Computers** OU, and then reboot the first test machine in the OU.

If you're assigning an application to a Windows XP or Windows 2000 machine, you'll see this during startup as shown in Figure 11.6.

If you're assigning an application to a Windows Vista machine, by default you won't see anything during startup except a "Please wait…" and a lot of disk activity. However, you can enable the policy setting called **Verbose vs normal status messages** located within Computer Configuration ➢ Administrative Templates ➢ System, you'll see more information during startup, such as the application's title, as seen in Figure 11.7

Go ahead and get a cup of coffee while this is installing. It takes a while. Really. Go ahead. I'll wait.

Once the application is fully installed, you can log on as any user in the domain (or the local computer) and see the application's icons on the Start Menu as seen later in Figure 11.10.

FIGURE 11.6   Applications Assigned to computers install completely upon reboot.

If you're deploying Office 2003 (or earlier), the icons will show up right away on the Start Menu for all users who log in.

However, if you've just assigned Office 2007 to a Windows Vista computer—the first user who uses Office 2007 on that computer needs to w-a-i-t. When I deployed Office 2007 to Windows Vista computer and then immediately logged in as Frank Rizzo when the Ctl+Alt+Del prompt was available, I got what's seen in Figure 11.8.

Strangely, the message basically states that Office 2007's setup isn't compatible with Windows Vista. How odd. If we can get past that, we can see what's happening behind the scenes is that Office 2007 is *still* setting up. If you click "Show me the message" (which would be better if it said "Show me the money" in one guy's opinion), you'll see what's going on "under the hood." You'll see this in Figure 11.9.

FIGURE 11.7 If you enable the Verbose vs Normal status messages policy setting to affect your Windows Vista machines, you'll see the name of the software installing instead of a lousy "Please wait..." message

FIGURE 11.8 Users don't actually see all of Office 2007's icons until it has finished deploying itself in the background.

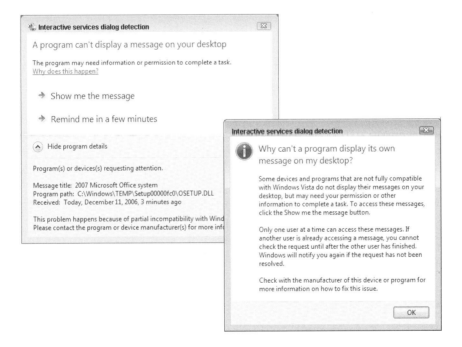

Eventually, this does finish. Or, if I chose not to immediately log in as Frank Rizzo, say, by getting a cup of coffee (maybe two) before logging in, Office 2007 would have completed on its own in the background. But, yes, you're reading this right; Office 2007 continues to install in the background even after you log in if you don't wait long enough.

FIGURE 11.9 You can watch Office 2007's display progress when installed via GPSI on a Windows Vista machine.

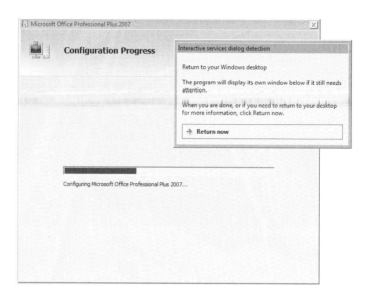

So, when completed, you'll see your newly installed items on the Start ≻ All Programs menu. These are nicely highlighted for Windows XP and Windows Vista, as shown in Figure 11.10. If you try this experiment with a Windows 2000 client, you'll notice that the new icons and program titles are not highlighted.

This "extra setup time" after a user quickly logs on is new for Office 2007 and not very welcome, in my opinion. And, it seems that multiple users sometimes have to sit through at least some installation time to get Office 2007 configured the first time.

At this point, any user can select any Office application, and the application is briefly prepared and then displayed for the user.

Stay tuned for more information on Assigning and Publishing .MSI applications (particularly to users). For now, however, let's switch gears and look at another deployment option.

Understanding .ZAP Files

Using .MSI files is one way to distribute software to your computers and users, but one disadvantage is associated with this process: you must actually have an .MSI package that you deploy. Indeed, some applications don't come with .MSI packages, and repackaging them with a third-party tool doesn't always work as expected. If you already have your own Setup.exe (or similar program), you can leverage a different type of installation: .ZAP files, which invoke your currently working Setup.exe program.

FIGURE 11.10   The Office icons and program names will appear on the Start Menu (more specifically on the Start ≻ All Programs menu).

Sounds great—but there is a downside: `.ZAP` files are not as robust as `.MSI` files. This "unrobustness" comes in several forms:

- They do not take advantage of the Windows Installer, and therefore they are not self-repairing should something go awry on the client.

- You can Publish but can't Assign `.ZAP` files. Their icons are available only in the Control Panel, and the application is installed all at once. And since `.ZAP` files are always Published, they can only be Published to users, not computers.

- The user is in full control of the install, unless you've magically scripted `Setup.exe`. This can create trouble for end users.

- The `.ZAP` files run with the user's privileges. They cannot run with elevated privileges. Again, only `.MSI` applications (not `.ZAP` files) automatically run elevated even for non-privileged users once deployed via GPSI.

Like `.MSI` files, `.ZAP` files (and their corresponding setup executables) can also be automatically invoked when a specific extension (or set of extensions) is chosen via *Document Invocation* (also called *Auto-Installer)*. Auto-Install is described in more detail in the "Advanced Published or Assigned" section, later in this chapter.

Creating Your Own *.ZAP* file

A .ZAP file resembles an .INI file. That is, it is a simple file created with a text editor such as Notepad, and it has headings and values. Instead of repackaging WinZip 8 with WinINSTALL LE (or any of the third-party applications), you can simply create a .ZAP file for a WinZip 8 setup executable, WinZip80.exe.

A sample WinZip 8 .ZAP file might look like this:

```
[Application]
FriendlyName = "Winzip 8.0 ZAP Package"
SetupCommand = "WINZIP80.exe"
DisplayVersion = 8.0
Publisher = WinZip Computing


[EXT]
.ZIP=
.ARC=
```

Let's briefly break down each entry. The [Application] heading is required, and the only other required elements are the FriendlyName and the SetupCommand, which are self-explanatory.

The entry pointed to the SetupCommand should be in the same folder as the .ZAP file itself. If it isn't, you can use UNC paths to specify, such as:

```
SetupCommand = "\\DC01\winzipsource\winzip8.exe"
```

Everything else is completely optional but might help you and your users sort things out. The [EXT] heading can list the file extensions that can fire off this particular .ZAP installation and the corresponding WINZIP80.exe setup executable. Listed in this sample file are .ZIP and .ARC, but you can also add file types such as .TAR and .Z. The [EXT] heading is not required and may not even be desired, depending on the application and its setup routine.

Publishing Your Own *.ZAP* File

If you want to Publish your own .ZAP file, you'll need to bring all the steps you've learned together:

1. Place the setup executable (in this case, WINZIP80.exe) in a subfolder (say, WINZIPSOURCE) underneath a shared folder (in this case APPS).

2. Lock down the WINZIPSOURCE subfolder with NTFS permissions.

3. Create the WINZIP8.zap file as directed earlier using Notepad.

4. Copy the .ZAP file to the distribution subfolder (WINZIPSOURCE).

5. Finally, distribute (Publish) the .ZAP package to your users.

Testing Your *.ZAP* File

Test your .ZAP file and distribution point by logging on to a workstation to which the GPSI policy applies. Open the "Add or Remove Programs" folder in Control Panel (or "Install a program from the network" for Windows Vista), and click Add New Programs in the column on the left. The application should appear in the list of programs available to add, named according to the entry in the FriendlyName field that you specified in the .ZAP file, as shown in Figure 11.11.

Once you've selected it and clicked Add, the WinZip setup program will launch and can be set up in any desired fashion.

Alternatively, you can double-click either a .ZIP or an .ARC file to automatically launch the .ZAP file setup application via document invocation (also known as auto-install).

FIGURE 11.11   .ZAP files are always published to Control Panel.

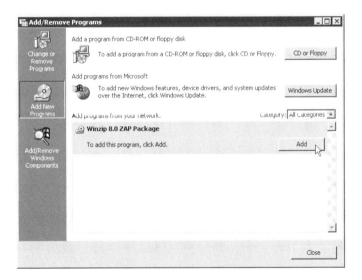

Testing Publishing Applications to Users

You can also test Publishing applications before continuing. Recall that the icons of Published applications appear in the "Add or Remove Programs" folder (or "Install a program from the network" for Windows Vista) in Control Panel. However, the usefulness of Published applications is minimal, which is why it's relegated to such a small section for discussion. Users must be specifically told there's something waiting for them, hunt it down themselves, and install it. And, applications can only be published to users, not computers; so a user who is getting a published application must be logged in.

To test this for yourself, simply select "Publish" when adding a new application, or right-click an existing package Assigned to users and choose "Publish" from the shortcut menu.

To see a Published application in action on a Windows XP or Windows 2000 machine, follow these steps from a client who is receiving a Published application:

1. Choose Start ➤ Control Panel ➤ Add or Remove Programs to open the "Add or Remove Programs" applet in Control Panel.

2. Click the "Add New Programs" button to display those applications that have been Published for the user as seen above in Figure 11.11.

3. Ask the user to click the Add button next to the application, and it will be fully loaded upon the machine.

The applications will then appear on the Start ➤ All Programs menu as seen previously in Figure 11.10, ready to be utilized.

To see a Published application in action on a Windows Vista machine, follow these steps:

1. Choose Start ➤ Control Panel ➤ Programs ➤ Get Programs ➤ Install a program from the network.

2. Select the application and select Install, as seen in Figure 11.12.

FIGURE 11.12 A Published application in Vista can be seen in Control Panel.

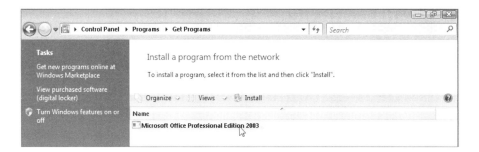

A Published application needn't be fully relegated to lying dormant until a user selects it. Indeed, the default is to specify that the application automatically launch via Document Invocation (also known as Auto-Install) as soon as an associated file type is opened. In this way, you can have the application available for use but just not have the application's icons appear on the Start Menu as you do when you Assign it. However, you can turn off document invocation by clearing the "Auto install this application by file extension activation" check box as specified in the section "The Deployment Options Section" a bit later.

WARNING You'll need to adjust the deployment properties before certain applications will deploy properly to users. (More on this in the "Advanced Published or Assigned" section later in this chapter.)

What Happens if You Try to Assign Office 2007 to Users?

In short: it doesn't work. Why not? The Office 2007 MSI files are (apparently) written to be more "modular." And, in doing so, they couldn't guarantee that one MSI would be able to call another MSI when initiated as a user install. It works as a computer-side install; but not a user side.

This deployment to a user has worked since Office 2000 but is simply not available as an option to Assign Office 2007 to Users.

If you try it, the applications icons install on the Start Menu. However, when you try to run it, you get this (at least helpful) error message.

So, long story short—don't deploy Office 2007 to your users. It just won't work. It's an application which only works when Assigned to Computers as we did in our example.

Application Isolation

In many circumstances, applications are *isolated* for their intended use. Here are some examples:

- Users do not share Assigned or Published applications that an administrator has set up. For instance, User A is Assigned an application and installs it. User B can use User A's machine, but is not Assigned the application via Group Policy. Therefore, when User B logs on to that machine, they do not see the Assigned icons for User A.

- Users require their own "instance" of the application. If User A and User B are Assigned the same application, each user must contact the source and perform a one-time per-user customization that some applications require. In most circumstances, this will not double the used disk space, and the time for installation for the second user would not be very long because portions of the application are already installed for User A.

- If two users are assigned different applications that register the same file types, the correct application is always used. For instance, Joe and Dave share the same machine. Joe is assigned Word 2000, and Dave is Assigned Office XP. When Joe opens a .DOC file, Office 2000's Word 2000 launches. When Dave opens a .DOC file, Office XP's Word 2002 launches. I even tried deploying Office 2007 to the computer and Office 2003 to a user, and the "user" side won. But, Office 2007's icons were available for selection, of course, via the Start Menu.

- Depending on the .MSI application, users might not be able to go "under the hood" and select the .exes of installed programs. For instance, if User A is Assigned an application, User B (who is not Assigned the application) cannot just use Explorer, locate the application on the hard drive, and double-click the application to install it. This is not a hard-and-fast rule and is based on how the .MSI application itself is coded. In Figure 11.13, you can see what happens when a user who is not specifically Assigned Office 2000 (yes, Office 2000) tries to run Winword.exe from Program Files. However, I tried this again with Office 2003, and, well, it let me run it just fine as another user.

- Users can uninstall applications that they have access to in the "Add or Remove Programs" folder (or "Uninstall or change a program" in Windows Vista parlance). This has a two-part implication. First, by default, all Assigned applications are also Published, and thus users can remove them using the "Add or Remove Programs" folder. The icons for the applications will still be on the Start ≻ All Programs menu the next time the user logs on. The first time the user attempts to run one of these applications by choosing Start ≻ All Programs ≻ *application*, the application reinstalls itself from the distribution point. The second implication deals with who, precisely, can remove Assigned (or Published) applications. First, users cannot delete applications that are directly Assigned to computers. Next, users cannot delete applications that aren't directly Assigned to their user account.

 Office 2000 and later can prevent users from just clicking their installed .exes. These applications use .MSI APIs to verify the application state. For more information about how an application can become "installer-aware," see www.microsoft.com/msj/0998/windowsinstaller.aspx.

FIGURE 11.13 Some applications prevent users from just clicking the actual .exe of the installed file. Again, this behavior is entirely application specific.

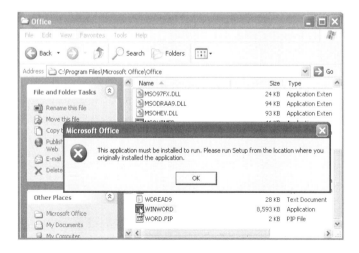

Advanced Published or Assigned

When you attempt to Publish or Assign an application to your users or computers, you are given an additional selection of "Advanced." If you didn't choose "Advanced" when you initially deployed the application, that's not a problem. You can simply right-click the package and choose Properties from the shortcut menu to open the Properties dialog box. The only option that is not available in this "after the fact" method is the ability to add *Microsoft Transform Files*, which I'll describe in the "Modifications Tab" section later in this chapter.

The Properties dialog box has six tabs: General, Deployment, Upgrades, Categories, Modifications, and Security. In Figure 11.14, the Properties dialog box is focused on the Deployment tab, which is discussed in detail in this section.

FIGURE 11.14   These are the options on the Deployment tab when Assigning to computers. Note how just about everything is grayed out when Assigning to computers.

The General Tab

This tab contains the basic information about the package: the name that is to be displayed in the "Add or Remove Programs" folder (or "Install a program from the network" for Windows Vista), the publisher, and some language and support information. All this is extracted from the .MSI package.

If you're using the Windows 2003 administrative tools to deploy your package, you'll get another little goodie: you can specify the URL of a web page that contains support information for the application. For instance, if you have specific setup instructions for the user, you can place the instructions on a page on one of your intranet servers and include the URL with the package. The client's "Add or Remove Programs" folder displays a hyperlink to the URL next to the package. Although .ZAP files also display this information, you can't configure these files once they are Published.

The Deployment Tab

This tab, as shown in Figure 11.14, has three sections: "Deployment type," "Deployment options," and "Installation user interface options." There is also an Advanced button at the bottom of the tab. Depending on how you wish to deploy, the options on the Deployment tab depend on how you want to deploy the application and whether you are Assigning to computer or Assigning or Publishing to users. In our first example, Figure 11.14 shows the options when Assigning to computers.

Figure 11.15 shows the options on the Deployment tab when Assigning an application to users. You'll notice that many more options are available than when Assigning to computers. The options in the "Installation user interface options" section are critical, and you will likely need to change them before applications are correctly Assigned or Published to users.

FIGURE 11.15 These are the options on the Deployment tab when Assigning or Publishing to users.

The Deployment Type Section

The options in this section let you instantly change the deployment type from Published to Assigned and vice versa, and it is available only when you are deploying applications to users. When you are deploying applications to computers, Assigning is the only option. If you're deploying to user accounts, you can also change the deployment type by right-clicking the package definition (as seen in the Group Policy Object Editor dialog box in Figure 11.5) and selecting the deployment type, Assign or Publish, from the shortcut menu.

The Deployment Options Section

This section has four check boxes:

Auto-Install this application by file extension activation   When .MSI applications are Published or Assigned (or .ZAP packages are Published), each of their definitions contain a list of supported file types. Those file types are actually loaded inside Active Directory.

When a GPO applies to a user or a computer and this check box is selected, the application is automatically installed based on the extension. This is, essentially, application execution via document invocation. Note, this option is always automatically selected (and cannot be unselected) if you Assign the application. That is, document invocation is only optional when Publishing.

Document invocation is most handy when new readers and file types are released, such as Adobe Acrobat Reader and its corresponding .PDF file type. Simply Assign or Publish an application with this check box enabled, and Acrobat Reader is automatically shot down to anyone who opens a .PDF file for the first time. This check box is selected by default when you are Assigning applications to users or computers.

Uninstall this application when it falls out of the scope of management   GPOs can be applied to sites, domains, or OUs. If a user is moved out of the scope to which this GPO applies, what happens to the currently deployed software? For instance, if a user or computer is moved from one OU to another, what do you want to happen with this specific software package? If you don't want the software to remain on the workstation, click this check box. Remember—the applications aren't removed immediately if a user or computer leaves the scope of the GPO. As you'll see shortly, computers receive a *signal* to remove the software. (This is described in the "Removing Applications" section later in this chapter.)

Do not display this package in the Add/Remove Programs control panel   As mentioned, icons and program names for Assigned applications appear in the Start ➢ All Programs menu, but, by default, they also appear as Published icons in the "Add or Remove Programs" applet in Control Panel. Thus, users may choose to install the application all at once or perform an en masse repair. However, the dark side of this check box is that users can remove any application they want. To prevent the application from appearing in the "Add or Remove Programs" folder or "Install a program from the network" for Windows Vista, check this check box. When the application is then earmarked for being Published, the application is available only for loading through document invocation.

Install this application at logon   This option is new and applies only to Windows XP, Windows Vista, and Windows 2003 Server clients. See the section "Assigning Applications to Users over Slow Links Using Windows XP, Windows Vista, and Windows 2003" later in this chapter for a detailed explanation.

The Installation User Interface Options Section

Believe it or not, the two little innocuous buttons in this section make a world of difference for many applications when Assigning or Publishing applications to users. Some .MSI packages can recognize when Basic or Maximum is set and change their installation behavior accordingly. Others don't. Consult your .MSI package documentation to see if the package uses this option and what it does.

Assigning applications like Office 2003 to users can be disastrous if you retain the default of Maximum. Instead of the application automatically and nearly silently loading from the source upon first use, the user is prompted to step through the Office 2003 Installation Wizard (the first screen of which is shown in Figure 11.16).

FIGURE 11.16   The default of "Maximum" results in many applications (like Office 2003) no longer being a silent install.

Simply choosing Basic remedies this problem. That is, Office 2003 is magically downloaded and installed for every user targeted in the OU. Why is Maximum the default? I wish I knew. It wasn't the default in Windows 2000. For now, if you're Assigning applications to users, be sure the Basic check box is checked. For information about how to change the defaults, see the "Default Group Policy Software Installation Properties" section later in this chapter.

The Advanced Button

Clicking the Advanced button opens the Advanced Deployment Options dialog box, as shown in Figure 11.17. This dialog box has two sections: "Advanced deployment options" and "Advanced diagnostic information."

FIGURE 11.17 The options in the Advanced Deployment Options dialog box in Windows 2003 Server

The Advanced Deployment Options Section

In Windows 2003 Server, this section has three options, and in Windows 2000 Server, it has four options:

Ignore language when deploying this package If the .MSI package definition is coded to branch depending on the language, selecting this option can force one version of the language. Normally, if the language of the .MSI package doesn't match the language of the operating system, Windows will not install it. The exceptions are if the application is in English, if the application is language neutral, or if this check box is checked. If there are multiple versions of the application in different languages, the .MSI engine chooses the application with the best language match.

Remove Previous Installs of This Product for Users, If the Product Was Not Installed by Group Policy-Based Software Installation (older version of Windows 2000 only) If you use older Windows 2000 administrative tools to deploy your application, you'll see this option. However, in Figure 11.17, there is just an empty hole. For each .MSI application, a unique product code (which is shown in Figure 11.17) is embedded in the .MSI. If your users somehow get their own copy of the .MSI source and the product code matches the .MSI application, they can forcibly uninstall their copy before loading the copy you specified.

This can come in handy if the folks in your organization run out to CompUSA and buy a version of a program you weren't ready to deploy using Group Policy—say, Office 2003. If users acquire and install their own copy of Office 2003 before you're really ready to officially deploy it using Group Policy, you can forcibly remove the copy they install. Once you are ready to deploy Office 2003 using Group Policy, be sure to check this check box to remove all copies of Office 2003 that you did not deploy using Group Policy. The copy you're shooting down from on high will then be installed. In this way, you can ensure that all copies you deploy using Group Policy are consistent, even if your users try to sneak around the system.

This works because the unique product code you're sending via Group Policy matches the product code of the .MSI package the user loaded on the machine. The Office 2003 you deploy is essentially the same as the Office 2003 they deploy. The product codes match, and the application you deliver "wins" if you select this check box.

Why is this option absent from the later versions of the Windows 2000 tools or the Windows 2003 Server version of the Adminpak tools? Because this feature is built in to the latest Windows 2000 Service Pack (SP4) and standard issue for Windows 2003 Server. This procedure is performed automatically and is no longer required as an option.

> Even if you repackage your own applications (such as WinZip, Adobe Acrobat Reader 6, and so on) using a third-party tool (such as WinINSTALL LE), a product code is automatically generated when the package is created, However, if you deploy those repackaged applications with Group Policy (in conjunction with this check box in Windows 2000), this procedure does not remove copies of applications that users installed with Setup.exe-style programs. It removes only applications on the target machine that have an .MSI product code.

Make this 32-bit x86 application available to Win64 machines   Software distribution with Windows 2003 Server gets a little more complex because of the support for 64-bit computers. The 64-bit version of Windows XP supports 32-bit applications by running them in a special Win32-on-Win64 emulator. This is similar to the way NT and Windows 2000 support 16-bit Windows applications. In general, 32-bit applications should run fine on x64 platforms, but you can encounter an ill-behaved application that does not function correctly in the emulator. Additionally, Service Pack 1 for Windows 2003 Server and Windows XP Service Pack 2 make 32-bit applications run even more stably on x64 computers.

Include OLE class and product information   This feature allows applications that contain COM services to be deployed such that COM clients can find their deployed applications. Basically, check with your application vendor to see if you need this switch; generally you don't. Enabling the switch increases the likelihood that the application will fail to deploy unless the application specifically requires this setting.

The Advanced Diagnostic Information Section

You can't modify anything in this section, but it does have some handy information.

Product code   As mentioned, if the unique product code of the application you are deploying matches an existing installed product, the application will be removed from the client.

Deployment Count   A bit later in this chapter, you'll learn why you might need to redeploy an application to a population of users or computers. When you do, this count is increased.

See the section "Using MSIEXEC to Patch a Distribution Point" a bit later in this chapter for more information.

Script name   Whenever an application is Published or Assigned, a pointer to the application, also known as an .AAS file, is placed in the SYSVOL in the Policies container within the GPT (Group Policy Template). The .AAS files are application advertisement script files and are critical to an application's ability to install-on-first-use. This entry shows the name of the .AAS file, which can be useful information if you're chasing down a GPO replication problem between Domain Controllers.

The Upgrades Tab

You can deploy a package that upgrades an existing package. For instance, if you want to upgrade from Office XP to Office 2003, you can prepare the Office 2003 installation (as we did earlier) and then specify that you want an upgrade, which can be either mandatory or optional.

 There is no Upgrades tab for .ZAP package definitions.

Moreover, you can "upgrade" to totally different programs. For instance, if your corporate application for .ZIP files is WinZip but changes to UltraZip, follow these steps to upgrade:

1. Create the UltraZip .MSI package, Assign or Publish the application, open the Properties dialog box, and click the Upgrades tab.

2. Click the Add button to open the "Add Upgrade Package" dialog box, as shown in Figure 11.18.

3. In the "Package to upgrade" section, select the package definition (in this case WINZIP 8). Note that WINZIP doesn't specifically appear in our example in Figure 11.18; it's just the dialog box.

 Although you can click the Browse button to open the Browse dialog box and select another GPO for this to apply to, it's easier to keep the original package and upgrade in the same GPO scope.

4. Use the options at the bottom of the "Add Upgrade Package" window to choose either to uninstall the application first or to plow on top of the current installation, and then click OK.

5. Back in the Upgrades tab, check the "Required upgrade for existing packages" check box and click OK to force the upgrade.

If the "Required upgrade for existing packages" check box is cleared, users can optionally add the program using the "Add or Remove Programs" applet in Control Panel. This can cause grief for some applications, such as Office 97 and Office 2000 together on the same machine. Moreover, if the check box is not checked, the old application is started whenever an associated file extension (such as .DOC) is invoked.

It is best if your package is specifically written to upgrade earlier (or different) products; sometimes, it may not actually remove the previous application.

When Assigning to computers, the "Required upgrade for existing package" check box is always checked and not available for selection.

FIGURE 11.18 Use the Upgrades tab to migrate from one application to another.

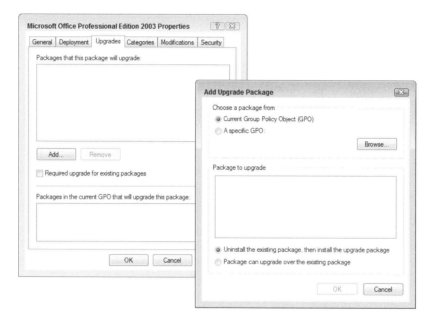

The Categories Tab

The Categories tab allows administrators to give headings to groups of software, which are then displayed in the "Add or Remove Programs" applet in Control Panel. Users can select the category of software they want to display and then select a program within the category to install. (See earlier Figure 11.11 above the mouse cursor, which shows the Category drop-down box.)

For example, you might want to create the category "Archive Programs" for WinZip and UltraZip and the category "Doc Readers" for Adobe Acrobat Reader and GhostScript. If you want, you can list a package in multiple categories. You can also create categories. For information on how to do so, see the "Default Group Policy Software Installation Properties" section later in this chapter.

The Modifications Tab

The Modifications tab is used to support .MST files, or *Microsoft Transform* Files, or just "Transform Files" for short. Transform Files are applied upon current .MSI packages either to filter the number of options available to the end user or to specify certain answers to questions usually brought up during the .MSI package installation.

Each vendor's .MST transform-creation program is unique. Ask your application vendor if they have a transform-generation utility for your package. If not, you might have to step up to a third-party .MSI/.MST tool, such as Wise Package Studio or AdminStudio by InstallShield. Some applications, such as Office 2000, Office XP, and Office 2003 come with their own .MST generation tool.

Note that Office 2007 does not. See the sidebar "Installing and Customizing Office 2007 via GPSI" for more information on how to modify Office 2007 installations.

In Figure 11.19, you can see I've loaded an .MST file named NOMSACCESS.MST. This .MST will prohibit the use of Microsoft Access 2003 from Office 2003 but allow all other functions of Office 2003 to run.

FIGURE 11.19   You can only add .MST files during the package definition.

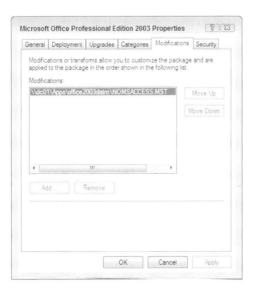

The Modifications tab is only available for use when "Advanced" is selected when an application is to be initially Published or Assigned. If a package is already Published or Assigned, the Modifications tab is not usable. As you can see in Figure 11.19, all of the buttons on the Modifications tab are grayed out. Again, this is because the .MST file was loaded at package deployment time, and afterward there is no way to add or remove .MST files after deployment. We'll reiterate and reexamine this issue a bit later.

There is no Modifications tab for .ZAP package definitions because Transform Files apply only to .MSI files.

You might be wondering how you can create your own .MST files for Office—and that's what the next section is about. After you're done, you'll have the chance to load your .MST file as well to test it out.

Office 2007 doesn't seem to use Transform Files, and hence, you wouldn't use the Modifications tab. Office 2007 has its own wacky way of describing settings during installation time. See the sidebar "Installing and Customizing Office 2007 via GPSI."

Installing and Customizing Office 2007 via GPSI

Earlier, we mentioned the fact that Office 2007 isn't like its predecessors. It's made up of smaller .MSI files. Doesn't sound like much of a change, but in practice this really throws a monkey wrench into what was a really beautiful system.

Recall: To deploy earlier versions of Office, you'd usually Assign the MSI to the user or computer. Then, you'd use the Office Custom Installation Wizard to create an .MST file and add that .MST file to the "Modifications" area when deploying the software.

Easy.

But not Office 2007. As we've already seen, you cannot deploy Office 2007 to Users. Nope. Only Computers. And we also saw that if you don't wait awhile before logging in, Office 2007 keeps installing—even after the user has logged on.

Bah.

Oh wait, this gets worse. So, there's no more Custom Installation Wizard tool that you download.

Customization and deployment happens in four steps.

Step 1: Create a config.xml File.

This file is to be placed in the root directory of the installation location so certain parameters can be set when the computer gets the assignment. There are two documents from Microsoft which have steps for producing a `config.xml`. This document, located at `http://tinyurl.com/umxoc`, shows all the available options normally available in a `config.xml` file. Buuuut, here's the trick. The document `http://tinyurl.com/327dnx` was removed from Microsoft's site, so I'm linking to a Google-cached version of it that tells the whole truth: The available configurable elements are pitiful for Group Policy installations—only four options can be set (Installation Location, Options and Features, Product Key, and Languages). Though one person on the `GPanswers.com` forum also suggested that Company might work, too. This affects every installation you use from this particular source. So, in our examples, we used the `Office2007Source` directory to perform our deployment to our client computers. If we deployed to Sales, Marketing, Human Resources, and Facilities, all these people would get these same four options because our `config.xml` file is rooted to this source. If you're only going to customize with `config.xml` files (to deploy to various categories of computers with different requirements), then you will need to maintain separate install locations per group of computers.

Step 2: Create a Custom MSP File

The `config.xml` file in Step 1 can only take us so far. In fact, not very far at all when it comes to customization. However, the tool to create more Office customizations is built in to the Office 2007 setup tool. Simply run `setup.exe /admin`, and <poof> instant customization tool. (Nice touch!) Note that trial and non-enterprise versions will not show the customization tool.

So, you might expect this new Office 2007 customization tool to produce `.MST` files like all the previous versions of Office before it.

Nope.

It produces `.MSP` files. A document at `http://tinyurl.com/39ru47` describes the way to produce `custom.msp` files.

`.MSP` files? Does that mean we can't use the Modifications tab to deploy our customization? That's exactly what it means.

Grrr.

So, take a big, deep breath, read the next two steps, then scream out the nearest window.

Step 3: Deploy Your MSI file Using GPSI

No big deal here. You're just using the information in this chapter to get Office 2007 installed. Remember, it only Assigns to the computer. At this point, it should pick up the `config.xml` configuration changes you made in Step 2.

Step 4: Patch Your Target Machines

Now that you've installed Office 2007 to your zillions of machines, here's the painful part. Use a logon script, batch file, or manually walk around to each machine to have it embrace your .MSP customization. Use the same information found in the section "Using MSIEXEC to Patch a Distribution Point." Except you don't update the distribution point. Instead, you patch the specific machines, individually.

Ow. Ow ow ow. That means you cannot use GPSI as a "unified" way of delivering Office 2007, and also customize it. This makes me spittin' mad, because, Group Policy is "the way" to do oh so much goodness in the world.

What I've just described is likely your best option for deploying a custom installation of Office 2007, even if it isn't pretty. But there is another way.

The Office 2007 team suggests that you use a technology (any technology) which allows you to run the setup.exe program from Office 2007, because the setup.exe will call all the .MSI files it needs for the installation you desire.

Well, a little later, you'll learn about .ZAP files.

.ZAP files really just run the underlying setup.exe of an application. Well, Office 2007 has a setup.exe. And, if you put your .MSP files (that you created by running setup /admin) in the Updates directory on your distribution source and then deploy using a .ZAP file, you should be able to install a customized Office 2007 in one fell swoop.

But don't forget— .ZAP files make the application's installation icons appear only in the "Add or Remove Programs" applet in Control Panel (or "Install a program from the network" for Windows Vista). And, .ZAP applications aren't "manageable." So, if you wanted to update Office 2007 later with more patches, you're basically asking the user to handle it on their own.

As you'll read later, in the "Removing Published .ZAP Applications" section, once you've deployed an application using a .ZAP file, you have no way to really upgrade it or revoke it. Once you've deployed it, consider it gone and basically "unmanaged" using Group Policy.

So, the "right" answer (from the Office 2007 team) is to deploy Office 2007 using (you know what's coming…) Microsoft SMS (or the next version, known as Microsoft SCCM 2007). I've got some feelings about where SMS or SCCM might fit into your organization, and you can read about those a bit later. But for now, the idea of spending a lot of money just to deploy a package because it has a lot of .MSI files upsets me a little bit.

If you've found a creative way to work around these issues, I want to hear about it. Be sure to email me at jeremym@moskowitz-inc.com and let me know your best techniques for deploying a customized Office 2007 using Group Policy.

Using the Office .*MST* Generation Tool (pre-Office 2007)

You can deploy Office 2000, Office XP, and Office 2003, for instance, whole hog by using their included .MSI package. Indeed, you saw this earlier. All applications of Office were available when our users chose to use Office. But what if we didn't want, say, Access available to our users? Or what if we want to adjust an Office property at a global level?

Using the Custom Installation Wizards from the Office Resource Kit, you can create an .MST Transform File that can limit which options can be installed, as well as specify all sorts of custom options, including the default installation path, the organization name, the custom Outlook behavior, and more! The tool has the same name in all three versions of Office (but the application is unique to each). Table 11.1 shows you where to find the downloads.

TABLE 11.1   Location of Office Resource Kit Downloads

Office Version	Where to Find the Resource Kit
Office 2000	www.microsoft.com/office/ork/2000/default.htm in the Toolbox folder
Office XP	www.microsoft.com/office/ork/xp/default.htm in the Toolbox folder
Office 2003	www.microsoft.com/office/ork/2003/default.htm in the Toolbox folder
Office 2007	http://tinyurl.com/vf9e3 (goes to Microsoft website). But remember, there is no tool to create .MST files for Office 2007. You create .MSP files (yes, .MSP files) with setup /admin. (See sidebar entitled "Installing and Customizing Office 2007 via GPSI.")

The procedure to create an .MST is straightforward but quite long, and I simply don't have room available to dedicate to each and every step. In this example, I'll assume you're using the Office 2003 Custom Installation Wizard (CIW). Here is the basic overview:

1. Choose Start ➤ All Programs ➤ Microsoft Office Tools ➤ [*the version of the tool you loaded*] ➤ Custom Installation Wizard to start the CIW.

2. Tell the CIW where your administrative installation of that version of Office is. Remember, you created an administrative installation of Office 2003 in the section "Setting Up an Administrative Installation (for .*MSI* Files that Need Them)" earlier in this chapter.

3. Give your .MST file a creative name, for example, nomsaccess.mst.

4. Continue to follow the wizard's instruction, choosing your specific installation options. In this example, on screen 7 (of 24), as shown in Figure 11.20, we'll tell Office 2003 that we don't want Access available to users.

5. At the final screen, click Finish and save the .MST file to a handy location.

As the CIW presents the final wizard screen, it will give you information about how to run the .MSI file along with the .MST file manually. But you can ignore this because you're about to use the .MST file in a Group Policy Software Installation GPO.

FIGURE 11.20   Use the CIW to choose the options you want and create the .MST file.

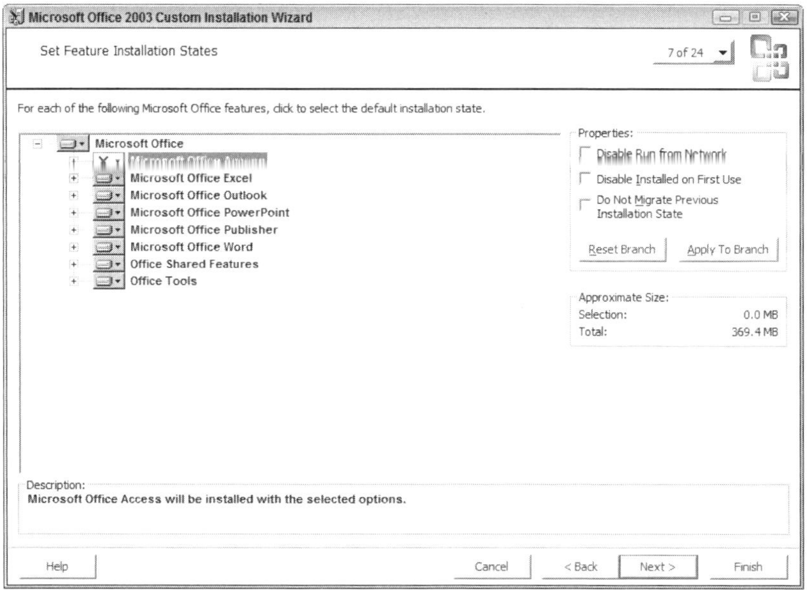

Applying Your .*MST* File to the Installation

As previously stated, you can add .MST files only when you're initially Assigning or Publishing a package. .MST files are valid, say, for Office 2003, but, it turns out, like I said, Office 2007 doesn't support them. See the sidebar "Installing and Customizing Office 2007 via GPSI" for the details.

You previously performed these steps in the "Creating and Editing the GPO to Deploy Office" section as shown in Figure 11.3. When you follow those steps, the "Select deployment method" dialog box will appear. Afterward, follow these steps:

1.   In the "Select deployment method" dialog box, click "Advanced" to open the Properties dialog box.

2.   Click the Modifications tab, and click Add to open the "Open" dialog box.

3.   In the "File name" field, enter the full UNC path of the .MST file, for instance, **\\DC01\ apps\office2003distro\nomsaccess.mst**.

NOTE   The .MST file needn't be in the same location as the .MSI distribution, as long as the path is available via the UNC name.

---

4.   Click OK.

Your screenshot should be similar to what is seen in Figure 11.19 in the "Modification Tab" section.

Once you click OK, the .MST file will be locked in and cannot be changed. You have only two options if you are unhappy with the .MST file:

- Remove the package and deploy it again.
- Create an upgrade package as described earlier.

Removing the entire Office suite and reinstalling it can be a pain for your users, so, if you want to deploy Office with (or without) .MST files, be sure to test in the lab before you really get started in your actual deployment.

What's with the Up and Down Buttons in the Modifications Tab?

If you wanted to, you could add multiple .MST files before clicking the OK button to lock in your selection. But why would you do this?

Multiple, autonomous administrators can individually create .MST files and layer them such that each Transform File contains some of the configuration options. These files are then ordered so that the options are applied from the top down. If configured options overlap, the last-configured option wins.

However, in my travels I really haven't seen administrators choose to add multiple .MST files for the same .MSI. Typically, only one .MST file is used as we did in this previous example.

The Security Tab

Individual applications can be filtered based on computer, user, or Security group membership. For instance, if you Assign Office 2003 to all members of the **Human Resources Users** OU, you set it up normally, as described earlier.

 If a user who happens to administer the application in the GPO is not given Read access, they will no longer be able to administer the application. Therefore, don't use filtering based on user or Security group membership on the administrators of the application.

If, however, you want to exclude a specific member, say, Frank Rizzo, you can deny Frank Rizzo's account permissions to "Read" the package. A better strategy is to create a Security group—say, DenyOffice2003—and put those people not allowed to receive the application inside that group. You can then set the permissions to "Deny" the entire Security group the ability to read the package as shown in Figure 11.21.

FIGURE 11.21   Use the Security tab to specify who can and cannot run applications.

Default Group Policy Software Installation Properties

Each GPSI node (one for users and one for computers) has some default installation properties that you can modify. In the Group Policy Object Editor, simply right-click the GPSI node and choose Properties from the shortcut menu, as shown in Figure 11.22, to open the Software Installation Properties dialog box (also shown on Figure 11.22), which has four tabs: General, Advanced, File Extensions, and Categories.

FIGURE 11.22   Use the GPSI Properties dialog box to set up general deployment settings.

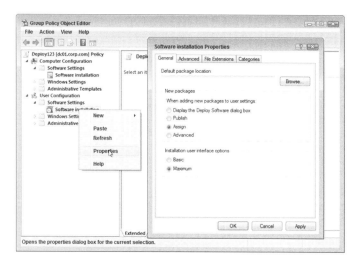

The General Tab

Most settings on the General tab are self-explanatory. Do note that you can specify a default package location, such as \\DC01\apps, so that you can then use the GUI when adding packages. Avoid using direct paths such as C:\apps\, since C:\apps probably won't exist on the client at runtime.

You can also specify the behavior for when you add in new packages; where Assign is the default action.

Last, you can establish the critical setting of Basic vs. Maximum here (when Assigning applications to users). The bummer is that these default setting changes are local only for this specific GPO. That is, the next GPO you create that uses GPSI will not adhere to the defaults you set in this GPO.

The Advanced Tab

The Advanced tab, as shown in Figure 11.23, allows you to set some default settings for all the packages you want to deploy in this GPO. You saw some of these settings with similar names before in the Advanced Deployment Options dialog box (Figure 11.17).

FIGURE 11.23 You can set up some default settings for new packages in this GPO.

Uninstall the applications when they fall out of the scope of management I'll discuss this setting in the "Removing Applications" section later in this chapter.

Include OLE information when deploying applications As stated earlier, this feature allows applications that contain COM services to be deployed such that COM clients can find their deployed applications. Again, check with your application vendor to see if you need this switch; generally you don't.

The "32-Bit applications on 64-Bit platforms" Section   As stated, it's possible to run x64 versions of Windows 32-bit applications on Windows XP 64-bit edition. You can set the defaults to block x64 machines from downloading 32-bit software packages. If you want to find out more about Windows XP 64-Bit Edition just check out `www.microsoft.com/ WindowsXP/64bit/default.asp`.

The File Extensions Tab

As stated earlier, you can install and start applications by double-clicking or by invoking their document type. For instance, double-clicking a `.ZIP` file can automatically deploy a Published or Assigned WinZip application. The correspondence of a file type to a package is found in either the `.ZAP` file definition or the `.MSI` file database. Once the application is set to be deployed, the file types are automatically entered into Active Directory.

Occasionally, two Published or Assigned applications are called by the same file extension. This can occur if you're upgrading a package from, say, WinZip to UltraZip, and both are using the `.ZIP` extension, or if you're upgrading from Office 2003 to Office 2007 and both Word applications use the `.DOC` extension.

In those cases, you need to specify which extension fires off which application. To do so, follow these steps:

1. In the Software Installation Properties dialog box, click the File Extensions tab, as shown in Figure 11.24.

2. Click the "Select file extension" drop-down list box, and select the extension to display all the applicable Assigned or Published applications in the Application Precedence list.

3. Select an application, and then click the Up or Down button to change the order.

FIGURE 11.24   Use the File Extensions tab to set the priority for conflicting file extensions.

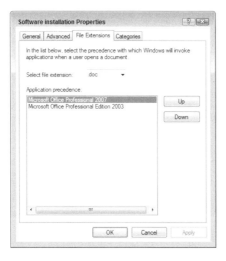

The Categories Tab

Categories is a domain-wide property that puts Published or Assigned software into bite-sized chunks instead of one giant-sized alphabetized list in the "Add or Remove Programs folder" or "Install a program from the network" for Windows Vista. As noted earlier, you might want to group WinZip and UltraZip in the "Archive Programs" category or put Adobe Acrobat Reader and GhostScript in the "Doc Readers" category. On this tab, simply click the Add button to enter the names of the categories in the "Enter new category" dialog box.

This whole business of Categories is a bit strange, as it lets any OU administrator add categories into Active Directory. Oddly, there appears to be no way to centrally manage this property.

Therefore, if possible, select one administrator to control this property, set it up to be centrally managed, and then use the Properties dialog box to associate a package with a category or categories.

Removing Applications

You can remove applications from users or computers in several ways. First, under some circumstances, users can manually remove applications, but, as an administrator, you hold the reigns. Therefore, you can set applications to automatically or forcefully be removed.

Users Can Manually Change or Remove Applications

If an application is Assigned (and also Published to a user), they can use Control Panel to change the installed options or remove the bits to save space. However, Microsoft's position is that it provides the best of both worlds: the user can remove the binaries, but if the application is Assigned, the icons and program names are forced to appear on the Start ➤ All Programs menu.

But, in practice, I've found that this is a bad thing. Users remove their applications and then go on the road with their laptops. Well, on the other hand, if they do this, they deserve what's coming to them. Note, however, that applications Assigned to the computer cannot be changed or uninstalled by anyone but local computer administrators. This is a good thing.

Automatically Removing Assigned or Published .*MSI* Applications

Applications can be automatically uninstalled when they no longer apply to the user. Earlier in the "Advanced Published or Assigned" section, you saw that in the Deployment tab of the Software Installation Properties dialog box you can check the "Uninstall this application when it falls out of the scope of management" check box. This was back in Figure 11.15. You can specify that the application is to be uninstalled if any of the following occurs:

- The user or computer is moved out of the OU to which this software applies.
- The GPO containing the package definition is deleted.
- The user or computer no longer has rights to read the GPO.

The software is never actually forcibly removed while the user is logged on to the current session but is removed a bit later in the following manner.

- Applications Published to users are removed upon next logon.
- Applications Assigned to users are removed upon next logon.
- Applications Assigned to computers are removed upon next reboot.
- Applications Assigned to computers that are currently not attached to the network are removed the next time the computer is plugged in to the network, rebooted, and the computer account "logs on" to Active Directory.
- Applications Assigned or Published to users on computers that are currently not attached to the network are removed the next time they log on and are validated to Active Directory.

In these cases, the software is automatically removed upon next logon (for users) or upon next reboot (for computers). For example, Figure 11.25 shows what happens when a computer is moved out of an OU and then rebooted. Moving users and computers in and out of OUs might not be such a hot idea if lots of applications are being Assigned.

These rules assume that the target system is Windows 2000, Windows 2003, Windows Vista, or Windows XP and Fast Boot is not enabled. If Fast Boot is enabled (the default), these rules don't apply; expect two logons or two reboots for the change to take effect.

FIGURE 11.25　When applications fall out of the scope of management, they uninstall.

One final warning about the automatic removal of applications. GPSI cannot remove the icons and programs names for the application if the GPO has been deleted and the user has a Roaming Profile and has roamed to a machine after the application was uninstalled. In this case, there is not enough uninstall information on the machine, and, hence, the icons and program names will continue to exist, though they will be nonfunctional.

Forcefully Removing Assigned or Published *.MSI* Applications

You have seen how applications can be automatically removed from users or computers when the user or computer object moves out the scope of management. But what if you want to keep the user or computer in the scope of management and still remove an application? You can manually remove Published or Assigned applications. To do so, simply right-click the package definition, and choose All Tasks ➤ Remove, as seen in Figure 11.26. This will open the "Remove Software" dialog box. The options presented in this dialog box depend on whether you deployed .MSI or .ZAP applications.

FIGURE 11.26   You can revoke deployed applications by selecting Remove.

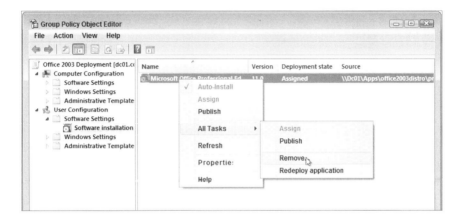

If you are removing an .MSI file, you have two options, as discussed in the next sections.

Immediately Uninstall the Software from Users and Computers

If you choose this option, all connected computers receive a signal to uninstall the software, and they follow the rules for uninstalling as in the previous section.

The signal to remove an application (such as Office XP) lives in the actual GPO definition. Therefore, if you're looking for success in the forceful removal of applications, don't delete the GPO right after selecting this option. If you do, the signal to remove the application won't be available to the workstations. Rather, remove the application, and leave the GPO definition around for a while to ensure that the computers get the signal to remove the software. If you remove the GPO before the target user receives the signal (upon next logon) or the computer receives the signal (upon next reboot), the application is orphaned on the Desktop and must be manually unloaded via Control Panel or by some other means (for instance, MSIEXEC, as described later in this chapter).

This is a second warning in case you overlooked the ominous message in the previous paragraph: if you remove the GPO definition before a target user or computer receives the signal, the application is orphaned on the Desktop. You can, however, likely get out of this trap if the application was specified with the "Uninstall this application when it falls out of the scope of management" check box. You can move the user or computer out of the scope of management to remove the application and then bring it back in when the application removal is completed. It's a bit rough, but it should work.

Allow Users to Continue to Use the Software, but Prevent New Installations

When you remove applications using this option, current installations of the software remain intact. Users to which this edict applies, however, will no longer be able to install new copies of the software. Therefore, those who do not have the software will not be able to install it. Those who do have it installed will be able to continue to use it.

The self-repair features of the Windows Installer will still function (for example, if Winword.exe gets deleted, it will come back from the dead), but the application cannot be fully reinstalled via Control Panel for fixing an application en masse.

Once you use this option, you will no longer be able to manage the application and force it to uninstall from the machines on which it is installed.

Removing Published *.ZAP* Applications

You have only one option for removing .ZAP applications. When you right-click the package definition and select Remove (as seen in Figure 11.26), you'll have to answer but one question: "Remove the Package but Leave the Application Installed Everywhere It Is Already Installed?"

Remember that since the .ZAP file really calls only the original Setup.exe program, and ultimately, that Setup.exe is in charge of how the application is uninstalled. Therefore, once applications are deployed using .ZAP files, the power to forcibly uninstall them is out of your hands.

Troubleshooting the Removal of Applications

Sometimes, applications refuse to leave the target system gracefully. Usually, this is because an application has been Published or Assigned, and the user has "double-dipped" by throwing in the CD and installing a program on top of itself. Sometimes, the Windows Installer becomes confused. When you then try to remove the application from being Published or Assigned, the application doesn't know what to do.

If an application refuses to go away (or you're left with entries in the "Add or Remove Programs" applet in Control Panel), you have two tools at your disposal: The Windows Installer Clean Up Utility (also known as MSICUU) and MSIZAP. Both were originally in the Windows 2000 Support Tools located in the \SUPPORT folder of the Windows 2000 Server CD. Updates are now available at Microsoft's download site. Both do essentially the same thing: they manually hunt down all Registry settings for an application and delete them. This should remove all vestigial entries in the "Add or Remove Programs" applet in Control Panel.

Windows Installer Clean Up Utility (also known as MSICUU)   This tool has a GUI. Programs displayed in the Installed Products list, as shown in Figure 11.27, are the same as those in the "Add or Remove Programs" applet in Control Panel. At last check, more information about the tool was available at http://tinyurl.com/9cml4, but the actual download for the tool was at http://support.microsoft.com/kb/290301.

MSIZAP   MSIZAP is a command-line tool with a similar function. You must specify a specific .MSI product code (GUID) to hunt down and destroy. At last check, additional reference and download for MSIZAP is at http://tinyurl.com/l9eb. However, you'll have to download and install the monstrous Windows Installer SDK just to get it.

FIGURE 11.27   The MSICUU program in the Windows 2000 Support Tools can whack entire programs off your system.

Using Group Policy Software Installation over Slow Links

First things first: applications Assigned to computers cannot ever be installed over a slow dial-up link or a VPN (virtual private network) connection. Why? Because the computer must see the network, log on to it, and then start to actually download the program. If you're using a dial-in or other slow connection, manual intervention to connect to the network must be involved. Hence, in general, no applications Assigned to computers will ever install unless the computer is connected to the LAN.

I say "in general" in the previous sentence, because it does depend a bit on your VPN technology. For instance, you could have a hardware VPN, separate from the client, and a computer assignment could work over that should a slow-link not be detected.

However, when applications are Assigned or Published to users (not computers), it's a different story. When a user connects via a slow link, they will not see new Assignment offers. By default, only users connected at 500Kbps or greater will see new Assignments on the Start ➢ All Programs menu. This is a good thing too, as you wouldn't want someone dialing in over a 56Kbps modem to try to accept the offer of Office XP.

You can change this behavior by modifying the GPO at Computer Configuration ➢ Administrative Templates ➢ System ➢ Group Policy ➢ **Software Installation Policy Processing**, as shown in Figure 11.28.

Checking the "Allow processing across a slow network connection" check box forces all clients, regardless of their connection speed, to adhere to the policy setting. If you want to be a bit less harsh, you can change the definition of a "slow link" and modify the **Group Policy Slow Link Detection** policy setting. After you Enable the policy setting, set a value in the "Connection speed (Kbps)" spin box.

FIGURE 11.28   Use Group Policy to change the default slow-link behavior.

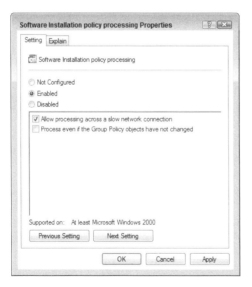

One word of warning with regard to slow links: users who are Assigned or Published applications can find other ways to install applications over slow links. First, they can trot out to the "Add or Remove Programs" applet and select the application. Sure, the offer isn't displayed on the Start ➤ All Programs menu, but it's still going to be available in the "Add or Remove Programs" applet in Control Panel. To prevent this, select the "Do not display this package in the Add/Remove Programs control panel" check box, which is found on the Deployment tab of the application's Properties (see Figure 11.15).

Last, check out this scenario. Imagine that while on a fast link, a user named Fred accepted the offer for Excel. Super-duper—Excel is now installed. Now, Fred is dialed up and receives a Word document in e-mail. And, Fred hasn't yet installed Word. Look out! Because .DOC is a registered file type for Microsoft Office, Word will attempt to install over a slow link (if assigned to a User). This happens because Fred has accepted the "offer" for Office (he got Excel over a fast link) and now selects to get Word via document invocation. To prevent this, simply clear the "Auto-install this application by file extension activation" option in the Deployment tab in the Properties dialog box of the application (again, seen in Figure 11.15).

Assigning Applications to Users over Slow Links Using Windows 2000

If you are planning on utilizing GPSI with Windows 2000 laptops, there are two things to keep in mind. Here they are.

Dealing with Already-Assigned Applications

Here's a scenario that illustrates the problem with Assigning an application, such as Office, to users. While at headquarters in Washington, D.C., Wally, on his Windows 2000 Professional laptop, sees and accepts your offer for Office. Specifically, Wally clicks Word on the Start ➤ All Programs menu. Because Wally is connected over a fast link, the download is quick and painless. Wally is shipped off from Washington, D.C. to Walla Walla, WA.

 Oh, by the way, to learn more about the fine city of Walla Walla, WA, be sure to visit www.ci.walla-walla.wa.us/.

While on the airplane from Washington, D.C. to Walla Walla, WA, Wally decides to accept the offer for Excel and clicks that item on the Start ➤ All Programs menu. He gets the message shown in Figure 11.29.

This is a major problem for Wally because the source files are only available on the server from which he originally receive the installation (or from a DFS share, if that's available). Long story short, Wally is woeful. Wally calls the help desk, and the help desk calls you. Worst part of the story—there's not a whole lot you can do to help him now.

You can ask Wally to dial in, but that's likely going to be fruitless. Trying to install Excel over a dial-up connection won't be painless. Can Wally with his Windows 2000 laptop be helped? Not easily, now that he's on the road. He really needs to connect using a fast link to download the rest of Excel.

FIGURE 11.29   This is what happens when a user tries to use a program that isn't fully installed.

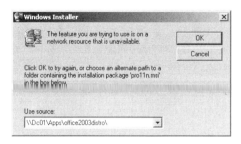

However, Wally could have been helped *before* he set out on the road in two ways:

- The application could have been Assigned to his computer (instead of to his user account), which would have ensured that the entire application was available and ready to go when he hit the road. You saw this earlier when we installed Office 2003. The entirety of Office 2003 was installed on the next reboot. Sure, it took a long time, but when it was done, it was done.

- Even though the application was Assigned to Wally's user account, the application could have been fully installed via a little scripting magic. We'll explore that option right now.

"Fully Installing" New Applications to Users on Windows 2000 When Using Assign

As I stated earlier, users dialed up over a slow link will not see *new* Assignment offers. The key word here is *new*.

However, this wasn't Wally's problem. He wasn't accepting a new offer over a slow link; rather, Wally had already accepted an offer before he left. Therefore, his problem could have been prevented if the application were already fully installed. But I already said that when you Assign applications to users, the .MSI file is downloaded in chunks—not all at once—which is precisely why Wally had problems when he tried to download Excel. He had the "chunk" for Word, but not for Excel. Hence, he needed to reach the original source for a download.

To that end, you can install a special logon script for users on Windows 2000 laptops. Here's the gist. When users connect at a high speed, the computer sees the new offer. This special logon script downloads and installs each "chunk" of the .MSI—all at once to ensure that the application is fully installed. Hence, even though the application is Assigned to Wally's user account, the entirety of the application is available.

Sure, the application takes a while to download the first time the offer is available, and, of course, all the disk space the application will ever use is used right away. But it's a darn good idea to set up this logon script for your Windows 2000 laptop users. You don't want them to get the message seen in Figure 11.29.

Space doesn't permit me to print the script right here, but you can download it from my website, www.GPanswers.com. One warning about this script: if the user has already accepted any part of the offer (that is, already downloaded Word, but not Excel), this script won't work for them. You need to set up the script *before* you start Assigning applications to users, that is, before they start accepting your offers. If you've already deployed applications in this way, you'll need to remove them (see the section "Removing Applications" earlier in this chapter) and then Assign the applications again after the special logon script is in place.

Assigning Applications to Users over Slow Links Using Windows XP, Windows Vista, and Windows 2003

Microsoft has fixed the problem that plagued Wally. However, the solution is only available when the client system is greater than Windows 2000 (say, Windows XP, Windows Vista, or Windows 2003). However, it's doubtful you'll have many Windows 2003 systems for use "on the road."

When a modern machine sees an offer for a newly Assigned application for a user (which it will only see when connected over a fast link), the entirety of the application can be installed—instead of waiting for it to come down in chunks.

Ideally, you'll set this up for packages you want to Assign to users using Windows XP laptops. When you Assign this application to users, in the Deployment tab of the Properties dialog box, click the "Install this application at logon" check box (as seen in Figure 11.15). This setting is only valid for Windows XP, Windows Vista, or Windows 2003 clients when applications are Assigned to users. Windows 2000 machines simply ignore it.

WARNING

If the user opens the "Add or Remove Programs" folder or "Install a program from the network" for Windows Vista and manually uninstalls the application, neither the logon script nor the "Install this application at logon" setting will kick back into high gear and install the application. This might be a big deal if your users dink around trying to add or remove stuff. You might also want to select the "Do not display this package in the Add/Remove Programs control panel" check box also located on the Deployment tab in the Properties dialog box.

Managing *.MSI* Packages and the Windows Installer

Users might occasionally want to install their own .MSI packages, which can be on CDs from vendors, such as Office 2003 and GPMC.msi (from Microsoft); other vendors; or applications that you create using WinINSTALL LE, for example. To manually install an .MSI application on a workstation, you can either double-click the application from the CD or shared folder or use a command-line tool called MSIEXEC to kick off (or repair) the installation.

This section explores the options when manually installing existing .MSI packages that you've deployed via Group Policy. As we've learned throughout the chapter, most of the things we need in order to deploy applications can be performed using the GPSI GUI. However, some functions are available only in the command-line tool.

Inside the *MSIEXEC* Tool

MSIEXEC is a command-line tool, which helps you get applications installed. There are three versions of MSIEXEC, but you're likely to encounter only two versions.

If your machine is Windows XP (pre-SP2), simply typing **MSIEXEC /?** on the command line is no help at all. In this case, to get the full syntax of MSIEXEC, you'll need to use the Windows help file and search for MSIEXEC.

However, if your machine is Windows XP/SP2, MSIEXEC has been upgraded to version 3. Now, if you type **MSIEXEC /?**, you'll get some useful feedback about how to use it.

For the purposes of this book, MSIEXEC for Windows XP/SP2 (that is, MSIEXEC version 3) and the non-Windows XP/SP2 versions of MSIEXEC (that is, MSIEXEC versions prior to 3) will act functionally equivalent. However, you might be interested in precisely what MSIEXEC 3 has to offer. And, if you like what you see, you'll be happy to know that MSIEXEC 3 is redistributable to your Windows XP (non-SP2) and Windows 2000 clients! Specifically, you can load Windows Installer 3 on Windows 2000 Service Pack 3, Windows 2000 Service Pack 4, Windows Server 2003, Windows XP, and Windows XP Service Pack 1. Note, however, you'll need to find some non–Group Policy way to deploy the update because you can't update the .MSI engine while in use (very clear chicken-and-egg problem). You should be able to update these systems with Microsoft WSUS.

You can find out about what MSIEXEC 3 is all about at MS KB 884016 with the plucky little title "Windows Installer 3.0 is Available."

You can use MSIEXEC in several ways, but here we're going to look at how to use it to manage existing .MSI packages. Indeed, you can use MSIEXEC to script an installation of an .MSI package at a workstation, but why bother? You're already using the power of Group Policy. However, you might need to check out how an installation works by hand or enable additional logging for deeper troubleshooting. Or you could trigger a preemptive repair of an application at specific times. You can even use MSIEXEC to remove a specific application.

You can also use MSIEXEC as a maintenance tool for existing packages on distribution points. We'll explore a bit of both uses.

Instead of diving into every MSIEXEC command here, I'll simply highlight some of the most frequently used. Indeed, you may never find yourself using MSIEXEC unless specifically directed to do so by an application vendor's Install program.

Using *MSIEXEC* to Install an Application

The first function of MSIEXEC is to initiate an installation from a source point. This is essentially the same as double-clicking the .MSI file, using the /I switch (for Install). The syntax for your application might be as follows:

```
Msiexec /I \\DC01\apps\yourapp.msi
```

Using *MSIEXEC* to Repair an Application

You can script the repair of applications by using MSIEXEC with the /f switch and an additional helper-switch, as indicated in the Windows help file. For instance, you might want to ensure that Pro11n.msi (Office 2003) is not corrupted on the client. You can do so by forcing all files from inside the Office 2003 .MSI to be reinstalled on the client. Use the following command from the client (which overwrites older or equally versioned files):

Msiexec /fe \\DC01\apps\office2003distro\pro11n.msi

If you simply want to ensure that no older version is installed, you can execute the following command:

Msiexec /fo \\DC01\apps\office2003distro\pro11n.msi

Again, be sure to consult the Windows help file for the complete syntax of MSIEXEC in conjunction with adhering to your specific application vendor's directions.

Using *MSIEXEC* to Patch a Distribution Point

You can also use MSIEXEC to *patch*; that is to incorporate vendor-supplied bug fixes and the like to the code base of an existing package. The vendor supplies the patches by using an .MSP file, or *Microsoft Patch* file. Office XP's service packs, for instance, come with several .MSP files that update the original .MSI files.

Office 2003 has multiple service packs. You can download the latest one (SP2) from http://support.microsoft.com/kb/887616. It contains Mainsp2ff.msp and Owc11sp2ff.msp.

Microsoft seems to have changed their tune midway with this technology. In some instances, you needed to apply each successive service pack's .MSP files to be sufficiently protected. However, Office XP's Service Pack 3, for instance, expressly states that it contains all the fixes contained within all previous service packs. So, be sure to read your manufacture's instructions on whether or not to install every .MSP file from every update, or if you can make due with just the most recent.

Throughout this chapter, we've leveraged our Office 2003 administration point. We'll continue with that trend. In the following example, the Office 2003 distribution, located at \\DC01\apps\office2003distro, is to be patched with the MAINSP2ff.msp patch that comes with Office 2003 Service Pack 1. The resulting log file will be called logfile.txt.

Because each vendor may have a different way of patching, be sure to check out the Readme file that comes with the patch files.

The following command line is written as directed from the Office 2003 SP1 Whitepaper:

```
Msiexec.exe /a \\dc01\apps\office2003distro\PRO11n.MSI /p MAINSP2ff.msp
SHORTFILENAMES=True /qb- /L*v c:\Logfile.txt
```

 Again, you'll have to run the command for each and every patch. This means you'll have to run the command three times to update an Office 2003 distribution point to SP2. The Office 2003 SP2 whitepaper expressly states that it includes all updates that were previously contained in the previous service pack, so there is no need to first update Office 2003 to SP1.

This next step is a point of order that I left out of the 2nd (and 1st) edition of this book. That is, once the .MSI is patched, all your users (or computers) need to reinstall the application. The underlying application has changed, and the client system doesn't know about the change until you tell it. You can see how to redeploy an application in Figure 11.30. Again, this is only required after an .MSI source is patched.

Users also need to do this because of what is termed the "client-source-out-of-sync" problem. Until the client reaches and reinstalls from the updated administrative image, it won't be able to use the administrative image for repairs or on-demand installations. This is because a source location is validated by the Windows Installer before use. The criteria for validation are the name of the package file and the package code (seen as a GUID) of the package. When you patch the administrative image, you change the underlying package code GUID. Thus, the client needs the recache and reinstall in order to pick up the updated package code information.

So, specifically, after you patch a distribution point (or otherwise change the underlying .MSI package in a distribution point), you need to right-click the offer and choose All Tasks ≻ Redeploy application, as shown in Figure 11.30.

FIGURE 11.30 Once you patch an .MSI source, be sure to select "Redeploy application."

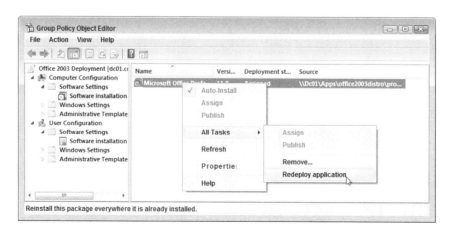

Affecting Windows Installer with Group Policy

You can use several policy settings to tweak the behavior of the Windows Installer. Most tweaks do not involve how software is managed or deployed via GPSI because there's not much to it. You deploy the application, and users (or computers) do your bidding. Rather, these settings tweak the access the user has when software is not being Assigned or Published.

There are two collections of policy settings for the Windows Installer; one is under Computer Configuration, and the other is under User Configuration. As usual, to utilize these policy settings, just create a new GPO, Enable the policy settings you like, then ensure that the corresponding user or computer account is in the scope of management of the GPO.

Computer Side Policy Settings for Windows Installer

To display the settings in Computer Configuration, as shown in Figure 11.31, choose Computer Configuration ➢ Administrative Templates ➢ Windows Components ➢ Windows Installer.

Note that Windows Installer 3 has four specific Computer side policy settings. That is, for these four settings to work, your machine needs to be running Windows Installer 3. As stated, Windows XP/SP2 and Windows 2003/SP1 both have Windows Installer 3 already loaded. And, as also stated, the Windows Installer 3 redistributable is available for Windows XP (no Service Pack), Windows 2003, and Windows 2000 (SP3 and later). Again, check out MS KB 884016. Once your client has Windows Installer 3, it will respond to the newest settings. These are specifically called out and listed in the next sections.

FIGURE 11.31   Use Group Policy to affect the Windows Installer settings.

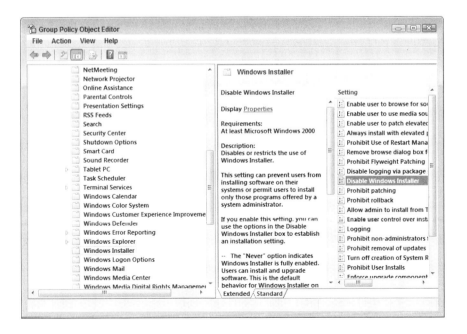

Disable Windows Installer

Once enabled, this setting lets you specify one of four options:

Not Configured   Uses the settings at a higher level.

Enabled/Never   Always keeps the Windows Installer active.

Enabled/For Nonmanaged Apps Only   Turns off the Windows Installer when users try to manually install their own applications. This is useful if you want to guarantee no foreign .MSI packages are making it through the door. This option permits users to install only those programs that a system administrator Assigns or Publishes.

Enabled/Always   Essentially turns off all methods (managed and unmanaged) for loading .MSI packages.

These settings specify only settings for .MSI packages—not other programs that users can install, such as those from SETUP.EXEs and the like.

Always Install with Elevated Privileges

Deploying applications with GPSI is awesome: we do all the work with .MSI files, and we don't have to worry about users having administrative privileges. As we've already seen, we can deploy applications to users, and have the system take care of the installation in the system context (not the user context).

And, what's more, mere-mortals cannot just download an .MSI application and necessarily expect it to install correctly. Many .MSI applications will fail installation if attempted in the user context. You can, however, bypass the normal security mechanism so that users can install .MSI files by Enabling this policy setting. You'll need to do the same with the corresponding policy setting in the User Configuration, as discussed in the "User Side Policy Settings for Windows Installer" section.

    If you are deploying .MSI applications with Group Policy, you need not use and enable this setting.

Prohibit Rollback

As stated, .MSI files can be "rolled back"—during the actual installation of the application. For instance, a user can click "Cancel" during an installation or the computer could suddenly be turned off.

If you enable this policy setting, you're effectively telling the system not to maintain "backup files" in the case of an on-the-fly rollback. Since a rollback can be initiated during the actual installation, a "fractured" and, hence, nonworking program could remain on the system.

Personally, I would never use this policy setting.

Remove Browse Dialog Box for New Source

Recall that, at any given point, only the components required to run an .MSI application are actually downloaded. For instance, the help files in Word are downloaded the first time it is used from the installation source (usually the server), not necessarily the first time Word runs. But what happens if you move the source?

When you move an application from one shared folder to another, the application can become confused, and users need to specify a different installation point to get to the source. By default, users can browse to any source.

If you Enable this setting, users are only allowed to use specific sources.

Prohibit Patching

If users can install some .MSI applications under their own security context, by default, they can also patch their own .MSI files with .MSP (Microsoft Patch) files by using the MSIEXEC command-line application. Enabling this setting prevents users from patching even their own installed .MSI applications.

Prohibit Flyweight Patching

This setting is new when a GPO is created from a Windows Vista management station. However, it is valid on machines that have Windows Installer 3. Windows Installer 4 is not required.

If you enable this setting, you're instructing the engine to be meticulous during its patching of applications. If you disable this setting (or leave it Not Configured), you are telling the system to utilize a faster algorithm when patching is needed.

Disable IE Security Prompt for Windows Installer Scripts

Recall that users can manually install .MSI applications from a CD or a shared folder or a web page. The default behavior before executing any downloaded application via Internet Explorer is to warn the user about potentially damaging content. Enabling this setting squelches this warning.

This scenario should be rare, because normally you Publish or Assign applications in order to install them to your users' Desktops. At times, however, some applications may be best suited for downloading via Internet Explorer, and, hence, a warning message could appear and frighten your users.

Enable User Control over Installs

When an administrator Publishes or Assigns applications, all the settings specified in the .MSI application are forced upon the user. Sometimes this behavior is undesirable. For example, you might want to let the user specify the destination folder or decide which features to download. If you enable this setting, you grant users the ability to change the default .MSI application settings.

 This policy setting affects all applications installed on the client system. However, if you want to let the user set up a specific product in their own way, you can use a transform that sets special properties inside the .MSI. You can use the .MST tool to set the EnableUserControl property to 1 or add specific properties to the SecureCustomProperties list (using a customization transform). If your application doesn't have a way to create .MST files, you can create them with third-party .MSI creation tools.

Enable User to Browse for Source While Elevated

When an administrator Publishes or Assigns applications, all the settings specified in the .MSI application are forced upon the user from the installation point the administrator specifies. Sometimes this behavior is undesirable because the user knows of a closer source to the application in their branch office. In cases like this, you might want to let the user specify the source to locate a closer source point. If you enable this setting, you grant users the ability to change the default .MSI source location.

WARNING   Once users are affected by this policy setting, they can basically browse anywhere they like, including the local system. If you have locked down the Desktop to prevent such behavior, enabling this setting could be a potential security hole during .MSI application install times.

Enable User to Use Media Source While Elevated

When users install .MSI packages under their own security context, they can choose whatever source they desire for the software. But when you, the administrator, Assign or Publish an application, you are essentially dictating the source of the .MSI file. If you enable this setting, you permit the user to choose a nonnetworked source, such as a CD or floppy drive, from which to install a program you specify. Enable this setting only if the **Enable the User to Browse for Source While Elevated** is enabled.

Enable User to Patch Elevated Products

By default, only the administrator who Assigns or Publishes the application can use an .MSP file (in conjunction with MSIEXEC) to patch a program. If you enable this setting, users can use MSIEXEC to patch their local versions of Published or Assigned applications.

Allow Admin to Install from Terminal Services Session

By default, administrators using the Terminal Services "Remote Administration Mode" on Windows 2000 or Windows 2003 Server are prevented from installing additional Published or Assigned applications.

   If you want Administrators to be able to install .MSI applications while logged in via Terminal Services session, just Enable this setting so that servers and Domain Controllers download the setting and, hence, reverse this default.

Cache Transforms in Secure Location on Workstation

Recall that you can specifically customize an .MST file to hone an .MSI application. Transform Files are applied on .MSI packages either to filter the number of options available to the end user or to specify certain answers to questions usually raised during the .MSI package installation.

   Once a user starts using an .MSI application applied with an .MST file, that .MST file follows them in the Roaming Profile—specifically, in the Application Data folder, as described in Chapter 9. You can change this default behavior by enabling this setting, which takes the .MST file out of the Roaming Profile and puts it in a secure place on the workstation. On the one hand, this closes a small security hole that sophisticated users might use to hack into their own .MST files in their profiles. On the other hand, users are forced to return to the machine that has their .MST files in order to additionally modify their application.

Avoid using this setting unless specifically directed to do so by your application vendor, a security bulletin, or Microsoft.

Logging

Applications Assigned or Published using Windows Installer do not provide much information to the administrator about the success of their installation. By default, several key tidbits of information are logged about managed applications that fail. The log files are named .MSI*.LOG; the * represents additional characters that make the log file unique for each application downloaded.

Per-computer logs are in c:\windows\temp and per-user logs are in %temp%.

Thus, centralized logging and reporting is an arduous, if not impossible, task for anything more than a handful of users who are using Windows Installer. For additional logging and reporting, Microsoft recommends their Systems Management Server, as described in the section titled "Do You Need a 'Big' Management Tool for Your Environment?" later in the chapter.

To add logging entries, modify the Logging setting. Some settings that might come in handy are Out of Memory and Out of Disk—two common reasons for Windows Installer applications failing to load.

 You can also turn on Application Management debugging logs by manually editing the Registry of the client machine. Simply run regedit or regedt32 and edit the following key: HKEY_LOCAL_MACHINE\Software\Microsoft\ Windows NT\CurrentVersion. Create a key called "Diagnostics," then add a Reg_DWORD value called AppMgmtDebugLevel and set it to 4b in hexadecimal. You'll then find a log in the local %windir%debug\usermode folder named appmgmt.log, which can also aid in finding out why applications fail to load.

Prohibit User Installs

On occasion an administrator might dictate that a user is Assigned Office 2003, and another administrator dictates that a computer gets Office 2003 (but perhaps without Access). What if the user who is Assigned Office 2003 sits down at a computer that is Assigned Office 2003 without Access? Which one "wins"? The application (and settings therein) Assigned to the user takes precedence.

This policy setting has three options (once enabled): "Allow User Installs," "Hide User Installs," or "Prohibit User Installs." Computers that are affected by "Hide User Installs" display only the applications Assigned to the computer. However, the user can still install the applications assigned to them using the "Add or Remove Programs" applet in Control Panel (hence, overriding the applications assigned to the computer).

If you set **Prohibit User Installs**, the user won't get the applications Assigned to them on the machines to which this policy setting applies. And the user cannot load Assigned applications to their user account via the "Add or Remove Programs" folder or "Install a program from the net-work" for Windows Vista. If they do so, they'll get an error message. If this policy setting is set somewhere else, you can also return the default behavior by setting "Allow User Installs."

This policy setting can be especially handy in Terminal Services sessions or Kiosk settings (for example, lab machines) where you want all users of the machine to get the applications Assigned only to computers (not to users).

This setting is valid for Windows XP and Windows 2000 machines (with Windows Installer 2 or later loaded). See the section "The Windows Installer Service" earlier in this chapter.

Turn off Creation of System Restore Checkpoints

On a Windows XP machine, a System Restore Checkpoint is created when users load their own .MSI files unless there is no user interface. The .MSI system creates System Restore Checkpoints on first installation and uninstall. System Restore Checkpoints are not created when deploying (or repairing) applications via GPSI.

Enable this setting if you want to ensure that no System Restore Checkpoints are created when .MSI files are loaded.

This setting is only valid on Windows XP and Windows Server 2003 machines.

Prohibit Removal of Updates

Windows Installer 3 has new technology to help roll back patches once installed. If you enable this policy, no one can remove software updates and patches once installed—not even an administrator. You might want to do this if your environment has special security require-ments. That is, if, by unloading a patch, you might be putting the system and your company in harm's way, you might want to enable this setting. This will ensure that no one can uninstall installed patches.

If this policy setting is disabled, a user can remove updates from the computer if the user has been granted privileges to remove the update. This all depends on how the patch was deployed. Read the Explaintext on this policy setting for more information.

This setting is valid only on machines that have Windows Installer 3.

Enforce Upgrade of Component Rules

Windows Installer 3 can be stricter about how applications allow themselves to be updated, via .MSP files, for example. That is, some .MSP files can perform some no-no's that could inad-vertently render an application to malfunction once updated.

The Explaintext of this policy setting describes two of these no-no's: when an .MSP changes the GUID of a function and when a new component is added in the wrong place of the .MSI tree. These have to do with the way an .MSI file is represented internally to the system. If these things are changed, the application could fail to function.

To that end, Enabling this policy setting forces the .MSI engine to ensure that certain safe-guards are in place and that the .MSP file doesn't actually perform these no-no's.

If you disable this policy setting, Windows Installer is allowed to perform these no-no's.

This setting is valid only on machines that have Windows Installer 3.

Prohibit Nonadministrators from Applying Vendor Signed Updates

When a patch comes out from an application vendor, how do you want to handle it? Application vendors can come out with patches that only the administrator can install—or conversely, they can also come out with patches that theoretically even the user should be able to install. And these patches are digitally signed, so you can be sure that they're not really coming from EvilSoftware, Inc. You can then just allow the user to just patch their own applications, but this is likely fraught with peril.

However, this policy setting controls just that. If you Enable it, you're forcing only administrators to install updates that have been digitally signed by the application vendor.

If you disable this policy setting, mere-mortal users can install these nonadministrator updates without needed administrative access.

This setting is valid only on machines that have Windows Installer 3.

Baseline File Cache Maximum Size

Don't you just hate it when you're asked for the original installation media when an update is available? In theory, this is silly: The application is already installed on my hard drive, why on earth do I need the original media?

Well, with Windows Installer 3, this policy setting tries to help fix that. It sets the percentage of disk space available to the Windows Installer "baseline file cache." The idea is that you can have these required files hanging around, ready for whenever an update is ready to go. Then, when the original source is needed, it goes to the baseline file cache and doesn't ask for the original installation source.

If you enable this policy setting, you can then modify the maximum size of the Windows Installer baseline file cache. Note that if the baseline cache size is set to 0, Windows Installer cannot store new files. Previously stored files will stay in place (until the application that uses it is uninstalled), but new applications (if loaded in the future) cannot store information here. Windows Installer will stop populating the baseline cache for new updates. The existing cached files will remain on disk and will be deleted when the product is removed.

Setting the baseline cache to 100 means "Use as much space as you need!"

By default, 10 percent of the hard drive is used for this purpose. Disabling this policy setting forces the value at 10 percent.

This setting is valid only on machines that have Windows Installer 3.

Prohibit Use of Restart Manager

The Restart Manager is a very, very cool new addition to Windows Installer 4. The idea is that applications can basically save their currently open files, get upgraded, and then present the saved document in the newly upgraded program. I saw a demo of this and it blew my socks off. This policy setting controls the Restart Manager. Why you would want to turn this neat thing off is a mystery to me; so leave it on unless instructed not to.

This setting is valid only on machines that have Windows Installer 4 (like Windows Vista, which has it installed by default).

User Side Policy Settings for Windows Installer

To display the Group Policy settings that affect the Windows Installer, as shown in Figure 11.32, choose User Configuration ➢ Administrative Templates ➢ Windows Components ➢ Windows Installer. These settings affect the behavior of the users in the scope.

One for the Road—Leave Windows Installer and Group Policy Software Installation Data

Back in Chapter 9, we discussed a specific problem with regard to GPSI and roaming user profiles. That is, if you chose to enable the **Delete Cached Copies of Roaming Profiles** policy setting, the machine "cleans up" as a user logs off.

This has an unintended consequence with regard to GPSI.

Specifically, if the Roaming Profiles data is deleted at logoff time, the information regarding applications deployed via Group Policy Software Installation is also lost (by default). To that end, you should enable a new policy that affects users on Windows XP/SP2 (or Windows 2003/SP1) called **Leave Windows Installer and Group Policy Software Installation Data**, which addresses this. Once enabled, the Group Policy Software Installation data remains on the hard drive, so subsequent logins for users are much faster.

Again, enable this setting if you're also choosing to wipe the Roaming Profile away when the user logs out. Note that it is not a Windows Installer setting, per se, so it's located in a different area. Specifically, you'll find the policy you need at Administrative Templates ➢ System ➢ User Profiles ➢ **Leave Windows Installer and Group Policy Software Installation Data**.

If you're interested, this problem is specifically discussed in MS KB 828452 "An Assigned Package Is Reinstalled Every Time Clients Log on to the Domain."

FIGURE 11.32 The Windows Installer user settings

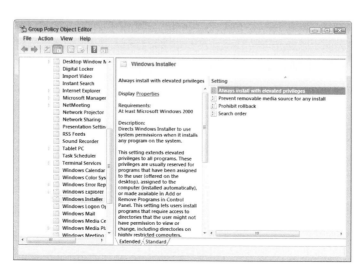

Always Install with Elevated Privileges

Enabling this policy setting allows users to manually install their own .MSI files and bypass their own insufficient and lowly user rights in order to correctly install applications. Some applications install correctly in the users' context, but many don't.

After you enable this setting, you'll also need to set the corresponding setting in the Computer half, as noted in the "Computer Side Policy Settings for Windows Installer" section.

Search Order

By default, applications that are Published or Assigned using the Windows Installer search their original location for updates or repairs. If that original location is not available, the application tries other locations.

This policy setting allows you to specify any or all of the following locations: Network, removable media, or URL (website).

Prohibit Rollback

See the **Prohibit Rollback** policy setting in the "Computer Side Policy Settings for Windows Installer" section.

This setting is found in both User Configuration and Computer Configuration. Recall that computer settings have precedence over user settings.

Prevent Removable Media Source for Any Install

If you enable this setting, which works only for .MSI application, users cannot install applications under their own context from removable media. Rather, only administrators can install applications, or applications must be Published or Assigned for users to use them. This prevents users from running down to the computer store, obtaining the latest version of a program, and installing it via CD.

GPO Targeting with WMI Filters

In Chapter 2, I alluded to a power called WMI filters. I like to think of WMI filters as adding laser-sighting to the gun of Group Policy. With WMI filters, you can dive into and inspect the soul of your client machines, and if certain criteria are met, you can then apply the GPO to them.

You might be asking yourself why I waited so long to talk about WMI filters and, why, of all places, am I talking about WMI filters in the GPSI chapter? Because, although WMI filters can be used on any GPOs in your Active Directory, I'm predicting you'll usually use them for targeting GPSI when you use Group Policy.

Before we jump headlong into ferreting out the power of WMI filters, let's make sure we have the machinery necessary to wield this power:

- The domain is a Windows 2003 domain or a Windows 2000 domain with an updated Windows 2003 schema. You update a Windows 2000 Active Directory domain's schema to the Windows 2003 domain schema via the command prompt. This is performed via the command ADPREP /Domainprep.

- Your target clients are Windows XP, Windows Vista, or Windows 2003 clients.

Windows 2000 clients ignore WMI filters; for Windows 2000 clients, the GPO is always applied—regardless of the evaluation of the WMI filter.

WMI is a huge animal, and you can choose to filter on thousands of items. Hot items to filter on typically include the following:

- The amount of memory
- The available hard-drive space
- CPU speed
- A hotfix

But you don't have to stop there. You can get creative and filter GPOs on obscure items (if they exist and are supported by the hardware) such as the following:

- BIOS revision
- Manufacturer of the CD drive
- Whether a UPS is connected
- The rotational speed of the fan

The potential esoteric criteria you can query for, and then filter on, goes on and on. If this example, I'll limit our Office 2007 distribution to client machines that have at least 128MB or more memory. To do this, we'll first need some tools to help us figure out which pieces of WMI to query. We'll then take what we've learned and use the GPMC to create a WMI filter to specifically target the systems we want.

Unfortunately, I don't have room to dive into how or why WMI works on a molecular level. If you're unfamiliar with WMI, take a peek at www.microsoft.com/whdc/system/pnppwr/wmi/default.mspx and other documentation at www.dtmf.org.

Tools (and References) of the WMI Trade

To master WMI, you have to do a lot of work. You'll have to read up on and master four crucial key pieces of WMI documentation, which are found at the following websites:

- http://msdn.microsoft.com/library/default.asp?url=/library/en-us/dnclinic/html/scripting06112002.asp (shortened to http://tinyurl.com/1sok)
- http://msdn.microsoft.com/library/default.asp?url=/library/en-us/dnclinic/html/scripting08132002.asp (shortened to http://tinyurl.com/6berp)
- http://msdn.microsoft.com/library/default.asp?url=/library/en-us/dnclinic/html/scripting01142003.asp (shortened to http://tinyurl.com/b9nxp)

And you'll have to get the accompanying "Windows 2000 Scripting Guide" from Microsoft—the de facto (and very large-o) book on scripting—and work through all the hundreds of examples (at Amazon at http://tinyurl.com/7yypc).

What? You don't have time for that? No problem! You can do the next best thing and "wing it." We'll use two tools to create WMI queries, and then we'll manually bend them into WMI filters.

- WMI CIM Studio is available on Microsoft's website. At last check, it was at `www` `.microsoft.com/downloads/release.asp?releaseid=40804` (shortened to `http://` `tinyurl.com/8zot`).

- The WMI Scriptomatic version 1 tool is also available from Microsoft. At last check, it was at `www.microsoft.com/technet/scriptcenter/tools/wmimatic.mspx` (shortened to `http://tinyurl.com/cmcdl`).

- And there's also available the Scriptomatic version 2 tool available at `http://tinyurl` `.com/5wdup`.

My choice is to use one of the two Scriptomatic tools, made by my pals the "Microsoft Scripting Guys." Both versions of the Scriptomatic tool basically do the same thing. That is, they zip through all the available WMI classes and then make them available for an easy-breezy query.

In Figure 11.33, the WMI class `Win32_PhysicalMemory` is selected. Then, scriptomagically, all the WMI attributes in that class are exposed in a ready-to-run VBScript application. You can see them in Figure 11.33, including `FormFactor`, `HotSwappable`, and the one we're after, `Capacity`. Just click the Run button and you can see the output with the values on *this* machine.

FIGURE 11.33   The Scriptomatic 2 tool from the "Microsoft Scripting Guys"

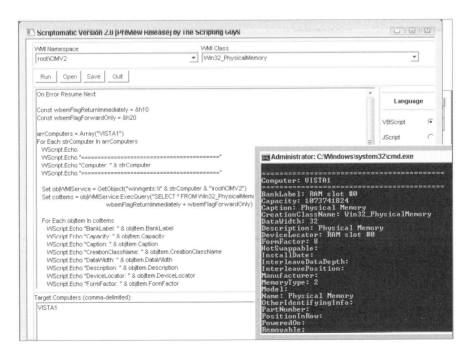

When you click Run, the script runs in a little prompt window. You can see that the `TotalPhysicalMemory` of this box is 1073741824, which is 1GB. The point here, however, is that the unit measurement and expected output of this field is expressed in thousands of bytes. We'll leverage this information when we bend this WMI query into a WMI filter.

WMI Filter Syntax

You can start nearly all the WMI filters you'll create using Scriptomatic. All that's left is to wrap a little logic around the output. All the WMI filters we'll create have the following syntax:

```
SELECT * from Win32_{something} WHERE {variable} [=,>,<,is, etc] {desired result}
```

Now, all we have to do is plug in the stuff we already know, and we're off and running. In this example, we're using `Win32_PhysicalMemory`. We know the variable we want is *Capacity*, and we know that we want it to be greater than 128MB, which we can represent as > 128000. Yes, I know 128000 isn't exactly 128MB of memory, but it's close enough. Anyway, when you put it all together, you get:

```
SELECT * from Win32_PhysicalMemory WHERE Capacity > 128000
```

Easy as pie. However, not all WMI filters are this easy. Some WMI variable entries have text, and you must use quotes to specifically match what's inside the string to what's inside the WMI variable.

Creating and Using a WMI Filter

Once your WMI filter is in the correct syntax, you're ready to inject it into an existing GPO for filtering. Again, this can be any GPO you want—not just GPOs that control GPSI. Again, we're using GPSI as an example because I think you'll get the most use of it this way. Creating and using a WMI filter is a two-step process: creating and then using. (I guess that makes sense.)

WMI Filter Creation

Before you can filter a specific GPO, you need to define the filter in Active Directory. Follow these steps:

1. Fire up the GPMC, then drill down to Forest ➤ Domain ➤ WMI Filters node.

2. Right-click the WMI Filters node and select New as seen in Figure 11.34.

3. When you do, you'll be presented with the New WMI Filter dialog box as seen in Figure 11.35. You'll be able to type in a name and description of your new filter. Then, click the Add button, and in the Query field, just enter in the full SELECT statement from before.

4. When done, click Save. Your query is now saved into Active Directory and can be leveraged for any GPO you want. We'll explore how to do that next.

FIGURE 11.34 Right-click the WMI Filters node to create a WMI filter

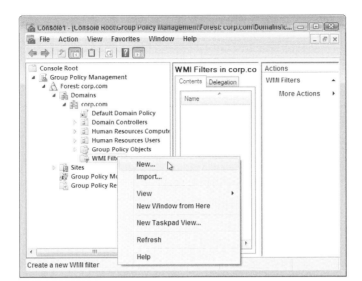

FIGURE 11.35 Enter in a name and description, then click the Add button to enter in your WMI filter.

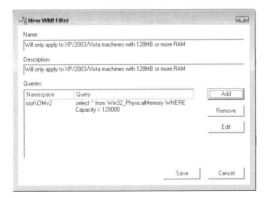

WMI Filter Usage

Using the GPMC, it's easy to find the GPO you want and then leverage the WMI filter you just made. Follow these steps:

1. Locate the "Deploy Office XP (to computers)" GPO you created (which should be within the **Human Resources Computers** OU).

2. Click the Scope tab of the GPO.

3. In the WMI Filtering section, select the WMI filter you just created, as shown in Figure 11.36.

4. At the prompt, confirm your selection.

FIGURE 11.36   Choose the GPO (or GPO link) and select a WMI filter.

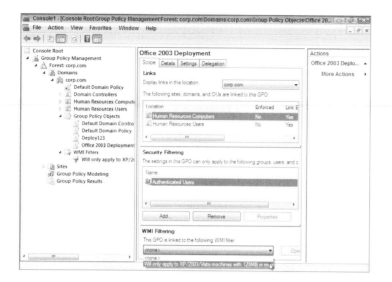

Now this GPO applies to Windows XP, Windows 2003, and Windows Vista computers with 128MB of RAM or more. Windows 2000 machines simply ignore WMI filters, and this GPO still applies to them.

Final WMI Filter Thoughts

WMI filters can be a bit tough to create, but they're worth it. You can filter target machines that meet specific criteria for GPOs that leverage GPSI or any other Group Policy function. But keep two things in mind.

WMI Performance Impact   WMI filters take some percentage of performance away each and every time Group Policy processing is evaluated. That is, at every logon, at startup, and every 90 minutes thereafter, you'll take a little performance hit because WMI filters are re-evaluated. So, if you link a GPO to the domain that leverages WMI filters, every single Windows Vista, Windows XP, and Windows 2003 machine works hard to evaluate that WMI query. The upshot: be careful where you link GPOs with WMI queries. You could seriously affect GPO processing performance. You'll definitely want to test your WMI filters first in the lab for performance metrics before you roll them out companywide.

WMI Filters Don't Apply to Windows 2000   Windows 2000 machines are left out of the mix. They simply ignore the WMI filters placed on GPOs. When a Windows 2000 machine processes a GPO that leverages a WMI filter, it's as if the query always evaluates to "True." However, with a little downloadable magic, you can hack Windows 2000 machines to play in the WMI filter game. A free, quasi-supported download, called "WMI Filtering for Windows 2000," is available at www.mml.ru/WMIF2K/, and it can inject the necessary code to support WMI filters. It's a little unwieldy to set up, but afterward you should be able to have a unified WMI scheme across your environment. Darren Mar-Elia, the Technical Editor for this edition adds: "While this solution is 'neat' it's pretty hokey—basically adding users and computers to groups on the fly. Not only is it kind of scary but, of course, also requires reboots or relogons to pick up new tokens." In short, use at your own risk.

 Return to Chapter 2 some time when you can review how to back up and restore WMI filters as well as how to delegate their creation and use. Also, don't forget about Chapter 8, which also discusses how to script the backup and restore of WMI filters.

Do You Need a "Big" Management Tool for Your Environment?

Microsoft's *SMS*, or *Systems Management Server*, is a component in the Windows Server System. Recently, SMS 2003 R2 was released, and it is steadily gaining more robustness than its older SMS 2 cousin. The next iteration will not be called SMS 4, but rather, System Center Configuration Manager 2007, or SCCM 2007 for short. However, because I'm an "old school" kind of guy, I'll just call it SMS in this brief discussion.

SMS costs an arm and a leg, has a thoroughly esoteric licensing scheme, and requires a client component on every Windows PC and server on your network. But, if you can get over these drawbacks, it houses a pretty amazing collection of core features:

- Software and Hardware Inventory
- Remote Control
- Software Metering
- Software Deployment
- Patch Management

Most of these features would be a welcome addition to any managed environment.

There are, of course, other management systems that don't ship from Microsoft. Companies like Altiris and LanDesk make their living selling similar tools. These all have one thing in common: more moving parts on your client and usually additional servers and components to move things around. They get the moniker of "Enterprise Management Systems" because they scale pretty well.

But what's also true about these tools is that they don't, fundamentally, use the Group Policy infrastructure that's already there. In other words, the "moving parts" to Group Policy are already installed on every client computer.

So, the question often comes up—do I need a "big" management tool if I'm already using Group Policy? To answer this question, we'll do a brief head-to-head comparison with, say, Microsoft SMS versus Standard Group Policy. However, when available, I'll also mention some third-party tools which hook right into Group Policy—leveraging the "moving parts" you already have deployed.

SMS vs. GPOs: A Comparison Rundown

Each feature of SMS is meant to chip away at that golden nugget of Total Cost of Ownership. I often get asked which has more power, SMS or GPSI. Let's take a look at how SMS stacks up against the stuff we get in the box, that is, all the stuff we've looked at thus far.

Hardware and Software Inventory

Hardware inventory and software inventory are two critical elements that administrators need to keep in touch with what's currently out there in their environment. With this information in hand, they can reign in rogue installations of software and hardware.

Without SMS, once software is added via GPSI (or by hand or otherwise), there is no native way, using just Active Directory with GPSI, to really know who has installed what software. Although using GPSI to set up an OU, a package, and an Assignment is a "pretty good" yardstick for measuring what's out there, you're never certain until an actual inventory of the machine is performed.

No hardware or software inventory is built in to Windows. You could build your own WMI scripts to pull out the hardware and software inventory data you want, but, in doing so you'd go insane. So installing SMS would seem like a slam dunk.

It should be noted, though that a nice pay tool is available that hooks in to Group Policy to do this function. It's called Specops Inventory (`www.specopssoft.com`). So, if you wanted to do this function with Group Policy, it's now, basically, an even playing field. And, it can be argued that Hardware and Software Inventory is the most popular part of SMS, and it's not available a la carte: you have to buy the entirety of SMS to get this most requested feature. With a product like Specops Inventory, you're able to just buy the functionality you need.

Remote Control

The Remote Control feature is Microsoft's version of Symantec's pcAnywhere, but it is extremely lightweight and takes up nearly no disk space. However, it could be argued that having a program such as SMS that specifically contains Remote Control is becoming less important. You can implement remote control "on the cheap" with various other options. In Windows 2000, you can use Netmeeting, which is workable, if not optimal. Or you can use the 100 percent–free multiplatform VNC from `www.realvnc.com`.

Additionally, Windows XP and Windows Vista have quite decent remote control built in via its Remote Assistance facilities. Oh, and Terminal Services has its own version of Remote Control called "shadowing."

So, although Remote Control is a great feature, it isn't as important as it used to be. So, who wins in this category? SMS or "In the Box"? It's a tie.

Software Metering

The Software Metering component has two methods of operation: Lock Out and Log Only.

Lock Out   This method (only available in SMS 2 and dropped from SMS 2003) is for strict license compliance. With this option, you can lock out users from applications if the number of licenses dries up across the environment. For example, if you purchased only 25 copies of DogFood Maker 4.5, the 26th person cannot run it.

Log Only This version doesn't lock users out of applications; rather, it simply logs the amount of copies in use. This is useful for gauging licensing compliance but not quite as intensive as the Lock Out method.

Without SMS, there is no way to gauge who's using what or to force users into compliance. Winner: SMS (if you really need this feature at all).

Software Deployment

The Software Deployment feature does overlap with the Active Directory IntelliMirror feature of GPSI. As we explored in this chapter, Group Policy has a decent set of features when it comes to deploying software to clients.

In the first edition of this book, I said that "SMS's Software Deployment features trounce the built-in features of Active Directory." I don't know if I would still agree with that. SMS does have quite a robust deployment mechanism, and one reason is that it can leverage the WMI query data to target to machines' CPU speeds, amount of RAM, BIOS revision, and so on. But we just did the same thing several pages ago with our Windows XP clients, so GPSI is certainly catching up!

Several facets of SMS software deployment are better than the GPSI. Specifically, SMS can do the following that GPSI cannot:

- Deploy software to users or computers any time of the day or night—not just on logon or reboot.

- Compress the application and send it to a distribution point close to the user. Even if we set up GPSI with DFS, we cannot do this.

- Target software to all Windows 32-bit platforms, including Windows 9*x*, Windows NT, and Windows 2000 clients and servers. GPSI works only with Active Directory and Windows 2000, Windows XP, and Windows 2003 clients.

- Once a machine is targeted for a delivery and the package is received, the machine can send back detailed status messages describing success or failure of the transaction.

- Dribble the applications to clients over slow links without slowing down the connection. Only when the software is fully downloaded is the install initiated.

- Get detailed, central logs about which users or computers did or did not get the package.

So, against Group Policy alone, SMS wins in this category. However, with a little elbow grease you can really get an amazing amount of mileage out of GPSI—even in really big environments. The big hit Group Policy takes in GPSI seems to be that the Office 2007 team really suggests that you don't use it for deploying their app. Again, for the gory details here, see the sidebar entitled "Installing and Customizing Office 2007 via GPSI."

However, those guys at Specops Software have another product which competes here, and, you guessed it—it hooks right in to Group Policy. It's called Specops Deploy (www .specopssoft.com). And it overcomes some of the thorniest problems that Group Policy out the box cannot solve. Specifically Specops Deploy can:

- Deploy .MSIs and .EXEs to client computers or users (where normal GPSI only targets .MSIs)

- Target based on time of day

- Deploy applications without requiring a reboot
- Use the "BITS" protocol to dribble applications to clients over slow links
- Give you detailed reports about which machines and users received the software and which ones don't

So, SMS versus "naked" Group Policy, SMS wins.

But add a moderately priced third-party tool which hooks directly in to Group Policy, and it's a much closer horse race.

Patch Management

SMS also has decent patch management support, which is really just a customized extension of its Software Deployment feature. It's really, really good. You can target specific machines with specific patches. Once the patches are received, you can dictate how to react: wait for reboot, reboot now, and so on.

However, Microsoft has just released Windows Server Update Services (WSUS), found here: `www.microsoft.com/windowsserversystem/updateservices/default.mspx`. The old way was to use SUS to do the patch management, but it had some major drawbacks. That is, SUS can't target specific machines with specific patches; rather, all machines that use the SUS server get the same packages.

However, now that WSUS is available, the major drawbacks are basically gone. You can dictate specific patches for specific machines—all in a very slick interface.

Winner? SMS, by some margin. But WSUS 3 is on the way, and who knows.

GPSI and SMS Coexistence

So, who wins?

If we're talking about SMS versus "naked" Group Policy, then, yes, I'm forced to admit it—SMS does have more raw power. However, I would argue that with a little finesse, you can squeeze quite a lot out of the IntelliMirror tools you have come to learn about with Group Policy. And, add a third-party tool or two to Group Policy and you've got some serious competition—with a very lightweight back-end infrastructure.

Some organizations use either GPSI or a "big" management tool for software deployment. And some shops use both. Although no two organizations ever do anything exactly the same way, there does seem to be a general trend in those places where SMS and GPSI coexist.

First, SMS is generally used in heterogeneous environments—that is, where there's a mix of Windows 2000 and non–Windows 2000 workstations and servers. Because GPSI works only with Active Directory and Windows 2000, Windows XP, and Windows 2003 clients, SMS makes sense in these cases.

If whether to use GPSI or SMS is a toss-up, GPSI is generally used to deploy smaller applications that need to be rapidly fired off due to document invocation. For example, if a user is sent an Adobe Acrobat PDF file via e-mail but doesn't have the reader, double-clicking the document automatically installs the application on the machine.

SMS, on the other hand, is typically used to deploy larger applications, such as the Office suite, when you need definitive feedback about what went wrong (if anything). This philosophy provides a good balance between the "on demand" feel of GPSI and the "strategic targeted deployment" feel of SMS.

As you've seen, most of the features do not overlap, making a bigger management tool, like an SMS a solid addition to any medium or large environment. However, before you invest in a bigger management tool, be sure to check out the kinds of add-ons available which hook directly in to Group Policy which can match the feature set. And, again, you can get those features "a la carte" instead of "all in one" as only available in a bigger management tool.

Final Thoughts

In this chapter we inspected Software Installation using Group Policy, or just GPSI for short. GPSI works with Active Directory and Windows clients. Use Microsoft SMS (or another tool) for non–Windows 2000, Windows 2003, and Windows XP clients. Use WSUS for patch management because patches to Windows are not deployable using GPSI.

In order to make the most of GPSI, you really need to leverage .MSI applications. You can either get .MSI applications from your software vendor, or wrap up your own with third-party tools (listed in this chapter and also in the Appendix and "Third-Party Group Policy Tools" on this book's website).

Share a folder on a server you want to send the package from. Plop the application in its own subfolder, and use both share and NTFS permissions to crank down who can read the executables and install files. Remember, though, that not all .MSI applications are ready to be deployed. Some are, indeed, ready-to-go (like the .NET Framework, or Office 2007), others require an Administrative Installation (like Office 2003), and still others ship as .MSI files but cannot be deployed via GPSI (such as older versions of Adobe Acrobat Writer).

Once you have your package, you can Assign or Publish your applications.

Assign applications when you want application icons to appear on the Start ➤ All Programs menu; Publish applications when you want users to dive into the "Add or Remove Programs" folder or "Install a program from the network" for Windows Vista to get the application. You can leverage Microsoft Transform files (.MST files) to hone an .MSI and customize it. (Though do note that Office 2007 doesn't use .MST files.) You can patch existing .MSI applications with Microsoft Patch Files (.MSP files) but afterward, you need to redeploy the application.

Try not to orphan applications by removing the GPO before the target computer gets the "signal" upon the next reboot (for computer) or logon (for user). If you think you might end up doing this, it's best to ensure that the "Uninstall this application when it falls out of the scope of management" check box is checked, as seen in Figure 11.15.

WMI filters are used to change the scope of management for when a GPO will apply. You can use WMI filters for any GPO you create—not just ones that leverage GPSI. However, the most common use for WMI filters is usually for GPOs that leverage GPSI. Don't forget that Windows 2000 clients don't honor WMI filters. Additionally, Windows XP and Windows 2003 clients set to evaluate a WMI filter will take some extra processing time for each filter they need to work through. Be sure to test all your WMI filters in the test lab first.

Additionally, Darren Mar-Elia, on his GPOguy.com website has a nice WMI tester tool available at `www.gpoguy.com/WMIFTest.htm` which you should check out.

He's also got a free tool called GPSIViewer that provides a nifty list view of all deployed applications in a domain and has some printout and `.CSV` reporting capability as well. Check it out at `www.gpoguy.com/gpsiviewer.htm`.

12

More to Love: Deploying Printers, Shadow Copies, and Using Windows Deployment Services

Technically, this book is over. You could put it down right now and feel that you've explored and conquered every major Group Policy and managed desktop function and that you've got the bulk of the managed desktop in gear. We started with Roaming Profiles and then moved on to Redirected Folders, Offline Folders, and Disk Quotas. We technically wrapped up what used to be known as the IntelliMirror functions with Software Distribution in the previous chapter. If you take a look back at Chapter 10, Figure 10.1, you'll see just how far we've come in our journey.

All these desktop management technologies are terrific, and they chip away at the TCO (Total Cost of Ownership) by preventing administrators from having to run out to a workstation to make a specific tweak or configuration changes or to fix something when users hop from machine to machine. Implementing a managed desktop can help when it comes to a user needing to be sure their user data and applications stay with them. But there are several unanswered questions:

- What happens if a user overwrites a key file (or deletes it)?

- What happens if the machine (usually a laptop) goes belly-up, catches fire, or gets stolen?

We spent the last several chapters ensuring that our critical data is safely stored on the server. But how can we further protect our users from disaster? Actually, more realistically, how can we protect our users from themselves?

To answer these questions, we'll investigate two more features: Shadow Copies and Windows Deployment Services. The Shadow Copies feature helps users restore data by themselves, without requiring us to grab the restore tapes. I mean, part of the whole idea of implementing the functions of Group Policy to make a managed desktop is all about data protection, and that's some of what we'll tackle here.

The last major feature, as seen in Figure 10.1, is under the broader heading of Change and Configuration Management. That feature is Windows Deployment Services (WDS). After a crash or other loss, you can get the PC back up and running with WDS. Then, all the data protection features we've implemented spring into action and return the user's configuration to exactly where they left off. Why? Because all the goodies are really just being brought down from the network!

Presto!

 If you had previous editions of this book, you'll note I talked about Remote Installation Services, or RIS. RIS is being deprecated for WDS. However, if you have an existing RIS server with existing RIS images, you might want to make special note of the section "Converting Existing RIS Images to WDS Images (or, Capturing Windows XP Machines for WDS Deployment)" so you can get a feel for how to leverage your existing RIS servers in today's WDS world.

Before we go all "doom and gloom" with backup and recovery, however, I want to explore a "fun" Group Policy feature that I'm sure you'll love. Because I simply cannot resist, I'll show you how to zap printers down to your users using Group Policy. C'mon—you know you want to!

So, in this chapter, I want you to implement a "holistic medicine practice" for your Windows environment. You'll implement features that ensure your user's safety and productivity. And a little Zen.

Assigning Printers via Group Policy

Let me guess what one of your biggest headaches is.

Printers.

Earlier in the book (Chapter 3, in the sidebar entitled "Setting All Who Log on to a Specific Computer to Use a Specific Printer"), we leveraged a Group Policy trick, called loopback policy, to take a script which assigns printers and ensure that all users who log on to a specific machine get a specific set of printers.

That's all super-cool. Except it forces the computer to be in Loopback mode, which might not be desirable. Remember—Loopback mode makes the computer process all user-side GPOs as well as computer-side GPOs.

So, wouldn't it be great if we could just zap printers down to our Windows 2000, Windows XP, and Windows Vista client machines? Or, whenever Sally roams from Desktop to Desktop, she got the same printers? That's two different goals and what we're about to approach here.

Before we get too far along, let me express how the goal is the same: deploying printers to our Windows 2000, Windows XP, and Windows Vista clients. However, the underlying bits and pieces of just how we get there is a little bit different. We'll see in a bit how we need to "shim" the Windows 2000 and Windows XP clients by using a specific executable in the login script, but how Windows Vista just has this functionality built in. Stay tuned, you're about to learn all about it.

Updating Our Schema (to at Least Level 31)

To zap printers down to our Windows XP and Windows Vista machines, we need to first update the Active Directory schema. You'll recall that in Chapter 7 we also had to update our Active Directory schema, but that was to support the new Windows Vista wireless policy.

Updating the schema is likely the hardest part of the job, because you'll need approval from your Active Directory bigwigs that this is an okay procedure to do. Once you have approval, this operation is best performed directly upon the Schema Master Domain Controller in your domain.

The reason for the schema upgrade is that our printer connection objects get a new "fast query" lookup via LDAP in Active Directory. This way, tools like Windows Server 2003/R2's Print Management Console (which we really won't be going into here) don't have to inspect every GPO in the domain to figure out where printers are currently deployed.

In short, you need to run the command `adprep /forestprep`, which is located in the Windows Vista DVD in the `\cmpnents\r2\adprep` directory. You can see this in Figure 12.1.

FIGURE 12.1   In order to get the ability to zap printers down to your users, you need to extend the schema with the Windows Server 2003/R2 schema.

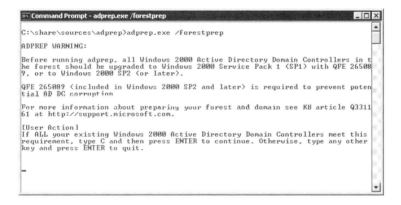

Zap Printers Down from Your (Vista) Management Station

Once again, leveraging a Windows Vista management station will save you time. You can do all the magic we're about to explore from, say, a Windows Server 2003 server or a Windows XP management station. But that requires extra components which I don't really want to explore here. (For a full rundown of these components, check out an article I wrote about these new print management features available at Microsoft Technet Magazine at `http://tinyurl.com/ymawtq`.)

From here, we'll assume you want to test drive this on your Windows Vista management station. We'll also assume you have a test printer connected on a server somewhere. You can follow along by running through the Add Printer Wizard on Windows Server 2003 and sharing out a (fake) printer if you like.

To zap a printer down to your users or computers, you start out by creating a GPO and linking it to an OU containing either users or computers. Say, the Human Resources OU.

You can see where to zap printers down in the two "Deployed Printers" nodes in the Group Policy Object Editor. One is under Computer Configuration ➢ Windows Settings ➢ Deployed Printers and the other is under User Configuration ➢ Windows Settings ➢ Deployed Printers.

Once you select User Configuration ➢ Deployed Printers ➢ Deploy Printers (as seen in Figure 12.2) or Computer Configuration ➢ Deployed Printers ➢ Deploy Printers, you'll be ready to blast new printer assignments down. Just type **\\server\printer** into the "Enter printer name" dialog, click Add, and you're done.

Now, if you didn't actually upgrade the schema, you'll see what's seen in Figure 12.2. That is the "Connection Status" field will say "Addition failed."

But, if the schema was successfully upgraded, you'll see what's shown in Figure 12.3.

FIGURE 12.2 If you didn't upgrade the schema and try to zap a printer down, you'll get an "Addition failed" message.

FIGURE 12.3 If the schema was upgraded properly, there is no Connection Status information.

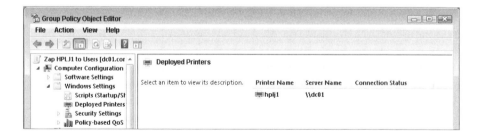

Verifying Printer Assignment on a Windows Vista and Windows XP Target

If you have all Windows Vista client machines, you're done. If you wait until Group Policy refreshes, you'll see the printer just pop into place, as in Figure 12.4. Just logoff and back on (for users) or reboot (for computers) and like magic, you'll have printers assigned.

FIGURE 12.4   Group Policy will naturally just pop this printer into place.

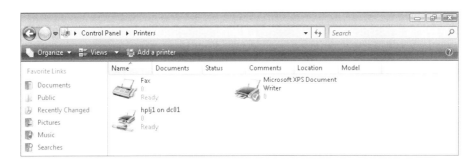

However, if you try this on a Windows XP machine, you won't see this work. That's because Windows Vista has a CSE (Client-Side Extension) which does the work. Windows XP doesn't have this CSE, and, hence, won't do it—automatically. To do this, we need a little "helper" application.

Adding PushPrinterConnections to the GPO

To make Windows XP (and Windows 2000 for that matter) "wake up and smell the printers" you need to have it run a little program. This trick is done through an executable program that you have to kick off via a Login script (for printers assigned to users) or Startup script (for printers assigned to computers).

The "moving part" to make the printer assignment work on Windows XP and Windows 2000 is a little .EXE called pushprinterconnections.exe. Here's the bad news (so brace yourself). This little .EXE is only available if you own a copy of Windows Server 2003/R2. If you own one copy, you can use it in your domain. If you don't own Windows Server 2003/R2, you cannot download this little executable anywhere else.

You'll find the pushprinterconnections.exe on your R2 server in the \windows\PMCSnap directory along with some other bits associated with the Print Management Console. Once you've located pushprinterconnections.exe from a Windows Server 2003/R2 server, here's the use:

- If you're deploying printers to users, the .EXE needs to be run in the user's Login Script.

- If you're deploying printers to computers, it needs to be run in the computer's Startup Script.

  Here are the rough steps to do this (as seen in Figure 12.5):

1. While editing the GPO, drill down to the script type (User Login or Computer Startup).

2. Click the Show Files button.

3. Copy the pushprinterconnections.exe into the window that opens up.

4. Back at the properties of the script, click Add and locate and select the pushprinterconnections.exe file.

5. Optionally, you can enter **-log** in the "Script Parameters" field to start a log file on the Windows XP or Windows 2000 client.

6. Click OK.

FIGURE 12.5 Add in pushprinterconnections.exe as part of the Logon Script for this user (or Startup Script for this computer).

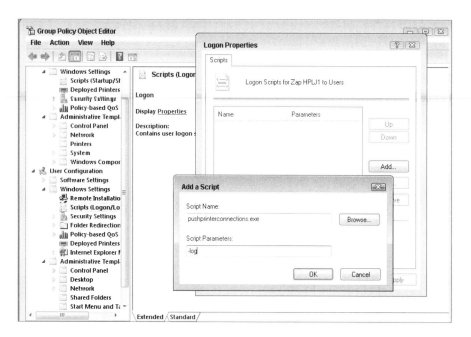

The key point is that the location where it starts out isn't the location where you need to run it from. Your job is to take the file and plunk it directly into the GPO itself.

Optionally, you can put the pushprinterconnections.exe program in a shared place that everyone can get to.

A troubleshooting log file is generated with a -log typed in the Script Parameters box. A per-user debug log file will be written to %temp%. A per-machine debug log will be written to %windir%\temp. (Note that these are totally different directories.)

It's worth noting that you shouldn't use the -log parameter in a production environment—you wouldn't want the utility filling up your client machine hard disks with megabytes of log files.

So what happens if a Windows Vista machine runs pushprinterconnections.exe? Absolutely nothing. The first thing that pushprinterconnections.exe does when you run it is to check if it is running on Windows Vista. If it is running on a Vista machine, the utility exits without doing anything—so network administrators don't have to worry if they accidentally push out the pushprinterconnections.exe utility down to Windows Vista clients.

In other words, you can use the same GPO to assign printers to Windows Vista and Windows XP or Windows 2000 machines.

Verifying Printer Assignment (Again) for Windows XP Machines

If you log in as Frank Rizzo on your Windows XP machine, you should see a printer in the "Printers and Faxes" section of Control Panel.

Note that Windows XP printers won't "change" during background refresh after you're already logged in. That's because the `pushprinterconnections.exe` only runs at login or startup.

Final Thoughts on Zapping Printers

Two more notes about all this printer stuff before we move on:

- Windows 2000 machines only support per-user printer connections.
- Windows Vista, Windows XP, and Windows 2003 support per-user or per-computer printer connections.

Additionally, there are two alternate methods: using the Print Management Console or deploying from a non-Vista management station.

The Print Management Console gives a "one stop shop view" of printers deployed via GPOs. Again, space prevents us from walking through the Print Management Console. However, you can read my full article here: `http://tinyurl.com/ymawtq` or read Microsoft's guide to the Printer Management Console at `http://tinyurl.com/n2pvh`.

Additionally, if for some reason you didn't want to use a Windows Vista management station (and you really should want to) then you could still get access to the Deployed Printers node. Provided you have first updated the schema as previously described, it'll be there—if you take one more step. It will appear as a new node underneath Administrative Templates. However, if you don't see it while editing a GPO on a Windows Server 2003 or Windows XP machine, it's likely that you don't have the updated Adminpak tools on your management station (the computer from which you're editing this GPO). To get the latest tools, get the R2 Adminpak here: `http://tinyurl.com/e9jm4`. This isn't "one big .MSI" like `Adminpak.msi`. Rather, this is a collection of smaller files for specific updated components like the Print Console.

Again, however, you're going to want to use Windows Vista management station whenever possible to deploy those printers.

Shadow Copies (aka Previous Versions)

The idea behind Shadow Copies is awesome: preserve some number of copies of the user's precious files on the server. When the user performs a CLM (Career-Limiting Move) by deleting a file or overwriting a file with data that cannot be undone, they can simply get that file back from a point in time. Microsoft's code name for this feature was "Time Warp," and I think that pretty much says it all.

Technically, the system doesn't precisely store "copies" of a file. Really, this current magic preserves a "point-in-time" copy of a file—not a copy of all the bytes that compose the entire file. Sometimes, this magic is referred to as "Snapshots," though, technically again, it's not a direct bitwise snapshot of the file.

There are two versions of this feature:

- One works when the data is stored on a Windows Server 2003 machine. The clients can be Windows 2000, Windows XP, or Windows Vista.

- The other version is built in locally to Windows Vista. So, if a user whacks a file on the local computer (and it wasn't ever saved on the network), you've still got them covered.

Setting up and Using Shadow Copies for Local Windows Vista Machines

By default, Windows Vista's "System Protection" is enabled. This system allows you to restore to a point-in-time backup if the operating system should have problems. This system existed in Windows XP as well but didn't capture the changes to data files. In Windows Vista, that's changed.

Again, "System Protection" is enabled, so Windows Vista is automatically "doing its thing" and protecting the files. There isn't really anything to "set up." System Protection *restore points* are created once every day and before a new driver is installed. You can also create a manual snapshot from the "System Protection" section of the System applet in Control Panel. Or, disable System Protection altogether. Again, do this at Control Panel ➢ System ➢ System Protection.

When ready to restore a previous version of a file, you'll use the same interface we're about to explore. As you'll see a bit later, it's as simple as right-clicking the file and selecting Previous Versions to get a file back.

Because we only have so much space, we're just going to show the version when files are stored on the server.

Setting Up Shadow Copies on the Server

You must take care of two tasks before the user can use Shadow Copies:

- Set up the Windows 2003 server to start creating these snapshots.

- Deliver the Shadow Copies client piece to the desktops. You need to do this for Windows 2000 and Windows XP (pre-SP2). The Shadow Copies client piece is already integrated into Windows XP/Service Pack 2 and Windows Vista.

So, let's do that now.

Shadow Copies work because you're making a *point-in-time* copy of the users' data files, which preserves them in case of a future calamity. The best place to do this is on the volume to which you've redirected Documents/My Documents. However, first you need to ask yourself several questions:

- How much junk, I mean, data, are my users taking up on each drive on the server?

- How much more space on this drive am I willing to cordon off to preserve previous versions of files?

- How often do I want to take a snapshot to preserve user data?

Once you answer these questions, follow these steps:

1. Right-click a drive letter on a server and choose Properties from the shortcut menu to open the Propcrtics dialog box, as shown in Figure 12.6.

2. Click the Shadow Copies tab, select a drive letter, and click the Settings button to open the Settings dialog box, as shown in Figure 12.7.

FIGURE 12.6　You set the Shadow Copies characteristics on a per-volume basis.

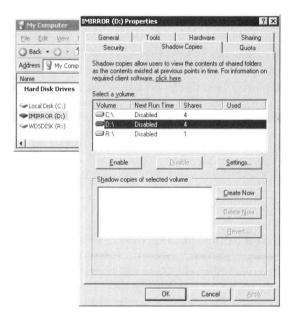

FIGURE 12.7　You can specify how much space to dedicate when files change, set a schedule to make Shadow Copies, and specify where to locate the storage area

Here you can specify how much space you want to set aside for this particular volume. My recommendation is to set aside about 20–30 percent. The point of Shadow Copies isn't to keep backup copies of *all* user files forever; rather, similar to the Offline Caching mechanism, user files that get old will be flushed out of this space to make room for new files. Although Shadow Copies are a great preventive measure, they're not a substitute or replacement for general backups should the file turn out not to be available for restore.

1. In the Use Limit spin box, specify the size, and then click the Schedule button to open up the Schedule tab for the volume.

2. The Schedule tab is pretty self-explanatory. You might just wish to leave the defaults for now. When ready, click OK to confirm a changed schedule, or click Cancel to return to the Settings tab. Click OK or Cancel again to return to the Properties tab.

The default schedule for any enabled volume is at 7:00 a.m. and 12:00 p.m. workdays (Monday through Friday). The idea is that you'll snag points in time of the data before the workday begins and again at the halfway point in the workday. If a user screws up and deletes a file, you've got at least two potentially restorable files from just today! If you have even more space available, you can store days or weeks of restorable data! Set the schedule however you want, but note two things:

- Shadow Copies keep a maximum of 64 previous versions of a file. Every time you take a snapshot, you're *potentially* dumping older files. The default schedule is usually pretty good for most organizations; it's estimated that it should provide about a month's worth of previous versions.

- The server will be hammered for a bit while the Shadow Copy snapshot is being made. Consequently, taking multiple snapshots during the day might not be such a hot idea. Therefore, you might want to perform fewer snapshots, say, once a day.

Delivering Shadow Copies to the Client

Once you set up the server, you're ready to deploy the client piece. If your clients are already using Windows Vista or Windows XP/Service Pack 2, they have got the client piece built in, and you can skip this section.

The good news is that the Shadow Copy client is valid for Windows XP (pre-SP2) and Windows 2000. Although a version of the Shadow Copies client is on the Windows 2003 Server CD, it's better to download the update, which you'll find at www.microsoft.com/windowsserver2003/downloads/shadowcopyclient.mspx.

To do the deployment, simply take what you learned in the previous chapter and use it to your advantage:

- Share the file out on a shared folder or DFS.

- Round up the computers you want to get the Shadow Copy client into an OU.

- Create a GPO, link it to the OU, and then use GPSI to deploy the .MSI file.

Figure 12.8 demonstrates how to assign the application to your Windows 2000 and Windows XP computers.

FIGURE 12.8   You can simply use GPSI to deploy the Shadow Copy client to your Windows 2000 and Windows XP (pre-SP2) machines.

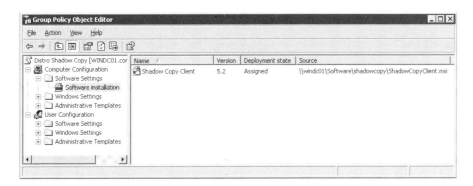

Restoring Files with the Shadow Copies Client

Before you can restore a file, the data must be Shadow Copied at least once, changed, and then Shadow Copied again. This process maintains a point in time of the volume—in its changed state and ready to be reverted to a previous version or restored if it was deleted altogether.

Reverting to a Previous Version of a File

Oftentimes, users inadvertently overwrite their documents with data. As a result, you have now given them the ability to revert to a previous version of the file. To do so, users follow these steps:

1. Open the Documents folder, right-click any file, and choose Properties from the shortcut menu to open the Properties dialog box, as shown in Figure 12.9. And, in Windows Vista, right-clicking a file in most cases will also have a "Restore previous versions" option which goes to the same place.

2. Click the Previous Versions tab.

3. Select the version you want, and then click Open, Copy, or Restore:

   Open (was View pre-Vista)   Clicking Open or View launches the program associated with the file type, and you can view the file. You might be able to make temporary changes in the document, but you cannot save them back to the same place on the server as the original document. You can do a Save As and save the file somewhere else.

   Copy   You can copy the file to an alternate location. A popular location is the Desktop, but any locations that users have access to are equally valid.

   Restore   The title of this button is sort of a misnomer. When I think of the word *Restore*, I think of restoring a deleted file, but the file needn't be fully deleted in order to use this option. Clicking this button will cause the selected file to revert to the previous version. Note, however, that it will overwrite the current version. So, use this Restore button with caution, because any changes in the document since a Shadow Copy was performed are deleted.

FIGURE 12.9   After at least one change is preserved, users can revert to a point-in-time file.

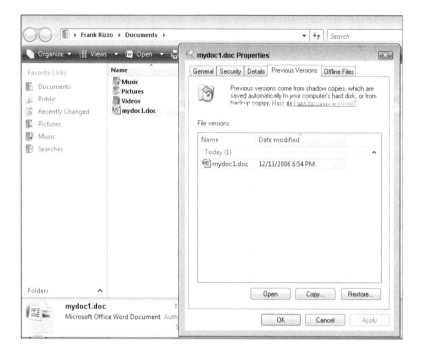

Restoring a Previous Version of a File

If a user actually deletes a copy of a preserved file you or they can restore it. Since we're using Shadow Copies on the volume that houses our redirected My Documents/Documents, we can leverage this magic.

Off the Start Menu, locate My Documents or Documents. Then right-click the user's My Documents folder, choose Properties from the shortcut menu to open the Properties dialog box, and click the Previous Versions tab, as shown in Figure 12.9.

WARNING   This doesn't seem to work if you're already in Windows Vista's *Documents* and then right-click Favorite Links in the left pane and select "Use Previous Versions." Seems like a bug. Seemingly, in Windows Vista this only works when right-clicking directly off the Start Menu.

You'll have the same three options as before: Open, Copy, or Restore. My suggestion is to select View and then drag the file you need to the intended location. Restore is quite dangerous, actually. It will restore the *entire contents of the folder* upon the live copy. This is not a good idea. In Windows XP, it just lets you do this. In Windows Vista, it gets a little smarter and UAC pops up and asks for administrative credentials before restoring the whole shootin' match, as shown in Figure 12.11.

FIGURE 12.10   You can restore the entire contents of the folder, or just use View to drag and drop the file to be restored to an alternate location.

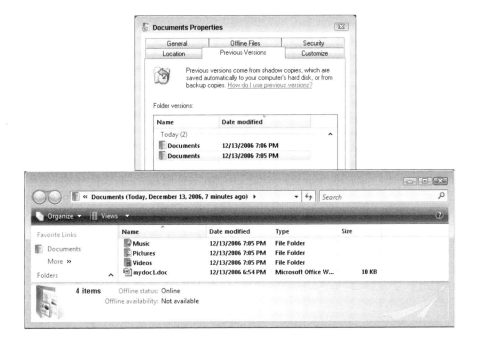

FIGURE 12.11   In Windows Vista, users are prevented from overwriting their entire Documents until admin credentials are provided.

Clicking Copy copies the entirety of the folder to a specific location; this is not all that useful either, as the user might not want to restore the entirety of the point in time of the folder.

Shadow Copies complete the circle of user data protection. Without it, the only data protection (other than normal, regularly scheduled backups) is Offline Files. Offline Files is a good piece of technology, but ultimately not enough if the data on the server is deleted or inadvertently overwritten.

Windows Deployment Services

In the previous section, you set out to protect users' files if they are deleted or overwritten. But what if a user leaves their laptop at the airport? Or the Desktop malfunctions due to a lightning strike? You can leverage Active Directory to help roll out new machines or replacements for old machines using *Windows Deployment Services*, or WDS.

 WDS can also mean "Windows Desktop Search" in other books and papers.

Its goal is to provide the administrator with the ability to roll out any number of Windows XP and Windows Vista (and Windows 2003) configurations in a short amount of time. In a nutshell, you simply prepare your server for WDS, leverage the built-in hardware your client machine already has to connect to the network, answer a few questions, and away the installation goes.

WDS is available in several forms. It will be included with Longhorn Server when ready. But you can get it today. Windows Server 2003/SP2 will upgrade your server so it supports WDS. Windows Server 2003/SP2 can be found here: `www.microsoft.com/technet/windowsserver/sp2.mspx`. You can also get the update for Windows Server 2003/SP1 as part of the Windows Vista Windows Automated Installation Kit (WAIK) here: `http://tinyurl.com/ykoo3x`. (Note: Those are Ohs, not zeros in that URL.)

WDS is the descendant of RIS, Remote Installation Services. Under the hood, they've got some similarities. And, if you're still using RIS, that's okay, WDS will upgrade your existing RIS server so it will just keep on acting like an RIS server. However, we're not going to go into RIS here. If you'd like my take on RIS, you'll have to chase up an older copy of this book (revisions 3 and earlier).

Here, we'll assume you don't have RIS yet installed on your Windows Server 2003 but have just installed Windows Server 2003/SP2 to get the WDS functionality.

After you create your first WDS-based client machine, you can customize it with commercial or homegrown apps and save that configuration to the server as well, making that machine appear as another downloadable "image."

Server Components

Before you can use WDS, you need to make sure several components are present on your network.

DHCP Server The DHCP server is the first place the client machines look to get a temporary TCP/IP address while the system is being installed.

DNS Server DNS server is also required, because not only is it the key ingredient for Active Directory, but, more specifically, it points the clients to servers running WDS.

WDS Server At least one server in your environment needs to be running WDS. We'll set up this service later in the chapter.

Although you can run all these services on just one server, in practice you probably wouldn't want to due to the potential heavy processor and disk load the WDS server will have to shoulder. Most real-world configurations run the DHCP and DNS servers on separate boxes but configure one or more specific servers solely for the purpose of running WDS server and dishing out WDS images. You must also authorize your DHCP server to participate in Active Directory if you want it to dish out any TCP/IP addresses.

For the sake of this learning example, however, you can use one server to run it all: DNS, DHCP, and WDS. In this case, we'll use DC01.

What Does WDS Have that RIS Doesn't?

If you're wondering if you should make the switch from RIS to WDS, the answer is "Yes." But here's a quick rundown of what you'll get when you do:

- Native support for Windows PE as a boot operating system
- Native support for the Windows Imaging (WIM) file format
- An extensible and higher-performing PXE server component
- A new client menu for selecting boot operating systems

We'll get to see these items as we progress during this chapter.

Client Components

Rolling out your workstations via WDS will usually be performed by leveraging the workstations' network cards. To do this, they'll need to be PXE Boot ROM–capable. *PXE (Preboot eXecution Environment)* is a newer architecture type for network cards that lets them pre-execute and talk to the network before the system itself or the hard drive becomes active.

> If you don't have PXE-compatible network cards, you can still likely use WDS. You may boot client machines directly to Windows PE 2 and still "bootstrap" into the WDS process. See the help topics for creating a WDS Client Discover image.

A client can connect to WDS servers in only two ways:

PXE Boot ROM   If your network card actually has the PXE Boot ROM code embedded, you can boot directly to the network. You might need to turn this feature on in the network card's BIOS or in the PC's BIOS—or both.

PXE Boot ROM Floppy   Remember that the specifications state that the network card must be PXE-capable. Some cards, which are technically non–PXE compliant, are still capable but just don't have the boot ROM code itself. Other network cards (such as the older Compaq NetFlex 3 cards) have the PXE boot ROM code, but it's older code so it's incompatible with WDS. Windows 2000 Server or Windows 2003 Server can create a PXE Boot ROM emulator floppy that can kick-start your network card into thinking it actually has a PXE Boot ROM that's up to snuff.

Not all network cards are PXE-capable. Indeed, only a handful are. First, if the card doesn't fit into a PCI slot, it's not PXE-capable—period. Therefore, by definition no ISA (Integrated Systems Architecture) cards are PXE-capable. Next, you can check with the manufacturer to see if the card is indeed PXE-capable. Some cards that are not on the list might also work, but there's certainly no guarantee.

> If your card isn't specifically listed as PXE-compliant, you might still be able to use the boot floppy generator program. Just click the Adapter List button in the RBFG.EXE application (see the section "Creating a Remote Boot Disk," later in this chapter).

The good news is that more and more laptops are WDS-capable. Generally, laptop network cards come in two flavors:

- Built in
- Credit card–style PC Card (or PCMCIA, Personal Computer Memory Card International Association) adaptors

In general, those with the PC Card network adaptors cannot leverage WDS (though I have seen exceptions). However, most laptops that have built-in on-board network cards generally are compatible with WDS. These on-board NICs (network interface cards) are considered "mini-PCI" network cards, and I've seen many of them that are indeed capable of running WDS.

If your laptop is not PXE-capable, you might be able to use a docking station that has a PXE-capable network card. However, don't try to deploy all your laptops with one PXE-capable docking station. WDS machines are registered in Active Directory based on a *globally unique identifier*, or *GUID*. The GUID is either hard-coded or based on the MAC address. If you deploy all your machines with a single docking station, you'll have multiple machines appearing to have the same GUID. Active Directory requires that machines have a GUID to function properly.

> If you're shopping around for new laptops, I recommend that you get only those that have mini-PCI cards that are PXE-capable, and verify that they work with WDS before buying a slew of them.

As a last-ditch effort, you might be able to buy some special boot-ROM software from a company named Argon Technology (`www.argontechnology.com`). The idea is that they have a floppy which can PXE boot cards that otherwise wouldn't be PXE capable.

Setting Up WDS Server

You can easily add the WDS to any Windows Server 2003 installation. (WDS is not available in Windows 2003 Server, Web Edition). In the following examples, I'll add a Windows Vista image for distribution.

Before you set it up, you'll need a decently sized NTFS partition that is *not* the system or boot partition for the WDS components and the WDS images. I'll use drive letter R: for my WDS server components and images, but you can use any drive letter.

> Although you can use a second partition on the same hard disk as your system or boot partition, this results in poor performance of both WDS and the system as a whole. The recommendation is to place the WDS partition on a separate physical disk from that on which Windows resides.

Loading WDS

These steps apply only to Windows Server 2003/SP2. For SP1, you would install RIS, then install the WDS update (noted earlier).

So, if you did not select WDS as an optional component when you created the server, you can load it now. Follow these steps:

1. Choose Start ➢ Control Panel to open Control Panel.

2. Click Add or Remove Programs to open the Add or Remove Programs window.

3. Click Add/Remove Windows Components to start the Windows Components Wizard, as shown in Figure 12.12.

4. In the Components list, scroll down, click the Windows Deployment Services check box, click Next, and then click OK. You'll then be asked to reboot your server.

FIGURE 12.12 Adding the WDS components is easy via Add/Remove Windows Components on a Windows Server 2003/SP2 server

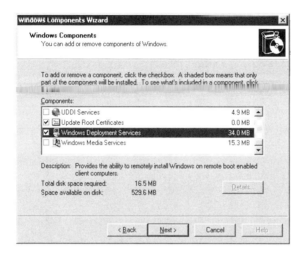

Setting Up the WDS Server

Once WDS is installed and the server is rebooted, you're ready to fire up WDS and get started with initial setup.

1. Choose Start ≻ Program Files ≻ Administrative Tools ≻ Windows Deployment Services. Note that there's a Windows Deployment Services Legacy icon right underneath, which can be used to make WDS act like an RIS server.

2. In the WDS console, right-click Servers and select Add Server. Add in the local server.

3. The new server will appear under Servers but isn't set up yet. Right-click the server and select "Configure server." The first page of the WDS Configuration Wizard appears.

4. Walk through the wizard to answer the questions. Choose a folder on an NTFS volume that is not the system drive. In this example, I'm choosing R:\RemoteInstall. Click Next to open the "DHCP Option 60" screen. Note you'll only see the "DHCP Option 60" screen if you have WDS and Microsoft DHCP on the same machine.

5. The WDS server needs to configure DHCP somewhat differently if the WDS machine is also a DHCP server. If it is, select "Do not listen on port 67" and "Configure DHCP option 60 to 'PXEClient'" when asked.

6. The WDS server must be turned on to accept client connections. For our quick example, click the "Respond to all (known and unknown) client computers." For now, do not select the "For unknown clients, notify administrator and respond after approval."

Clicking the "Do Not Respond to Unknown Client Computers Requesting Service" check box lets you lock down a computer's GUID to a specific WDS server. Make this connection when manually adding a computer to Active Directory Users and Computers by selecting "This Is a Managed Computer" and then entering the computer's GUID. You can find the computer's GUID either in the computer's BIOS or in the MAC address of the network card—it's the 12 zeros padded with 20; for example, 00000000000000000000A309CDE24601.

Installing Your First WDS *Images*

Once your server is initially configured, you need to introduce it to the images you'll want to deploy. Let's first get a grip on the kinds of image files available to us, then we'll go forth and install the image types we need.

Understanding WDS's Image Types

WDS has three types of images.

Boot Image   When your target machine performs a PXE boot to connect to the WDS server, this is what will be run on the client to "get it going." This is a cut-down version of windows called WinPE to help you (stay with me here) load the big version of Windows in the "Install Image" section (coming up next).

Install Image   This is the actual image you'll be downloading to your target machine. You might have an image for Sales, for Marketing, and so on. However, a best practice is to have (get this) just one image which does it all. Note that images can be Vista, Windows XP, or Windows Server 2003. The file format is a little special here, and it's called the .WIM file format. We'll talk more about this a bit later.

Legacy Images   If you want to make your WDS machine at like RIS, this is the place to do it. If you've upgraded an existing RIS server with RIS-style images, they will appear here. Ultimately, you'll want to convert these to the WIM file format. The WDS help file, under the topic "Legacy Images" gives tips for how to do just that.

To use WDS successfully, you will leverage these images. If you're going to use WDS in "native" mode, you'll start out by booting a Boot Image then loading an Install image. If you're going to use WDS in "legacy" mode, you'll leverage Legacy Images only.

Adding the Boot Image

Let's start out by adding the Boot Image first. Again, the Boot Image is a cut-down version of Windows to help you get started with your installation. Right-click the Boot Images node and select Install Image. Then, the Boot Image you'll need is right on the Windows Vista DVD in the \sources directory. Enter the path to the Windows Vista DVD's \sources directory and specify boot.wim as seen in Figure 12.13.

FIGURE 12.13   The boot.wim file gets your clients started with WDS.

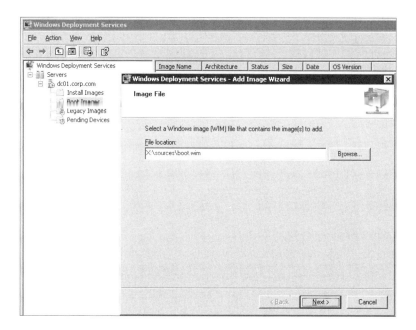

Once you click Next, you'll be able to enter in the Image name. I'm not wild about the default name "Microsoft Windows Longhorn Setup (x86)," so I've changed it to "Vista Boot WIM" so it's much clearer.

Adding the Install Image

Before we install the first image, we need to understand the concept of Image Groups. Image Groups are like folders that contain similar images.

Here's the idea: within an Image Group, all the data is "single instance stored." That means if you have multiple images, and they're very, very similar, you're only saving a copy of the differences. This is huge! Because the differences between the Sales and Marketing images might really only be very small!

The other advantage of Image Groups is that you can lock out who has access to Image Groups. So, you can say that "Server Installers" have access to an Image Group for servers, but "Desktop Installers" have access just to an Image Group for desktops.

For our working examples, we're not going to have more than one image, so, setting up multiple Image Groups isn't necessary.

So, when you right-click Install Images and select "Add Install Image" you'll be prompted for your first Image Group. I'm naming mine VistaGroup, but you can call it anything you like. Then, in the Image File dialog, you're going to point WDS toward the file called `install.wim` in the `\sources` directory of the Windows Vista DVD. When you do, you'll be presented with the List of Available Images as seen in Figure 12.14.

FIGURE 12.14 You can select which versions of Windows Vista you want to put in the Image Group.

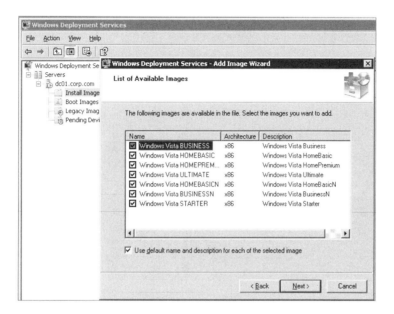

Remember: Because the images in the Image Group are single instance stored, you're not burning 4GB for each Vista image. It's 4GB plus a littttle more for each image you select. So, don't worry about leaving them all (or deselecting those you won't use). In most cases, you'll likely only need Windows Vista Business and Windows Vista Ultimate.

Click Next until the images are added. This could take a while to complete.

Managing the WDS Server

Before you roll out your first client, you might want to tweak WDS. To do this, right-click the server name (dc01.corp.com) inside the WDS management tool and select Properties. Inside, you'll find various tabs.

There is nothing configurable on the General tab. It is information only.

Directory Services

Space prevents us from diving into each option, but the one you'll likely want to explore is "Directory Services," as seen in Figure 12.15, where you can change the computer name of newly born computers as well as where to place newly born computers in Active Directory.

FIGURE 12.15 You can customize some WDS defaults, such as the client's computer name and where to drop it into Active Directory.

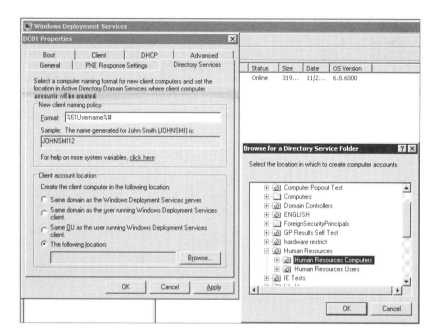

There are certainly lots of other options here as well, including associating unattended installation files to your WDS client installations to make them hands off. Space prevents us from showing how to do this task; it's a rather large (but worthwhile) endeavor. This is done via the Windows System Image Manager (WSIM) tool to create the unattended files. Microsoft docs on the process can be found here: `http://tinyurl.com/y2sdbd`. The tool is found in the Windows Automated Installation Kit download (about 800MB!) and can be found here: `http://go.microsoft.com/fwlink/?LinkID=53552`.

PXE Response Settings

This tab instructs the server how to respond to known and unknown clients. A known computer is one that already has a record in Active Directory. When you create a new computer account in Active Directory, you can pre-stage it using the wizard when creating new computers.

You can also use this tab to help "load balance" servers as described a bit later in the "Setting up a Distributed WDS Infrastructure" section.

Boot

This tab is the PXE program that's downloaded right after you hit F12 for network boot. Under normal circumstances, it is not necessary to change this.

Client

Customizations in this area affect all clients when loading via WDS. You can basically customize the WDS Client installation here.

Jamming Your Own Network Drivers into the *boot.wim*

I do a lot of testing using VMware Workstation and server. It's a great cheap way to emulate a lot of computers quickly. And it's also great for when I need to take screenshots of the boot process. However, when you try to spawn a new Windows Vista machine via WDS, it turns out that the network card that VMware emulates isn't part of the boot.wim (the file that's downloaded before you kick off WDS).

What you need is the WAIK (Windows Automated Install Kit) (http://tinyurl.com/ykoo3x), which can help you "jam in" the VMware network card driver. The tool you'll leverage is the imagex.exe utility, which can "crack into" an existing .WIM file, mount it in the file system, and allow you to put new drivers right into the file. Then, once completed, you can sew it up and use those drivers!

Here are the steps:

1. Install the Windows AIK.

2. Create a new directory on your hard drive. This will be a temporary directory to "mount" the boot.wim file. For this example I will use C:\6000 (the build number for Windows Vista). While you're here, create a subfolder under that called Mount (so the final path is C:\6000\Mount).

3. Copy the boot.wim file from the Windows Vista DVD (in the \sources directory) to the C:\6000 folder.

4. The point is to jam in the network drivers you'll need that WDS doesn't natively support. In my case, I needed the VMware drivers. To get them, leverage an .ISO reading program (such as VCD, Daemon Tools, WinISO, and so on) to mount the "C:\Program Files\VMWare\ VMWare Workstation\Windows.iso" file. You could also grab these files while telling VMware Workstation (or Server) that you want to "Install VMware Tools" from the VM menu. You'll then be able to see these files for copying (and you don't actually have to reinstall VMware Tools if you already have them installed).

5. From that ISO copy the following: <root>\Program Files\VMWare\VMWare Tools\Drivers\ vmxnet\win2k. Copy all the files in that folder to a new directory C:\6000\vmnet.

6. Now it's time to use imagex.exe from the WAIK. Start a command prompt to run imagex.exe. Type in and execute "**C:\Program Files\Windows AIK\Tools\x86\imagex.exe**" **/mountrw c:\6000\boot.wim 2 c:\6000\mount**. Note the number 2 between boot.wim and c:\6000\ mount. This designates the second image contained within the boot.wim.

---

7. Now in the command prompt execute the next three lines which will jam in the drivers and commit the drivers into the .WIM:

```
"C:\Program Files\Windows AIK\Tools\PETools\peimg.exe" /inf=c:\6000\vmnet\vmxnet
.inf c:\6000\mount\windows

"C:\Program Files\Windows AIK\Tools\PETools\peimg.exe" /inf=c:\6000\vmnet\
vmware-nic.inf c:\6000\mount\windows

"C:\Program Files\Windows AIK\Tools\x86\imagex.exe" /unmount /commit c:\6000\mount
```

1. Once that finishes, your boot.wim will have the network drivers it needs inside the second image (the one Windows Vista uses when setup runs).

2. Now, use the WDS server manager to right-click the Boot Images folder and select "Add Boot Image." Import your newly updated boot.wim (c:\6000\boot.wim) into your WDS server and give it a unique name, like "Vista Boot WIM with Custom Network Drivers."

This is the boot.wim selection to choose when you boot and need those custom drivers.

Installing and Managing Clients via WDS

You're almost ready to start rolling out your clients. Remember that your clients need network cards that are PXE Boot ROM–capable. To use the NICs that have the ROM code built right onto the card, watch for the PC to flash "Hit F12 for Network Boot" upon reboot. If your computer doesn't flash that message (or something similar), you'll need to check the network card's BIOS, the PC's BIOS, or both to see if the PXE feature is disabled; or you can create the PXE Boot ROM emulator disk as described in the sidebar "Creating a Remote Boot Disk."

Installing Your First Client

Once you're sitting down at your target machine, you're ready to install your first client.

 WARNING   Running WDS on your workstations completely formats the first hard drive.

To use WDS to install a client, follow these steps:

1. Turn on the target system.

2. When prompted, immediately press F12 to see the boot menu as seen in Figure 12.16.

3. Select the boot WIM you want. (We created the "Vista Boot WIM with Custom Network Drivers" using the information in the "Jamming in Your Own Network Drivers into the boot.wim" sidebar.)

Creating a Remote Boot Disk

Most network cards are PXE compliant and can be enabled to PXE boot using F12 at boot time. However, there are some older cards which are PXE compliant but are unable to boot using F12 at boot time.

If you have that situation, you might need a PXE boot disk to jumpstart your process. The code to write a WDS boot disk is less than 1KB. Therefore, creating a remote boot disk takes only a moment. Moreover, the PXE boot disk supports a slew of network cards. If you have multiple cards that you need to boot from, it doesn't matter what brand the NIC is, since all are supported by the same floppy. To create your PXE Remote boot disk, follow these steps:

1. Run the RBFG.EXE program from the \Admin\i386 directory where you installed WDS. Click Start ➢ Run, and type `R:\RemoteInstall\Admin\i386\rbfg.exe` in the Open dialog box.

2. Put a blank floppy in the floppy drive and click the Create Disk button to start the boot disk generation.

3. When prompted to create another disk, click No, and click Close to close the Microsoft Windows Remote Boot Disk Generator.

If your card isn't listed, you still have a ray of hope. Check out Argon Technologies at www .argontechnology.com/mbadisk/index.shtml and http://www.emboot.com/products_mba_ on_disk5.htm.

These companies make special PXE boot floppies (and CD-ROMs, and so on) that could support your hardware!

4. It will take some time to download the boot.wim and present the next screen. That's because the boot.wim is about 120MB, so, be patient. When the first information screen appears, press Enter to open the Client Installation Wizard Logon screen.

5. The first WDS screen you'll see is entitled "Windows Deployment Services," and you simply select a Locale (like English/United States) and a Keyboard Input Method (US). Click Next.

6. Enter a valid username, password, and domain. You'll have to enter it as **DOMAIN\ username** or **username@domain.com**. Just about any username and password combination will work, like Frank Rizzo and our default password (if you chose to use it) of p@ssw0rd. In other words, users don't need to be Domain Administrators to perform this function.

7. You can then select the Windows Vista image you want to install, as seen in Figure 12.17.

FIGURE 12.16 Start WDS by hitting F12 and selecting which boot option you want. Note that Remote Installation Services will not be an option unless you've upgraded an existing RIS server.

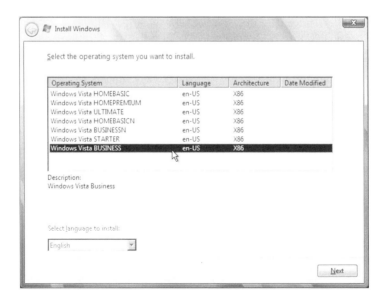

FIGURE 12.17 Select the Windows Vista image you want to deploy and select Next.

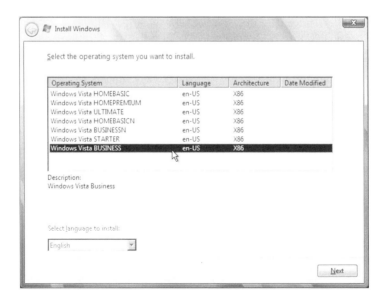

You'll then be able to partition the hard drive if you like, click Next and be off to the races. If all goes well, the computer will be left at a logon prompt, waiting for the user to log on for the first time.

Mere-Mortals Can Add Only 10 Workstations

In Windows NT, only administrators can add computer accounts to the domain. Now, under Active Directory, the Authenticated Users group can add computer accounts to the domain via the Add Workstation to Domain user right. But there's a catch. Each authenticated user can add only 10 new computer accounts. On the next try, the user is presented with the error message: "The machine account for this computer either does not exist or is unavailable."

This is a little-known problem that has three little-known solutions.

Administrators can pre-create the computer accounts.

Administrators can create as many accounts as they like. They are exempt from the "10 strikes and you're out" rule.

You can grant the "Create Computer Objects" (and if desired) the "Delete Computer Objects" rights to the *Computers* folder in Active Directory.

These rights are different from the Add Workstation to Domain user right that all Authenticated Users are given. To make this change, follow these steps:

1. Choose Start ➢ Programs ➢ Administrative Tools ➢ Active Directory Users and Computers.

2. Choose View ➢ Advanced to enable the Advanced view.

3. Right-click the Computers folder, and choose Properties from the shortcut menu to open the Properties dialog box.

4. Click the Security tab, and then click the Advanced button to open the Advanced Settings for Computers properties.

5. On the Permissions tab, click Authenticated Users, and then click the Edit button to open the Permissions Entry for Authenticated Users.

6. Before proceeding, make sure the "This Object and All Child Objects" option is displayed in the "Apply Onto" box.

7. In the Permissions list, click the Allow check box for "Create Computer Objects" and, optionally, "Delete Computer Objects" as seen here.

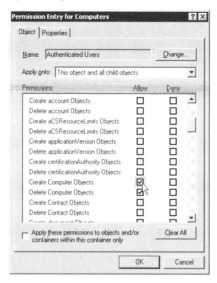

Use ADSI edit to manipulate the ms-DS-MachineAccountQuota to increase (or decrease) the value to the desired number of times a user can create a computer account.

1. Load an MMC console with the "ADSI Edit" snap-in.

2. Expand the Domain NC partition to expose the first level, which is the domain. Right-click the domain and choose Properties to open the Properties dialog box.

3. Ensure that you have the Attribute Editor tab selected.

4. In the Select a Property to View drop-down list box, select `ms-DS-Machine-AccountQuota`.

5. Click Edit to open the Integer Attribute Editor dialog box.

6. In the Value field enter the desired number of times a user can create computer accounts, and then click OK.

7. Click OK to close the Domain Properties dialog box.

Converting Existing RIS Images to WDS Images (or, Capturing Windows XP Machines for WDS Deployment)

If you chose to upgrade your RIS server to a WDS server, you'll see your old RIS images in a folder called `Legacy Images` as seen in Figure 12.13 (though in that figure, we're not expressly showing the contents of the Legacy Images folder). Should you then boot a new client machine and press F12 at boot time, you would see the ability to select "Remote Installation Services" as seen earlier in Figure 12.16.

There's no penalty for leaving these RIS images here like this—other than leveraging extra disk space. So, don't feel obligated to perform this procedure to convert your existing RIS images to WDS images (in the `.WIM` file format).

Additionally, you might have a Windows XP machine (or Windows Vista machine for that matter) that you want to deploy. But what about your applications? How you will get those onto the target systems?

To make that decision, you need to choose to do one of the following:

- Put your applications inside your WDS image.

- Use the techniques described in the previous chapter and have clients pull down the software to your users and/or computers.

- Use a combination of the previous two techniques such that a bunch of general applications are in the image and the remainder of the applications are deployed via Group Policy Software Installation (GPSI).

On the one hand, it's certainly faster to load an application, such as Office 2003 or Office 2007, inside the WDS image and then deploy the image all at once rather than deploying a base WDS image and then using GPSI to shoot down Office 2007. But remember, our GPSI features have the added ability to upgrade packages and perform magic such as applying MSP (Microsoft Patch) and MST (Microsoft transform files) into packages; these abilities are lost if the applications are embedded inside the WDS image.

Therefore, you'll need to analyze each application to determine if it's better to embed it inside the WDS image or deploy the package after the fact using GPSI. In my experience, in almost all cases, it's better to use GPSI to deploy your applications. Later, if you want to do some of the stuff we explored in Chapter 11, such as upgrading an existing package or revoking existing applications, you can do so only if you've originally deployed the applications via GPSI—and not by installing the applications in an embedded fashion via WDS. So, for the record, if you do choose to embed applications in your WDS images, I'm presenting that information here. Again, however, *I encourage you not to do this.*

After you install the applications on your target machine, you need to first run SYSPREP upon it which prepares the machine for imaging. However, you won't be imaging it; you'll be capturing it, using the tools in the next steps.

We don't have room to go in to all the SYSPREP steps here, but you can see a screenshot of Windows XP when it is being SYSPREP-ed in Figure 12.18. However, if you want a quick SYSPREP primer, check out http://support.microsoft.com/kb/302577 or Christa Anderson's *Windows 2000 Automated Deployment and Remote Administration* (Sybex, 2001—in the same series as this book).

FIGURE 12.18   You need to have a Windows XP machine (or Windows Vista machine) SYSPREP-ed in order to capture it.

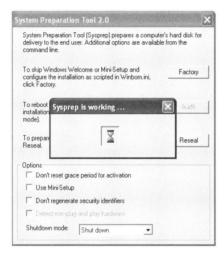

Creating Your Capture Boot Image

To get started, you need to first create a "Capture Image" and introduce that into your WDS Boot Images. The idea is that once you press F12, then boot from the Capture Image, you'll be able to "push up" any machine (Windows XP, Windows Server 2003, or Windows Vista) that you want to deploy via WDS. Again, these machines can have no applications or a zillion applications preloaded. (Again, I'm a fan of not preloading any applications.)

The Capture Boot Image is required so that the target machine can find a WDS server and push up the existing machine into an image. You'll leverage an existing Boot Image to make your Capture Boot Image. Simply right-click one of your Boot Images and select "Create Capture Boot Image" as seen in Figure 12.19.

When you do, you'll be prompted for a name and location. Select any temporary location for now. Once the Capture Image is completely written, you'll then need to right-click Boot Images and suck it in from this temporary location. It's a bit convoluted, but it gets the job done.

FIGURE 12.19   Right-click an existing Boot Image to Create Capture Boot Image.

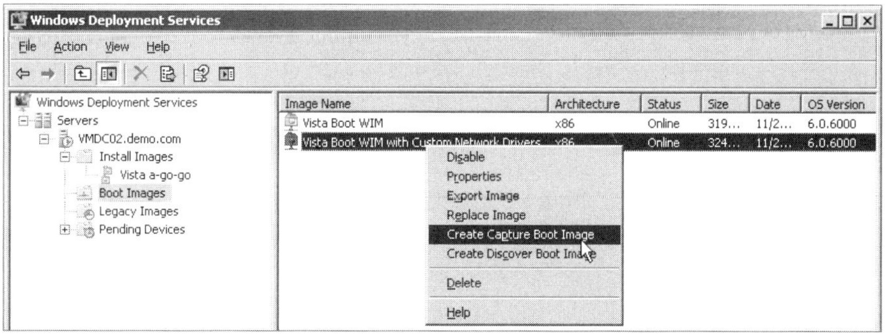

When complete, you should see your new Capture Image as listed in Boot Images.

Leveraging Your Capture Boot Image

Let's assume you have a Windows XP machine you want to make as an available Install Image. Again, you have to have pre-SYSPREP the machine in order to go on to the next steps. Without having SYSPREP-ed your Windows XP machine (or Windows Vista for that matter), the Capture Wizard (described next) won't be able to see the partition.

Once you Press F12 and select your new Capture Image Boot Image, you'll be presented with what's seen in Figure 12.20.

FIGURE 12.20   The WDS Capture Wizard can "upload" a SYSPREP-ed Windows XP machine.

When you click Next, you'll be able to select a drive letter to capture, as well as name the image. I'll be calling this a "Nurse's Station" as seen in Figure 12.21.

You'll then be able to specify the name of the server and the Image Group to plunk this in, and you're off to the races.

This image will then be available for deploying using WDS.

FIGURE 12.21   You can name your image anything you like.

Converting Existing "RIPREP" Images to .*WIM*

If you chose to upgrade your RIS server to a WDS server, you'll see your old RIS images in a folder called Legacy Images as seen in Figure 12.13. Some of these could be "RIPREP" images, which are RIS images you made that already had the base applications inside the image. There's an alternate way to covert these to .WIM format.

The command-line wdsutil.exe (which is on your Windows Server 2003 WDS server) can do the conversion job to take an RIS image and make it a .WIM file.

Your legacy RIS images are likely in a directory called

```
<driveletter>\RemoteInstall\Setup\English\Images\<imagename>\i386\templates\
<something>.sif
```

For example:

```
R:\RemoteInstall\Setup\English\Images\WindowsXPSP2\
\i386\templates\myriprepedimage.sif
```

And there will be additional .SIF files for every RIS image with an answer file.

So, to convert the RIPREP image directly to .WIM format we'll leverage the wdsutil /convert-riprepimage command.

Now, a quick word about the `WDSutil.exe` command before we actually run the thing. It depends upon some libraries and .DLLs in the WAIK tools, and, well, those .DLLs aren't in the "path." So, you'll need to add in `c:\Program Files\Windows AIK\Tools\x86\servicing` into the Windows path using the System applet. If you don't, running `WDSutil.exe` will fail when trying to convert the RIS image.

Once you've properly added in the aforementioned path, here's an example command line which should do the trick:

```
wdsutil /verbose /progress /convert-riprepimage /FilePath:"r:\remoteinstall\
setup\english\images\windowsxpsp2\i386\templates\xpsp2_unattended.sif"
/DestinationImage /FilePath:"r:\XPSP2_fully_unattended.WIM" /Name:"Windows XP
Unattended Image" /Description:"XP/SP2 Fully Unattended Converted RIPREP Image"
```

Again, this trick only works for RIPREP images, not "flat" images where you just gave it the CD-ROM media.

Beyond the Basics: Care and Feeding of WDS and Your Images

By this point, you're able to do the basics of WDS. You can create your own new Windows Vista clients and you can zap up your existing Windows XP machines into .WIM files into the WDS server and zap those down too.

But there are several ways to go beyond the basics of WDS. That's what this section is about.

One of the key takeaways about WDS and the .WIM format (and their resulting WIM files) is that you can maintain an image—even after it's captured. The idea is that if you have a mere driver update, a hotfix to add, or a whole service pack—it's a piece of cake to add those to an existing image. This idea of "maintaining an image" once captured is really only for Windows Vista WIMs, even though we've explored how to also capture Windows XP as a WIM as well. We'll spend most of our time here talking about how to perform these maintenance steps for Windows Vista WIMs.

Additionally, we'll cover how to associate an answer file with a .WIM image, how to set up a "larger" WDS infrastructure, and finally, how to speed up WDS (under some specific circumstances).

Understanding Image Groups

As we've already discussed, WDS maintains .WIM images in Image Groups. Image groups serve two functions: performing "single instancing" and maintaining security.

The .WIM file itself is *also* a unit of single-instancing. A single .WIM file can contain multiple images. However, putting multiple images inside a WIM file isn't recommended if you use WDS, because, again, WDS Image Groups already perform the function of performing single instancing. So, even though you can put multiple images inside a single .WIM file, why bother? WDS's Image Groups goes the extra mile and does the work for you.

Single Instance Storing

Windows Vista is about 2GB compressed on the DVD. So, you might think that if you had seven versions of Windows Vista in an Image Group, you might expect that Image Group to be as large as 14GB! But it's not.

Again, that's because WDS will single instance store all the images. Think about it: the differences between each Windows Vista version is ever-so-slight. And that's all that's captured between the various images.

So, if you dive into the actual image store via command line or Explorer, you'll see the images inside the image store as various .WIM files, with a big ol' Res.RWM file alongside it. Ninety-eight percent of all the images are contained inside that big file. The rest of the files are stored as the differences inside the remaining .WIM files.

 The Res.RWM file is really a .WIM file, too. But, technically, it's called a "Resource WIM" and it gets distinguished by a different filename.

You can see a list of my available images inside my VistaGroup Image Group and the corresponding underlying files in Figure 12.22.

FIGURE 12.22   WDS will perform "Single Instancing" inside an Image Group.

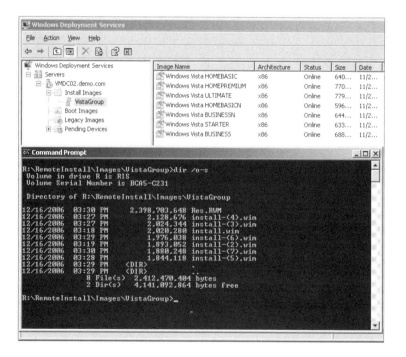

Setting Security for an Image Group

The other benefit of Image Groups is the ability to set security upon the Image Group. By default, anyone who provides credentials when booting from a boot .WIM can see the available images for download, format their machine, and get a fresh image.

I'll let that last sentence sink in for a while.

Go ahead and re-read that if you need to.

The key word is "anyone"; specifically, "Authenticated Users."

So, the takeaway here is that if you want to ensure that only the "right people" have access to WDS Install Images, you need to set permissions on an Image Group.

To do this, right click the Image Group, say, VistaGroup, and select Security. Remove Authenticated Users' ability to "Read & execute," "List folder contents," and "Read." Add in a group of people you trust, like DesktopAdmins or something similar, and give them those rights. You can see the default Image Group rights in Figure 12.23.

You'll need to get rid of Authenticated Users and add in just the group you want. However, Authenticated Users is being inherited at a higher level. So, you'll need to click the Advanced security button and uncheck the "Allow inheritable permissions from the parent to propagate to this object and all child objects" check box as seen in Figure 12.24. When asked, select to "Copy" the permissions from the parent, also seen in Figure 12.24.

FIGURE 12.23   By default, users can Read and leverage the list of images inside an Image Group.

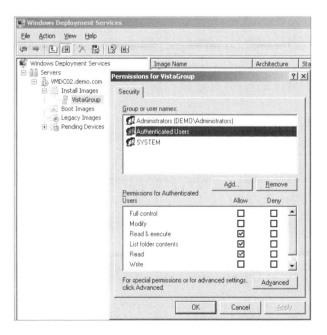

FIGURE 12.24 Remove the inheritable permissions and copy them from the parent.

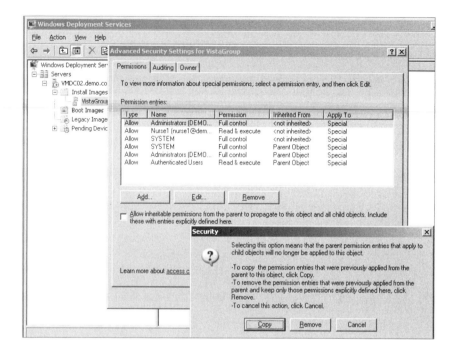

Then, you'll be able to remove Authenticated Users and select just the users and groups you want.

When a user tries with their credentials, it will succeed and only present images that you've enabled them to see.

Servicing a WDS *.WIM* Image

As I'm writing this, there aren't any Windows Vista service packs or hotfixes. I'm not worried though; I'm sure they're around the corner any minute. And, when they come, you'll want to just jam those hotfixes or that service pack in to your existing image.

And, when you're done, you could either save the image out to another image (preserving the original one) or overwrite the original one. Here's the short version of how to do this procedure:

1. Use the WDS MMC snap-in to mark the image as "disabled" (just right-click the Image Name and select "Disabled").

2. Right-click the disabled image and select "Export Image" to export the image to a "whole" .WIM file. This can take a while.

3. Mount the image using the `imagex.exe` utility. Usually, the command will be `imagex /mountrw <image.wim> 1 <mountpoint>`, where *mountpoint* is a directory somewhere you can write to.

4. Service the image with the hotfix, service pack, or driver. An example of how to add a driver can be found earlier in the "Jamming Your Own Network Drivers into the *boot.wim*" sidebar. It's basically the same procedure.

5. Import the image back in to the Image Group. If you want to completely replace the image, then right-click the existing image and select "Replace-Image." If you want to add it as a new image while preserving the existing one, then just right-click the Image Group and select "Add Install Image."

Adding Drivers to an Existing Image

There's some extra beauty in WDS images. That is, you can easily add in new network, audio, video, and modem drivers. To do this, you create subdirectories with specific names within your Image Group's directory structure.

So, in my examples, all the WDS stuff is being stored in `r:\RemoteInstall` in the `\images` directory. My first (and only) Image Group is named "VistaGroup."

```
\Images
    \VistaGroup
        RES.RWM
        Install-(2).WIM
        Install-(3).WIM
        Install-(4).WIM
```

and so on.

To add drivers to any particular image, you just create a subdirectory with the same name as the `.WIM` file, say, `Install-(2)`. Yep, that's the name of the directory `Install-(2)` (if that's the name of the `.WIM` file).

Then, create a `$OEM$` subdirectory and within that subdirectory create `\$$` and `\$1`, as seen here:

```
\Images
    \VistaGroup
        RES.RWM
        Install-(2).WIM
        \Install-(2)
            \$OEM$
                \$$
                    \Drivers
                        \NIC
                        \Audio
                        \SCSI
                \$1
```

Finally, to make use of this, you'll need an `unattend.xml` file (created with the Windows System Image Manager utility). Use that utility to modify the `DriverPaths` entry in the `unattend.xml` to point to installing these drivers.

The Windows AIK for Vista has the rest of the story here. Be sure to read the Windows AIK, specifically the section on `DriverPaths` and unattend settings to see how to best make use of this technique.

Associating an Answer File with a WDS Image

Associating an answer file with a specific WDS image is easy. The hard part is creating the answer files first. Again, I'm sorry, dear reader, that topic is simply too huge to go into in these pages. The tool you'll use to create an `unattend.xml` file is the Windows System Image Manager (WSIM), part of the WAIK tools you downloaded earlier. Inside the WAIK tools is guidance you'll need to understand the WSIM and create a working `unattend.xml` file.

In WDS (unlike RIS) there is a one-to-one mapping between images and unattend files. So, you can immediately associate a single answer file with a single image. That's great—but then everyone is using the exact same answer file with that image.

If you want to deploy, say, Windows Vista for Business to both Doctors and Nurses, you'll need two Windows Vista Business images—each with their own answer file. This isn't a big deal, nor does it take up very much disk space. Remember: images are single instance stored, so making a copy of any existing image is quick, small, and painless.

So, in this example, we'll copy our Windows Vista Business image twice, once for Doctors and another for Nurses. Then we'll pretend to associate answer files to them. But, if we take a look inside the `\images\<imagegroup>` directory (in my case, it's `\imaged\VistaGroup`), we'll notice lots of `.WIM` files, which don't exactly tell you which `.WIM` is associated with which image.

Directory of `R:\RemoteInstall\Images\VistaGroup`:

```
12/16/2006  03:29 PM    <DIR>          .
12/16/2006  03:29 PM    <DIR>          ..
12/16/2006  03:19 PM         1,893,052 install-(2).wim
12/16/2006  03:27 PM         2,024,344 install-(3).wim
12/16/2006  03:27 PM         2,128,676 install-(4).wim
12/16/2006  03:28 PM         1,844,118 install-(5).wim
12/16/2006  03:29 PM         1,976,038 install-(6).wim
12/16/2006  03:30 PM         1,880,248 install-(7).wim
12/16/2006  03:18 PM         2,020,280 install.wim
12/16/2006  03:30 PM     2,398,703,648 Res.RWM
               8 File(s)  2,412,470,404 bytes
               2 Dir(s)   4,136,259,584 bytes free

R:\RemoteInstall\Images\VistaGroup>
```

To figure out which .WIM you need to copy, run the command

```
wdsutil /get-allimages /show:install
```

This will show you the relation to the "friendly name" of the image and the filenames (which aren't so friendly). In my case, Windows Vista Business is install.wim (no numbers).

So, now I need to copy install.wim to, say, doctorsbusiness.wim and nursesbusiness.wim so I can then associate an answer file to each of these.

```
wdsutil /copy-image /Image:"Windows Vista Business" /ImageType:Install
/DestinationImage /Name:"Vista-Business-Doctors"
/filename:"VistaBusinessDoctors.wim"
```

and again for Nurses

```
wdsutil /copy-image /Image:"Windows Vista Business" /ImageType:Install
/DestinationImage /Name:"Vista-Business-Nurses"
/filename:"VistaBusinessNurses.wim"
```

When complete, you should have two more images (one for Doctors and Nurses) in the Vista-Group install group. You might not see them until you close and reopen the WDS management MMC snap-in.

When ready, right-click the image and select Properties. On the General tab, select "Select File" and give the answer filename. The process can be seen in Figure 12.25 (though no answer file is shown).

FIGURE 12.25   Once you have created a copy of your image for your scenario, you can associate an answer file directly with that image.

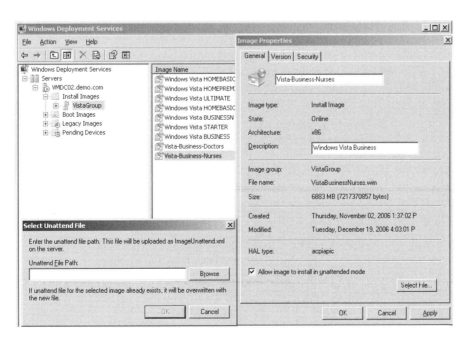

RIS saw an "image" as an unattended answer file (`ristndrd.sif`). RIS didn't actually know that you only had one version of the binaries, it simply looked for the `.SIF` files to figure out how many "images" you had. So, in the case where you had a single RISETUP image and two `.SIF` files, RIS saw that as two separate images.

Setting up a Distributed WDS Infrastructure

What if you have branch offices and want to enable the ability to deploy workstations at those remote sites? If your goal is to load balance image downloads, I recommend using DFS. We don't have enough room to go into all the steps, so here's the "high-level" advice (assuming you have two branch offices):

1. Create three WDS Servers: Server1, Server2, and Server3. Server 1 will be the "load balancing" server and redirect traffic to Server2 and Server3.

2. Set the PXE Answer Policy such that Server1 answers PXE requests and Server2 and Server3 do not. All clients will network boot against Server1. To tell Server1 to respond to all client computers, ensure "Respond to all (known and unknown) client computers" is checked. To tell Server2 and Server3 to ignore client requests, select "Do not respond to any client computer." You can see this in Figure 12.26, which shows the Properties of the server's "PXE Response Settings" tab.

3. Add in your `.WIM` installation images as we did previously. Do this on Server2 and Server3. You can optionally keep the two servers' `\images` directories in synch via DFS-R (which only comes with Windows Server 2003/R2).

4. Create Image Groups on Server1 mirroring those on Server2 and Server3. You don't need the actual contents, just the groups (which, you'll recall just look like folders).

5. Set up DFS redirection such that any requests for the contents of the Image Groups on Server1 get redirected to Server2 and Server3. In that manner, clients will automatically load balance between the two servers.

In practice, the network segments tend to get overloaded *way* before an actual server does. As such, if you really want to speed up imaging time and load balance you'll need to have lots of WDS servers and you'll need to segment your network.

Use at Your Own Risk: Speeding Up the Download Time of a *boot.wim* Image

For me, the only big drawback in WDS is the slow boot time of the `boot.wim` file. That's because it's about 167MB, which, well, is still pretty big, even on most networks. Actually, the problem really isn't that the file itself is that big, it's the underlying protocols used to transfer that `boot.wim` from the server to your Windows Vista-machine-to-be.

That's because it uses the TFTP (Trivial FTP) protocol, which really stinks. The major limitation is the TFTP block size used when downloading an image. The default block size is around 1000 bytes; small enough to still fit in an Ethernet frame without causing packet fragmentation.

FIGURE 12.26   Set how a server should or should not respond to client requests.

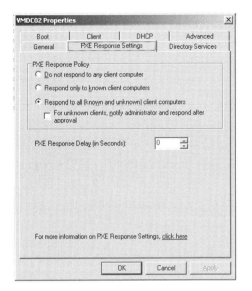

However, and I need to stress this here: what I'm about to show you how to do only works if your network cards support it, and the switches and routers support it. That is, you can bump up the frame size WDS uses when sending the boot.wim file via TFTP.

Now, let's say you have two kinds of network cards and three kinds of network switches and four kinds of routers. All of the equipment (from the server's network card through the switch through the router to the target machine's network card) has to be able to support the increased block size trick I'm about to show you. That is, you'll tell the WDS server to increase the frame size from 1000 to another number of bytes per block.

The program you need to run, bcdedit.exe is only available on a Windows Vista machine. So, to do this trick, you'll need to start on a Windows Vista machine, then map a drive to the REMINST\Boot\x86 on the server. Then, the bcdedit.exe utility will edit the WDS configuration database directly, named default.bcd.

```
Bcdedit -store default.bcd -set
{68d9e51c-a129-4ee1-9725-2ab00a957daf} ramdisktftpblocksize
 <yourblock size here>
```

Just go up in even multiples: 4096, 8192, 16384. I wouldn't set it any higher than 16384. I've tried a lot of values. The two values that worked best were 4096 and 8192.

Finally, run this command while back on the server:

```
Sc control wdsserver 129
```

The next time you boot a client it will use the new TFTP block size to download the Windows PE image.

Again, the maximum value isn't a function of your network bandwidth, it's a function of the maximum buffer size your PXE ROM allocates for UDP packets.

Final Thoughts

In the beginning, Microsoft created Group Policy, and it was good. Now, you can take this goodness and leverage it to protect and serve your subjects.

At the beginning of this book, you learned the ins and outs of Group Policy. You learned how to get around in the GPMC and how to script Group Policy operations. You went on and leveraged your Group Policy knowledge to implement a secure environment with Group Policy and a robust managed desktop environment to allow your users to roam freely—*online and offline*—and maintain the same user experience.

This, the final chapter, talked about what happens after you get Group Policy implemented and want a truly managed desktop. Here, you used Shadow Copies to further ensure that users' data is protected should they inadvertently delete or overwrite it. You zapped printers down to users and computers, and you used Windows Deployment Services to bring back a Windows machine from the dead. And you learned you can automate it even further with answer files.

I hope you can fully appreciate the beauty in this holistic approach to user settings and data management. No longer are users tied to a specific desktop or laptop as a single point of failure. If a machine gets lost or dies, the user environment (Profile), the data (`Documents/My Documents` with Redirected Folders), and the applications (via GPSI) are always preserved on the server for when that new machine arrives.

Dropping a new machine on the desk (perhaps with WDS) is like magic: Roaming Profiles, Redirected Folders, Offline Folders, Disk Quotas, and Group Policy Software Installation perform exactly as they did before the machine blew up. You'll bring it all back for the user with the press of F12.

You'll be a hero.

A Look into the Future...

Before we close the door on this edition of the book, I want to take a moment and put on my prognosticator's hat (I just love that word) and look into the future. While I was in the middle of writing this book, some key developments happened that will be very interesting for the next generation of Group Policy and the managed desktop.

On the Group Policy front, Microsoft recently bought out the popular Group Policy product company DesktopStandard. They had multiple products which hooked in directly to Group Policy. The two big packages of note were PolicyMaker Professional and GPOVault.

PolicyMaker Professional added 21 additional Client-Side-Extension "goodies" to Group Policy. For instance, if you wanted to set up power management or set up Outlook profiles or create Desktop shortcuts or map drive letters, you could do this with PolicyMaker Professional. Now, that technology is owned by Microsoft.

GPOVault is a "check-in/check-out" Group Policy change-management system which hooks right into the GPMC. So, if you wanted to have certain people create GPOs and other people verify that those GPOs were A-OK before putting them into the Group Policy swimming pool, GPOvault was a cool tool to let you do that. Again, now that technology is owned by Microsoft.

On the desktop management front, Microsoft also recently bought out a company called Softricity. Softricity's main product, called SoftGrid, helped rapidly deploy applications to existing desktops. As we saw, GPSI did a great job in deploying the applications we needed. But, GPSI does have some limitations. First, when an application was deployed via GPSI, it was really *installed* onto our system. This is great, but if we only need the application for a one-time use, we have to wait for the application to really install itself into our computer. And, even though the MSI file type helps resolve .DLL conflicts and the like, it's not perfect. Indeed, it's certainly not recommended to deploy multiple versions of Office to the same computer. It could be unpredictable which .DLLs will take over. So, Softricity's goal is to (stay with me here) zap applications down to the target machine—but not actually install them (in the traditional sense of the word). They get installed into a "sandbox." Users use the applications as *if they were installed*, but they're really not. They're *virtually* installed. This gives us several advantages: because the application isn't really installed, cleanup is a snap. Just chuck out the sandbox, and the application is removed. And, also because each application is running in its own sandbox, you run multiple (normally conflicting) applications side-by-side. In a word: wow.

So, how do these pieces fit together for the future? Well, for a percentage of what I've just described, the future is now. That is, you can already get your hands on both GPOvault and SoftGrid if you have Microsoft's Software Assurance. This is being delivered as part of a licensing program called the Microsoft Desktop Optimization Pack for Software Assurance, or "MDOP" for short. You can learn more about all the pieces here: `www.microsoft.com/windowsvista/getready/optimizeddesktop.mspx`. As of this writing, these applications are available in their "non-Microsoft rebranded" form. That is, they're the last version that was available before Microsoft bought them. Stay tuned for real Microsoft versions of these packages when MDOP is fully released. Note, they may or may not even have many (or any!) new features upon their debut as Microsoft products.

But what about the PolicyMaker Professional add-ons? At this point, I don't know. I could make a guess as to what might come of it, but it's only a guess. I expect to see this as a free add-on pack once Longhorn Server is shipped. Maybe even a little after Longhorn Server is shipped—maybe Longhorn SP1 or Windows Vista/SP2. If Microsoft really works extra hard, they might be able to make this part of Windows Vista/SP1, but I would be really surprised. PolicyMaker Professional was compatible for Windows 2000 and Windows XP (but not Windows Vista clients) when it was bought out by Microsoft. I'm not sure if it will remain compatible across *all* those client types, perhaps just Windows XP, but almost assuredly Windows Vista. Regardless, when this is released, there will be a lot more Group Policy goodies to talk about. And then you can look for the next edition of this book, and learn about developments as they happen by staying in touch with me at `www.GPanswers.com/newsletter`.

Until then...

Thank you for reading this book and using it to its fullest! Let's keep the information flowing! Come join your peers at www.GPanswers.com for ongoing support of the material in this book. You'll find free downloads, training services, a third-party tools listing, and a community discussion forum regarding all Group Policy, Profiles, the managed desktop, Printers, Shadow Copies, and WDS topics! See you online!

Jeremy

Moskowitz

Appendix

Group Policy Tools

Obviously, the power of Group Policy is awesome, but some aspects of Group Policy and Desktop Management are better suited to additional tools. In this appendix, we're going to leverage a variety of tools to perform several key duties. We'll also finish the functionality of what the GPMC has to offer, specifically, migrating existing GPOs between domains. We'll then dive into the other free Group Policy management tools from Microsoft.

Last, we'll round up third-party Group Policy tools, third-party Profiles tools, third-party ADM editing tools, and third-party Microsoft Installer (MSI) repackaging tools. However, it should be noted that Group Policy tool manufacturers constantly create and innovate. To that end, some manufacturers choose to show off their products on www.GPanswers.com, so be sure to check out my website for updated information (if available).

Migrating Group Policy Objects between Domains

For years, I had stood in front of large audiences and recommended testing the power of GPOs in a test forest. In return, I'd get blank stares because this advice was inherently impractical. Sure, it was safe—safer than testing GPOs in production—but ultimately my advice was doomed. How can you do the hard work in a test domain, test it, debug it, get it all right, and then lift it out of its home domain and put it in production? Answer? You couldn't. Until now.

These examples will continue with our fictional multidomain environment. You can flip back to Figure 3.6 to see the relationship between our three domains: Corp.com, Widgets.corp.com, and the Cross-Forest Trust between bigu.edu and Corp.com.

Basic Interdomain Copy and Import

Now using the GPMC, you can take existing GPOs from any domain and copy them to another domain. The target domain can be a parent domain, a child domain, a cross-forest domain, or a completely foreign domain that has no trusts! Both the Copy and the Import operations transfer only the policy settings; these operations do not modify either the source or the destination links of the GPOs.

The Copy Operation

The interdomain Copy operation is meant to be used when you want to copy live GPOs from one domain to another. That is, you have two domains, connectivity between them, and appropriate rights to the GPOs. To copy the GPO, you need "Read" rights on the source GPO you want to copy and "Write" rights in the target domain.

First, you want to tweak your GPMC console so that you can see the two domains you want.

Recall that to add new domains to the GPMC, you simply right-click "Domains" and choose "Show Domains" from the shortcut menu to open up the Show Domains dialog box. Then simply select the domains you want to see. To add other forests, right-click "Group Policy Management" and choose "Add Forest" from the shortcut menu to open the "Add Forest" dialog box. You can then enter the name of the forest in the field labeled "Domain" (yes, domain!).

In this first example, we'll copy a GPO from Corp.com to Widgets.corp.com. An enterprise administrator will have rights in all domains. Since we're logged in as an enterprise administrator, we have rights in both Corp.com (to read) and Widgets.corp.com (to write). Follow these steps:

1. In the Group Policy Objects container, right-click the GPO you want to copy, as shown in Figure A.1. For this example, I've chosen the "Hide Settings Tab/Restore Screen Saver Tab" GPO.

FIGURE A.1   You can copy a GPO from the Group Policy Objects container.

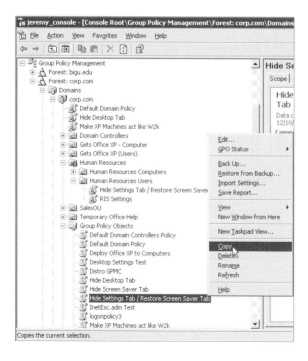

2. Adjust your view of the GPMC so that you can see the target domain. In Figure A.2, I've minimized the view of Corp.com and expanded Widgets.corp.com—especially the Group Policy Objects container.

3. Right-click the target domain's Group Policy Objects container, and choose "Paste" to start the "Cross-Domain Copying Wizard."

4. Click Next to bypass the initial splash screen and open the Specifying permissions screen, as shown in Figure A.2.

FIGURE A.2 When you paste a GPO, you can choose how to handle permissions.

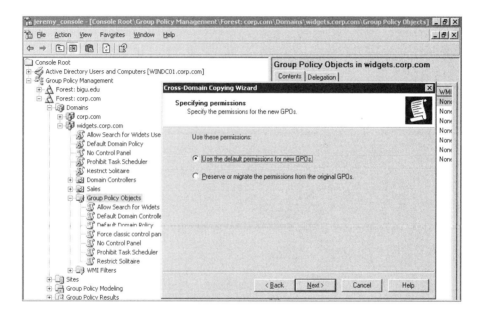

You can now choose to create a GPO with the default permissions or copy the original permissions to the new GPO. The latter might be useful if you've delegated some special permissions to that GPO and don't want to go through the hassle of redoing your efforts. Most of the time, however, the first option is fine. You can now zip through the rest of the wizard.

 You might see a message about Migration tables. Don't fret; they're right around the corner. For this specific GPO, you won't need Migration tables, so it won't be an issue.

 If you copy a GPO between domains, the WMI filtering is lost because the WMI filter won't necessarily exist in the target domain.

The Import Operation

In the previous scenario, we copied a GPO from Corp.com to Widgets.corp.com. We did this when both domains were online and accessible. But if you are working on an isolated testing network, this won't be possible. How then do you take a GPO you created in the isolated test lab and bring it into production? First, create a backup as described in Chapter 2. You'll then have a collection of files that you can put on a floppy, a CD, and so on and take out the door of your test lab into the real world. You can then create a brand new GPO (or overwrite an existing GPO) and perform the import! Follow these steps:

A Word about Drag and Drop

Dragging and dropping a GPO from one domain into another domain can be hazardous! For example, your intention is to copy a GPO named "Restrict Solitaire" from the GPO container in Widgets.corp.com to the **Human Resources Users** OU in Corp.com. It looks like it's going to make sense: you set up your view in the GPMC to show both domains, you can see the Group Policy Objects container in Widgets.corp.com, and you can see the **Human Resources Users** OU in Corp.com. Then, you drag and drop, and you're asked the following question:

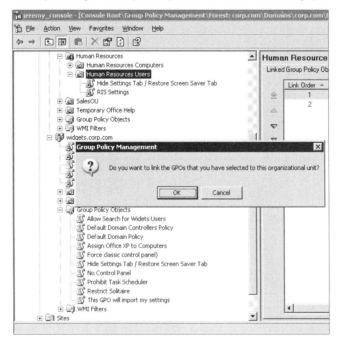

If you click OK, you're not actually copying! Indeed, you're performing a no-no! You are creating a cross-domain link to the GPO, as you can see when you click the Details tab of the GPO:

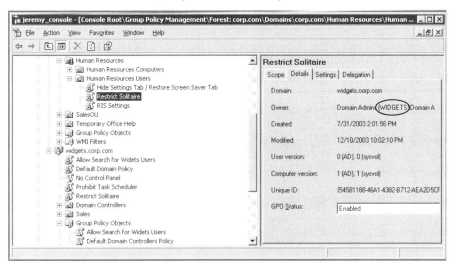

In this example, the "Domain" field shows that it "lives" in Widgets.corp.com, even though the GPO is linked to an OU in Corp.com.

Whenever a GPO is linked from across a domain, the GPO must be pulled from a Domain Controller that actually houses it. If it's across the WAN, so be it. And that could mean major slowdowns.

The moral of the story is to be sure you're copying (as described earlier) and not just linking.

1. Right-click the Group Policy Objects container, choose New from the shortcut menu to open the "New GPO" dialog box, and in the Name Field enter the name of a new GPO.

2. Right-click that GPO and choose Import Settings from the shortcut menu, as shown in Figure A.3. This then starts the Import Settings Wizard.

Anyone with "Edit" rights on the GPO can perform an Import.

You can choose to overwrite an existing GPO, but that's just it. It's an overwrite, not a merge. So, be careful!

FIGURE A.3 You can import the settings and overwrite an existing GPO.

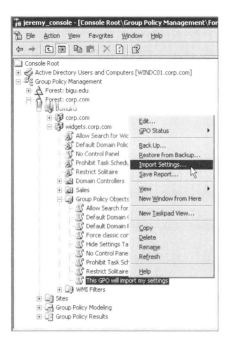

3. The wizard then presents the "Backup GPO" screen, which allows you to back up the newly created GPO; however, this is unnecessary. This is a safety measure should you decide to overwrite an existing GPO. You can then click Next to see the "Backup Location" screen.

4. In the "Backup Location" screen, use the Backup folder field to input the path to where your backup set is and select Next. The "Source GPO" screen will appear as seen in Figure A.4.

5. At the "Source GPO" screen, select the GPO from which you want to import settings, as shown in Figure A.4 and click Next.

You should now be able to zip through the rest of the wizard. Ignore any references to Migration tables; they're coming up next.

Copy and Import with Migration Tables

In the previous examples, we migrated the very simple GPO named "Hide Settings Tab/Restore Screen Saver Tab." That particular GPO contained only Administrative Template settings that affected the desktop. Nothing fancy, for sure.

FIGURE A.4   Select a GPO from which you want to import settings.

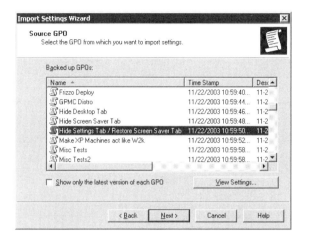

However, certain policy settings do perform some fancy footwork. Some GPOs can include references to security groups, such as "Allow Log on Locally." Other GPOs can include references to UNC paths, such as Folder Redirection. Indeed, an Advanced Folder Redirection policy setting contains both security group references and UNC path references! Other possibilities include Restricted Groups, Group Policy Software Installation policy settings, and pointers to scripts.

When you migrate GPOs across domains, you need to take care of these references. Copying a GPO in one domain that redirects folders to the \\WinDC01\Data share will not likely make much sense when used in another domain.

With that in mind, both the Copy and Import functions can leverage *Migration tables*. Migration tables let you rectify both security group and UNC references that exist in a GPO when you transfer the GPO to another domain. You'll be given the opportunity to use the Migration tables automatically if your Copy or Import operation detects that a policy setting needs it! After the GPO is ready to be copied or imported, you'll be notified that some adjustments are needed. It's that easy!

In the Migrating References screen of the wizard (as shown in Figure A.5), you can choose two paths here:

- Selecting "Copying them identically from the source" can be risky. Again, you won't know what the source is using for security groups or UNC paths. The existing security groups and UNC paths may be valid, but they may not be.

- Selecting "Using this migration table to map them in the destination GPO" gives you the opportunity to choose an existing Migration table (if you have one), or you can click the New button to open the Migration Table Editor and create on the fly.

To start, use a new blank Migration table (after pressing the New button) and follow these steps:

1. If you're performing a Copy, choose Tools ➢ Populate from GPO to open the Select GPO screen, then simply select the live GPO. If you're performing an Import, choose Tools ➢ Populate from Backup to open the "Select Backup" dialog, which allows you to select a GPO from backup.

2. Choose the GPO you're copying or importing to display a list of all the references that need to be corrected.

FIGURE A.5   A Migration table can smooth the bumps between domains.

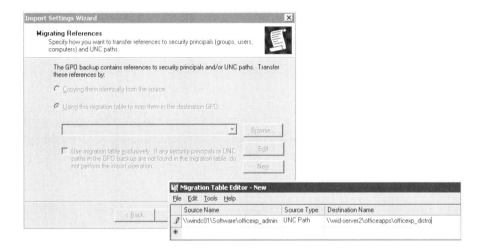

3. In Figure A.5, you can see both the Source Name and Destination Name fields. The Source Name field will automatically be filled in. All that's left is to enter in the Destination Name UNC path for the new environment and you're done!

4. Save the file (with a `.migtable` extension), and close the "Migration Table Editor— New" screen.

5. Back at the Migrating References page, simply click Browse and choose the Migration table you just made.

Before clicking the Next button, you can optionally choose the check box that begins with "Use migration table exclusively." In this example, we have but one UNC reference that needs to be rectified. You might have a meaty GPO with 30 UNC paths and another 50 security principles that need to be cleared up. Perhaps you can't locate all the destination names. If you select this check box, the wizard will not proceed unless all the paths in the destination name are valid. Use this setting if you really need to be sure all settings will be verified successfully.

When ready, click Next, click Next again past the summary screen, and you're finished.

Microsoft has a detailed white paper you'll want to check out if you're planning to do a lot of this. You'll find it at `www.microsoft.com/windowsserver2003/gpmc/migrgpo.mspx`.

Wholesale Backup and Restore of Your Test Lab (or an Easy Way to Migrate to Production)

One more tip before we leave this section. That is, when you're working in your test lab, you might find it necessary to completely demolish and rebuild your test lab for any variety of reasons. However, as noted in Chapter 2, when a GPO is restored, the links are not restored along with the GPO. Again, this is a protection mechanism for your benefit. However, as they say in the hallowed IT halls, "What you do in the test lab, stays in the test lab." So the test lab is a different animal. And, to that end, you might want to back up a whole gaggle of stuff for safekeeping, such as:

- GPOs

- Group Policy links

- Security groups

- OUs

- Users

- Permissions on GPOs

Then, if you need to demolish your test lab and put it back in order, you'll need a way to perform a wholesale restore of all these objects. The GPMC has a built-in script that will back up all these things into one little package. Then, when you're ready, you run another script that takes the package and expands it back into these objects.

The script that does all the backup stuff is called `CreateXMLFromEnvironment.vbs`. The one that does all the restoring is `CreateEnvironmentFromXML.vbs`. Both scripts are located in `C:\Program Files\GPMC\scripts` (when the GPMC is downloaded). The scripts are not present by default on Vista machines; you'll need to download them from the Scripting Center at Microsoft.

The other reason to use these scripts is to do a wholesale migration from the test lab into the real production environment. Personally, I'm not all that keen on a wholesale backup and restore of my test lab into the real world, but I guess if you had nothing at all in the real world this could be a useful way to get things over lock-stock-and-barrel. These scripts are a little too far-reaching for that purpose for my taste, but perhaps you'll find them just the thing.

Microsoft has a document about the ins and outs of both of these scripts. Be sure to check it out before you jump headlong into using it, though, at `http://tinyurl.com/ahen8`.

Microsoft Tools Roundup

As might be expected, Microsoft has a slew of tools to help manage your Group Policy infrastructure as well as your user profiles. In this section, we'll check out the Microsoft tools and where to find them.

Group Policy Tools from Microsoft

Except for Active Directory Monitor and GPInventory, you can download the remainder of the Microsoft tools for free from the Windows 2003 Resource Kit. As of this writing, you can find it at `www.microsoft.com/windowsserver2003/downloads/tools/default.mspx` under the heading "Windows Server 2003 Resource Kit Tools." After you install the Resource Kit, you'll find the tools in the `\Program Files\Windows Resource Kits\Tools` folder. Some of these tools are ready to use; others require additional installation.

Active Directory Monitor and GPOTOOL

These tools help to troubleshoot GPOs if the GPC and GPT get out of sync. See Chapter 4 for information.

admX (within *ADMX.MSI*)—ADM Template Comparison Utility

This tool has an unfortunate name; it was born before the advent of ADMX files, so don't be confused and think that admX really has anything to do with ADMX files (that we explored in Chapter 5).

   This tool prints (or redirects) an ADM template into a nice readable format for documentation. It will parse an ADM file and list Registry path, Symbolic Policy Name, Full Policy Name, Registry Settings, and the `Supported on` keyword. You can also use it to show the differences between two similar ADM files.

   This tool requires additional installation. Be sure the latest .NET Framework is installed (the one built into Windows 2003 is not sufficient). Next, run the ADMX.MSI to install and follow the wizard. After installation, the default location for admX is `c:\Program Files\Microsoft\admx`. You'll need to execute `admX.exe` from there.

GPMonitor—Group Policy Monitor Tool

The purpose of GPMonitor, which is shown in Figure A.6, is to perform historical analysis of what has changed between different Group Policy refresh intervals on your clients and servers. This tool requires an armload of additional installation; it unpacks to a set of files that need to stay together. You deploy the MSI (Microsoft Installer) to two locations: the clients you want to monitor and a management station that you'll use to see your results. After you unpack the MSI, you deploy the MSI file via GPSI (Group Policy Software Installation) to the clients. Additionally, this package comes with an ADM template, which you need to import into the Group Policy Object Editor. The point of the ADM file is to push the data about the client's Group Policy application to a central shared folder location.

Once your clients start pushing up the data, you can run the GPMonitorUI at your management station to see what's going on. The clients will upload their historical data every *N* Group Policy refreshes. (The default is every 8.) From your management station, you can then see which GPOs have or have not applied yesterday, but are applying today—among other possibilities.

FIGURE A.6   GPMonitor

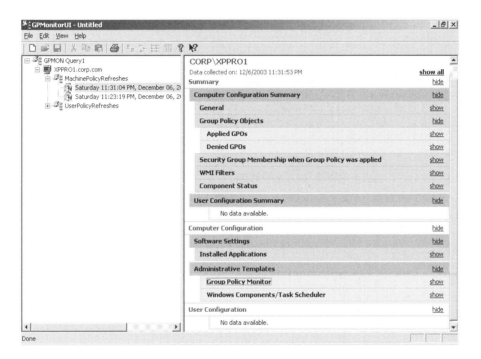

 Your management station needs the GPMC loaded in order to display the data as seen in Figure A.6, but the clients you want to monitor do not.

GPInventory—Group Policy Inventory Tool

GPInventory is a late addition to the Windows 2003 Server Resource Kit. You must download and install it separately. To find it, search for "Group Policy Inventory" on Microsoft's website. At last check, however, it could be found here: `http://tinyurl.com/b38lu`.

GPInventory can reach out across the network and query your clients and servers for a list of attributes you want to document in Excel or a text file. Simply point GPInventory toward a list of clients, select the attributes you want to gather, and then let it do its thing. Afterward, just save the resulting file.

In Figure A.7, I can easily find out how much memory my Windows XP clients have by selecting the "WMI: Computer Memory" field and documenting the RSoP (Resultant Set of Policy) status of all my clients with some of the other attributes.

You can even change the default attributes that GPInventory will inventory for via the XML file. Read the included documentation for a how-to.

FIGURE A.7 Group Policy Inventory

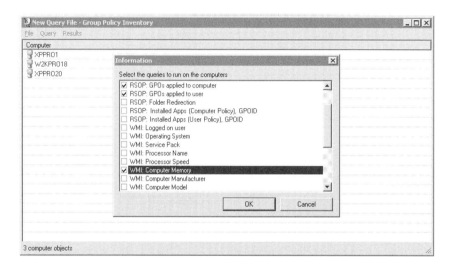

 There's a great little article on GPInventory in Microsoft Technet Magazine found here: http://tinyurl.com/2gw2ry

The WinPolicies Tool

WinPolicies, which is shown in Figure A.8, is also known as the "Policy Spy" (which happens to be what my next costume for Halloween will be, coincidentally). Anyway, WinPolicies can perform lots of the ultra-propeller head client-side troubleshooting stuff you saw in Chapter 4, without having to get your fingers too dirty.

Specifically, you can enable verbose logging, perform tracing, refresh policies (enforced, or not enforced), and get additional troubleshooting information. Typically, you run this tool on the client system experiencing the problem. You can run it as a mere-mortal user or as an administrator. Several features let you enter alternative credentials so you can use it, mostly, as a mere-mortal, but still see log files that are for admins only. That's a nice touch.

WinPolicies doesn't really add any new features to the Group Policy troubleshooting arsenal, but it does consolidate them. And you still need to understand what you're looking at in order to make heads or tails of the output. Hopefully, the information in Chapter 4 gets you off to the right start.

FIGURE A.8   WinPolicies

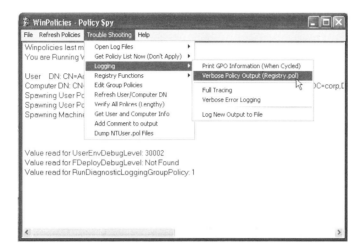

Note that not all features will work when run on Windows Vista machines.

The Group Policy Management Pack for MOM

If you use MOM to manage your environment, there are two MOM management packs you should be aware of. The first is an Active Directory health MOM snap-in which is found here:

`http://tinyurl.com/anatx`

However, this didn't focus specifically on Group Policy. So, Microsoft introduced the Group Policy Management Pack for MOM (as seen in Figure A.9). Organizations needed a mechanism to monitor the health of the Group Policy system. Many of the things, if not all of the things, that we do in Group Policy are mission critical. In the event that one of these pieces decides to go south we need to know about it. The Group Policy Management Pack monitors both Group Policy core processing and individual Client Side extensions. There are some limitations to the Management Pack. It does not represent all of the extensions but does represent Core, Software Installation, Folder Redirection, Quotas, and others. Additionally, there is quite a bit of knowledge built into the Pack to aid in troubleshooting. The Group Policy Management Pack can be downloaded from `http://tinyurl.com/6mqy9`.

ADMX Migrator

The ADMX Migrator is actually, two tools in one: an ADMX Migrator tool and an ADMX Editor tool. We discussed these tools in the section "ADMX Migrator and ADMX Editor Tools" in Chapter 5. Additional information can be found in the online appendix at `GPanswers.com`

Group Policy Log View

A new tool for Windows Vista, Group Policy Log View helps you quickly view operational log results and put them in file types of your choice. We saw this tool in Chapter 4.

FIGURE A.9   Group Policy Management Pack for MOM

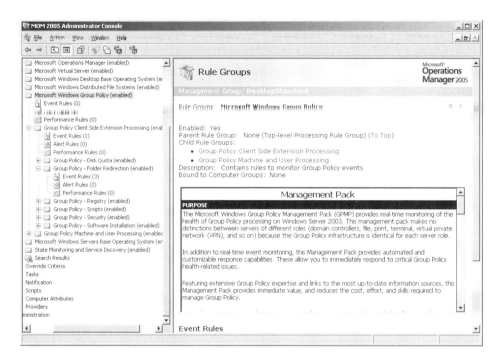

Profile Tools from Microsoft

Microsoft also has two tools to help manipulate Profiles if they need a kick in the pants. Here they are.

The Delprof Tool

You use this utility to bulk-delete profiles—either locally or remotely. An update is available at www.microsoft.com/windowsserver2003/techinfo/reskit/tools/default.mspx. This is a command-line tool, so be careful, you can get in a lot of trouble in a hurry. Microsoft has a nice Knowledge Base article on this tool, 315411, that discusses how to eliminate profiles if they are not used in, say, 30 days.

The Proquota Tool

You can use this tool to limit the size that the roaming user profile can become. This isn't a tool you can run, per se. It's part of the operating system. It is invoked whenever the **Limit profile size** policy setting in User Configuration ➢ Administrative Templates ➢ System ➢ User Profiles is set to Enabled.

Utilities and Add-ons

There are utilities which pop up all the time to help with Group Policy management and configuration. Instead of listing them here, however, I suggest you go to www.GPanswers .com/solutions, which has a current list of utilities which you might want to check out. Here's a sampling of what you'll find:

- Killpol: Temporarily stops the application of policy to help troubleshoot a system.

- RGPrefresh: Command-line Group Policy refresh utility.

- GPSIViewer: GUI utility for viewing and printing information on all software installation packages in a domain (www.gpoguy.com/gpsiviewer.htm).

- WMIFTest: GUI utility for testing WMI filters on a given Windows system prior to implementation (www.gpoguy.com/wmiftest.htm).

- Specops GPUpdate: A Group Policy refresh utility that hooks in to Active Directory Users and Computers.

- PolicyReporter: Helps analyze both Windows XP and Windows Vista logs to help find Group Policy problems.

Third-Party Vendors List

When I wrote the first edition of this book, only one or two vendors were really doing interesting stuff with Group Policy. By the time I wrote the second edition of this book, I had a handful of vendors with a handful of products.

Vendors are now recognizing the power that Group Policy provides. Some vendors are adding to the management capabilities of GPOs, others help in GPO troubleshooting, and still others take the next logical step and extend Group Policy to harness even more power!

In this third edition, I'll list all the vendors I know that make third-party products. Do note that names of products change, and features change all the time. To that end, it's better to simply visit the company's websites to get a rundown of their current offerings.

Additionally, some vendors showcase their products on www.GPanswers.com/solutions.

Tables A.1, A.2, and A.3 list tools that can help you in your Group Policy journey. In these tables, I provide an incredibly short description of the product. On www.GPanswers.com, some vendors have chosen to showcase their tools. Otherwise, you can go to the vendors' websites to check out their products.

TABLE A.1   Group Policy Management Tools

Vendor	Product	Company Website	Brief Description
BeyondTrust	Privilege Manager	www.beyondtrust.com	Helps you set applications to run as admins and users to run with least privilege.

TABLE A.1   Group Policy Management Tools *(continued)*

Vendor	Product	Company Website	Brief Description
Centrify	DirectControl	www.centrify.com	Extends Group Policy to Linux systems.
Configuresoft	Enterprise Configuration Manager	www.configuresoft.com	Centralizes and automates the labor-intensive task of planning, auditing, and monitoring changes in Group Policy objects on Windows systems deployed in large enterprise networks or Web server farms.
FullArmor	Group Policy Anywhere	www.fullarmor.com	Separates Group Policy from Active Directory, allowing you to start using Group Policy today, even if you are still planning for Active Directory or Group Policy.
FullArmor	PolicyPortal	www.fullarmor.com	Enforces and audits Group Policy on all machines on your network and over the Internet.
PolicyPak Software	PolicyPak line of products (such as PolicyPak for Adobe Acrobat Reader and PolicyPak for Exchange Server 2003)	www.policypak.com	Group Policy enables the applications you already have with specific client-side extensions.
Special-Operations-Software	Special Operations Suite	www.specopssoft.com	A broad and deeply Active Directory integrated Desktop Management suite for all sizes of organizations.
Special-Operations-Software	SpecOps Deploy	www.specopssoft.com	Enhances the native Group Policy Software Installation functions.

TABLE A.1   Group Policy Management Tools *(continued)*

Vendor	Product	Company Website	Brief Description
Special-Operations-Software	SpecOps Password Policy	www.specopssoft.com	Sets individual password requirements per OU.
Special-Operations-Software	SpecOps Inventory	www.specopssoft.com	Provides Hardware and Software Inventory via Group Policy.
SDM Software	GPHealth Reporter	www.SDMsoftware.com	Reports on the health of Group Policy processing and helps with troubleshooting.
SDM Software	GPLog Analyzer	www.SDMsoftware.com	Integrates with GPHealth Reporter to provide consolidated reporting and expert advice on GP processing logs.
NetPro	Change Auditor	www.netpro.com	Performs auditing of Group Policy changes.
NetPro	GPOadmin	www.netpro.com	Provides Group Policy Version Control and Group Policy comparison
Attachmate/NetIQ	IntelliPolicy (Created by FullArmor)	www.netiq.com	Provides additional functionality to Group Policy via extensions
Attachmate/NetIQ	Group Policy Administrator (Created by FullArmor)	www.netiq.com	Provides change-management capabilities to Group Policy.
Attachmate/NetIQ	Group Policy Guardian (Created by FullArmor)	www.netiq.com	Performs auditing of Group Policy changes
SecureVantage	Policy Controls Management Pack for MOM	www.securevantage.com	Performs auditing and discovery of Group Policy inside Microsoft MOM.

TABLE A.1   Group Policy Management Tools *(continued)*

Vendor	Product	Company Website	Brief Description
Scriptlogic	Active Administrator	www.scriptlogic.com	Provides Group Policy auditing and change management.
NVAPᵢₙ	Pᵤₗᵢₘₘₙ	www.ꞀyₐPₒₒNₒPₒ.com	A Pᵤℓₕ y Mₐₙₐₑₘₑₙₜ tool; more easily interprets Policy settings.
Quest	Group Policy Manager	www.quest.com	Provides change management capabilities to Group Policy.
Quest	Group Policy Extensions for Desktops	www.quest.com	A set of Group Policy extensions; performs common administration tasks.
Quest's Vintela	VAS (Vintela Authentication Services)	www.quest.com/unix_linux/	Extends Group Policy to Linux.

You might wonder what happened to DesktopStandard. They were bought out by Microsoft. The status of their three products is as follows: PolicyMaker Standard Edition and Share Manager will likely be incorporated into a future version or add-on pack for Windows; PolicyMaker Software Update will not be resold or repurposed by Microsoft; PolicyMaker Application Security became BeyondTrust Corporation. Finally, GPOVault is already being resold by Microsoft as part of their Desktop Optimization Pak for Software Assurance customers (MDOP). Information can be found here: http://tinyurl.com/ud3uk.

TABLE A.2   Third-Party ADM Template-Creation Tools

Vendor	Product Name	Website	Brief Description
Advanced Toolware	Policy Template Editor 2	www.advtoolware.com/t4e/pte/pte_default.htm	Eases the creation of ADM templates.

TABLE A.2   Third-Party ADM Template-Creation Tools *(continued)*

Vendor	Product Name	Website	Brief Description
SYSPRO	ADM Template Editor	www.SysProSoft.com	Eases the creation of ADM templates. They may have an ADMX editor by the time you read this.
Microsoft/FullArmor	ADMX Migrator	Download directly at http://tinyurl.com/yjnptj	For migrating from ADM to ADMX and for creating new ADMX from scratch.

TABLE A.3   Third-Party MSI Repackaging Tools

Vendor	Product Name	Website
InstallAware	InstallAware	www.installaware.com
Installshield/Macrovision	AdminStudio	www.installshield.com
Scriptlogic	DesktopAuthority MSI Studio	www.scriptlogic.com
New Boundary	PrismPack	www.newboundary.com
OnDemand Software	WinInstall (many versions)	www.ondemandsoftware.com
Wise Solutions/Altiris	Wise Package Studio	www.wise.com

Index

Note to the reader: Page numbers in **bold** indicate the principle discussion of a topic or the definition of a term. Page numbers in *italic* indicate illustrations.

O

Q

R

S